595/אוx

THE JOHN HARVARD LIBRARY

Howard Mumford Jones
Editor-in-Chief

LECTURES
ON
REVIVALS OF RELIGION

By

CHARLES GRANDISON FINNEY

Edited by William G. McLoughlin

THE BELKNAP PRESS OF
HARVARD UNIVERSITY PRESS
Cambridge, Massachusetts
1960

© Copyright 1960 by the President and Fellows of Harvard College
All Rights Reserved

Distributed in Great Britain by Oxford University Press, London

Library of Congress Catalog Card Number 60-11558

Printed in the United States of America

CONTENTS

Introduction and Notes by William G. McLoughlin　　VII

LECTURES

I	WHAT A REVIVAL OF RELIGION IS	9
II	WHEN A REVIVAL IS TO BE EXPECTED	24
III	HOW TO PROMOTE A REVIVAL	38
IV	PREVAILING PRAYER	52
V	THE PRAYER OF FAITH	72
VI	SPIRIT OF PRAYER	89
VII	BE FILLED WITH THE SPIRIT	107
VIII	MEETINGS FOR PRAYER	124
IX	MEANS TO BE USED WITH SINNERS	140
X	TO WIN SOULS REQUIRES WISDOM	156
XI	A WISE MINISTER WILL BE SUCCESSFUL	174
XII	HOW TO PREACH THE GOSPEL	194
XIII	HOW CHURCHES CAN HELP MINISTERS	223

XIV	MEASURES TO PROMOTE REVIVALS	250
XV	HINDRANCES TO REVIVALS	277
XVI	NECESSITY AND EFFECT OF UNION	310
XVII	FALSE COMFORTS FOR SINNERS	333
XVIII	DIRECTIONS TO SINNERS	361
XIX	INSTRUCTIONS TO CONVERTS	381
XX	INSTRUCTION OF YOUNG CONVERTS	410
XXI	BACKSLIDERS	431
XXII	GROWTH IN GRACE	447

INTRODUCTION

This book, first published in 1835, has an important place not only in American religious history but in American social and intellectual history as well. Its importance to religious history has two dimensions. In the realm of theology it clearly marks the end of two centuries of Calvinism and the acceptance of pietistic evangelicalism as the predominant faith of the nation. In the realm of applied religion, as a textbook on how to promote revivals of religion, this book is the perennial classic to which all succeeding generations of revivalists have turned for authority and inspiration.

The volume's importance to American social and intellectual history lies in the fact that it constitutes a vigorous and dramatic expression of the religious side of the Era of the Common Man. In its underlying assumptions about nature, man, and society, it was in its way as ebullient an embodiment of the spirit of Jacksonian democracy as the speeches of Andrew Jackson, the editorials of John L. O'Sullivan and William Leggett, or the essays of Ralph Waldo Emerson. For in these lectures Finney gave characteristic expression to the views of those sincere believers in Christianity who took a middle ground between the ambitions of clerical Whigs, who hoped to erect a national church as a bulwark against atheistic mobocracy, and the efforts of those anticlerical Democrats who were trying to reduce Christianity to little more than an exalted system of ethics. Finney spoke particularly for those far-flung sons of New England who eventually abandoned both the Whigs and the Democrats to vote for the Republican Party of Abraham Lincoln. Opposing both the ecclesiastical pretensions of the conservatives and the freethinking propensities of the radicals, Finney stood for the evangelical outlook that became the prevailing one among middle-class churchgoers in mid-nineteenth century America. He believed, as the lectures in this book clearly testify, that a Christian nation must be based upon the devout personal faith in the revealed truth of God of each individual citizen. In this respect it might justly be claimed that he was more truly a spokesman of his age than any of the religious liberals or churchly Whigs who have commonly been granted that role.

Charles Grandison Finney, the son of a Revolutionary veteran and an heir of the Pilgrim tradition of seventeenth-century Massachusetts, was born in Warren, Connecticut, in 1792. He moved west with his family two years later, grew up in the "burnt-over district" of western New York, and in 1821, as the result of an intense religious experience, he gave up a promising career as a lawyer in order to become an itinerant evangelist. He was a tall, slim, handsome man with piercing blue eyes, sandy hair, and a burning conviction that he was "led by God" in his effort to convert and reform the nation. Because he was ordained as a Presbyterian minister and because orthodox Presbyterianism at this time was Calvinistic, many who have not read his works erroneously assume that Finney was a preacher of hellfire and damnation who excoriated the moral depravity of man and exalted the wrath of God. Because he ardently espoused such moral reforms as temperance, abolition, and Sabbatarianism, and because of his close association with such wealthy Whig merchants as Lewis and Arthur Tappan, David and William E. Dodge, and Anson G. Phelps, it has been commonly assumed that Finney was totally out of sympathy with the Jacksonian temper of his times. His famous revival meetings, conducted in towns and cities across the country in the second quarter of the nineteenth century, are mistaken for manifestations of a resurgent ecclesiasticism, a "Protestant Counter-Reformation" designed to put down the deistic radicalism of Tom Paine and Thomas Jefferson and to reassert Christian orthodoxy and clerical domination in the new nation. And despite the fact that in 1851 Finney became the President of Oberlin College, it is sometimes assumed that his evangelical theology brands him as anti-intellectual, antiscientific, and antiliberal.

Even a cursory reading of the *Lectures on Revivals* will soon dispel these misconceptions. Unlike the majority of his clerical colleagues, Finney was a child of his age, not an enemy of it. He had little use for Calvinism, and the basic philosophical and social principles underlying his thought were essentially the same as those associated with Jacksonian democracy. Like the Jacksonians, Finney had an ardent faith in progress, in the benevolence of God, and in the dignity and worth of the common man. Like the Jacksonians, he believed that the restrictive clerical and aristocratic traditions of the seventeenth and eighteenth centuries were out of date and that they must give way to a new and more liberal outlook if the nation was to continue to grow in peace, liberty, and prosperity under God. Finney was no backward-looking fundamentalist exhorter, longing for the good old days of Puritanism and inculcating a fear of hell to keep the wickedness of the common man in check. He was in fact just the opposite of a theocrat — he was a pietist. And that is why he spent his life at odds with the Calvinists of his day. He disliked man-made creeds; he saw no need for institutionalized denominational systems; he believed in the priesthood of all believers. His mission, as he saw it, was to create a universal Church based upon the fundamentals of the gospel. He sought to cut away the bonds of customs and liberate men from their blind obedience to the past. He wanted to help men free themselves from sin and learn to grow in wisdom and love as free Christian men and women. And he believed that the millennial age was about to dawn in the United States of America.

It is true that Finney never took the stump for Andrew Jackson. His antislavery convictions were sufficient to prevent this. Moreover, like Emerson, he preferred to vote against the party that shared his broad principles because he was convinced the other side had the more honest men. His pietistic evangelicalism made him see politics through moralistic eyes, and he cast his vote in terms of particular moral issues rather than in terms of party politics.

The clue to Finney's Jacksonian temper lies not in his attitude toward politics but in his attitude toward Calvinism. The first thing that strikes the reader of the *Lectures on Revivals* is the virulence of Finney's hostility toward traditional Calvinism and all it stood for. He denounced its doctrinal dogmas (which, as embodied in the Westminster Confession of Faith, he referred to elsewhere as "this wonderful theological fiction"); he rejected its concept of nature and the structure of the universe (especially its exaltation of the sovereign and miraculous power of God in regard to conversions and the promotion of revivals); he scorned its pessimistic attitude toward human nature and progress (particularly in regard to the freedom of the will); and he thoroughly deplored its hierarchical and legalistic polity (as embodied in the ecclesiastical system of the Presbyterian Church). Or to put it more succinctly, John Calvin's philosophy was theocentric and organic; Charles Finney's was anthropocentric and individualistic. It is little wonder that Finney was considered a renegade, a radical, and a "revolutionary" by so many of his strait-laced church brethren throughout his career. As one prominent Calvinist editor wrote in 1838 of Finney's revivals, "Who is not aware that the Church has been almost revolutionized within four or five years by means of such excitements?"[1]

But this volume is more than a destructive attack upon "the traditions of the elders," as Finney scornfully referred to the old Calvinistic doctrines. It is a positive, ringing statement of the new religious, social, and intellectual philosophy that came to dominate popular American thought until well into the twentieth century — a philosophy that, however inconsistently, blended reason and faith, science and revelation, self-reliance and divine guidance, pragmatism and intuition, head and heart, moral self-denial and spiritual freedom, social reform and rugged individualism, humanitarianism and piety in a form perfectly adapted to the needs of the expanding and prospering American society. Within the broader frame of western civilization, Finney's faith, like that of the Jacksonians, was part and parcel of Thomas Reid's "Scottish Common Sense School" of philosophy, Jeremy Bentham's "philosophical radicalism," John Stuart Mills' "utilitarianism," Adam Smith's "laissez faire," plus that spongey modification of Jonathan Edwards' Calvinism in terms of John Wesley's Arminianism that is commonly called "evangelicalism." The one element that produced the tensile strength of this miscellaneous compound, and the strongest note in Finney's preaching, was the pietistic sectarianism he got from his separatist Pilgrim forebears.

Finney struck the keynote of the intellectual revolution for which this volume speaks in the very first lecture, when he stated it as axiomatic that a revival of religion "is not a miracle or dependent on a miracle. It is a purely philosophical result of the right use of the constituted means." This was obviously a direct contradiction of the theocentric cosmology of John Calvin and especially of the doctrines of God's arbitrary grace and inscrutable sovereignty that John Cotton and Jonathan Edwards had so vigorously upheld in America. Jonathan Edwards had described the famous revival in Northampton, Massachusetts, in 1734 as "a marvelous work of God," a "shower of divine blessing," which, like a shower of rain in a parched land, came miraculously through the divine hand of Providence. Finney, writing one hundred years later, insisted that the revivals with which he was so prominently connected in the years 1825–1835 were simply the result of cause and effect in which the revival preacher was the principal agent:

[1] Charles Pigeon, "Thoughts on the New Haven Theology," *Literary and Theological Review*, 5: 158 (March 1838).

"The connection between the right use of means for a revival and a revival is as philosophically sure as between the right use of means to raise grain and a crop of wheat." And as Finney went on to claim, the physical, psychological, and physiological laws of nature were now so well known (as perhaps they were not in Edwards' day) that it was clearly God's intention that men should make use of them to evangelize the world. Therefore, for the better advancement of God's kingdom, Finney designed the *Lectures on Revivals* to be a handbook, a how-to-do-it book, for ministers interested (as all ministers should be) in promoting revivals and winning souls.

Finney was so far from Edwards in his philosophical outlook that it may seem odd that he frequently quotes Edwards to buttress his views on specific aspects of revival preaching. But it is no more strange than the fact that Finney was himself a Presbyterian minister at the time he wrote this book and that as such he still claimed to believe in the tenets of Calvinism (as he defined them). This is not the place to indulge in an exhaustive explanation of the decline of Calvinism, but it is necessary, if this book is to be fully appreciated, that readers should recognize the broad implications of these lectures for American religious and intellectual history in terms of the specific theological and ecclesiastical problems Finney faced in his career. The Calvinists, or rather, the churches that claimed to believe in the tenets of the Westminster Confession of Faith were still the predominant religious bodies in America at the time Finney wrote. The Presbyterian churches, the Congregational churches, the Associate Reformed churches, and the various Reformed Churches all adhered to the Westminster Confession and most Baptist churches were generally in agreement with its doctrines. At the time Finney wrote his *Lectures on Revivals* he was at the storm center of a bitter quarrel that had wracked these Calvinistic churches for over a decade. As a result of these lectures many Presbyterian leaders demanded that Finney get out of their church (which he did a year after the book was published), and within two years after the lectures were published the Presbyterian and Congregational denominations split over the proper definition of Calvinism. The old Calvinistic tradition had withstood many hard battles in the preceding centuries, but it was in its death throes when Finney wrote, and it is not too farfetched to say that through him it received its *coup de grâce*.

Dr. Oliver Wendell Holmes, the famous "Autocrat of the

Breakfast Table," wrote the epitaph of Calvinism in 1858. But his claim that the deacon's wonderful "One Hoss Shay" disintegrated on November 1, 1855, "All at once and nothing first,/ Just as bubbles do when they burst," carried poetic license a bit too far. Since 1836 the good doctor had himself been indirectly whittling away at the shay in his essays, having taken up medicine instead of the ministry, because he was in rebellion against the Calvinism of his father, the pastor of the First Congregational Church of Cambridge, Massachusetts. And certainly the termite work of Taylor and Beecher at Yale had badly damaged the ancient chariot by 1828. It might even be justly claimed that the shay collapsed (or at least lost a front wheel) when Harvard College was captured by the Unitarians in 1805. Or, to push the matter back to its real *fons et origo*, the springs of the shay were irreparably broken upon the rocky road of Lockean rationalism that justified the War for Independence in terms of the natural rights of man. The "Spirit of Seventy-six" was a far cry from the "Spirit of the Puritans."

The truth of the matter is that the breakdown of Calvinism was one of the two or three great intellectual revolutions in American history, and a chronicle of its decline would constitute a history of almost a century of American civilization. Dr. Holmes's career indicated the revolution in science and medicine that accompanied the more naturalistic outlook of the post-Calvinistic era. In American literature a large segment of the romantic movement sprang from the nineteenth century's faith in man and nature and gave rise to a literary outburst later critics have called "the flowering of New England" and "the American renaissance." In philosophy the Transcendentalists produced their unique and talented contribution by inverting every tenet of Calvinism and making a virtue out of each inversion. The repudiation of the doctrines of original sin and an arbitrary God of wrath had its eccentric side in the perfectionist, the communitarian, and the physiological fads of the pre-Civil War era. And it had its ugly side in the spread-eagle oratory about "manifest destiny" and the "Order of the Star-Spangled Banner." Like all great intellectual revolutions the overthrow of Calvinism broke through the crust of custom and unleashed an uncontrollable flood of human energy in all areas of life. It is perhaps not too much to say that it provided the driving power which thrust the United States into the forefront of western civilization.

Finney's contribution to this revolution was made in the field of theology and ecclesiasticism. But he was not primarily a theo-

INTRODUCTION

logian or an ecclesiastic. He was primarily an evangelist, and as such he can best be understood in terms of the shifts in American religious life embodied in the first and second Great Awakenings.

To put the matter briefly, the first Great Awakening of 1725–1750, in which Edwards, Whitefield, Frelinghuysen, and the Tennents played major roles, had resulted in a restatement of seventh-century Calvinism in terms that made the individual more responsible than formerly for working out his salvation, without quite asserting that he could effectively attain it by any act of his own. As the theologians of the time put it, man had the natural ability to act rightly but he was morally unable to do so unless God, through the Holy Spirit, transformed or infused his soul with supernatural grace. The followers of Edwards in the Congregational and Presbyterian churches maintained the legalistic rigidity of his theology after 1750 without maintaining his homiletic fervor. The theology of the neo-Edwardeans, like Samuel Hopkins, Jonathan Edwards, Jr., Joseph Bellamy, Nathaniel Emmons, and Asa Burton, hardened into a series of arid formulae that produced endless quibbling among the clergy and increasing tedium, frustration, and skepticism among the churchgoers.[2] The deistic ideology that underlay the Revolutionary zeal for human or natural rights aroused more fervor after 1765 than anything the churches were espousing. The demand for separation of church and state that began in Virginia in 1776 and ended in Massachusetts in 1833 was made easier by the desiccated state of theology in this period.

But the deistic anticlericalism of Ethan Allen, Thomas Paine, and Thomas Cooper went too far for the average American, who continued to respect the Word of God even when he found the words of His ministers incomprehensible. Toward the end of the eighteenth century, as the new nation stabilized its domestic and international position, a new interest in religion was stimulated by a group of itinerant evangelists — Presbyterians, Methodists, and Baptists — who rode through the newly settled frontier regions across the Appalachians preaching a new theology and holding four-day camp meetings under the trees to promote it. The Presbyterian Church in the Southwest was galvanized by great excitement and by grave schisms in 1804–1810 as a result of the new

---

[2] The best discussions of the breakdown of Calvinism are to be found in: Joseph Haroutunian, *Piety Versus Moralism* (New York, 1932); Frank H. Foster, *A Genetic History of the New England Theology* (Chicago, 1907); Sidney E. Mead, *Nathaniel William Taylor* (Chicago, 1942); and Conrad Wright, *Beginnings of Unitarianism in America 1735–1805* (Boston, 1955).

doctrines of Barton W. Stone, Finis Ewing, and Thomas Campbell. New Englanders also had a return to religious interest in the opening decades of the nineteenth century under the spirited but restrained preaching of Timothy Dwight, Lyman Beecher, and Asahel Nettleton, whose subtle modifications in New England Calvinism avoided the quarrels that rent the Presbyterian Church. And then in 1821 Finney began his astounding career as a revivalist in the middle colonies, starting in western New York and gradually moving eastward to the big cities of Philadelphia, New York, and Boston. He brought the Presbyterian and Congregational churches to their great schism of 1837 and completed the downfall of Calvinism.

The significant fact about this second Great Awakening (which can roughly be dated as 1795–1835) was that from the outset it minimized or denied entirely the arbitrary grace of God, which elected some to heaven but most to hell. The preachers of this awakening proceeded on the assumption that every individual had the free will and the moral ability to work out his own salvation. The five points of Calvinism, with their stress upon predestination and total depravity, were kept in the background even by revivalists who claimed to believe in the Westminster Confession. Instead, these revivalists concentrated upon putting new life into the dry bones of the churches by calling upon sinners to repent and submit to God without offering any clear doctrinal interpretations of what these terms meant. The average American, who had never been very fond of the mechanistic God of the deists, was ready to return to church when he found that an arbitrary God of wrath was being replaced by a comprehensible God of love and when he was told that religion was a reasonable service in which God merely asked the acceptance of a freely proffered salvation for all. It was an especial relief to be told that the Word of God plus the experience of receiving His Spirit was more important than adherence to any denominational creed or doctrinal confession. Between 1800 and 1835 church membership in America increased more than fivefold, considerably outdistancing the threefold increase in population.³

To the more rigid Calvinist ministers who adhered closely to

---

³ See the estimates of church growth in Charles C. Cole, Jr., *The Social Ideas of the Northern Evangelists* (New York, 1954), p. 13. According to his figures, church membership increased from 365,000 in 1800 to about 1,875,000 in 1835; the population in these years increased from about 5,000,000 to 15,000,000.

the standards of Edwards and the Westminster Confession the new revival was a mixed blessing. They were delighted at the multitude of new church members and the manifest evidence of divine blessings, but they soon began to question whether the bars of doctrine were not being lowered too far by some revivalists in their overzealous efforts to fill the fold. By 1830 it was evident to the defenders of the Edwardean view of Calvinism that a stand would have to be taken against innovations all along the line if the faith of the founding fathers was to be maintained. The quarrel naturally centered in the Presbyterian Church, which since 1801 had been affiliated with the Congregationalists. These two denominations combined represented the most learned, numerous, and influential religious bodies in the nation. Their Plan of Union was consummated when the second Great Awakening was just getting under way. Its purpose was to prevent denominational quarreling among Calvinists over new converts in the West. Since Congregationalists and Presbyterians both claimed allegiance to the Westminster Confession and to the theology of Edwards there was thought to be no reason for competition between them. And since the Presbyterian form of church government was considered better suited to bringing order and stability to the frontier areas, most of the families that moved west from New England gave up their Congregationalism to form Presbyterian churches, especially in western New York, Ohio, Michigan, and Indiana. Nevertheless, these new Plan of Union (or "Presbygational") churches in the West more often chose pastors who had been trained at Yale, Andover, Williams, Middlebury, Hamilton, or in the home of some honored Congregational divine in New England than ministers trained at Princeton, Glasgow, Edinburgh, or under the guidance of the Scotch-Irish presbyteries of the Middle and Southern states.

As a result the doctrines taught in the Plan of Union territory were flavored with certain New England modifications of Calvinism that qualified the doctrines taught in strict Presbyterian churches. The neo-Edwardean theologians of New England honored Jonathan Edwards, as they did John Calvin, but they considered it possible to reinterpret his teachings in the light of further study and spiritual insight. And by 1830 many of the leading ministers of New England, particularly Lyman Beecher and Nathaniel W. Taylor, had so far departed from the old interpretations of Calvinism that they were openly being accused of heresy by their more rigid colleagues. However, Beecher and Taylor were not only adroit theological disputants, they were also ardent and successful revival preachers. By disclaiming any heretical tendencies in their views and by pointing to their revival converts as signs of divine approval of their ministries they made it very difficult for heresy-hunting Congregationalists and Presbyterians to bring them to account. And this was where Finney entered the drama.

Finney was a Plan of Union minister from Western New York.[4] Ordained by a liberal "Presbygational" presbytery and not having been trained in any theological school, he was unable and unwilling to split theological hairs in expressing his own divergence from what he called "hyper-Calvinism," whether it was of the Congregational or Presbyterian variety. Although he had been trained for the ministry by a graduate of Princeton Seminary, Finney had disavowed his belief in a strict interpretation of the Westminster Confession shortly after his ordination in 1824. His immediate and astounding success as a revivalist, preaching what came to be called "New School" theology (or the "New Divinity" or "New Haven theology") convinced him and many others in western New York that the Lord approved of his modifications of hyper-Calvinism or "Old School" Calvinism. Unfortunately Finney was somewhat intemperate in his zeal during his early years as an itinerant evangelist. As he testified himself in his *Memoirs*, his revival meetings in the small towns of Oneida and St. Lawrence counties in New York in the 1820's were scenes of physical and emotional hysteria such as these transplanted Yankees had never believed themselves capable of. Prior to Finney's day only the "ignorant Methodist and Baptist exhorters" (as Finney called them) had aroused such enthusiasm in New York. But these itinerants had never been accepted by the respectable Congregational and "Presbygational" churchgoers in the region. Nevertheless, when Finney poured out his New School Calvinism upon them with all the fiery vigor of his dramatic rhetoric and dynamic per-

---

[4] For biographical data about Finney, see his *Memoirs* (New York, 1876) and George F. Wright, *Charles Grandison Finney* (New York, 1891). Additional useful information about his career and theology can be found in Robert S. Fletcher, *A History of Oberlin College*, 2 vols. (Oberlin, Ohio, 1943); Whitney R. Cross, *The Burned-Over District* (Ithaca, New York, 1950); Gilbert H. Barnes, *The Anti-Slavery Impulse 1830–1844* (New York, 1933); and W. G. McLoughlin, *Modern Revivalism: Charles Grandison Finney to Billy Graham* (New York, 1959). The best sources of primary material are the Finney Papers in the Oberlin College Library, the Lewis Tappan Papers in the Library of Congress, and the *Letters of Theodore Weld, Angelina Grimke Weld, and Sarah Grimke*, ed. Gilbert H. Barnes and Dwight L. Dumond, 2 vols. (New York, 1934).

sonality, they too fell into fainting fits or writhed in agony on the floors of their meetinghouses. "The Lord let me loose upon them in a wonderful manner," Finney wrote of his meetings in one town in 1824, and soon "the congregation began to fall from their seats in every direction and cry for mercy."[5]

Certain Old School Calvinists in western New York took offense at Finney's preaching — especially when he and his followers invaded their parishes and denounced them as "enemies of revivals" if they opposed him or his views. The Rev. William R. Weeks of Paris Hill, near Utica, was one of the most vigorous of Finney's opponents, and in 1826 he wrote to Lyman Beecher and Asahel Nettleton back in New England to ask them to use their influence to quiet this wild man who was wreaking havoc with the churches in the West. Weeks made two principal charges against Finney: first, that he did not adhere to orthodox Calvinism, and second, that he employed radical "new measures" in revivals in order to stir up emotional excitement. Zealous for the good name of Congregationalism and of New England revivals, Beecher and Nettleton decided to put all the pressure they could upon Finney in order to mollify him or, failing that, to turn the "Presbygational" ministers and church people of the West against him. The reasons for the actions of Beecher and Nettleton were complex, but it is important to understand them. Vanity would be too simple a motive for their opposition. It was unfortunate for the cause they represented, however, that they underestimated both Finney and the impulses behind the success of his revivals.

Nettleton's great interest in quieting Finney was to preserve the tradition of conservative revivalism that since 1811 he had practiced with good success as an itinerant evangelist among New England Congregationalists. Beecher's concern was more sophisticated. He too wished to keep revivalism respectable so that he could continue to use it as a counterforce against Unitarianism in Boston. But he also feared that Finney's rash attacks upon Calvinism would hinder the subtle attempts he and Nathaniel W. Taylor of Yale Seminary were making, to modify the tenets of Calvinism so as to allow a greater amount of free will to individuals in effecting their own salvation. In the third place, Beecher had been for some time mulling over in his mind a vague but elaborate scheme for what he called "a great evangelical assimilation" among the nation's churches. Finney's provocative and sensational

[5] Finney, *Memoirs*, p. 103.

revival measures would not be conducive to the sort of ecclesiastical maneuvering that would be necessary for the success of this ecumenical endeavor among Calvinists. But there was more to Beecher's opposition to Finney than these matters of ecclesiastical politics. There was also a question of party politics. Much of the antagonism between Beecher and Finney stemmed from Beecher's inherent political conservatism and Finney's inherent political or pietistic radicalism.

Beecher has been called a latter-day theocrat who, when Congregationalism was disestablished in Connecticut in 1818, sought to re-establish a clerically dominated social order by means of voluntary social and moral reform societies that would give the clergy an influential role in forming public opinion and molding public legislation.[6] The many "benevolent societies" of the period, which sought to evangelize the unchurched, to save the heathen, to sober the drunkard, to rescue the wayward female, to purify the Sabbath, to end dueling, to inaugurate Sunday schools, and to send freed slaves back to Africa, were all dear to Beecher's heart, and he was a prime mover in their activities. These were interdenominational in character and voluntary in principle. But it was the ministers and leading laymen and women of the Congregational churches who formed the bulk of their membership. There is little doubt that Beecher and many of his colleagues hoped that through these societies the clergy could reassert their proper influence as vicegerents of God, in order to make the United States a Christian nation rather than a secular one. There is also little doubt that Beecher never lost his Federalist political philosophy, which maintained that the political, social, and moral life of any decent society should be controlled by the educated, the wellborn, and the well-to-do. At the root of this was the old corporate theory of society, imbedded in Calvinism, that could not bear the separatist and individualistic antistatism of the pietists. Beecher never became reconciled to the rise of Jeffersonian and Jacksonian democracy, and there is abundant evidence, especially in his "Sermons on Political Atheism" of 1852, that he greatly feared government of, by, and for the common man.

It is not surprising therefore that Beecher and his friend Nettleton saw in Finney's revivalism certain social overtones that

---

[6] See John R. Bodo, *The Protestant Clergy and Public Issues 1812–1848* (Princeton, 1954); R. J. Purcell, *Connecticut in Transition 1775–1818* (Washington, 1918); and S. J. Baird, *A History of the New School* (Philadelphia, 1868), p. 369.

seemed to them to portend the worst aspects of mob rule. In *Letters of the Rev. Dr. Beecher and Rev. Mr. Nettleton on the "New Measures" in Conducting Revivals of Religion*, which was published by Nettleton with Beecher's permission in 1828 as a direct rebuke to Finney, Nettleton in several places referred to Finney and his followers as "the ragamuffins," "the irregulars," the "ignorant," "the insurgents," and "the *ignobile vulgus*," thus revealing his distaste for anyone who tried to arouse the lower orders against their betters. Beecher likewise, in these letters, spoke of the western revivalists as producing "impudent young men . . . poured out as from the hives of the north to obliterate civilization and roll back the wheels of time to semi-barbarism." [7] Beecher seems to have suspected in 1827 that a popular wave of democratic feelings was about to lift Andrew Jackson over John Quincy Adams to the White House, and he apparently feared that Finney's revivalism might well aid and abet mobocracy. "We are on the confines of universal misrule and moral desolation," he wrote in a letter warning ministers about Finney, "and no time is to be lost in forestalling and holding public sentiment correctly before the mass shall be put in motion by fierce winds before which nothing can stand. . . ." [8] Like most Federalists Beecher never forgot the fright which the Jacobins of the French Revolution had aroused in the pious aristocrats of old England and New England. And in his fulminations against Finney he took occasion to recall the horrors of mob rule under the atheism of the First Republic. One of the most startling rumors about Finney's preaching that had reached Beecher in Boston was that he and his fellow revival ministers treated all sinners alike, "without respect to age or station in society." Here was the essence of the quarrel between the Whigs and the Jacksonians: the fight against aristocracy and privilege in politics had a clear parallel in religion. Finney in Beecher's eyes was an uneducated frontier evangelist who relied simply upon his own feelings of divine guidance and, turning upon his betters, dared to denounce them publicly as sinners. Beecher pointed out that to rebuke respectable citizens and officeholders as sinners would be dangerous in any society, but "how much more in republican governments where public opinion is the only law

[7] Lyman Beecher to N. S. S. Beman, January 1827, in *Letters of the Rev. Dr. Beecher and Rev. Mr. Nettleton on the "New Measures" in Conducting Revivals of Religion* (New York, 1828), p. 98.

[8] From a letter by Beecher to Nettleton quoted in the *Christian Examiner and Theological Review* (Unitarian, Boston), 4:265 (May-June 1827).

and a levelling of all distinctions of society would be the sure presage of anarchy and absolute destruction. Such as in France existed for a time . . . [under] the mob." [9] Finney's lack of respect for tradition, for learned doctors of divinity, for the social proprieties, for those in power, for the ancient and honorable institutions (civil and ecclesiastical) of the East, was as evident in 1827 as in his *Lectures on Revivals* of 1835.

But what made Beecher's task of subduing Finney particularly difficult in 1827 was that Finney was preaching virtually the same theological doctrines in western New York that Beecher was preaching in Boston. Nettleton, no theologian, didn't know about the ecclesiastical machinations brewing in Beecher's brain and thought the situation could be settled easily by holding a conference in which Beecher and his friends confronted Finney face-to-face and literally overawed him into submission to the more conservative ways of the East. Beecher also underestimated Finney and the force of the western revivals. The famous New Lebanon Convention in July 1827 brought together nine Eastern and nine Western ministers (Congregational, "Presbygational," and Presbyterian) to discuss the whole problem. But the confrontation proved inconclusive. It left Finney free to continue as before, and it so angered Nettleton that he never regained confidence in Beecher. In fact, five years later Nettleton turned against Beecher and sided with the Old School Calvinists in forming East Windsor Seminary (later Hartford Theological Seminary) as a rival to Yale Seminary, which was dominated by Beecher's friend, Taylor.

This whole imbroglio of 1827 had several ironic consequences in the ensuing years. Finney slowly came to realize that Beecher was really his ally rather than his enemy in renovating Calvinist theology. Beecher came to see that Finney was not so fanatical or crude as he had been reputed to be. In 1831 Beecher actually signed an invitation to Finney to come to Boston to conduct a series of revival meetings. During these meetings Finney delivered his famous sermon, "Sinners Bound to Change Their Own Hearts," which the Old School Calvinists at once pounced upon as heretical and used to belabor Beecher and all his New School friends who had invited Finney to Boston. And finally, in 1835, when Beecher was on trial for heresy and was asked his opinion of Finney, he

[9] Lyman Beecher to N. S. S. Beman, January 1827, in *Letters of the Rev. Dr. Beecher*, p. 89.

responded that he had heard more truth from Finney than from any other man in the same space of time, "I have felt the beatings of his great, warm heart before God." [10] In subsequent years, after Finney had left the Presbyterian Church and begun to espouse what was known as "Oberlin Perfectionism," Beecher became once again his enemy, but by then the schism that Beecher had worked so hard to prevent was an accomplished fact.

At the time Finney published his *Lectures on Revivals* in 1835, however, he and Beecher were still on good terms. The principal opposition to this book came from the Old School Calvinists of Princeton and Philadelphia, especially from those who wrote for and supported the *Biblical Repertory and Theological Review*. This quarterly scholarly journal, which advertised on its cover that it was "conducted by an association of gentlemen in Princeton, New Jersey," was founded in 1825, and for fifty years it remained the foremost Calvinist journal in the United States — if not in the world. Its editor, Charles Hodge, was Professor of Oriental and Biblical Literature at Princeton Seminary, and by 1835 he had established a reputation for himself as the outstanding leader of Old School Presbyterianism, a position he held until his death in 1878. Hodge was later to write a devastating attack upon Finney's *Systematic Theology*, but in 1835 he assigned the task of demolishing Finney's *Lectures on Revivals* to his able friend and colleague, the Rev. Albert Baldwin Dod.

Dod, who was born in Mendham, New Jersey, in 1805, was a graduate of Princeton College and Seminary, but because of his intense interest in mathematics he had given up the ministry to become Professor of Mathematics at Princeton at the age of twenty-five. He remained an ardent churchman, however, as most Princeton professors were, and he put his keen analytical mind and his trenchant pen at the service of the Old School wing of his church for the remaining fifteen years of his short life. His contributions to the *Biblical Repertory and Theological Review* rival those of Hodge for the scorn that, in the name of orthodoxy and the honor of the Presbyterian Church, they heaped upon Beecher, Taylor, Finney and all that the "New Divinity" stood for. (He also exhibited his conservatism in the areas of philosophy and science by vigorously attacking the Transcendentalists and the sensational forerunner of Darwinism, Robert Chambers' *Vesti-*

---

[10] Quoted in Albert Dod, "Finney's Lectures," *Biblical Repertory and Theological Review*, 7: 659 note (October 1835).

ges of Creation.) Inasmuch as Dod, like Hodge, was an authoritative spokesman not only for the associated gentlemen of Princeton but also for the Old School Calvinists across the nation, his review of the *Lectures on Revivals* can and should be properly considered the official and definitive counterattack upon the theological revolution that Finney led. It was so considered by contemporaries, and it merits careful consideration here.

Dod reviewed the lectures simultaneously with Finney's *Sermons on Various Subjects*, which had appeared piecemeal in the early months of 1835. The review consisted of ninety-seven pages of biting sarcasm in two installments in the July and October issues of the *Biblical Repertory and Theological Review*. Dod began it by remarking, in the orotund style so dear to the learned theologians of the era:

We congratulate the friends of truth and order on the appearance of these publications. We have never had any doubt what would be the decision of the public mind respecting the new divinity and new-measure system of our day if its distinctive features could be brought out to the light and exposed to general observation. History warrants us in cherishing this our confidence. The truth is, that this system contains but little that is *new*. It is mainly, if not entirely, composed of exploded errors and condemned heresies. The church has already once and again pronounced judgment upon it; and we have no doubt therefore that the same sentence of condemnation will be repeated by the Presbyterian church of the present day whenever the case is fairly presented for decision.

And the review ended:

We conclude this article . . . by pointing out to Mr. Finney his duty to leave our church. It is an instructive illustration of the fact that fanaticism debilitates the conscience, that this man can doubt the piety of anyone who uses coffee and call him a *cheat* who sends a letter to another on his own business without paying the postage, while he remains apparently without remorse with the sin of broken vows upon him. In this position we leave him before the public. Nor will we withdraw our charges against him until he goes out from among us, for he is not of us.[11]

Finney's broken vow, of course, was the affirmation of his belief

---

[11] Albert Dod in his reviews, "Finney's Sermons" and "Finney's Lectures," *Biblical Repertory and Theological Review*, 7: 482–527, 626–674 (July and October 1835).

in the Westminster Confession of Faith, which he made at the time he was licensed to preach in 1824. (He later claimed in his *Memoirs* that he had made the affirmation without having read the Confession and was not fully aware of how much he disagreed with it. He also claimed, like many Plan of Union and Congregational ministers, that the Confession was capable of a wide variety of interpretations and that it was perfectly possible for him to construe his own theological outlook so as to conform to it. The New School Presbyterians all made this latter claim when they were exscinded from the church by the Old School majority two years later.)

While few of the New School Calvinists had departed quite so far from orthodoxy as Finney did in his *Lectures on Revivals* and his *Sermons on Various Subjects*, it was nevertheless apparent that in this review the Rev. Mr. Dod was throwing down the gauntlet to the whole group of theologians who were trying to pour the new wine of pietistic evangelicalism into the old bottles of Calvinism. "We tender him our thanks," said Dod of Finney, "for the substantial service he has done the church by exposing the naked deformities of the New Divinity." [12] And he took every occasion to connect Finney with Beecher and Taylor during the course of his review.

Dod spelled out his complaints against Finney's theology (and the New Divinity in general) under three headings: the nature of God's government; the nature of sin and depravity; and the nature of regeneration and conversion. In each case he concluded that Finney was guilty of the heresy of Pelagianism. Pelagianism, the fifth-century heresy in opposition to which Augustine had formulated the predestinarian theory that constituted the basis of Calvinism, became the predominant heresy of the nineteenth century and is still deeply imbedded in Protestantism. Dod may have been unfair in laying the blame for its resurgence thus heavily upon Finney, nevertheless the fact that, as a responsible spokesman for the orthodox viewpoint, he did so, is another reason why Finney must rank as an important figure in American intellectual history. The charge is worth examining in some detail.

Finney's great error in relation to "the government of God," said Dod, was that he adopted the view (earlier put forward and then qualified by Nathaniel W. Taylor) "that God could not prevent the introduction of sin" in the world. This view was, as

[12] *Ibid.*, p. 527.

Dod saw it, advanced by Finney for the primary purpose of exalting the self-reliance of man at the expense of the sovereignty and omnipotence of God. Finney naturally claimed that his view was commensurate with God's sovereignty and that, more clearly than Calvinism, it placed upon men the responsibility for sinning against the moral law of God's government. This point of divine sovereignty arose in the very first lecture on revivals, where Finney defended the view that revivals are not miracles but are subject to the operations of cause and effect in which man has as important a part to play as God. The Calvinistic doctrine of God's sovereignty, Finney said, had been misunderstood. Many "supposed it to be such an arbitrary disposal of events, and particularly of the gift of his Spirit, as precluded rational employment of means for promoting a revival of religion." [13] Finney denied that this view was justified either by Scripture or by experience. "Everything goes to show that God has connected means with the end through all the departments of his government — in nature and in grace." Of course, Finney went on, this does not justify the deistic concept of God as the great clockmaker of the universe. "He has not built the creation like a vast machine that will go on alone without his further care. He has not retired from the universe, to let it work for itself. This is mere atheism. . . . And yet every event in nature has been brought about by means. He neither administers providence nor grace with that sort of sovereignty that dispenses with the use of means." [14] In short, the deists were wrong but so also were those Calvinists who talked about the arbitrary grace of God, which, like the wind, bloweth where it listeth and no man knows how or why.

The question of divine sovereignty came up again in even more significant form when Finney discussed the regeneration and conversion of individuals. Here, as Dod pointed out, Finney went so far in his theory of means and ends that he actually gave to the sinner the power to thwart the will of God by hardening his heart against the converting power of the Holy Spirit: "When the Son of God approaches you, gathering motives from heaven, earth, and hell and pours them in a focal blaze upon your mind, how is it that you are strong enough to resist? You . . . can exert such a giant strength, I had almost said the strength of Omnipo-

---

[13] Finney, *Lectures on Revivals of Religion*, p. 21. [All references to *Lectures on Revivals* are to the pagination of this edition.]
[14] *Idem.*

tence, in resisting the infinite weight of motive that rolls upon you from every quarter of the universe to obey God." [15] Could anything be more diametrically opposed to the Calvinist doctrine of irresistible grace?

Dod was particularly wroth with Finney's statement on the very first page of the *Lectures on Revivals* that (and the italics are Dod's) "God has found it *necessary to take advantage* of the excitability there is in mankind to produce powerful excitements among them before he *can* lead them to obey." If this were true, Dod noted, then "God, thwarted in his wishes and plans by the obstinacy of the human will, is literally grieved by the perverse conduct of men; and sinners may properly be exhorted, as they have been, to forsake their sins from compassion for their suffering Maker!" [16] This was to become a very common argument in evangelical preaching later in the century, but to Dod, as to any seventeenth-or eigthteenth-century Calvinist, the idea was little short of blasphemy: "We know of nothing which ought more deeply to pain and shock the pious mind" than this, he said; "If the perverseness of man has been able in one instance to prevent God from accomplishing what he preferred, then may it in any instance obstruct the working of his preferences. Where then is the infinite and immutable blessedness of the Diety? . . . We can see, indeed, but little to decide our choice between such a God as this and no God."

What, in the broad range of intellectual history, is most significant about Finney's assault upon the Calvinist doctrine of God's unlimited and arbitrary sovereignty is that it so clearly made man and not God the measure of all things. Finney, like the deists of the Enlightenment, preferred to think of God simply as the Creator and Governor of the universe, the God of nature, who works according to the fixed laws of physics and of psychology that he has made known to man. In presenting God to the sinner, as Dod rightly pointed out, Finney "takes his stand amid the wonders of creation" and, having pointed out the benevolence of God, the reasonableness of his commands, the utility of his moral law, and the wisdom of cause and effect, he then chastises the selfish, unreasonable, hardhearted sinner with having "set his unsanctified feet upon the principles of eternal righteousness, lifted up his hands against the throne of the Almighty, set

---
[15] Finney, *Sermons on Various Subjects* (New York, 1835), p. 14.
[16] Dod, "Finney's Sermons," p. 491.

at naught the authority of God and the rights of man!"[17] When Presbyterian revivalists began to chastise sinners for setting God at naught and interfering with the rights of man, Calvinism was clearly dead. Finney was in effect saying that while God "proposes" the general terms of earthly and eternal life, it is man who "disposes." God offers the possibility for a happy universe, but man rejects it. Thus man is the captain of his fate, not God. And by this means Christianity was made to conform to the nineteenth century's optimistic belief in human progress, humanly controlled, toward an eventual utopian society, a New Eden, in which all men could voluntarily and joyfully live and work in harmony with all God's moral and spiritual laws, provided they would only "accept" or "get right with" God.

This self-reliant, optimistic outlook, which pervades all Finney's work, naturally collided with another basic tenet of Calvinism, and that was the doctrine of original sin, or the innate depravity of man. On this point Finney and Dod clashed swords over the interpretation of the prevailing theory of pure and applied psychology. Twentieth-century readers of Dod's review will at this point be apt to cry "a plague on both your houses," for the terminology of the old "faculty psychology" in which they argued is now as antiquated as it was inadequate. Even a novice in Freudian theory can punch holes in it. But it is not necessary to plunge into the ancient quagmire of nineteenth-century "mental science" in order to understand the importance of the intellectual issues at stake. Finney and Dod were here arguing the age-old question of the freedom of the will and with it the problem of whether human nature is basically and irremediably bad or whether it is basically good or reasonable and capable of improvement. Finney took the eighteenth-century view, the view of the Enlightenment (which he glossed over with a Christian veneer) that human nature is (with God's help) perfectible. Dod took the older view that even with God's help men are incurably sinful and while they remain on earth will always be so.

Theologically they were arguing over whether God was or was not the author of sin; psychologically they were trying to define the basis of human volition or motivation. Finney argued, with some justice, that as Calvinism was generally preached and understood, its doctrine of innate or natural depravity made God the author of sin because it defined man as a creature incapable

[17] Finney, *Sermons on Various Subjects*, p. 47.

of acting rightly. Hyper-Calvinists, said Finney, "have spoken of depravity, and of the pollutions of our nature, as if there were some moral depravity cleaving to, or incorporated with, the very substance of our being." [18] To which Dod answered that Finney was confusing the sinner's moral inability (which Calvinists did believe in) with the theory of physical inability (which they did not believe in). According to Jonathan Edwards, men were physically capable of obeying God's laws but they were, because of Adam's sin, born with an innate or constitutional preference or disposition for evil (that is, for satisfying selfish or animal desires) that made them morally incapable of obeying God's laws or accepting His grace. Finney insisted that this theory of an innate constitutional preference or disposition toward evil in effect denied men freedom of will and thereby failed to make men morally responsible for their actions. He claimed that the Calvinists preached a theory of physical inability, whether they called it that or not, because they implied that the nature of man was so deformed at birth that only the supernatural action of the Holy Spirit could convert the mind (or the heart or the soul) into a state where it could (the Calvinist's said "would") act rightly.

Dod was forced to admit that "our dispositions or states of heart, including the original disposition by which we are biassed to evil . . . are the proximate sources of all the good and evil in our conduct." But he denied that these dispositions deserved "the epithet physical." Finney, he said, "shows himself here, as on all occasions when he ventures upon the field of mental science, a perfect novice," for he failed to see that a disposition to sin was not a physical "act of mind," a volition, a flexing of some distorted mental muscle. It was simply a "taste," a preference, a craving for evil. Dod acknowledged that "at first sight" the existence of any "such antecedent disposition as we are contending for, formed previous to any action of the mind" must be the "effect of" some "creative power"; and "if it possess any moral character, as we shall offer some reasons for believing it does, then God is the immediate author of sin." But at second sight, he went on, "Does it follow that a primitive disposition such as we speak of, must be the direct product of the agency of the Deity? Is it not evident on the contrary that this is only one out of an infinite number of modes in which it may possibly have been produced?" He then made the rather weak explanation that "a primitive disposition of

[18] *Ibid.*, p. 84.

the mind may be produced in an infinite number of ways and the mode of its formation may be such that it cannot be considered the effect of the divine power in any other sense than that in which all the movements and actions both of matter and mind throughout the universe are said to be of God." [19]

Dod's strong point, however, was that he could quote a large number of Biblical passages that do indicate men are born sinful by nature, such as that we are "by nature children of wrath" and "the carnal mind is enmity against God, for it is not subject to the law of God, neither indeed can be" and "I was shapen in iniquity, and in sin did my mother conceive me." Finney was forced to reply by interpreting these texts to mean simply that "we are always sinners from the commencement of our moral existence" and "the only sense in which sin is natural to man is that it is natural for the mind to be influenced in its individual exercises by a supreme preference or choice" of selfish rather than virtuous or benevolent objects. In other words, for Finney, depravity whether innate or natural, consisited entirely in actions. "Dispositions" to evil were not in and of themselves sins, he maintained; only the actions men took were sins. At this point Dod cried out "Pelagianism!" For if, as Finney said, the commencement of sin in a child "is entirely the result of temptation to selfishness arising out of the circumstances under which the child comes into being," then all that was necessary was for mankind to remove the temptation and alter the circumstances of life, and human nature would grow up without sinning.[20]

Finney retorted that Calvinists were all guilty of "Antinomianism," or, as he more commonly called it, "cannot-ism." Antinomianism or cannot-ism, as Finney defined it in Lecture XII of the *Lectures on Revivals*, was the perverted view of total depravity, predestination, and divine sovereignty held by persons who said they had "no power to do anything but must wait God's time" before they could be converted. This was, said Finney, the view held by Old School Calvinists who lulled churchgoers into inaction and gave them a sense of false security and perhaps even of vain complacency by preaching the doctrine that God had created them with a nature that was incapable of doing good until God first sent the Holy Spirit to transform their hearts. If a man were predestined to be saved, he would, so the Old Calvinists were

---

[19] Dod, "Finney's Sermons," pp. 504, 496, 497, 498.
[20] *Ibid.*, pp. 504–505, 498.

understood to preach, be saved "in God's own good time." Meanwhile it was worse than useless, perhaps it was even sinful, for a sinner to try to exert himself against God's will or against his own dispositions. "No doubt," Finney commented, "more than five thousand millions have gone down to hell while the church has been dreaming and waiting for God to save them. . . . It has been the devil's most successful means of destroying souls." The danger of Antinomianism or cannot-ism was the central burden of all Finney's early preaching, and it occurs upon page after page of the *Lectures on Revivals*: "Sinners ought to be made to feel that they have something to do, and that is to repent; that it is something which no other being can do for them, neither God nor man, and something which they can do and do now. Religion is something to do, not something to wait for." [21]

This was the crux of the whole reaction against "the traditions of the elders," against the dead or dying hand of a dessicated Calvinism. And it was also the crux of the new spirit of religious activism that lay at the heart of nineteenth-century evangelicalism. The quarrel between Finney and Dod therefore passed naturally from the question of the nature of sin to the nature of regeneration. For if sin lay in actions, as Finney claimed, and if men could do something to effect their salvation, then Finney was broaching the ultimate doctrine of Pelagianism, the doctrine that men can lift themselves by their own bootstraps from sin to virtue.

The clearest statement Finney ever made of his theory of regeneration appeared in the sermon, "Sinners Bound to Change Their Own Hearts," which was the first in his *Sermons on Various Subjects*. Finney repeated verbatim the central portion of this sermon in Lecture XII of his *Lectures on Revivals*; this is the famous metaphor in which he compared the conversion of a sinner to the way in which a man, walking in a reverie near Niagara Falls, was saved from falling over the cliff by a passer-by who shouted "Stop!" just in the nick of time. In explaining the metaphor Finney pointed out that there were four agencies at work saving the life of this foolish day-dreamer: there was the passer-by, there was the word "Stop," there was "the force" of the word acting upon the dulled mind of the daydreamer to awaken him to his danger, and there was the action of the daydreamer himself in stopping short and turning back from the brink of destruction. Obviously the

[21] Finney, *Lectures on Revivals*, pp. 379–380, 203, 14, 227.

daydreamer is the sinner, the passerby the revivalist, the word is the Scripture, and the force behind the word is the Holy Spirit.

In his review of Finney's books Dod rightly pointed out that Finney's theory of regeneration and conversion explicitly reduced the roles of God and the Holy Spirit to positions of equality with those of the revivalist and the sinner, while implicitly it almost pushed them out of the picture entirely. Finney's description of the agency of the Holy Spirit in regeneration, said Dod, was so limited that "it is strictly parenthetical" if not in fact "superfluous." Instead of supernaturally transforming the heart by "imparting a new relish for spiritual objects" or "implanting a new principle" into it, as the Calvinists taught, "the Spirit" in Finney's theory, said Dod, "merely presents the truth and the moral suasion of the truth regenerates the sinner, or rather, induces him to regenerate himself." This is the heart of Pelagianism, said Dod, and "we do utterly deny that man is able, in the sense which Mr. Finney contends for, to obey the divine commands" until such time as his heart is "renewed" by God. "Nor are we able to see," he went on, still speaking for all the Old School Calvinists, how a sinner can be turned from selfishness to benevolence, from sin to virtue, from enmity toward God to love of God "unless his mind be illuminated, his heart renewed, by the influence of the Holy Spirit." If 'Mr. Finney asserts the perfect, unqualified ability of man to regenerate himself," Dod concluded, then he has forgotten the Bible. For Christ said, "No man can come to me except the Father which hath sent me, draw him," and Paul taught, "The natural man receiveth not the things of the spirit of God; neither can he know them, for they are spiritually discerned." [22]

Finney's attempts to utilize such texts as "make to yourself a new heart" and "my son, give me thy heart" were distortions of the Bible, according to Dod. In order to make these texts support his view Finney was required to rely not upon the words themselves but upon an appeal to "our natural sense of justice" or to "the common sense of mankind" (an appeal, Dod might have added, often used by Paine and the deists when they sought to discredit the Bible). Finney maintained that the text "make you a new heart and a new spirit, for why will ye die," and others like it, were direct commands from God to all sinners ordering them to effect their own salvation. If God, said Finney, commands His creatures to do something, it is only common sense to believe

---

[22] Dod, "Finney's Sermons," pp. 524, 522, 508, 523, 509, 521, 510, 516, 517.

that he gives them the ability to obey. "Obligation and ability are commensurate" was Finney's famous phrase for it. And he insisted that if the Calvinists taught that men could not change their own hearts then they were either denying the word of God or else were making "God an infinite tyrant." [23]

Although Dod maintained that "the Bible does not inform us that there is any tyranny in God's commanding men to do what they cannot do" and although he claimed that "the common sense of mankind" substantiated the Calvinist view of inability (as for example in such cases as that of "a man under the influence of any dominant passion," such as drink or gluttony, who knows he ought to reform but cannot), nevertheless Finney's argument was clearly more in harmony with the spirit of the age than Dod's. Americans who had wrested their political freedom from the British Empire and their economic self-sufficiency from the seas and the forests of the New World were ready to believe with Finney that God had endowed them with the intelligence, the conscience, and the will power to wrest their spiritual freedom from the grip of Satan. And as good democrats who had, under Jacksonian leadership, won control of American politics from the Federalist aristocrats by laws granting universal manhood suffrage, "the common sense people" (as Finney called them) were persuaded rather than shocked, as Dod was, by Finney's declaration that "the object of the ministry is to get all the people to feel that the devil has no right to rule this world but that they ought all to give themselves to God and vote in the Lord Jesus Christ as the governor of the universe." [24]

In emphasizing this rationalistic and Pelagian aspect of Finney's doctrines, however, it is necessary to remember, as Dod did not do, that there was also a strong pietistic strain in Finney's theology. This is amply demonstrated in the *Lectures on Revivals* by his three lectures on prayer and his lecture on the need for being "filled with the Spirit." For all his lawyer-like logic, for all his comparisons of the Holy Ghost to an advocate arguing before a jury, and his carefully reasoned arguments taken step by step, there was a strong element of mysticism about Finney. (In this regard he again resembles Jonathan Edwards, whom he quotes.)

Time and again in his lectures he speaks of prayer as a means of obtaining close communion with God. He even speaks of

[23] Finney, *Lectures on Revivals*, pp. 108, 206–207.
[24] *Ibid.*, p. 181.

prophecies and coincidences bordering on miracles that were brought about by "the prayer of faith." Finney's revivals, like those of the second Great Awakening in general, were evidence of a resurgent pietism in American Protestantism, a pietism that had been dormant but not dead since the first Great Awakening. The hysterical outbursts in the frontier camp meetings demonstrated just how emotionally and spiritually starved by the arid legalism and formalism of Old School Calvinism the average, unsophisticated churchgoers were. Among the more devout, continual fasting and agonizing all-night prayer meetings became common. The ultimate limit of pietism came with the various perfectionist movements after 1830 and the adventist movement led by William Miller. To most Old School Calvinists, and even to such dignified New School ministers as Beecher and Taylor, pietism was far too powerful an explosive to be trusted. To their minds Finney was guilty of encouraging the worst excesses of the camp meeting exhorters when he spoke approvingly (as he does in Lecture IV of this volume) of a person who prayed so fervently that his nose bled. Finney himself, in the early days of his ministry prayed and fasted so rigorously, "without ceasing," that he frequently had visions in which "a light perfectly ineffable, shone in my soul" and "almost prostrated me to the ground." [25] And throughout his career Finney continually spoke of his being "led by the Spirit" or "instructed by God." He implored his readers in the *Lectures on Revivals* to learn to watch for "leadings of the Spirit," and when these came to follow them without hesitation. If you wish to be filled with the Spirit, he said, "you must yield to his softest and gentlest motions and watch to learn what he would have you do, and yield yourself up to his guidance." [26] This deep emotional reliance upon the leadings of God's Spirit distinguishes the radical pietistic evangelical from the conservative ecclesiastical evangelical and indicates why both Beecher and Dod considered Finney a revolutionary. It also indicates a common bond between Finney's anti-ecclesiasticism and the Jacksonian's anticlericalism. Egalitarian reliance upon the innate common sense of the common man is, after all, only a secular form of the doctrine of the priesthood of all believers.

The implications of Finney's pietism in terms of his perfectionism, his millennialism, and his individualistic social philosophy

---

[25] Finney, *Memoirs*, p. 34.
[26] Finney, *Lectures on Revivals*, p. 123.

are of particular importance in seeing him as a spokesman of his age. But before leaving Dod's review it is important to point out two other criticisms that he launched against Finney in 1835. The first of these was his attack upon Finney's lack of regard for the ecclesiastical system of the Presbyterian Church, and the second was his caustic denunciation of Finney's system of "new measures" in revivals.

In the seventeenth century the Puritans of Massachusetts Bay had fought off the pietists of their day, the Antinomians, Quakers, and Baptists, who challenged the ecclesiastical standing order, by calling them "separatists" possessed of a "desperate enthusiasm." The favorite epithet for pietism employed by Dod and the Old School Calvinists against Finney and the New School radicals was "fanaticism." Not only was Finney fanatical in his theology, his rejection of the doctrines of Calvinism and the tenets of the Westminster Confession that formed the creedal standards of the faith, but he was also fanatical in his disrespect for established ecclesiastical authority and polity. As Dod noted, "the coarse, blustering fanaticism" of Finney's activities and those of his followers had virtually destroyed ecclesiastical order in western New York during the preceding decade. "Ministers who have opposed them have been forced to abandon their charges; and those who have yielded to them have been unsettled . . . it is now a difficult matter among the western churches of New York to find a pastor who has been with his present flock more than two or three years. . . . Rash and reckless men have every where rushed in and pushed matters to extremes." Dod quoted the letters that Nettleton and Beecher had written against Finney in 1827 and, like them, compared Finney's work to that of James Davenport in 1742: "It is well known that Davenport, against whose extravagant fanaticism Edwards wrote at length, is *redivivus* in Mr. Finney. . . ." [27]

Dod was not only concerned with the havoc Finney's revival cohorts were wreaking with church discipline in western New York. He was also annoyed that Finney showed so little respect for the learned theologians of the Eastern seminaries. The eleventh of the lectures on revivals constitutes a serious indictment of the whole system of ministerial education of that day. To a Calvinist there was no more certain sign of dangerous fanaticism than an attack upon a learned ministry, and Finney's *Lectures on Revivals* is full of assertions, explicit and implicit, concerning the in-

[27] Dod, "Finney's Lectures," pp. 661, 657.

adequacies of the average seminary graduate and particularly of the "eminent doctors of divinity." To Finney, "those are the best educated ministers who win the most souls." The "grand defect in educating" ministers was that when they got finished with their seminary training they were not "fit to go into a revival." In these schools the young theologues were "shut out from intercourse with the common people" and had their minds directed "too much to irrelevant matters." "I would say nothing to undervalue or lead you to undervalue a thorough education for ministers. But I do not call that a thorough education which they get in our colleges and seminaries. It does not fit them for their work. I appeal to all experience, whether our young men in seminaries are thoroughly educated for the purpose of winning souls? DO THEY DO IT? Everybody knows they do not." To Finney, a pious young man who had been truly converted and who was "filled with the Spirit" was worth five hundred educated ministers: "So learned students may understand their *hic*, *haec*, *hoc* very well and may laugh at the humble Christian, and call him ignorant, although he may know how to win more souls than five hundred of them." The responsibility for this fell squarely upon the shoulders of the "learned D.D.'s" who are the professors at these schools: "Those fathers who have the training of our young ministers are good men, but they are ancient men, men of another age and stamp from what is needed in these days of excitement when the church and world are rising to new thought and action. . . . Some of them are getting back toward second childhood and ought to resign and give place to younger men who are not rendered physically incapable by age of keeping pace with the onward movements. . . . It is as dangerous and ridiculous for our theological professors, who are withdrawn from the field of conflict to be allowed to dictate, in regard to the measures and movements of the church, as it would be for a general to sit in his bed-chamber and attempt to order a battle." [28]

 This is the perennial argument around which revivals center. It is well to remember that Finney was a pragmatist as well as a pietist. If the church was to fulfil its divinely appointed mission, it must evangelize the world. Those who were winning souls were doing God's work, and those who did not were not. The proof that the New School doctrines and methods were right and those of the Old School wrong was the fact that God blessed the

[28] Finney, *Lectures on Revivals*, pp. 186, 191–192.

work of the New School ministers through revivals and a rich harvest of souls.

Finney carried his "fanatical" opposition to the "traditions of the elders" to its logical anti-ecclesiastical conclusion when he assaulted the judicatures of the Presbyterian Church for putting New School ministers on trial for heresy. In his lecture, "Hindrances to Revivals," he wrote, "Some of the most efficient ministers in the church have been called off from their direct efforts to win souls to Christ to attend day after day and in some instances week after week to charges preferred against them" by heresy hunters. Finney went on specifically to criticize the trials for New School heresy of Nathaniel Beman, George Duffield, and Alfred Barnes. Barnes's trials twice reached the General Assembly, the highest tribunal of the Presbyterian Church and twice were the cause of violent quarreling within that body. Dod was particularly shocked that Finney assaulted even that august assemblage with the blunt remark, "No doubt there is a jubilee in hell every year about the time of the meeting of the General Assembly." [29] On which Dod could only comment, "how to the very life is the fanaticism of" remarks like this.[30]

Dod was less worried about the extremism evident in these frontal assaults upon church polity than he was about the more insidious undermining of good order and sound doctrine that might result from the introduction into the church of Finney's "new measures" for revivalism. "Nothing can be more evident," said Dod, "than that these new measures are remarkably adapted to form and propagate a false religion." [31] In one sense the primary purpose of the *Lectures on Revivals* was to defend the new measures for which Finney had been so violently attacked ever since he began his career. And Dod was perfectly correct in saying that the new measures and the New School theology were "in entire keeping" with each other. Of course, Nathaniel Taylor and Lyman Beecher had been preaching the New School theology long before Finney began his career [32] and Beecher had at first

---

[29] *Ibid.*, pp. 290–292.
[30] Dod, "Finney's Lectures," p. 671.
[31] *Ibid.*, p. 650.
[32] In his excellent study of Nathaniel Taylor, Sidney Mead shows that Taylor was preaching the New School views to his congregation in New Haven in the years 1812–1822. Mead, *Taylor*, pp. 62ff. Taylor actually preached a sermon in this period with the title "The Sinner's Duty to Make Himself a New Heart," which is very similar to Finney's in regard to free will, but it is doubtful whether Fin-

disliked the sensational methods used by the crude western revivalists. But by 1835 it was apparent that the new measures and the new theology would proceed together, for, as Beecher and Finney both knew, they were a natural complement to each other. The New Divinity called upon men to change their own hearts "at once" and the new measures provided the stimulus and the procedures by which they were to do it.

No precise list of what the new measures were was ever made nor could be made, for as Dod rightly pointed out, "The only novelty in the matter is that these measures should be employed in the Presbyterian church in combination with a false theology and a fanatical spirit." [33] Dod claimed that most of Finney's measures originated with the fanatics of the first Great Awakening or with the rude camp meetings exhorters in the second Great Awakening. A few of the "new" measures had been employed by Whitefield or Nettleton or other respectable revivalists but had not been carried to such lengths as Finney carried them. Among the more frequently mentioned and deprecated revival measures that were called new in the 1830's were the following: the setting aside of a period of days for "protracted meetings" during which all other regular and sacred activities ceased while churchgoers devoted themselves entirely to prayer meetings and preaching services; the use of the anxious bench or anxious seat (sometimes called the mourner's bench) to which those particularly anxious or awakened or convicted concerning their need for salvation would repair in order to be specifically exhorted by the minister at the conclusion of his sermon; the use of anxious meetings, held in the lecture room or basement of the church or in private homes, at which the revivalist and local ministers and laymen spoke personally with the anxious and tried to convert them; the frequent use of prayer meetings, sometimes lasting all night, during which individual and congregational prayers were offered both for a general outpouring of the Spirit and for the conversion of specific sinners; the practice of permitting women to offer prayer publicly in mixed or "social" prayer meetings; the employment of a dramatic, colloquial, extemporaneous, and often vituperative preaching style by the revivalist in order to impress the congregation with the necessity for complete and immediate submission to God;

---

ney ever read it, for it was not published until 1858. See Nathaniel W. Taylor, *Practical Sermons* (N.Y., 1858), pp. 397–410.

[33] Dod, "Finney's Lectures," p. 626–627.

itinerant preaching by revival preachers who were "filled with the Spirit" and "felt the call" to preach, whether they were ordained or not.

The abuses arising from these various measures were obvious. Protracted meetings, which were at first called "four-day meetings," quickly were extended to seven, ten, and twenty days during which a whole community was turned upside down by continual concentration on revival excitement. Prayer meetings, all night or otherwise, turned into religious orgies or community mudslinging as officious revivalists and laymen prayed for the conversions of their sin-hardened neighbors and called down wrath upon those "enemies of God and revivals" who failed to cooperate heartily in the meetings. Itinerant revival preachers entered a town or city and having won over a few fervent souls proceeded to denounce local ministers for not having had frequent revivals and for failing to cooperate in this new visitation. Finney admitted in his *Memoirs* that he had frequently taken ministers to task who had not been willing to follow his doctrines or methods. He also told of ministers who were dismissed from their churches as a result of their failure to keep pace with the revival enthusiasm of a majority of their parishioners.

The new measure upon which Dod vented most of his sarcasm and denunciation, however, was the use of the anxious seat. In his lectures Finney ardently defended the practice, because he believed that it compelled the hesitant and hypocritical to prove their desire to be Christians by publicly coming forward and making their decision to be "on the Lord's side." It "breaks the chains of pride," said Finney, and "uncovers the delusions of the human heart," for if the anxious sinner "is not willing to do so small a thing as that, then he is not willing to do anything" for Christ.[34] In a paragraph which shocked Dod into astonishment Finney compared the practice of requiring a sinner to go forward and sit on the anxious seat to the practice of baptism in the days of the apostles. According to Dod, not only was it blasphemous to compare such an innovation to an ordinance of the church, but it implied to sinners that like "a pilgrimage to Mecca" this act was "a necessary step towards their salvation" and that by it "they were rendering to Christ an acceptable service." This requiring the sinner to make an immediate decision for or against Christ, said Dod, would surely lead to the belief among unso-

---

[34] Finney, *Lectures on Revivals*, p. 268.

phisticated people that there is "some wonder-working power in the person's rising before the congregation and taking the assigned place." As such, the anxious seat could only "foster delusion and create false hopes," and its use "should be deprecated as fraught with almost certain evil." [35]

In the light of the subsequent careers of revivalists like Billy Sunday and Billy Graham, whose calls for decisions often brought forward as many as two or three thousand at one meeting, Dod was certainly making an accurate prediction of the formalization of this practice.

Of course what rankled Dod most in the *Lectures on Revivals* was Finney's notion that excitement and innovation were essential to the progress of religion. And Finney himself did not realize that he had exalted into a fundamental dogma what in reality was simply the temporary result of the desiccated state of Calvinism. Because the people of western New York and elsewhere were spiritually and emotionally starved by the stereotyped Old School Calvinism that had for so long constituted their only conception of religion, they had reacted enthusiastically to his vigorous and uninhibited revival methods. Finney thereupon assumed that what had worked for him in Oneida County, New York, in the mid-1820's was part of God's divine economy. Extrapolating from his own experience he worked out a theory of revivalism that for better or for worse, became the accepted basis for one hundred years or more of evangelistic work in the Protestant churches of the United States. On the other hand, Dod and the opponents of Finney generally were so fearful of any innovation whatsoever that they inevitably went down to defeat.

The weaknesses of Finney's reliance upon novelty and excitement were perfectly evident, however, in 1835, and Dod satirized them to good effect. If Finney's view of the need for constant novelty is correct, Dod said, then "the house of God becomes transformed into a kind of religious laboratory." And "would anyone, save the preacher and the trumpeter who are said to have actually tried the trick, approve of stationing a man in the belfry of the church to give emphasis, by a blast from his horn, to the preacher's account of the blowing of the archangel's trump? Phosphoric paintings might be drawn upon the walls of the church, which being rendered suddenly visible by the extinguishment of the lights at the proper point in the preacher's discourse,

[35] Dod, "Finney's Lectures," pp. 644, 637, 643, 641.

would most powerfully aid in the impression of the truth he was delivering. A thousand devices equally effective and equally objectionable might be invented by the exercise of a little ingenuity. . . . ." [36] If Dod had lived long enough he would have seen evangelists who were very ingenious indeed on this score. His retort to Finney's statement that revivalists should, like "the politicians, get up meetings, circulate handbills and pamphlets, blaze away in the newspapers . . . all to gain attention to their cause and elect their candidate" was the logical one: "Where then is the contrast which Paul so often draws between the weapons of our warfare and those with which the world contends" (II Corinthians, 10:4, "for the weapons of our warfare are not carnal . . ."). To which Finney would answer, "means will not produce a revival, we all know, without the blessing of God," but nevertheless God always used worldly means to effect his ends.[37] Advertising and ballyhoo are merely to get the crowds; vigorous preaching is merely to awaken them to the sense of their sinfulness; the anxious bench is merely to compel them to act; but in the last analysis, said Finney, only by the grace of God are men saved.

One final remark is worth making about the Rev. Albert Dod's definitive critique of Finney's *Lectures on Revivals* from the Old School point of view. There can be no doubt that Dod, like Beecher and Nettleton in 1827, saw Finney as a "revolutionary" in more ways than in terms of theology and new measures. Fanaticism to all of these men was demagoguery, and demagoguery had social and political overtones that, as conservatives, these men feared and disliked. Dod noted that Finney's revivalism had already spread desolation through western New York, the "burnt-over region." In his review he expressed the fear that "if it should affect still larger masses . . . it will spread desolation and ruin" throughout the nation for ages to come.[38] The association of gentlemen at Princeton were not great admirers of the self-reliant common men who heard Finney so gladly. They suspected that the lower classes throughout the United States were somehow getting out of hand under Jacksonian leadership. "The great improvements in the mechanic arts and the wide diffusion of knowledge have given a strong impulse to the popular mind," said Dod, "and everywhere the social mass is seen to be in such a state of agitation

---

[36] *Ibid.*, p. 636.
[37] Finney, *Lectures on Revivals*, p. 13.
[38] Dod, "Finney's Lectures," p. 673.

that the slightest breath may make it heave and foam. This being the case, should religion fall in with the excitement and institute measures for fostering it up to a certain point that she may gain a favorable moment for presenting her claims? We had thought that one great object of religion was to allay this undue excitement of the human mind; to check its feverish outgoings towards earthly objects and to teach it without hurry or distraction, in self-collectedness, to put forth its energies in a proper direction and to their best advantage." [39]

These sentences provide a kind of key to the growing gap between the outlook of the Old School Calvinists and the New School Calvinists. It would be too much to say that the Old School looked upon religion as the opiate of the masses or even as a utilitarian method by which the better classes might keep "the social masses" in check. But it would not be wholly inaccurate to see the Old School as defenders of the status quo, aristocratic in temper, and generally unsympathetic to the democratic egalitarianism and optimistic self-reliance that characterized the spirit of the second quarter of the nineteenth century.[40] The Old School clung to the ideal of an organic Christian society guided by the spiritual leadership of the clergy; the New School stood for the individualistic view of society in which each citizen made his own peace with God and went his own way in life. And to this extent Finney's "revolutionary" theology and revival measures, formed on the frontier and based upon the common-sense reasoning of the common man, deserve to be considered as part and parcel of the Jacksonian revolution in American social and intellectual history. This estimate of his work receives strong substantiation from the social philosophy revealed in the *Lectures on Revivals* as well as in all his other writings.

If the essence of Finney's Jacksonian temper lies in his attitude toward progress, this in turn is closely connected with his doctrines of millennialism, disinterested benevolence, and perfectionism. Progress Finney defined as the working out of God's will, and since God was by definition benevolent, His ultimate aim was to produce the great possible happiness in the universe. Because Finney no longer accepted the Calvinist view of God's inscrutable sovereignty and of man's ineradicable depravity and because he

---

[39] *Ibid.*, pp. 633–634.
[40] See Arthur M. Schlesinger, Jr., chap. xxvii, "Jacksonian Democracy and Religion," *The Age of Jackson* (New York, 1945).

INTRODUCTION

did not believe that the Bible justified the view that only a few predestined elect were eligible for salvation, he saw no reason why the whole world might not someday be made up of converted Christians living in brotherly love. Nor did he doubt that as the world became increasingly Christian through the conversion of more and more individuals it would become increasingly happy and prosperous. Men, especially regenerated men, would grow in wisdom, learn all the laws of science, and someday create a perfect utopia which would start the millennium of God's kingdom on earth. When he accepted the post as professor of theology at Oberlin early in 1835 (while still in the midst of writing his lectures on revivalism), he expressly did so in order to help educate "a new race of revival ministers," who would constitute the advance guard of the world-wide evangelistic movement.

Finney was sufficiently patriotic to believe that the United States was to be the first nation in which the whole population would be completely converted. Unlike those theocratically inclined Calvinists (Old School and New School) who saw an inevitable conflict between democracy and religion, Finney believed that democracy was the form of government most approved by God. There is an illuminating chapter on "Human Government" in his *Systematic Theology* (a book based upon his lectures at Oberlin and first published in 1846). In this chapter he stated explicitly that a republic is a "less pure form of self-government" than a democracy, and "a democracy is in many respects the most desirable form of government." In 1776 God, who controls the outcome of all revolutions (as John Locke said), permitted Americans to establish a republican form of government instead of continuing as subjects of a monarchy, because "God always allows his children as much liberty as they are prepared to enjoy" and "the intelligence and virtue of our Puritan forefathers rendered a monarchy an unnecessary burden." [41] Consequently, if Americans continued to grow still more intelligent and virtuous, it was probable that God, in his benevolence, would someday grant them a democratic form of complete self-government that would be tantamount to a withering away of the state. Finney of course recognized the possibility of a nation's backsliding in virtue and hence slipping into a monarchy or a despotism, but he did not think

---

[41] I have taken these quotations from the one-volume edition of *Lectures on Systematic Theology*, revised and edited by the Rev. George Redford of Worcester, England (London, 1851), pp. 362ff.

this would happen in the United States where revivals were flourishing, education was expanding, and social reform was overcoming one evil after another.

Finney clearly did not share the view of Dwight L. Moody and most other revivalists of the post-Civil War period that only the cataclysm of Christ's Second Coming could bring about the millennium. However, this premillennial pessimism was advanced in Finney's day by William Miller, the Baptist preacher who predicted the return of Christ and the end of the world in the year 1843. Finney flatly rejected Miller's views. "I have examined Mr. Miller's theory," Finney wrote, "and am persuaded that what he expects to come after the judgment will come before it. Read the sixty-fifth chapter of Isaiah. The Prophet there speaks of the advancement to be made as the creation of a new heaven and a new earth." [42] Scattered throughout the *Lectures on Revivals* there are continual references to the millennial hope. Perhaps the most striking of these, and one that doubtless astonished the less optimistic Albert Dod, was Finney's statement in Lecture XV that "if the church will do her duty the millennium may come in this country in three years." [43]

Probably Finney did not believe that the church would or could do its duty until all ministers were New School "revival ministers" and all Christians were dedicated to the doctrines of disinterested benevolence and perfectionism. In some ways it is odd that Finney should have preached the doctrine of disinterested benevolence, for it was originally put forth by Jonathan Edwards and his pupil, Samuel Hopkins, as a complement to the doctrine of God's absolute sovereignty. Samuel Hopkins was a hero of the Old School Calvinists of New England, many of whom referred to themselves as "Hopkinsians." And Finney devoted much of his time to attacking "Hopkinsianism" as a particularly malevolent form of "hyper-Calvinism." It is probable that Finney adopted the doctrine of disinterested benevolence without realizing who its authors were.

Hopkins set forth the doctrine in 1773 in his book *An Inquiry into the Nature of True Holiness* (a gloss upon Edwards' book on *The Nature of True Virtue*). The key to the doctrine is Hopkins' statement that true holiness is "disinterested benevolent affection" toward "God and our neighbor" and "true benevolence

[42] Oberlin *Evangelist* April 12, 1843, p. 58.
[43] Finney, *Lectures on Revivals*, p. 306.

always seeks the greatest good of the whole." [44] Hopkins meant by this to define virtue or holiness in terms of cosmic altruism. But Finney transformed the doctrine into cosmic utilitarianism. He defined benevolence in terms of the greatest happiness of the greatest number and spoke of "the utility of benevolence" as the fact that benevolent actions increased both the happiness of our neighbors, of God, and of the universe in general. Hence, in his *Lectures on Revivals* he insisted that all young converts "should set out with a determination to aim at being useful in the highest degree" and "if they can see an opportunity where they can do more good, they must embrace it whatever may be the sacrifice to themselves." [45] This is the heart and core of nineteenth-century evangelical activism, and as Finney's comments on the various social issues of the day indicate in these lectures, he and his converts embraced the great reform movements of the day with the passion of crusaders. It is not surprising that in his *Systematic Theology* he said of all true Christians that "their spirit is necessarily that of the reformer. To the universal reformation of the world they stand committed." [46]

Among the many reforms of the day in which Finney expressed interest in his *Lectures on Revivals* were abolition, temperance, dietary regulations (especially the disuse of all stimulants, including tea and coffee), education, gambling, dueling, and hygiene (see his remarks in Lecture III on the evils of "that filthy poison, tobacco"). In addition he attacked the sins of fashionable display, luxury, idleness, novel-reading, theater-going, card-playing, dancing, and gluttony. There is a close relationship between Finney's moral code and Victorian prudery. Although the twentieth century mislabeled this evangelical moralizing "puritanism," most of it was simply lower-middle-class pietism reacting against what Finney called "the starch and flattery of high life." An historically inclined sociologist could discover much about the class structure and the social code of the 1830's by reading these lectures. The general reader will doubtless find these passages among the most amusing, especially his remarks about the evils of tightly laced corsets.

But it is important to note that Finney's attitude toward social

---

[44] See Samuel Hopkins, *An Inquiry into the Nature of True Holiness* (Newport, Rhode Island, 1773), pp. 41, 57, 68, 71.
[45] Finney, *Lectures on Revivals*, p. 404.
[46] Finney, *Systematic Theology*, p. 450.

reform, like his attitude toward politics and economics, was a distinctly moralistic one. That is, he believed that personal moral reform rather than political or legislative action was the surest and fastest way to improve the social order. The first step toward the millennium was to convert men to Christ; the rest would follow automatically from this. And herein lies the conservative side of Finney's preaching. For there is an inevitable tendency among pietistic evangelicals to limit their horizon entirely to the regeneration of individuals and to deny or ignore the complexities of custom, prejudice, and sectional or class conflict that lie at the root of so much social injustice. Pessimistic, premillennial revivalists since the Civil War have usually opposed efforts toward social reform on a broad scale, because they maintain that nothing but the return of Christ can possibly solve the major problems of this world. But Finney erred on the optimistic side. He believed that revivals could produce such sweeping results, could reform so many individuals so completely and rapidly, that legislative attempts at reform paled in comparison. In any case, his words spoke louder than his actions on the crucial reform movements of his day. Finney's stand on the question of slavery, for example, on which issue he was more radical than most Jacksonian democrats but not nearly so radical as an extreme pietist like William Lloyd Garrison, typifies this conservative element in his outlook.

As he states in Lecture XV in this volume, Finney firmly believed in 1835 that slavery was not only a sin which all Christians should oppose but that it was a problem with which the churches also must be concerned. As a pastor he refused to admit anyone to membership in his church who owned or trafficked in slaves. And yet Finney showed the prevailing prejudice of his day about social equality between Negroes and whites. He segregated Negro members from whites in his New York church, and he wished the Negro students at Oberlin to sit separately from whites. When his friend Lewis Tappan expostulated with him concerning this lack of Christian charity, Finney gave the standard answer that social equality was not a Christian duty, and he asked Tappan whether he would want his daughter to marry a Negro.[47]

But more important in this regard was Finney's cautious attitude toward carrying antislavery agitation too far and too fast — especially in terms of legislative activity. When mobs in New

[47] For a more detailed discussion of these points, see McLoughlin, *Modern Revivalism*, pp. 108ff.

York City attacked the home of his friend Arthur Tappan in July 1834, Finney began to retreat from his outspoken endorsement of the movement. He wrote to his wife that fall, "I don't believe that it would do to say too much about abolition here in publick."[48] And in his revival lectures delivered that winter he repeatedly urged his abolitionist friends "to avoid a censorious spirit," to "consider it calmly," and to "act judiciously."[49] Perhaps the most active and effective leader of the abolition movement in the 1830's was the brilliant and energetic young Theodore Weld, who had been converted by Finney in Utica in 1826. Weld always looked up to Finney as his "father in Christ," but when Weld tried to persuade the students at Oberlin to become abolitionist lecturers, Finney took the students aside and urged them not to do it. As one student wrote to Weld in August 1836: Finney "poured out his soul before us in agony in view of our continuing in the abolition field" and said that "the only hope of the country, the church, the oppressor, and the slave was in *wide spread* revivals."[50] And Finney himself wrote to Weld about this time to try to persuade him that the whole slavery problem could be solved "in 2 years" if only "the publick mind can be engrossed with the subject of salvation and make abolition an appendage [of revivals] just as we made temperance an appendage of revival in Rochester."[51] To an ardent social reformer such an attitude smacks of blind escapism, but to a pietist like Finney it is simply reliance upon God.

Much the same attitude exhibited itself in Finney's statements about politics. As he wrote in Lecture XV in this volume, it did not seem to him important whether a political candidate was for or against Andrew Jackson, whether he favored the National Bank or not, whether he was a Whig or a Democrat. The only important question was whether he was a Christian and an honest man or not. And in the field of economics, Finney, like most revivalists ever since, expressed more concern over the evils of indebtedness and the spiritual welfare of factory workers than over whether the incipient industrial revolution in the United States placed new social responsibilities upon Christian businessmen and

---

[48] Finney to his wife, November 24, 1834, in the Finney Papers, Oberlin College Library.
[49] Finney, *Lectures on Revivals*, pp. 299ff.
[50] James A. Thome to Weld, August 9, 1836, in *Weld Letters*, ed. Barnes and Dumond, I, 327–328.
[51] Finney to Weld, July 21, 1836, *ibid.*, I, 318–319.

upon the churches. Finney was so far from understanding the whole system of laissez faire capitalism that he condemned the practice of doing business on credit and echoed the old Puritan demand for a just price and a just wage.[52]

There is a close connection between this pietistic attitude toward reform and Finney's doctrine of perfectionism. His emphasis upon personal regeneration as the only basis for social reform, his belief in progress, and his doctrine that "obligation and ability are commensurate" all combined to push him to the conclusion that the most desperate need of the age was a higher degree of consecration among professing Christians. For a perfect society must consist of perfect men. Finney did not evolve the view that came to be known as "Oberlin Perfectionism" (but which he preferred to call "entire consecration" or "sanctification") until after the *Lectures on Revivals* was completed. His *Lectures to Professing Christians*, published in 1837, was the first clear-cut statement of this doctrine — a doctrine that at once caused almost all of his New School colleagues to disown him. But there are several passages in the *Lectures on Revivals* that clearly indicate that this point of view had always been implicit in his preaching. For example, he states in Lecture XIX, all converts "should aim at being holy and not rest satisfied till they are as perfect as God."[53] If this statement is taken in conjunction with his theory that God never commands any action with which man is not capable of complying, then the conclusion follows that all Christians can become perfect, for Christ declared, "Be ye therefore perfect even as your Father which is in heaven is perfect." Albert Dod saw this, perhaps even before Finney, and pointed it out in his review of the *Lectures on Revivals*. But Dod assumed that Finney's perfectionism (which was to him but the proof of the absurdity of New School Pelagianism) was precisely the same as that of John Humphrey Noyes and various other New England and western New York perfectionists in these years. It is necessary to point out that Finney expressly repudiated what he called the "antinomian perfectionism" of Noyes, because its purpose was to release the inhibitions and permit the perfected Christian complete freedom. To Noyes one of the most important freedoms for the perfected was sexual freedom and in the communistic community which he

---

[52] See McLoughlin, *Modern Revivalism*, pp. 113ff., for a discussion of Finney's political and economic views.

[53] Finney, *Lectures on Revivals*, p. 403.

founded at Oneida, New York, Noyes and his associates practised a form of free love called "complex marriage," which thoroughly shocked Finney. Finney's perfectionism was based upon precisely the opposite approach to behavior. He believed that an entirely consecrated or sanctified Christian would become more perfect as he learned how to practice self-denial and to avoid self-indulgence. Declaring that "a self-indulgent Christian is a contradiction," Finney spoke of attaining "perfect obedience to the law of God." [54] And of course the law of God implied conformity to the entire code of Victorian prudery and small-town morality that played so prominent a part in his exhortatory preaching. To Finney a Christian who gave up drinking tea and coffee was on the road to perfection, while one who took up "complex marriage" was on the primrose path to hell. But at least he and Noyes agreed that men were perfectible and that a perfect social order was well within the realm of possibility for Americans who were alive in the year 1835.

In the light of Finney's theology and social philosophy it is of some interest to compare briefly his views with those of a typical Jacksonian spokesman like John L. O'Sullivan in order to see how much they had in common. O'Sullivan, who was the part-owner and editor of the *United States Magazine and Democratic Review* is generally acknowledged to have been a particularly articulate and representative spokesman of the Jacksonian spirit. In the first number of his newspaper, in October 1837, he issued a statement of his political and social philosophy that is often quoted as a manifesto of the age.[55] Among the beliefs that O'Sullivan here espoused were "the principle of democratic republicanism," "an abiding confidence in the virtue, intelligence, and full capacity for self-government of the great mass of our people," and a deep-seated dislike for those "aristocratic interests" or "better classes" who claim a "more enlightened wisdom" than the average man and therefore a greater right to govern. Finney would have agreed with all of these beliefs. O'Sullivan then went on to advocate "the general diffusion of knowledge" among all classes, to acknowledge "the moral elements implanted by its Creator in human society," and to profess "a true and living faith in the existence and attributes of

---

[54] Finney, *Systematic Theology* (Oberlin, 1878), pp. 312–316.
[55] See, for example, *Social Theories of Jacksonian Democracy: Representative Writings of the Period 1825–1850*, ed. Joseph L. Blau (New York, 1954), which includes this editorial.

that Creator." Finney used more theological and Scriptural terminology, but he would have endorsed all of this. In his argument for the view that that government is best which governs least, O'Sullivan, like Finney, saw "the democratic principle walking hand in hand with the sister spirit of Christianity" down through time until "our theory and practice of government shall be sifted and analyzed down to the lowest point of simplicity consistent with the preservation of some degree of national organization." O'Sullivan attacked men, like Beecher and Dod, who "cast the weight of their social influence against the cause of democracy under the false prejudice of an affinity between it and infidelity." The cause of Democracy "is the cause of Christianity" he asserted. And just as Finney attacked the dead hand of Calvinism for trying to preserve the outmoded "traditions of the elders," so O'Sullivan argued that progress depended upon avoiding "that specious sophistry by which old evils always struggle to perpetuate themselves by appealing to our veneration for the wisdom of our fathers." Like Finney, O'Sullivan praised the great step forward made by those who led the American Revolution and declared that Americans were "a chosen people" with a "glorious destiny," which would be guided by the unseen hand of Providence. The whole of this manifesto breathes the optimistic faith in God, in man, in America, and in the future that underlies Finney's fervent pietism. Both men saw God as a benevolent Creator who has endowed human kind with moral principles and who requires of all men the abandonment of selfish desires and a devotion to the reformation of the world. There is even in O'Sullivan something of Finney's distrust of the wealth and social pretensions of the *nouveaux riches* of the wicked cities. O'Sullivan deprecates the rising "cities, where wealth accumulates, where luxury gradually unfolds its corrupting tendencies, where aristocratic habits and social classifications form and strengthen themselves, where the congregation of men stimulates and exaggerates all ideas."

There is no denying, of course, that there was a strong tinge of rationalism, free thought, and anticlericalism in the Jacksonian spirit, which runs directly counter to Finney's evangelical temper. And, too, the Jacksonian politicians were opposed to such moral reforms as temperance, Sabbath legislation, and abolition, just as Finney was uninterested in the political and economic reforms of the party platform. Finney probably shared the view of his close friend — Lewis Tappan regarding Andrew Jackson. Tappan stated that the General was "a very unfit man to be at the head of the government." [56] But there were many reasons why a pietist might dislike Jackson without disliking the principles of Jacksonian democracy. And it can be said that Finney and Jackson, each in his own way, were striving for much the same kind of free, individualistic, and egalitarian society.[57]

In concluding this introduction it is only fair to Finney to point out that ten years after publishing his *Lectures on Revivals* he had some serious second thoughts about many of the extreme things he had written in 1835. Consequently he wrote a series of thirty-two short "Letters on Revivals," which appeared in the Oberlin *Evangelist* every fortnight from January 29, 1845, through June 24, 1846. Some publisher will render a service to evangelical and historical literature by resurrecting these pithy, personal comments on revivalism by the nineteenth century's foremost evangelist. Finney realized by 1846 that he had been over-optimistic about the progress of revivalism. "For the last ten years revivals of religion have been gradually becoming more and more superficial," he wrote. Ministers "have seen the disastrous results of modern revivals so frequently that they honestly entertain the doubt whether they are upon the whole desirable." [58] Recognizing the considerable influence his own career and publications had had in establishing the theory and practise of modern revivalism Finney offered some apologies and corrections to rescue revivalism from

[56] Quoted in Charles C. Cole, Jr., *The Social Ideas of the Northern Evangelists 1826–1860* (New York, 1954), p. 140. It may be worth noting here, however, that another of Finney's close friends, the ardent New School leader, Nathaniel S. S. Beman, was an ardent supporter and friend of Andrew Jackson. See Robert E. Thompson, *A History of the Presbyterian Church in the United States* (New York, 1895) p. 109, note 1.

[57] In contrast to the constantly expressed fear and distrust of democracy in the writings of Old School Calvinists and of New School conservatives (like Lyman Beecher) I have found almost no such statements by Finney apart from a pious doubt now and then about "a government of mere opinions like ours, in the hands of a people who fear not God, with a temporizing ministry, a licentious press" etc., etc. (Oberlin *Evangelist*, February 18, 1846, p. 27.) Perhaps the most conservative statement by Finney about politics was made in a letter to the Oberlin *Evangelist* (September 24, 1845, p. 155) in which he protested that while he had no objection to ministers preaching about political matters, "If lay members of the church who have property, talents and influence will put forth the appropriate exertions to scatter light on political questions . . . it will save the minister the necessity. . . ." See also, Oberlin *Evangelist*, May 21, 1845, p. 83, for a remark about the "ultra-democratic tendency of mind" among some fanatical reformers — presumably men like William Lloyd Garrison who were willing to trample on the Bible and the Constitution in order to attain their goal.

[58] Oberlin *Evangelist*, February 12, 1845, p. 27.

disrepute. "I erred in manner and in spirit," he wrote of his early career, saying that in many respects "I fell short of securing all the desirable results which might have been secured had I been free from the faults" that "ripening" knowledge and experience had now made clear. He did not, however, offer to retract any of his basic theological doctrines nor reverse any of the basic principles for promoting revivals that he had formerly espoused. But he did admit that some of the new measures and methods he had sanctioned were liable to grave abuse. And he also saw that his overemphasis upon obtaining the immediate conversion of sinners had overlooked the necessity for cultivating in young Christians the means of spiritual growth that would prevent backsliding.

The "Letters on Revivals" contain too much material to be summarized adequately here. But the general tenor of their argument can be disclosed by quoting some of Finney's more revealing comments upon his own practices: "I have laid . . . too much stress upon the natural ability of sinners to the neglect of showing them the nature and extent of their dependence upon the grace of God," he said in one of the first letters.[59] Perhaps because of this there has been of late too much preaching "the philosophy of religion [rather] than the great facts of revelation. Into this mistake I am sure that I have often fallen myself. Where the preacher is so metaphysical and philosophical as to leave the impression that everything about religion can be comprehended and that nothing can be received which cannot be explained . . . great mischief is a certain result."[60] Albert Dod, if he read the Oberlin *Evangelist*, must have been pleased to see this change of heart.

But Dod would have been even more pleased by other comments: "The more I have seen of revivals," Finney went on, "the more I am impressed with the importance of keeping excitement down. . . . I have learned to . . . feel much more confidence in apparent conversions that occur where there is greater calmness of mind."[61] "Efforts to promote revivals of religion have become so mechanical, there is so much policy and machinery, so much dependence upon means and measures, so much of man and so little of God, that the character of revivals has greatly changed within the last few years."[62] And not only were the new professional

---
[59] *Idem.*
[60] *Ibid.*, April 9, 1845, p. 59.
[61] *Ibid.*, April 23, 1845, p. 69.
[62] *Ibid.*, December 17, 1845, p. 205.

revivalists making a business of excitement but the church was forgetting its duty to reform society. "The Church with a great many ministers, have resorted to the plea of using more suasion as the means of ridding the world of intemperance, licentiousness, slavery," etc., but it is necessary "to secure legislation that shall put these abominations away. They are afraid to employ government lest it should be a departure from the system of moral suasion." [63] In his dismay at the waning of the reform fever that had made the preceding decades so full of schemes for world reformation and had given to revivals such a powerful stimulus Finney began to lean more and more toward government coercion upon those conservatives who were thwarting the purification of society. As for the state of revival preaching itself, he offered the significant comment (which Asahel Nettleton would have heartily endorsed), "There are comparatively few men well qualified for Evangelists." [64]

It is apparent that Finney had lived to regret the direction revivalism was taking under the authority of his handbook on the subject. But in spite of these frank acknowledgments of the shortcomings and misplaced emphases in the *Lectures on Revivals*, Finney by no means repudiated his earlier work. In fact, the main burden of the "Letters on Revivals" in 1845–1846 was to the effect that a few incompetent and overzealous evangelists had carried his methods to extremes, while the regular ministers had been either too fearful to correct the abuses or else had become too involved in ecclesiastical and social activities. Too many ministers "have given their attention to Church-politics, Church-government, and Ecclesiastical proceedings" instead of working to save souls, he wrote.[65] And too many church members had come to believe that religion consisted primarily in religiosity; "To visit and talk and bustle about and do the work of the Lord" on a strictly businesslike basis, he said wryly, has become the characteristic of most religious activity.[66] There was, he complained in 1846, too much sectarianism, too much heresy-hunting, too much policy-making.

---

[63] *Ibid.*, January 21, 1846, p. 11. This is a clear departure from Finney's earlier view that all reform should come about as an appendage of revivals. Disappointed perfectionists often have a tendency to enact by force what they formerly thought could come about by spiritual means. By 1864 Finney was so rabid against the South that he wanted to see Benjamin Butler elected President in order that all the traitors might be hung. See Cole, *Northern Evangelists*, pp. 204–211, 219, 227.

[64] Oberlin *Evangelist*, March 4, 1846, p. 35.

[65] *Ibid.*, February 26, 1845, p. 34.

[66] *Ibid.*, July 16, 1845, p. 115.

At the root of it, the cause of the falling-off in revivals after 1835 was that the ministers and church members had grown cold and formal and needed to "be quickened" with the old zeal. There was nothing wrong with revivalism except that there was not enough of the genuine article around: "I do not believe that this government could exist in its present form fifty years without revivals." [67]

In 1868 Finney was asked to edit a revised and enlarged edition of his *Lectures on Revivals*. Looking back over the course of his long life he did not decide to retract his earlier views. He did not even decide to include in this new edition some of the second thoughts he had had in 1845–1846. Instead he re-issued the first edition of 1835 almost unchanged (except for rewriting the last two lectures in more ample, but not doctrinally different, form). The world had altered greatly in those thirty-three years, and the revivalists who were currently holding the field preached that it was getting steadily worse and worse. But Finney retained his faith to the end. He died in 1875 without ever having lost the buoyant spirit of the days of America's adolescence in which he had played so large a part.

[67] *Ibid.*, February 18, 1846, p. 27.

*Chronology of the Life of
Charles Grandison Finney (1792–1875)*

1792 — born August 29 in Warren, Connecticut. Seventh child of Sylvester and Rebecca Finney. Father a farmer and Revolutionary veteran whose ancestors were early settlers in Plymouth Plantation.

1794 — moved with his family to Oneida County, New York. Attended common schools and Hamilton Oneida Academy (1806–1808).

1808 — moved with his family to Henderson, New York, near the shore of Lake Ontario.

1808–1812 — taught district school near Henderson.

1812–1814 — returned to Warren, Connecticut, to attend high school and prepare for Yale.

1814–1816 — having decided against entering Yale, taught school in New Jersey.

1816 — returned to Henderson, New York.

1818 — entered law office of Benjamin Wright of Adams, New York, to study for the bar.

1820 — admitted to the bar.

1821 — had intense conversion experience on October 10. Gave up his career as a lawyer to study for the ministry.

1821–1824 — studied theology and languages with the Rev. George Gale, pastor of the Presbyterian church in Adams, New York. Licensed to preach by the Presbytery of St. Lawrence, December 30, 1823. Ordained as an evangelist by the Oneida Presbytery, July, 1824. Married, October, 1824.

1824–1826 — conducted sensational revival meetings in small towns of western New York.

1826–1827 — conducted revivals in Utica and Troy. Converted Theodore Weld in Utica. Attacked by Asahel Nettleton for using "new measures" in revivalism. Attended New Lebanon Convention in July, 1827, where Lyman Beecher and other New England ministers tried to persuade him and his friends to modify their revival methods.

1827–1829 — conducted revival meetings in Wilmington, Philadelphia, Lancaster, Reading. Signed peace treaty with Beecher in Philadelphia, May 27, 1828.

1829–1830 — conducted first revival in New York City at the invitation of Anson G. Phelps and David L. Dodge. The *New York Evangelist* founded March 6, 1830, to publicize his views. (Joshua Leavitt made editor in 1832).

1830–1831 — conducted the most successful revival of his career in Rochester, New York.

1831–1832 — conducts revivals in Providence and Boston. Lyman Beecher cooperated in the latter. Preached "New Heart" sermon in October, 1831, and was attacked for heresy by Asa G. Rand.

1832 — accepted pastorate of Chatham Street Chapel (the Second Free Presbyterian Church) in New York City at the request of Arthur and Lewis Tappan. Stricken with cholera at his installation service, October 5, 1833.

1833 — New York Anti-Slavery Society formed in Chatham Street Chapel, October 2.

1834 — took ocean voyage to Mediterranean for his health, January-July. Persuaded his church to refuse to admit slaveholders to communion in November. The first of his twenty-two Friday night lectures on "Revivals of Religion" published in the *New York Evangelist*, December 6.

1835 — accepted position as Professor of Theology at Oberlin Collegiate Institute (later Oberlin College) in February and held this post until his death. Published *Lectures on Revivals of Religion* in May and *Sermons on Various Subjects* in June or July. Left New York City for Oberlin in May but continued to be pastor of Chatham Street Chapel where he preached in the winter months.

1836 — withdrew from the Presbyterian Church on March 2 to accept pastorate of Broadway Tabernacle (Congregational) in New York City. Published *Sermons on Important Subjects*. Began series of lectures to professing Christians in Broadway Tabernacle in December in which he first expounded his perfectionist views.

1837 — gave up New York pastorate, April 6. Became pastor of Oberlin Congregational Church (until 1872). Published *Lectures to Professing Christians*.

1838 — helped to found the Oberlin *Evangelist*, October.

1840 — published *Skeletons of a Course of Theological Lectures* and *Views of Sanctification*.

1842 — conducted particularly successful revival in Rochester.

1843 — attacked William Miller's theory of the Second Coming of Christ.

1845 — published *Letters on Revivals*, which first appeared in the Oberlin *Evangelist*.

1846 — published *Lectures on Systematic Theology*.

1849–1850 — conducted a series of revival meetings in various towns and cities in England including Birmingham, London, and Worcester.

1851 — conducted revival meetings in Hartford, Connecticut, in which Horace Bushnell cooperated.

1851–1866 — served as President of Oberlin College.

1857 — conducted revival meetings in Boston and Providence during the Great Prayer Meeting Revival that swept the country.

1859–1860 — conducted second revival tour in England and Scotland; held meetings in Manchester, Edinburgh, and London.

1868 — completed manuscript of his memoirs, which was published posthumously in 1876.

1869 — published *The Character, Claims, and Practical Workings of Freemasonry*.

1875 — died in Oberlin, August 16.

The following works were published posthumously: *Memoirs* (New York, 1876); *Sermons on Gospel Themes* (Oberlin, 1876); *Sermons on the Way of Salvation* (Oberlin, 1891).

Bibliographical Note on This Edition

This volume of Finney's *Lectures on Revivals of Religion* is based upon the first edition, which was published on May 15, 1835, by Leavitt, Lord and Company, publishers, 180 Broadway, New York. The lectures had been published previously in the columns The *New York Evangelist* had been founded in March 1830 by May 2, 1835. It was the heavy demand for back numbers of this weekly newspaper by those who wished to have a complete set of the lectures that led to the decision to publish them in book form.

The origin of the lectures is in itself of some interest. Finney told the story in his *Memoirs*, and there is no reason to doubt it. The *New York Evangelist* had been founded in March 1830 by some of Finney's well-to-do lay supporters in the city. As its subhead read, the *New York Evangelist* was "Devoted to Revivals of Religion, Doctrinal Discussion, Practical Godliness, and Religious Intelligence." More specifically it was designed to be a mouthpiece of the New School theology and "New Measure" revival movement, which Finney and his friends felt were not being fairly represented in either the religious or secular press of the East. The paper was non-denominational, although its main support came from Presbyterians, Congregationalists, and "Presbygationalists," or Plan of Union churches. Its peak circulation was probably about 7,500. In 1832 the Rev. Joshua Leavitt became its editor.

Leavitt was a graduate of Yale and an ordained minister, but he spent most of his life as an editor and a promoter of reform movements (after leaving the *New York Evangelist* he edited the *Emancipator* and the *Independent*). He was an able editor, but he had a tendency to espouse his views on moral reform so strongly as to antagonize many of the paper's subscribers. The antislavery cause was a particularly delicate subject in New York City in the mid-1830's and when Finney departed for an ocean voyage to recoup his health after a seige of cholera in January 1834, he urged Leavitt to be more "prudent" about pushing abolitionism in the paper than he had been. But when Finney returned from his cruise in July 1834, he was met at the boat by a distraught Leavitt who cried, "Brother Finney, I have ruined the *Evangelist*. I have not been as prudent as you cautioned me to be. . . ." The paper was losing subscribers at the rate of sixty per day, and Leavitt feared that unless something was done quickly it would soon have to cease publication.

However, Leavitt had an idea. Finney was just returned from a long absence, and he was acknowledged to be one of the foremost revival preachers of his day. If Finney would consent to "write a series of articles on revivals," said Leavitt, he had "no doubt it would restore the paper immediately to favor." Finney mulled the idea over, and then told Leavitt that he would preach a series of Friday night lectures on revivals to his church members in the Chatham Street Chapel that Leavitt, if he liked, could take down and report in the columns of the *Evangelist*. And so it began.

Finney did not write out these lectures any more than he ever wrote out his sermons. He merely prepared a brief skeleton or outline and preached extemporaneously from that. Leavitt did not know shorthand, but he had a good ear, a quick pencil, and a retentive memory. He attended every lecture, taking the words down in an abbreviated form, and the next morning he would sit down and rewrite the lecture from his notes and rush it off to the printer. Finney did not see the lectures in this form until they appeared in the newspaper on the following Saturday. However, he always maintained that Leavitt had caught both the spirit and the content of them very well. The only criticism Finney offered was that the lectures averaged "not less than an hour and three quarters in their delivery. But all that he [Leavitt] could catch and report could be read probably in thirty minutes." Nevertheless the public was well pleased, and those who had heard Finney speak said that Leavitt had done an excellent job in every respect in capturing the essence of Finney's subject matter and style. Subscriptions to the newspaper quickly increased, and Leavitt stated that by the time the twenty-two lectures were completed the *Evangelist* had obtained 2,600 new subscribers — far more than he had previously lost. (He shrewdly printed up 3000 extra copies of the sermons on newsprint, which he offered free to all new subscribers.)

When it was decided to publish the sermons in book form Finney agreed to revise the versions as printed in the *Evangelist*. The two men also agreed to split the royalties between them. (The 438 page volume sold at retail for one dollar.) It is worth noting that Finney is correct in stating in his preface that he had little time in which to make his revisions, for it was not decided to publish the book until the middle of March 1835, and it was ready for the public by the middle of May. However, it should also be pointed out that thirty-three years later, when an Oberlin publisher persuaded Finney to issue a new revised and enlarged edition of the volume, Finney made almost no changes in the 1835 edition except to rewrite the last two lectures. (He did however change "ain't" to "is not" and "can't" to "cannot," thereby losing some of the informal quality of the first edition.)

In preparing this edition for the John Harvard Library I have seen no reason to use the later edition (nor any of the English editions). The first edition was the most popular and the most widely read. Twelve thousand copies of it were sold within the first three months after publication. According to the custom of the day the publishers marked "Second edition" or "Third edition" on the title pages whenever they ran off an additional set of reprints (each printing consisted of 2000 copies). But I have checked these other "editions" and found that they were obviously printed from the same plates for they contain exactly the same pagination and the same typographical errors. Finney reports that the book was printed by two different publishers in England (one of whom issued 80,000 copies within Finney's lifetime) and that it was translated into Welsh, French, and German for editions in those countries. But Finney had no connection with any of these foreign editions. I have looked at one of the English editions and have occasionally annotated changes by its editor where they seemed of interest. The most amusing change I noted was that the London edition published by Simpkin, Marshall, Co. in 1840, omitted the paragraph in Lecture XX in which Finney called tea a "useless stimulant" and insisted that no true Christian would drink it.

In order to avoid excessive annotation, I have not indicated every variation between the sermons as printed in the *New York Evangelist* and the first edition. Nor have I tried to include every variation that was made in the edition of 1868. I have tried, however, to note any variations among editions that seemed of significance in evaluating Finney's doctrines, style, social philosophy, or revival methods. I have also included some references to the thirty-two "Letters on Revivals" that Finney published in the Oberlin *Evangelist* in 1845–1846 as a kind of supplement to the lectures. On the whole Finney's views changed very little after 1835 except in regard to perfectionism or sanctification. But this doctrine is relevant to his views on revivalism only in that Finney came to espouse it when he became disillusioned with the failure of the converts of his early revivals to live up to the high pitch of

Christian consecration that they had embraced at the time they were converted under his preaching.

Because I believe that the punctuation, capitalization, italicizing, and subheadings of the lectures are an intrinsic part of their style and their historical interest, I have left them unchanged. Except for obvious cases of misspelling or typographical error this edition is exactly the same as the first edition of 1835. In a few instances the paragraph numbering proved too much for both Leavitt and Finney and they either left out numbers or printed the same number twice. I have corrected this. I have also retained Finney's own footnotes, indicating which are his and which are mine.

Finally it ought to be mentioned that books about revivals were not at all uncommon in this period. The two most important and influential of these, next to Finney's, were Calvin Colton's *History and Character of American Revivals* (2d. ed., London, 1832) and William B. Sprague's *Lectures on Revivals of Religion* (Albany, 1832). Sprague's book is of particular interest because it was written by a moderate Old School Calvinist who was alarmed at the new measures being introduced at this time by Finney and his friends. Finney's lectures may be seen in part as a rebuttal to Sprague's book. It is also a painful duty to point out that Finney evidently had been reading Calvin Colton's book on this subject prior to delivering his lectures (or else Leavitt turned to it to fill out some passages he had missed), for there are parallels between the two volumes that are too similar to be coincidental. (Compare particularly pp. 63–64 and 204–220 in Colton's book with pp. 12–14, 21–22, 174–175, 206–207, 347–350, 362–375 in this volume.

It should also be pointed out that the whole problem of revivalism was thrashed out in countless articles in periodicals during the years 1825–1840, which should be consulted by any serious student of the question. Perhaps the most important and famous of these was Horace Bushnell's "The Spiritual Economy of Revivals of Religion," *Quarterly Christian Spectator*, X (February 1838), pp. 131–147. Bushnell, though somewhat equivocal in his reservations about revivalism in this article, did put forth many of the ideas that later appeared in his book, *Christian Nurture*, and the article is therefore significant as the first tentative argument against revivals by a New School theologian. However, as I have tried to spell out in some detail elsewhere, Finney's book remains the single most important work in understanding the nature of modern revivalism.

LECTURES

ON

REVIVALS OF RELIGION

A daguerreotype of Finney and his second wife, Elizabeth Atkinson, taken during their evangelistic tour of Britain in 1850 during which Mrs. Finney conducted the "female prayer meetings."

Courtesy of Oberlin College Library

Interior of Broadway Tabernacle, the Congregational Church built for and in part designed by Finney in New York, 1835.

Courtesy of Oberlin College Library

THE LECTURER'S PREFACE

Let it be remembered, that these Lectures were delivered to *my own congregation*. They were entered upon, without my having previously marked out any plan or outline of them, and have been pursued, from week to week, as one subject naturally introduced another, and as, from one lecture to another, I saw the state of our people seemed to require.

I consented to have the Editor of the Evangelist report them, upon his own responsibility, because he thought that it might excite a deeper interest in, and extend the usefulness of his paper. And as I am now a Pastor, and have not sufficient health to labour as an Evangelist, and as it has pleased the Head of the Church to give me some experience in revivals of religion, I thought it possible, that, while I was doing the work of a Pastor in my own church, I might, in this way, be of some little service to the churches abroad.[1]

I found a particular inducement to this course, in the fact, that on my return from the Mediterranean, I learned, with pain, that the spirit of revival had greatly declined in the United States, and that a spirit of jangling and controversy alarmingly prevailed.

The peculiar circumstances of the church, and the state of revivals, was such, as *unavoidably* to lead me to the discussion of some points, that I would gladly have avoided, had the omission been consistent with my main design, to reach and arouse the church, when she was fast settling down upon her lees.

I am far from setting up the claim of *infallibility* upon this or

---

[1] Finney had contracted cholera in New York City in October 1832, and in January 1834 he had taken a six-month's cruise to the Mediterranean to speed his recovery. He was not yet in good health when he wrote this preface in April 1835. However, he lived to the age of eighty-three and conducted numerous revivals after 1835 throughout the United States and in the British Isles. The best source of biographical data about Finney is his *Memoirs* (New York, 1876). For necessary corrections and additions see also, George F. Wright, *Charles Grandison Finney* (New York, 1891); Robert S. Fletcher, *A History of Oberlin College* (Oberlin, Ohio, 1943), 2 vols.; Whitney R. Cross, *The Burned-Over District* (Ithaca, New York, 1950); Gilbert H. Barnes, *The Anti-Slavery Impulse 1830-1844* (New York, 1933); and W. G. McLoughlin, *Modern Revivalism: Charles Grandison Finney to Billy Graham* (New York, 1959). Valuable primary material is available in the Finney Papers in the Oberlin College Library, and in the *Letters of Theodore Weld, Angelina Grimke Weld, and Sarah Grimke*, ed. Gilbert H. Barnes and Dwight L. Dumond (New York, 1934).

any other subject. I have given my own views, so far as I have gone, without pretending to have exhausted the subject, or to have spoken in the best possible manner upon the points I have discussed.

I am too well acquainted with the state of the church, and especially with the state of some of its ministers, to expect to escape without censure. I have felt obliged to say some things, that I fear will not, in all instances, be received as kindly as they were *intended*. But whatever may be the result of saying the truth as it respects *some*, I have reason to believe that the great body of *praying* people, will receive and be benefited by what I have said.

What I have said upon the subject of prayer, will not, I am well aware, be understood and received by a certain portion of the church, and all I can say is, "*He that hath an ear to hear, let him hear*."

I had not the most distant idea until recently, that these Lectures, in this, or any other form, would ever grow into a book: but the urgent call for their publication, in a volume, and the fact that I have repeated assurances that the reading of them in the Evangelist, has been owned and blessed, to the quickening of individuals and churches, and has resulted in the conversion of many sinners, have led me to consent to their publication in this imperfect form.

The Reporter has succeeded, in general, in giving an *outline* of the Lectures, as they were delivered. His report, however, would, in general make no more than a full *skeleton* of what was said on the subject, at the time. In justice to the Reporter, I would say, that on reading his reports, in his paper, although there were some mistakes and misapprehensions, yet I have been surprised that, without stenography, he could so nearly report my meaning.

As for literary merit, they have none; nor do they claim to any. It was no part of my design to deliver *elegant* Lectures. They were my most familiar Friday evening discourses; and my great, and I may add my only object, was to have them understood and felt.

In correcting the Lectures for a volume, I have not had time, nor was it thought advisable to remodel them, and change the style in which they had been reported. I have, in some few instances, changed the phraseology, when a thought had been very awkwardly expressed, or when the true idea had not been given. But I have, in nearly every instance, left the sentences as they were reported, when the thought was *perspicuously* expressed, although the style might have been improved by emendation. They were the editor's reports, and as such they must go before the public; with such little additions and alterations, as I have had time to make. Could I have written them out in full, I doubt not but they might have been more acceptable to many readers. But this was impossible, and the only alternative was, to let the public have them as they are, or refuse to let them go out in the form of a volume at all. I am sorry they are not better Lectures, and in a more attracting form; but I have done what I could under the circumstances; and, as it is the wish of many whom I love, and delight to please and honour, to have them, although in this imperfect form, they must have them.

C. G. FINNEY.

ADVERTISEMENT BY THE REPORTER

The work of reporting these Lectures was undertaken for the purpose of increasing the interest and usefulness of the New-York Evangelist. The Reporter is wholly unacquainted with short hand, and has, therefore, only aimed to give a *sketch* of the leading thoughts of the Discourse. It is hardly necessary to mention, that Mr. Finney never writes his sermons; but guides his course of argument by a skeleton, or brief, carefully prepared, and so compact, that it can be written on one side of a card, about half as large as one of these printed pages. His manner is direct, and his language colloquial and Saxon, and his illustrations are drawn from the commonest incidents and maxims of life. The Reporter has aimed to preserve, as much as he could, the style of the speaker, and is thought to have been in some degree successful. If, in any cases, by letting his language run in a colloquial strain, he has made the copy more simple and homely than the original, he hopes to be pardoned easily for a fault by no means prevalent.

If any one should attempt to criticise the style of these Reports, he will assuredly lose his labour; for the only ambition of the Reporter has been, to make such a use of language as should fully convey the meaning, and fairly exhibit the manner of the Lecturer. When words have done this, they have done their great work. The notes were taken with a pencil, and transcribed in great haste, and sent to the printer without revision. In preparing them for publication, in this form, Mr. Finney has reviewed them, with reference only to this point — the correct expression of the sentiment. The style of an off-hand sketch has been preserved, partly of choice, and partly from necessity. There was no time to remodel the work, and the public voice seemed to be, that it was more attractive, and more useful, in its present condensed form. Mr. Finney has therefore done little more than to amend where the Reporter misapprehended the meaning, or did not express it with sufficient distinctness. He has enlarged in a few places where the illustrations, as given by the Reporter, seemed to be incomplete.

My labour with these Sketches is now done; and its results are sent forth in this permanent form, with the prayer, that God would employ the book, as he has already done the newspaper edition, to rouse, and teach, and strengthen his people, and to guide, unite, and encourage zealous Christians of all classes, in the great duty of saving sinners.

J. L.

New-York, April, 1835.

LECTURES

I

WHAT A REVIVAL OF RELIGION IS

Text. — O Lord, revive thy work in the midst of the years, in the midst of the years make known; in wrath remember mercy. — Hab. iii. 2.

It is supposed that the prophet Habakkuk was contemporary with Jeremiah, and that this prophecy was uttered in anticipation of the Babylonish captivity. Looking at the judgments which were speedily to come upon his nation, the soul of the prophet was wrought up to an agony, and he cries out in his distress, "O Lord, revive thy work." As if he had said, "O Lord, grant that thy judgments may not make Israel desolate. In the midst of these awful years, let the judgments of God be made the means of reviving religion among us. In wrath remember mercy."

Religion is the work of man. It is something for man to do. It consists in obeying God. It is man's duty. It is true, God induces him to do it. He influences him by his Spirit, because of his great wickedness and reluctance to obey. If it were not necessary for God to influence men — if men were disposed to obey God, there would be no occasion to pray, "O Lord, revive thy work." The ground of necessity for such a prayer is, that men are wholly indisposed to obey; and unless God interpose the influence of his Spirit, not a man on earth will ever obey the commands of God.

A "Revival of Religion" presupposes a declension. Almost all the religion in the world has been produced by revivals. God has found it necessary to take advantage of the excitability there is in mankind, to produce powerful excitements among them, before he can lead them to obey. Men are so sluggish,[1] there are so many things to lead their minds off from religion, and to oppose the influence of the gospel, that it is necessary to raise an excitement

---

[1] In the revised edition of these lectures published in Oberlin in 1868 Finney inserted the world "spiritually" before "sluggish."

among them, till the tide rises so high as to sweep away the opposing obstacles. They must be so excited that they will break over these counteracting influences, before they will obey God.[2]

Look back at the history of the Jews, and you will see that God used to maintain religion among *them* by special occasions, when there would be a great excitement, and people would turn to the Lord. And after they had been thus revived, it would be but a short time before there would be so many counteracting influences brought to bear upon them, that religion would decline, and keep on declining, till God could have time — so to speak — to shape the course of events so as to produce another excitement, and then pour out his Spirit again to convert sinners. Then the counteracting causes would again operate, and religion would decline, and the nation would be swept away in the vortex of luxury, idolatry, and pride.

There is so little *principle* in the church, so little firmness and stability of purpose, that unless they are greatly excited,[3] they will not obey God. They have so little knowledge, and their principles are so weak, that unless they are excited, they will go back from the path of duty, and do nothing to promote the glory of God. The state of the world is still such, and probably will be till the millennium is fully come, that religion must be mainly promoted by these excitements.[4] How long and how often has the experiment been tried, to bring the church to act steadily for God, without these periodical excitements! Many good men have supposed, and still suppose, that the best way to promote religion, is to go along *uniformly*, and gather in the ungodly gradually, and without excitement. But however such reasoning may appear

[2] In the revised edition of 1868 Finney added here, "Not that excited feeling is religion, for it is not; but it is excited desire, appetite, and feeling that prevents religion. The will is, in a sense, enslaved by the carnal and worldly desires. Hence it is necessary to awaken men to a sense of guilt and danger, and thus produce an excitement of counter-feeling and desire which will break the power of carnal and worldly desire and leave the will free to obey God."

[3] In the revised edition of 1868 Finney substituted for "unless they are greatly excited" the words, "unless the religious feelings are awakened and kept excited, counter worldly feelings and excitements will prevail, and men will not obey God."

[4] Throughout these lectures it is evident that Finney was a convinced postmillennialist. He believed that through revivals, soul-winning, and moral reform movements the world was getting better and better and that some day, in the not too distant future, everyone would be converted to Christianity. Then a utopian world would be ready for Christ's second return. For a discussion of this in relation to Finney's theological and social outlook, see the Introduction to this edition, pp. xl–xlix.

in the abstract, *facts* demonstrate its futility. If the church were far enough advanced in knowledge, and had stability of principle enough to *keep awake*, such a course would do; but the church is so little enlightened, and there are so many counteracting causes, that the church will not go steadily to work without a special excitement. As the millennium advances, it is probable that these periodical excitements will be unknown. Then the church will be enlightened, and the counteracting causes removed, and the entire church will be in a state of habitual and steady obedience to God. The entire church will stand and take the infant mind, and cultivate it for God. Children will be trained up in the way they should go, and there will be no such torrents of worldliness, and fashion, and covetousness, to bear away the piety of the church, as soon as the excitement of a revival is withdrawn.

It is very desirable it should be so. It is very desirable that the church should go on steadily in a course of obedience without these excitements. Such excitements are liable to injure the health. Our nervous system is so strung that any powerful excitement, if long continued, injures our health and unfits us for duty. If religion is ever to have a pervading influence in the world, it can't be so; this spasmodic religion must be done away. Then it will be uncalled for. Christians will not sleep the greater part of the time, and once in a while wake up, and rub their eyes, and bluster about, and vociferate, a little while, and then go to sleep again. Then there will be no need that ministers should wear themselves out, and kill themselves, by their efforts to roll back the flood of worldly influence that sets in upon the church. But as yet the state of the Christian world is such, that to expect to promote religion without excitements is unphilosophical and absurd.[5] The great political, and other worldly excitements that agitate Christendom, are all unfriendly to religion, and divert the mind from the interests of the soul. Now these excitements can only be counteracted by *religious* excitements. And until there is religious principle in the world to put down irreligious excitements, it is in

[5] Finney lived in the era when there was no academic distinction between the humanities and the sciences. Consequently he uses the adjective "philosophical" throughout these lectures in the old sense of "logical," "rational," or "scientific." And he includes in the word "philosophy" what would now be designated as the science of psychology. Finney would accept Webster's first definition of philosophy as "the science which investigates the facts and principles of reality and of human nature and conduct." The crux of Finney's attack on Calvinism in these lectures is that its doctrines are contrary to the laws of philosophy and to "the laws of mind" and hence, in modern terms, Calvinism is "unscientific."

vain to try to promote religion, except by counteracting excitements. This is true in philosophy, and it is a historical fact.

It is altogether improbable that religion will ever make progress among *heathen* nations except through the influence of revivals. The attempt is now making to do it by education, and other cautious and gradual improvements. But so long as the laws of mind remain what they are, it cannot be done in this way. There must be excitement sufficient to wake up the dormant moral powers, and roll back the tide of degradation and sin. And precisely so far as our own land approximates to heathenism, it is impossible for God or man to promote religion in such a state of things but by powerful excitements. — This is evident from the fact that this has always been the way in which God has done it. God does not create these excitements, and choose this method to promote religion for nothing, or without reason. Where mankind are so reluctant to obey God, they will not act until they are excited. For instance, how many there are who know that they ought to be religious, but they are afraid if they become pious they shall be laughed at by their companions. Many are wedded to idols, others are procrastinating repentance, until they are settled in life, or until they have secured some favorite worldly interest. Such persons never will give up their false shame, or relinquish their ambitious schemes, till they are so excited that they cannot contain themselves any longer.

These remarks are designed only as an introduction to the discourse. I shall now proceed with the main design, to show,

I. What a revival of religion is not;

II. What it is; and,

III. The agencies employed in promoting it.

I. A REVIVAL OF RELIGION IS NOT A MIRACLE.

1. A miracle has been generally defined to be, a Divine interference, setting aside or suspending the laws of nature. It is not a miracle, in this sense.[6] All the laws of matter and mind remain in force. They are neither suspended nor set aside in a revival.

2. It is not a miracle according to another definition of the

---

[6] Typical of the type of revision that Finney made in preparing these lectures for publication in book form is the way in which he broke up into the first two sentences in this paragraph what Joshua Leavitt had written in the *New York Evangelist* as one sentence, namely: "1. It is not a miracle in the sense of a suspension or setting aside of the laws of nature."

term miracle — *something above the powers of nature*. There is nothing in religion beyond the ordinary powers of nature. It consists entirely in the *right exercise* of the powers of nature. It is just that, and nothing else. When mankind become religious, they are not *enabled* to put forth exertions which they were unable before to put forth. They only exert the powers they had before in a different way, and use them for the glory of God.

3. It is not a miracle, or dependent on a miracle, in any sense. It is a purely philosophical result of the right use of the constituted means — as much so as any other effect produced by the application of means.[7] There may be a miracle among its antecedent causes, or there may not. The apostles employed miracles, simply as a means by which they arrested attention to their message, and established its Divine authority. But the miracle was not the revival. The miracle was one thing; the revival that followed it was quite another thing. The revivals in the apostles' days were connected with miracles, but they were not miracles.

I said that a revival is the result of the *right* use of the appropriate means. The means which God has enjoyed for the production of a revival, doubtless have a natural tendency to produce a revival. Otherwise God would not have enjoined them. But means will not produce a revival, we all know, without the blessing of God. No more will grain, when it is sowed, produce a crop without the blessing of God. It is impossible for us to say that there is not as direct an influence or agency from God, to produce a crop of grain, as there is to produce a revival. What are the laws of nature, according to which, it is supposed, that grain yields a crop? They are nothing but the constituted manner of the operations

---

[7] Anyone who has read Jonathan Edwards' *Faithful Narrative of the Surprising Work of God* or his *Some Thoughts Concerning the Present Revival of Religion in New England* will see at once how different his view of a revival was from that expressed here. Edwards constantly marvels at "this shower of divine blessing," which is "a very extraordinary dispensation of providence; God has in many respects gone out of, and much beyond, his usual and ordinary way." And he applies the words "strange," "remarkable," "wonderful," "uncommon," "amazing" to the revival to indicate its miraculous character: "It is a great and wonderful event, a strange revolution, an unexpected, surprising overturning of things, suddenly brought to pass." In fact, Edwards went out of his way to chastise those who sought to explain in human terms how and why revivals came about: "This is too much for the clay to take upon it with respect to the potter," for "The wind bloweth where it listest" and "We know not the work of God who maketh all." See Jonathan Edwards, *Works*, ed. Sereno E. Dwight (New York, 1829–1830), IV, 27, 80, 120–121, and *passim*. (Of course, it should be noted that although Finney denies the miraculous aspect of revivals, he by no means denies that miracles can and do happen.)

of God. In the Bible, the word of God is compared to grain, and preaching is compared to sowing seed, and the results to the springing up and growth of the crop. And the result is just as philosophical in the one case, as in the other, and is as naturally connected with the cause.[8]

I wish this idea to be impressed on all your minds, for there has long been an idea prevalent that promoting religion has something very peculiar in it, not to be judged of by the ordinary rules of cause and effect; in short, that there is no connection of the means with the result, and no tendency in the means to produce the effect. No doctrine is more dangerous than this to the prosperity of the church, and nothing more absurd.

Suppose a man were to go and preach this doctrine among farmers, about their sowing grain. Let him tell them that God is a sovereign, and will give them a crop only when it pleases him, and that for them to plow and plant and labor as if they expected to raise a crop is very wrong, and taking the work out of the hands of God, that it interferes with his sovereignty, and is going on in their own strength; and that there is no connection between the means and the result on which they can depend. And now, suppose the farmers should believe such doctrine. Why, they would starve the world to death.

Just such results will follow from the church's being persuaded that promoting religion is somehow so mysteriously a subject of Divine sovereignty, that there is no natural connection between the means and the end. What *are* the results? Why, generation after generation have gone down to hell. No doubt more than five thousand millions have gone down to hell, while the church has been dreaming, and waiting for God to save them without the use of means.[9] It has been the devil's most successful means of

---

[8] In the revised edition of 1868 Finney added here, "or more correctly, a revival is as naturally a result of the use of the appropriate means as a crop is of the use of its appropriate means. It is true that religion does not properly belong to the category of cause and effect; but although it is not *caused* by means, yet it has its occasion, and may as naturally and certainly result from its *occasion* as a crop does from its *cause*."

[9] In the more rigid expositions of Calvinistic predestination, especially as preached by the New England Congregationalists who followed the theology of Samuel Hopkins, sinners were considered passive in their regeneration. They were told to "wait God's time" and if they were among the predestined elect, God would send the Holy Spirit to infuse grace or impart grace to them when He was ready. If they were not among the elect, then nothing they could do would keep them out of hell. Finney's whole career was devoted to tearing down this generally accepted notion of salvation.

destroying souls. The connection is as clear in religion as it is when the farmer sows his grain.

There is one fact under the government of God, worthy of universal notice, and of everlasting remembrance; which is, that the most useful and important things are most easily and certainly obtained by the use of the appropriate means. This is evidently a principle in the Divine administration. Hence, all the *necessaries* of life are obtained with great *certainty* by the use of the simplest means. The luxuries are more difficult to obtain; the means to procure them are more intricate and less certain in their results; while things absolutely hurtful and poisonous, such as alcohol and the like, are often obtained only by torturing nature, and making use of a kind of infernal sorcery to procure the death-dealing abomination. This principle holds true in moral government, and as spiritual blessings are of surpassing importance, we should expect their attainment to be connected with *great certainty* with the use of the appropriate means; and such we find to be the fact; and I fully believe that could facts be known, it would be found that when the appointed means have been *rightly* used, spiritual blessings have been obtained with greater uniformity than temporal ones.[10]

II. I AM TO SHOW WHAT A REVIVAL IS.[11]

It presupposes that the church is sunk down in a backslidden state, and a revival consists in the return of the church from her backslidings, and in the connversion of sinners.

1. A revival always includes conviction of sin on the part of the church. Backslidden professors cannot wake up and begin right away in the service of God, without deep searchings of heart.[12]

[10] This paragraph does not appear in the vision of this lecture that appeared in the *New York Evangelist*, December 6, 1834, p. 194. This "philosophical" justification for teetotalism was often used by later revivalists. The whole paragraph is eloquent proof of Finney's pietistic love of simplicity and his optimistic view of the benevolence of Nature and of Nature's God.

[11] In the revised edition of 1868 Finney inserted a paragraph here, which reads: "It is the renewal of the first love of Christians resulting in the awakening and conversion of sinners to God. In the popular sense, a revival of religion in a community is the arousing, quickening, and reclaiming of the more or less backslidden church and the more or less general awakening of all classes and insuring attention to the claims of God."

[12] By the term "professor" of religion Finney usually means a church member as opposed to a "Christian" or a "pious man" who has had a conversion experience and who is an active, soul-winning, servant of God. Finney's frequent casti-

The fountains of sin need to be broken up. In a true revival, Christians are always brought under such convictions; they see their sins in such a light, that often they find it impossible to maintain a hope of their acceptance with God. It does not always go to that extent; but there are always, in a genuine revival, deep convictions of sin, and often cases of abandoning all hope.

2. Backslidden Christians will be brought to repentance. A revival is nothing else than a new beginning of obedience to God. Just as in the case of a converted sinner, the first step is a deep repentance, a breaking down of heart, a getting down into the dust before God, with deep humility, and forsaking of sin.

3. Christians will have their faith renewed. While they are in their backslidden state they are blind to the state of sinners. Their hearts are as hard as marble. The truths of the Bible only appear like a dream. They admit it to be all true; their conscience and their judgment assent to it; but their faith does not see it standing out in bold relief, in all the burning realities of eternity. But when they enter into a revival, they no longer see men as trees walking, but they see things in that strong light which will renew the love of God in their hearts. This will lead them to labor zealously to bring others to him. They will feel grieved that others do not love God, when they love him so much. And they will set themselves feelingly to persuade their neighbors to give him their hearts. So their love to men will be renewed. They will be filled with a tender and burning love for souls. They will have a longing desire for the salvation of the whole world. They will be in agony for individuals whom they want to have saved; their friends, relations, enemies. They will not only be urging them to give their hearts to God, but they will carry them to God in the arms of faith, and with strong crying and tears beseech God to have mercy on them, and save their souls from endless burnings.

4. A revival breaks the power of the world and of sin over Christians. It brings them to such vantage ground that they get a fresh impulse towards heaven. They have a new foretaste of heaven, and new desires after union to God; and the charm of the world is broken, and the power of sin overcome.

5. When the churches are thus awakened and reformed, the reformation and salvation of sinners will follow, going through the same stages of conviction, repentance, and reformation. Their

---

gation of cold, dead, formal, or lukewarm "professors" of religion is characteristic of all revivalists.

hearts will be broken down and changed. Very often the most abandoned profligates are among the subjects. Harlots, and drunkards, and infidels, and all sorts of abandoned characters, are awakened and converted. The worst part of human society are softened, and reclaimed, and made to appear as lovely specimens of the beauty of holiness.

III. I AM TO CONSIDER THE AGENCIES EMPLOYED IN CARRYING FORWARD A REVIVAL OF RELIGION.

Ordinarily, there are three agents employed in the work of conversion, and one instrument. The agents are God, — some person who brings the truth to bear on the mind, — and the sinner himself. The instrument is the truth. There are *always two* agents, God and the sinner, employed and active in every case of genuine conversion.[13]

1. The agency of God is two-fold; by his Providence and by his Spirit.

(1.) By his providential government, he so arranges events as to bring the sinner's mind and the truth in contact. He brings the sinner where the truth reaches his ears or his eyes. It is often interesting to trace the manner in which God arranges events so as to bring this about, and how he sometimes makes every thing seem to favor a revival. The state of the weather, and of the public health, and other circumstances concur to make every thing just right to favor the application of truth with the greatest possible efficacy. How he sometimes sends a minister along, just at the time he is wanted! How he brings out a particular truth, just at the particular time when the individual it is fitted to reach is in the way to hear!

(2.) God's special agency by his Holy Spirit. Having direct access to the mind, and knowing infinitely well the whole history and state of each individual sinner, he employs that truth which is best adapted to his particular case, and then sets it home with Divine power. He gives it such vividness, strength, and power, that the sinner quails, and throws down his weapons of rebellion, and turns to the Lord. Under his influence, the truth burns and cuts its way like fire. He makes the truth stand out in such aspects, that it crushes the proudest man down with the weight of a

[13] Compare Finney's discussion of regeneration on pp. 195–197, where he indicates that there can be four possible agencies in the work of conversion.

mountain. If men were *disposed* to obey God, the truth is given with sufficient clearness in the Bible; and from preaching they could learn all that is necessary for them to know. But because they are wholly *disinclined* to obey it, God clears it up before their minds, and pours in a blaze of convincing light upon their souls, which they cannot withstand, and they yield to it, and obey God, and are saved.

2. The agency of men is commonly employed. Men are not mere *instruments* in the hands of God. Truth is the instrument. The preacher is a moral agent in the work; he acts; he is not a mere passive instrument; he is voluntary in promoting the conversion of sinners.

3. The agency of the sinner himself. The conversion of a sinner consists in his obeying the truth. It is therefore impossible it should take place without his agency, for it consists in *his* acting right. He is influenced to this by the agency of God, and by the agency of men. Men act on their fellow-men, not only by language, but by their looks, their tears, their daily deportment. See that impenitent man there, who has a pious wife. Her very looks, her tenderness, her solemn, compassionate dignity, softened and moulded into the image of Christ, are a sermon to him all the time. He has to turn his mind away, because it is such a reproach to him. He feels a sermon ringing in his ears all day long.

Mankind are accustomed to read the countenances of their neighbors. Sinners often read the state of a Christian's mind in his eyes. If his eyes are full of levity, or worldly anxiety and contrivance, sinners read it. If they are full of the Spirit of God, sinners read it; and they are often led to conviction by barely seeing the countenance of Christians.

An individual once went into a manufactory to see the machinery. His mind was solemn, as he had been where there was a revival. The people who labored there all knew him by sight, and knew who he was. A young lady who was at work saw him, and whispered some foolish remark to her companion, and laughed. The person stopped and looked at her with a feeling of grief. She stopped, her thread broke, and she was so much agitated she could not join it. She looked out at the window to compose herself, and then tried again; again and again she strove to recover her self-command. At length she sat down, overcome with her feelings. The person then approached and spoke with her; she soon manifested a deep sense of sin. The feeling spread through the establishment like fire, and in a few hours almost every person employed there was under conviction, so much so, that the owners, though worldly men, were astounded, and requested to have the works stop and have a prayer meeting; for they said it was a great deal more important to have these people converted than to have the works go on. And in a few days, the owners and nearly every person employed in the establishment were hopefully converted. The eye of this individual, his solemn countenance, his compassionate feeling, rebuked the levity of the young woman, and brought her under conviction of sin; and this whole revival followed, probably in a great measure, from so small an incident.[14]

If Christians have deep feeling on the subject of religion themselves, they will produce deep feeling wherever they go. And if they are cold, or light and trifling, they inevitably destroy all deep feeling, even in awakened sinners.

I knew a case, once, of an individual who was very anxious, but one day I was grieved to find that her convictions seemed to be all gone. I asked her what she had been doing. She told me she had been spending the afternoon at such a place, among some professors of religion, not thinking that it would dissipate her convictions to spend an afternoon with professors of religion. But they were trifling and vain, and thus her convictions were lost. And no doubt those professors of religion, by their folly, destroyed a soul, for her convictions did not return.

The church is required to use the means for the conversion of sinners. Sinners cannot properly be said to use the means for their own conversion. The church uses the means. What sinners do is to submit to the truth, or to resist it. It is a mistake of sinners, to think they are using means for their own conversion. The whole drift of a revival, and every thing about it, is designed to present the truth *to* your mind, for your obedience or resistance.

REMARKS.

1. Revivals were formerly regarded as miracles. And it has been so by some even in our day. And others have ideas on the subject so loose and unsatisfactory, that if they would only *think*, they would see their absurdity. For a long time, it was supposed

---

[14] The "individual" in this story was Finney himself; the manufactory was the Oriskany Woolen Mill in Oriskany, New York; the year was 1826. Finney tells the story in his *Memoirs*, pp. 183–184.

by the church, that a revival was a miracle, an interposition of Divine power which they had nothing to do with, and which they had no more agency in producing, than they had in producing thunder, or a storm of hail, or an earthquake. It is only within a few years that ministers generally have supposed revivals were to be *promoted*, by the use of means designed and adapted specially to that object. Even in New England, it has been supposed that revivals came just as showers do, sometimes in one town, and sometimes in another, and that ministers and churches could do nothing more to produce them, than they could to make showers of rain come on their own town, when they are falling on a neighboring town.

It used to be supposed that a revival would come about once in fifteen years, and all would be converted that God intended to save, and then they must wait until another crop came forward on the stage of life. Finally, the time got shortened down to five years, and they supposed there might be a revival about as often as that.

I have heard a fact in relation to one of these pastors, who supposed revivals might come about once in five years. There had been a revival in his congregation. The next year, there was a revival in a neighboring town, and he went there to preach, and staid several days, till he got his soul all engaged in the work. He returned home on Saturday, and went into his study to prepare for the Sabbath. And his soul was in an agony. He thought how many adult persons there were in his congregation at enmity with God — so many still unconverted — so many persons *die* yearly — such a portion of them unconverted — if a revival does not come under five years, so many adult heads of families will be in hell. He put down his calculations on paper, and embodied them in his sermon for the next day, with his heart bleeding at the dreadful picture. As I understood it, he did not do this with any expectation of a revival, but he felt deeply, and poured out his heart to his people. And that sermon awakened *forty heads of families*, and a powerful revival followed; and so his theory about a revival once in five years was all exploded.

Thus God has overthrown, generally, the theory that revivals are miracles.[15]

---

[15] Notice that Finney takes no credit for discovering the fact that revivals can be and should be promoted by means. God has revealed it, and Finney is here simply calling the fact to the attention of tradition-bound Calvinists who have failed to see the new light that has been shed. Finney takes the same view

2. Mistaken notions concerning the sovereignty of God, have greatly hindered revivals.

Many people have supposed God's sovereignty to be something very different from what it is. They have supposed it to be such an arbitrary disposal of events, and particularly of the gift of his Spirit, as precluded a rational employment of means for promoting a revival of religion. But there is no evidence from the Bible, that God exercises any such sovereignty as that. There are no facts to prove it. But every thing goes to show, that God has connected means with the end through all the departments of his government — in nature and in grace. There is no *natural* event in which his own agency is not concerned. He has not built the creation like a vast machine, that will go on alone without his further care. He has not retired from the universe, to let it work for itself. This is mere atheism. He exercises a universal superintendence and control. And yet every event in nature has been brought about by means. He neither administers providence nor grace with that sort of sovereignty, that dispenses with the use of means. There is no more sovereignty in one than in the other.

And yet some people are terribly alarmed at all direct efforts to promote a revival, and they cry out, "You are trying to get up a revival in your own strength. Take care, you are interfering with the sovereignty of God. Better keep along in the usual course, and let God give a revival when he thinks it is best. God is a sovereign, and it is very wrong for you to attempt to get up a revival, just because *you think* a revival is needed." This is just such preaching as the devil wants. And men cannot do the devil's work more effectually, than by preaching up the sovereignty of God, as a reason why we should not put forth efforts to produce a revival.

3. You see the error of those who are beginning to think that religion can be better promoted in the world without revivals, and who are disposed to give up all efforts to produce religious excitements. Because there are evils arising in some instances out of great excitements on the subject of religion, they are of opinion that it is best to dispense with them altogether. This cannot, and must not be. True, there is danger of abuses. In cases of great *religious* as well as all other excitements, more or less incidental evils may be expected of course. But this is no reason why they should be given up. The best things are always liable to abuses. Great

---

(which has been called the doctrine of progressive revelation) about the new light recently shed upon the question of slavery in his discussion on pp. 287–289.

and manifold evils have originated in the providential and moral governments of God. But these *foreseen* perversions and evils were not considered a sufficient reason for giving them up. For the establishment of these governments was on the whole the best that could be done for the production of the greatest amount of happiness. So in revivals of religion, it is found by experience, that in the present state of the world, religion cannot be promoted to any considerable extent without them. The evils which are sometimes complained of, when they are real, are incidental, and of small importance when compared with the amount of good produced by revivals. The sentiment should not be admitted by the church for a moment, that revivals may be given up. It is fraught with all that is dangerous to the interests of Zion, is death to the cause of missions, and brings in its train the damnation of the world.[16]

FINALLY — I have a proposal to make to you who are here present. I have not commenced this course of Lectures on Revivals to get up a curious theory of my own on the subject. I would not spend my time and strength merely to give you instructions, to gratify your curiosity, and furnish you something to talk about. I have no idea of preaching *about* revivals. It is not my design to preach so as to have you able to say at the close, "We *understand* all about revivals now," while you do *nothing*. But I wish to ask you a question. What do you hear lectures on revivals for? Do you mean that whenever you are convinced what your duty is in promoting a revival, you will go to work and practise it?

Will you follow the instructions I shall give you from the word of God, and put them in practice in your own hearts? Will you bring them to bear upon your families, your acquaintances, neighbors, and through the city? Or will you spend the winter in learning *about* revivals, and do nothing *for* them? I want you, as fast as you learn any thing on the subject of revivals, to put it in practice, and go to work and see if you cannot promote a revival among sinners here. If you will not do this, I wish you to let me know at the beginning, so that I need not waste my strength. You ought to decide *now* whether you will do this or not. You know that we call sinners to decide on the spot whether *they* will obey the gospel. And we have no more authority to let you take time to deliberate whether *you* will obey God, than we have to let sinners do so.

---

[16] This paragraph does not appear in the version of this lecture that was printed in the *New York Evangelist*, December 6, 1834, p. 194.

We call on you to unite now in a solemn pledge to God, that you will do your duty as fast as you learn what it is, and to pray that He will pour out his Spirit upon this church and upon all the city this winter.[17]

[17] Like all true revival preachers Finney lost no opportunity to call upon sinners to come forward and make their peace with God "on the spot." These lectures were not simply for edification; they were also designed to save souls and to start a revival in the Chatham Street Chapel.

II

WHEN A REVIVAL IS TO BE EXPECTED

TEXT. — Wilt thou not revive us again; that thy people may rejoice in thee? — PSALM lxxxv. 6.

THIS Psalm seems to have been written soon after the return of the people of Israel from the Babylonish captivity; as you will easily see from the language at the commencement of it. The Psalmist felt that God had been very favorable to the people, and while contemplating the goodness of the Lord in bringing them back from the land where they had been carried away captive, and while looking at the prospects before them, he breaks out into a prayer for a Revival of Religion. "Wilt thou not revive us again, that thy people may rejoice in thee?" Since God in his providence had re-established the ordinances of his house among them, he prays that there may be also a revival of religion, to crown the work.

Last Friday evening I attempted to show what a Revival of Religion is not; what a Revival is; and the agencies to be employed in promoting it. The topics to which I wish to call your attention to-night, are,

I. When a Revival of Religion is needed.
II. The importance of a Revival when it is needed.
III. When a Revival of Religion may be expected.

I. WHEN IS A REVIVAL OF RELIGION NEEDED?

1. When there is a want of brotherly love and Christian confidence among professors of religion, then a revival is needed. Then there is a loud call for God to revive his work. When Christians have sunk down into a low and backslidden state, they neither have, nor ought to have, nor is there reason to have, the same love and confidence toward each other, as when they are all alive, and active, and living holy lives. The love of benevolence may be the same, but not the love of complacency. God loves all men with the love of benevolence, but he does not feel the love

of complacency toward any but those who live holy.[1] Christians do not and cannot love each other with the love of complacency, only in proportion to their holiness. If Christian love is the love of the image of Christ in his people, then it never can be exercised only where that image really or apparently exists. A person must reflect the image of Christ, and show the spirit of Christ, before other Christians can love him with the love of complacency. It is in vain to call on Christians to love one another with the love of complacency, as Christians, when they are sunk down in stupidity. They see nothing in each other to produce this love. It is next to impossible that they should feel otherwise toward each other, than they do toward sinners. Merely knowing that they belong to the church, or seeing them occasionally at the communion table, will not produce Christian love, unless they see the image of Christ.

2. When there are dissensions, and jealousies, and evil speakings among professors of religion, then there is great need of a revival. These things show that Christians have got far from God, and it is time to think earnestly of a revival. — Religion cannot prosper with such things in the church, and nothing can put an end to them like a revival.

3. When there is a worldly spirit in the church. It is manifest that the church is sunk down into a low and backslidden state, when you see Christians conform to the world in dress, equipage, parties, seeking worldly amusements, reading novels, and other books such as the world read. It shows that they are far from God, and that there is a great need of a Revival of Religion.

4. When the church finds its members falling into gross and scandalous sins, then it is time for the church to awake and cry to God for a Revival of Religion. When such things are taking place, as give enemies of religion an occasion for reproach, it is time for the church to ask God, "What will become of thy great name?"

5. When there is a spirit of controversy in the church or in the land, a revival is needful.[2] The spirit of religion is not the spirit of controversy. There can be no prosperity in religion, where the spirit of controversy prevails.

[1] Finney uses "complacency" in its original sense of "contentment" or of "being pleased with."
[2] The two great controversies that Finney had particularly in mind as detriments to revivalism in 1834–1835 were abolitionism and the New School-Old School quarrel among the Calvinists.

6. When the wicked triumph over the church, and revile them, it is time to seek for a Revival of Religion.

7. When sinners are careless and stupid, and sinking into hell unconcerned, it is time the church should bestir themselves. It is as much the duty of the church to awake, as it is for the firemen to awake when a fire breaks out in the night in a great city. The church ought to put out the fires of hell which are laying hold of the wicked. Sleep! Should the firemen sleep, and let the whole city burn down, what would be thought of such firemen? And yet their guilt would not compare with the guilt of Christians who sleep while sinners around them are sinking stupid into the fires of hell.

II. I AM TO SHOW THE IMPORTANCE OF A REVIVAL OF RELIGION IN SUCH CIRCUMSTANCES.

1. A Revival of Religion is the only possible thing that can wipe away the reproach which covers the church, and restore religion to the place it ought to have in the estimation of the public. Without a revival, this reproach will cover the church more and more, until it is overwhelmed with universal contempt. You may do any thing else you please, and you can change the aspects of society in some respects, but you will do no real good; you only make it worse without a Revival of Religion. You may go and build a splendid new house of worship, and line your seats with damask, put up a costly pulpit, and get a magnificent organ, and every thing of that kind, to make a show and dash, and in that way you may procure a sort of respect for religion among the wicked, but it does no good in reality. It rather does hurt. It misleads them as to the real nature of religion; and so far from converting them, it carries them farther away from salvation. Look wherever they have surrounded the altar of Christianity with splendor, and you will find that the impression produced is contrary to the true nature of religion. There must be a waking up of energy on the part of Christians, and an outpouring of God's Spirit, or the world will laugh at the church.

2. Nothing else will restore Christian love and confidence among church members. Nothing but a Revival of Religion can restore it, and nothing else *ought* to restore it. There is no other way to wake up that love of Christians for one another, which is

sometimes felt, when they have such love as they cannot express. You cannot have such love without confidence; and you cannot restore confidence without such evidence of piety as is seen in a revival. If a *minister* finds he has lost in any degree the confidence of his people, he ought to labor for a revival as the only means of regaining their confidence. I do not mean that this should be his *motive* in laboring for a revival, to regain the confidence of his people, but that a revival through his instrumentality, and ordinarily nothing else, will restore to him the confidence of the praying part of his people. So if an elder or private member of the church finds his brethren cold towards him, there is but one way to restore it. It is by being revived himself, and pouring out from his eyes and from his life the splendor of the image of Christ. This spirit will catch and spread in the church, and confidence will be renewed, and brotherly love prevail again.

3. At such a time a Revival of Religion is indispensable to avert the judgments of God from the church. This would be strange preaching, if revivals are only miracles, and if the church has no more agency in producing them, than it has in making a thunder storm. To say to the church, that unless there is a revival you may expect judgments, would then be as ridiculous as to say, If you don't have a thunder storm, you may expect judgments. The fact is, that *Christians* are more to blame for not being revived, than *sinners* are for not being converted. And if they are not awakened, they may know assuredly that God will visit them with his judgments. How often God visited the Jewish church with judgments, because they would not repent and be revived at the call of his prophets! How often have we seen churches, and even whole denominations, cursed with a curse, because they would not wake up and seek the Lord, and pray, "Wilt thou not revive us again, that thy people may rejoice in thee?"

4. Nothing but a Revival of Religion can preserve such a church from annihilation. A church declining in this way cannot continue to exist without a revival. If it receives new members, they will, for the most part, be made up of ungodly persons. Without revivals there will not ordinarily be as many persons converted as will die off in a year. There have been churches in this country where the members have died off, and there were no revivals to convert others in their place, till the church has run out, and the organization has been dissolved.

A minister told me that he once labored as a missionary in

Virginia, on the ground where such a man as Samuel Davies[3] once flashed and shone like a flaming torch; and that Davies's church was so reduced as to have but one male member, and he, if I remember right, was a colored man. The church had got proud, and was all run out. I have heard of a church in Pennsylvania, that was formerly flourishing, but neglected revivals, and it became so reduced that the pastor had to send to a neighboring church for a ruling elder when he administered the communion.*

5. Nothing but a Revival of Religion can prevent the means of grace from doing a great injury to the ungodly. Without a revival, they will grow harder and harder under preaching, and will experience a more horrible damnation than they would if they had never heard the gospel. Your children and your friends will go down to a much more horrible fate in hell, in consequence of the means of grace, if there are no revivals to convert them to God. Better were it for them if there were no means of grace, no sanctuary, no Bible, no preaching, and if they had never heard the gospel, than to live and die where there is no revival. The gospel is the savor unto death, if it is not made a savor of life unto life.

6. There is no other way in which a church can be sanctified, grow in grace, and be fitted for heaven. What is growing in grace? Is it hearing sermons and getting some new *notions* about religion? No — no such thing. The Christian who does this, and nothing more, is getting worse and worse, more and more hardened, and every week it is more difficult to rouse him up to duty.

III. I AM TO SHOW WHEN A REVIVAL OF RELIGION MAY BE EXPECTED.

1. When the providence of God indicates that a revival is at hand. The indications of God's providence are sometimes so plain as to amount to a revelation of his will. There is a conspiring of events to open the way, a preparation of circumstances to favor

---

* Why not, in such a case, let any member of the church, male or female distribute the elements? Is it indispensable to have an elder.[4]

[3] Samuel Davies (1723–1761) was a Presbyterian evangelist in Virginia from 1747 to 1759. Although Angelicanism was the established religion of that colony, Davies established the Hanover Presbytery in 1755, the first presbytery in Virginia. In 1759 he succeeded Jonathan Edwards as the fourth President of Princeton College.

[4] Finney added this note in revising his lectures for publication in book form. It is typical of his egalitarian and pietistic belief in the priesthood of all believers that he should suggest giving a larger role in church affairs to the laity.

a revival, so that those who are looking out can see that a revival is at hand, just as plainly as if it had been revealed from Heaven. Cases have occurred in this country, where the providential manifestations were so plain, that those who are careful observers, felt no hesitation in saying, that God was coming to pour out his Spirit, and grant a revival of religion. There are various ways for God to indicate his will to a people — sometimes by giving them peculiar means, sometimes by peculiar and alarming events, sometimes by remarkably favoring the employment of means, by the weather, health, &c.

2. When the wickedness of the wicked grieves and humbles and distresses Christians. Sometimes Christians do not seem to mind any thing about the wickedness around them. Or if they talk about it, it is in a cold, and callous, and unfeeling way, as if they despaired of a reformation: they are disposed to scold at sinners — not to feel the compassion of the Son of God for them. But sometimes the conduct of the wicked drives Christians to prayer, and breaks them down, and makes them sorrowful and tender-hearted, so that they can weep day and night, and instead of scolding and reproaching them, they pray earnestly for them. Then you may expect a revival. Sometimes the wicked will get up an opposition to religion. And when this drives Christians to their knees in prayer to God, with strong crying and tears, you may be certain there is going to be a revival. The prevalence of wickedness is no evidence at all that there is not going to be a revival. That is often God's time to work. When the enemy cometh in like a flood, the Spirit of the Lord lifts up a standard against him. Often the first indication of a revival, is the devil's getting up something new in opposition. It will invariably have one of two effects. It will either drive Christians to God, or it will drive them farther away from God, to some carnal policy or other that will only make things worse. Frequently the most outrageous wickedness of the ungodly is followed by a revival. If Christians are made to feel that they have no hope but in God, and if they have sufficient feeling left to care for the honor of God and the salvation of the souls of the impenitent, there will certainly be a revival. Let hell boil over if it will, and spew out as many devils as there are stones in the pavements, if it only drives Christians to God in prayer — they can't hinder a revival.[5] Let Satan get up a row, and sound his horn as

---

[5] Language like this caused many conservative ministers to feel that Finney was letting down the dignity of the pulpit.

loud as he pleases; if Christians will only be humbled and pray, they shall soon see God's naked arm in a revival of religion. I have known instances where a revival has broken in upon the ranks of the enemy, almost as sudden as a clap of thunder, and scattered them — taken the very ringleaders as trophies, and broken up their party in an instant.

3. A revival may be expected when Christians have a spirit of prayer for a revival. That is, when they pray as if their hearts were set upon a revival. Sometimes Christians are not engaged in prayer for a *revival*, not even when they are warm in prayer. Their minds are upon something else; they are praying for something else — the salvation of the heathen and the like — and not for a revival among themselves. But when they feel the want of a revival, they pray for it; they feel for their own families and neighborhoods, and pray for them as if they could not be denied. What constitutes a spirit of prayer? Is it many prayers and warm words? No. Prayer is the state of the heart. The spirit of prayer is a state of continual desire and anxiety of mind for the salvation of sinners. It is something that weighs them down. It is the same, so far as the philosophy of the mind is concerned, as when a man is anxious for some worldly interest. A Christian who has this spirit of prayer feels anxious for souls. It is the subject of his thoughts all the time, and makes him look and act as if he had a load on his mind. He thinks of it by day, and dreams of it by night. This is properly praying without ceasing. The man's prayers seem to flow from his heart liquid as water — "O Lord, revive thy work." Sometimes this feeling is very deep; persons have been bowed down, so that they could neither stand nor sit. I can name men in this state, of firm nerves, who stand high in character, who have been absolutely crushed with grief for the state of sinners. They have had an actual travail of soul for sinners, till they were as helpless as children. The feeling is not always so great as this, but such things are much more common than is supposed. In the great revivals in 1826, they were common.[6] This is by no means enthusiasm. It is just what Paul felt, when he says, "My little children, of whom I travail in birth." I heard of a person in this state, who prayed for sinners, and finally got into such a state of mind, that she could not live without prayer. She could not rest day nor night, unless there

---

[6] By the great revivals of 1826 Finney means those revivals in which he played the predominant part in and around Oneida County in western New York. He describes these revivals at some length in his *Memoirs*.

was somebody praying. Then she would be at ease; but if they ceased, she would shriek in agony till there was prayer again. And this continued for two days, until she prevailed in prayer, and her soul was relieved. This travail of soul, is that deep agony, which persons feel when they lay hold on God for such a blessing, and will not let him go till they receive it. I do not mean to be understood that it is essential to a spirit of prayer, that the distress should be so great as this. But this deep, continual, earnest desire for the salvation of sinners, is what constitutes the spirit of prayer for a revival.

When this feeling exists in a church, unless the Spirit is grieved away by sin, there will infallibly be a revival. This anxiety and distress increases till the revival commences. A clergyman in W——n [7] told me of a revival among his people, which commenced with a zealous and devoted woman in the church. She became anxious about sinners, and went to praying for them, and she prayed and her distress increased; and she finally came to her minister, and talked with him, and asked him to appoint an anxious meeting, for she felt that one was needed. The minister put her off, for he felt nothing of it. The next week she came again, and besought him to appoint an anxious meeting; she knew there would be somebody to come, for she felt as if God was going to pour out his Spirit. He put her off again. And finally she said to him, "If you don't appoint an anxious meeting I shall die, for there is certainly going to be a revival." The next Sabbath he appointed a meeting, and said that if there were any who wished to converse with him about the salvation of their souls, he would meet them on such an evening. He did not know of one, but when he went to the place, to his astonishment he found a large number of anxious inquirers. Now don't you think that woman knew there was going to be a revival? Call it what you please, a new revelation or an old revelation, or any thing else. I say it was the Spirit of God that taught that praying woman there was going to be a revival. "The secret of the Lord" was with her, and she knew it. She knew God had been in her heart, and filled it so full that she could contain no longer.

Sometimes ministers have had this distress about their congregations, so that they felt as if they could not live unless they could see a revival. Sometimes elders and deacons, or private members of the church, men or women, have the spirit of prayer for a re-

[7] Probably Western or Watertown, New York.

vival of religion, so that they will hold on and prevail with God, till he pours out his Spirit. The first ray of light that broke in upon the midnight which rested on the churches in Oneida county, in the fall of 1825, was from a woman in feeble health, who, I believe, had never been in a powerful revival. Her soul was exercised about sinners. She was in an agony for the land. She did not know what ailed her, but she kept praying more and more, till it seemed as if her agony would destroy her body. At length she became full of joy, and exclaimed, "God has come! God has come! There is no mistake about it, the work is begun, and is going over all the region." And sure enough, the work began, and her family were almost all converted, and the work spread all over that part of the country. Now, do you think that woman was deceived? I tell you, no. She knew she had prevailed with God in prayer.[8] She had travailed in birth for souls, and she knew it. This was not the only instance, by many, that I knew in that region.

Generally, there are but few professors of religion that know any thing about this spirit of prayer which prevails with God. I have been amazed to see such accounts as are often published about revivals, as if the revival had come without any cause — nobody knew why or wherefore. I have sometimes inquired into such cases; when it had been given out that nobody knew any thing about it until one Sabbath they saw in the face of the congregation that God was there; or they saw it in their conference room, or prayer meeting, and were astonished at the mysterious sovereignty of God, in bringing in a revival without any apparent connection with means. Now mark me. Go and inquire among the obscure members of the church, and you will always find that somebody had been praying for a revival, and was expecting it — some man or woman had been agonizing in prayer, for the salvation of sinners, until they gained the blessing. It may have found the minister and the body of the church fast asleep, and they would wake up all of a sudden, like a man just rubbing his eyes open, and running round the room pushing things over, and wondering where all this excitement came from. But though few knew it, you may be sure there has been somebody on the watch-tower, constant in prayer till the blessing came. Generally, a revival is more or less extensive, as there are more or less persons who have the spirit of prayer. But

[8] See Lecture IV, pp. 52ff., for further discussion of Finney's doctrine of prevailing prayer.

I will not dwell on this subject any further at present, as the subject of prayer will come up again in this course of lectures.

4. Another sign that a revival may be expected, is when the attention of ministers is especially directed to this *particular object*, and when their preaching and other efforts are aimed particularly for the conversion of sinners. Most of the time the labors of ministers are, it would seem, directed to other objects. They seem to preach and labor with no particular design to effect the *immediate* conversion of sinners. And then it need not be expected that there will be a revival under their preaching. There never will be a revival till *somebody* makes particular efforts for this end. But when the attention of a minister is directed to the state of the families in his congregation, and his heart is full of feeling of the necessity of a revival, and when he puts forth the proper efforts for this end, then you may be prepared to expect a revival. As I explained last week, the connection between the right use of means for a revival, and a revival, is as philosophically sure as between the right use of means to raise grain, and a crop of wheat. I believe, in fact, it is more certain, and that there are fewer instances of failure. The effect is more certain to follow. Probably the law connecting cause and effect is more undeviating in spiritual than in natural things, and so there are fewer exceptions, as I have before said. The paramount importance of spiritual things makes it reasonable that it should be so. Take the Bible, the nature of the case, and the history of the church, all together, and you will find fewer failures in the use of means for a revival, than in farming, or any other worldly business. In worldly business there are sometimes cases where counteracting causes annihilate all a man can do. In raising grain, for instance, there are cases which are beyond the control of man, such as drought, hard winter, worms, and so on. So in laboring to promote a revival, there may things occur to counteract it, something or other turning up to divert the public attention from religion, which may baffle every effort. But I believe there are fewer such cases in the moral than in the natural world. I have seldom seen an individual fail, when he used the means for promoting a revival in earnest, in the manner pointed out in the word of God. I believe a man may enter on the work of promoting a revival, with as reasonable an expectation of success, as he can enter on any other work with an expectation of success; with the same expectation as the farmer has of a crop when he sows his grain.

I have sometimes seen this tried and succeed under circumstances the most forbidding that can be conceived.

The great revival in Rochester begun under the most disadvantageous circumstances that could well be imagined.[9] It seemed as though Satan had interposed every possible obstacle to a revival. The three churches were at variance; one had no minister, one was divided about their minister, and they were just going to have a trial before the presbytery between an elder and the other minister. After the work begun, one of the first things was, the great stone church gave way, and created a panic. Then one of the churches went on and dismissed their minister right in the midst of it. Another church nearly broke down. Many other things occurred, so that it seemed as if the devil was determined to divert the public attention from the subject of religion. But there were a few remarkable cases of the spirit of prayer, which assured us that God was there, and we went on; and the more Satan opposed, the Spirit of the Lord lifted up the standard higher and higher, till finally a wave of salvation rolled over the place.

5. A revival of religion may be expected when Christians begin to confess their sins to one another. At other times, they confess in a general manner, as if they were only half in earnest. They may do it in eloquent language, but it does not mean any thing. But when there is an ingenuous breaking down, and a pouring out of the heart in making confession of their sins, the flood-gates will soon burst open, and salvation will flow over the place.

6. A revival may be expected whenever Christians are found willing to make the sacrifice necessary to carry it on. They must be willing to sacrifice their feelings, their business, their time, to help forward the work. Ministers must be willing to lay out their strength, and to jeopard their health and life. They must be willing to offend the impenitent by plain and faithful dealing, and perhaps offend many members of the church who will not come up to the work. They must take a decided stand with the revival, be the consequences what they may. They must be prepared to go on with the work, even though they should lose the affections of all the impenitent, and of all the cold part of the church. The minister must be prepared, if it is the will of God, to be driven away from his place. He must be determined to go straight forward, and leave the entire event with God.

[9] For a thorough discussion of the details of the Rochester revival, see Cross, *Burned-Over District*, pp. 154ff.

I knew a minister who had a young man laboring with him in a revival. The young man preached pretty plain, and the wicked did not like him. They said, We like *our* minister, and we wish to have him preach. They finally said so much that the minister told the young man, "Mr. Such-a-one, that gives so much towards my support, says so and so. Mr. A. says so, and Mr. B. says so. They think it will break up the society if you continue to preach, and I think you had better not preach any more." The young man went away, but the Spirit of God immediately withdrew from the place, and the revival stopped short. The minister, by yielding to the wicked desires of the wicked, drove him away. He was afraid the devil would drive *him* away from his people, and by undertaking to satisfy the devil, he offended God. And God so ordered events, that in a short time he had to leave his people after all. He undertook to go between the devil and God, and God spewed him out.[10]

So the people, also, must be willing to have a revival, let the sacrifice be what it may. It won't do for them to say, "We are willing to attend so many meetings, but we can't attend any more." Or, "We are willing to have a revival if it will not disturb our arrangements about our business, or prevent our making money." I tell you, such people will never have a revival, till they are willing to do any thing, and sacrifice any thing, that God indicates to be their duty. Christian merchants must feel willing to lock up their stores for six months, if it is necessary to carry on a revival. I do not mean to say any such thing is called for, or that it is their duty to do so. But if there should be such a state of feeling as to call for it, then it would be their duty, and they ought to be willing to do it. They ought to be willing to do it if God calls, for he can easily burn down their stores if they don't. In fact, I should not be sorry to see such a revival in New York, as would make every merchant in the city lock up his store till spring, and say he had sold goods enough, and now he would serve God all this winter.[11]

7. A revival may be expected when ministers and professors are willing to have God promote it by what instruments he pleases. Sometimes ministers are not willing to have a revival unless *they* can have the management of it, or unless *their* agency can be con-

---

[10] In the revised edition of 1868 Finney modified his language from "God spewed him out" to "God dismissed him."

[11] In the revised edition of 1868 Finney altered "he would serve God all this winter" to "he would give up his whole time to lead sinners to Christ."

spicuous in promoting it. They wish to prescribe to God what he shall direct and bless, and what men he shall put forward. They will have no new measures. They can't have any of this new-light preaching,[12] or of these *evangelists* that go about the country preaching. They have a great deal to say about God's being a sovereign, and that he will have revivals come in his own way and time. But then he must choose to have it just in their way, or they will have nothing to do with it. Such men will sleep on till they are awakened by the judgment trumpet, without a revival, unless they are willing that God should come in his own way — unless they are willing to have any thing or any body employed, that will do good.[13]

REMARKS.

1. Brethren, you can tell from our subject, whether you need a revival here or not, in this church, and in this city; and whether you are going to have one or not. Elders of the church, men, women, any of you, and all of you — what do you say?

Do you need a revival here?

Do you expect to have one?

Have you any reason to expect one?

You need not make any mist about it;[14] for you know, or can know if you will, whether you have any reason to look for a revival here.

2. You see why you have not a revival. It is only because you don't want one. Because you are not praying for it, nor anxious for it, nor putting forth efforts for it. I appeal to your own consciences. Are you making these efforts now, to promote a revival?

---

[12] "New-light preaching" was another term for New School or New Divinity Calvinism.

[13] In the revised edition of 1868 Finney added the following paragraph: "8. Strictly I should say that when the foregoing things occur, a revival to the same extent already exists. In truth a revival should be *expected* whenever it is *needed*. If we need to be revived it is our duty to be revived. If it is duty, it is possible, and we should set about being revived ourselves, and, relying on the promise of Christ to be with us in making disciples always and everywhere, we ought to labor to revive Christians and convert sinners with confident expectation of success. Therefore, whenever the church needs reviving, they ought and may expect to be revived, and to see sinners converted to Christ. When those things are seen which are named under the foregoing, let Christians and ministers be encouraged and know that good is already begun. Follow it up."

[14] To "make a mist" about something was a colloquialism for "raise doubts and queries" or "see difficulties where there are none."

You know, brethren, what the truth is about it. Will you stand up and say that you have made the efforts for a revival and been disappointed — that you have cried to God, "Wilt thou not revive us?" and God would not do it?

3. Do you wish for a revival? Will you have one? If God should ask you this moment, by an audible voice from heaven, "Do you want a revival?" would you dare to say, Yes? "Are you willing to make the sacrifices?" would you answer, Yes? "When shall it begin?" would you answer, Let it begin tonight — let it begin here — let it begin in my heart NOW? Would you dare to say so to God, if you should hear his voice to-night?

III

HOW TO PROMOTE A REVIVAL

Text. — Break up your fallow ground; for it is time to seek the Lord, till he come and rain righteousness upon you. — Hosea x. 12.

The Jews were a nation of farmers, and it is therefore a common thing in the Scriptures to refer for illustrations to their occupation, and to the scenes with which farmers and shepherds are familiar. The prophet Hosea addresses them as a nation of backsliders, and reproves them for their idolatry, and then threatens them with the judgments of God. I have showed you in my first lecture what a revival is not — what it is — and the agencies to be employed in promoting it; and in my second, when it is needed — its importance — and when it may be expected. My design in this lecture is to show,

HOW A REVIVAL IS TO BE PROMOTED.

A revival consists of two parts; as it respects the church, and as it respects the ungodly. I shall speak to-night of a revival in the church. Fallow ground is ground which has once been tilled, but which now lies waste, and needs to be broken up and mellowed, before it is suited to receive grain. I shall show, as it respects a revival in the church,

1. What it is to break up the fallow ground, in the sense of the text.
2. How it is to be performed.

I. WHAT IS IT TO BREAK UP THE FALLOW GROUND?

To break up the fallow ground, is to *break up your hearts* — to prepare your minds to bring forth fruit unto God. The mind of man is often compared in the Bible to ground, and the word of God to seed sown in it, and the fruit represents the actions and affections of those who receive it. To break up the fallow ground, therefore, is to bring the mind into such a state, that it is fitted to receive the word of God. Sometimes your hearts get matted down hard and dry, and all run to waste, till there is no such thing as getting fruit from them till they are all broken up, and mellowed down, and fitted to receive the word of God. It is this softening of the heart, so as to make it feel the truth, which the prophet calls breaking up your fallow ground.

II. HOW IS THE FALLOW GROUND TO BE BROKEN UP?

1. *It is not by any direct efforts to feel.* People run into a mistake on this subject, from not making the laws of mind the object of thought. There are great errors on the subject of the laws which govern the mind. People talk about religious feeling, as if they thought they could, by direct effort, call forth emotion. But this is not the way the mind acts. No man can make himself feel in this way, merely by *trying* to feel. The *emotions* of the mind are not *directly* under our control. We cannot by willing, or by direct volition, call forth our emotions. We might as well think to call spirits up from the deep. The emotions are purely involuntary states of mind. They naturally and necessarily exist in the mind under certain circumstances calculated to excite them. But they can be controlled *indirectly*. Otherwise there would be no moral character in our emotions, if there were not a way to control them. We cannot say, "Now I will feel so and so towards such an object." But we can command our *attention* to it, and look at it intently, till the proper feeling arises. Let a man who is away from his family, bring them up before his mind, and will he not feel? But it is not by saying to himself, "Now I will feel deeply for my family." A man can direct his attention to any object, about which he ought to feel and wishes to feel, and in that way he will call into existence the proper emotions. Let a man call up his enemy before his mind, and his feelings of enmity will rise. So if a man thinks of God, and fastens his mind on any parts of God's character, he will feel — emotions will come up, by the very laws of mind. If he is a friend of God, let him contemplate God as a gracious and holy being, and he will have emotions of friendship kindled up in his mind. If he is an enemy of God, only let him get the true character of God before his mind, and look at it, and fasten his attention on it, and his enmity will rise against God.[1]

[1] It was such passages as this (and those that follow), in which Finney tries to redefine the psychology of the Scottish Common Sense School in order to

If you wish to break up the fallow ground of your hearts, and make your minds feel on the subject of religion, you must go to work just as you would to feel on any other subject. Instead of keeping your thoughts on every thing else, and then imagine that by going to a few meetings you will get your feelings enlisted, go the common sense way to work, as you would on any other subject. It is just as easy to make your minds feel on the subject of religion as it is on any other subject. God has put these states of mind just as absolutely under your control, as the motions of your limbs. If people were as unphilosophical about moving their limbs, as they are about regulating their emotions, you would never have gotten here to meeting to-night.

If you mean to break up the fallow ground of your hearts, you must begin by looking at your hearts — examine and note the state of your minds, and see where you are. Many never seem to think about this. They pay no attention to their own hearts, and never know whether they are doing well in religion or not — whether they are gaining ground or going back — whether they are fruitful, or lying waste like fallow ground. Now you must draw off your attention from other things, and look into this. Make a business of it. Don't be in a hurry. Examine thoroughly the state of your hearts, and see where you are — whether you are walking with God every day, or walking with the devil — whether you are serving God or serving the devil most — whether you are under the dominion of the prince of darkness, or the Lord Jesus Christ.

To do all this, you must set yourself at work to consider your sins. You must examine yourselves. And by this I do not mean, that you must stop and look directly within to see what is the present state of your feelings. That is the very way to put a stop to all feeling. This is just as absurd as it would be for a man to shut his eyes on the lamp, and try to turn his eyes inward to find out whether there was any image painted on the retina. The man complains that he don't see any thing! And why? Because he has turned his eyes away from the objects of sight. The truth is, our moral feelings are as much an object of consciousness as our senses. And the way to find them out is to go on acting, and employing our minds. Then we can tell our moral feelings by consciousness,

---

fit his own theory of free will, that caused Professor Albert Dod of Princeton to call him "a perfect novice in mental science." See the Introduction to this edition, pp. xxvi–xxix.

just as I could tell my natural feelings by consciousness, if I should put my hand in the fire.

Self-examination consists in looking at your lives, in considering your actions, in calling up the past, and learning its true character. Look back over your past history. Take up your individual sins one by one, and look at them. I do not mean that you should just cast a glance at your past life, and see that it has been full of sins, and then go to God and make a sort of general confession, and ask for pardon. That is not the way. You must take them up one by one. It will be a good thing to take a pen and paper, as you go over them, and write them down as they occur to you. Go over them as carefully as a merchant goes over his books; and as often as a sin comes before your memory, add it to the list. General confessions of sin will never do. Your sins were committed *one by one*; and as far as you can come at them, they ought to be reviewed and repented of one by one. Now begin; and take up first what are commonly, but *improperly*, called your

SINS OF OMISSION.

1. *Ingratitude.* Take this sin, for instance, and write down under it all the instances you can remember, wherein you have received favors from God, for which you have never exercised gratitude.[2] How many cases can you remember? Some remarkable providence, some wonderful turn of events, that saved you from ruin. Set down the instances of God's goodness to you when you were in sin, before your conversion. Then the mercy of God in the circumstances of your conversion, for which you have never been half thankful enough. The numerous mercies you have received since. How long the catalogue of instances, where your ingratitude is so black that you are forced to hide your face in confusion! Now go on your knees, and confess them one by one to God, and ask forgiveness. The very act of confession, by the laws of suggestion, will bring up others to your memory. Put down these. Go over these three or four times in this way, and you will find an astonishing amount of mercies, for which you have never thanked God. Then take another sin. Let it be,

2. *Want of love to God.* Write that down, and go over all the

[2] There is something so mechanical about Finney's piety at this point that he seems closer to the utilitarian ethics of Benjamin Franklin than to the pietism of a revivalist. The juxtaposition of the practical with the mystical appears throughout Finney's works.

instances you can remember, when you did not give to the blessed God that hearty love which you ought.

Think how grieved and alarmed you would be, if you discovered any flagging of affection for you, in your wife, husband, or children; — if you saw somebody else engrossing their hearts, and thoughts, and time. Perhaps, in such a case, you would well nigh die with a just and virtuous jealousy. Now, God styles himself a jealous God; and have you not given your heart to other loves; played the harlot, and infinitely offended him?

3. *Neglect of the Bible.* Put down the cases, when for days, and perhaps for weeks — yea, it may be, even for months together, you had no pleasure in God's word. Perhaps you did not read a chapter, or if you read it, it was in a way that was still more displeasing to God. Many people read over a whole chapter in such a way, that if they were put under oath when they have done, they could not tell what they have been reading. With so little attention do they read, that they cannot remember where they have read from morning till evening, unless they put in a string or turn down a leaf. This demonstrates that they did not lay to heart what they read, that they did not make it a subject of reflection. If you were reading a novel, or any other piece of intelligence that greatly interests you, would you not remember what you read last? And the fact that you fold a leaf or put in a string, demonstrates that you read rather as a task, than from love or reverence for the word of God. The word of God is the rule of your duty. And do you pay so little regard to it as not to remember what you read? If so, no wonder that you live so at random, and that your religion is such a miserable failure.

4. *Unbelief.* Instances in which you have virtually charged the God of truth with lying, by your unbelief of his express promises and declarations. God has promised to give the Holy Spirit to them that ask him. Now, have you believed this? Have you expected him to answer? Have you not virtually said in your hearts, when you prayed for the Holy Spirit, "I do not believe that I shall receive it?" If you have not believed nor expected you should receive the blessing, which God has expressly promised, you have charged him with lying.

5. *Neglect of prayer.* Times when you omitted secret prayer, family prayer, and prayer meetings, or have prayed in such a way as more grievously to offend God, than to have neglected it altogether.

6. *Neglect of the means of grace.* When you have suffered trifling excuses to prevent your attending meetings, have neglected and poured contempt upon the means of salvation, merely from disrelish of spiritual duties.

7. *The manner in which you have performed* those duties — want of feeling — want of faith — worldly frame of mind — so that your words were nothing but the mere chattering of a wretch, that did not deserve that God should feel the least care for him. When you have fallen down upon your knees, and *said your prayers*, in such an unfeeling and careless manner, that if you had been put under oath five minutes after you left your closet, you could not have told what you had been praying for.

8. *Your want of love for the souls of your fellow-men.* Look round upon your friends and relations, and remember how little compassion you have felt for them. You have stood by and seen them going right to hell, and it seems as though you did not care if they did. How many days have there been, in which you did not make their condition the subject of a single fervent prayer, or even an ardent desire for their salvation?

9. *Your want of care for the heathen.* Perhaps you have not cared enough for them to attempt to learn their conditions; perhaps not even to take the *Missionary Herald*.[3] Look at this, and see how much you do really care for the heathen, and set down honestly the real amount of your feelings for them, and your desire for their salvation. Measure your desire for their salvation by the self-denial you practise, in giving of your substance to send them the gospel. Do you deny yourself even the hurtful superfluities of life, such as tea, coffee, and tobacco? Do you retrench your style of living, and really subject yourself to any inconvenience to save them? Do you daily pray for them in your closet? Do you statedly attend the monthly concert?[4] Are you from month to month laying by something to put into the treasury of the Lord, when you go up to pray? If you are not doing these

---

[3] The *Missionary Herald* was a Congregationalist journal edited in Boston by Jeremiah Evarts and devoted to the promotion of home and foreign missions. It grew out of the merger between the *Panoplist* and the *Massachusetts Missionary Magazine* and was at this time dominated by moderate Calvinists at Andover Theological Seminary in Massachusetts.

[4] The monthly concert was a monthly prayer meeting commonly held in Presbyterian and Congregational churches throughout the United States in the 1830's for the purpose of praying for the success of missionary work and for the conversion of the heathen. It was common to take collections for home and foreign missions at these concerts.

things, and if your soul is not agonized for the poor benighted heathen, why are you such a hypocrite, as to pretend to be a Christian? Why, your profession is an insult to Jesus Christ!

10. *Your neglect of family duties.* How you have lived before them, how you have prayed, what an example you have set before them. What direct efforts do you habitually make for their spiritual good? What duty have you *not* neglected?

11. Neglect of social duties.

12. *Neglect of watchfulness over your own life.* Instances in which you have hurried over your private duties, and not taken yourself to task, nor honestly made up your accounts with God. Where you have entirely neglected to watch your conduct, and have been off your guard, and have sinned before the world, and before the church, and before God.

13. *Neglect to watch over your brethren.* How often have you broken your covenant, that you would watch over them in the Lord! How little do you know or care about the state of their souls! And yet you are under a solemn oath to perform it. What have you done to make yourself acquainted with them? How many of them have you interested yourself for, to know their spiritual state? Go over the list, and wherever you find there has been a neglect, write it down. How many times have you seen your brethren growing cold in religion, and have not spoken to them about it? You have seen them beginning to neglect one duty after another, and you did not reprove them in a brotherly way. You have seen them falling into sin, and you let them go on. And yet you pretend to love them. What a hypocrite! Would you see your wife or child going into disgrace, or into the fire, and hold your peace? No, you would not. What do you think of yourself, then, to pretend to love Christians, and love Christ, while you can see them going into disgrace, and say nothing to them?

14. *Neglect of self-denial.* There are many professors who are willing to do almost any thing in religion, that does not require self-denial. But when they are called to do any thing that requires them to deny themselves, O! that is too much. They think they are doing a great deal for God, and doing about as much as he ought to ask in reason, if they are only doing what they can do about as well as not; but they are not willing to deny themselves any comfort or convenience whatever, for the sake of serving the Lord. They will not willingly suffer reproach for the name of Christ. Nor will they deny themselves the *luxuries* of life, to save a

world from hell. So far are they from remembering that self-denial is a *condition of discipleship*, that they don't know what self-denial is. They never have really denied themselves a riband or a pin for Christ, and for the gospel. O, how soon such professors will be in hell! Some are giving of *their abundance*, and are giving much, and are ready to complain that others don't give more; when, in truth, they do not give any thing that they *need*, any thing that they could enjoy, if they kept it. They only give of their surplus wealth; and perhaps that poor woman, who puts in twelve and a half cents at the monthly concert, has exercised more self-denial than they have in giving thousands.

From these we now turn to

SINS OF COMMISSION.

1. *Worldly mindedness*. What has been the state of your heart in regard to your worldly possessions? Have you looked at them as really *yours* — as if you had a right to dispose of them as your own, according to your own will? If you have, write that down. If you have loved property, and sought after it for its own sake, or to gratify lust or ambition, or a worldly spirit, or to lay it up for your families, you have sinned, and must repent.

2. *Pride*. Recollect all the instances you can, in which you have detected yourself in the exercise of pride. Vanity is a particular form of pride. How many times have you detected yourself in consulting vanity, about your dress and appearance? How many times have you thought more, and taken more pains, and spent more time, about decorating your body to go to church, than you have about preparing your mind for the worship of God? You have gone to the house of God caring more how you appear outwardly in the sight of mortal men, than how your soul appears in the sight of the heart-searching God. You have in fact set up yourself to be worshipped by them, rather than prepared to worship God yourself. You came to divide the worship of God's house, to draw off the attention of God's people to look at your pretty appearance. It is in vain to pretend now, that you don't care any thing about having people look at you. Be honest about it. Would you take all this pains about your looks if every body was blind?

3. *Envy*. Look at the cases in which you were envious at those who you thought were above you in any respect. Or perhaps

you have envied those who have been more talented or more useful than yourself. Have you not so envied some, that you have been pained to hear them praised? It has been more agreeable to you to dwell upon their faults, than upon their virtues, upon their failures, than upon their success. Be honest with yourself, and if you have harbored this spirit of hell, repent deeply before God, or *he will never forgive you.*

4. *Censoriousness.* Instances in which you have had a bitter spirit, and spoken of Christians in a manner entirely devoid of charity and love — charity, which requires you always to hope the best the case will admit, and to put the best construction upon any ambiguous conduct.

5. *Slander.* The times you have spoken behind people's backs of their faults, real or supposed, of members of the church or others, unnecessarily or without good reason. This is slander. You need not *lie* to be guilty of slander; — to tell the truth with the design to injure, is slander.

6. *Levity.* How often have you trifled before God, as you would not have dared to trifle in the presence of an earthly sovereign? You have either been an Atheist, and forgotten that there was a God, or have had less respect for him, and his presence, than you would have had for an earthly judge.

7. *Lying.* Understand now what lying is. Any species of *designed* deception. If the deception is not designed it is not lying. But if you design to make an impression contrary to the naked truth, you lie. Put down all those cases you can recollect. Don't call them by any soft name. God calls them LIES, and charges you with LYING, and you had better charge yourself correctly.

How innumerable are the falsehoods perpetrated every day, in business, and in social intercourse, by words, and looks, and actions — designed to make an impression on others contrary to the truth!

8. *Cheating.* Set down all the cases in which you have dealt with an individual, and done to him that which you would not like to have done to you. *That* is cheating. God has laid down a rule in the case; "All things whatsoever ye would that men should do to you, do ye even so to them." That is the rule; and now if you have not done so you are a cheat. Mind, the rule is not that you should do what you might reasonably expect them to do to you. That is a rule which would admit of every degree of wickedness. But it is "As ye WOULD they should do to you."

9. *Hypocrisy*. For instance, in your prayers and confessions to God. Set down the instances in which you have prayed for things you did not really want. And the evidence is, that when you had done praying, you could not tell what you had prayed for. How many times have you confessed sins that you did not mean to break off, and when you had no solemn purpose not to repeat them? Yes, have confessed sins when you knew you as much expected to go and repeat them as you expected to live.

10. *Robbing God*. Instances in which you have misspent your time, and squandered hours which God gave you to serve him and save souls, in vain amusements or foolish conversation, reading novels, or doing nothing; cases where you have misapplied your talents and powers of mind; where you have squandered money on your lusts, or spent it for things you did not need, and which neither contributed to your health, comfort or usefulness. Perhaps some of you who are here to-night have laid out God's money for TOBACCO. I will not speak of rum, for I presume there is no professor of religion here to-night that would drink rum. I hope there is no one that uses that filthy poison, tobacco. Think of a professor of religion, using God's money to poison himself with tobacco!

11. *Bad temper*. Perhaps you have abused your wife, or your children, or your family, or servants, or neighbors. Write it all down.

12. *Hindering others from being useful*. Perhaps you have weakened their influence by insinuations against them. You have not only robbed God of your own talents, but tied the hands of somebody else. What a wicked servant is he that loiters himself, and hinders the rest! This is done sometimes by taking their time needlessly; sometimes by destroying Christian confidence in them. Thus you have played into the hands of Satan, and not only showed yourself an idle vagabond, but prevented others from working.

If you find you have committed a fault against an individual, and that individual is within your reach, go and confess it immediately, and get that out of the way. If the individual you have injured is too far off for you to go and see him, sit down and write him a letter, and confess the injury, *pay the postage*, and put it into the mail immediately. I say, pay the postage, or otherwise you will only make the matter worse. You will add to the former injury, by making him a bill of expense. The man that writes a letter on his own business, and sends it to another without paying the postage, is dishonest, and has cheated him out of so much. And if he would cheat a man out of a sixpence or shilling, when the temptation is so small, what would he not do were the temptation greater, and he had the prospect of impunity? [5] If you have defrauded any body, send the money, the full amount and the interest.

Go thoroughly to work in all this. Go *now*. Don't put it off; that will only make the matter worse. Confess to God those sins that have been committed against God, and to man those sins that have been committed against man. Don't think of getting off by going round the stumbling blocks. Take them up out of the way. In breaking up your fallow ground, you must remove every obstruction. Things may be left that you may think little things, and you may wonder why you do not feel as you wish to in religion, when the reason is that your proud and carnal mind has covered up something which God required you to confess and remove. Break up all the ground and turn it over. Don't balk it, as the farmers say; don't turn aside for little difficulties; drive the plow right through them, beam deep, and turn the ground all up, so that it may all be mellow and soft, and fit to receive the seed and bear fruit a hundred fold.

When you have gone over your whole history in this way, thoroughly, if you will then go over the ground the second time, and give your solemn and fixed attention to it, you will find that the things you have put down will suggest other things of which you have been guilty, connected with them, or near them. Then go over it a third time, and you will recollect other things connected with these. And you will find in the end that you can remember an amount of your history, and particular actions, even in this life, which you did not think you should remember in eternity. Unless you do take up your sins in this way, and consider them in detail, one by one, you can form no idea of the amount of your sins. You should go over it as thoroughly and as solemnly, as you would if you were just preparing yourself for the judgment.

As you go over the catalogue of your sins, be sure to resolve upon present and entire reformation. Wherever you find any thing wrong, resolve at once, in the strength of God, to sin no more in

---

[5] It was customary for the receiver not the sender to pay the postage on United States mail. It was also still common in the 1830's, especially among New Englanders, to use the old English designations for money; even American coins were evaluated in shillings.

that way. It will be of no benefit to examine yourself, unless you determine to amend in *every particular* that you find wrong in heart, temper, or conduct.

If you find, as you go on with this duty, that your mind is still all dark, cast about you, and you will find there is some reason for the Spirit of God to depart from you. You have not been faithful and thorough. In the progress of such a work you have got to do violence to yourself, and bring yourself as a rational being up to this work, with the Bible before you, and try your heart till you *do* feel. You need not expect that God will work a miracle for you to break up your fallow ground. It is to be done by means. Fasten your attention to the subject of your sins. You cannot look at your sins long and thoroughly, and see how bad they are, without feeling, and feeling deeply. Experience abundantly proves the benefit of going over our history in this way. Set yourself to the work now; resolve that you never will stop till you find you can *pray*. You never will have the spirit of prayer, till you examine yourselves, and confess your sins, and break up your fallow ground. You never will have the Spirit of God dwelling in you, till you have unraveled this whole mystery of iniquity, and spread out your sins before God. Let there be this deep work of repentance, and full confession, this breaking down before God, and you will have as much of the spirit of prayer as your body can bear up under. The reason why so few Christians know any thing about the spirit of prayer, is because they never would take the pains to examine themselves properly, and so never knew what it was to have their hearts all broken up in this way.

You see I have only begun to lay open this subject to-night. I want to lay it out before you, in the course of these lectures, so that if you will begin and go on to do as I say, the results will be just as certain as they are when the farmer breaks up a fallow field, and mellows it, and sows his grain. It will be so, if you will only begin in this way, and hold on till all your hardened and callous hearts break up.

REMARKS.

1. It will do no good to preach to you while your hearts are in this hardened, and waste, and fallow state. The farmer might just as well sow his grain on the rock. It will bring forth no fruit. This is the reason why there are so many fruitless professors in

the church, and why there is so much outside machinery, and so little deep-toned feeling in the church. Look at the Sabbath school for instance, and see how much machinery there is, and how little of the power of godliness. If you go on in this way, the word of God will continue to harden you, and you will grow worse and worse, just as the rain and snow on an old fallow field makes the turf thicker, and the clods stronger.

2. See why so much preaching is wasted, and worse than wasted. It is because the church will not break up their fallow ground. A preacher may wear out his life, and do very little good, while there are so many stony-ground hearers, who have never had their fallow ground broken up. They are only half converted, and their religion is rather a change of opinion than a change of the feeling of their hearts. There is mechanical religion enough, but very little that looks like deep heart-work.

3. Professors of religion should never satisfy themselves, or expect a revival, just by starting out of their slumbers, and blustering about, and making a noise, and talking to sinners. They must get their fallow ground broken up. It is utterly unphilosophical to think of getting engaged in religion in this way. If your fallow ground is broken up, *then* the way to get more feeling, is to go out and see sinners on the road to hell, and talk to them, and guide inquiring souls, and you will get more feeling. You may get into an *excitement* without this breaking up; you may show a kind of zeal, but it won't last long, and it won't take hold of sinners, unless your hearts are broken up. The reason is, that you go about it mechanically, and have not broken up your fallow ground.

4. And now, finally, will you break up your fallow ground? Will you enter upon the course now pointed out, and persevere till you are thoroughly awake? If you fail here, if you don't do *this*, and get prepared, you can go no further with me in this course of lectures. I have gone with you as far as it is of any use to go, until your fallow ground is broken up. Now, you must make thorough work upon this point, or all I have further to say will do you little good. Nay, it will only harden and make you worse. If, when next Friday night arrives, it finds you with unbroken hearts, you need not expect to be benefited by what I shall say. If you don't set about this work immediately, I shall take it for granted that you don't mean to be revived, that you have forsaken your minister, and mean to let him go up to battle alone. If you don't do this, I charge you with having forsaken Christ, with refusing to

repent and do your first work. But if you will be prepared to enter upon the work, I propose, God willing, next Friday evening, to lead you into the work of saving sinners.[6]

[6] This final paragraph was added by Finney for the first edition. It does not appear in the lecture as printed in the *New York Evangelist*, December 20, 1834, p. 202.

IV

PREVAILING PRAYER[1]

TEXT. — The effectual, fervent prayer of a righteous man availeth much. — JAMES v. 16.

THE last lecture referred principally to the confession of sin. To-night my remarks will be chiefly confined to the subject of intercession, or prayer. There are two kinds of means requisite to promote a revival; one to influence men, the other to influence God. The truth is employed to influence men, and prayer to move God. When I speak of moving God, I do not mean that God's mind is changed by prayer, or that his disposition or character is changed. But prayer produces such a change *in us* as renders it consistent for God to do as it would not be consistent for him to do otherwise. When a sinner repents, that state of feeling makes it proper for God to forgive him. God has always been ready to forgive him on that condition, so that when the sinner changes his feelings, and repents, it requires no change of feeling in God to pardon him. It is the sinner's repentance that renders his forgiveness proper, and is the occasion of God's acting as he does. So when Christians offer effectual prayer, their state of feeling renders it proper for God to answer them. He was always ready to bestow the blessing, on the condition that they felt right, and offered the right kind of prayer. Whenever this change takes place in them, and they offer the right kind of prayer, then God, without any change in himself, can answer them. When we offer effectual fervent prayer for

---

[1] Finney's doctrine of prevailing prayer (sometimes called by him "effectual prayer" or "agonizing prayer") seems to have originated with him or with his friend Daniel Nash (see Cross, *Burned-Over District*, p. 179). It aroused a great deal of opposition among orthodox Calvinists. One objection was that it seemed to put prayer on a cause-and-effect basis in which God allowed himself to be importuned by the aggressively pious. Another objection was that it seemed to allow for the possibility of direct revelations in answer to prayer. A third objection was that in practice it led to an overbearing and censorious attitude on the part of those who believed that they possessed the power of prevailing with God. Finney's mystical attitude toward prayer represents the more pietistic side of his personality. Modern revivalism since 1835 has been a curious combination of pietism and pragmatism.

others, the fact that we offer such prayer renders it consistent for him to do what we pray for, when otherwise it would not have been consistent.

Prayer is an essential link in the chain of causes that lead to a revival; as much so as truth is. Some have zealously used truth to convert men, and laid very little stress on prayer. They have preached, and talked, and distributed tracts with great zeal, and then wondered that they had so little success. And the reason was, that they forgot to use the other branch of the means, effectual prayer. They overlooked the fact, that truth by itself will never produce the effect, without the Spirit of God.[2]

Sometimes it happens that those who are the most engaged in employing truth, are not the most engaged in prayer. This is always unhappy. — For unless they, or somebody else, have the spirit of prayer, the truth by itself will do nothing but harden men in impenitence. Probably in the day of judgment it will be found that nothing is ever done by the truth, used ever so zealously, unless there is a spirit of prayer somewhere in connection with the presentation of truth.

Others err on the other side. Not that they lay too much stress on prayer. But they overlook the fact that prayer might be offered for ever, by itself, and nothing would be done. Because sinners are not converted by direct contact of the Holy Ghost, but by the truth, employed as a means. To expect the conversion of sinners by prayer alone, without the employment of truth, is to tempt God.

The subject of discourse this evening, is

PREVAILING PRAYER.

I. I propose to show what is effectual or prevailing prayer.
II. State some of the most essential attributes of prevailing prayer.
III. Give some reasons why God requires this kind of prayer.
IV. Show that such prayer will avail much.

I. I proceed to show what is prevailing prayer.
1. Effectual, prevailing prayer, does not consist in benevolent desires merely. Benevolent desires are doubtless pleasing to God.

---

[2] In the revised edition of 1868 Finney added here, "and that Spirit is given in answer to earnest prayer."

Such desires pervade heaven, and are found in all holy beings. But they are not prayer. Men may have these desires as the angels and glorified spirits have them. But this is not the effectual, prevailing prayer, spoken of in the text. Prevailing prayer is something more than this.

2. Prevailing, or effectual prayer, is that prayer which attains the blessing that it seeks. It is that prayer which effectually moves God. The very idea of *effectual* prayer is, that it effects its object.

II. I will state some of the most essential attributes of prevailing prayer. I cannot detail in full all the things that go to make up prevailing prayer. But I will mention some things that are essential to it; some things which a person must do in order to prevail in prayer.

1. *He must pray for a definite object.* He need not expect to offer such prayer, if he prays at random, without any distinct or definite object. He must have an object distinctly before his mind. I speak now of secret prayer. Many people go away into their closets, because they must *say* their prayers. The time has come that they are in the habit of going by themselves for prayer, in the morning, or at noon, or at whatever time of day it may be. And instead of having any thing to say, any definite object before their mind, they fall down on their knees, and pray for just what comes into their minds, for every thing that floats in their imagination at the time, and when they have done, they could not tell hardly a word of what they had been praying for. This is not effectual prayer. What should we think of any body who should try to move a legislature so, and should say, "Now it is winter, and the legislature is in session, and it is time to send up petitions," and should go up to the legislature and petition at random, without any definite object? Do you think such petitions would move the legislature?

A man must have some definite object before his mind. He cannot pray effectually for a variety of objects at once. The mind of man is so constituted that it cannot fasten its desires intensely upon many things at the same time. All the instances of effectual prayer recorded in the Bible were of this kind. Wherever you see that the blessing sought for in prayer was attained, you will find that the prayer which was offered was prayer for that definite object.

2. Prayer, to be effectual, must be in accordance with the revealed will of God. To pray for things contrary to the revealed

will of God, is to tempt God. There are three ways in which God's will is revealed to men for their guidance in prayer.

(1.) By express promises or predictions in the Bible, that he will give or do certain things. Either by express promises in regard to particular things, or promises in general terms, so that we may apply them to particular things. For instance, there is this promise: "Whatsoever things ye desire, when ye pray, believe that ye receive them, and ye shall have them."

(2.) Sometimes God reveals his will by his providence. When he makes it clear that such and such events are about to take place, it is as much a revelation as if he had written it in his word. It would be impossible to reveal every thing in the Bible. But God often makes it clear to those who have spiritual discernment, that it is his will to grant such and such blessings.

(3.) By his Spirit. When God's people are at a loss what to pray for, agreeable to his will, his Spirit often instructs them. Where there is no particular revelation, and providence leaves it dark, and we know not what to pray for as we ought, we are expressly told, that "the Spirit also helpeth our infirmities," and "the Spirit itself maketh intercession for us with groanings that cannot be uttered." A great deal has been said on the subject of praying in faith for things not revealed. It is objected, that this doctrine implies a new revelation. I answer, that, new or old, it is the very revelation that Jehovah says he makes. It is just as plain here, as if it were now revealed by a voice from heaven, that the Spirit of God helps the people of God to pray according to the will of God, when they themselves know not what things they ought to pray for. "And he that searcheth the heart knoweth the mind of the Spirit," because he maketh intercession for the saints according to the will of God, and he leads Christians to pray for just those things, with groanings that cannot be uttered. When neither the word nor providence enables them to decide, then let them be filled with the Spirit, as God commands them to be. He says, "Be ye filled with the Spirit." And *He* will lead their mind to such things as God is willing to grant.

3. To pray effectually, you must pray with submission to the will of God. Don't confound submission with indifference. No two things are more unlike. I once knew an individual come where there was a revival. He himself was cold, and did not enter into the spirit of it, and had no spirit of prayer; and when he heard the brethren pray as if they could not be denied, he was shocked at

their boldness, and kept all the time insisting on the importance of praying with submission; when it was as plain as any thing could be, that he confounded submission with indifference

So again, don't confound submission in prayer with a general confidence that God will do what is right. It is proper to have this confidence that God will do what is right in all things. But this is a different thing from submisison. What I mean by submission in prayer, is, acquiescence in the revealed will of God. To submit to any *command* of God is to obey it. Submission to some supposable or possible, but secret decree of God, is not submission. To submit to any dispensation of Providence is impossible till it comes. For we never can know what the event is to be, till it takes place. Take a case: David, when his child was sick, was distressed, and agonized in prayer, and refused to be comforted. He took it so much to heart, that when the child died, his servants were afraid to tell him that the child was dead, for fear he would vex himself still worse. But as soon as he heard that the child was dead, he laid aside his grief, and arose, and asked for food, and ate and drank as usual. While the child was yet alive, he did not know what was the will of God, and so he fasted and prayed, and said, "Who can tell whether God will be gracious to me, that my child may live?" He did not know but that his prayer and agony was the very thing on which it turned, whether the child was to live or not. He thought that if he humbled himself and entreated God, perhaps God would spare him this blow. But as soon as God's will appeared, and the child was dead, he bowed like a saint. He seemed not only to acquiesce, but actually to take a satisfaction in it. "I shall go to him, but he shall not return to me." This was true submission. He reasoned correctly in the case. While he had no revelation of the will of God, he did not know but what the child's recovery depended on his prayer. But when he had a revelation of the will of God, he submitted. While the will of God is not known, to submit, without prayer, is tempting God. Perhaps, and for aught you know, the fact of your offering the right kind of prayer, may be the thing on which the event turns. In the case of an impenitent friend, the very condition on which he is to be saved from hell, may be the fervency and importunity of your prayer for that individual.

4. Effectual prayer for an object implies a desire for that object commensurate with its importance. If a person *truly* desires any blessing, his desires will bear some proportion to the greatness

of the blessing. The desires of the Lord Jesus Christ for the blessing he prayed for, were amazingly strong, and amounted even to agony. If the desire for an object is strong, and is a benevolent desire, and the thing not contrary to the will and providence of God, the presumption is, that it will be granted. There are two reasons for this presumption:

(1.) From the general benevolence of God. If it is a desirable object; if, so far as we can see, it would be an act of benevolence in God to grant it, his general benevolence is presumptive evidence that he will grant it.

(2.) If you find yourself exercised with benevolent desires for any object, there is a strong presumption that the Spirit of God is exciting these very desires, and stirring you up to pray for that object, so that it may be granted in answer to prayer. In such a case no degree of desire or importunity in prayer is improper. A Christian may come up, as it were, and take hold of the hand of God. See the case of Jacob, when he exclaimed in an agony of desire, "I will not let thee go, except thou bless me." Was God displeased with his boldness and importunity? Not at all; but he granted him the very thing he prayed for. So in the case of Moses. God said to Moses, "Let me alone, that I may destroy them, and blot out their name from under heaven, and I will make of thee a nation mightier and greater than they." What did Moses do? Did he stand aside and let God do as he said? No, his mind runs back to the Egyptians, and he thinks how they will triumph. "Wherefore should the Egyptians say, For mischief did he bring them out." It seemed as if he took hold of the uplifted hand of God, to avert the blow. Did God rebuke him for his interference, and tell him he had no business to interfere? No; it seemed as if he was unable to deny any thing to such importunity, and so Moses stood in the gap, and prevailed with God.

It is said of Xavier, the missionary, that he was once called to pray for a man who was sick, and he prayed so fervently that he seemed as it were to do violence to heaven — so the writer expresses it.[3] And he prevailed, and the man recovered.

---

[3] Finney refers again to Francis Xavier in commendatory terms in Lecture IX, p. 147. There is no doubt that Finney shared the antipathy of most Protestant ministers in the 1830's toward the Roman Catholic Church and its priests, but in his zeal for converting the world, Finney could not help paying some tribute to the devoted Jesuit who first brought Christianity to India, the East Indies, and Japan in 1542–1552. I have been unable to locate the writer to whom Finney refers here as describing Xavier's method of prayer.

Such prayer is often offered in the present day, when Christians have been wrought up to such a pitch of importunity and such a holy boldness, that afterwards, when they looked back upon it, they were frightened and amazed at themselves, to think they should dare to exercise such importunity with God. And yet these prayers have prevailed, and obtained the blessing. And many of these persons, that I am acquainted with, are among the holiest persons I know in the world.

5. Prayer, to be effectual, must be offered from right motives. Prayer should not be selfish, but dictated by a supreme regard for the glory of God. A great deal of prayer is offered from pure selfishness. Women sometimes pray for their husbands, that they may be converted, because they say, "It would be so much more pleasant, to have my husband go to meeting with me," and all that. And they seem never to lift up their thoughts above self at all. They do not seem to think how their husbands are dishonoring God by their sins, and how God would be glorified in their conversion. So it is with parents very often. They can't bear to think that *their children* should be lost. They pray for them very earnestly indeed. But if you go to talk with them, they are very tender, and tell you how good their children are, how they respect religion, and they think they are almost Christians now; and so they talk as if they were afraid you would hurt their children if you tell them the truth. They do not think how such amiable and lovely children are dishonoring God by their sins; they are only thinking what a dreadful thing it will be for them to go to hell. Ah! unless their thoughts rise higher than this, their prayers will never prevail with a holy God. The temptation to selfish motives is so strong, that there is reason to fear a great many parental prayers never rise above the yearnings of parental tenderness. And that is the reason why so many prayers are not heard, and why so many pious, praying parents have ungodly children. Much of the prayer for the heathen world, seems to be based on no higher principle than sympathy. Missionary agents, and others, are dwelling almost exclusively upon the six hundred millions of heathens going to hell, while little is said of their dishonoring God. This is a great evil; and until the church have higher motives for prayer and missionary effort than sympathy for the heathen, their prayers and efforts will never amount to much.

6. Prayer, to be effectual, must be by the intercession of the Spirit. You never can expect to offer prayer according to the will

of God without the Spirit. In the first two cases, it is not because Christians are unable to offer such prayer, where the will of God is revealed in his word, or indicated by his providence. They are able to do it, just as they are able to be holy. But the fact is, that they are so wicked, that they never do offer such prayer, without they are influenced by the Spirit of God. There must be a faith, such as produced by the effectual operation of the Holy Ghost.

7. It must be persevering prayer. As a general thing, Christians who have backslidden and lost the spirit of prayer, will not get at once into the *habit* of persevering prayer. Their minds are not in a right state, and they cannot fix their minds, and hold on till the blessing comes. If their minds were in that state, that they would persevere till the answer comes, effectual prayer might be offered at once, as well as after praying ever so many times for an object. But they have to pray again and again, because their thoughts are so apt to wander away, and are so easily diverted from the object to something else. Until their minds get imbued with the spirit of prayer, they will not keep fixed to one point, and push their petition to an issue on the spot. Do not think you are prepared to offer prevailing prayer, if your feelings will let you pray once for an object, and then leave it. Most Christians come up to prevailing prayer by a protracted process. Their minds gradually become filled with anxiety about an object, so that they will even go about their business, sighing out their desires to God. Just as the mother whose child is sick, goes round her house, sighing as if her heart would break. And if she is a praying mother, her sighs are breathed out to God all the day long. If she goes out of the room where her child is, her mind is still on it; and if she is asleep, still her thoughts are on it, and she starts in her dreams, thinking it is dying. Her whole mind is absorbed in that sick child. This is the state of mind in which Christians offer prevailing prayer.

What was the reason that Jacob wrestled all night in prayer with God? He knew that he had done his brother Esau a great injury, in getting away the birthright a long time ago. And now he was informed that his injured brother was coming to meet him, with an armed force altogether too powerful for him to contend against. And there was great reason to suppose he was coming with a purpose of revenge. There were two reasons then why he should be distressed. The first was, that he had done this great injury, and had never made any reparation. The other was, that Esau was coming with a force sufficient to crush him. Now, what does he do? Why, he first arranges everything in the best manner he can to meet his brother, sending his present first, then his property, then his family, putting those he loved most farthest behind. And by this time his mind was so exercised that he could not contain himself. He goes away alone over the brook, and pours out his very soul in an agony of prayer all night. And just as the day was breaking, the angel of the covenant said, "Let me go;" and his whole being was, as it were, agonized at the thought of giving up, and he cried out, "I will not let thee go except thou bless me." His soul was wrought up into an agony, and he obtained the blessing, but he always bore the marks of it, and showed that his body had been greatly affected by this mental struggle. This is prevailing prayer.

Now, do not deceive yourselves with thinking that you offer effectual prayer, unless you have this intense desire for the blessing. I don't believe in it. Prayer is not effectual unless it is offered up with an agony of desire. The apostle Paul speaks of it as a travail of the soul. Jesus Christ, when he was praying in the garden, was in such an agony, that he sweat as it were great drops of blood falling down to the ground. I have never known a person sweat blood; but I have known a person pray till the blood started from the nose. And I have known persons pray till they were all wet with perspiration, in the coldest weather in winter. I have known persons pray for hours, till their strength was all exhausted with the agony of their minds. Such prayers prevailed with God.[4]

This agony in prayer was prevalent in President Edwards' day, in the revivals that then took place. It was one of the great stumbling blocks in those days, to persons who were opposed to the revival, that people used to pray till the body was overpowered with their feelings. I will read a paragraph of what President Edwards says on the subject, to let you see that this is not a new thing in the church, but has always prevailed wherever revivals prevailed with power. It is from his Thoughts on Revivals.

We cannot determine that God never shall give any person so much of a discovery of himself, not only as to weaken their bodies, but to take away their lives. It is supposed by very learned and judicious divines, that Moses' life was taken away after this manner; and this has also been supposed to be the case with some other saints. Yea, I do not

---

[4] Finney refers frequently in his *Memoirs* to his own sessions of agonizing prayer and how they prevailed.

see any solid, sure grounds any have to determine, that God shall never make such strong impressions on the mind by his Spirit, that shall be an occasion of so impairing the frame of the body, and particularly that part of the body, the brain, that persons shall be deprived of the use of reason. As I said before, it is too much for us to determine, that God will not bring an outward calamity in bestowing spiritual and eternal blessings: so it is too much for us to determine, how great an outward calamity he will bring. If God give a great increase of discoveries of himself, and of love to him, the benefit is infinitely greater than the calamity, though the life should presently after be taken away; yea, though the soul should not immediately be taken to heaven, but should lie some years in a deep sleep, and then be taken to heaven; or, which is much the same thing, if it be deprived of the use of its faculties, and be inactive and unserviceable, as if it lay in a deep sleep for some years, and then should pass into glory. We cannot determine how great a calamity distraction is, when considered with all its consequences, and all that might have been consequent, if the distraction had not happened; nor indeed whether (thus considered) it be any calamity at all, or whether it be not a mercy, by preventing some great sin, or some more dreadful thing, if it had not been. It was a great fault in us to limit a sovereign, all-wise God, whose judgments are a great deep, and his ways past finding out, where he has not limited himself, and things concerning which he has not told us what his way shall be. It is remarkable, considering in what multitudes of instances, and to how great a degree, the frame of the body has been overpowered of late, that persons' lives have, notwithstanding, been preserved, and that the instances of those that have been deprived of reason, have been so very few, and those, perhaps all of them, persons under the peculiar disadvantage of a weak, vapory habit of body. A merciful and careful Divine hand is very manifest in it, that in so many instances where the ship has begun to sink, yet it has been upheld, and has not totally sunk. The instances of such as have been deprived of reason are so few, that certainly they are not enough to cause us to be in any fright, as though this work that has been carried on in the country, was like to be of baneful influence; unless we are disposed to gather up all that we can to darken it, and set it forth in frightful colors.

There is one particular kind of exercise and concern of mind, that many have been overpowered by, that has been especially stumbling to some; and that is, the deep concern and distress that they have been in for the souls of others. I am sorry that any put us to the trouble of doing that which seems so needless, as defending such a thing as this. It seems like mere trifling in so plain a case, to enter into a formal and particular debate, in order to determine whether there be any thing in the greatness and importance of the case, that will answer, and bear a proportion to the greatness of the concern that some have manifested. Men may be allowed, from no higher a principle than common ingenuity and humanity, to be very deeply concerned, and greatly exercised in mind, at seeing others in great danger of no greater a calamity than drowning, or being burnt up in a house on fire. And if so, then doubtless it will be allowed to be equally reasonable, if they saw them in danger of a calamity ten times greater, to be still much more concerned; and so much more still, if the calamity was still vastly greater. And why then should it be thought unreasonable, and looked upon with a very suspicious eye, as if it must come from some bad cause, when persons are extremely concerned at seeing others in very great danger of suffering the fierceness and wrath of Almighty God to all eternity? And besides, it will doubtless be allowed that those that have very great degrees of the Spirit of God, that is, a spirit of love, may well be supposed to have vastly more of love and compassion to their fellow-creatures, than those that are influenced by common humanity. Why should it be thought strange that those that are full of the Spirit of Christ, should be proportionably, in their love to souls, like to Christ? who had so strong a love to them and concern for them, as to be willing to drink the dregs of the cup of God's fury for them; and at the same time that he offered up his blood for souls, offered up also, as their high priest, strong crying and tears, with an extreme agony, wherein the soul of Christ was, as it were, in travail for the souls of the elect; and therefore in saving them he is said to see of the travail of his soul. As such a spirit of love to and concern for souls was the spirit of Christ, so it is the spirit of the church; and therefore the church, in desiring and seeking that Christ might be brought forth in the world, and in the souls of men, is represented, Rev. xii., as 'a woman crying, travailing in birth, and pained to be delivered.' The spirit of those that have been in distress for the souls of others, so far as I can discern, seems not to be different from that of the apostle, who travailed for souls, and was ready to wish himself accursed from Christ for others. And that of the Psalmist, Psalm cxix. 53, 'Horror hath taken hold upon me, because of the wicked that forsake the law.' And v. 136, 'Rivers of waters run down mine eyes, because they keep not thy law.' And that of the prophet Jeremiah, Jer. iv. 19, 'My bowels! my bowels! I am pained at my very heart! My heart maketh a noise in me! I cannot hold my peace! because thou hast heard. O my soul, the sound of the trumpet, the alarm of war!' And so, chap. ix. 1, and xiii. 17, and Isa. xxii. 4. We read of Mordecai, when he saw his people in danger of being destroyed with a temporal destruction, Esther iv. 1, that he 'rent his clothes, and put on sackcloth with ashes, and went out into the midst of the city, and cried with a loud and bitter cry.' And why then should persons be thought to be distracted, when they cannot forbear crying out at the consideration of the misery of those that are going to eternal destruction? *

I have read this to show that this thing was common in the great revivals of those days. It has always been so in all great revivals, and has been more or less common in proportion to the greatness, and extent, and depth of the work. It was so in the great revivals in Scotland, and multitudes used to be overpowered, and some almost died, by the depth of their agony.

9. If you mean to pray effectually, you must pray a great deal. It was said of the apostle James, that after he was dead it was found his knees were callous like a camel's knees, by praying so much. Ah! here was the secret of the success of those primitive ministers. They had callous knees.

10. If you intend prayer to be effectual, it must be offered in the name of Christ. You cannot come to God in your own name. You cannot plead your own merits. But you can come in a name that is always acceptable. You all know what it is to *use the name* of a man. If you should go to the bank with a draft or note, endorsed by John Jacob Astor, that would be giving you his name, and you know you could get the money from the bank just as well as he could himself. Now, Jesus Christ gives you the use of his name. And when you pray in the name of Christ, the meaning of

---

* Edwards' Works, vol. iv, p. 85, New York edition.[5]

[5] Finney probably used the edition of Edwards' works published in ten volumes by G. & C. & H. Carvill in New York in 1829–1830 and edited by Sereno E. Dwight. This quotation is from Edwards' *Some Thoughts Concerning the Present Revival of Religion in New England* in the above edition, IV, 88–90. It should not be surprising that Finney quotes from Edwards wherever he can to substantiate his views, for Edwards was the great theologian to whom both Old School and New School ministers turned for justification. Because Edwards was accepted as an orthodox Calvinist and because he had taken part in and condoned many of the most sensational aspects of the First Great Awakening, Finney found him a particularly helpful ally. Although Finney nowhere makes a direct comparison of his theological views with those of Edwards, it was no doubt apparent to him that further light had been shed since Edwards' day that made their differences understandable. To those Old School Calvinists who pointed out that Edwards had converted hundreds of souls without departing from orthodoxy Finney answered that Edwards and the other revival preachers of the First Great Awakening had been "inconsistent" and had preached the New School views whether they knew it or not. See Finney's *Sermons on Various Subjects* (New York, 1835), p. 80. And to those who pointed out that Edwards did not use the new measures Finney found indispensable, Finney devoted Lecture XIV of this volume. It was unfortunate for Finney that Edwards had also devoted a considerable portion of his books on revivals to deploring some of the excesses of the First Great Awakening, and these passages could be, and were, quoted against the New School and New Measure revivalists of 1825–1835.

it is, that you can prevail just as well as he could himself, and receive just as much as God's well-beloved Son would if he were to pray himself for the same things. But you must pray in faith. His name has all the virtue in your lips that it has in his own, and God is just as free to bestow blessings upon you, when you ask in the name of Christ, and in faith, as he would be to bestow them upon Christ, if he should ask.

11. You cannot prevail in prayer, without renouncing all your sins. You must not only recall them to mind, and repent of them, but you must actually renounce them, and leave them off, and in the purpose of your heart renounce them all *for ever.*

12. You must pray in faith. You must expect to obtain the things you ask for. You need not look for an answer to prayer, if you pray without an expectation of obtaining it. You are not to form such expectations without any reason for them. In the cases I have supposed, there is a reason for the expectation. In case the thing is revealed in God's word, if you pray without an expectation of receiving the blessings, you just make God a liar. If the will of God is indicated by his providence, you ought to depend on it, according to the clearness of the indication, so far as to expect the blessing if you pray for it. And if you are led by his Spirit to pray for certain things, you have just as much reason to expect the thing to be done as if God had revealed it in his word.

But some say, "Will not this view of the leadings of the Spirit of God lead people into fanaticism?" I answer, that I know not but many may deceive themselves in respect to this matter. — Multitudes have deceived themselves in regard to all the other points of religion. And if some people should think they are led by the Spirit of God, when it is nothing but their own imagination, is that any reason why those who know that they are led by the Spirit should not follow? Many people suppose themselves to be converted when they are not. Is that any reason why we should not cleave to the Lord Jesus Christ? Suppose some people are deceived in thinking they love God, is that any reason why the pious saint who knows he has the love of God shed abroad in his heart, should not give vent to his feelings in songs of praise? So I suppose some may deceive themselves in thinking they are led by the Spirit of God. But there is no need of being deceived. If people follow impulses, it is their own fault. I do not want you to follow impulses. I want you to be sober minded, and follow the sober, rational leadings of the Spirit of God. There *are those* who understand what I mean, and who know very well what it is to give themselves up to the Spirit of God in prayer.

III. I will state some of the reasons why these things are essential to effectual prayer. Why does God require such prayer, such strong desires, such agonizing supplications?

1. These strong desires strongly illustrate the strength of God's feelings. They are like the real feelings of God for impenitent sinners. When I have seen, as I sometimes have, the amazing strength of love for souls that has been felt by Christians, I have been wonderfully impressed with the amazing love of God, and his desires for their salvation. The case of a certain woman, of whom I read, in a revival, made the greatest impression on my mind. She had such an unutterable compassion and love for souls, that she actually panted for breath. What must be the strength of the desire which God feels, when his Spirit produces in Christians such amazing agony, such throes of soul, such *travail* — God has chosen the best word to express it — it is travail — travail of the soul.

I have seen a man of as much strength of intellect and muscle as any man in the community, fall down prostrate, absolutely overpowered by his unutterable desires for sinners. I know this is a stumbling block to many; and it always will be as long as there remain in the church so many blind and stupid professors of religion. But I cannot doubt that these things are the work of the Spirit of God. O that the whole church could be so filled with the Spirit as to travail in prayer, till a nation should be born in a day!

It is said in the word of God, that as soon "as Zion *travailed*, she brought forth." What does that mean? I asked a professor of religion this question once. He was making exceptions about our ideas of effectual prayer, and I asked him what he supposed was meant by Zion's travailing. "O," said he, "it means that as soon as the church walk together in the fellowship of the gospel, then it will be said that Zion *travels!* This walking together is called *travelling*." Not the same term, you see. So much he knew.[6]

2. These strong desires that I have described, are the natural results of great benevolence and clear views of the danger of

[6] It was said that early in his career Finney had occasionally indulged in "wit" and "levity" in the pulpit until some of his friends warned him against it. If this pun on the word "travails" is typical of his humor, his change of manner need hardly be regretted. See the letter from Nathaniel S. S. Beman to Finney, October 23, 1829 in the Finney Papers, Oberlin College Library, in which Beman warns Finney against "the indulgence of anything like wit in the pulpit." Later revivalists have pretty generally ignored this warning.

sinners. It is perfectly reasonable that it should be so. If the women who are in this house should look up there, and see a family burning to death in the fire, and hear their shrieks, and behold their agony, they would feel distressed, and it is very likely that many of them would faint away with agony. And nobody would wonder at it, or say they were fools or crazy to feel so much distressed at such an awful sight. They would think it strange if there were not some expressions of powerful feeling. Why is it any wonder, then, if Christians should feel as I have described, when they have clear views of the state of sinners, and the awful danger they are in? The fact is, that those individuals who never have felt so, have never felt much real benevolence, and their piety must be of a very superficial character. I do not mean to judge harshly, or to speak unkindly. But I state it as a simple matter of fact; and people may talk about it as they please, but I know that such piety is superficial. This is not censoriousness, but plain truth.

People sometimes wonder at Christians' having such feelings. Wonder at what! Why, at the natural, and philosophical, and necessary results of deep piety towards God, and deep benevolence towards man, in view of the great danger they see sinners to be in.

3. The soul of a Christian, when it is thus burdened, must have relief. God rolls this weight upon the soul of a Christian, for the purpose of bringing him near to himself. Christians are often so unbelieving, that they will not exercise proper faith in God, till he rolls this burden upon them, so heavy that they cannot live under it, and then they must go to God for relief. It is like the case of many a convicted sinner. God is willing to receive him at once, if he will come right to him, with faith in Jesus Christ. But the sinner will not come. He hangs back, and struggles, and groans under the burden of his sins, and will not throw himself upon God, till his burden of conviction becomes so great that he can live no longer; and when he is driven to desperation, as it were, and feels as if he was ready to sink into hell, he makes a mighty plunge, and throws himself upon God's mercy as his only hope. It was his duty to come before. God had no delight in his distress, for its own sake. It was only the sinner's obstinacy that created the necessity for all this distress. He would not come without it. So when professors of religion get loaded down with the weight of souls, they often pray again and again, and yet the burden is not gone, nor their distress abated, because they have never thrown it all upon God in faith.

But they can't get rid of the burden. So long as their benevolence continues it will remain and increase, and unless they resist and quench the Holy Ghost they can get no relief, until at length, when they are driven to extremity, they make a desperate effort, roll the burden off upon the Lord Jesus Christ, and exercise a child-like confidence in him. Then they feel relieved; then they feel as if the soul they were praying for would be saved. The burden is gone, and God seems in kindness to sooth down the mind to feel a sweet assurance that the blessing will be granted. Often, after a Christian has had this struggle, this agony in prayer, and has obtained relief in this way, you will find the sweetest and most heavenly affections flow out — the soul rests sweetly and gloriously in God, and rejoices, "with joy unspeakable and full of glory."

Do any of you think now, that there are no such things in the experience of believers? I tell you, if I had time, I could show you from President Edwards, and other approved writers, cases and descriptions just like this. Do you ask why we never have such things here in New York? I tell you, it is not at all because you are so much wiser than Christians are in the country, or because you have so much more intelligence or more enlarged views of the nature of religion, or a more stable and well regulated piety. I tell you, no; instead of priding yourselves in being free from such extravagances, you ought to hide your heads, because Christians in New York are so worldly, and have so much starch, and pride, and fashion, that they cannot *come down* to such spirituality as this. I wish it could be so. O that there might be such a spirit in this city, and in this church! I know it would make a noise, if we had such things done here. But I would not care for that. Let them say, if they please, that the folks in Chatham Chapel [7] are getting deranged. We need not be afraid of that, if we could live near enough to God to enjoy his Spirit in the manner I have described.

4. These effects of the Spirit of prayer upon the body are themselves no part of religion. It is only that the body is often so weak that the feelings of the soul overpower it. These bodily effects are not at all essential to prevailing prayer, but only a natural or physical result of highly excited emotions of the mind. It is not at all unusual for the body to be weakened and even overcome by any

[7] Finney was pastor of the Chatham Street Chapel (the Second Free Presbyterian Church) in New York City from April 1832 to March 1836, when he left the Presbyterian Church to become pastor of the Congregational Broadway Tabernacle in New York. The Chatham Street Chapel had been a theater before the Tappan brothers converted it into a church for Finney.

powerful emotion of the mind, on other subjects besides religion. The door-keeper of Congress in the time of the revolution fell down dead on the reception of some highly cheering intelligence. I knew a woman in Rochester, who was in a great agony of prayer for the conversion of her son-in-law. One morning he was at an anxious meeting, and she remained at home praying for him. At the close of the meeting, he came home a convert, and she was so rejoiced that she fell down and died on the spot. It is no more strange that these effects should be produced by religion than by strong feeling on any other subject. It is not essential to prayer, but the natural result of great efforts of the mind.

5. Doubtless one great reason why God requires the exercise of this agonizing prayer is, that it forms such a bond of union between Christ and the Church. It creates such a sympathy between them. It is as if Christ came and poured the overflowings of his own benevolent heart into his church, and led them to sympathize and to co-operate with him, as they never do in any other way. They feel just as Christ feels — so full of compassion for sinners that they cannot contain themselves. Thus it is often with those ministers who are distinguished for their success in preaching to sinners; they often have such compassion, such overflowing desires for their salvation, that it shows itself in their speaking, and their preaching, just as though Jesus Christ spoke through them. The words come from their lips fresh and warm, as if from the very heart of Christ. I do not mean that he dictates their words; but he excites the feelings that give utterance to them. Then you see a movement in the hearers, as if Christ himself spoke through lips of clay.

6. This travailing in birth for souls creates also a remarkable bond of union between warm-hearted Christians and the young converts. Those who are converted appear very dear to the hearts that have had this spirit of prayer for them. The feeling is like that of a mother for her first-born. — Paul expresses it beautifully, when he says, "My little children!" His heart was warm and tender to them. "My little children, of whom I travail in birth *again*." They had backslidden, and he has all the agonies of a parent over a wandering child. "I travail in birth again, till Christ be formed in you, the hope of glory." In a revival, I have often noticed how those who have had the spirit of prayer, love the young converts. I know this is all algebra to those who have never felt it. But to those who have experienced the agony of wrestling, prevailing

prayer, for the conversion of a soul, you may depend upon it, that soul, after it is converted, appears as dear as a child is to the mother who has brought it forth with pain. He has agonized for it, and received it in answer to prayer, and can present it before the Lord Jesus Christ, saying, "Here, Lord, am I, and the children thou hast given me."

7. Another reason why God requires this sort of prayer is, that it is the only way in which the church can be properly prepared to receive great blessings without being injured by them. When the church is thus prostrated in the dust before God, and is in the depth of agony in prayer, the blessing does them good. While at the same time, if they had received the blessing without this deep prostration of soul, it would have puffed them up with pride. But as it is, it increases their holiness, their love, their humility.

IV. I am to show that such prayer as I have described will avail much. But time fails me to go into a particular detail of the evidence which I intended to bring forward under this head.

Elijah the prophet mourned over the declensions of the house of Israel, and when he saw that no other means were likely to be effectual, to prevent a perpetual going away into idolatry, he prayed that the judgments of God might come upon the guilty nation. He prayed that it might not rain, and God shut up the heavens for three years and six months, till the people were driven to the last extremity. And when he saw that it was time to relent, what does he do? See him go up to the mountain and bow down in prayer. He wished to be alone; and he told his servant to go seven times, while he was agonizing in prayer. The *last* time, the servant told him there was a little cloud appeared, like a man's hand, and he instantly arose from his knees — the blessing was obtained. The time had come for the calamity to be turned back. "Ah, but," you say, "Elijah was a prophet." Now don't make this objection. They made it in the apostle's days, and what does the apostle say? Why he brought forward this very instance, and the fact that Elijah was a man of like passions with ourselves, as a case of prevailing prayer, and insisted that they should pray so too.

John Knox was a man famous for his power in prayer, so that bloody Queen Mary used to say she feared his prayers more than all the armies of Europe. And events showed that she had reason to do it. He used to be in such an agony for the deliverance of his country that he could not sleep. He had a place in his garden where he used to go to pray. One night he and several friends were praying together, and as they prayed, Knox spoke and said that deliverance had come. He could not tell what had happened, but he felt that something had taken place, for God had heard their prayers. What was it? Why the next news they had was, that Mary was dead!

Take a fact which was related, in my hearing, by a minister. He said, that in a certain town there had been no revival for many years; the church was nearly run out, the youth were all unconverted, and desolation reigned unbroken. There lived in a retired part of the town, an aged man, a blacksmith by trade, and of so stammering a tongue, that it was painful to hear him speak. On one Friday, as he was at work in his shop, alone, his mind became greatly exercised about the state of the church, and of the impenitent. His agony became so great, that he was induced to lay by his work, lock the shop door, and spend the afternoon in prayer.

He prevailed, and on the Sabbath called on the minister, and desired him to appoint a conference meeting. After some hesitation, the minister consented, observing, however, that he feared but few would attend. He appointed it the same evening, at a large private house. When evening came, more assembled than could be accommodated in the house. All was silent for a time, until one sinner broke out in tears, and said, if any one could pray, he begged him to pray for *him*. Another followed, and another, and still another, until it was found that persons from every quarter of the town were under deep conviction. And what was remarkable was, that they all dated their conviction at the hour when the old man was praying in his shop. A powerful revival followed. Thus this old stammering man prevailed, and, as a prince, had power with God. I could name multitudes of similar cases, but, for want of time, must conclude with a few.[8]

REMARKS.

1. A great deal of prayer is lost, and many people never prevail in prayer, because, when they have *desires* for particular blessings, they do not follow them up. They may have had desires, benevolent and pure, which were excited by the Spirit of God; and when they have them, they should persevere in prayer, for if they turn off their attention to other objects, they will quench the

[8] This paragraph and the one preceding it did not appear in the lecture as originally printed in the *New York Evangelist*, December 27, 1834, p. 206.

Spirit. We tell sinners not to turn off their minds from the one object, but to keep their attention fixed there, till they are saved. When you find these holy desires in your minds, take care of two things:

(1.) Don't quench the Spirit.

(2.) Don't be diverted to other objects.

Follow the leadings of the Spirit, till you have offered that effectual fervent prayer than availeth much.

2. Without the spirit of prayer, ministers will do but little good. A minister need not expect much success, unless he prays for it. *Sometimes* others may have the spirit of prayer, and obtain a blessing on his labors. Generally, however, those preachers are the most successful who have the most of a spirit of prayer themselves.

3. Not only must ministers have the spirit of prayer, but it is necessary that the church should unite in offering that effectual fervent prayer which can prevail with God. You need not expect a blessing, unless you ask for it. "For all these things will I be inquired of by the house of Israel, to do it."

Now, my brethren, I have only to ask you, in regard to what I have preached to-night, "Will you do it?" Have you done what I preached to you last Friday evening? Have you gone over with your sins, and confessed them, and got them all out of the way? Can you pray now? And will you join and offer prevailing prayer, that the Spirit of God may come down here?

V

THE PRAYER OF FAITH

Text. — "Therefore I say unto you, What things soever ye desire when ye pray, believe that ye receive them, and ye shall have them." — Mark xi. 24.

These words have been by some supposed to refer exclusively to the faith of miracles. But there is not the least evidence of this. That the text was not designed by our Savior to refer exclusively to the faith of miracles, is proved by the connection in which it stands. If you read the chapter, you will see that Christ and his apostles were at this time very much engaged in their work, and very prayerful; and as they returned from their place of retirement in the morning, faint and hungry, they saw a fig-tree at a little distance. It looked very beautiful, and doubtless gave signs as if there was fruit on it; but when they came nigh, they found nothing on it but leaves. And Jesus said, "No man eat fruit of thee hereafter for ever.

"And in the morning, as they passed by, they saw the fig-tree dried up from the roots.

"And Peter, calling to remembrance, saith unto him, Master, behold the fig-tree which thou cursedst is withered away.

"And Jesus answering, saith unto them, have faith in God.

"For verily I say unto you, that whosoever shall say unto this mountain, Be thou removed, and be thou cast into the sea; and shall not doubt in his heart, but shall believe that those things which he saith shall come to pass; he shall have whatsoever he saith."

Then follow the words of the text:

"Therefore I say unto you, What things soever ye desire when ye pray, believe that ye receive them, and ye shall have them."

Our Savior was desirous of giving his disciples instructions respecting the nature and power of prayer, and the necessity of strong faith in God. He therefore stated a very strong case, a miracle — one so great as the removal of a mountain into the sea. And he tells them, that if they exercise a proper faith in God, they might do such things. But his remarks are not to be limited to faith merely a regard to working miracles, for he goes on to say,

"And when ye stand praying, forgive, if ye have aught against any: that your Father also which is in heaven may forgive you your trespasses.

"But if ye do not forgive, neither will your Father which is in heaven forgive you your trespasses."

Does that relate to miracles? When you pray, you must forgive. Is that required only when a man wishes to work a miracle? There are many other promises in the Bible nearly related to this, and speaking nearly the same language, which have been all disposed of in this short-hand way, as referring to the faith employed in miracles. Just as if the faith of miracles was something different from faith in God!

In my last lecture, I dwelt upon the subject of "prevailing prayer;" and you will recollect that I passed over the subject of *faith* in prayer very briefly, because I wished to reserve it for a separate discussion. The subject to-night is,

THE PRAYER OF FAITH.

I propose,

I. To show that faith is an indispensable condition of prevailing prayer.

II. Show what it is that we are to believe when we pray.

III. Show when we are bound to exercise this faith, or to believe that we shall receive the thing that we ask for.

IV. That this kind of faith in prayer always does obtain the blessing sought.

V. Explain how we are to come into the state of mind, in which we can exercise such faith.

VI. Answer several objections, which are sometimes alleged against these views of prayer.

I. That faith is an indispensable condition of prevailing prayer, will not be seriously doubted. There is such a thing as offering benevolent desires, which are acceptable to God as such, that do not include the exercise of faith in regard to the actual reception of those blessings. But such desires are not prevailing prayer, the prayer of faith. God may see fit to grant the things desired, as an act of kindness and love, but it would not be properly in answer to prayer. I am speaking now of the kind of faith that *insures* the blessing. Do not understand me as saying that there is nothing in prayer that is acceptable to God, or that even obtains the blessing sometimes, without *this* kind of faith. But I am speaking of the faith which secures the very blessing it seeks. To prove that faith is indispensable to prevailing prayer, it is only necessary to repeat what the apostle James expressly tells us: "If any of you lack wisdom, let him ask of God, that giveth to all men liberally, and upbraideth not; and it shall be given him. — But let him ask in faith, nothing wavering. For he that wavereth is like a wave of the sea, driven with the wind and tossed."

II. We are to inquire *what we are to believe when we pray*.

1. We are to believe in the existence of God — "He that cometh to God must believe that he *is*" — and in his willingness to answer prayer — "that he is, and that he is the rewarder of them that diligently seek him." There are many who believe in the existence of God, and do not believe in the efficacy of prayer. They profess to believe in God, but deny the necessity or influence of prayer.

2. *We are to believe that we shall receive* — something — what? Not something, or any thing, as it happens, but some particular thing we ask for. We are not to think that God is such a being, that if we ask a fish, he will give us a serpent, or if we ask bread, he will give us a stone. But he says, "*What things soever ye desire*, when ye pray, believe that ye receive *them*, and ye shall have them." With respect to the faith of miracles, it is plain that they were bound to believe they should receive just what they asked for — that the very thing itself should come to pass. That is what they were to believe. Now what ought men to believe in regard to other blessings? Is it a mere loose idea, that if a man prays for a specific blessing, God will by some mysterious sovereignty give something or other to him, or something to somebody else, somewhere? — When a man prays for his children's conversion, is he to believe that either his children will be converted, or somebody's else children, and it is altogether uncertain which? All this is utter nonsense, and highly dishonorable to God. No, we are to believe that we shall receive the *very* things that we ask for.

III. When are we bound to make this prayer? When are we bound to believe that we shall have the very things we pray for? I answer, When we have evidence of it. Faith must always have evidence. A man cannot believe a thing, unless he sees something which he supposes to be evidence. He is under no obligation to

THE PRAYER OF FAITH

believe, and has no right to believe, a thing will be done, unless he has evidence. It is the height of fanaticism to believe without evidence. The kinds of evidence a man may have are the following:

1. Suppose that God has *especially promised* the thing. As for instance, God says he is more ready to give his Holy Spirit to them that *ask* him, than parents are to give bread to their children. Here we are bound to believe that we shall receive it when we pray for it. You have no right to put in an *if*, and say, "Lord, *if it be thy will*, give us thy Holy Spirit." This is to insult God. To put an *if* into God's promise, where God has put none, is tantamount to charging God with being insincere. It is like saying, "O God, if thou art in earnest in making these promises, grant us the blessing we pray for."

I heard of a case where a young convert was the means of teaching a minister a solemn truth on the subject of prayer. She was from a very wicked family, and went to live with a minister. While there, she was hopefully converted, and appeared well. One day she came to the minister's study, while he was in it — a thing she was not in the habit of doing; and he thought there must be something the matter. So he asked her to sit down, and kindly inquired into the state of her religious feelings; she said, she was distressed at the manner in which the old church members prayed for the Spirit. They would pray for the Holy Spirit to come, and would seem to be very much in earnest, and plead the promises of God, and then say, "O Lord, *if it be thy will*, grant us these blessings for Christ's sake." She thought that saying, "if it be thy will," when God has expressly promised it, was questioning whether God was sincere in his promises. The minister tried to reason her out of it, and of course he succeeded in confounding her. But she was distressed and filled with grief, and said, "I can't argue the point with you, sir, but it is impressed on my mind that it is wrong, and dishonoring God." — And she went away weeping with anguish. The minister saw she was not satisfied, and it led him to look at the matter again, and finally he saw that it was putting in an *if* where God had put none, and where he had revealed his will expressly, and that it was an insult to God. And he went and told his church they were bound to believe that God was in earnest when he made them a promise. And the spirit of prayer came down upon that church, and a most powerful revival followed.[1]

---

[1] This is one of numerous illustrations used by Finney in these lectures to demonstrate that humble but devout Christians are often wiser than educated

2. Where there is a *general promise* in the Scriptures, which you may reasonably apply to the particular case before you. If its real meaning includes the particular thing for which you pray, or if you can reasonably apply the principle of the promise to the case, there you have evidence. For instance, suppose it is a time when wickedness prevails greatly, and you are led to pray for God's interference. What promise have you? Why, this one: "When the enemy shall come in like a flood, the Spirit of the Lord shall lift up a standard against him." Here you see is a general promise, laying down a principle of God's administration, which you may apply to the case before you, as a warrant for exercising faith in prayer. And if the case comes up, to inquire as to the *time* in which God will grant blessings in answer to prayer, you have this promise: "While they are yet speaking, I will hear."

There is a vast amount of general promises and principles laid down in the Bible, which Christians might make use of, if they would only *think*. Whenever you are in circumstances to which the promises or principles apply, there you are to use them. A parent finds this promise: "The mercy of the Lord is from everlasting to everlasting upon them that fear him, and his righteousness unto children's children, to such as keep his covenant, and to those that remember his commandments to do them." Now, here is a promise made to those that possess a certain character. If any parent is conscious that this is his character, he has a rightful ground to apply it to himself and his family. If you have this character, you are bound to make use of this promise in prayer, and believe it, even to your children's children.

If I had time to-night, I could go from one end of the Bible to the other, and produce an astonishing variety of texts that are applicable as promises; enough to prove, that in whatever circumstances a child of God may be placed, God has provided in the Bible some promise, either general or particular, which he can apply, that is precisely suited to his case. Many of God's promises are very broad on purpose to cover much ground. What can be broader than the promise in the text: "Whatsoever things ye desire when ye pray?" What praying Christian is there who has not been surprised at the length, and breadth, and fullness, of the promises

---

ministers and that in such disputed questions God will give his judgment to settle the issue by producing a conversion or a revival to indicate which is correct. In Finney's stories God always sides with the humble against the learned, the devout against the formal, the New School against the Old School.

of God, when the Spirit has applied them to his heart? Who that lives a life of prayer, has not wondered at his own blindness, in not having before seen and felt the extent of meaning and richness of those promises, when viewed under the light of the spirit of God? At such times he has been astonished at his own ignorance, and found the Spirit applying the promises and declarations of the Bible in a sense in which he had never dreamed of their being applicable before. The manner in which the apostles applied the promises, and prophecies, and declarations of the Old Testament, places in a strong light the breadth of meaning, and fullness, and richness of the word of God. He that walks in the light of God's countenance, and is filled with the Spirit of God as he ought to be, will often make an appropriation of promises to himself, and an application of them to his own circumstances, and the circumstances of those for whom he prays, that a blind professor of religion would never dream of.

3. Where there is any *prophetic declaration*, that the thing prayed for is agreeable to the will of God. When it is plain from prophecy that the event is certainly to come, you are bound to believe it, and to make it the ground for your special faith in prayer. If the time is not specified in the Bible, and there is no evidence from other sources, you are not bound to believe that it shall take place now, or immediately. But if the time is specified, or if the time may be learned from the study of the prophecies, and it appears to have arrived, then Christians are under obligation to understand and apply it, by offering the prayer of faith. For instance, take the case of Daniel, in regard to the return of the Jews from captivity. What does he say? "I Daniel understood by books the number of the years whereof the word of the Lord came to Jeremiah the prophet, that he would accomplish seventy years in the desolations of Jerusalem." Here he learned from books, that is, he studied his Bible, and in that way understood that the length of the captivity was to be seventy years. What does he do then? Does he sit down upon the promise, and say, "God has pledged himself to put an end to the captivity in seventy years, and the time has expired, and there is no need of doing any thing?" O no; he says, "And I set my face unto the Lord God, to seek by prayer and supplications, with fasting, and sackcloth, and ashes." He set himself at once to pray that the thing might be accomplished. He prayed in faith. But what was he to believe? What he had learned from prophecy. There are many prophecies yet unfulfilled, in the

Bible, which Christians are bound to understand, as far as they are capable of understanding them, and then make them the basis of believing prayer. Do not think, as some seem to, that because a thing is foretold in prophecy it is not necessary to pray for it, or that it will come whether Christians pray for it or not. There is no truth in this. God says, in regard to this very class of events, which are revealed in prophecy, "Nevertheless, for all these things will I be inquired of by the house of Israel to do it for them."

4. When the signs of the times, or the providence of God, indicate that a particular blessing is about to be bestowed, we are bound to believe it. The Lord Jesus Christ blamed the Jews, and called them hypocrites, because they did not understand the indications of Providence. They could understand the signs of the weather, and see when it was about to rain, and when it would be fair weather; but they could not see, from the signs of the times, that the time had come for the Messiah to appear, and build up the house of God. There are many professors of religion, who are always stumbling and hanging back, whenever any thing is proposed to be done. They always say, The time has not come — the time has not come; when there are others who pay attention to the signs of the times, and who have spiritual discernment to understand them. These pray in faith for the blessing, and it comes.

5. When the *Spirit of God is upon you*, and excites strong desires for any blessing, you are bound to pray for it in faith. You are bound to infer, from the fact that you find yourself drawn to desire such a thing while in the exercise of such holy affections as the Spirit of God produces, that these desires are the work of the Spirit. People are not apt to desire with the right kind of desires, unless they are excited by the Spirit of God. The apostle refers to these desires, excited by the Spirit, in his epistle to the Romans, where he says — "Likewise the Spirit also helpeth our infirmities; for we know not what we should pray for as we ought; but the Spirit itself maketh intercession for us with groanings which cannot be uttered. And he that searcheth the heart knoweth what is the mind of the Spirit, because he maketh intercession for the saints, according to the will of God." Here, then, if you find yourself strongly drawn to desire a blessing, you are to understand it as an intimation that God is willing to bestow that particular blessing, and so you are bound to believe it. God does not trifle with his children. He does not go and excite in them a desire for one blessing, to turn them off with something else. But he excites

the very desires he is willing to gratify. And when they feel such desires, they are bound to follow them out till they get the blessing.

IV. I will proceed to show that this kind of faith *always obtains the object*. The text is plain here, to show that you shall receive the very thing prayed for. It does not say, "Believe that ye shall receive, and ye shall either have that or something else equivalent to it." To prove that this faith obtains the very blessing asked, I observe,

1. That otherwise we could never know whether our prayers were answered. And we might continue praying and praying, long after the prayer was answered by some other blessing equivalent to the one we ask for.

2. If we are not bound to expect the very thing we ask for, it must be that the Spirit of God deceives us. Why should he excite us to desire a certain blessing, when he means to grant something else?

3. What is the meaning of this passage, "If a man ask bread, will he give him a stone?" Does not our Savior rebuke the idea that prayer may be answered by giving something else? What encouragement have we to pray for any thing in particular, if we are to ask for one thing and receive another? Suppose a Christian should pray for a revival here — he would be answered by a revival in China. Or he might pray for a revival, and God would send the cholera, or an earthquake. All the history of the church shows that when God answers prayer, he gives his people the very thing for which their prayers are offered. God confers other blessings, on both saints and sinners, which they do not pray for at all. He sends his rain both upon the just and the unjust. But when he *answers prayer*, it is by doing what they ask him to do. To be sure, he often *more* than answers prayer. He grants them not only what they ask, but often connects other blessings with it.

4. Perhaps you may feel a difficulty here about the prayers of Jesus Christ. People may often ask, "Did not he pray in the garden for the cup to be removed, and was his prayer answered?" I answer that this is no difficulty at all, for the prayer was answered. The cup he prayed to be delivered from was removed. This is what the apostle refers to, when he says — "Who in the days of his flesh, when he had offered up prayers and supplications with strong crying and tears unto him that was able to save him from death, was heard in that he feared." Now I ask, On what occasion was he saved from death, if not on this? Was it the death of the cross he

prayed to be delivered from? Not at all. But the case was this. A short time before he was betrayed, we hear him saying to his disciples, "My soul is exceedingly sorrowful, even unto death." Anguish of mind came rolling in upon him, till he was just ready to die, and he went out into the garden to pray, and told his disciples to watch, and then he went by himself and prayed; "O my Father," said he, "if it be possible, let this cup pass from me; nevertheless not as I will, but as thou wilt." In his agony he rose from his knees, and walked the garden, till he came where his disciples were, and there he saw them fast asleep. He awakend them and said, "What, could ye not watch with me one hour?" And then he went again, for he was in such distress that he could not stand still, and again he poured out his soul. And the third time he goes away and prays, "Father, if thou be willing, remove this cup from me; nevertheless, not my will, but thine be done." And now the third time of praying, there appeared an angel unto him from heaven, strengthening him. And his mind became composed, and calm, and the *cup was gone*. Till then, he had been in such an agony that his sweat was as it were great drops of blood, but now it was all over.

Some have supposed that he was praying against the cross, and begging to be delivered from dying on the cross! Did Christ ever shrink from the cross? Never. He came into the world on purpose to die on the cross, and he never shrunk from it. But he was afraid he should die in the garden before he came to the cross. The burden on his soul was so great, and produced such an agony, that he felt as if he was on the point of dying. His soul was sorrowful even unto death. But after the angel appeared unto him, we hear no more of his agony of soul. He had prayed for relief from *that cup*, and his prayer was answered. He became calm, and had no more mental suffering till just as he expired. This case, therefore, is no exception. He received the very thing for which he asked, as he says, "I knew thou always hearest me."

But there is another case often brought up, where the apostle Paul prayed against the thorn in the flesh. He says, "I be-sought the Lord thrice, that it might depart from me." And God answered him, "My grace is sufficient for thee." It is the opinion of Dr. Clarke [2] and others, that Paul's prayer was answered in the very

---

[2] It is not clear which Dr. Clarke Finney is referring to here, but in all probability it was to Dr. Samuel Clarke (1626–1701), the noted English Presbyterian whose annotated edition of the Bible (1690) was often quoted by Calvinist ministers.

thing for which he prayed. That "the thorn in the flesh, the messenger of Satan," of which he speaks, was a false apostle who had distracted and perverted the church at Corinth. That Paul prayed against his influence, and the Lord answered him by assuring him, "My grace is sufficient for thee." Who does not know that it was, and that Paul's influence ultimately triumphed?

But admitting that Paul's prayer was not answered by granting the particular thing for which he prayed, in order to make out this case as an exception to the prayer of faith, they are obliged to assume the very thing to be proved; and that is, that the apostle *prayed in faith*. There is no reason to suppose that Paul would always pray in faith, any more than that any other Christian does. The very manner in which God answered him shows that it was not in faith. He virtually tells him, "That thorn is necessary for your sanctification, and to keep you from being exalted above measure. I sent it upon you in love, and in faithfulness, and you have no business to pray that I should take it away. — LET IT ALONE."

There is not only no evidence that he prayed in faith, but a strong presumption that he did not. From the history it is evident that he had nothing on which to repose faith. There was no express promise, no general promise, that could be applicable, no providence of God, no prophecy, no teaching of the Spirit that God would remove this thorn; but the presumption was that God would not remove it. He had given it to him for a particular purpose. His prayer appears to have been selfish, praying against a mere personal inconvenience. This was not any personal suffering that retarded his usefulness, but on the contrary it was given him to increase his usefulness by keeping him humble; and because on some account he found it inconvenient and mortifying, he set himself to pray out of his own heart, evidently without being *led to it by the Spirit of God*. But did Paul pray in faith without the Spirit of God, any more than any other man? And will any one undertake to say that the Spirit of God led him to pray that this might be removed, when God himself had given it for a particular purpose, which purpose could not be answered only as the thorn continued with him?

Why then is this made an exception to the general rule laid down in the text, that a man shall receive whatsoever he asks in faith? I was once amazed and grieved at a public examination at a Theological Seminary, to hear them darken counsel by words without knowledge on this subject. This case of Paul, and that of Christ just adverted to, were both of them cited as instances to prove to their students that the prayer of faith would not be answered in the particular thing for which they prayed. Now to teach such sentiments as these in or out of a Theological Seminary, is to trifle with the word of God, and to break the power of the Christian ministry. Has it come to this, that our grave doctors in our seminaries, are employed to instruct Zion's watchmen, to believe and teach that it is not to be expected that the prayer of faith is to be answered in granting the object for which we pray? Oh, tell it not in Gath, nor let the sound reach Askalon. What is to become of the church while such are the views of its gravest and most influential ministers? I would not be unkind nor censorious, but as one of the ministers of Jesus Christ, I feel bound to bear testimony against such a perversion of the word of God.

5. It is evident that the prayer of faith will obtain the blessing, from the fact that our faith rests on evidence that to grant *that* thing is the will of God. Not evidence that something else will be granted, but that this particular thing will be. But how, then, can we have evidence that *this* thing will be granted, if *another* thing is to be granted? People often receive more than they pray for. Solomon prayed for wisdom, and God granted him riches and honor in addition. So a wife sometimes prays for the conversion of her husband, and if she offers the prayer, of faith, God may not only grant that blessing, but convert her child, and her whole family. Blessings sometimes seem to hang together, so that if a Christian gains one he gets them all.

V. I am to show how we are to come into this state of mind, in which we can offer such prayer. People sometimes ask, "How shall I offer such prayer? Shall I say, Now I will pray in faith for such and such blessings?" No, the human mind is not moved in this way. You might just as well say, "Now I will call up a spirit from the bottomless pit." I answer,

1. You must first obtain *evidence* that God will bestow the blessing. How did Daniel make out to offer the prayer of faith? He searched the Scriptures. Now, you need not let your Bible lie on a shelf, and expect God to reveal his promises to you. Search the Scriptures, and see where you can get either a general or special promise, or a prophecy, on which you can plant your feet when you pray. Go through the Bible, and you will find it full of such things — precious promises, which you may plead in faith. You

never need to want for objects of prayer, if you will do as Daniel did. Persons are staggered on this subject, because they never make a proper use of the Bible.

A curious case occurred in one of the towns in the western part of this state. There was a revival there. A certain clergyman came to visit the place, and heard a great deal said about the Prayer of Faith. He was staggered at what they said, for he had never regarded the subject in the light they did. He inquired about it of the minister that was laboring there. The minister requested him, in a kind spirit, to go home, and take his Testament, look out the passages that refer to prayer, and go round to his most praying people, and ask them how they understood these passages. He said he would do it, for though these views were new to him, he was willing to learn. He did it, and went to his praying men and women, and read the passages without note or comment, and asked what they thought. He found their plain common sense had led them to understand these passages, and to believe that they mean just as they say.[3] This affected him, and then the fact of his going round and presenting the promises before their minds awakened the spirit of prayer in them, and a revival followed.

I could name many individuals, who have set themselves to examine the Bible on this subject, and before they got half through with it, have been filled with the spirit of prayer. They found that God meant by his promises just what a plain, common sense man would understand them to mean. I advise you to try it. You have Bibles; look them over, and whenever you find a promise that you can use, fasten it in your mind, before you go on; and I venture to predict you will not get through the book without finding out that God's promises mean just what they say.

2. Cherish the good desires you have. Christians very often lose their good desires, by not attending to this; and then their prayers are mere words, without any desire or earnestness at all. The least longing of desire must be cherished. If your body was likely to freeze, and you had even the least spark of fire, how you would cherish it! So if you have the least desire for a blessing, let it be ever so small, don't trifle it away. Don't grieve the Spirit. Don't be diverted. Don't lose good desires, by levity, by censorious-

---

[3] Finney's belief that the "plain common sense" of the average man is sufficient to discern the correct interpretation of Scripture was not only a typical pietistic assault upon a learned clergy, but it was also a long step down the road from Calvinism to Biblical fundamentalism.

ness, by worldly-mindedness. Watch, and pray, and follow it up, or you will never pray the prayer of faith.

3. *Entire consecration to God is indispensable to the prayer of faith.* You must live a holy life, and consecrate all to God — your time, talents, influence — all you have, and all you are, to be his entirely. Read the lives of pious men, and you will be struck with this fact: that they used to set apart times to renew their covenant and dedicate themselves anew to God, and whenever they have done so, a blessing has always followed immediately. If I had Edwards here to-night, I could read passages showing how it was in his days.

4. *You must persevere.* You are not to pray for a thing once, and then cease, and call that the prayer of faith. Look at Daniel. He prayed twenty-one days, and did not cease till he had obtained the blessing. He set his heart and his face unto the Lord, to seek by prayer and supplications, with fasting, and sackcloth, and ashes; and he held on three weeks, and then the answer came. And why did not it come before? God sent an Archangel to bear the message, but the devil hindered him all this time. See what Christ says, in the parable of the unjust judge, and the parable of the loaves. What does he teach us by them? Why, that God will grant answers to prayer when it is importunate. "Shall not God avenge his own elect, who *cry day and night unto him*?"

5. If you would pray in faith, be sure to *walk every day with God.* If you do, he will tell you what to pray for. Be filled with his Spirit, and he will give you objects enough to pray for. He will give you as much of the spirit of prayer as you have strength of body to bear.

Said a good man to me, "O, I am dying for the want of strength to pray. My body is crushed, the world is on me, and how can I forbear praying?" I have known that man go to bed absolutely sick, for weakness and faintness under the pressure. And I have known him pray as if he would do violence to heaven, and then seen the blessing come as plainly in answer to his prayer, as if it was revealed, so that no person would doubt it, any more than if God had spoken from heaven. Shall I tell you how he died? He prayed more and more, and he used to take the map of the world before him, and pray, and look over the different countries, and pray for them, till he absolutely expired in his room, praying. Blessed man! He was the reproach of the ungodly, and of carnal, unbelieving professors, but he was the favorite of heaven, and a prevailing prince in prayer.

VI. I will refer to some objections, which are brought forward, against this doctrine.

1. "It leads to fanaticism, and amounts to a new revelation." Why should this be a stumbling block? They must have evidence to believe, before they can offer the prayer of faith. And if God gives other evidence besides the senses, where is the objection? True, there is a sense in which this is a new revelation; it is making known a thing by his Spirit. But it is the very revelation which God has promised to give. It is just the one we are to expect, if the Bible is true; that when we know not what we ought to pray for, according to the will of God, his Spirit helps our infirmities, and teaches us the very thing to pray for. Shall we deny the teaching of the Spirit?

2. It is often asked, "Is it our duty to pray the prayer of faith for the salvation of all men?" I answer, No, for that is not a thing according to the will of God. It is directly contrary to his revealed will. We have no evidence that all will be saved. We should feel benevolently to all, and in itself considered, desire their salvation. But God has revealed it to us that many of the human race shall be damned. And it cannot be a duty to *believe* that they shall all be saved, in the face of a revelation to the contrary.

3. But, say some, "If we *were* to offer this prayer for all men, would not all men be saved?" I answer, Yes, and so they would be saved, if they would all repent. But they will not. Neither will Christians offer the prayer of faith for all, because there is no evidence on which to ground a belief that God intends to save all men.

4. But you ask, "For whom are we to offer this prayer? We want to know in what cases, for what persons, and places, and at what times, &c. we are to make the prayer of faith." I answer, as I already answered, When you have evidence, from promises, or prophecies, or the leadings of the Spirit, that God will do the things you pray for.

5. "How is it that so many prayers of pious parents for their children are not answered? Did you not say there was a promise which pious parents may apply to their children? Why is it then, that so many pious praying parents have had impenitent children, that died in their sins?" Granted that it is so, what does it prove? Let God be true, but every man a liar. Which shall we believe,

that God's promise has failed, or that these parents did not do their duty? Perhaps they did not believe the promise, or did not believe there was any such thing as the prayer of faith. Wherever you find a professor that does not believe in any such prayer, you find, as a general thing, that he has children and domestics yet in their sins. And no wonder, unless they are converted in answer to the prayers of somebody else.

6. "Will not these views lead to fanaticism? Will not many people think they are offering the prayer of faith when they are not?" That is the same objection that the Unitarians make against the doctrine of regeneration — that many people think they have been born again when they have not. It is an argument against all spiritual religion whatever. Some think they have it, when they have not, and are fanatics. But there are those who *know* what the prayer of faith is, just as there are those who know what spiritual experience is, though it may stumble cold-hearted professors who know it not. Even ministers often lay themselves open to the rebuke which Christ gave to Nicodemus: "Art thou a master in Israel, and knowest not these things?"

REMARKS.

1. Persons who have not known by experience what this is, have great reason to doubt their piety. This is by no means uncharitable. Let them examine themselves. It is to be feared that they understand prayer as Nicodemus did the new birth. They have not walked with God, and you cannot describe it to them, any more than you can describe a beautiful painting to a blind man, who cannot see colors. Many professors can understand about the prayer of faith, just as much as a blind man does of colors.

2. There is reason to believe millions are in hell because professors have not offered the prayer of faith. When they had promises under their eye, they have not had faith enough to use them. Thus parents let their children, and even *baptized* children, go down to hell, because they would not believe the promises of God.[4] Doubtless many women's husbands have gone to hell, when

[4] Although Finney seems here to be putting a great load of guilt upon parents and threatening them with the responsibility for sending their children to hell if they do not adapt his views, it is worth remembering the terrible anxiety many parents felt under the strict interpretation of orthodox Calvinism in which they were helpless to do anything to save their children. Finney's doctrines were actually a great boon to God-fearing parents. See, for example, his statement on

they might have prevailed with God in prayer, and saved them. The signs of the times, and the indications of Providence, were favorable, perhaps, and the Spirit of God prompted desires for their salvation, and they had evidence enough to believe that God was ready to grant a blessing, and if they had only prayed in faith, God would have granted it; but God turned it away, because they would not discern the signs of the times.

3. You say, "This leaves the church under a great load of guilt." True, it does; and no doubt multitudes will stand up before God, covered all over with the blood of souls that have been lost through their want of faith. The promises of God, accumulated in their Bibles, will stare them in the face, and weigh them down to hell.

4. Many professors of religion live so far from God, that to talk to them about the prayer of faith, is all unintelligible. Very often the greatest offence possible to them, is to preach about this kind of prayer.

5. I want to ask the professors who are here a few questions. Do you know what it is to pray in faith? Did you ever pray in this way? Have you ever prayed, till your mind was assured the blessing would come — till you felt that rest in God, that confidence, as perfect as if you saw God come down from heaven to give it to you? If not, you ought to examine your foundation. How can you live without praying in faith at all? How do you live in view of your children, while you have no assurance whatever that they will be converted? One would think you would go deranged. I knew a father at the west; he was a good man, but he had erroneous views respecting the prayer of faith; and his whole family of children were grown up, and not one of them converted. At length his son sickened, and seemed about to die. The father prayed, but the son grew worse, and seemed sinking into the grave without hope. The father prayed, till his anguish was unutterable. He went at last and prayed — (there seemed no prospect of his son's life) — but he poured out his soul as if he would not be denied, till at length he got an assurance that his son would not only live, but be converted; and not only this one, but his whole family, would be converted to God. He came into the house, and told his family his son would not die. They were astonished at him. "I tell you,"

---

p. 331, "We see that pious parents can render the salvation of their children certain. Only let them pray in faith . . . and God has promised them the desire of their hearts."

says he, "he won't die. And no child of mine will ever die in his sins." That man's children were all converted years ago.

What do you think of that? Was that fanaticism? If you believe so, it is because you know nothing about the matter. Do you pray so? Do you live in such a manner that you *can* offer such prayer for your children? I know that the children of professors may sometimes be converted in answer to the prayers of somebody else. But ought you to live so? Dare you trust to the prayers of others, when God calls *you* to sustain this most important relation to your children?

Finally — See what combined effort is made to dispose of the Bible. The wicked are for throwing away the threatenings of the Bible, and the church the promises. And what is there left? Between them, they leave the Bible a blank. I say it in love: What are our Bibles good for, if we do not lay hold on their precious promises, and use them as the ground of our faith when we pray for the blessing of God? You had better sent your Bibles to the heathen, where they will do some good, if you are not going to believe and use them. I have no evidence that there is much of this prayer now in this church, or in this city. And what will become of it? What will become of your children? your neighbors? the wicked?

VI

SPIRIT OF PRAYER

Text. — Likewise the Spirit also helpeth our infirmities: for we know not what we should pray for as we ought: but the Spirit itself maketh intercession for us with groanings which cannot be uttered. And he that searcheth the hearts knoweth what is the mind of the Spirit, because he maketh intercession for the saints, according to the will of God. — Romans viii. 26, 27.

My last lecture but one, was on the subject of Effectual Prayer; in which I observed that one of the most important attributes of effectual or prevailing prayer is Faith. This was so extensive a subject that I reserved it for a separate discussion. And accordingly, I lectured last Friday evening on the subject of Faith in Prayer, or, as it is termed, the Prayer of Faith. It was my intention to discuss the subject in a single lecture. But as I was under the necessity of condensing so much on some points, it occurred to me, and was mentioned by others, that there might be some questions which people would ask, that ought to be answered more fully, especially as the subject is one on which there is so much darkness. One grand design in preaching, is, to exhibit the truth in such a way as to answer the questions which would naturally arise in the minds of those who read the Bible with attention, and who want to know what it means, so that they can put it in practice. In explaining the text, I propose to show,

I. What Spirit is here spoken of, "The Spirit also helpeth our infirmities."

II. What that Spirit does for us.

III. Why he does what the text declares him to do.

IV. How he accomplishes it.

V. The degree in which he influences the minds of those who are under his influence.

VI. How his influences are to be distinguished from the influences of evil spirits, or from the suggestions of our own minds.

VII. How we are to obtain this agency of the Holy Spirit.

VIII. Who have a right to expect to enjoy his influences in this matter — or for whom the Spirit does the things spoken of in the text.

1. What Spirit is it, that is spoken of in the text?

Some have supposed that the Spirit spoken of in the text means our own spirit — our own mind. But a little attention to the text will show plainly that this is not the meaning. "The Spirit helpeth our infirmities," would then read, "Our own spirit helpeth the infirmities of our own spirit," — and "Our own spirit likewise maketh intercession for our own spirit." You see you can make no sense of it on that supposition. It is evident from the manner in which the text is introduced, that the Spirit referred to is the Holy Ghost. "For if ye live after the flesh, ye shall die: but if ye through the Spirit do mortify the deeds of the body, ye shall live. For as many as are led by the Spirit of God, they are the sons of God. For ye have not received the spirit of bondage again to fear; but ye have received the spirit of adoption, whereby we cry, Abba, Father. The Spirit itself beareth witness with our spirit, that we are the children of God." And the text is plainly speaking of the same Spirit.

II. What the Spirit does.[1]

Answer — He intercedes for the saints. "He maketh intercession for us," and "helpeth our infirmities," when "we know not what to pray for as we ought." He helps Christians to pray according to the will of God, or for the things that God desires them to pray for.

III. Why is the Holy Spirit thus employed?

Because of our ignorance. Because we know not what we should pray for as we ought. We are so ignorant both of the will of God, revealed in the Bible, and of his unrevealed will, as we ought to learn it from his providence. Mankind are vastly ignorant both of the promises and prophecies of the Bible, and blind to the providence of God. And they are still more in the dark about those points of which God has said nothing but by the leadings of his Spirit. You recollect that I named these four sources of evidence on which to ground faith in prayer — promises, prophecies, providences, and the Holy Spirit. When all other means fail of leading us to the knowledge of what we ought to pray for, the Spirit does it.

IV. How does he make intercession for the saints? In what mode does he operate, so as to help our infirmities?

Not by superseding the use of our faculties. It is not by pray-

[1] Finney insisted that the agency of the Holy Spirit as described in the following paragraphs proved that he was not a Pelagian.

ing for us, while we do nothing. He prays for us, by exciting our own faculties. Not that he immediately suggests to us words, or guides our language. But he enlightens our minds, and makes the truth take hold of our souls. He leads us to consider the state of the church, and the condition of sinners around us. The *manner* in which he brings the truth before the mind, and keeps it there till it produces its effect, we cannot tell. But we can know as much as this — that he leads us to a deep consideration of the state of things; and the results of this, the natural and philosophical result, is, deep feeling. When the Spirit brings the truth up before a man's mind, there is only one way in which he can keep from deep feeling. That is, by turning away his thoughts, and leading his mind to think of other things. Sinners, when the Spirit of God brings the truth before them, must feel. They feel wrong, as long as they remain impenitent. So if a man is a Christian, and the Holy Spirit brings a subject into warm contact with his heart, it is just as impossible he should not feel, as it is that your hand should not feel if you put it into the fire. If the Spirit of God leads him to dwell on things calculated to excite warm and overpowering feelings, and he is not excited by them, it proves that he has no love for souls, nothing of the Spirit of Christ, and knows nothing about Christian experience.

2. The Spirit makes the Christian feel the value of souls, and the guilt and danger of sinners in their present condition. It is amazing how dark and stupid Christians often are about this.[2] Even Christian parents let their children go right down to hell before their eyes, and scarcely seem to exercise a single feeling, or put forth an effort to save them. And why? Because they are so blind to what hell is, so unbelieving about the Bible, so ignorant of the precious promises which God has made to faithful parents. They grieve the Spirit of God away, and it is in vain to try to make them pray for their children, while the Spirit of God is away from them.

3. He leads Christians to understand and apply the promises of Scripture. It is wonderful that in no age have Christians been able fully to apply the promises of Scripture to the events of life, as they go along. This is not because the promises themselves are obscure. The promises themselves are plain enough. But there has always been a wonderful disposition to overlook the Scriptures,

---

[2] By "stupid" or "stupidity" Finney always means "lacking in understanding" or "spiritually sluggish," and not "foolish" or "imbecilic."

as a source of light respecting the passing events of life. How astonished the apostles were at Christ's application of so many prophecies to himself! They seemed to be continually ready to exclaim, "Astonishing! Can it be so? We never understood it before." Who, that has witnessed the manner in which the apostles, influenced and inspired by the Holy Ghost, applied passages of the Old Testament to gospel times, has not been amazed at the richness of meaning which they found in the Scriptures? So it has been with many a Christian; while deeply engaged in prayer, he has seen that passages of Scripture are appropriate which he never thought of before, as having any such application.

I once knew an individual who was in great spiritual darkness. He had retired for prayer, resolved that he would not desist till he had found the Lord. He kneeled down and tried to pray. All was dark, and he could not pray. He rose from his knees, and stood for a while, but he could not give it up, for he had promised that he would not let the sun go down before he had given himself to God. He knelt again, but it was all dark, and his heart was hard as before. He was nearly in despair, and said in agony, "I have grieved the Spirit of God away, and there is no promise for me. I am shut out from the presence of God." But his resolution was formed not to give over, and again he knelt down. He had said but a few words when this passage came into his mind as fresh as if he had just read it. It seemed as if he had just been reading the words, "Ye shall seek me, and find me, when ye shall search for me with all your heart." Jer. xxix. 13. He saw that though this promise was in the Old Testament, and was addressed to the Jews, it was still as applicable to him as to them. And it broke his heart, like the hammer of the Lord, in a moment. And he prayed, and rose up, happy in God. Thus it often happens when professors of religion are praying for their children. Sometimes they pray, and are in darkness and doubt, feeling as if there was no foundation for faith, and no special promises for the children of believers. But while they are pleading, God has shown them the full meaning of some promises, and their soul has rested on it as on the mighty arm of God. I once heard of a widow who was greatly exercised about her children, till this passage was brought powerfully to her mind: "Leave thy fatherless children with me, I will preserve them alive." She saw it had an extended meaning, and she was enabled to lay hold on it, as it were with her hands; and then she prevailed in prayer, and her children were converted. — The Holy

Spirit was sent into the world by the Savior, to guide *his people*, and instruct them, and bring things to their remembrance, as well as to convince the world of sin.

4. The Spirit leads Christians to desire and pray for things of which nothing is specifically said in the word of God. Take the case of an individual. That God is willing to save is a general truth. So it is a general truth that he is willing to answer prayer. But how shall I know the will of God respecting that individual, whether I can pray in faith according to the will of God for the conversion and salvation of that individual, or not? Here the agency of the Spirit comes in, to lead the minds of God's people to pray for those individuals, and at those times, when God is prepared to bless them. When we know not what to pray for, the Holy Spirit leads the mind to dwell on some object, to consider its situation, to realize its value, and to feel for it, and pray, and travail in birth, till the person is converted. This sort of experience I know is less common in cities, than it is in some parts of the country, because of the infinite number of things to divert the attention and grieve the Spirit in cities. — I have had much opportunity to know how it has been in some sections.[3] I was acquainted with an individual who used to keep a list of persons that he was specially concerned for; and I have had the opportunity to know a multitude of persons for whom he became thus interested, who were immediately converted. I have seen him pray for persons on his list, when he was literally in an agony for them; and have sometimes known him call on some other person to help him pray for such a one. I have known his mind to fasten thus on an individual of hardened, abandoned character, and who could not be reached in any ordinary way. In a town in the north part of this state, where there was a revival, there was a certain individual who was a most violent and outrageous opposer. He kept a tavern, and used to delight in swearing at a desperate rate, whenever there were Christians within hearing, on purpose to hurt their feelings. He was so bad, that one man said he believed he should have to sell his place, or give it away, and move out of town, for he could not live near a man that swore so. This good man, that I was speaking of, was passing through the town, and heard of the case, and was very much grieved and distressed for the individual. He took him on his pray-

---

[3] This is the first of many references in these lectures to the superior piety of rural dwellers over city dwellers, a view shared by all revivalists since Finney's day.

ing list. The case weighed on his mind, when he was asleep and when he was awake. He kept thinking about him, and praying for him for days. And the first we knew of it, this ungodly man came into a meeting, and got up and confessed his sins, and poured out his soul. His bar-room immediately became the place where they held prayer meetings. In this manner the Spirit of God leads individual Christians to pray for things which they would not pray for, unless they were led by the Spirit. And thus they pray for things according to the will of God.

By some, this may be said to be a revelation from God. I do not doubt that great evil has been done by saying that this kind of influence amounts to a new revelation. And many people will be afraid of it if they hear it called a new revelation, so that they will not stop to inquire what it means, or whether the Scriptures teach it or not. They suppose it to be a complete answer to the idea. But the plain truth of the matter is, that the Spirit leads a man to pray. And if God leads a man to pray for an individual, the inference from the Bible is, that God designs to save that individual. If we find by comparing our state of mind with the Bible, that we are *led by the Spirit* to pray for an individual, we have good evidence to believe that God is prepared to bless him.

6. By giving to Christians a spiritual discernment respecting the movements and developments of Providence. Devoted, praying Christians often see these things so clearly, and look so far ahead, as greatly to stumble others. They sometimes almost seem to prophecy. No doubt persons may be deluded, and sometimes are so, by leaning to their own understanding when they think they are led by the Spirit. But there is no doubt that a Christian may be made to see and discern clearly the signs of the times, so as to understand, by providence, what to expect, and thus to pray for it in faith. Thus they are often led to expect a revival, and to pray for it in faith, when nobody else can see the least signs of it.

There was a woman in New Jersey, in a place where there had been a revival. She was very positive there was going to be another. She insisted upon it that they had had the former rain, and were now going to have the latter rain. She wanted to have conference meetings appointed. But the minister and elders saw nothing to encourage it, and would do nothing. She saw they were blind, and so she went forward and got a carpenter to make seats for her, for she said she would have meetings in her own house. There was certainly going to be a revival. She had scarcely opened her doors for meetings, before the Spirit of God came down in great power. And these sleepy church members found themselves surrounded all at once with convicted sinners. And they could only say, "Surely the Lord was in this place, and we knew it not." The reason why such persons understand the indication of God's will is not because of the superior wisdom that is in them, but because the Spirit of God leads them to see the signs of the times. And this, not by revelation, but they are led to see that converging of providences to a single point, which produces in them a confident expectation of a certain result.

V. In what degree are we to expect the Spirit of God to affect the minds of believers? The text says, "The Spirit maketh intercession with groanings that cannot be uttered." The meaning of this I understand to be, that the Spirit excites desires too great to be uttered except by groans. Something that language cannot utter — making the soul too full to utter its feelings by words, where the person can only groan them out to God, who understands the language of the heart.

VI. How are we to know whether it is the Spirit of God that influences our minds or not?

1. Not by feeling that some external influence or agency is applied to us. We are not to expect to feel our minds in direct physical contact with God. If such a thing can be, we know of no way in which it can be made sensible. We know that we exercise our minds freely, and that our thoughts are exercised on something that excites our feelings. But we are not to expect a miracle to be wrought, as if we were led by the hand, sensibly, or like something whispered in the ear, or any miraculous manifestation of the will of God. Individuals often grieve the Spirit away, because they do not harbor him and cherish his influences. Sinners often do this ignorantly. They suppose that if they were under conviction by the Spirit, they should have such and such mysterious feelings, a shock would come upon them, which they could not mistake. Many Christians are so ignorant of the Spirit's influences, and have thought so little about having his assistance in prayer, that when they have them they do not know it, and so do not cherish, and yield to them, and preserve them. We are sensible of nothing in the case, only the movement of our own minds. There is nothing else that *can* be felt. We are merely sensible that our thoughts are intensely employed on a certain subject. Christians are often unnecessarily misled and distressed on this point,

for fear they have not the Spirit of God. They feel intensely, but they know what makes them feel. They are distressed about sinners; but why should they not be distressed, when they think of their condition? They keep thinking about them all the time, and why shouldn't they be distressed? Now, the truth is, that the very fact that you are *thinking* upon them is evidence that the Spirit of God is leading you. Do you not know that the greater part of the time these things do not affect you so? The greater part of the time you do not think much about the case of sinners. You know their salvation is always equally important. But at other times, even when you are quite at leisure, your mind is entirely dark, and vacant of any feeling for them. But now, although you may be busy about other things, you think, you pray, and feel intensely for them, even while you are about business that at other times would occupy all your thoughts. Now, almost every thought you have is, "God have mercy on them." Why is this? Why, their case is placed in a strong light before your mind. Do you ask what it is, that leads your mind to exercise benevolent feelings for sinners, and to agonize in prayer for them? What can it be but the Spirit of God? There are no devils that would lead you so. If your feelings are truly benevolent, you are to consider it as the Holy Spirit leading you to pray for things according to the will of God.

2. Try the spirits by the Bible. People are sometimes led away by strange fantasies and crazy impulses. If you compare them faithfully with the Bible, you never need be led astray. You can always know whether your feelings are produced by the Spirit's influences, by comparing your desires with the spirit and temper of religion, as described in the Bible. The Bible commands you to try the spirits. "Beloved, believe not every spirit, but try the spirits, whether they be of God."

VII. How shall we get this influence of the Spirit of God?

1. It must be sought by fervent, believing prayer. Christ says, "If ye then, being evil, know how to give good gifts to your children, how much more shall your heavenly Father give the Holy Spirit to them that ask it!" Does any one say, I have prayed for it, and it does not come? It is because you do not pray aright. "Ye ask and receive not, because ye ask amiss, that ye may consume it upon your lusts." You do not pray from right motives. A professor of religion, and a principal member in a church, once asked a minister what he thought of his case; he had been praying week

after week for the Spirit, and had not found any benefit. The minister asked him what his motive was in praying. He said he wanted to be happy. He knew those who had the Spirit were happy, and he wanted to enjoy his mind as they did. Why, the devil himself might pray so. That is mere selfishness. The man turned away in anger. He saw that he had never known what it was to pray. He was convinced he was a hypocrite, and that his prayers were all selfish, dictated only by a desire for his own happiness. David prayed that God would uphold him by his free Spirit, that he might teach transgressors and turn sinners to God. A Christian should pray for the Spirit, that he may be the more useful and glorify God more; not that he himself may be more happy. This man saw clearly where he had been in error, and he was converted. Perhaps many here have been just so. You ought to examine and see if all your prayers are not selfish.

2. Use the means adapted to stir up your minds on the subject, and to keep your attention fixed there. If a man prays for the Spirit, and then diverts his mind to other objects; uses no other means, but goes right away to worldly objects, he tempts God, he swings loose from his object, and it would be a miracle if he should get what he prays for. How is a sinner to get conviction? Why, by thinking of his sins. That is the way for a Christian to obtain deep feeling, by thinking on the object. God is not going to pour these things on you, without any effort of your own. You must cherish the slightest impressions. Take the Bible, and go over the passages that show the condition and prospects of the world. Look at the world, look at your children, and your neighbors, and see their condition while they remain in sin, and persevere in prayer and effort till you obtain the blessing of the Spirit of God to dwell in you. This was the way, doubtless, that Dr. Watts [4] came to have the feelings which he has described in the second Hymn of the second Book, which you would do well to read after you go home.

> My thoughts on awful subjects roll,
>   Damnation and the dead:
> What horrors seize the guilty soul
>   Upon a dying bed!

---

[4] Isaac Watts (1674–1748) was the first and best known of all English hymn writers.

> Lingering about these mortal shores,
>   She makes a long delay,
> Till, like a flood, with rapid force
>   Death sweeps the wretch away.
>
> Then, swift and dreadful, she descends
>   Down to the fiery coast,
> Amongst abominable fiends,
>   Herself a frighted ghost.
>
> There endless crowds of sinners lie,
>   And darkness makes their chains;
> Tortured with keen despair they cry,
>   Yet wait for fiercer pains.
>
> Not all their anguish and their blood
>   For their past guilt atones,
> Nor the compassion of a God
>   Shall hearken to their groans.
>
> Amazing grace, that kept my breath,
>   Nor bid my soul remove,
> Till I had learned my Savior's death,
>   And well insured his love!

Look, as it were, through a telescope that will bring it up near to you; look into hell, and hear them groan; then turn the glass upwards and look at heaven, and see the saints there, in their white robes, with their harps in their hands, and hear them sing the song of redeeming love; and ask yourself — Is it possible, that I should prevail with God to elevate the sinner there?[5] Do this, and if you are not a wicked man, and a stranger to God, you will soon have as much of the spirit of prayer as your body can sustain.

3. You must watch unto prayer. You must keep a look out, and see if God grants the blessing when you ask him. People sometimes pray, and never look to see if the prayer is granted. Be careful also, not to grieve the Spirit of God. Confess and forsake your sins. God will never lead you as one of his hidden ones, and let you into his secrets, unless you confess and forsake your sins. Not be always confessing and never forsake, but confess and forsake too. Make redress wherever you have committed an injury. You cannot expect to get the spirit of prayer first, and then repent. You can't fight it through so. Professors of religion, who are proud

---

[5] This image of heaven as a place where saints wear white robes and play harps dropped out of revival preaching after the Civil War.

and unyielding, and justify themselves, never will force God to dwell with them.

4. Aim to obey perfectly the written law. In other words, have no fellowship with sin. Aim at being entirely above the world; "Be ye perfect even as your Father in heaven is perfect." If you sin at all, let it be your daily grief. The man who does not aim at this, means to live in sin. Such a man need not expect God's blessing, for he is not sincere in desiring to keep all his commandments.

VIII. For whom does the Spirit intercede?

Answer — He maketh intercession for the saints, for all saints, for any who are saints.

REMARKS.

1. Why do you suppose it is, that so little stress is laid on the influences of the Spirit in prayer, when so much is said about his influences in conversion? Many people are amazingly afraid the Spirit's influences will be left out. They lay great stress on the Spirit's influences in converting sinners. But how little is said, how little is printed, about his influence in prayer! How little complaining that people do not make enough of the Spirit's influences in leading Christians to pray according to the will of God! Let it never be forgotten, that no Christian ever prays aright, unless led by the Spirit. He has natural power to pray, and so far as the will of God is revealed, is able to do it; but he never does, unless the Spirit of God influences him. Just as sinners are able to repent, but never do, unless influenced by the Spirit.

2. This subject lays open the foundation of the difficulty felt by many persons on the subject of the Prayer of Faith. They object to the idea that faith in prayer is a belief that we shall receive the very things for which we ask; and insist that there can be no foundation or evidence upon which to rest such a belief. In a sermon published a few years since, upon this subject, the writer brings forward this difficulty, and presents it in its full strength. I have, says he, no evidence that the thing prayed for will be granted, *until* I have prayed in faith; because, praying in faith is the condition upon which it is promised. And of course I cannot claim the promise, until I have fulfilled the condition. Now, if the condition is, that I am to believe I shall receive the very blessing for which I ask, it is evident that the promise is given upon the performance of an *impossible* condition, and is of course a mere

nullity. The promise would amount to just this: You shall have whatsoever you ask, upon the condition that you first believe that you shall receive it. Now, I must fulfill the condition before I can claim the promise. But I can have no evidence that I shall receive it, until I have believed that I shall receive it. This reduces me to the necessity of believing that I shall receive it *before* I have any evidence that I shall receive it — which is impossible.

The whole force of this objection arises out of the fact, that the *Spirit's influences* are entirely overlooked, which he exerts in leading an individual to the exercise of faith. It has been supposed that the passage in Mark xi. 22 and 24, with other kindred promises on the subject of the Prayer of Faith, relate exclusively to miracles. But suppose this were true. I would ask, What were the apostles to believe, when they prayed for a miracle? Were they to believe that the precise miracle would be performed for which they prayed? It is evident that they were. In the verses just alluded to, Christ says, "For verily I say unto you, that whosoever shall say unto this mountain, Be thou removed, and be thou cast into the sea, and shall not doubt in his heart, but SHALL BELIEVE THAT THESE THINGS WHICH HE SAITH SHALL COME TO PASS, he shall have whatsoever he saith. Therefore I say unto you, what things soever ye desire, when ye pray, BELIEVE THAT YE RECEIVE THEM, and ye shall have them." Here it is evident, that the thing to be believed, and which they were not to doubt in their heart, was, that they should have the very blessing for which they prayed. Now the objection above stated, lies in all its force against this kind of faith, when praying for the performance of a miracle. If it be impossible to believe this in praying for any other blessing, it was equally so in praying for a miracle. I might ask, Could an apostle believe that the miracle would be wrought, before he had fulfilled the condition? inasmuch as the condition was, that he should believe that he should receive that for which he prayed. Either the promise is a nullity and a deception, or there is a possibility of performing the condition.

Now, as I have said, the whole difficulty lies in the fact that the Spirit's influences are entirely overlooked, and that faith which is of the operation of God, is left out of the question. If the object is good against praying for any object, it is as good against praying in faith for the performance of a miracle. The fact is, that the Spirit of God could give evidence, on which to believe that any particular miracle would be granted; could lead the mind to a firm reliance upon God, and trust that the blessing sought would be obtained. And so at the present day he can give the same assurance, in praying for any blessing that we need. Neither in the one case or the other, are the *influences of the Spirit* miraculous. Praying is the same thing, whether you pray for the conversion of a soul, or for a miracle. Faith is the same thing in the one case as in the other; it only terminates on a different object; in the one case on the conversion of a soul, and in the other on the performance of a miracle. Nor is faith exercised in the one more than in the other, without reference to a promise; and a *general* promise may with the same propriety be applied to the conversion of a soul as to the performance of a miracle. And it is equally true in the one case as the other, that no man ever prays in faith without being influenced by the Spirit of God. And if the Spirit could lead the mind of an apostle to exercise faith in regard to a miracle, he can lead the mind of another Christian to exercise faith in regard to receiving any other blessing, by a reference to the same general promise.

Should any one ask, "When are we *under an obligation* to believe that we shall receive *the blessing* for which we ask?" I answer:

(1.) When there is a particular promise, specifying the particular blessing: as where we pray for the Holy Spirit. This blessing is particularly named in the promise, and here we have evidence, and are bound to believe, whether we have any Divine influence or not; just as sinners are bound to repent whether the Spirit strives with them or not. Their obligation rests, not upon the Spirit's influences, but upon the powers of moral agency which they possess; upon their ability to do their duty. And while it is true that not one of them ever will repent without the influences of the Spirit, still they have power to do so, and are under obligation to do so, whether the Spirit strives with them or not. So with the Christian. He is bound to believe where he has evidence. And although he never does believe, even where he has an express promise, without the Spirit of God, yet his obligation to do so rests upon his ability, and not upon the Divine influence.

(2.) Where God makes a revelation by his providence, we are bound to believe in proportion to the clearness of the providential indication.

(3.) So where there is a prophecy, we are bound also to believe. But in neither of these cases *do we*, in fact, believe, without the Spirit of God.

But where there is neither promise, providence, nor prophecy, on which to repose our faith, we are under no obligation to believe unless, as I have shown in this discourse, *the Spirit* gives us evidence, by creating desires, and by leading us to pray for a particular object. In the case of those promises of a general nature, where we are honestly at a loss to know in what *particular* cases to apply them, it may be considered rather as our privilege than as our *duty*, in many instances, to apply them to particular cases; but whenever the Spirit of God leads us to apply them to a particular object, then it becomes *our duty* so to apply them. In this case, God explains his own promise, and shows how he designed it should be applied. And then our obligation to make this application, and to believe in reference to this particular object, remains in full force.

3. Some have supposed that Paul prayed in faith for the removal of the thorn in the flesh, and that is was not granted. But they cannot prove that Paul *prayed in faith*. The presumption is all on the other side, as I have shown in a former lecture. He had neither promise, nor prophecy, nor providence, nor the Spirit of God, to lead him to believe. The whole objection goes on the ground that the apostle might pray in faith without being led by the Spirit. This is truly a shorthand method of disposing of the Spirit's influences in prayer. Certainly, to assume that he prayed in faith, is to assume either that he prayed in faith without being led by the Spirit, or that the Spirit of God led him to pray for that which was not according to the will of God.

I have dwelt the more on this subject, because I want to have it made so plain, that you will all be careful not to grieve the Spirit. I want you to have high ideas of the Holy Ghost, and to feel that nothing good will be done without his influences. No praying or preaching will be of any avail without him. If Jesus Christ were to come down here and preach to sinners, not one would be converted without the Spirit. Be careful then not to grieve him away, by slighting or neglecting his heavenly influences when he invites you to pray.

4. In praying for an object, it is necessary to persevere till you obtain it. O, with what eagerness Christians sometimes pursue a sinner in their prayers, when the Spirit of God has fixed their desires on him! No miser pursues his gold with so fixed a determination.

5. The fear of being led by impulses has done great injury, by not being duly considered. A person's mind *may be* led by an

ignis fatuus. But we do wrong, if we let the fear of impulses lead us to resist the *good* impulses of the Holy Ghost. No wonder Christians don't have the spirit of prayer, if they are unwilling to take the trouble to distinguish; and so reject or resist all impulses, and all leadings of invisible agents. A great deal has been said about fanaticism, that is very unguarded, and that causes many minds to reject the leadings of the Spirit of God. "As many as are the sons of God, are led by the Spirit of God." And it is our duty to "try the spirits, whether they be of God." We should insist on a close scrutiny, and an accurate discrimination. There *must be* such a thing as being led by the Spirit. And when we are convinced it is of God, we should be sure to follow — follow on, with full confidence that he will not lead us wrong.

6. We see from this subject the absurdity of using forms of prayer. The very idea of using a form, rejects, *of course*, the leadings of the Spirit. Nothing is more calculated to destroy the spirit of prayer, and entirely to darken and confuse the mind, as to what constitutes prayer, than to use forms. Forms of prayer are not only absurd in themselves, but they are the very device of the devil to destroy the spirit and break the power of prayer. It is of no use to say the form is a good one. Prayer does not consist in words. And it matters not what the words are, if the heart is not led by the Spirit of God. If the desire is not enkindled, the thoughts directed, and the whole current of feeling produced, and led by the Spirit of God, it is not prayer. And set forms are, of all things, best calculated to keep an individual from praying as he ought.[6]

7. The subject furnishes a test of character. — The Spirit maketh intercession — for whom? For the saints.[7] Those who are saints are thus exercised. If you are saints, you know by experience what it is to be thus exercised, or it is because you have grieved the Spirit of God, so that he will not lead you. You live in such a manner, that this Holy Comforter will not dwell with you, nor give you the spirit of prayer. If this is so, you must repent. Whether you are a Christian or not, don't stop to settle that, but repent, as if you never had repented. Do your first works. Don't

---

[6] This paragraph is not included in the version of the lecture that appeared in the *New York Evangelist*, January 10, 1835, p. 6. It is a cardinal point of pietists that extempore prayers and sermons are superior to written ones for they come more directly from the heart and are more apt to be inspired by the Holy Spirit.

[7] A "saint" is any person destined for heaven and hence any truly converted Christian.

take it for granted that you are a Christian, but go like a humble sinner, and pour out your heart unto the Lord. You never can have the spirit of prayer in any other way.

8. The importance of understanding this subject.

(1.) In order to be useful. Without this spirit there can be no such sympathy between you and God, that you can either walk with God or work with God. You need to have a strong beating of your heart with his, or you need not expect to be greatly useful.

(2.) As important as your sanctification.[8] Without such a spirit you will not be sanctified, you will not understand the Bible, you will not know how to apply it to your case. I want you to feel the importance of having God with you all the time. If you live as you ought, he says he will come unto you, and make his abode with you, and sup with you, and you with him.

9. If people know not the spirit of prayer, they are very apt to be unbelieving in regard to the results of prayer. They don't see what takes place, or don't see the connection, or don't see the evidence. They are not expecting spiritual blessings. When sinners are convicted, they think they are only frightened by such terrible preaching. And when people are converted, they feel no confidence, and only say, "We'll see how they turn out."

10. Those who have the spirit of prayer know when the blessing comes. It was just so when Jesus Christ appeared. Those ungodly doctors did not know him. Why? Because they were not praying for the redemption of Israel. But Simeon and Anna knew him. How was that? Mark what they said, how they prayed, and how they lived. They were praying in faith, and so they were not surprised when he came. So it is with such Christians. If sinners are convicted or converted, they are not surprised at it. They were expecting just such things. They know God when he comes, because they were looking out for his visits.

11. There are three classes of persons in the church who are liable to error, or have left the truth out of view, on this subject.

(1.) Those who place great reliance on prayer, and use no other means. They are alarmed at any special means, and talk about your "getting up a revival."

---

[8] Sanctification is the step beyond conversion in which a Christian attains to a more mature state of grace and hence of closer communion with God. As Finney later developed this doctrine along the lines of John Wesley, he came to associate it with a "second blessing" or a "second baptism of the Holy Ghost," and this led him to his doctrine of perfectionism. His *Systematic Theology* (Oberlin, 1846) has a long section devoted to "Sanctification."

(2.) Over against these are those who use means, and pray, but never think about the influences of the Spirit in prayer. They talk about prayer for the Spirit, and feel the importance of the Spirit in the conversion of sinners, but do not realize the importance of the Spirit in prayer. And their prayers are all cold talk, nothing that any body can feel, or that can take hold of God.

(3.) Those who have certain strange notions about the sovereignty of God, and are waiting for God to convert the world without prayer or means.

There must be in the church a deeper sense of the need of the spirit of prayer. The fact is that, *generally*, those who use means most assiduously, and make the most strenuous efforts for the salvation of men, and who have the most correct notions of the manner in which means should be used for converting sinners, also pray most for the Spirit of God, and wrestle most with God for his blessing. And what is the result? Let facts speak, and say whether these persons do or do not pray, and whether the Spirit of God does not testify to their prayers, and follow their labors with his power.

10. A spirit very different from the spirit of prayer appears to prevail in the Presbyterian church.[9] Nothing will produce an excitement and opposition so quick as the spirit of prayer. If any person should feel burdened with the case of sinners, in prayer, so as to groan in his prayer, why, the women are nervous, and he is visited at once with rebuke and opposition. From my soul I abhor all affectation of feeling where there is none, and all attempts to work one's self up into feeling by groans. But I feel bound to defend the position, that there is such a thing as being in a state of mind, in which there is but one way to keep from groaning; and that is, by resisting the Holy Ghost. I was once present where this subject was discussed.[10] It was said that groaning ought to be discountenanced. The question was asked, whether God *could not* produce such a state of feeling, that to abstain from groaning was impossible? and the answer was, "Yes, but he never does." Then the apostle Paul was egregiously deceived, when he wrote about groanings that cannot be uttered. Edwards was deceived, when he wrote his book upon revivals. Revivals are all in the dark. Now,

---

[9] This is the first of many attacks in these lectures upon the cold, dead formality of the Old School element that still dominated the Presbyterian Church.

[10] Finney refers here to the New Lebanon Convention with Lyman Beecher in 1827, which is discussed in the Introduction to this edition, p. xx.

no man who reviews the history of the church will adopt such a sentiment. I don't like this attempt to shut out, or stifle, or keep down, or limit the spirit of prayer. I would sooner cut off my right hand, than rebuke the spirit of prayer, as I have heard of its being done by saying, "Don't let me hear any more groaning."

But then, I hardly know where to end this subject. I should like to discuss it a month, and till the whole church could understand it, so as to pray the prayer of faith. Beloved, I want to ask you if you believe all this? Or do you wonder that I should talk so? Perhaps some of you have had some glimpses of these things. Now, will you give yourselves up to prayer, and live so as to have the spirit of prayer, and have the spirit with you all the time? O, for a praying church! I once knew a minister who had a revival fourteen winters in succession. I did not know how to account for it, till I saw one of his members get up in a prayer meeting, and make a confession. "Brethren," said he, "I have been long in the habit of praying every Saturday night till after midnight, for the descent of the Holy Ghost among us. And now, brethren," and he began to weep, "I confess that I have neglected it for two or three weeks." The secret was out. That minister had a praying church. Brethren, in my present state of health, I find it impossible to pray as much as I have been in the habit of doing, and continue to preach. It overcomes my strength. Now, shall I give myself up to prayer, and stop preaching? That will not do. Now, will not you, who are in health, throw yourselves into this work, and bear this burden, and lay yourselves out in prayer, till God will pour out his blessing upon us?

VII

BE FILLED WITH THE SPIRIT

TEXT. — Be filled with the Spirit. — EPH. v. 18.

SEVERAL of my last lectures have been on the subject of prayer, and the importance of having the spirit of prayer, of the intercession of the Holy Ghost. Whenever the necessity and importance of the Spirit's influences are held forth, there can be no doubt that persons are in danger of abusing the doctrine, and perverting it to their own injury. For instance, when you tell sinners that without the Holy Spirit they never will repent, they are very liable to pervert the truth, and understand by it that they *cannot* repent, and therefore are under no obligation to do it until they feel the Spirit. It is often difficult to make them see that all the "cannot" consists in their unwillingness, and not in their inability.[1] So again, when we tell Christians that they need the Spirit's aid in prayer, they are very apt to think they are under no obligation to pray the prayer of faith, until they feel the influences of the Spirit. They can't be made to see that in all those cases, where they have any means of ascertaining the mind and will of God, they are dependent on the Spirit's aid in prayer for precisely the same reason that sinners are dependent, and in the same sense. They often make it a matter of self-justification, as if it was a necessity arising out of an inability, instead of an unwillingness to do that which lies within their power.

Before we come to consider the other department of means for promoting a revival, that is, *the means to be used with sinners*, I wish to show you, that if you live without the Spirit, you are without excuse. Obligation to perform duty never rests on the condition, that we shall first have the influence of the Spirit, but on the powers of moral agency. We, as moral agents, have the power to obey God, and are perfectly bound to obey, and the

---

[1] This is the first of many references in this volume to what Finney called "cannot-ism," the view allegedly held by Old School Calvinists that the sinner could do nothing to effect his own conversion but must wait for the Holy Spirit to take the first step by infusing a new principle in his heart. For a discussion of this point, see the Introduction to this edition, pp. xxviii–xxxi.

reason we do not is, that we are unwilling. The influences of the Spirit are wholly a matter of grace. If they were indispensable to *enable* us to perform duty, the bestowment of them would not be a gracious act, but a mere matter of common justice. Sinners are not bound to repent because they have the Spirit's influence, or because they can obtain it, but because they are moral agents, and have the powers which God requires them to exercise. So in the case of Christians. They are not bound to pray in faith because they have the Spirit, (except in those cases where his influences in begetting desire constitute the evidence that it is God's will to grant the object of desire,) but because they have evidence. They are not bound to pray in faith at all, except when they have evidence as the foundation of their faith. They must have evidence from promises, or principle, or prophecy, or providence. And where they have evidence independent of his influences, they are bound to exercise faith, whether they have the Spirit's influence or not. They are bound to see the evidence, and to believe. The Spirit is given not to enable them to see and believe, but because without it they *will not* look, nor feel, nor act, as they ought. I purpose this evening to show from the text,

I. That individuals may have the Spirit of God, or be filled with the Spirit.

II. That it is their duty to be filled with the Spirit.

III. Why they do not have the Spirit.

IV. The guilt of those who have not the Spirit of God, to lead their minds in duty and prayer.

V. The consequences that will follow if they do have the Spirit.

VI. The consequences if they do not have the Spirit.

I. I am to show you that you may have the Spirit. Not because it is a matter of justice for God to give you his Spirit, but because he has promised to give it to those that ask. "If ye then, being evil, know how to give good gifts to your children, *how much more* shall your Father which is in heaven give the Holy Spirit to them that ask him?" If you ask the Holy Spirit, God has promised to give it.

But again, God has commanded you to have it. He says in the text, "Be filled with the Spirit." When God commands us to do a thing, it is the highest possible evidence that we can do it. For God to command, is equivalent to an oath that we can do it. He has no right to command, unless we have power to obey. There is no stopping short of the conclusion that God is an infinite tyrant, if he commands that which is impracticable.

II. I am to show, secondly, that it is your duty.

1. Because you have a promise of it.
2. Because God has commanded it.
3. It is essential to your own growth in grace that you should be filled with the Spirit.
4. It is as important as it is that you should be sanctified.
5. It is as necessary as it is that you should be useful and do good in the world.
6. If you do not have the Spirit of God in you, you will dishonor God, disgrace the church, and die and go to hell.

III. Why many do not have the Spirit. There are some, even professors of religion, who will say, "I don't know any thing about all this; I never had any such experience; either it is not true or I am all wrong." No doubt you are all wrong, if you know *nothing* about the influence of the Spirit. I want to present you with a few of the reasons that may prevent you from being filled with the Spirit.

1. It may be that you live a hypocritical life. Your prayers are not earnest and sincere. Not only is your religion a mere outside show, without any heart, but you are insincere in your intercourse with others. Thus you do many things to grieve the Spirit, so that he cannot dwell with you.

A minister was once boarding in a certain family, and the lady of the house was constantly complaining that she did not enjoy her mind, and nothing seemed to help her. One day some ladies called to see her, and she protested that she was very much offended because they had not called before, and pressed them to stay and spend the day, and declared she *could not* consent to let them go. — They excused themselves, however, and left the house, and as soon as they were gone, she said to her servant, she wondered these people had so little sense as to be always troubling her, and taking up her time. The minister heard it, and immediately rebuked her, and told her she could now see why she did not enjoy religion. It was because she was in the daily habit of insincerity that amounted to downright lying. And the Spirit of truth could not dwell in such a heart.

2. Others have so much levity that the Spirit will not dwell with them. The Spirit of God is solemn, and serious, and will not dwell with those who give way to thoughtless levity.

3. Others are so proud that they cannot have the Spirit. They are so fond of dress, high life, equipage, fashion, &c., that it is no wonder they are not filled with the Spirit. And yet such persons will pretend to be at a loss to know why it is that they do not enjoy religion!

4. Some are so worldly-minded, love property so well, and are trying so hard to get rich, that they cannot have the Spirit. How can he dwell with them, when their thoughts are all on things of the world, and all their powers absorbed in procuring wealth? And they hold on to it when they get it, and they are pained if pressed by conscience to do something for the conversion of the world. They show how much they love the world, in all their intercourse with others. Little things show it. They will screw down a poor man, who is doing a little piece of work for them, to the lowest penny. If they are dealing on a large scale, very likely they will be liberal and fair, because it is for their advantage. But if it is a person they care not about, a laborer, or a mechanic, or a servant, they will grind him down to the last fraction, no matter what it is really worth; and they actually pretend to make conscience of it, that they cannot possibly give any more. Now they would be ashamed to deal so with people of their own rank, because it would be known and injure their reputation.[2] But God knows it, and has it all written down, that they are covetous and unfair in their dealings, and will not do right, only when it is for their interest. Now how can such professors have the Spirit of God? It is impossible.

There are a multitude of such things, by which the Spirit of God is grieved. People call them little sins, but God will not call them little. I was struck with this thought, when I saw a little notice in the *Evangelist*. The publishers stated that they had many thousand dollars in the hands of subscribers, which was justly due, and that it would cost them as much as it was worth to send an agent to collect it. I suppose it is so with all the other religious papers, that subscribers either put the publisher to the trouble and expense of sending an agent to collect his due, or else they cheat him out of it. There are doubtless, I don't know how many, thousands of dollars held back in this way by professors of religion, just because it is in such small sums, or they are so far off

---

[2] This and other passages in the lectures offer good internal evidence that Finney's audiences were for the most part middle-class citizens on their way up in the world and not mechanics or laborers. Note also his frequent castigations of social climbing, as on p. 123.

that they can't be sued. And yet these people will pray, and appear very pious, and wonder why they cannot enjoy religion, and have the Spirit of God! It is this looseness of moral principle, this want of conscience about little matters, prevailing in the church, that grieves away the Holy Ghost. Why, it would be disgraceful to God to dwell and have communion with such persons, who will take an advantage and cheat their neighbor out of his dues, because they can do it and not be disgraced.

5. Others do not *fully* confess and *forsake* their sins, and so cannot enjoy the Spirit's presence. They will confess their sins in general terms, perhaps, and are ready always to acknowledge that they are sinners. Or they will confess partially some particular sins. But they do it reservedly, proudly, guardedly, as if they were afraid they should say a little more than is necessary; that is, when they confess to men the injuries done to them. They do it in a way which shows that, instead of bursting forth from an ingenuous heart, the confession is wrung from them, by the hand of conscience griping them. If they have injured any one, they will make a *partial* recantation, which is hard-hearted, cruel, and hypocritical, and then they will ask, "Now, brother, are you satisfied?" And you know it would be very difficult for a person to say that he was not satisfied, even if the confession is cold and heartless. But I tell you God is not satisfied. He knows whether you have gone the full length of honest confession, and taken all the blame that belongs to you. If your confessions have been constrained and wrung from you, do you suppose you can cheat God? "He that covereth his sins shall not prosper, but whoso confesseth and forsaketh shall find mercy." "He that humbleth himself shall be exalted." Unless you come quite down, and confess your sins honestly, and remunerate where you have done injury, you have no right to expect the spirit of prayer.

6. Others are neglecting some known duty, and that is the reason why they have not the Spirit. One does not pray in his family, though he knows he ought to do it, and yet he is trying to get the spirit of prayer! There is many a young man who feels in his heart that he ought to prepare for the ministry, and he has not the spirit of prayer because he has some worldly object in view, which prevents his devoting himself to the work. He has known his duty, and refuses to do it, and now he is praying for direction from the Spirit of God. He can't have it. One has neglected to make a profession of religion. He knows his duty, but he refuses

to join the church. He once had the spirit of prayer, but neglecting his duty, he grieved the Spirit away. And now he thinks, if he could once more enjoy the light of God's countenance, and have his evidences renewed, he would do his duty, and join the church. And so he is praying for it again, and trying to bring God over to his terms, to grant him his presence. You need not expect it. You will live and die in darkness, unless you are willing *first* to do your duty, *before* God manifests himself as reconciled to you. It is in vain to say, you will come forward if God will *first* show you the light of his countenance. He never will do it as long as you live; he will let you die without it, if you refuse to do your duty.

I have known women who felt that they ought to talk to their unconverted husbands, and pray with them, but they have neglected it, and so they get into the dark. They knew their duty and refused to do it; they went round it, and there they lost the spirit of prayer.

If you have neglected any known duty, and thus lost the spirit of prayer, you must yield first. God has a controversy with you; you have refused obedience to God, and you must retract it. You may have forgotten it, but God has not, and you must set yourself to recall it to mind, and repent. God never will yield nor grant you his Spirit, till you repent. Had I an omniscient eye now, I could call the names of the individuals in this congregation, who had neglected some known duty, or committed some sin, that they have not repented of, and now they are praying for the spirit of prayer, but they cannot succeed in obtaining it.

To illustrate this I will relate a case. A good man in the western part of this state, had been a long time an engaged Christian, and he used to talk to the sleepy church with which he was connected. By and by the church was offended and got out of patience, and many told him they wished he would let them alone, they did not think he could do them any good. He took them at their word, and they all went to sleep together, and remained so two or three years. By and by a minister came among them and a revival commenced, but this elder seemed to have lost his spirituality. He used to be forward in a good work, but now he held back. Every body thought it unaccountable. Finally, as he was going home one night, the truth of his situation flashed upon his mind, and he went into absolute despair for a few minutes. At length his thoughts were directed back to that sinful resolution to let the church alone in their sins. He felt that no language could describe the blackness of that sin. He realized that moment what it was to be lost, and to find that God had a controversy with him. He saw that it was a bad spirit which caused the resolution: the same that caused Moses to say, "You rebels." He humbled himself on the spot, and God poured out his Spirit on him. Perhaps some of you that hear me are in just this situation. You have said something provoking or unkind to some person. Perhaps it was peevishness to a servant that was a Christian. Or perhaps it was speaking censoriously of a minister or some other person. Perhaps you have been angry because your opinions have not been taken, or your dignity has been encroached upon. Search thoroughly, and see if you cannot find out the sin. Perhaps you have forgotten it. But God has not forgotten it, and never will forgive your unchristian conduct until you repent. God cannot overlook it. It would do no good if he should. What good would it do to forgive, while the sin is rankling in your heart?

7. Perhaps you have resisted the Spirit of God. Perhaps you are in the *habit* of resisting the Spirit. You resist conviction. In preaching, when something has been said that reached your case, your heart has risen up against it and resisted. Many are willing to hear plain and searching preaching so long as they can apply it all to others; a misanthropic spirit makes them take a satisfaction in hearing others searched and rebuked; but if the truth touch *them*, they directly cry out that it is personal and abusive. Is this your case?

8. The fact is that you do not *on the whole* desire the Spirit. This is true in every case in which you do not have the Spirit. Let me not be mistaken here. I want you should carefully discriminate. Nothing is more common than for people to desire a thing on some accounts, which they do not choose *on the whole*. A person may see an article in a store which he desires to purchase, and he goes in and asks the price, and thinks of it a little, and on the whole concludes not to purchase it. He desires the article, but does not like the price, or does not like to be at the expense, so that, upon the whole, he prefers not to purchase it. That is the reason why he does not purchase it. So persons may desire the Spirit of God on some accounts; from a regard to the comfort and joy of heart which it brings. If you know what it is by former experience to commune with God, and how sweet it is to dissolve in penitence and to be filled with the Spirit, you cannot but desire a return of those joys. And you may set yourself to pray earnestly for it, and

to pray for a revival of religion. But on the whole you are unwilling it should come. You have so much to do that you cannot attend to it. Or it will require so many sacrifices, that you cannot bear to have it. There are some things you are not willing to give up. You find that if you wish to have the Spirit of God dwell with you, you must lead a different life, you must give up the world, you must make sacrifices, you must break off from your worldly associates, and makes confession of your sins. And so on the whole you do not choose to have him come, unless he will consent to dwell with you and let you live as you please. But that he never will do.

9. Perhaps you do not pray for the Spirit; or you pray and use no other means, or pray and do not act consistently with your prayers. Or you use means calculated to resist them. Or you ask, and as soon as he comes and begins to affect your mind, you grieve him right away, and will not walk with him.

IV. I am to show the great guilt of not having the Spirit of God.

1. Your guilt is just as great as the authority of God is great, which commands you to be filled with the Spirit. God commands it, and it is just as much a disobedience of God's commands, as it is to swear profanely, or steal, or commit adultery, or break the Sabbath. Think of that. And yet there are many people who do not blame themselves at all for not having the Spirit. They even think themselves quite pious Christians, because they go to prayer meetings, and partake of the sacrament, and all that, though they live year after year without the Spirit of God. Now, you see the same God who says, "Do not get drunk," says also, "Be filled with the Spirit." You all say, if a man is an habitual murderer, or a thief, he is no Christian. Why? Because he lives in habitual disobedience to God. So if he swears, you have no charity for him. You won't allow him to plead that his heart is right, and words are nothing. God does not care any thing about words. You would think it outrageous to have such a man in the church, or to have a company of such people pretend to call themselves a church of Christ. And yet they are not a whit more absolutely living in disobedience to God, than you are, who live without the spirit of prayer, and without the presence of God.

2. Your guilt is equal to all the good you might do if you had the Spirit of God in as great measure as it is your duty to have it, and as you might have it. You elders of this church! how much good you might do, if you had the Spirit. And you Sunday school

teachers, how much good you might do; and you church members too, if you were filled with the Spirit, you might do vast good, infinite good. Well, your guilt is just as great. Here is a blessing promised, and you can have it by doing your duty. You are entirely responsible to the church and to God for all this good that you might do. A man is responsible for all the good he can do.

3. Your guilt is further measured by all the evil which you do in consequence of not having the Spirit. You are a dishonor to religion. You are a stumbling block to the church, and to the world. And your guilt is enhanced by all the various influences you exert. And it will prove so in the day of judgment.

V. The consequences of having the Spirit.

1. You will be called eccentric; and probably you will deserve it. Probably you will really be eccentric.[3] I never knew a person who was filled with the Spirit, that was not called eccentric. And the reason is, that they are unlike other people. This is always a term of comparison. There is therefore the best of reasons why such persons should appear eccentric. They act under different influences, take different views, are moved by different motives, led by a different spirit. You are to expect such remarks. How often I have heard the remark respecting such and such persons, "He is a very good man — but he is rather eccentric." I have sometimes asked for the particulars; in what does his eccentricity consist? I hear the catalogue, and the amount is, that he is spiritual. Make up your mind for this, to be eccentric. There is such a thing as affected eccentricity. Horrible! But there is such a thing as being so deeply imbued with the Spirit of God, that you must and will act so as to appear strange and eccentric, to those who cannot understand the reasons of your conduct.

2. If you have much of the Spirit of God, it is not unlikely you will be thought deranged, by many. We judge men to be deranged, when they act differently from what we think to be prudent and according to common sense, and when they come to conclusions for which we can see no good reasons. Paul was accused of being deranged, by those who did not understand the views of things under which he acted. No doubt Festus thought the man was crazy, and that much learning had made him mad. But Paul said, "I am not mad, most noble Festus." His conduct was so strange

---

[3] True pietists glory in being called "eccentric," for it shows that they are not of this world. This same outlook causes Finney to warn his followers to expect persecution and martyrdom. See pp. 117–118.

so novel, that Festus thought it must be insanity. But the truth was, he only saw the subject so clearly, that he threw his whole soul into it. They were entirely in the dark in respect to the motive by which he was actuated. This is by no means uncommon. Multitudes have appeared, to those who had no spirituality, as if they were deranged. Yet *they* saw good reasons for doing as they did. God was leading their minds to act in such a way, that those who were not spiritual could not see the reasons. You must make up your mind to this, and so much the more, as you live more above the world and walk with God.

3. If you have the Spirit of God, you must expect to feel great distress in view of the church and the world. Some spiritual epicures ask for the Spirit because they think it will make them so perfectly happy. Some people think that spiritual Christians are always very happy and free from sorrow.

There never was a greater mistake. Read your Bibles, and see how the prophets and apostles were always groaning and distressed in view of the state of the church and the world. The apostle Paul says he was always bearing about in his body the dying of the Lord Jesus. I protest, says he, that I die daily. You will know what it is to sympathize with the Lord Jesus Christ, and be baptized with the baptism that he was baptized with. O how he agonized in view of the state of sinners! how he travailed in soul for their salvation! The more you have of his Spirit, the more clearly you will see the state of sinners, and the more deeply you will be distressed about them. Many times you will feel as if you could not live in view of their situation; your distress will be unutterable.

4. You will be often grieved with the state of the ministry. Some years since I met a woman belonging to one of the churches in this city. I inquired of her the state of religion here. She seemed unwilling to say much about it, made some general remarks, and then choked, and her eyes filled, and she said, "O, our minister's mind seems to be very dark." Spiritual Christians often feel like this, and often weep over it. I have seen much of it, and often found Christians who wept and groaned in secret, to see the darkness on the minds of ministers in regard to religion, their earthliness and fear of man; but they dared not speak of it, lest they should be denounced and threatened, and perhaps turned out of the church. I do not say these things censoriously, to reproach my brethren, but because they are true. And ministers ought to know, that nothing is more common than for spiritual Christians to feel

burdened and distressed at the state of the ministry. I would not wake up any wrong feeling towards ministers, but it is time it should be known, that Christians do often get spiritual views of things, and their souls are kindled up, and then they find that their minister does not enter into their feelings, that he is far below the standard of what he ought to be, and in spirituality far below some of the members of his church. This is one of the most prominent, and deeply to be deplored evils of the present day. The *piety* of the ministry, though *real*, is so superficial, in many instances, that the spiritual part of the church feel that ministers cannot, do not, sympathise with them. Their preaching does not meet their wants, it does not feed them, it does not meet their experience. The ministers have not depth enough of religious experience, to know how to search and wake up the church; to help those under temptation, to support the weak, to direct the strong, and lead them through all the labyrinths and mazes with which their path may be beset. When a minister has gone with a church as far as his experience in spiritual exercises goes, there he stops; and until he has a renewed experience, until he is reconverted, his heart broken up afresh, and he set forward in the divine life and Christian experience, he will help them no more. He may preach sound doctrine, and so may an unconverted minister; but, after all, his preaching will want that searching pungency, that practical bearing, that unction which alone will reach the case of a spiritually-minded Christian. It is a fact over which the church is groaning, that the piety of young men suffers so much in the course of their education, that when they enter the ministry, however much intellectual furniture they may possess, they are in a state of *spiritual babyhood*. They want nursing, and need rather to be fed, than to undertake to feed the church of God.

5. If you have much of the Spirit of God, you must make up your mind to have much opposition, both in the church and the world. Very likely the leading men in the church will oppose you. There has always been opposition in the church. So it was when Christ was on earth. If you are far above their state of feeling, church members will oppose you. If any man will live godly in Christ Jesus, he must expect persecution. Often the elders, and even the minister will oppose you, if you are filled with the Spirit of God.

6. You must expect very frequent and agonizing conflicts with Satan. Satan has very little trouble with those Christians who are

not spiritual, but lukewarm, and slothful, and worldly-minded. And such do not understand what is said about spiritual conflicts. Perhaps they will smile when such things are mentioned. And so the devil lets them alone. They don't disturb him, nor he them. But spiritual Christians, he understands very well, are doing him a vast injury, and therefore he sets himself against them. Such Christians often have terrible conflicts. They have temptations that they never thought of before, blasphemous thoughts, atheism, suggestions to do deeds of wickedness, to destroy their own lives, and the like. And if you are spiritual, you may expect these terrible conflicts.

7. You will have greater conflicts with yourself than you ever thought of. You will sometimes find your own corruptions making strange headway against the Spirit. "The flesh lusteth against the Spirit, and the Spirit against the flesh." Such a Christian is often thrown into consternation at the power of his own corruptions. One of the Commodores in the United States was, as I have been told, a spiritual man; and his pastor told me he had known that man lie on the floor and groan a great part of the night, in conflict with his own corruptions, and to cry to God in agony that he would break the power of the temptation. It seemed as if the devil was determined to ruin him; and his own heart, for the time being, was almost in league with the devil.

8. But you will have peace with God. If the church and sinners, and the devil, oppose you, there will be one with whom you will have peace. Let those who are called to these trials, and conflicts and temptations, and who groan, and pray, and weep, and break your hearts, remember this consideration: your peace, so far as your feelings towards God are concerned, will flow like a river.

9. You will likewise have peace of conscience, if you are led by the Spirit. You will not be constantly goaded and kept on the rack by a guilty conscience. Your conscience will be calm and quiet, unruffled as the summer's lake.

10. If filled with the Spirit, you will be useful. You cannot help being useful. Even if you were sick and unable to go out of your room, or to converse, and saw nobody, you would be ten times more useful than a hundred of those common sort of Christians who have no spirituality. To give you an idea of this, I will relate an anecdote. A pious man in the western part of this state was sick with a consumption. He was a poor man, and sick for

years. An unconverted merchant in the place, had a kind heart, and used to send him now and then some things for his comfort, or for his family. He felt grateful for the kindness, but could make no return, as he wanted to do. At length he determined that the best return he could make would be to pray for his salvation; he began to pray, and his soul kindled, and he got hold of God. There was no revival there, but by and by, to the astonishment of every body, this merchant came right out on the Lord's side. The fire kindled all over the place, and a powerful revival followed, and multitudes were converted.

This poor man lingered in this way for several years, and died. After his death, I visited the place, and his widow put into my hands his diary. Among other things, he says in his diary, "I am acquainted with about thirty ministers and churches." He then goes on to set apart certain hours in the day and week to pray for each of these ministers and churches, and also certain seasons for praying for the different missionary stations. Then followed, under different dates, such facts as these: "To-day," naming the date, "I have been enabled to offer what I call the prayer of faith for the outpouring of the Spirit on ——— church, and I trust in God there will soon be a revival there." Under another date, "I have to-day been able to offer what I call the prayer of faith for such a church, and trust there will soon be a revival there." Thus he had gone over a great number of churches, recording the fact that he had prayed for them in faith that a revival might soon prevail among them. Of the missionary stations, if I recollect right, he mentions in particular the mission at Ceylon. I believe the last place mentioned in his diary, for which he offered the prayer of faith, was the place in which he lived. Not long after noticing these facts in his diary, the revival commenced, and went over the region of country, nearly, I believe, if not quite, in the order in which they had been mentioned in his diary; and in due time news came from Ceylon that there was a revival of religion there. The revival in his own town did not commence till after his death. Its commencement was at the time when his widow put into my hands the document to which I have referred. She told me that he was so exercised in prayer during his sickness, that she often feared he would pray himself to death. The revival was exceedingly great and powerful in all the region; and the fact that it was about to prevail had not been hidden from this servant of the Lord. According to his word, the secret of the Lord is with them that fear him. Thus this man, too feeble in body to go out of his house, was yet more useful to the world and the church of God, than all the heartless professors in the country. Standing between God and the desolations of Zion, and pouring out his heart in believing prayer, as a prince he had power with God, and prevailed.

11. If you are filled with the Spirit, you will not find yourselves distressed, and galled, and worried, when people speak against you. When I find people irritated and fretting at any little thing that touches them, I am sure they have not the Spirit of Christ. Jesus Christ could have every thing said against him that malice could invent, and yet not be in the least disturbed by it. If you mean to be meek under persecution, and exemplify the temper of the Savior, and honor religion in this way, you need to be filled with the Spirit.

12. You will be wise in using means for the conversion of sinners. If the Spirit of God is in you, he will lead you to use means wisely, in a way adapted to the end, and to avoid doing hurt. No man who is not filled with the Spirit of God, is fit to be employed in directing the measures adopted in a revival. Their hands will be all thumbs, unable to take hold, and they will act as if they had not common sense. But a man who is led by the Spirit of God, will know how to *time* his measures right, and how to apportion Divine truth, so as to make it tell to the best advantage.

13. You will be calm under affliction; not thrown into confusion or consternation when you see the storm coming over you. People around will be astonished at your calmness and cheerfulness under heavy trials, not knowing the inward supports of those who are filled with the Spirit.

14. You will be resigned in death; you will always feel prepared to die, and not afraid to die, and after death you will be proportionately more happy for ever in heaven.

VI. Consequences of not being filled with the Spirit.

1. You will often doubt, and reasonably doubt, whether you are Christians. You will have doubts, and you ought to have them. The sons of God are led by the Spirit of God. And if you are not led by the Spirit, what reason have you to think you are sons? You will try to make a little evidence go a great way to bolster up your hopes, but you can't do it, unless your conscience is seared as with a hot iron. You cannot help being plunged often into painful doubt and uncertainty about your state.

2. You will always be unsettled in your views about the prayer

of faith. The prayer of faith is something so spiritual, so much a matter of experience and not of speculation, that unless you are spiritual yourselves, you will not understand it fully. You may talk a great deal about the prayer of faith, and for the time get thoroughly convinced of it. But you will never feel so settled on it as to retain the same position of mind concerning it, and in a little while you will be all uncertainty. I knew a curious instance in a brother minister. He told me, "When I have the Spirit of God, and enjoy his presence, I believe firmly in the prayer of faith; but when I have it not, I find myself doubting whether there is any such thing, and my mind is full of objections." I know, from my own experience, what this is, and when I hear persons raising objections to that view of prayer which I have presented in these lectures, I understand very well what their difficulty is, and have often found it impossible to satisfy their minds, while so far from God; when at the same time they would understand it themselves, without argument, whenever they had experienced it.

3. If you have not the Spirit, you will be very apt to stumble at those who have. You will doubt the propriety of their conduct. If they seem to feel a good deal more than yourself, you will be likely to call it animal feeling.[4] You will perhaps doubt their sincerity when they say they have such feelings. You will say, "I don't know what to make of brother such-a-one; he seems to be very pious, but I don't understand him, I think he has a great deal of animal feeling." Thus you will be trying to censure them, for the purpose of justifying yourself.

4. You will be had in reputation with the impenitent, and with carnal professors. They will praise you, as a rational, orthodox, consistent Christian. You will be just in the frame of mind to walk with them, because you are agreed.

5. You will be much troubled with fears about fanaticism. Whenever there are revivals, you will see in them a strong tendency to fanaticism, and will be full of fears and anxiety.

6. You will be much disturbed by the measures that are used in revivals. If any measures are adopted, that are decided and direct, you will think they are all "new," and will be stumbled at them just in proportion to your want of spirituality. You do not see

---

[4] The term "animal feeling" was opposed to "spiritual feeling" or "religious affections" to indicate the difference between mere passion or emotional excitement and the higher sensitivity of a truly spiritual exaltation. The line between the two was admittedly often difficult to perceive, but Finney, like Edwards, thought he could do it.

their appropriateness. You will stand and cavil at the measures, because you are so blind that you cannot see their adaptedness, while all heaven is rejoicing in them as the means of saving souls.

7. You will be a reproach to religion. The impenitent will sometimes praise you because you are so much like themselves, and sometimes laugh about you because you are such a hypocrite.

8. You will know but little about the Bible.

9. If you die without the Spirit, you will fall into hell. There can be no doubt of this.

REMARKS.

1. Christians are as guilty for not having the Spirit, as sinners are for not repenting.

2. They are even more so. As they have more light, they are so much the more guilty.

3. All beings have a right to complain of Christians who have not the Spirit. You are not doing work for God, and he has a right to complain. He has placed his Spirit at your disposal and if you have it not, he has a right to look to you and to hold you responsible for all the good you might do, did you possess it. You are sinning against all heaven, for you ought to be adding to their happy ranks.[5] Sinners, the church, ministers, have a right to complain.

4. You are right in the way of the work of the Lord. It is in vain for a minister to try to work over your head. Ministers often groan and struggle, and wear themselves out in vain, trying to do good where there is a church who live so that they do not have the Spirit of God. If the Spirit is poured out at any time, the church will grieve him right away. Thus you may tie the hands and break the heart of your minister, and break him down, and perhaps kill him, because you will not be filled with the Spirit.

5. You see the reason why Christians need the Spirit, and the degree of their dependence. This cannot be too strongly exhibited.

6. Do not tempt God, by waiting for his Spirit, while using no means to procure his presence.

7. If you mean to have the Spirit, you must be childlike, and

---

[5] From Finney's day onward the primary duty of all Christians was considered by pietistic evangelicals to be saving souls. This outlook colored the whole nature of nineteenth-century Protestantism. See Sidney E. Mead, "The Rise of the Evangelical Conception of the Ministry in America, 1607–1850," *The Ministry in Historical Perspective* (New York, 1956), ed. H. R. Niebuhr and Daniel D. Williams, pp. 207–249.

yield to his influences — just as yielding as air. If he is drawing you to prayer, you must quit every thing to yield to his gentle strivings. No doubt you have sometimes felt a desire to pray for some object, and you have put it off and resisted, and God left you. If you wish him to remain, you must yield to his softest and gentlest motions, and watch to learn what he would have you do, and yield yourself up to his guidance.

8. Christians ought to be willing to make any sacrifice to enjoy the presence of the Spirit. Said a woman in high life, a professor of religion, "I must either give up hearing such a minister (naming him) preach, or I must give up my gay company." She gave up the preaching and staid away. How different from another case!

A woman in the same rank of life heard the same minister preach, and went home resolved to abandon her gay and worldly manner of life — dismissed most of her attendants — changed her whole mode of dress, of equipage, of living, and of conversation; so that her gay and worldly friends were soon willing to leave her to the enjoyment of communion with God, and free to spend her time in doing good.

9. You see from this, that it must be very difficult for those in fashionable life to go to heaven. What a calamity to be in such circles! Who can enjoy the presence of God in them?

10. See how crazy those are who are scrambling to get up to these circles, enlarging their houses, changing their style of living, furniture, &c. It is like climbing up mast-head to be thrown off into the ocean. To enjoy God, you must come down, not go up there. God is not there, among all the starch and flattery of hell.

11. Many professors of religion are as ignorant of spirituality as Nicodemus was of the new birth. They are ignorant, and I fear unconverted. If any body talks to them about the spirit of prayer, it is all algebra to them. The case of such professors is awful. How different was the character of the apostles! Read the history of their lives, read their letters, and you will see that they were always spiritual, and walked daily with God. But now how little is there of such religion! "When the Son of Man cometh, will he find faith on the earth?" Set some of these professors to work in a revival, and they don't know what to do, have no energy, no skill, and make no impression. When will professors of religion set themselves to work, filled with the Spirit? If I could see this church filled with the Spirit, I would ask nothing more to move this whole mighty mass of minds. Not two weeks would pass before the revival would spread all over this city.

VIII

MEETINGS FOR PRAYER[1]

TEXT. — Again I say unto you, That if two of you shall agree on earth as touching any thing that they shall ask, it shall be done for them of my Father which is in heaven. — MATTHEW xviii. 19.

HITHERTO, in treating of the subject of PRAYER, I have confined my remarks to secret prayer. I am now to speak of social prayer, or prayer offered in company, where two or more are united in praying. Such meetings have been common from the time of Christ, and even hundreds of years before. And it is probable that God's people have always been in the habit of making united supplication, whenever they had the privilege. The propriety of the practice will not be questioned here. I need not dwell now on the duty of social prayer. Nor is it my design to discuss the question, whether any two Christians agreeing to ask any blessing, will be sure to obtain it. My object is to make some remarks on

MEETINGS FOR PRAYER.

I. The design of Prayer Meetings.
II. The manner of conducting them.
III. Mention several things that will defeat the design of holding them.

I. THE DESIGN OF PRAYER MEETINGS.

1. One design of assembling several persons together for united prayer, is to promote union among Christians. Nothing tends more to cement the hearts of Christians than prayer together. Never do they love one another so well as when they witness the outpouring of each other's hearts in prayer. Their spirituality begets a feeling of union and confidence, highly important to the prosperity of the church. It is doubtful whether Christians can ever be otherwise than united, if they are in the habit of really praying together. And

[1] This lecture is an excellent example of the pragmatic or practical side of Finney's temperament, as contrasted with the mystical side expressed in his lectures on prayer.

where they have had hard feelings and differences among themselves, they are all done away, by uniting in prayer. The great object is gained, if you can bring them *really to unite* in prayer. If this can be done, the difficulties vanish.

2. To extend the spirit of prayer. God has so constituted us, and such is the economy of his grace,[2] that we are sympathetic beings, and communicate our feelings to each other. A minister, for instance, will often as it were breathe his own feelings into his congregation. The Spirit of God that inspires his soul, makes use of his *feelings* to influence his hearers, just as much as he makes use of the words he preaches. So he makes use of feelings of Christians. Nothing is more calculated to beget a spirit of prayer, than to unite in social prayer, with one who has the spirit himself; unless this one should be so far ahead that his prayer will repel the rest. His prayer will awaken them, if they are not *so far* behind, as to revolt at it and resist it. If they are any where near the standard of his feelings, his spirit will kindle, and burn, and spread all around. — One individual in a church, that obtains a spirit of prayer, will often arouse a whole church, and extend the same spirit through the whole, and a general revival follows.

3. Another grand design of social prayer, is *to move God*. Not that it changes the mind and feelings of God. When we speak of moving God, as I have said in a former lecture, we do not mean that it alters the will of God. But when the right kind of prayer is offered by Christians, they are in such a state of mind, that it becomes proper for God to bestow a blessing. They are then prepared to receive it, and he gives because he is always the same, and always ready and happy to show mercy. When Christians are united, and praying as they ought, God opens the windows of heaven, and pours out his blessing, till there is not room to receive them.

4. Another important design of prayer meetings is the *conviction and conversion of sinners*. When properly conducted, they are eminently calculated to produce this effect. Sinners are apt to be solemn, when they hear Christians pray. Where there is a spirit of prayer, sinners must feel. An ungodly man, a Universalist, once said respecting a certain minister, "I can bear his preaching very well, but when he prays, I feel awfully; I feel as if God was coming down upon me." Sinners are often convicted by hearing prayer.

[2] Finney uses "economy" in the broad sense of "arrangement" or "management" and not of "thrift."

A young man of distinguished talents, known to many of you, said concerning a certain minister to whom before his conversion he had been very much opposed, "As soon as he began to pray, I began to be convicted, and if he had continued to pray much longer, I should not have been able to contain myself." Just as soon as Christians begin to pray as they ought, sinners then know that they pray, and they feel awfully. They don't understand what spirituality is, because they have no experience of it. But when such prayer is offered, they know there is something in it; they know God is in it, and it brings them near to God; it makes them feel awfully solemn, and they cannot bear it. And not only is it calculated to impress the minds of sinners, but when Christians pray in faith, the Spirit of God is poured out, and sinners are melted down and converted on the spot.

II. THE MANNER OF CONDUCTING PRAYER MEETINGS.

1. It is often well to open a prayer meeting by reading a short portion of the word of God; especially if the person who takes the lead of the meeting, can call to mind any portion that will be applicable to the object or occasion, and that is impressive, and to the point. If he has no passage that is applicable, he had better not read any at all. Do not drag in the word of God to make up part of the meeting as a mere matter of form. This is an insult to God. It is not well to read any more than is applicable to the subject before the meeting, or the occasion. Some people think it always necessary to read a whole chapter, though it may be ever so long, and have a variety of subjects. It is just as impressive and judicious to read a whole chapter, as it would be for a minister to take a whole chapter for his text, when his object was to make some particular truth bear on the minds of his audience. The design of a prayer meeting should be to bring Christians to the point, to pray for a definite object. Wandering over a large field, hinders and destroys this design.

2. It is proper that the person who leads should make some short and appropriate remarks, calculated to explain the nature of prayer, and the encouragements we have to pray, and to bring *the object to be prayed for*, directly before the minds of the people.

A man can no more pray without having his thoughts concentrated, than he can do any thing else. The person leading, should therefore see to this, by bringing up before their minds the object they came to pray for. If they came to pray for *any* object he can do this. And if they did not, they had better go home. It is of no use to stay there and mock God, by pretending to pray, when they have nothing on earth to pray for.

After stating the object, he should bring up some promise or some principle, as the ground of encouragement to expect an answer to their prayers. If there is any indication of Providence, or any promise, or any principle in the Divine government, that affords a ground of faith, let him call it to mind, and not let them be talking out of their own hearts at random, without knowing any solid reason to expect an answer. One reason why prayer meetings mostly accomplish so little, is because there is so little common sense exercised about them. Instead of looking round for some solid footing on which to repose their faith, they just come together and pour forth their *words*, and neither know nor care whether they have any reason to expect an answer. If they are going to pray about any thing concerning which there can be any doubt or any mistake, in regard to the ground of faith, they should be shown the reason there is for believing that their prayers will be heard and answered. It is easy to see, that unless something like this is done, three fourths of them will have no idea of what they are doing, or of the ground on which they should expect to receive what they pray for.

3. In *calling on persons to pray* it is always desirable to let things take their own course, wherever it is safe. If it can be left so with safety, let those pray who are most inclined to pray. It sometimes happens that even those who are ordinarily the most spiritual, and most proper to be called on, are not at the time in a suitable frame; they may be cold and worldly, and only freeze the meeting. But if you let those pray, who desire to pray, you avoid this. But often this cannot be done with safety, especially in large cities, where a prayer meeting might be liable to be interrupted by those who have no business to pray; some fanatic or crazy person, some hypocrite or enemy, who would only make a noise. In most places, however, this course may be taken with perfect safety. Give up the meeting to the Spirit of God. Those who desire to pray, let them pray. If the leader sees anything that needs to be set right, let him remark, freely and kindly, and put it right, and then go on again. Only, he should be careful to *time* his remarks, so as not to interrupt the flow of feeling, or to chill the meeting, or turn off the minds from the proper subject.

4. If it is necessary to name the individuals who are to pray, it is best to call on those who are most spiritual first. And if you do not know who they are, then those whom you would naturally suppose to be most alive. If they pray at the outset, they will be likely to spread the spirit of prayer through the meeting, and elevate the tone of the whole. Otherwise, if you call on those who are cold and lifeless at the beginning, they will be likely to diffuse a chill throughout the meeting. The only hope of having an efficient prayer meeting is when at least a part of the church is spiritual, and they infuse their spirit into the rest. This is the very reason why it is often best to let things take their course, for then those who have the most feeling are apt to pray first, and give character to the meeting.

5. The prayers should always *be very short.* — When individuals suffer themselves to pray long, they forget where they are, that they are only the mouth of the congregation, and that the congregation cannot be expected to sympathise with them, so as to go along and feel united in prayer, if they are long and tedious, and go all around the world, and pray for every thing that they can think of. Commonly, those who pray long in meeting, do it not because they *have* the spirit of prayer, but because they *have* not. And they go round and round, not because they are full of prayer. Some men will spin out a long prayer in telling God who and what he is, or they exhort God to do so and so. — Some pray out a whole system of divinity. Some preach, some exhort the people, till every body wishes they would stop, and God wishes so too, undoubtedly. They should keep to the point, and pray for what they came to pray for, and not follow the imagination of their own foolish hearts all over the universe.

6. Each one should pray for *some one object.* — It is well for every individual to have one object for prayer: two or more may pray for the same thing, or each a separate object. If the meeting is convened to pray for some specific thing, let them all pray for that. If its object is more general, let them select their subjects, according as they feel interested in them. If one feels particularly disposed to pray for the church, let him do it. If the next feels disposed to pray for the church, he may do so too. Perhaps the next will feel inclined to pray for sinners, for the youth, to confess sin; let him do it, and as soon as he has got through, *let him stop.* Whenever a man has deep feeling, he always feels on some particular point, and if he prays for that, he will speak out of the abundance

of his heart, and then he will naturally stop when he is done. Those who feel most, will be most ready to confine their prayers to that point, and stop when they have done, and not pray all over the world.

7. If in the progress of the meeting it becomes necessary to change the object of prayer, let the man who leads state the fact, and explain it in a few words. If the object is to pray for the church, or for backsliders, or sinners, or the heathen, let him state it plainly, and then turn it over and hold it up before them, till he brings them to think and feel deeply before they pray. Then state to them the grounds on which they may repose their faith in regard to obtaining the blessings they pray for, if any such statement is needed, and so lead them right up to the throne, and let them take hold of the hand of God. This is according to the philosophy of the mind. People always do it for themselves, when they pray in secret, if they really mean to pray to any purpose. And so it should be in prayer meetings.

8. It is important that the *time should be fully occupied*, so as not to leave long seasons of silence. This always makes a bad impression, and chills the meeting. I know that sometimes churches have seasons of silent prayer. But in those cases they should be specially requested to pray in silence, so that all may know why they are silent. This often has a most powerful effect, where a few moments are spent by a whole congregation in silence, while all lift up their thoughts to God. This is very different from having long intervals of silence because there is nobody to pray. Every one feels that such a silence is like the cold damp of death over the meeting.

9. It is exceedingly important that he who leads the meeting should press sinners who may be present, to immediate repentance. He should crowd this hard, and urge the Christians present to pray in such a way as to make sinners feel that they are expected to repent immediately. This tends to inspire Christians with compassion and love for souls. The remarks made to sinners are often like pouring fire upon the hearts of Christians, to awaken them to prayer and effort for their conversion. Let them see and feel the guilt and danger of sinners right among them, and then they will pray.

III. I am to mention several things, which *may defeat the design of a prayer meeting*.

1. When there is an unhappy want of confidence in the leader,

there is no hope of any good. Whatever the cause may be, whether he is to blame or not, the very fact that *he* leads the meeting will cast a damp over it, and prevent all good. I have witnessed it in churches, where there was some offensive elder or deacon, perhaps justly offensive and perhaps not, set to lead the prayer meeting, and the meeting would all die under his influence. If there is a want of confidence in regard to his piety, or in his ability, or in his judgment, or in any thing connected with the meeting, every thing he says or does will fall to the ground. The same thing often takes place, where the church have lost their confidence in the minister.

2. Where the leader *lacks spirituality*, there will be a dryness and coldness in his remarks and prayers, and every thing will indicate his want of unction, and his whole influence will be the very reverse of what it ought to be. I have known churches where a prayer meeting could not be sustained, and the reason was not obvious but those who understood the state of things knew that the leader was so notorious for his want of spirituality, that he would inevitably freeze a prayer meeting to death. In many Presbyterian churches, the elders are so far from being spiritual men, that they always freeze a prayer meeting. And then they are often amazingly jealous for their dignity, and can't bear to have any body else lead the meeting. And if any member that is spiritual takes the lead of a prayer meeting, they will take him to task for it: "Why, you are not an elder, and ought not to lead a prayer meeting in presence of an elder." And thus they stand in the way, while the whole church is suffering under their blighting influence.[3]

A man who knows he is not in a spiritual frame of mind has no business to conduct a prayer meeting; he will kill it. There are two reasons. — First, he will have *no spiritual discernment*, and will not know what to do, or when to do it. A person who is spiritual can see the movements of Providence, and can feel the Spirit of God, and understand what he is leading them to pray for, so as to time his subjects, and take advantage of the state of feeling among Christians. He will not overthrow all the feeling in a meeting, by

---

[3] Since the elders were apt to be the more well-to-do and respectable members of a church, it is evident why they would be inclined to take a more formal and conservative or "dignified" approach to prayer meetings and revivals than Finney thought proper. Finney, like all revivalists, condoned and even urged rebellion against church officers in the name of piety and zeal. Note, however, that Finney was opposed only to stereotyped formalism, not to good order. See pp. 136–137 where he wants no behavior in revivals that will offend "persons of taste."

introducing other things that are incongruous or ill-timed. He has spiritual discernment to understand the leadings of the Spirit, and his workings in those who pray, and to follow on as the Spirit leads. Suppose an individual leads, who is not spiritual, and there are two or three prayers, and the spirit of prayer rises, but the leader has no spiritual discernment to see it, and he makes some remarks on another point, or reads a piece out of some book, that is as far from the feeling of the meeting as the north pole. It may be just as evident to others what they are called to pray for, as if the Son of God himself had come into the meeting and named the subject; but the leader will overthrow it all, because he is so stupid that he does not know the indications of the meeting.

And then, if the leader is not spiritual, he will very likely be *dull and dry* in his remarks, and in all his exercises. He will read a long hymn in a dreamy manner, and then read a long passage of Scripture, in a tone so cold and wintry, that he will spread a wintry pall over the meeting, and it will be dull, as long as his cold heart is placed up in front of the whole thing.

3. A want of *suitable talents* in the leader. If he is wanting in that kind of talents which are fitted to make a meeting useful, he will injure the meeting. If he can say nothing, or if his remarks are so out of the way as to produce levity or contempt, or if they have nothing in them that will impress the mind, or are not guided by good sense, or not appropriate, he will injure the meeting. A man may be pious, but so weak that his prayers do not edify, but rather disgust the people present. When this is so, he had better keep silence.

4. Sometimes the benefit of a prayer meeting is defeated by a bad spirit in the leader. For instance, when there is a revival, and great opposition, if a leader gets up in a prayer meeting and speaks of instances of opposition, and comments upon them, and thus diverts the meeting away from the object they come to pray for, he knows not what spirit he is of. Its effect is always ruinous to a prayer meeting. Let a minister in a revival come out and preach against the opposition, and he will infallibly destroy the revival, and turn the hearts of Christians away from their proper object. Let the man who is set to lead the church be careful to guard his own spirit, lest he should mislead the church, and diffuse a wrong temper. The same will be true, *if any one* who is called upon to speak or pray, introduces in his remarks or prayers any thing controversial, impertinent, unreasonable, unscriptural, ridiculous or

irrelevant. Any of these things will quench the tender breathings of the spirit of prayer, and destroy the meeting.

5. Persons *coming late* to the meeting. This is a very great hinderance to a prayer meeting. When people have begun to pray, and their attention is fixed, and they have shut their eyes and closed their ears, to keep out every thing from their minds, in the midst of a prayer somebody will come bolting in and walk up through the room. Some will look up, and all have their minds interrupted for the moment. Then they all get fixed again, and another comes in, and so on. Why, I suppose the devil would not care how many Christians went to a prayer meeting, if they will only go after the meeting is begun. He would be glad to have ever so many go scattering along so, and dodging in very piously after the meeting is begun.

6. When persons make cold prayers, and cold confessions of sin, they are sure to quench the spirit of prayer. When the influences of the Spirit are enjoyed, in the midst of the warm expressions that are flowing forth, let an individual come in who is cold, and pour his cold breath out, like the damp of death, and it will make every Christian that has any feeling want to get out of the meeting.

7. In some places it is common to begin a prayer meeting by reading a long portion of Scripture. Then the deacon or elder gives out a long hymn. Next, they sing it. Then he prays a long prayer, praying for the Jews and the fullness of the Gentiles, and many other objects that have nothing to do with the occasion of the meeting. After that perhaps he reads a long extract from some book or magazine. Then they have another long hymn and another long prayer, and then they go home. I once heard an elder say, they had kept up a prayer meeting so many years, and yet there had been no revival in the place. The truth was, that the officers of the church had been accustomed to carry on the meetings in just such a dignified way, and their dignity would not allow any thing to be altered. No wonder there was no revival. Such prayer meetings are enough to hinder a revival. And if ever so many revivals should commence, the prayer meeting would destroy them. There was a prayer meeting once in this city, as I have been told, where there appeared to be some feeling, and some one proposed that they should have two or three prayers in succession, without rising from their knees. One dignified man present opposed it, and said that they never had done so, and he hoped

there would be no innovations. He did not approve of innovations. And that was the last of the revival. Such persons have their prayer meetings stereotyped, and they are determined not to turn out of their track, whether they have the blessing or not. To allow any such thing would be a new measure, and they never like new measures.

8. A *great deal of singing* often injures a prayer meeting. The *agonizing spirit of prayer* does not lead people to sing. There is a time for every thing; a time to sing, and a time to pray. But if I know what it is to *travail in birth* for souls, Christians never feel less like it, than when they have the spirit of prayer for sinners. Singing is the natural expression of feelings that are joyful and cheerful. The spirit of prayer is not a spirit of joy. It is a spirit of travail, and agony of soul, supplicating and pleading with God with strong cryings, and groanings that cannot be uttered. This is more like any thing else than it is like singing. I have known states of feeling, where you could not distress the people of God more than to begin to sing. It would be so entirely different from their feelings. Why, if you knew your house was on fire, would you first stop and sing a hymn before you put it out? How would it look here in New York, when a building was on fire, and the firemen are all collected, for the foreman to stop and sing a hymn? It is just about as natural for the people to sing when exercised with a spirit of prayer. When people feel like pulling men out of the fire, they don't feel like singing. I never knew a singing revival amount to much. Its tendency is to do away all deep feeling. It is true that singing a hymn has sometimes produced a powerful effect upon *sinners* who are convicted, but in general it is the perfect contrast there is between their feelings and those of the happy souls who sing, that produces the effect. If the hymn be of a joyful character it is not *directly* calculated to benefit sinners, and is highly fitted to relieve the mental anguish of the Christian, so as to destroy that travail of soul which is indispensable to his prevailing in prayer.

When singing is introduced in a prayer meeting, the hymns should be short, and so selected as to bring out something solemn; some striking words, such as the Judgment Hymn, and others calculated to produce an effect on sinners; or something that will produce a deep impression on the minds of Christians; but not that joyful kind of singing, that makes every body feel comfortable, and turns off the mind from the object of the prayer meeting.

I once heard a celebrated organist produce a remarkable effect in a protracted meeting. The organ was a powerful one, and the double bass pipes were like thunder. The hymn was given out that has these lines:

> See the storm of vengeance gathering
> O'er the path you dare to tread;
> "Hear the awful thunder rolling,
> Loud and louder o'er your head."

When he came to these words, we first heard the distant roar of thunder, then it grew nearer and louder, till at the word "louder," there was a crash that seemed almost to overpower the whole congregation.[4]

Such things in their proper place do good. But common singing dissipates feeling. It should always be such as not to take away feeling, but to deepen it.

Often a prayer meeting is injured by calling on the young converts to sing joyful hymns. This is highly improper in a prayer meeting. It is no time for them to let feeling flow away in joyful singing, while so many sinners around them, and their own former companions, are going down to hell. A revival is often put down by the church and minister all giving themselves up to singing with young converts. Thus by stopping to rejoice, when they ought to feel more and more deeply for sinners, they grieve away the Spirit of God, and they soon find that their agony and travail of soul are all gone.

9. Introducing *subjects of controversy* into prayer will defeat a prayer meeting. Nothing of a controversial nature should be introduced into prayer, unless it is the object of the meeting to *settle that thing*. Otherwise, let Christians come together in their prayer meetings, on the broad ground of offering united prayer for a common object. And let controversies be settled somewhere else.

10. Great pains should be taken, both by the leader and others, to *watch narrowly the motions of the Spirit of God*. Let them not pray without the Spirit, but follow his leadings. Be sure not to quench the Spirit for the sake of praying according to the regular custom. Avoid every thing calculated to divert attention away from the object. All affectation, of feeling that is not real, should be par-

---

[4] This theatrical use of an organ for "sound effects" typifies what Albert Dod referred to as Finney's willingness to transform the house of God into "a kind of religious laboratory." See *Biblical Repertory and Theological Review*, VII (October 1835), 636.

ticularly guarded against. If there is an affectation of feeling, most commonly others see and feel that it is affectation, not reality. At any rate, the Spirit of God knows it, and will be grieved, and leave the place. On the other hand, all resistance to the Spirit will equally destroy the meeting. Not infrequently it happens, that there are some so cold that if any one should break out in the spirit of prayer, they would call it fanaticism, and perhaps break out in opposition.

11. If individuals *refuse to pray when they are called on* it injures a prayer meeting. There are some people, who always pretend they have no gifts. Women sometimes refuse to take their turn in prayer, and pretend they have no ability to pray. But if any one else should say so, they would be offended. Suppose they should know that any other person had made such a remark as this, "Don't ask her to pray, she can't pray, she has not talents enough;" would they like it? So with a man who pretends he has no gifts, let any one else report that he has not talents enough to make a decent prayer, and see if he will like it. The pretence is not sincere; it is all a sham.

Some say they cannot pray in their families, they have no gift. But a person could not offend them more than to say they cannot pray a decent prayer before their own families. They would say, "Why, the man talks as if he thought nobody else had any gifts but himself." People are not apt to have such a low opinion of themselves. I have often seen the curse of God follow such professors. They have no excuse. God will take none. The man has got a tongue to talk to his neighbor, and he can talk to God if he has any heart for it. You will see their children unconverted, their son a curse, their daughter — tongue cannot tell. God says he will pour out his fury on the families that call not on his name. If I had time, I could mention a host of facts to show that God MARKS those individuals with his disapprobation and curse who refuse to pray when they ought. Until professors of religion will repent of this sin and take up the cross (if they choose to call *praying a cross!*) and do their duty, they need not expect a blessing.

12. Prayer meetings are often *too long*. They should always be dismissed while Christians have feeling, and not be spun out until all feeling is exhausted, and the spirit is gone.

13. Heartless confessions. People confess their sins and don't forsake them. Every week they will make the same confession over again. A long, cold, dull, stupid confession this week, and then the next week another just like it, without forsaking any sins. Why,

they have no intention to forsake their sins! It shows plainly that they do not mean to reform. All their religion consists in these confessions. Instead of getting a blessing from God by such confessions they will get only a curse.

14. When Christians spend all the time in praying for themselves. They should have done this in their closets. When they come to a prayer meeting, they should be prepared to offer effectual intercessions for others. If Christians pray in their closets as they ought, they will feel like praying for sinners. If they pray exclusively *in their closets* for themselves, they will not get the spirit of prayer. I have known men shut themselves up for days to pray for themselves, and never get any life, because their prayers are all selfish. But if they will just forget themselves, and throw their hearts abroad, and pray for others, it will wake up such a feeling, that they can pour forth their hearts. And then they can go to work for souls. I knew an individual in a revival, who shut himself up seventeen days, and prayed as if he would have God come to his terms, but it would not do, and then he went out to work, and immediately he had the Spirit of God in his soul. It is well for Christians to pray for themselves, and confess their sins, and then throw their hearts abroad, till they feel as they ought.

15. Prayer meetings are often defeated by the *want of appropriate* remarks. The things are not said which are calculated to lead them to pray. Perhaps the leader has not prepared himself; or perhaps he has not the requisite talents, to lead the church out in prayer, or he does not lead their minds to dwell on the appropriate topics of prayer.

16. When individuals who are justly obnoxious for any cause, are forward in speaking and praying. Such persons are sometimes very much set upon taking a part. They say it is their duty to get up and testify for God on all occasions. They will say, they know they are not able to edify the church, but nobody else can do their duty, and they wish to testify. Perhaps the only place they ever did testify *for God*, was in a prayer meeting; all their lives, out of the meeting, testify against God. — They had better keep still.

17. Where persons take a part who are so illiterate that it is impossible persons of taste should not be disgusted. Persons of intelligence cannot follow them, and their minds are unavoidably diverted. I do not mean that it is necessary a person should have a liberal education in order to lead in prayer. All persons of common education, especially if they are in the habit of praying, can lead

in prayer, if they have the spirit of prayer. But there are some persons who use such absurd and illiterate expressions, as cannot but disgust every intelligent mind. They cannot help being disgusted. The feeling of disgust is an involuntary thing, and when a disgusting object is before the mind, the feeling is irresistible. Piety will not keep a person from feeling it. The only way is to take away the object. If such persons mean to do good, they had better remain silent. Some of them may feel grieved at not being called to take a part. But it is better that they should be kindly told the reason than to have the prayer meeting regularly injured, and rendered ridiculous by their performances.

18. A want of union in prayer. When one leads the others do not follow, but are thinking of something else. Their hearts do not unite, do not say, Amen. It is as bad as if one should make a petition and another remonstrate against it. One asks God to do a thing, and the others ask him not to do it, or to do something else.

19. Neglect of secret prayer. Christians who do not pray in secret, cannot unite with power in a prayer meeting, and cannot have the spirit of prayer.

REMARKS.

1. An illy conducted prayer meeting often does more hurt than good. In many churches, the general manner of conducting prayer meetings is such that Christians have not the least idea of the design or the power of such meetings. It is such as tends to keep down rather than to promote pious feeling and the spirit of prayer.

2. A prayer meeting is an index to the state of religion in a church. If the church neglect the prayer meetings, or come and have not the spirit of prayer, you know of course that religion is low. Let me go into the prayer meeting, and I can always see the state of religion there.

3. Every minister ought to know that if the prayer meetings are neglected, all his labors are in vain. Unless he can get Christians to attend the prayer meetings, all he can do will not bring up the true religion.

4. A great responsibility rests on him who leads a prayer meeting. If the prayer meeting be not what it ought to be, if it does not elevate the state of religion, he should go seriously to work and see what is the matter, and get the spirit of prayer, and prepare himself to make such remarks as are calculated to do good and set things

right. A leader has no business to lead prayer meetings, if he is not prepared, both in head and heart, to do this. I wish you, who lead the district prayer meetings of this church, to notice this point.

5. Prayer meetings are the most difficult meetings to sustain as they ought to be. They are so spiritual, that unless the leader be peculiarly prepared, both in heart and mind, they will dwindle. It is in vain for the leader to complain that members of the church do not attend. In nine cases out of ten, it is the leader's fault, that they do not attend. If he felt as he ought, they would find the meetings so interesting, that they would attend of course. If he is so cold, and dull, and without spirituality, as to freeze every thing, no wonder people don't come to the meeting. Church officers often complain and scold because people don't come to the prayer meeting, when the truth is, they themselves are so cold that they freeze everybody to death that comes.

6. Prayer meetings are most important meetings for the church. It is highly important for Christians to sustain the prayer meetings: —

(1.) To promote union.
(2.) To increase brotherly love.
(3.) To cultivate Christian confidence.
(4.) To promote their own growth in grace.
(5.) To cherish and advance spirituality.

7. Prayer meetings should be so numerous in the church, and be so arranged, as to exercise the gifts of every individual member of the church — male and female. Every one should have the opportunity to pray, and to express the feelings of his heart, if he has any. The sectional prayer meetings [5] of this church are designed to do this. And if they are too large for this, let them be divided, so as to bring the entire mass into the work, to exercise all gifts, and diffuse union, confidence, and brotherly love through the whole.

8. It is important that impenitent sinners should always attend prayer meetings. If none come of their own accord, go out and invite them. Christians ought to take great pains to induce their impenitent friends and neighbors to come to prayer meetings. They can pray better for impenitent sinners when they have them right before their eyes. I have know female prayer meetings exclude sinners from the meeting. And the reason was, they were so proud they were ashamed to pray before sinners. What a spirit! Such

---

[5] "Sectional prayer meetings" of the devout were conducted weekly in private homes or the church by groups divided by age, sex, or place of abode.

prayers will do no good. They insult God. You have not done enough, by any means, when you have gone to the prayer meeting yourself. You can't pray, if you have invited no sinner to go. If all the church have neglected their duty so, and have gone to the prayer meeting, and taken no sinners along with them, no subjects of prayer — what have they come for?

9. The great object of all the means of grace is to aim directly at the conversion of sinners. You should pray that they may be converted *there*. Not pray that they may be awakened and convicted, but pray that they may be converted on the spot. No one should either pray or make any remarks, as if he expected a single sinner would go away without giving his heart to God. You should all make the impression on his mind, that NOW he must submit. And if you do this, while you are yet speaking God will hear. If Christians make it manifest that they have really set their hearts on the conversions of sinners, and are bent upon it, and pray as they ought, there would rarely be a prayer meeting held without souls being converted, and sometimes every sinner in the room. That is the very time, if ever, that sinners *should be* converted in answer to those prayers. I do not doubt but that you may have sinners converted in every sectional prayer meeting, if you do your duty. Take them there, take your families, your friends, or your neighbors there with that design, give them the proper instruction, if they need instruction, and pray for them as you ought, and you will save their souls. Rely upon it, if you do your duty, in a right manner, God will not keep back his blessing, and the work will be done.

IX

MEANS TO BE USED WITH SINNERS

TEXT. — "Ye are my witnesses, saith the Lord, and my servant whom I have chosen." — ISAIAH xliii: 10.

IN the text it is affirmed of the children of God, that they are his witnesses. In several preceding lectures I have been dwelling on the subject of Prayer, or that department of means for the promotion of a revival, which is intended to move God to pour out his Spirit. I am now to commence the other department:

MEANS TO BE USED FOR THE CONVICTION AND CONVERSION OF SINNERS.

It is true, in general, that persons are affected by the subject of religion, in proportion to their conviction of its truth. Inattention to religion is the great reason why so little is felt concerning it. No being can look at the great truths of religion, *as truths*, and not feel deeply concerning them. The devil cannot. He feels and trembles. Angels in heaven feel in view of these things. God feels. An intellectual *conviction* of truth, is always accompanied with feeling of some kind.

One grand design of God in leaving Christians in the world after their conversion, is that they may be *witnesses for God*. It is that they may call the attention of the thoughtless multitude to the subject, and make them see the difference in the character and destiny of those who believe and those who reject the gospel. This inattention is the grand difficulty in the way of promoting religion. And what the Spirit of God does is to awaken the attention of men to the subject of their sin and the plan of salvation. Miracles have sometimes been employed to arrest the attention of sinners. And in this way, miracles may become instrumental in conversion, although conversion is not itself a miracle, nor do miracles themselves ever convert any body. They may be the means of awakening. Miracles are not always effectual even in that. And if continued or made common, they would soon lose their power. What is wanted in the world is something that can be a sort of omnipresent miracle, able not only to arrest attention but to fix it, and keep the mind in warm contact with the truth, till it yields.

Hence we see why God has scattered his children everywhere, in families and among the nations. He never would suffer them to be all together in one place, however agreeable it might be to their feelings. He wishes them scattered. When the church at Jerusalem herded together, neglecting to go forth as Christ had commanded, to spread the gospel all over the world, God let loose a persecution upon them and scattered them abroad, and then "they went every where preaching the gospel." In examining the text, I purpose to inquire,

I. To what particular points Christians are to testify for God.
II. The manner in which they are to testify.

1. To what points are the children of God required to testify?

Generally, they are to testify to the truth of the Bible. They are competent witnesses to this, for they have experience of its truth. The experimental Christian has no more need of external evidence to prove the truth of the Bible to his mind, than he has to prove his own existence.[1] The whole plan of salvation is so fully spread out and settled in his conviction, that to undertake to reason him out of his belief in the Bible would be a thing as impracticable as to reason him out of the belief in his own existence. Men have tried to awaken a doubt of the existence of the material world. But they cannot succeed. No man can doubt the existence of a material world. To doubt it, is against his own consciousness. You may use arguments that he cannot answer, and may puzzle and perplex him, and shut up his mouth; he may be no logician or philosopher, and unable to detect your fallacies. But what he knows he knows.

So it is in religion. The Christian is conscious that the Bible is true. The veriest child in religion knows by his experience the truth of the Bible. He may hear objections from infidels, that he never thought of, and that he cannot answer, and he may be confounded, but he cannot be driven from his ground. He will say, "I cannot answer you, but I know the Bible is true."

As if a man should look in a mirror, and say, "That's my face." How do you know it is your face? "Why, by its looks." So when

---

[1] Throughout the nineteenth century the terms "experimental religion" or "experience religion" were commonly used to designate the conversion-centered evangelicalism that prevailed among Protestants.

a Christian sees himself drawn and pictured forth in the Bible, he sees the likeness to be so exact, that he knows it is true. But more particularly, Christians are to testify—

1. To the immortality of the soul. This is clearly revealed in the Bible.

2. The vanity and unsatisfying nature of all earthly good.

3. The satisfying nature and glorious sufficiency of religion.

4. The guilt and danger of sinners. On this point they can speak from experience as well as the word of God. They have seen their own sins, and they understand more of the nature of sin, and the guilt and danger of sinners.

5. The reality of hell, as a place of eternal punishment for the wicked.

6. The love of Christ for sinners.

7. The necessity of a holy life, if we think of ever getting to heaven.

8. The necessity of self-denial, and living above the world.

9. The necessity of meekness, heavenly-mindedness, humility, and integrity.

10. The necessity of an entire renovation of character and life, for all who would enter heaven. These are the subjects on which they are to be witnesses for God. And they are bound to testify in such a way as to constrain men to believe the truth.

II. How are they to testify?

By *precept and example*, on every proper occasion, by their lips, but mainly by their lives. Christians have no right to be silent with their lips; they should rebuke, exhort, and entreat with all long-suffering and doctrine. But their main influence as witnesses is by their example.

They are required to be witnesses in this way, because example teaches with so much greater force than precept. This is universally known. Actions speak louder than words. But where both precept and example are brought to bear, it brings the greatest amount of influence to bear upon the mind. As to the manner in which they are to testify; the way in which they should bear witness to the truth of the points specified; in general — they should live in their daily walk and conversation, as if they believed the Bible.

1. As if they believed the soul to be immortal, and as if they believed that death was not the termination of their existence, but the entrance into an unchanging state. They ought to live so as to

make this impression full upon all around them. It is easy to see that precept without example on this point will do no good. All the arguments in the world will not convince mankind that you really believe this, unless you live as if you believed it. Your reasoning may be unanswerable, but if you do not live accordingly, your practice will defeat your arguments. They will say you are an ingenious sophist, or an acute reasoner, and perhaps admit that they cannot answer you; but then they will say, it is evident that your reasoning is all false, and that you know it is false, because your life contradicts your theory. Or that, if it is true, you don't believe it, at any rate. And so all the influence of your testimony goes to the other side.

2. The vanity and unsatisfying nature of the things of this world. You are to testify this by your life. The failure in this is the great stumbling block in the way of mankind. Here the testimony of God's children is needed more than any where else. Men are so struck with the objects of sense, and so constantly occupied with them, that they are very apt to shut out eternity from their minds. A small object, that is held close to the eye, may shut out the distant ocean. So the things of the world, that are near, magnify so in their minds, that they overlook every thing else. One important design in keeping Christians in the world is to teach people on this point, *practically*, not to labor for the meat that perisheth. But suppose professors of religion teach the vanity of earthly things by precept, and contradict it in practice. Suppose the women are just as fond of dress, and just as particular in observing all the fashions, and the men as eager to have fine houses and equipage, as the people of the world. Who does not see that it would be quite ridiculous for them to testify with their lips, that this world is all vanity, and its joys unsatisfying and empty? People feel this absurdity, and it is this that shuts up the lips of Christians. They are ashamed to speak to their neighbors, while they cumber themselves with these gewgaws, because their daily conduct testifies to every body the very reverse. How it would look for some of the church members in this city, male or female, to go about among the common people, and talk to them about the vanity of the world! — Who would believe what they say? [2]

3. The satisfying nature of religion. Christians are bound to show, by their conduct, that *they are* actually satisfied with the

[2] This distinction between church members and "the common people" indicates again that Finney's congregation was middle class.

enjoyments of religion, without the pomps and vanities of the world; that the joys of religion and communion with God keep them above the world. They are to manifest that this world is not their home. Their profession is, that heaven is a reality, and that they expect to dwell there for ever. But suppose they contradict this by their conduct, and live in such a way as to prove that they cannot be happy unless they have a full share of the fashion and show of the world, and that as for going to heaven, they had much rather remain on earth, than to die and go there! What do the world think, when they see a profession of religion just as much afraid to die as an infidel? Such Christians perjure themselves — they swear to a lie, for they testify that there is nothing in religion for which a person can afford to live above the world.

4. The guilt and danger of sinners. Christians are bound to warn sinners of their awful condition, and exhort them to flee from the wrath to come, and lay hold on everlasting life. But who does not know that *the manner* of doing this is every thing? Sinners are often struck under conviction by the very manner of doing a thing. There was a man once very much opposed to a certain preacher. On being asked to specify some reason, he replied, "I can't bear to hear him, for he says the word HELL in such a way that it rings in my ears a long time afterwards." He was displeased with the very thing that constituted the power of speaking that word. The manner may be such as to convey an idea directly opposite to the meaning of the words. A man may tell you that your house is on fire in such a way as to make directly the opposite impression, and you will take for granted that it is not *your* house that is on fire. The watchman might sing out FIRE, FIRE, in such a way that every body would think he was either asleep or drunk. A certain manner is so usually connected with the announcement of certain things, that they cannot be expressed without that manner. The words themselves never alone convey the meaning, because the idea can only be fully expressed by a particular manner of speaking. Go to a sinner, and talk with him about his guilt and danger; and if in your manner you make an impression that does not correspond, you in effect bear testimony the other way, and tell him he is in no danger of hell. If the sinner believes at all that he is in danger of hell, it is wholly on other grounds than your saying so. If you live in such a way as to show that you do not feel compassion for sinners around you; if you show no tenderness, by your eyes, your features, your voice; if your manner is not solemn and earnest, how can they believe you are sincere?

Woman, suppose you tell your converted husband, in an easy, laughing way, "My dear, I believe you are going to hell;" will he believe you? If your life is gay and trifling, you show that either you do not believe there is a hell, or that you wish to have him go there, and are trying to keep off every serious impression from his mind. Have you children that are unconverted? Suppose you never say any thing to them about religion, or when you do talk to them it is in such a cold, hard, dry way, as shows you have no feeling; do you suppose they believe you? They don't see the same coldness in you in regard to other things. They are in the habit of seeing all the mother in your eye, and in the tones of your voice, your emphasis, and the like, and feeling the warmth of a mother's heart as it flows out from your lips on all that concerns them. If, then, when you talk to them on the subject of religion, you are cold and trifling, can they suppose you believe it? If your deportment holds up before your child this careless, heartless, prayerless spirit, and then you talk to him about the importance of religion, the child will go away and laugh, to think you should try to persuade him there is a hell.

5. The love of Christ. You are to bear witness to the reality of the love of Christ, by the regard you show for his precepts, his honor, his kingdom. You should act as if you believed that he died for the sins of the whole world, and as if you blamed sinners for rejecting his great salvation. This is the only legitimate way in which you can impress sinners with the love of Christ. Christians, instead of this, often live so as to make the impression on sinners that Christ is so compassionate that they have very little to fear from him. I have been amazed to see how a certain class of professors want ministers to be always preaching about the *love* of Christ. If a minister preaches up duty, and urges Christians to be holy, and to labor for Christ, they call it all legal preaching. They say they want to hear the gospel. Well, suppose you present the love of Christ. How will they bear testimony in their lives? How will they show that they believe? Why, by conformity to the world they will testify, point blank, that they don't believe a word of it, and that they care nothing at all for the love of Christ, only to have it for a cloak, that they can talk about it, and so cover up their sins. They have no sympathy with his compassion, and no belief in it as a reality, and no concern for the feelings of Christ, which fill his mind when he sees the condition of sinners.[3]

[3] Revivalists have always faced a fundamental decision as to whether they should emphasize the love of Christ or the wrath of God. Their choice depends

6. The necessity of holiness in order to enter heaven. It will not do to depend on talking about this. They must live holy, and thus testify that men need not expect to be saved, unless they are holy. The idea has so long prevailed, that we *cannot be perfect here*, that many professors do not so much as seriously aim at a sinless life. They cannot honestly say, that they ever so much as really meant to live without sin. They drift along before the tide, in a loose, sinful, unhappy and abominable manner, at which, doubtless, the devil laughs, because it is, of all others, the surest way to hell.

7. The necessity of self-denial, humility, and heavenly-mindedness. Christians ought to show by their own example what the religion is, which is expected of men. That is the most powerful preaching, after all, and the most likely to have influence on the impenitent, by showing them the *great difference* between them and Christians. Many people are trying to make men Christians by a different course, by copying as near as possible their present manner of life, and conforming to them as much as will possibly do. They seem to think they can make men fall in with religion best by bringing religion down to their standard. As if the nearer you bring religion to the world, the more likely the world would be to embrace it. Now all this is as wide as the poles from the true philosophy about making Christians. But it is always the policy of carnal professors. And they think they are displaying wonderful sagacity and *prudence*, by taking so much pains not to scare people at the mighty strictness and holiness of the gospel. They argue that if you exhibit religion to mankind as requiring such a great change in their manner of life, such innovations upon their habits, such a separation from their old associates, why, you will drive them all away. This seems plausible at first sight. But it is not true. Let professors live in this lax and easy way, and sinners say, "Why, I don't see but I am about right, or at least so near right, that it is impossible God should send me to hell for the difference between me and these professors. It is true, they do a little more than I do, they go to the communion table, and pray in their families, and a few such like little things, but they can't make any such great difference as heaven and hell." No, the true way is, to

---

upon whether they find from experience that those to whom they preach are more lax in faith or in conduct. Most nineteenth-century revivalists took the opposite side from Finney after 1835 and preached predominantly the love of Christ. Finney felt that most people believed in Christ but needed to be told to act upon those beliefs. Hence he generally emphasized obedience to God's laws.

exhibit religion and the world in strong contrast, or you never can make sinners feel the necessity of a change. Until the necessity of this fundamental change is embodied and held forth in a strong light by example, how can you make men believe they are going to be sent to hell if they are not wholly transformed in heart and life?[4]

This is not only true in philosophy, but it has been proved by the history of the world. Look at the missions of the Jesuits in Japan, by Francis Xavier and his associates.[5] How they lived, what a contrast they showed between their religion and the heathen, and what results followed! Now I was reading a letter from one of our missionaries, in the East, who writes, I believe, to this effect, that a missionary must be able to rank with the English nobility, and so recommend his religion to the *respect* of the natives. He must get away up above them, so as to show a superiority, and thus impress them with respect! Is this philosophy? Is this the way to convert the world? You can no more convert the world in this way, than by blowing a ram's horn. It has no tendency that way. What did the Jesuits do? They went about among the people in the daily practice of self-denial before their eyes, teaching, and preaching, and praying, and laboring, unwearied and unawed, mingling with every caste and grade, bringing down their instructions to the capacity of every individual. And in that way the mission carried idolatry before it like a wave of the sea, and all at once their religion spread over the vast empire of Japan. And if they had not meddled with politics and brought themselves in needless collision with the government, no doubt they would have held their ground till this day. I am not saying any thing in regard to the religion they taught, for I am not sure how much truth they preached with it. I speak only of their following the true policy of missions, by showing by their lives, the religion they taught in wide contrast with a worldly spirit, and the fooleries of idolatry. This one feature of their policy so commended itself to

[4] This pietistic or separatistic differentiation between the saved and the worldly is not only the mark of individualistic religion but also of a religion devoted to moral reform. The Calvinists put more emphasis upon the corporate life of the community in which visible and invisible saints were inevitably mixed and indistinguishable both within and without the church. They emphasized tradition and stability because they doubted the possibility of any sweeping reform either within individuals or within society. Finney's religious outlook took the opposite tack and thus conformed more closely to the spirit of change and of progress in the Jacksonian era.

[5] See Lecture IV, p. 57, note 3.

the consciences of the people, that it was irresistible. If Christians contradict this one point, and attempt to accommodate their religion to the worldliness of men, they render the salvation of the world impossible. How can you make people believe that self-denial and separation from the world are necessary, unless you practise them?

8. *Meekness, humility, and heavenly-mindedness.* The people of God should always show a temper like the Son of God, who when he was reviled, reviled not again. If a professor of religion is irritable, and ready to resent an injury, and fly in a passion, and take the same measures as the world do to get redress, by going to law and the like, how is he to make people believe there is any reality in a change of heart? They cannot recommend religion, while they have such a spirit. If you are in the habit of resenting injurious conduct; if you do not bear it meekly, and put the best construction that can be on it, you contradict the gospel. Some people always show a bad spirit, ever ready to put the worst construction on what is done, and take fire at any little thing. This shows a great want of that charity, which "hopeth all things, believeth all things, endureth all things." But if a man always shows meekness, under injuries, it will confound gainsaying. Nothing makes so solemn an impression on sinners, and bears down with such a tremendous weight on their consciences, as to see a Christian, Christlike, bearing affronts and injuries with the meekness of a lamb. It cuts like a two-edged sword.

I will mention a case to show this. A young man abused a minister to his face, and reviled him in an unprecedented manner. The minister possessed his soul in patience, and spoke mildly in reply, telling him the truth pointedly, but yet in a very kind manner. This only made him the more angry, and at length he went away in a rage, declaring that he was not going to stay and bear this vituperation. As if it was the minister, instead of himself, that had been scolding. The sinner went away, but with the arrows of the Almighty in his heart, and in less than half an hour he followed the minister to his lodgings in intolerable agony, wept, and begged forgiveness, and broke down before God, and yielded up his heart to Christ.[6] This calm and mild manner was more overwhelming to him than a thousand arguments. Now if that minister had been thrown off his guard, and answered harshly, no doubt he would

---

[6] Finney may be referring here to the conversion of Theodore Weld in Utica, New York, in 1826. See Finney's *Memoirs*, pp. 184-188.

have ruined the soul of that young man. How many of you have defeated every future effort you may make with your impenitent friends or neighbors, in some such way as this. On some occasion you have showed yourself so irascible, that you have sealed up your own lips, and laid a stumbling block over which that sinner will stumble into hell. If you have done it in any instance, don't sleep till you have done all you can to retrieve the mischief; till you have confessed the sin and done every thing to counteract it as far as possible.

9. The necessity of entire honesty in a Christian. O what a field opens here for remark! But I cannot go over it fully now. It extends to all the departments of life. Christians need to show the strictest regard to integrity in every department of business, and in all their intercourse with their fellow-men. If every Christian would pay a scrupulous regard to honesty, and always be conscientious to do exactly right, it would make a powerful impression on the minds of people, of the reality of religious principle.

A lady was once buying some eggs in a store, and the clerk made a miscount and gave her one more than the number. She saw it at the time, but said nothing, and after she got home it troubled her. She felt that she had acted wrong, and she went back to the young man and confessed it and paid the difference. The impression of her conscientious integrity went to his heart like a sword. It was a great sin in her in concealing the miscount, because the temptation was so small; for if she would cheat him out of an egg, it showed that she would cheat him out of his whole store, if she could do it and not be found out. But her prompt and humble confession showed an honest conscience.

I am happy to say, there are some men who deal on this principle of integrity. And the wicked hate them for it. They rail against them, and vociferate in bar-rooms, that they never will buy goods of such and such individuals, that such a hypocrite shall never touch a dollar of their money, and all that, and then they will go right away and buy of them, because they know they shall be honestly dealt with. This is a testimony to the truth of religion, that is heard from Georgia to Maine. Suppose all Christians did so. What would be the consequence? Christians would run away with the business of the city. The Christians would soon do the business of the world. The great argument which some Christians urge, that if they do not do business upon the common principle, of stating one price and taking another, they cannot compete with men of the world, is all false — false in philosophy and false in history. Only make it your invariable rule to do right, and do business upon principle, and you control the market. The ungodly will be obliged to conform to your standard. It is perfectly in the power of the church to regulate the commerce of the world, if they will only themselves maintain perfect integrity.[7]

And if Christians will do the same in *politics*, they will sway the destinies of nations, without involving themselves at all in the base and corrupting strife of parties. Only let Christians generally determine to vote for no man for any office, that is not an honest man and a man of pure morals, and let it be known that Christians are united in this, whatever may be their difference in political sentiments, and no man would be put up who is not such a character. In three years it would be talked about in taverns and published in newspapers, when any man is set up as a candidate for office, "What a good man he is, how moral, how pious," and the like. And any political party would no more set up a known Sabbath breaker, or a gambler, or a profane swearer, or a whoremonger, or a rum-seller, as their candidate for office, than they would set up the devil himself for president. The carnal policy of many professors, who undertake to correct politics by such means as wicked men employ, and who are determined to vote with a party, let the candidate be ever so profligate, is all wrong, wrong in principle, contrary to philosophy and common sense, and ruinous to the best interests of mankind. The dishonesty of the church is cursing the world. I am not going to preach a political sermon, I assure you. But I want to show you, that if you mean in impress men favorably to your religion by your lives, you must be honest, strictly honest, in business, politics, and every thing you do. What do you suppose those ungodly politicians, who *know themselves* to be playing a dishonest game in carrying an election, think of your religion when they see you uniting with them? They know you are a hypocrite!

REMARKS.

1. It is unreasonable for professors of religion to wonder at the thoughtlessness of sinners. — Every thing considered, the care-

---

[7] The essence of Finney's simplistic views of economics and politics is contained in these views that honesty is the best policy, that good will always triumph over evil, and that the practice of Christian love will solve all problems.

lessness of sinners is not wonderful. We are affected by testimony, and only by that testimony which is received to our minds. Sinners are so taken up with business, pleasure, and the things of the world, that they will not examine the Bible to find out what religion is. Their feelings are excited only on worldly subjects, because these only are brought into warm contact with their minds. — The things of the world make therefore a strong impression. But there is so little to make an impression on their minds in respect to eternity, and to bring religion home to them, that they do not feel on the subject. If they examined the subject they would feel. But they don't examine it, nor think upon it, nor care for it. And they never will, unless God's witnesses rise up and testify. But inasmuch as the great body of Christians in fact live so as to testify *on the other side* by their conduct, how can we expect that sinners will feel right on the subject? Nearly all the testimony and all the influence that comes to their minds tends to make them feel the other way. God has left his cause here before the human race, and left his witness to testify in his behalf, and behold, they all turn round and testify the other way! Is it any wonder that sinners are careless?

2. We see why it is that preaching does so little good; and how it is that so many sinners get gospel-hardened. Sinners that live under the gospel are often supposed to be gospel-hardened; but only let the church wake up, and act consistently, and they will feel. If the church were to live only one week as if they believed the Bible, sinners would melt down before them. Suppose I were a lawyer, and should go into court and spread out my client's case, the issue is joined, and I make my statements, and tell what I expect to prove, and then call in my witness. This first witness takes his oath, and then rises up and contradicts me to my face. What good will all my pleading do? I might address the jury a month, and be as eloquent as Cicero, but so long as my witnesses contradicted me, all my pleading would do no good. Just so it is with a minister who is preaching in the midst of a cold, stupid, and God-dishonoring church. In vain does he hold up to view the great truths of religion, when every member of the church is ready to swear he lies. Why, in such a church, their very manner of going out of the aisles contradicts the sermon. They press out as cheerful and as easy, bowing to one another, and whispering together, as if nothing was the matter. Let the minister warn every man daily with tears, it will produce no

effect. If the devil should come in and see the state of things, he would think he could not better the business for his interest.

Yet there are ministers who will go on in this way for years, preaching over the heads of such a people, that by their lives contradict every word they say, and they think it their duty to do so. Duty! To preach to a church that are undoing all his work, and contradicting all his testimony, and that will not alter! No. Let him shake off the dust from his feet for a testimony, and go to the heathen, or to the new settlements. The man is wasting his energies, and wearing out his life, and just rocking the cradle for a sleepy church, all testifying to sinners, there is no danger. Their whole-lives are a practical testimony that the Bible is not true. Shall ministers continue to wear themselves out so? Probably not less than ninety-nine hundredths of the preaching in this country is lost, because it is contradicted by the church. Not one truth in a hundred that is preached takes effect, because the lives of professors testify it is not so.

3. It is evident that the standard of Christian living must be raised, or the world will never be converted. If we had as many church members now, as there are families, and scattered all over the world, and a minister to every five hundred souls, and every child in a Sabbath school, and every young person in a Bible class; you would have all the machinery you want, but if the church contradict the truth by their lives, it would produce a revival.

They never will have a revival in any place, while the whole church in effect testify against the minister. Often it is the case that where there is the most preaching, there is the least religion, because the church contradict the preaching. I never knew means fail of a revival, where Christians live consistent. One of the first things is to raise the standard of religion, so as to embody and hang out in the sight of all men, the truth of the gospel. Unless ministers can get the church to wake up and act as if religion was true, and back their testimony by their lives, in vain will they attempt to promote a revival.

Many churches are depending on their minister to do every thing. When he preaches, they will say, "What a great sermon that was. He's an excellent minister. Such preaching must do good. We shall have a revival soon, I do not doubt." And all the while, they are contradicting the preaching by their lives. I tell you, if they are depending on preaching alone to carry on the work, they must fail. If Jesus Christ were to come and preach, and the church contradict it, he would fail. It has been tried once. Let an apostle rise from the dead, or an angel come down from heaven and preach, without the church to witness for God, and it would have no effect. The novelty might produce a certain kind of effect for a time, but as soon as the novelty was gone, the preaching would have no saving effect, while contradicted by the witnesses.

4. Every Christian makes an impression by his conduct, and witnesses either for one side or the other. His looks, dress, whole demeanor, make a constant impression on one side or the other. He cannot help testifying for or against religion. He is either gathering with Christ, or scattering abroad. Every step you take, you tread on cords that will vibrate to all eternity. Every time you move, you touch keys whose sound will re-echo over all the hills and dales of heaven, and through all the dark caverns and vaults of hell. Every movement of your lives, you are exerting a tremendous influence, that will tell on the immortal interests of souls all around you. Are you asleep, while all your conduct is exerting such an influence?

Are you going to walk in the street? Take care how you dress. What is that on your head? What does that gaudy ribbon, and those ornaments upon your dress, say to every one that meets you? It makes the impression that you wish to be thought pretty. Take care! You might just as well write on your clothes, "NO TRUTH IN RELIGION." It says, "GIVE ME DRESS, GIVE ME FASHION, GIVE ME FLATTERY, AND I AM HAPPY." The world understands this testimony as you walk the streets. You are "living epistles, known and read of all men." If you show pride, levity, bad temper, and the like, it is like tearing open the wounds of the Savior. How Christ might weep to see professors of religion going about hanging up his cause to contempt at the corners of streets. Only "let the women adorn themselves in modest apparel, with shamefacedness and sobriety, not with broidered hair, or gold, or pearls, or costly array, but (which becometh women professing godliness) with good works;" only let them act consistently, and their conduct will tell on the world, heaven will rejoice and hell groan at their influence. But O, let them display vanity, try to be pretty, bow down to the goddess of fashion, fill their ears with ornaments, and their fingers with rings. Let them put feathers in their hats, and clasps upon their arms, lace themselves up till they can hardly breathe. Let them put on their "round tires and walk mincing as they go," [8] and their influence is reversed. Heaven puts on the robes of mourning, and hell may hold a jubilee.

5. It is easy to see why revivals do not prevail in a great city. How can they? Just look at God's witnesses, and see what they are testifying to. They seem to be agreed together to tempt the Spirit of the Lord, and lie to the Holy Ghost. — They make their vows to God, to consecrate themselves wholly to him, and then go bowing down at the shrine of fashion, and then wonder there are no revivals. It would be more than a miracle to have a revival under such circumstances. How can a revival prevail in this church? Do you suppose I have such a vain imagination of my own ability, as to think I can promote a revival by preaching over your heads, while you live on as you do? Do you not know that so far as your influence goes, most of you are right in the way of a revival? Your spirit and deportment produce an influence on the world against religion. How shall the world believe religion, when the witnesses are not agreed among themselves? You contradict yourselves, you contradict one another, and you contradict your minister, and the sum of the whole testimony is, there is no need of being pious.

Do you believe the things I have been preaching are true, or are they the ravings of a disturbed mind? If they are true, do you recognize the fact that they have reference to *you*? You say, perhaps, "I wish some of the rich churches could hear it!" Why, I am not preaching to them, I am preaching to you. My responsibility is to you, and my fruits must come from you. Now are you contradicting it? What is the testimony on the leaf of the record that is now sealed for the judgment concerning *this day*? Have you manifested a sympathy with the Son of God, when his heart is bleeding in view of the desolations of Zion? Have your children, clerks, servants, seen it to be so? Have they seen a solemnity on your countenance, and tears in your eyes, in view of perishing souls?

FINALLY. — I must close by remarking, that God and all moral beings have great reason to complain of this false testimony. There is ground to complain that God's witnesses turn and testify

---

[8] "Round tires" was the popular term for hoop skirts, which were just coming into fashion. The last four sentences in this paragraph were not included in the version of the sermon that appeared in the *New York Evangelist*, January 31, 1835, p. 18.

point-blank against him. They declare by their conduct that there is no truth in the gospel. Heaven might weep and hell rejoice to see this. O how guilty! Here you are, going to the judgment, red all over with blood. Sinners are to meet you there, those who have seen how you live, many of them already dead, and many others you will never see again. What an influence you have exerted! Perhaps hundreds of souls will meet you in the judgment, and curse you (if they are allowed to speak) for leading them to hell, by practically denying the truth of the gospel. What will become of this city, and of the world, when the church is united in practically testifying that God is a liar? They testify by their lives, that if they make a profession and live a moral life, that is religion enough. O! what a doctrine of devils is that! Enough to ruin the whole human race.

X

TO WIN SOULS REQUIRES WISDOM

TEXT. — "He that winneth souls is wise." — PROVERBS xi. 30.

THE most common definition of wisdom is, that it is the selection of the most appropriate means for the accomplishment of an end — the best adaptation of means to secure a desired end. "He that winneth souls," God says, "is wise." The object of this evening's lecture is to direct Christians in the use of means for accomplishing their infinitely desirable end, the salvation of souls. To-night I shall confine my attention to the private efforts of individuals for the conversion and salvation of men. On another occasion, perhaps I shall use the same text in speaking of what is wise in the public preaching of the gospel, and the labors of ministers. In giving some directions to aid private Christians in this work, I propose,

I. To show Christians how they should deal with *careless* sinners.

II. How they should deal with *awakened* sinners.

III. How they should deal with *convicted* sinners.

I. The manner of dealing with careless sinners.

1. In regard to the *time*. It is important that you should select a proper *time to* try to make a serious impression on the mind of a careless sinner. Much depends on timing your efforts right. For if you fail of selecting the most proper time, very probably you will be defeated. True, you may say, it is our duty at all times to warn sinners, and try to awaken them to think of their souls. And so it is; yet if you do not pay due regard to the time and opportunity, your hope of success may be very doubtful.

(1.) It is desirable, if possible, to address a person that is careless, *when he is disengaged from other employments*. In proportion as his attention is taken up with something else, it will be difficult to awaken him to religion. People who are careless and indifferent to religion are often offended, rather than benefited, by being called off from important and lawful business. For instance, a minister perhaps goes to visit the family of a merchant, or mechanic, or farmer, and finds the man absorbed in his business; perhaps he calls him off from his work when it is urgent, and the man is uneasy and irritable, and feels as if it was an intrusion.[1] In such a case, there is little room to expect any good. Notwithstanding it is true that religion is infinitely more important than all his worldly business, and he ought to postpone every thing to the salvation of his soul, yet he does not feel it, for if he did he would no longer be a careless sinner, and therefore he regards it as unjustifiable, and gets offended. You must take him as you find him, a careless, impenitent sinner, and deal with him accordingly. He is absorbed in other things, and very apt to be offended if you take such a time to interfere and call his attention to religion.

(2.) It is important to take a person, if possible, at a time when he is *not strongly excited with any other subject*. If that is the case, he is in an unfit frame to be addressed on the subject of religion. In proportion to the strength of that excitement would be the probability that you would do no good. — You may possibly reach him; persons have had their minds arrested and turned to religion in the midst of a powerful excitement on other subjects. But it is not likely.

(3.) Be sure that the person is *perfectly sober*. It used to be more common that it is now, for people to drink spirits every day, and become more or less intoxicated. Precisely in proportion as they are so, they are rendered unfit to be approached on the subject of religion. If they have been drinking beer, or cider, or wine, so that you can smell their breath, you may know there is but little chance of producing any lasting effect on them. I have had professors of religion bring persons to me, pretending they were under conviction; for you know that people in liquor are often very fond of talking upon religion; but as soon as I came near them, so as to smell their breath, I have asked, Why do you bring this drunken man to me? Why, they say, he is not drunk, he has only drank a little. Well, that little has made him a little drunk. He *is* drunk, if you can smell his breath. The cases are exceedingly rare where a person has been truly convicted, who had any intoxicating liquor in him.

(4.) If possible, where you wish to converse with a man on the subject of salvation, take him *when he is in a good temper*.

---

[1] It is indicative of how seriously people took their religion in Finney's day that a farmer or businessman would drop his work to talk about his soul if the minister happened to call upon him during working hours.

If you find him out of humor, very probably he will get angry and abuse you. Better let him alone for that time, or you will be likely to quench the Spirit. It is possible you may be able to talk in such a way as to cool his temper, but it is not likely. The truth is, men hate God, and though their hatred may be dormant, it is easily excited, and if you bring God fully before their minds when they are already excited with anger, it will be so much the easier to arouse their enmity to open violence.

(5.) If possible, always take an opportunity to converse with careless sinners *when they are alone*. Most men are too proud to be conversed with freely respecting themselves in the presence of others, even with their own family. A man in such circumstances will brace up all his powers to defend himself, while if he was alone he would melt down under the truth. — He will resist the truth, or try to laugh it off, for fear that if he should manifest any feeling, somebody will go and report that he is serious.

In visiting families, instead of calling all the family together at the same time to be talked to, the better way is to see them all, *one at a time*. There was a case of this kind: Several young ladies, of a proud, gay, and fashionable character, lived together in a fashionable family. Two men were strongly desirous to get the subject of religion before them, but were at a loss how to accomplish it, for fear they would all combine, and counteract or resist every serious impression. At length they took this course. They called and sent up their card to one of the young ladies by name. She came down and they conversed with her on the subject of her salvation, and as she was alone, she not only treated them politely, but seemed to receive the truth with seriousness. A day or two after, they called in like manner on another, and then another, and so on, till they had conversed with every one separately. In a little time they were all, I believe, every one, hopefully converted. This was as it should be, for then they could not keep each other in countenance. And then the impression made on one was followed up with the others, so that one was not left to exert a bad influence over the rest.

There was a pious woman who kept a boarding house for young gentlemen; she had twenty-one or two of them in her family, and at length she became very anxious for their salvation; she made it a subject of prayer, but saw no seriousness among them. At length she saw that there must be something done besides praying, and yet she did not know what to do. One morning after breakfast, as they were retiring, she asked one of them to stop a few minutes. She took him to her room, and conversed with him tenderly on the subject of religion, and prayed with him. She followed up the impression made, and pretty soon he was hopefully converted. Then there were two, and they addressed another, and prayed with him, and soon he was prepared to join them. Then another, and so on, taking one at a time, and letting none of the rest know what was going on, so as not to alarm them, till every one of these young men were converted to God. Now if she had brought the subject before the whole of them together, very likely they would have turned it all into ridicule; or perhaps they would have been offended, and left the house, and then she could have had no further influence over them. But taking one alone, and treating him respectfully and kindly, he had no such motive for resistance as arises out of the presence of others.

(6.) Try to seize an opportunity to converse with a careless sinner, *when the events of Providence seem to favor your design.* If any particular event should occur, calculated to make a serious impression, be sure to improve the occasion faithfully.

(7.) Seize the *earliest opportunity* to converse with those around you who are careless. Don't put it off from day to day, thinking a better opportunity will come. You must *seek* an opportunity, and if none offers *make* one. Appoint a time and place, and get an interview with your friend or neighbor, where you can speak to him freely. Send him a note, go to him on purpose, make it look like a matter of business, as if you were in earnest in endeavoring to promote his soul's salvation. Then he will feel that it is a matter of importance, at least in your eyes. Follow it up till you succeed, or become convinced nothing can now be done.

(8.) If you have any feeling for a particular individual, take an opportunity to converse with that individual *while this feeling continues.* If it is a truly benevolent feeling, you have reason to believe the Spirit of God is moving you to desire the salvation of his soul, and that God is ready to bless your efforts for his conversion. In such a case, make it the subject of special and importunate prayer, and seek an early opportunity to pour out all your heart to him, and bring him to Christ.

2. In regard to the *manner* of doing all this.

(1.) When you approach a careless individual, to endeavor to awaken him to his soul's concerns, be sure to treat him *kindly.*

Let him see that you address him, not because you seek a quarrel with him, but because you love his soul, and desire his best good, in time and eternity. If you are harsh and overbearing in your manner, you will probably offend him, and drive him farther off from the way of life.

(2.) Be *solemn*. Avoid all lightness of manner or language. Levity will produce any thing but a right impression. You ought to feel that you are engaged in a very solemn work, which is going to affect the character of your friend or neighbor, and probably determine his destiny for eternity. Who could trifle and use levity in such circumstances if his heart was sincere?

(3.) Be *respectful*. Some seem to suppose it necessary to be abrupt, and rude, and coarse in their intercourse with the careless and impenitent. Nothing can be a greater mistake. The Apostle Paul has given us a better rule on the subject, where he says, "Be pitiful, be courteous, not rendering evil for evil, or railing for railing, but contrariwise blessing." A rude and coarse address is only calculated to give an unfavorable opinion both of you and of your religion.

(4.) Be sure to be *very plain*. Do not suffer yourself to cover up any circumstance of the person's character, and his relations to God. Lay it all open, not for the purpose of offending or wounding him, but because it is necessary. Before you can cure a wound, you must probe it to the bottom. Keep back none of the truth, but let it come out plainly before him.

(5.) Be sure to *address his conscience*. In public addresses, ministers often get hold of the feelings only, and thus awaken the mind. But in private conversation you cannot do so. You cannot pour out the truth in an impassioned and rousing manner. And unless you address the conscience pointedly, you get no hold of the mind at all.

(6.) Bring the *great and fundamental truths* to bear upon the person's mind.[2] Sinners are very apt to run off upon some pretext or some subordinate point, especially some point of sectarianism. For instance, if the man is a Presbyterian, he will try to turn the conversation on the points of difference between Presbyterians and Methodists. Or he will fall foul of old school divinity. Don't

---

[2] Of course Finney often did argue over the doctrinal points of Old School Calvinism, but this he considered simply clarifying the gospel. The importance of his emphasis upon "the fundamental truths" of religion is that it broke down denominational rivalry and helped to promote evangelical ecumenism, at least until the days of the fundamentalist-modernist schism.

yield to him, or talk with him on any such point; it will do more hurt than good. Tell him the present business is to save his soul, and not to settle controverted questions in theology. Hold him to the great fundamental points, by which he must be saved or lost.

(7.) Be *very patient*. If he has a real difficulty in his mind, be very patient till you find out what it is, and then clear it up. If what he alleges is a mere cavil, make him see that it is a cavil. Don't try to answer it by argument, but show him that he is not sincere in advancing it. It is not worth while to spend your time in arguing against a cavil, but make him feel that he is committing sin to plead it, and thus enlist his conscience on your side.

(8.) Be careful to *guard your own spirit*. There are many people who have not good temper enough to converse with those who are much opposed to religion. And such a person wants no better triumph than to see you angry. He will go away exulting because he has made one of these saints mad.

(9.) If the sinner is inclined to intrench himself against God, be careful *not to take his part in any thing*. If he says he can't do his duty, do not take sides with him, or say any thing to countenance his falsehood. Do not tell him he can't, or help him maintain himself in the controversy against his Maker. Sometimes a careless sinner will go to finding fault with Christians. Do not take his part or side with him against Christians. Just tell him he has not got their sins to answer for, and he had better see to his own concerns. If you fall in with him, he feels that he has you on his side. Show him that it is a censorious and wicked spirit that prompts him to make these remarks, and not a regard for the honor of religion or the laws of Jesus Christ.

(10.) Bring up the individual's *particular sins*. Talking in general terms against sin will produce no results. You must make a man feel that you mean *him*. A minister who cannot make his hearers feel that he means them, cannot expect to accomplish much. Some people are very careful to avoid mentioning the particular sins of which they know the individual to be guilty, for fear of hurting his feelings. This is wrong. If you know his history, bring up his particular sins, kindly but plainly, not to give offence, but to awaken conscience, and give full force to the truth.

(11.) It is generally *best to be short*, and not spin out what we have to say. Get the attention as soon as you can to the very point, say a few things and press them home, and bring the matter to an issue. If possible, get them to repent and give themselves to Christ at the time. This is the proper issue. Carefully avoid making an impression that you do not expect them to repent NOW.

(12.) If possible, when you converse with sinners, be sure to pray with them. If you converse with them, and leave them without praying, you leave your work undone.

II. The manner of dealing with *awakened sinners*.

1. You should be careful to distinguish between an awakened sinner, and one who is under conviction. When you find a person who feels a little on the subject of religion, do not take it for granted that he is *convicted of sin*, and thus omit to use means to show him his sin. Persons are often *awakened* by some providential circumstance, as sickness, a thunderstorm, pestilence, death in the family, disappointment, or the like, or by the Spirit of God, so that their ears are open, and they are ready to hear on the subject of religion with attention and seriousness, and some feeling. If you find a person awakened, no matter by what means, lose no time to pour in light upon his mind. Don't be afraid, but show him the breadth of the Divine law, and the exceeding strictness of its precepts. Make him see how it condemns his thoughts and life. Search out his heart, find what is there, and bring it up before his mind, as far as you can. If possible, melt him down on the spot. When once you have got a sinner's attention, very often his conviction and conversion is the work of a few moments. You can sometimes do more in five minutes, than in years or a whole life while he is careless or indifferent.

I have been amazed at the conduct of those cruel parents, and other heads of families, who will let an awakened sinner be in their families for days and weeks, and not say a word to him on the subject. Why, they say, if the Spirit of God has begun a work in him, he will certainly carry it on! Perhaps the person is anxious to converse, and puts himself in the way of Christians, as often as possible, expecting they will converse with him, and they do not say a word. Amazing! Such a person ought to be looked out immediately, as soon as he is awakened, and let a blaze of light be poured into his mind without delay. Whenever you have reason to believe that a person within your reach is awakened, do not sleep till you have poured in the light upon his mind, and tried to bring him to immediate repentance. Then is the time to press the subject with effect. If that favorable moment is lost, it can never be recovered.

I have often seen Christians in revivals, who were constantly on the look-out to see if any persons appeared to be awakened. And as soon as they saw any one begin to manifest feeling under preaching, they would mark him, and as soon as the meeting was out, invite him to a room and converse and pray with him, and if possible not leave him till he was converted. A remarkable case of this kind occurred in a town at the West. A merchant came to the place from a distance to buy goods. It was a time of powerful revival, but he was determined to keep out of its influence, and so he would not go to any meeting at all. At length he found every body so much engaged in religion that it met him at every turn, and he got vexed, and swore he would go home. There was so much religion there, he said, he could not do any business, and he would not stay. Accordingly he took his seat for the stage, which was to leave at four o'clock the next morning. As he spoke of going away, a gentleman belonging to the house, who was one of the young converts, asked him if he would not go to meeting once before he left town. He finally consented, and went to the meeting. The sermon took hold of his mind, but not with sufficient power to bring him into the kingdom. He returned to his lodgings, and called the landlord to pay his bill. The landlord, who had himself recently experienced religion, saw that he was agitated. He accordingly spoke to him on the subject of religion, and the man burst into tears. The landlord immediately called in three or four young converts, and they prayed and exhorted him, and at four o'clock in the morning, when the stage called, he went on his way *rejoicing in God!* When he got home, he called his family together, confessed to them his past sins, and avowed his determination to live differently, and prayed with them for the first time. It was so unexpected that it was soon noised abroad, people began to inquire, and a revival broke out in the place. Now, suppose these Christians had done as some do, been careless, and let the man go off, slightly impressed? It is not probable he ever could have been saved. Such opportunities are often lost for ever, when once the favorable moment is passed.

III. The manner of dealing with *convicted sinners*.

By a *convicted* sinner I mean one who feels himself condemned by the law of God, as a guilty sinner. He has so much instruction as to understand something of the extent of God's law, and he sees and feels his guilty state, and knows what his remedy is. To deal with these often requires great wisdom. There are some most trying cases occur, when it is extremely difficult to know what to do with them.

1. When a person is *convicted* and not *converted*, but remains in an anxious state, there is generally some specific reason for it. In such cases, it does no good to exhort him to repent, or to explain the law to him. He knows all that, he understands all these general points. But still he don't repent. Now there must be some particular difficulty to overcome. You may preach, and pray, and exhort till doomsday, and not gain any thing.

You must then set yourself to inquire what is that particular difficulty. A physician, when he is called to a patient, and finds him sick with a particular disease, first administers the general remedies that are applicable to that disease. If they produce no effect, and the disease still continues, he must examine the case, and learn the constitution of the individual, and his habits, diet, manner of living, &c., and see what the matter is that the medicine does not take effect. So it is with the case of a sinner convicted but not converted. If your ordinary instructions and exhortations fail, there must be a difficulty. The particular difficulty is often known to the individual himself, though he keeps it concealed. Sometimes it is something that has escaped even his own observations.

(1.) Sometimes the individual has some idol, something which he loves more than God, which prevents him from giving himself up. You must search out and see what it is that he will not give up. Perhaps it is wealth, perhaps some earthly friend, perhaps gay dress, or gay company, or some favorite amusement. At any rate there is something on which his heart is so set that he will not yield to God.

(2.) Perhaps he has done an injury to some individual, that calls for redress, and he is unwilling to confess it or to make a just recompense. Now, until he will confess and forsake this sin, he can find no mercy. If he has injured the person in property, or character, or has abused him, he must make it up. If you can find out, tell him plainly, and frankly, that there is no hope for him till he is willing to confess it, and to do what is right.

(3.) Sometimes there is some *particular sin*, which he will not forsake. He pretends it is only a small one, or tries to persuade himself it is no sin. No matter how small it is, he can never get into the kingdom of God till he gives it up. Sometimes an individual has seen it to be a sin to use tobacco, and he never can find true

TO WIN SOULS REQUIRES WISDOM

peace till he gives it up. Perhaps he is looking upon it as a small sin.

But God knows nothing about small sins in such a case. What is the sin? Why, it is injuring your health, setting a bad example, and taking God's money, which you are bound to employ in his service, and spending it for tobacco. What would a merchant say, if he found one of his clerks in the habit of going to the money drawer, and taking money enough to keep him in cigars? Would he call it a small offense? No, he would say he deserved to be sent to the state prison. I mention this particular sin, because I have found it to be one of the things to which men who are convicted will hold on when they know it is wrong, and then wonder why they do not find peace.

(4.) See if there is not some work of *remuneration*, which he is bound to do. Perhaps he has defrauded somebody in trade, or taken some unfair advantage, contrary to the golden rule of doing as you would be done by, and is unwilling to make satisfaction. This is a very common sin among merchants and men of business. I have known many melancholy instances, where men have grieved away the Spirit of God, or else have been driven well nigh to absolute despair, because they were unwilling to give satisfaction where they have done such things. Now it is plain that such persons never can have forgiveness until they do it.

(5.) They may have *intrenched* themselves somewhere, and fortified their minds in regard to some particular point, which they are determined not to yield. For instance, they may have taken strong ground that they will not do a particular thing. I knew a man who was determined not to go into a certain grove to pray. Several other persons during the revival had gone into the grove, and there, by prayer and meditation given themselves to God. His own clerk had been converted there. The lawyer himself was awakened, but he was determined that he would not go into the grove. He had powerful convictions, and went on for weeks in this way, with no relief. He tried to make God believe it was not pride that kept him from Christ; and so, when he was going home from meeting he would kneel down in the street and pray. And not only that, but he would look round for a mud-puddle in the street, in which he might kneel, to show that he was not proud. He once prayed *all night* in his parlor, but he would not go into the grove. His distress was so great, and he was so mad with God, that he was strongly tempted to make way with himself, and actually threw away his knife for fear he should cut his throat. At length he concluded he would go into the grove and pray, and as soon as he got there he was converted, and went and poured out his full heart to God.[3]

So individuals are sometimes intrenched in a determination that they will not go to a particular meeting, perhaps the inquiry meeting, or some prayer meeting, or they will not have a certain person pray with them, or they will not take a particular seat, such as the anxious seat. They say that they can be converted just as well without yielding this point, for religion don't consist in this, going to a particular meeting, or taking a particular attitude in prayer, or a particular seat. This is true, but by taking this ground they *make* it the material point. And so long as they are intrenched there, and determined to bring God to their terms, they never can be converted. Sinners will often yield any thing else, and do any thing in the world, but yield the point upon which they have committed themselves, and taken a stand against God. They cannot be humbled, until they yield this point, whatever it is. And if without yielding it, they get a hope, it will be a false hope.

(6.) Perhaps he has a prejudice against some one, a member of the church perhaps, on account of some faithful dealing with his soul, or something in his business that he did not like, and he hangs on this, and will never be converted till he gives it up. Whatever it be, you should search it out and tell him the truth, plainly and faithfully.

(7.) He may feel ill will towards some one, or be angry, and cherish strong feelings of resentment, which prevent him from obtaining mercy from God. "And when ye stand praying, forgive, if ye have aught against any: that your Father also which is in heaven may forgive you your trespasses. But, if ye do not forgive, neither will your Father which is in heaven forgive your trespasses."

(8.) Perhaps he entertains some errors in doctrine, or some wrong notions respecting the *thing to be done*, or the way of doing it, which may be keeping him out of the kingdom. Perhaps he is waiting for God. He is convinced that he deserves to go to hell, and that unless he is converted he must go there, but he is waiting for God to do something to him before he submits. He is in fact waiting for God to do for him what he has required the sinner to do.

---

[3] The man in this story was Squire Benjamin Wright; the clerk was Finney. The story is told in Finney's *Memoirs,* pp. 32–33.

He may be waiting for more conviction. People often do not know what conviction is, and think they are not under conviction when in fact they are under powerful conviction. They often think nothing is conviction unless they have great fears of hell. But the fact is, individuals often have strong convictions, who have very little fear of hell. Show them what is the truth, and let them see they have no need to wait.

Perhaps he may be waiting for certain feelings, which somebody else has had before he obtained mercy. This is very common in revivals, where some one of the first converts has told of remarkable experiences. Others who are awakened are very apt to think they must wait for just such feelings. I knew a young man thus awakened; his companion had been converted in a remarkable way, and this one was waiting for just such feelings. He said he was using the means, and praying for them, but finally found that he was a Christian, although he had not been through the course of feeling he expected.

Sinners often lay out a plan of the way they expect to feel, and how they expect to be converted, and in fact lay out the work for God, determined that they will go in that path or not at all. Tell them this is all wrong, they must not lay out any such path beforehand, but let God lead them as he sees to be best. God always leads the blind by a way they know not. There never was a sinner brought into the kingdom through such a course of feeling as he expected. Very often they are amazed to find that they are in, and have had no such exercises as they expected.

It is very common for persons to be waiting to be made subjects of prayer, or for some particular means to be used, or to see if they cannot make themselves better. They are so wicked, they say, that they can't come to Christ. They want to try, by humiliation, and suffering, and prayer, to fit themselves to come. You will have to hunt them out of all these refuges. It is astonishing into how many corners they will often run before they will go to Christ. I have known persons almost deranged for the want of a little correct instruction.[4]

Sometimes such people think their sins are too great to be forgiven, or that they have grieved the Spirit of God away, when that Spirit is all the while convicting them. They pretend their

---

[4] Finney may on occasion have driven unstable persons to insanity by his insistence upon immediate submission to the will of God, but it is also likely that his common-sense attitude toward conversion saved many unstable persons from driving themselves insane by dwelling upon the doctrine of predestination.

sins are greater than Christ's mercies, thus actually insulting the Lord Jesus Christ.

Sometimes sinners get the idea that they are given up of God, and that now they cannot be saved. It is often very difficult to beat persons off from this ground. Many of the most distressing cases I ever met with, have been of this character, where persons would insist upon it that they were given up, and nothing would change them.

In a place where I was laboring in a revival, I went one day into the meeting, and before the exercises commenced, I heard a low moaning, distressing, unearthly noise. I looked and saw several women gathered round the person who made it. They said it was a woman in despair. She had been a long time in that state. Her husband was a drunkard. He had brought her to meeting and gone himself to the tavern. I conversed with her, and saw her state, and that it was very difficult to reach her case. As I was going away to commence the exercises, she said she must go out, for she could not hear praying or singing. I told her she must not go, and told the ladies to detain her, if necessary by force. I felt that if the devil had hold of her, God was stronger than the devil, and could deliver her. The exercises began, and she made some noise at first. But by and by she looked up. The subject was chosen with special reference to her case, and as it proceeded, her attention was gained, her eyes were fixed — I never shall forget how she looked — her eyes and mouth open, her head up, and she almost rose from her seat as the truth poured in upon her mind. Finally, as the truth knocked away every foundation on which her despair had rested, she shrieked out, put her head down, and sat perfectly still till the meeting was out. I went to her, and found her perfectly calm and happy in God. I saw her long afterwards, and she remained so. Thus Providence threw her where she never expected to be, and compelled her to hear instruction adapted to her case. You may often do incalculable good by finding out precisely where the difficulty lies, and then bring the truth to bear right on that point.

Sometimes persons will strenuously maintain that they have committed the unpardonable sin.[5] When they get that idea into their minds, they will turn every thing you say against themselves.

[5] The unpardonable sin became a favorite topic of revival sermons in the nineteenth century. The most common definition of it was that it consisted in resisting the Spirit of God so many times that He was "grieved away," never to return.

In some such cases, it is a good way to take them on their own ground, and reason with them in this way; "Suppose you have committed the unpardonable sin, what then? It is reasonable that you should submit to God, and be sorry for your sins, and break off from them, and do all the good you can, even if God will not forgive you. Even if you go to hell you ought to do this." Press this thought and turn it over until you find they understand and consent to it.

It is common for persons in such cases to keep their eyes on themselves; they will shut themselves up, and keep looking at their own darkness, instead of looking away to Christ. Now if you can take their minds off from themselves, and get them to think of Christ, you may draw them away from brooding over their own present feelings, and get them to lay hold on the hope set before them in the gospel.

2. Be careful, in conversing with convicted sinners, not to *make any compromise* with them on any point where they have a difficulty. If you do, they will be sure to take advantage of it, and thus get a false hope.[6] Convicted sinners often get into a difficulty, in regard to giving up some darling sin, or yielding some point where conscience and the Holy Ghost are at war with them. And if they come across an individual who will yield the point, they feel better, and are happy, and think they are converted. The young man who came to Christ was of this character. He had one difficulty, and Jesus Christ knew just what it was. He knew he loved his money, and instead of compromising the matter and thus trying to comfort him, he just put his finger on the very place and told him, "Go sell all that thou hast, and give to the poor, and come follow me." What was the effect? Why the young man went away sorrowful. Very likely, if Christ had told him to do anything else, he would have felt relieved, and would have got a hope; would have professed himself a disciple, joined the church, and gone to hell.

[6] To "get a hope" or "entertain a hope" or "indulge a hope" was to believe that one was among the saved. Prior to Finney's day few if any church members felt certain enough of their salvation to state flatly that they were saved no matter how intense their conversion experience had been. Finney himself sometimes speaks of persons in his revivals as being "hopefully converted." But by and large Finney preached that a true Christian or saint could be certain of his salvation, and he implied that those who would say only that they "had a hope" were really not saved. Old School Calvinists charged that Finney's revivals produced proud hypocrites or self-deceived sinners who thought they were saved but were not.

People are often amazingly anxious to make a compromise. They will ask such questions as this, Whether you don't think a person may be a Christian and yet do such and such things; or if he may not be a Christian and not do such and such things. Now, do not yield an inch to any such questions. These questions themselves may often show you the very point that is laboring in their minds. They will show you that it is pride, or love of the world, or something of the kind, which prevents their becoming Christians.

Be careful to make thorough work on this point, the love of the world. I believe there have been more false hopes built on wrong instructions here, than in any other way. I once heard a Doctor of Divinity trying to persuade his hearers to give up the world; and he told them "if they would only give it up, God would give it right back to them again. He is willing you should enjoy the world." Miserable! God never gives back the world to the Christian, in the same sense that he requires a convicted sinner to give it up.[7] He requires us to give up the *ownership* of every thing to him, so that we shall never again for a moment consider it *as our own*. A man must not think he has a right to judge for himself how much of his property he shall lay out for God. One man thinks he may spend seven thousand dollars a year to support his family; he has a right to do it, because he has the means, of his own. Another thinks he may lay up fifty or a hundred thousand dollars. One man said the other day, that he had promised he never would give any of his property to educate young men for the ministry. When he is applied to, he just answers, "I have said I never will give to any such object, and I never will." Man! did Jesus Christ ever tell you to do so with *his money?* Has he laid down any such rule? Remember it is his money you are talking about, and if he wants it to educate ministers, you withhold it at your peril. That man has yet to learn the first principle of religion, that he is not his own, and that the money which he *possesses* is Jesus Christ's.

Here is the great reason why the church is so full of false hopes. Men have been left to suppose they could be Christians, while holding on to their money. And this has served as a clog to every enterprise. It is an undoubted fact, that the church has funds

---

[7] This "miserable" Doctor of Divinity was Lyman Beecher. The incident occurred when Finney was holding a prayer meeting in Beecher's Hanover Street Church in Boston in the winter of 1831–1832. See Finney's *Memoirs*, pp. 315–316.

enough to supply the world with Bibles, and tracts, and missionaries, immediately. But the truth is, that professors of religion do not believe that the "earth is the Lord's, and the fullness thereof." Every man supposes he has a right to decide what appropriation he shall make of his own money. And they have no idea that Jesus Christ shall dictate to them on the subject.

Be sure to deal thoroughly on this point. The church is now filled up with hypocrites, because they were never made to give up the world. They never were made to see that unless they made an entire consecration of all to Christ, all their time, all their talents, all their influence, they would never get to heaven. Many think they can be Christians, and yet dream along through life, and use all their time and property for themselves, only giving a little now and then, to save appearances, when they can do it with perfect convenience. But it is a sad mistake, and they will find it so, if they do not employ their energies for God. And when they die, instead of finding heaven at the end of the path they are pursuing, they will find hell there.

In dealing with a convicted sinner, be sure to drive him away from every refuge, and not leave him an inch of ground to stand on, so long as he resists God. This need not take a long time to do. When the Spirit of God is at work striving with a sinner, it is easy to drive him from his refuges. You will find the truth will be like a hammer, crushing wherever it strikes. Make clean work with it, so that he shall give up all for God.

Make the sinner see clearly the nature and extent of the Divine law, and press the *main question* of entire submission to God. Bear down on that point as soon as you have made him clearly understand what you aim at, and do not turn off upon any thing else.

Be careful, in illustrating the subject, not to mislead the mind so as to leave the impression that a selfish submission will answer, or a selfish acceptance of the atonement, or a selfish giving up to Christ and receiving him, as if a man was making a good bargain, giving up his sins and receiving salvation in *exchange*. This is mere barter, and not submission to God. Leave no ground in your explanations or illustrations, for such a view of the matter. Man's selfish heart will eagerly seize such a view of religion, if it be presented, and very likely close in with it, and thus get a false hope.

Another time I shall call your attention to certain things that are to be *avoided* in dealing with sinners.

REMARKS.

1. Make it an object of *constant study and of daily reflection and prayer*, to learn how to deal with sinners, so as to promote their conversion. It is the great business on earth of every Christian, to save souls. People often complain that they do not know how to take hold of this matter. Why, the reason is plain enough; they have never studied it. They never took the proper pains to qualify themselves for the work of saving souls. If people made it no more a matter of attention and thought to qualify themselves for their worldly business, than they do to save souls, how do you think they would succeed? Now, if you are thus neglecting the main business of life, what are you living for? If you do not make it a matter of study, how you may most successfully act in building up the kingdom of Christ, you are acting a very wicked and absurd part as a Christian.

2. Many professors of religion do *more hurt than good*, when they attempt to talk to impenitent sinners. They have so little knowledge and skill, that their remarks rather divert attention than increase it.

3. Be careful to find the *point where the Spirit of God is pressing* a sinner, and press the same point in all your remarks. If you divert his attention from that point, you will be in great danger of destroying his convictions. Take pains to learn the state of his mind, what he is thinking of, how he feels, and what he feels most deeply upon, and then press that thoroughly, and don't divert his mind by talking about any thing else. Do not fear to press that point, for fear of driving him to distraction. Some people fear to press a point to which the mind is tremblingly alive, lest they should injure the mind, notwithstanding the Spirit of God is evidently debating that point with the sinner. This is an attempt to be wiser than God. You should clear up the point, throw the light of truth all around it, and bring the soul to yield, and then the mind is at rest.

4. Great evils have arisen, and many false hopes have been created, by not *discriminating between an awakened and a convicted sinner*. For the want of this, persons who are only awakened are immediately pressed to submit; "you must repent," "submit to God," when they are not in fact convinced of their guilt, nor instructed so far as even to know what submission means. This is one way in which revivals have been greatly injured by indis-

criminate exhortations to repent, unaccompanied with proper instruction.

5. Anxious sinners are to be regarded as being in a very *solemn and critical state*. They have in fact come to a turning point. It is a time when their destiny is likely to be settled for ever. The Spirit of God will not strive always. Christians ought to feel deeply for them. In many respects their circumstances are more solemn than the judgment day. *Here* their destiny is *settled*. The judgment day reveals it. And the particular time when it is done is when *the Spirit is striving with them.* Christians should remember their awful responsibility at such times. The physician, if he knows any thing of his duty, sometimes feels himself under a very solemn responsibility. His patient is in a critical state, where a little error will destroy life, and he hangs quivering between life and death. If such responsibility is felt in relation to the body, what awful responsibility should be felt in relation to the soul, when it is seen to hang trembling on a point, and its destiny is now to be decided. One false impression, one indiscreet remark, one sentence misunderstood, a slight diversion of mind, may *wear* him the wrong way, and his soul is lost. Never was an angel employed in a more solemn work, than that of dealing with sinners who are under conviction. How solemnly and carefully then should Christians walk, how wisely and skillfully work, if they do not mean to be the means of damning a soul!

FINALLY. — If there is a sinner in this house, let me say to him, Abandon all your excuses. You have been hold to-night that they are all in vain. To-night it will be told in hell, and told in heaven, and echoed from the ends of the universe, what you decide to do. This very hour may seal your eternal destiny. Will you submit to God to-night — NOW?

XI

A WISE MINISTER WILL BE SUCCESSFUL

Text. — "He that winneth souls is wise." — Proverbs xi. 30.

I preached last Friday evening from the same text, on the method of dealing with sinners by private Christians. My object at this time is to take up the more public means of grace, with particular reference to the

DUTIES OF MINISTERS.

As I observed in my last lecture, wisdom is the appropriate adaptation of means for securing a desired end. The great end for which the Christian Ministry was appointed, is to glorify God in the salvation of souls.[1] In speaking on this subject I propose to show,

I. That a right discharge of the duties of a minister requires great wisdom.

II. That the amount of success in the discharge of his duties (*other things being equal*) decides the amount of wisdom employed by him in the exercise of his office.

I. I am to show that a right discharge of the duties of a minister requires great wisdom.

1. On account of the *opposition it encounters*. The very end for which the ministry is appointed is one against which is arrayed the most powerful opposition of sinners themselves. If men were willing to receive the gospel, and there were nothing needed to be done but to tell the story of redemption, a child might convey the news. But men are opposed to the gospel. They are opposed to their own salvation, *in this way*. Their opposition is often violent and determined. I once saw a maniac who had formed designs against his own life, and he would exercise the utmost sagacity and cunning to effect his purpose. He would be as artful, and make his keepers believe he had no such design, that he had given it all up, and would appear as mild and sober, and at the instant the keeper was off his guard he would lay hands on himself. So

[1] See Lecture VII, p. 122, note 5.

sinners often exercise great cunning in evading all the efforts that are made to save them. And to meet this dreadful cunning, and overcome it so as to save men, ministers need a great amount of wisdom.

2. The particular means appointed to be employed in the work, show the necessity of great wisdom in ministers. If men were converted by an act of physical omnipotence, creating some new taste, or something like that, and if sanctification were nothing but the same physical omnipotence rooting out the remaining roots of sin from the soul, it would not require so much sagacity and skill to win souls. Nor would there then be any meaning in the text. But the truth is, that regeneration and sanctification are to be effected by moral means — by argument and not by force.[2] There never was and never will be any one saved by any thing but truth as the means. Truth is the outward means, the outward motive, presented first by man and then by the Holy Spirit. Take into view the opposition of the sinner himself, and you see that nothing, after all, short of the wisdom of God and the moral power of the Holy Spirit, can break down this opposition, and bring him to submit to God. Still the means are to be used by men, and means adapted to the end, skillfully used. God has provided that the work of conversion and sanctification shall in all cases be done by means of that kind of truth, applied in that connection and relation, which is fitted to produce such a result.

3. He has the powers of earth and hell to overcome, and that calls for wisdom. The devil is constantly at work, trying to prevent the success of ministers, laboring to divert the attention from the subject of religion, and to get the sinner away from God and lead him down to hell.[3] The whole frame-work of society, almost, is hostile to religion. Nearly all the influences which surround a man, from cradle to his grave, in the present state of society, are calculated to defeat the design of the ministry. Does not a minister then need great wisdom, to conflict with the powers of darkness and the whole influence of the world, in addition to the sinner's own opposition?

4. The same is seen from the infinite importance of the end

[2] For a discussion of Finney's concept of regeneration as opposed to that of the Old School Calvinists, see the Introduction to this edition, pp. xxix–xxxii.

[3] Finney was perfectly convinced that the devil existed as a malevolent personal force upon the earth, and in his *Memoirs* he speaks several times of ways in which the devil tried to kill him or otherwise thwart his revivals. See especially, *Memoirs*, p. 228.

itself. The end of the ministry, is the salvation of the soul. When we consider the importance of the end, and the difficulties of the work, who will not say with the apostle, "Who is sufficient for these things?"

5. He must understand how to wake up the church, and get them out of the way of the conversion of sinners. This is often the most difficult part of a minister's work, and requires more wisdom and patience than any thing else. Indeed, to do this successfully, is a most rare qualification in the Christian ministry. It is a point where almost all ministers fail. They know not how to wake up the church, and raise the tone of piety to a high standard, and thus clear the way for the work of conversion. Many ministers can preach to sinners very well, but gain little success, while the counteracting influence of the church resists it all, and they have not skill enough to remove the difficulty. There is only here and there a minister in the country, who knows how to probe the church when they are in a cold, backslidden state, so as effectually to wake them up, and *keep them* awake. The members of the church sin against such light, that when they become cold it is very difficult to rouse them up. They have a form of piety which wards off the truth, while at the same time it is just that kind of piety which has no power nor efficiency. Such professors are the most difficult individuals to arouse from their slumbers. I do not mean that they are always more wicked than the impenitent. They are often employed about the machinery of religion, and pass for very good Christians, but are of no use in a revival.

I know ministers are sometimes amazed to hear it said that churches are not awake. No wonder such ministers do not know how to wake a sleeping church. There was a young licentiate heard brother Foote the other day, in this city, pouring out truth, and trying to wake up the churches, and he knew so little about it, that he thought it was abusing the churches.[4] So perfectly blind was he that he really thought the churches in New York were all awake on the subject of religion. So some years ago there was a great controversy and opposition raised, because so much was said about the churches being asleep.[5] It was all truth, yet many ministers knew nothing about it, and were astonished to hear such

---

[4] Horatio Foote was an itinerant Presbyterian evangelist who had assisted Finney during his Oneida revivals. In 1837 Foote was unfrocked for seducing a girl. See Cross, *Burned-Over District*, pp. 194–195.

[5] This is a reference to the opposition led by Nettleton and Beecher in 1826–1827 to the Oneida revivals. See the Introduction to this edition, p. xxvii.

things said about the churches. When it has come to this, that *ministers* do not know when the church is asleep, no wonder that we have no revivals. I was invited once to preach at a certain place. I asked the minister what was the state of the church. "O," says he, "to a man they are awake." I was delighted at the idea of laboring in such a church, for it was a sight I had never yet seen, to see every single member awake in a revival. But when I got there, I found the church sleepy and cold, and I doubt whether one of them was awake.

Here is the great difficulty in keeping up revivals, to keep the church thoroughly awake and engaged. It is one thing for a church to get up in their sleep, and bluster about and run over each other; and a widely different thing for them to have their eyes open, and their senses about them, and be wide awake, so as to know how to find God, and how to work for Christ.

6. He must know how *to set the church to work, when they are awake.* If a minister attempts to go to work alone, calculating to do it all himself, it is like attempting to roll a great stone up a hill alone. The church can do much to help forward a revival. Churches have sometimes had powerful revivals without any minister. But when a minister has a church who are awake, and knows how to set them to work, and how to sit at the helm and guide them, he may feel strong, and oftentimes may find that they do more than he does himself, in the conversion of sinners.

7. In order to be successful, a minister needs great wisdom to *know how to keep the church to the work.* Often the church seem just like children. You set children to work, and they appear to be all engaged, but as soon as your back is turned, they will stop and go to play. The great difficulty in *continuing* a revival, lies here. And to meet it requires great wisdom. To know how to break them down again, when their heart gets lifted up because they have had such a great revival; to wake them up afresh when their zeal begins to flag; to keep their hearts full of zeal for the work; these are some of the most difficult things in the world. Yet if a minister would be successful in winning souls, he must know when they first begin to grow proud, or to lose the spirit of prayer, and when to probe them, and how to search them over again, how to keep the church in the field, gathering the harvest of the Lord.

8. He must *understand the gospel.* But you will ask, Do not all ministers understand the gospel? I answer, that they certainly do not all understand it alike, for they do not all preach alike.

9. He must know how to *divide* it, so as to bring forward the particular truths, in that order, and to make them bear upon those points and at such times, as are calculated to produce a given result. A minister should understand the philosophy of the human mind, so as to know how to plan and arrange his labors wisely. Truth, when brought to bear upon the mind, is in itself calculated to produce corresponding feelings. The minister must know what feelings he wishes to produce, and how to bring such truth to bear as is calculated to produce these feelings. He must know how to present truth calculated to humble Christians, or to make them feel for sinners, or to awaken sinners, or to convert them.[6]

Often, when sinners are awakened, the ground is lost for the want of wisdom in following up the blow. Perhaps a rousing sermon is preached, Christians are moved, and sinners begin to feel, and the next Sabbath something will be brought forward that has no connection with the state of feeling in the congregation, and that is not calculated to lead the mind on to the exercise of right feelings. It shows how important it is that a minister should understand how to produce a given impression, at what time it may and should be done, and by what truth, and how to follow it up, till the sinner is broken down and brought in.

A great many good sermons preached, are all lost for the want of a little wisdom here. They are good sermons, and calculated, if well timed, to do great good; but they have so little connection with the actual state of feeling in the congregation, that it would be more than a miracle if they should produce a revival. A minister may preach in this random way till he has preached himself to death, and never produce any great results. He may convert here and there a scattering soul; but he will not move the mass of the congregation, unless he knows how to follow up his impressions, to carry out a plan of operations and execute it, so as to carry on the work when it is begun. He must not only be able to blow the trumpet so loud as to start the sinner up from his lethargy, but when he is waked, he must lead him by the shortest way to Jesus Christ. And not as soon as sinners are roused by a sermon, immediately begin to preach about some remote subject, that has no tendency to carry on the work.

[6] Finney is simply saying that ministers must be good psychologists. Most ministers knew this, but few of them practised psychology as adroitly and self-consciously as Finney wanted them to do. Ever since the days of George Whitefield revival preachers have been accused of manipulating crowds by applied psychology. Finney tried to blunt this charge by indicating that God wanted all ministers to use "the laws of mind" to save souls.

10. To reach *different classes of sinners successfully*, requires great wisdom on the part of a minister. For instance, a sermon on a particular subject may start a particular class of persons among his hearers. Perhaps they will begin to look serious, or perhaps talk about it, or perhaps they will begin to cavil about it. Now, if the minister is wise, he will know how to observe those indications, and to follow right on with sermons adapted to this class, until he leads them into the kingdom of God. Then let him go back and take another class, find out where they are hid, break down their refuges, and follow them up, till he leads them into the kingdom of God. He should thus beat about every bush where sinners hide themselves, as the voice of God followed Adam in the garden — "ADAM, WHERE ART THOU?" till one class of hearers after another are brought in, and so the whole community converted. Now a minister must be very wise to do this. It never will be done so, till a minister sets himself to hunt out and bring in every class of sinners in his congregation, the old and young, male and female, rich and poor.

11. A minister needs great wisdom to get sinners away from their present refuges of lies, *without forming new hiding places for them*. I once sat under the ministry of a man who had contracted a great alarm about heresies, and was constantly employed in confuting them.[7] And he used to bring up many such heresies as his people never heard of. He got his ideas chiefly from books, and mingled very little among the people to know what they thought. And the result of his labors often was, that the people would be taken with the heresy, more than with the argument against it. The novelty of the error attracted their attention so much that they forgot the answer. And in that way, he gave many of his people new objections against religion, such as they never thought of before. If a man does not mingle enough with mankind to know how people think *now-a-days*, he cannot expect to be wise to meet their objections and difficulties.

I have heard a great deal of preaching against Universalists, that did more hurt than good, because the preachers did not under-

---

[7] Finney sat under the ministry of only two men. The first was Peter Starr, pastor of the Congregational Church in Warren, Connecticut, while Finney was preparing for Yale at the academy there in 1812–1814. The second was the Rev. George Washington Gale, pastor of the Presbyterian Church in Adams, New York, where Finney studied law in 1818–1821. Of the two, Gale is the more likely to have been the heresy-hunter, although he eventually became a New School leader. Note once again Finney's scorn for bookish ministers who refuse to mingle with the people.

stand how Universalists of the present day reason. They have never mingled with Universalists, and know not what they believe and how they argue, *now*, but have got all they know of Universalism from books that were written long ago, and are now out of date among Universalists themselves. And the consequence, is that when they attempt to preach against Universalism they oppose a man of straw, and not Universalist sentiments as they are now found in the community. And people either laugh at them, or say it is all lies, for they know Universalists do not hold such sentiments as are ascribed to them by the preacher.

When ministers undertake to oppose a present heresy, they ought to know what it is at present. For instance, almost all those who write and preach against Universalism think they are called upon to oppose the idea that God is all mercy. They suppose Universalists hold the doctrine that God is all mercy, and that when they have refuted this doctrine, they have got Universalists down. But this is not true. They do not hold such doctrine. They deny it altogether. They reject the idea of *mercy* in the salvation of men, for they hold that every man is punished in full according to his just deserts. Of what use is it then, to argue against Universalists, that God is a God of justice and not a God all mercy, when they hold to the justice of God alone as the ground of salvation, and do not admit the idea of mercy at all? In like manner, I have heard men preach against the idea that men are saved *in* their sins, and they supposed they were preaching down Universalist doctrine. Universalists believe no such thing. They believe that all men will be made holy, and saved in that way. This shows the importance of knowing what people actually hold, before you try to reason them out of their errors. It is of no use to misrepresent a man's doctrines to his face, and then try to reason him out of them. You must state his doctrine *just as he holds it*, and state his arguments fairly. Otherwise, if you state them wrong, you either make him angry, or he laughs in his sleeve at the advantage you give him. He will say, That man can't argue with me on fair grounds; he has to misrepresent our doctrines in order to confute me. Great hurt is done in this way. Ministers do not intend to misrepresent their opponents; but the effect of it is, that the poor miserable creatures who hold these errors go to hell, because ministers do not take care to inform themselves what are their real errors. Errors are never torn away by such a process. I mention these cases, to show how much wisdom a minister must have to meet the cases that occur. He must be acquainted with the real views of men in order to meet them, and do away their errors and mistakes.

12. Ministers ought to know *what measures* are best calculated to aid in accomplishing the great end of their office, the salvation of souls. Some measures are plainly necessary. By measures I mean what things should be done to get the attention of the people, and bring them to listen to the truth. Building houses for worship, and visiting from house to house, &c. are all "measures," the object of which is to get the attention of people to the gospel. Much wisdom is requisite to devise and carry forward all the various measures that are adapted to favor the success of the gospel.

What do the politicians do? They get up meetings, circulate handbills and pamphlets, blaze away in the newspapers, send their ships about the streets on wheels with flags and sailors, send coaches all over town, with handbills, to bring people up to the polls, all to gain attention to their cause and elect their candidate. All these are their "measures," and for their *end* they are wisely calculated. The object is to get up an excitement, and bring the people out. They know that unless there can be an excitement it is in vain to push their end. I do not mean to say that their measures are pious, or right, but only that they are wise, in the sense that they are the appropriate application of means to the end.

The object of the ministry is to get all the people to feel that the devil has no right to rule this world, but that they ought all to give themselves to God, and vote in the Lord Jesus Christ as the governor of the universe. Now what shall be done? What measures shall we take? Says one, "Be sure and have nothing that is new." Strange! The object of our measures is to gain attention, and you *must have* something new. As sure as the effect of a measure becomes stereotyped, it ceases to gain attention, and then you must try something new. You need not make innovations in every thing. But whenever the state of things is such that any thing *more* is needed, it must be something *new*, otherwise it will fail. A minister should never introduce innovations that are not called for. If he does, they will embarrass him. He cannot alter the gospel; that remains the same. But new measures are necessary from time to time, to awaken attention, and bring the gospel to bear upon the public mind. And then a minister ought to know how to introduce new things, so as to create the least possible resistance or reaction. Mankind are fond of *form* in religion. They love to have their religious duties stereotyped, so as to leave them at ease. And they are therefore inclined to resist any new movement, designed to rouse them up to action and feeling. Hence it is all-important to introduce new things wisely, so as not to give needless occasion or apology for resistance.

13. Not a little wisdom is sometimes needed by a minister, to know *when to put a stop to new measures*. When a measure has novelty enough to secure attention to the truth, ordinarily no other new measure should be introduced. You have secured the great object of novelty. Any thing more will be in danger of *diverting* the public mind away from the great object, and fixing it on the measures themselves. And then, if you introduce novelties when they are not called for, you will go over so large a field, that by and by when you really want something new, you will have nothing else to introduce, without doing something that will give too great a shock to the public mind. The Bible has laid down no specific course of measures to promote revivals of religion, but has left it to ministers to adopt such as are wisely calculated to secure the end. And the more sparing we are of our new things, the longer we can use them, to keep public attention awake to the great subject of religion. By a wise course this may undoubtedly be done for a long series of years, until our *present* measures will by and by have sufficient novelty in them again, to attract and fix public attention. And so we shall never want for something *new*.

14. A minister, to win souls, must know how to deal with *careless*, with *awakened*, and with *anxious* sinners, so as to lead them right to Christ in the shortest and most direct way. It is amazing to see how many ministers there are who do not know how to deal with sinners, or what to say to them in their various states of mind. A good woman in Albany told me, that when she was under concern she went to her minister, and asked him to tell her what she must do to get relief. And he said God had not given him much experience on the subject, and advised her to go to such a deacon, who perhaps could tell her what to do. The truth was, he did not know what to say to a sinner under conviction, although there was nothing peculiar in her case. Now if you think this minister a rare case, you are quite deceived. There are many ministers who do not know what to say to sinners.

A minister once appointed an anxious meeting, and went to attend it, and instead of going round to the individuals, he began to ask them the catechism, "Wherein doth Christ execute the office of a priest?" About as much in point to a great many of their minds as any thing else.

I know a minister who held an anxious meeting, and went to attend it with a *written discourse*, which he had prepared for the occasion. Just as wise it would be if a physician, going out to visit his patients, should sit down at leisure and write all the prescriptions before he had seen them. A minister needs to know the state of mind of the individuals, before he can know what truth will be proper and useful to administer. I say these things, not because I love to do it, but because truth, and the object before me, requires them to be said. And such instances as I have mentioned are by no means rare.

A minister should know how to apply truth to all the situations in which he may find dying sinners going down to hell. He should know how to preach, how to pray, how to conduct prayer meetings, and how to use all the means for bringing the truth of God to bear upon the kingdom of darkness. Does not this require wisdom? And who is sufficient for these things?

II. The amount of a minister's success in winning souls (*other things being equal*) invariably decides the amount of wisdom he has exercised in the discharge of his office.[8]

1. This is plainly asserted in the text. "He that winneth souls is wise." That is, if a man wins souls, *he does* skillfully adapt means to the end, which is, to exercise wisdom. He is the more wise, by how much the greater is the number of sinners that he saves. A blockhead may indeed now and then stumble on such truth, or such a manner of exhibiting it, as to save a soul. It would be a wonder indeed if any minister did not sometimes have something in his sermons that would meet the case of some individual. But the amount of wisdom is to be decided, "other things being equal," by the *number* of cases in which he is successful in converting sinners.

Take the case of a physician. The greatest quack in New York may now and then stumble upon a remarkable cure, and so get his name up with the ignorant. But sober and judicious people judge of the skill of a physician by the *uniformity* of his success

---

[8] Finney's use of conversion totals as the criterion of success led inevitably to a statistical approach to evangelism, which became a great source of criticism in succeeding years. Professional evangelists have deplored this criterion but have seldom failed to utilize it.

in overcoming disease, the variety of diseases he can manage, and the number of cases in which he is successful in saving his patients. The most skillful saves the most. This is common sense. It is truth. And it is just as true in regard to success in saving souls, and true in just the same sense.

2. This principle is not only asserted in the text, but it is a *matter of fact*, a historical truth, that "He that winneth souls is wise." He has actually employed means adapted to the end, in such a way as to secure the end.

3. Success in saving souls is evidence that a man understands the gospel, and understands human nature, that he knows how to adapt means to his end, he has common sense, and that he has that kind of tact, that practical discernment, to know how to get at people. And if his success is extensive, it shows that he knows how to deal with a great variety of characters, in a great variety of circumstances, who are yet all the enemies of God, and to bring them to Christ. To do this, requires great wisdom. And the minister who does it, shows that he is wise.

4. Success in winning souls shows that a minister not only knows how to labor wisely for that end, but also, that he *knows where his dependence is*. You know that fears are often expressed respecting those ministers who are aiming most directly and earnestly for the conversion of sinners. People say, "Why, this man is going to work in his own strength; one would imagine he thinks he can convert himself." How often has the event showed that the man knows what he is about, very well, and knows where his strength is too. He went to work to convert sinners so earnestly, just as if he could do it all himself; but that was the very way he should do. He *ought* to reason with sinners, and plead with them, as faithfully and fully, as if he did not expect any interposition of the Spirit of God, or as if he knew there was no Holy Ghost. But whenever a man does this successfully, it shows that, after all, he knows he must depend on the Spirit of God alone for success.

OBJECTION. — There are many who feel an objection against this subject, arising out of the view they have taken of the ministry of Jesus Christ. They ask us, "What will you say about the ministry of Jesus Christ, was not he wise?" I answer, Yes, infinitely wise. But in regard to his alleged want of success in the conversion of sinners, you will observe the following things:

(1.) That his ministry was vastly more successful than is

generally supposed. We read in one of the sacred writers, that after his resurrection and before his ascension "he was seen by above five hundred brethren at once." If so many as five hundred brethren were found assembled together at one place, we see there must have been a vast number of them scattered over the country.

(2.) Another circumstance to be observed is, that his public ministry was *very short*, less than three years.

(3.) Consider the peculiar *design* of his ministry. His main object was to make atonement for the sins of the world. It was not aimed so much at promoting revivals. The "dispensation of the Spirit" was not yet given. He did not preach the gospel so fully as his apostles did afterwards. The prejudices of the people were so fixed and violent that they would not bear it. That he did not, is plain from the fact that even his apostles, who were constantly with him, did not understand the atonement. They did not get the idea that he was going to die, and consequently, when they heard he was actually dead, they were driven to despair, and thought the thing was all gone by, and their hopes blown to the winds. The fact was, that he had another object in view, to which every thing else was made to yield, and the perverted state of the public mind, and the obstinate prejudices prevailing, showed why results were not seen any more in the conversion of sinners. The state of public opinion was such, that they finally murdered him for what he did preach.

Many ministers who have little or no success, are hiding themselves behind the ministry of Jesus Christ, as if he was an unsuccessful preacher. Whereas, in fact, he was eminently successful, considering the circumstances in which he labored. This is the last place in all the world where a minister who has no success should think of hiding himself.

REMARKS.

1. A minister may be *very learned and not wise*. There are many ministers possessed of great learning; they understand all the sciences, physical, moral, and theological; they may know the dead languages, and possess all learning, and yet not be *wise*, in relation to the great end about which they are chiefly employed. Facts clearly demonstrate this. "He that *winneth souls* is wise."

2. An unsuccessful minister may be *pious* as well as learned,

and yet not wise. It is unfair to infer because a minister is unsuccessful, that therefore he is a hypocrite. There may be something defective in his education, or in his mode of viewing a subject, or of exhibiting it, or such a want of *common sense*, as will defeat his labors, and prevent his success in winning souls, while he himself may be saved — "yet so as by fire."

3. A minister may be *very wise*, though he is *not learned*. He may not understand the dead languages, or theology in its common acceptation; and yet he may know just what a minister of the gospel wants most to know, without knowing many other things. A learned minister and a wise minister are different things. Facts in the history of the church in all ages prove this. It is very common for churches, when looking out for a minister, to aim at getting a very learned man. Do not understand me to disparage learning. The more learning the better, if he is also wise in the great matter he is employed about. If a minister knows how to win souls, the more learning he has the better. But if he has any other kind of learning, and *not this*, he will infallibly fail of the end of his ministry.

4. Want of success in a minister (*other things being equal*) proves, (1.) either that he was never called to preach, and has taken it up out of his own head; or (2.) that he was badly educated, and was never taught the very things he wants most to know; or (3.) if he was called to preach, and knows how to do his duty, he is too indolent and too wicked to do it.

5. Those are the *best educated ministers*, who win the most souls. Ministers are sometimes looked down upon, and called very ignorant, because they do not know the sciences and languages; although they are very far from being ignorant of the *great thing* for which the ministry is appointed. This is wrong. Learning is important, and always useful. But after all, a minister may know how to win souls to Christ, without *great* learning, and he has the best education *for a minister*, who can win the most souls to Christ.

6. There is evidently a great defect in the present mode of educating ministers. This is a SOLEMN FACT, to which the attention of the whole church should be distinctly called; that the great mass of young ministers who are educated accomplish very little.

When young men come out from the seminaries, are they fit to go into a revival? Look at a place where there has been a revival in progress, and a minister is wanted. Let them send to a theological seminary for a minister. Will he enter into the work, and sustain it, and carry it on? Seldom. Like David with Saul's armor, he comes in with such a load of theological trumpery, that he knows nothing what to do. Leave him there for two weeks, and the revival is at an end. The churches know and feel, *that the greater part* of these young men do not know how to do any thing that needs to be done for a revival, and they are complaining that the young ministers are so far behind the church. You may send all over the United States, to theological seminaries, and find *but few* young ministers fitted to carry forward the work. What a state of things!

There is a grand defect in educating ministers. Education ought to be such, as to prepare young men for the *peculiar work to which they are destined*. But instead of this, they are educated for any thing else. The grand mistake is this. They direct the mind *too much to irrelevant matters*, which are not necessary to be attended to. In their courses of study, they carry the mind over too wide a field, which diverts their attention from the main thing, and so they get cold in religion, and when they get through, instead of being fitted for their work, they are *unfitted* for it. Under pretence of disciplining the mind, they in fact scatter the attention, so that when they come to their work, they are awkward, and know nothing how to take hold, or how to act, to win souls. This is not universally the case, but too often it is so.

It is common for people to talk loudly and largely about an educated ministry. God forbid that I should say a word against an educated ministry. But what do we mean by an education for the ministry? Do we mean that they should be so educated, as to be fitted for the work? If they are so educated, the more education the better. Let education be of the right kind, teaching a young man the things he wants to know, and not the very things he don't want to know. Let them be educated *for the work*. Do not let education be such, that when young men come out, after spending six, eight, or ten years in study, they are not worth half as much as they were before they went. I have known young men come out after what they call "a thorough course," who were not fit to take charge of a prayer meeting, and who could not manage a prayer meeting, so as to make it profitable or interesting. An elder of a church in a neighboring city, informed me recently of a case in point. A young man, before he went to the seminary, had labored as a layman with them, conducted their prayer meetings, and had been exceedingly useful among them. After he had been to the seminary, they sent for him and desired his help; but O, how changed! he was so completely transformed, that he made no impression; the church soon began to complain that they should die under his influences, and he left, because he was not prepared for the work.

It is common for those ministers who have been to the seminaries, and are now useful, to affirm that their course of studies there did them little or no good, and that they had to *unlearn* what they had there learned, before they could effect much. I do not say this censoriously, but it is a solemn fact, and I must say it in love.

Suppose you were going to make a man a surgeon in the navy. Instead of sending him to the medical school to learn surgery, would you send him to the nautical school to learn navigation? In this way, you might qualify him to navigate a ship, but he is no surgeon. Ministers should be educated to know what the Bible is, and what the human mind is, and know how to bring one to bear on the other. They should be brought into contact with mind, and made familiar with all the aspects of society. They should have the Bible in one hand, and the map of the human mind in the other, and know how to use the truth for the salvation of men.

7. A *want of common sense* often defeats the ends of the Christian ministry. There are many good men in the ministry, who have learning, and talents of a certain sort, but they have no common sense to win souls.

8. We see one great defect in our theological schools. — Young men are shut up in their schools, confined to books and shut out from intercourse with the common people, or contact with the common mind. Hence they are not familiar with the mode in which common people think. This accounts for the fact that some plain men, that have been brought up to business, and acquainted with human nature, are ten times better qualified to win souls than those who are educated on the present principle, and are in fact ten times as well acquainted with the proper business of the ministry. These are called "uneducated men." This is a grand mistake. They are not learned in science, but they are learned in the very things which they need to know *as ministers*. They are not ignorant ministers, for they know exactly how to reach the mind with truth. They understand the minds of men, and how

to adapt the gospel to their case. They are better furnished *for their work*, than if they had all the machinery of the schools.

I wish to be understood. I do not say, that I would not have a young man go to school. Nor would I discourage him from going over the field of science. The more the better, if together with it he learns also *the things* that the minister needs to know, in order to win souls, — if he understands his Bible, and understands human nature, and knows how to bring the truth to bear, and how to guide and manage minds, and to lead them away from sin and lead them to God.

9. The success of any measure designed to promote a revival of religion, demonstrates its wisdom; with the following exceptions:

(1.) A measure may be introduced *for effect* to produce excitement, and be such that when it is looked back upon afterwards, it will look nonsensical, and appear to have been a mere trick. In that case, it will re-act, and its introduction will do more hurt than good.

(2.) Measures may be introduced, and the revival be very powerful, and the success be attributed to the *measures*, when in fact other things made the revival powerful, and these very measures may have been a hinderance. The prayers of Christians, and the preaching, and other things may have been so well calculated to carry on the work, that it has succeeded *in spite* of these measures.

But when the blessing evidently follows the introduction of the *measure itself*, the proof is unanswerable, that the measure is wise. It is profane to say that such a measure will do more hurt than good. God knows about that. His object is, to do the *greatest amount* of good possible. And of course he will not add his blessing to a measure that will do more hurt than good. He may sometimes withhold his blessing from a measure that is calculated to do some good because it will be at the expense of a greater good. But he never will bless a pernicious proceeding. There is no such thing as *deceiving* God in the matter. He knows whether a given measure is on the whole, wise, or not. He may bless a course of labors notwithstanding some unwise or injurious measures. But if he blesses the *measure itself*, it is rebuking God to pronounce it unwise. He who undertakes to do this, let him look to the matter.

10. It is evident that much fault has been found with measures, which have been *pre-eminently and continually blessed* of God for the promotion of revivals. We know it is said that the horrid oaths of a profane swearer have been the means of awakening another less hardened sinner. But this is a rare case. God does not usually make such a use of profanity. But if a measure is *continually or usually* blessed, let the man who thinks he is wiser than God, call it in question. TAKE CARE! how you find fault with God.[9]

11. Christians should *pray for ministers*. Brethren, if you felt how much ministers need wisdom to perform the duties of their great office with success, and how ignorant they all are, and how insufficient they are of themselves, to think any thing as of themselves, you would pray for them a great deal more than you do; that is, if you cared any thing for the success of their labors. People often find fault with ministers, when they don't pray for them. Brethren, this is tempting God, for you ought not to expect any better ministers, unless you pray for them. And you ought not to expect a blessing on the labors of your minister, or to have your families converted by his preaching, where you do not pray for him. And so for others, the waste places, and the heathen, instead of praying all the time, only that God would sent out *more* laborers, you have need to pray that God would make ministers *wise to win souls*, and that those he sends out may be *properly* educated, so that they shall be scribes well instructed in the kingdom of God.

12. Those *laymen* in the church who know how to win souls are to be counted wise. They should not be called "ignorant laymen." And those church members who do not know how to convert sinners, and who cannot win souls, should not be called wise — *as Christians*. They are not wise Christians; only "he that winneth souls is wise." They may be learned in politics, in all sciences, or they may be skilled in the management of business, or other things, and they may look down on those who win souls, as nothing but plain, simple-hearted and ignorant men. If any of you are inclined to do this, and to undervalue those brethren who win souls, as being not so wise and cunning as you are, you deceive yourselves. They may not know some things which you know. But they know those things which a Christian is *most concerned* to know, and you do not.

[9] This arrogant assumption that to criticize a successful revivalist was to "find fault with God" was particularly resented by the Old School Calvinists.

It may be illustrated by the case of a minister that goes to sea. He may be learned in science, but he knows nothing how to sail a ship. And he begins to ask the sailors about this thing and that, and what is this rope for, and the like. "Why," say the sailors, "these are not *ropes*, we have only one rope in a ship, these are the rigging, the man talks like a fool." And so this learned man becomes a laughing-stock, perhaps, to the sailors, because he does not know how to sail a ship. But if he were to tell them one half of what he knows about science, perhaps they would think him a conjurer, to know so much. So learned students may understand their *hic, hac, hoc*, very well, and may laugh at the humble Christian, and call him ignorant, although he may know how to win more souls than five hundred of them.

I was once distressed and grieved at hearing a minister bearing down upon a young preacher, who had been converted under remarkable circumstances, and who was licensed to preach, without pursuing a regular course of study. This minister, who was never, or at least rarely known to convert a soul, bore down upon the young man in a very lordly, censorious manner, depreciating him because he had not had the advantage of a liberal education, when in fact he was instrumental in converting more souls than any five hundred ministers like himself.

I would say nothing to undervalue, or lead you to undervalue a thorough education for ministers. But I do not call that a *thorough education*, which they get in our colleges and seminaries. It does not fit them for *their work*. I appeal to all experience, whether our young men in seminaries are thoroughly educated for the purpose of winning souls. Do THEY DO IT? Every body knows they do not. Look at the reports of the Home Missionary Society.[10] If I recollect right, in 1830, the number of conversions in connection with the labors of the missionaries of that society did not exceed five to each missionary. I believe the number has increased since, but is still exceedingly small to what it would have been had they been fitted by a right course of training for their work. I do not

---

[10] The American Home Missionary Society was formed in 1826 as a part of the Plan of Union between the Presbyterian and Congregational Churches. Its principal function was to supply the ministers and ministerial salaries for new churches in the West. It tried to keep its standards for a learned ministry high and thus earned the enmity of Finney. But as it was dominated by Congregationalists it also lost the confidence of the Presbyterian Church. See Cross, *Burned-Over District*, pp. 22ff., and James H. Hotchkin, *A History of the Purchase and Settlement of Western New York* (New York, 1848), pp. 197ff.

say this to reproach them, for from my heart I pity them, and I pity the church for being under the necessity of supporting ministers so trained, or none at all. They are the best men the Missionary Society can obtain. I suppose, of course, that I shall be reproached for saying this. But it is too true and too painful to be concealed. Those fathers who have the training of our young ministers are good men, but they are ancient men, men of another age and stamp, from what is needed in these days of excitement, when the church and world are rising to new thought and action. Those dear fathers will not, I suppose, see this; and will perhaps think hard of me for saying it; but it is the cause of Christ. Some of them are getting back toward second childhood, and ought to resign, and give place to younger men, who are not rendered physically incapable, by age, of keeping pace with the onward movements of the church. And here I would say, that to my own mind, it appears evident, that unless our theological professors preach a good deal, mingle much with the church, and sympathise with her in all her movements, it is morally, if not naturally impossible, that they should succeed in training young men to the spirit of the age. It is a shame and a sin, that theological professors, who preach but seldom, who are withdrawn from the active duties of the ministry, should sit in their studies and write their letters, advisory, or dictatorial, to ministers and churches who are in the field, and who are in circumstances to judge what needs to be done. The men who spend all or at least a portion of their time in the active duties of the ministry, are the only men who are able to judge of what is expedient or inexpedient, prudent or imprudent, as to measures from time to time. And it is as dangerous and ridiculous for our theological professors, who are withdrawn from the field of conflict, to be allowed to dictate, in regard to the measures and movements of the church, as it would be for a general to sit in his bed-chamber and attempt to order a battle.

Two ministers were one day conversing about another minister whose labors were greatly blessed in the conversion of some thousands of souls. One of them said, "That man ought not to preach any more; he should stop and go to" a particular theological seminary which he named, "and go through a regular course of study." He said the man had "a good mind, and if he was thoroughly educated, he might be very useful." The other replied, "Do you think he would be more useful for going to that seminary? I challenge you to show by facts that any are more useful who have been there. No, sir, the fact is, that since this man has been in the ministry, he has been instrumental in converting more souls than all the young men who have come from that seminary in the time." This is logic! Stop, and go to a seminary, to prepare himself for converting souls, when he is now converting more than all who come from the seminary!

FINALLY — I wish to ask you, before I sit down, who among you can lay any claim to the possession of this Divine wisdom? Who among you, laymen? Who among you, ministers? Can any of you? Can I? Are we at work, wisely, to win souls? Or are we trying to make ourselves believe that success is no criterion of wisdom? *It is* a criterion. It is a safe criterion for every minister to try himself by. The amount of his successes, *other things being equal*, measures the amount of wisdom he has exercised in the discharge of his office.

How few of you have ever had wisdom enough to convert so much as a single sinner!

Don't say now, "I cannot convert sinners; how can I convert sinners? God alone can convert sinners." Look at the text, "He that winneth souls is wise," and do not think you can escape the sentence. It is true that God converts sinners. But there is a sense, too, in which ministers convert them. And you have something to do; something that requires wisdom; something which, if you do it wisely, will insure the conversion of sinners in proportion to the wisdom employed. If you never have done this, it is high time to think about yourselves, and see whether you have wisdom enough to save even your own souls.

Men — women — you are bound to be wise in winning souls. Perhaps already souls have perished; perhaps a friend, or a child is in hell, because you have not put forth the wisdom which you might, in saving them. The city is going to hell. Yes, the world is going to hell, and must go on, till the church finds out what to do, to win souls. Politicians are wise. The children of this world are wise, they know what to do to accomplish their ends, while we are prosing about, not knowing what to do, or where to take hold of the work, and sinners are going to hell.[11]

[11] This pessimism is part of Finney's peroration and is not typical of his outlook.

XII

HOW TO PREACH THE GOSPEL

Text. — "He that winneth souls is wise." — Proverbs xi. 30.

One of the last remarks in my last lecture, was this, that the text ascribes conversion to men. Winning souls is converting men. This evening I design to show,

I. That several passages of Scripture ascribe conversion to men.

II. That this is consistant with other passages which ascribe conversion to God.

III. I purpose to discuss several further particulars which are deemed important, in regard to the preaching of the gospel, and which show that great practical wisdom is necessary to win souls to Christ.

I. I am to show that the Bible ascribes conversion to men.

There are many passages which represent the conversion of sinners as the work of men. In Daniel, xii. 3, it is said, "And they that be wise, shall shine as the brightness of the firmament; and they that turn many to righteousness as stars for ever and ever." Here the work is ascribed to men. So also in 1 Cor. iv. 15. "For though ye have ten thousand instructors in Christ, yet have ye not many fathers: for in Christ Jesus I have begotten you through the gospel." Here the apostle explicitly tells the Corinthians that he made them Christians, with the gospel or truth which he preached. Again, in James, v. 19, 20, we are taught the same thing. "Brethren, if any of you do err from the truth, and one convert him; let him know that he which converteth the sinner from the error of his way shall save a soul from death, and shall hide a multitude of sins." I might quote many other passages, equally explicit. But these are sufficient abundantly to establish the fact, that the Bible does actually ascribe conversion to men.

II. I proceed to show that this is not inconsistent with those passages in which conversion is ascribed to God.

And here let me remark, that to my mind it often appears very strange that men should ever suppose there was an inconsistency here, or that they should ever have overlooked the plain common sense of the matter. How easy it is to see, that there is a sense in which *God* converts them, and another sense in which *men* convert them.

The Scriptures ascribe the conversion of a sinner to four different agencies — to *men*, to *God*, to the *truth*, and to the *sinner himself*. The passages which ascribe it to the truth are the largest class. That men should ever have overlooked this distinction, and should have regarded conversion as a work performed exclusively by God, is surprising. Or that any difficulty should ever have been felt on the subject, or that people should ever have professed themselves unable to reconcile these several classes of passages.

Why, the Bible speaks on this subject, precisely as we speak on common subjects. There is a man who has been very sick. How natural it is for him to say of his physician, "That man saved my life." Does he mean to say that the physician saved his life without reference to God? Certainly not, unless he is an infidel? God made the physician, and he made the medicine too. And it never can be shown but that the agency of God is just as truly concerned in making the medicine take effect to save life, as it is in making the truth take effect to save a soul. To affirm the contrary is downright atheism. It is true then, that the physician saved him, and it is also true that God saved him. It is equally true that the medicine saved his life, and that he saved his own life by taking the medicine; for the medicine would have done no good if he had not voluntarily taken it, or yielded his body to its power.

In the conversion of a sinner, it is true that God gives the truth efficiency to turn the sinner to God. He is an active, voluntary, powerful agent in changing the mind. But he is not the only agent. The one who brings the truth to his notice is also an agent. We are apt to speak of ministers and other men as only *instruments* in converting sinners. This is not exactly correct. Man is something more than an instrument. Truth is the mere unconscious instrument. But man is more, he is a voluntary, responsible agent in the business. In my printed sermon, No. 1. which some of you may have seen, I have illustrated this idea by the case of an individual standing on the banks of Niagara.[1]

---

[1] This sermon, entitled "Sinners Bound to Change Their Own Hearts," was first delivered in Boston in October 1831. For a discussion of the furor it aroused at that time see McLoughlin, *Modern Revivalism*, pp. 73ff. Finney first published

Suppose yourself to be standing on the banks of the Falls of Niagara. As you stand upon the verge of the precipice, you behold a man lost in deep reverie, approaching its verge unconscious of his danger. He approaches nearer and nearer until he actually lifts his foot to take the final step that shall plunge him in destruction. At this moment you lift your warning voice above the roar of the foaming waters, and cry out, *Stop*. The voice pierces his ear, and breaks the charm that binds him; he turns instantly upon his heel, all pale and aghast he retires, quivering, from the verge of death. He reels and almost swoons with horror; turns and walks slowly to the public house; you follow him; the manifest agitation in his countenance calls numbers around him; and on *your* approach, he points to you, and says, That man saved my life. Here he ascribes the work to you; and certainly there is a sense in which you had saved him. But, on being further questioned, he says, *Stop!* how that word rings in my ears. Oh, that was to me the word of life! Here he ascribes it to the *word* that aroused him, and caused him to turn. But, on conversing still further, he says, Had I not turned at that instant, I should have been a dead man. Here he speaks of it, and truly, as his own act; but directly you hear him say, O the mercy of God! if God had not interposed, I should have been lost. Now the only defect in this illustration is this: In the case supposed, the only interference on the part of God, was a *providential* one; and the only sense in which the saving of the man's life is ascribed to him, is in a providential sense. But in the conversion of a sinner, there is something more than the providence of God employed; for here not only does the providence of God so order it, that the preacher cries, *Stop*, but the Spirit of God urges the truth home upon him with such tremendous power as to induce him to turn.

Not only does the preacher cry, *Stop*, but through the living voice of the preacher, the Spirit cries, *Stop*. The preacher cries, "Turn ye, why will ye die." The Spirit pours the expostulation home with such power, that the sinner turns. Now in speaking of this change, it is perfectly proper to say, that the Spirit turned him, just as you would say of a man, who had persuaded another to change his mind on the subject of politics, that he had converted him, and brought him over. It is also proper to say that the truth converted him; as in a case when the political sentiments of a man were changed by a certain argument, we should say that argument brought him over. So also with perfect propriety may we ascribe the change to the living preacher, or to him who had presented the motives; just as we should say of a lawyer who had prevailed in his argument with a jury; he has got his case, he

---

the sermon in pamphlet form in December 1834 or January 1835. It also appeared as the first sermon in his volume, *Sermons on Various Subjects* (New York, 1835). For a discussion of the review of this sermon by the Princeton Calvinist, Albert Dod, see the Introduction to this edition.

has converted the jury. It is also with the same propriety ascribed to the individual himself whose heart is changed; we should say that he had changed his mind, he has come over, he has repented. Now it is strictly true, and true in the most absolute and highest sense: the act is his own act, the turning is his own turning, while God by the truth has induced him to turn; still it is strictly true that he has turned and has done it himself. Thus you see the sense in which it is the work of God, and also the sense in which it is the sinner's own work. The Spirit of God, by truth, influences the sinner to change, and in this sense is the efficient cause of the change. But the sinner actually changes, and is therefore himself, in the most proper sense, the author of the change. There are some who, on reading their Bibles, fasten their eyes upon those passages that ascribe the work to the Spirit of God, and seem to overlook those that ascribe it to man, and speak of it as the sinner's own act. When they have quoted Scripture to prove it is the work of God, they seem to think they have proved that it is that in which man is passive, and that it can in no sense be the work of man. Some months since a tract was written, the title of which was, *Regeneration, the effect of Divine Power*.[2] The writer goes on to prove that the work is wrought by the Spirit of God, and there stops. Now it had been just as true, just as philosophical, and just as scriptural, if he had said, that conversion was the work of man. It was easy to prove that it was the work of God, in the sense in which I have explained it. The writer, therefore, tells the truth, so far as he goes; but he has told only half the truth. For while there is a sense in which it is the work of God, as he has shown, there is also a sense in which it is the work of man, as we have just seen. The very title to this tract is a stumbling block. It tells the truth, but it does not tell the whole truth. And a tract might be written upon this proposition, that *Conversion or regeneration is the work of man*; which would be just as true, just as scriptural, and just as philosophical, as the one to which I have alluded. Thus the writer, in his zeal to recognise and honor God as concerned in this work, by leaving out the fact that a change of heart is the sinner's *own act*, has left the sinner strongly intrenched, with his weapons in his rebellious hands, stoutly resisting the claims of his Maker, and waiting passively for God to make him a new heart. Thus you see the consistency between the requirement of the text, and the declared fact that God is the author of the new heart. God commands you to do it, expects you to do it, and if it ever is done, you must do it.

And let me tell you, sinner, if you do not do it you will go to hell, and to all eternity you will feel that you *deserved* to be sent there for not having done it.

[2] I have been unable to discover the author of this tract.

III. As proposed, I shall now advert to several important particulars growing out of this subject, as connected with preaching the gospel, and which show that great practical wisdom is indispensable to win souls to Christ.

And FIRST, in regard to the MATTER OF PREACHING.

1. All preaching should be *practical*.

The proper end of all doctrine is practice. Any thing brought forward as doctrine, which cannot be made use of as practical, is not preaching the gospel. There is none of that sort of preaching in the Bible. That is all practical. "All Scripture is given by inspiration of God, and is profitable for doctrine, for reproof, for correction, for instruction in righteousness: that the man of God may be perfect, thoroughly furnished unto all good works." A vast deal of preaching in the present day, as well as in past ages, is called *doctrinal*, as opposed to *practical* preaching. The very idea of making this distinction is a device of the devil. And a more abominable device Satan himself never devised. You sometimes hear certain men tell a wonderful deal about the necessity of "indoctrinating the people." By which they mean something different from practical preaching; teaching them certain doctrines, as abstract truths, without any particular reference to practice. And I have known a minister in the midst of a revival, while surrounded with anxious sinners, leave off laboring to convert souls, for the purpose of "indoctrinating" the young converts, for fear somebody else should indoctrinate them before him. And there the revival stops! Either his doctrine was not true, or it was not preached in the right way. To preach doctrines in an abstract way, and not in reference to practice, is absurd. God always brings in doctrine to regulate practice. To bring forward doctrinal views for any other object is not only nonsense, but it is wicked.

Some people are opposed to *doctrinal* preaching. If they have been used to hear doctrines preached in a cold, abstract way, no wonder they are opposed to it. They ought to be opposed to such preaching. But what can a man preach, who preaches no doctrine? If he preaches no doctrine, he preaches no gospel. And if he does not preach it in a practical way, he does not preach the gospel. All preaching should be doctrinal, and all preaching should be practical. The very design of doctrine is to regulate practice. Any preaching that has not this tendency is not the gospel. A loose, exhortatory style of preaching, may affect the passions, and may produce excitement, but will never sufficiently instruct the people to secure sound conversions. On the other hand, preaching doctrine in an abstract manner, may fill the head with *notions*, but will never sanctify the heart or life.

2. Preaching should be *direct*. The gospel should be preached *to* men, and not *about* them. The minister must address his hearers. He must preach *to* them *about themselves*, and not leave the impression that he is preaching to them about others. He will never do them any good, farther than he succeeds in convincing each individual that he means him. Many preachers seem very much afraid of making the impression that they mean any body in particular. They are preaching against certain *sins*, not that have any thing to do with the *sinner*. It is the *sin*, and not the *sinner*, that they are rebuking; and they would by no means speak as if they supposed any of *their hearers* were guilty of these abominable practices. Now this is any thing but preaching the gospel. Thus did not the prophets, nor Christ, nor the apostles. Nor do those ministers do this, who are successful in winning souls to Christ.

3. Another very important thing to be regarded in preaching, is, that the minister should hunt after sinners and Christians, wherever they may have intrenched themselves in inaction. It is not the design of preaching, to make men easy and quiet, but to make them ACT. It is not the design of calling in a physician to have him give opiates, and so cover up the disease and let it run on till it works death; but to search out the disease wherever it may be hidden, and to remove it. So if a professor of religion has backslidden, and is full of doubts and fears, it is not the minister's duty to quiet him in his sins, and comfort him, but to hunt him out of his errors and backslidings, and show him just where he stands, and what it is that makes him full of doubts and fears.[3]

A minister ought to know the religious opinions of every sinner in his congregation. Indeed, a minister in the country is inexcusable if he does not. He has no excuse for not knowing the religious views of all his congregation, and of all that may come under his influence. How otherwise can he preach to them? How can he know how to bring forth things new and old, and adapt truth to their case? How can he hunt them out unless he knows where they hide themselves? He may ring changes on a few fundamental doctrines, Repentance and Faith, and Faith and Repentance, till the day of judgment, and never make any impression on many

---

[3] This paragraph did not appear in the version of this lecture printed in the *New York Evangelist*, February 21, 1835, p. 30.

minds. Every sinner has some hiding place, some intrenchment where he lingers. He is in possession of some darling LIE, with which he is quieting himself. Let the minister find it out and get it away, either in the pulpit or in private, or the man will go to hell in his sins, and his blood will be found in the minister's skirts.

4. Another important thing to observe, is that a minister should dwell most on those particular points which are most needed. I will explain what I mean.

Sometimes he may find a people who have been led to place great reliance on their own resolutions. They think they can consult their own convenience, and by and by they will repent, when they get ready, without any concern about the Spirit of God. Let him take up these notions, and show that they are entirely contrary to the Scriptures. Let him show that if the Spirit of God is grieved away, *however able* he may be, it is *certain he never will* repent, and that by and by, when it shall be convenient for him to do it, he will have no inclination. The minister who finds these errors prevailing, should expose them. He should hunt them out, and understand just how they are held, and then preach the class of truths which will show the fallacy, the folly, and the danger of these notions.

So on the other hand. He may find a people who have got such views of Election and Sovereignty, as to think they have nothing to do but to wait for the moving of the waters. Let him go right over against them, and crowd upon them their ability to obey God, and to show their obligation and duty, and press them with that until he brings them to submit and be saved. They have got behind a perverted view of these doctrines, and there is no way to drive them out of the hiding place but to set them right *on these points*. Wherever a sinner is intrenched, unless you pour light upon him *there*, you will never move him. It is of no use to press him with those truths which he admits, however plainly they may in fact contradict his wrong notions. *He supposes* them to be perfectly consistent, and does not see the inconsistency, and therefore it will not move him, or bring him to repentance.

I have been informed of a minister in New England, who was settled in a congregation which had long enjoyed little else than Arminian preaching, and the congregation themselves were chiefly Arminians.[4] Well, this minister, in his preaching, strongly insisted

---

[4] The terms "Arminian" and "Antinomian" are almost impossible to define precisely. Each generation and almost every minister uses the words in a dif-

on the opposite points, the doctrine of election, Divine sovereignty, predestination, &c. The consequence was, as might have been expected where this was done with ability; there was a powerful revival. Some time afterwards this same minister was called to labor in another field, in this state, where the people were all on the other side, and strongly tinctured with Antinomianism. They had got such perverted views of election, and Divine sovereignty, that they were continually saying they had no power to do any thing, but must wait God's time. Now, what does this minister do, but immediately go to preaching the doctrine of election. And when he was asked, how he could think of preaching the doctrine of election so much to that people, when it was the very thing that lulled them to a deeper slumber, he replied. "Why, that's the very class of truths by which I had such a great revival in ———;" not considering the difference in the views of the people. And if I am correctly informed, there he is to this day, preaching away at the doctrine of election, and wondering that it does not produce as powerful a revival as it did in the other place. Probably those sinners never will be converted. You must take things as they are, find out where sinners lie, and pour in truth upon them *there*, and START THEM OUT from their refuges of lies. It is of vast importance that a minister should find out where the congregation are, and preach accordingly.

I have been in many places in times of revival, and I have never been able to employ precisely the same course of preaching in one as in another. Some are intrenched behind one refuge, and some behind another. In one place, the church will need to be instructed, in another, sinners. In one place, one set of truths, in another, another set. A minister must find out where they are, and preach accordingly. I believe this is the experience of all preachers who are called to labor from field to field.

5. If a minister means to promote a revival, he should be very careful not to introduce controversy. He will grieve away the

---

ferent sense. Finney generally meant by an Arminian someone who overemphasized man's free will, and underemphasized or ignored the agency of God or the Holy Spirit in conversion. By Antinomian he generally meant a "hyper-Calvinist," who so emphasized predestination and the passivity of the sinner in regeneration that he denied freedom of the will. Finney did not consider himself an Arminian, although he considered the Methodists to be. Nevertheless he was willing to cooperate with Methodist ministers in revivals, and he believed them to be nearer the truth than the Old School Calvinists. The significant thing about this passage is Finney's willingness to be expedient in the emphasis he gave to his doctrine of free will.

Spirit of God. In this way probably more revivals are put down, than in any other. Look back upon the history of the church from the beginning, and you will see that *ministers* are generally responsible for grieving away the Spirit and causing declensions, by controversy. It is the ministers who bring forward controversial subjects for discussion, and by and by they get very zealous on the subject, and then get the church into a controversial spirit, and so the Spirit of God is grieved away.

If I had time to go over the history of the church from the days of the Apostles, I could show that all the controversies that have taken place, and all the great declensions in religion, too, were chargeable upon ministers. I believe the ministers of the present day are responsible for the present state of the church, and it will be seen to be true at the judgment. Who does not know that ministers have been crying out "Heresy," and "New Measures," and talking about the "Evils of Revivals," until they have got the church all in confusion? Look at the poor Presbyterian church, and see ministers getting up their Act and Testimony, and keeping up a continual war! [5] O God, have mercy on ministers. They talk about their days of fasting and prayer, but are these the men to call on *others* to fast and pray? They ought to fast and pray themselves. It is time that ministers should assemble together, and fast and pray over the evils of controversy, for they have caused it. The church itself never would get into a controversial spirit unless led into it by ministers. The body of the church are always averse to controversy, and will keep out of it, only as they are dragged into it by ministers. When Christians are revived they are not inclined to meddle with controversy, either to read or hear it. But they may be told of such and such "damnable heresies," that are afloat, till they get their feelings enlisted in controversy, and then farewell to the revival. If a minister, in preaching, finds it necessary to discuss particular points, about which Christians differ in opinion, let him BY ALL MEANS avoid a controversial *spirit and manner* of doing it.

[5] The Act and Testimony was a statement of belief drawn up in 1835 by a large and influential group of Old School Calvinists. Apparently its chief architect was Charles Hodge, the editor of the *Biblical Repertory and Theological Review*. Its purpose was to put the General Assembly on record against the New School by attacking certain theological "errors" that the signers believed had infiltrated the Presbyterian Church. The statement was presented to the General Assembly in 1835 and adopted by that body, but it merely hastened the schism that followed two years later. See Robert E. Thompson, *A History of the Presbyterian Church in the United States* (New York, 1895), pp. 111, 113.

6. The gospel should be preached in *those proportions*, that *the whole gospel* may be brought before the minds of the people, and produce its proper influence. If too much stress is laid on one class of truths, the Christian character will not have its due proportions. Its symmetry will not be perfect. If that class of truths be almost exclusively dwelt upon, that requires great exertion of intellect, without being brought home to the heart and conscience, it will be found that the church will be indoctrinated *in those views*, will have their heads filled with notions, but will not be awake, and active, and efficient in the promotion of religion. If, on the other hand, the preaching be loose, indefinite, exhortatory, and highly impassioned, the church will be like a ship, with too much sail for her ballast. It will be in danger of being swept away by a tempest of feeling, where there is not sufficient knowledge to prevent their being carried away with every wind of doctrine. If election and sovereignty are too much preached, there will be Antinomianism in the church, and sinners will hide themselves behind the delusion that they can do nothing. If the other doctrines of ability and obligation are too prominent, they will produce Arminianism in the church, and sinners will be blustering and self-confident.

When I entered the ministry, there had been so much said about the doctrine of election and sovereignty, that I found it was the universal hiding place, both of sinners and of the church, that they could not do any thing, or could not obey the gospel. And wherever I went, I found it indispensable to demolish these refuges of lies. And a revival would in no way be produced or carried on, but by dwelling on that class of truths, which hold up man's ability, and responsibility. This was the only class of truths that would bring sinners to submission.

It was not so in the days when President Edwards and Whitefield labored. Then the churches in New England had enjoyed little else than Arminian preaching, and were all resting in themselves and their own strength. These bold and devoted servants of God came out and declared those particular doctrines of grace, Divine sovereignty, and election, and they were greatly blessed. They did not dwell on these doctrines exclusively, but they preached them very fully. The consequence was, that because *in those circumstances* revivals followed from such preaching, the ministers who followed, *continued to preach these doctrines exclusively*. And they dwelt on them so long, that the church and the world got intrenched behind them, waiting for God to come and do what he required *them* to do, and so revivals ceased for many years.

Now, and for years past, ministers have been engaged in hunting them out from these refuges. And here it is all important for the ministers of this day to bear in mind, that if they dwell exclusively on ability and obligation, they will get their hearers back on the old Arminian ground, and then they will cease to promote revivals. Here are a body of ministers who have preached a great deal of truth, and have had great revivals, under God. Now let it be known and remarked, that the reason is, they have hunted sinners out from their hiding places. But if they continue to dwell on the same class of truths till sinners hide themselves behind their preaching, another class of truths must be preached. And then if they do not change their mode, another pall will hang over the church, until another class of ministers shall arise and hunt sinners out of those new retreats.

A right view of both classes of truths, election and free-agency, will do no hurt. They are eminently calculated to convert sinners and strengthen saints. It is a perverted view which chills the heart of the church, and closes the eyes of sinners in sleep, till they sink down to hell. If I had time I would remark on the manner in which I have sometimes heard the doctrines of Divine sovereignty, election, and ability preached. They have been exhibited in irreconcileable contradiction, the one against the other. Such exhibitions are any thing but the gospel, and are calculated to make a sinner feel any thing else rather than his responsibility to God.[6]

By preaching truth in proper proportions, I do not mean mingling all things together in the same sermon, in such a way that sinners will not see their connection or consistency. A minister once asked another, Why do you not preach the doctrine of election? Because, said the other, I find sinners here are intrenched behind *inability*. The first then said he once knew a minister who used to preach election in the forenoon, and repentance in the afternoon. Marvellous grace it must be, that would produce a

---

[6] Finney here and elsewhere makes the common New School statement that it is possible to reconcile the five points of Calvinism, or the Westminster Confession, with the New School theology if the terms are properly defined. When the New School and Old School reunited in 1870 after their thirty-three year schism this reconciliation was assumed. But few seventeenth- or eighteenth-century Calvinists would have accepted the interpretation of Calvinism made by the New School.

revival under such preaching! What connection is there in this? Instead of exhibiting to the sinner his sins in the morning, and then and in the afternoon calling on him to repent, he is first turned to the doctrine of election, and then commanded to repent. What is he to repent of? The doctrine of election? This is not what I mean by preaching truth in its proportion. Bringing things together, that only confound the sinner's mind, and overwhelm him with a fog of metaphysics, is not wise preaching. When talking of election, the preacher is not talking of the sinner's duty. It has no relation to the sinner's duty. Election belongs to the government of God. It is a part of the exceeding richness of the grace of God. It shows the love of God, not the duty of the sinner. And to bring election and repentance together in this way is diverting the sinner's mind away from his duty. It has been customary, in many places, for a long time, to bring the doctrine of election into every sermon. Sinners have been commanded to repent, and told that they could not repent, in the same sermon. A great deal of ingenuity has been exercised in endeavoring to reconcile a sinner's "inability" with his obligation to obey God. Election, predestination, free-agency, inability, and duty, have all been thrown together in one promiscuous jumble. And with regard to many sermons, it has been too true, as has been objected, that ministers have preached,

> You can and you can't,
> You shall and you shan't,
> You will and you won't
> And you'll be damned if you don't.[7]

Such a mixture of truth and error, of light and darkness, has confounded the congregation, been the fruitful source of Universalism, and every species of infidelity and error.

7. It is of great importance that the sinner should be made to *feel his guilt*, and not left to the impression that he is *unfortunate*. I think this is a very prevailing fault, particularly with printed books on the subject. They are calculated to make the sinner think more of his sorrows than of his sins, and feel that his state

---

[7] This jingle was common enough in the 1820's to give credence to Finney's view that the average churchgoer, especially in New England and in western New York, was utterly bewildered and frustrated by the theological arguments put forward by neo-Edwardean Calvinists. Like most such popular jingles its origin and author are unknown.

is rather *unfortunate* than *criminal*. Perhaps most of you have seen a very lovely little book recently published, entitled "Todd's Lectures to Children." [8] It is very fine, exquisitely fine, and happy in some of its illustrations of truth. But it has one very serious fault. Many of its illustrations, I may say most of them, are not calculated to make a correct impression respecting the *guilt* of sinners, or to make them feel how much they have been to *blame*. This is very unfortunate. If the writer had guarded his illustrations on this point, so as to make them impress sinners with a sense of their *guilt*, I do not see how a child could read through that book and not be converted.

Multitudes of the books written for children, and for adults too, within the last twenty-years, have run into this mistake to an alarming degree. Mrs. Sherwood's writings have this fault standing out upon almost every page.[9] They are not calculated to make the sinner blame and condemn himself. Until you can do this, the gospel will never take effect.

8. A prime object with the preacher must be to make *present obligation* felt. I have talked, I suppose, with many thousands of anxious sinners. And I have found that they had *never before felt* the pressure of present obligation. The impression is not commonly made by ministers in their preaching that sinners are expected to repent NOW. And if ministers suppose they make this impression, they deceive themselves. Most commonly any other impression is made upon the minds of sinners by the preacher, than that they are expected *now* to submit. But what sort of a gospel is this? Does God authorize such an impression? Is this according to the preaching of Jesus Christ? Does the Holy Spirit, when striving with the sinner, make the impression upon his mind that he is not expected to obey now? — Was any such impression produced by the preaching of the apostles? How does it happen that so many ministers now preach, so as in fact to make an impression on their hearers, that they are not expected to repent now? Until the sinner's conscience is reached on this subject, you preach to him in vain. And until ministers learn how to preach so as to make *the right* impression, the world never can be converted. O, to what an alarming extent does the impression now prevail among the im-

---

[8] The Rev. John Todd, *Lectures to Children Illustrating Important Truth*, 2d. ed. (Northampton, Massachusetts, 1834).

[9] Mrs. Mary Martha (Butt) Sherwood (1775–1851) was a prolific English writer of didactic and pious books for children.

penitent, that they are not expected to repent *now*, but must wait God's time!

9. Sinners ought to be made to feel that they have *something* to do, and that is *to repent*; that it is something which *no other* being can do for them, neither God nor man, and something which *they can* do, and do *now*. Religion is something to *do*, not something to *wait for*. And they must do it now, or they are in danger of eternal death.

10. Ministers should never rest satisfied, until they have ANNIHILATED every excuse of sinners. The plea of "inability" is the worst of all excuses. It slanders God so, charging him with infinite tyranny, in commanding men to do that which they have no power to do. Make the sinner see and feel that this is the very nature of his excuse. Make the sinner see that *all* pleas in excuse for not submitting to God, are an act of rebellion against him. Tear away the last LIE which he grasps in his hand, and make him feel that he is absolutely condemned before God.

11. Sinners should be made to feel that if they *now* grieve away the Spirit of God, it is very probable that they will be *lost for ever*. There is infinite danger of this. They should be made to understand *why* they are dependent on the Spirit, and that it is not because they *cannot* do what God commands, but because they are *unwilling*; but that they are so unwilling that it is just as certain they will not repent without the Holy Ghost, as if they were now in hell, or as if they were actually unable. They are so opposed and so unwilling, that they never will repent in the world, unless God sends his Holy Spirit upon them.

Show them, too, that a sinner under the gospel, who hears the truth preached, if converted at all, is generally converted young. And if not converted while young, he is commonly given up of God. Where the truth is preached, sinners are either gospel-hardened or converted. I know some old sinners are converted, but they are rather exceptions, and by no means common.

I wish now, SECONDLY, to make a few remarks on the MANNER OF PREACHING.[10]

---

[10] Although there is nothing original in Finney's theory of preaching that follows, it was new in the Presbyterian and Congregational churches. The long tradition of an educated ministry had discredited the more popular style of extempore preaching. Finney warns the Presbyterians and Congregationalists here and throughout this book that their system must become more democratic if their churches are to compete with those of other denominations. But his colleagues paid little heed to him and as a result the Baptist and Methodist churches

1. It should be *conversational*. Preaching, to be understood, should be colloquial in its style. A minister must preach just as he would talk, if he wishes to be fully understood. Nothing is more calculated to make a sinner feel that religion is some mysterious thing that he cannot understand, than this mouthing, formal, lofty style of speaking, so generally employed in the pulpit. The minister ought to do as the lawyer does when he wants to make a jury understand him perfectly. He uses a style perfectly colloquial. This lofty, swelling style will do no good. The gospel will never produce any great effects, until ministers *talk* to their hearers, in the pulpit, as they talk in private conversation.

2. It must be in the *language of common life*. Not only should it be colloquial in its style, but the *words* should be such as are in common use. Otherwise they will not be understood. In the New Testament you will observe that Jesus Christ invariably uses words of the most common kind. You scarcely find a word of his instructions, that any child cannot, understand. The language of the gospels is the plainest, simplest, and most easily understood of any language in the world.

For a minister to neglect this principle, is *wicked*. Some ministers use language that is purely *technical* in preaching. They think to avoid the mischief by explaining the meaning fully at the outset; but this will not answer. It will not effect the object in making the people understand what he means. If he uses a word that is not in common use, and that people do not understand, his explanation may be very full, but the difficulty is that people will forget his explanations, and then his words are all Greek to them. Or if he uses a word in common use, but employs it in an *un*common sense, giving his special explanations, it is no better: for the people will soon forget his special explanations, and then the impression actually conveyed to their minds will be according to their *common* understanding of the word. And thus he will never convey the right idea to his congregation. It is amazing how many men of thinking minds there are in congregations, who do not understand the most common technical expressions employed by ministers, such as regeneration, sanctification, &c.

Use words that can be perfectly understood. Do not, for fear of appearing unlearned, use language half Latin and half Greek, which the people do not understand. The apostle says the man is a

---

grew far more rapidly in the nineteenth century than either the Presbyterian or Congregational.

barbarian, who uses language that the people do not understand. And "if the trumpet give an uncertain sound, who shall prepare himself for the battle?" In the apostle's days there were some preachers, who were marvellously proud of displaying their command of language, and showing off the variety of tongues they could speak, which the common people could not understand. The apostle rebukes this spirit sharply, and says, "I had rather speak five words with my understanding, that by my voice I might teach others also, than ten thousand words in an unknown tongue."

I have sometimes heard ministers preach, even when there was a revival, when I have wondered what that part of the congregation would do, who had no dictionary. So many phrases were brought in, manifestly to adorn the discourse, rather than to instruct the people, that I have felt as if I wanted to tell the man, "Sit down, and not confound the people's minds with your *barbarian* preaching, that they cannot understand."

3. Preaching should be *parabolical*. That is, illustrations should be constantly used, drawn from incidents, real or supposed. Jesus Christ constantly illustrated his instructions in this way. He would either advance a principle and then illustrate it by a parable, that is, a short story of some event real or imaginary, or else he would bring out the principle *in* the parable. There are millions of facts that can be used to advantage, and yet very few ministers *dare* to use them, for fear somebody will reproach them. "Oh," says somebody, "he tells stories." Tells stories! Why, that is the way Jesus Christ preached. And it is the only way to preach. Facts, real or supposed, should be used to show the truth. Truths not illustrated, are generally just as well calculated to convert sinners as a mathematical demonstration. Is it always to be so? Shall it always be matter of reproach, that ministers follow the example of Jesus Christ, in *illustrating* truths by facts? Let them do it, and let fools reproach them as story-telling ministers. They have Jesus Christ and common sense on their side.

4. The illustrations should be drawn *from common life*, and the common business of society. I once heard a minister illustrate his ideas by the manner in which merchants transact business in their stores. Another minister who was present made some remarks to him afterwards. He objected to this illustration particularly, because, he said, it was too familiar, and was letting down the dignity of the pulpit. He said all illustrations in preaching should be drawn from ancient history, or from some elevated source, that would

keep up the dignity of the pulpit. Dignity indeed! Just the language of the devil. He rejoices in it. Why, the object of an illustration is, to make people *see the truth*, not to bolster up pulpit dignity. A minister whose heart is in the work, does not use an illustration to make people stare, but to make them see the truth. If he brought forward his illustrations from ancient history, it could not make the people *see*, it would not illustrate any thing. The novelty of the thing might awaken their attention, but then they would lose the truth itself. For if the illustration itself be a novelty, the attention will be directed to this fact as a matter of history, and the *truth itself*, which it was designed to illustrate, will be lost sight of. The illustration should, if possible, be a matter of common occurrence, and the *more* common the occurrence the more sure it will be, not to fix attention upon *itself*, but it serves as a *medium through* which the truth is conveyed. I have been pained at the very heart, at hearing illustrations drawn from ancient history, of which not one in a hundred of the congregation had ever heard. The very manner in which they were adverted to, was strongly tinctured, to say the least, with the appearance of vanity, and an attempt to surprise the people with an exhibition of learning.

The Savior always illustrated his instructions by things that were taking place among the people to whom he preached, and with which their minds were familiar. He descended often very far below what is now supposed to be essential to support the dignity of the pulpit. He talked about the hens and chickens, and children in market-places, and sheep and lambs, shepherds and farmers, and husbandmen and merchants. And when he talked about kings, as in the marriage of the king's son, and the nobleman that went into a far country to receive a kingdom; he had reference to historical facts, that were well known among the people at the time. The illustration should always be drawn from things so common, that the illustration itself will not attract attention away from the subject, but that people may *see through it* the truth illustrated.

5. Preaching should be *repetitious*. If a minister wishes to preach with effect, he must not be afraid of repeating whatever he sees is not perfectly understood by his hearers. Here is the evil of using notes. The preacher preaches right along just as he has it written down, and cannot observe whether he is understood or not. If he interrupts his reading, and attempts to catch the countenances of the audience, and to explain where he sees they do not

understand, he gets lost and confused, and gives it up. If a minister has his eyes on the people he is preaching to, he can commonly tell by their looks whether they understand him. And if he sees they do not understand any particular point, let him stop and illustrate it. If they do not understand one illustration, let him give another, and make it all clear to their minds, before he goes on. But those who write their sermons go right on, in a regular consecutive train, just as in any essay or a book, and do not repeat their thoughts till the audience fully comprehend them.

I was conversing with one of the first advocates in this country. He said the difficulty which preachers find in making themselves understood, is, that they do not repeat enough, Says he, "In addressing a jury, I always expect that whatever I wish to impress upon their minds, I shall have to repeat at least twice, and often I repeat it three or four times, and even more. Otherwise, I do not carry their minds along with me, so that they can feel the force of what comes afterwards." If a jury under oath, called to decide on the common affairs of this world, cannot apprehend an argument, unless there is so much repetition, how is it to be expected that men will understand the preaching of the gospel without it?

In like manner the minister ought to turn an important thought over and over before his audience, till even the children understand it perfectly. Do not say that so much repetition will create disgust in cultivated minds. It will not disgust. This is not what disgusts thinking men. They are not weary of the efforts a minister makes to be understood. The fact is, the more simple a preacher's illustrations are, and the more plain he makes every thing, the more men of mind are interested. I know that men of the first minds, often get ideas they never had before, from illustrations which were designed to bring the gospel down to the comprehension of a child. Such men are commonly so occupied with the affairs of this world, that they do not *think* much on the subject of religion, and they therefore need the plainest preaching, and they will like it.

6. A minister should always feel deeply his subject, and then he will suit the action to the word and the word to the action, so as to make the full impression which the truth is calculated to make. He should be in solemn earnest in what he says. I heard lately a most judicious criticism on this subject. "How important it is that a minister should feel what he says. Then his actions will of course correspond to his words. If he undertakes to *make* gestures, his arms may go like a windmill, and yet make no impres-

sion." It requires the utmost stretch of art on the stage for the actors to make their hearers feel. The design of elocution is to teach this skill. But if a man *feels* his subject fully, he will *naturally* do it. He will naturally do the very thing that elocution laboriously teaches. See any common man in the streets, who is earnest in talking. See with what force he gestures. See a woman or a child, in earnest. How natural. To gesture with their hands is as natural as it is to move their tongue and lips. It is the perfection of eloquence.

Let a minister, then, only feel what he says, and not be tied to his notes, to read an essay, or to speak a piece, like a school-boy, first on one foot and then on the other, put out first one hand and then the other. Let him speak as he feels, and act as he feels, and he will be eloquent.

No wonder that a great deal of preaching produces so little effect. Gestures are of more importance than is generally supposed. Mere words will never express the full meaning of the gospel. The *manner* of saying it is almost every thing. Suppose one of you, that is a mother, goes home to-night, and as soon as you get into the door, the nurse comes rushing up to you, with her whole soul in her countenance, and tells you that your child is burnt to death. You would believe it, and you would feel it too, at once. But suppose she comes and tells it in a cold and careless manner. Would that arouse you? No. It is the earnestness of her manner, and the distress of her looks, that *tells the story*. You know something is the matter, before she speaks a word.

I once heard a remark made, respecting a young minister's preaching, which was instructive. He was uneducated, in the common sense of the term, but well educated to win souls. It was said of him, "The manner in which he comes in, and sits in the pulpit, and rises to speak, is a sermon of itself. It shows that he has something to say that is important and solemn." That man's manner of saying some things I have known to move the feelings of a whole congregation, when the same things said in a prosing way would have produced no effect at all.

A fact which was stated by one of the most distinguished professors of elocution in the United States, ought to impress ministers on this subject. That man was an infidel. He said, "I have been fourteen years employed in teaching elocution to ministers, and I know they don't believe the Christian religion. The Bible may be true. I don't pretend to know as to that, but I do know these ministers don't believe it. I can demonstrate that they do not. The perfection of my art is to teach them to speak naturally on this subject. I go to their studies, and converse with them, and they speak eloquently. I say to them, Gentlemen, if you will preach just as you yourselves naturally speak on any other subject in which you are interested, you do not need to be taught. That is just what I am trying to teach you. I hear you talk on other subjects, with admirable force and eloquence. I see you go into the pulpit, and you speak and act as if you did not believe what you are saying. I have told them, again and again, to talk in the pulpit as they naturally talk to me. And I *cannot make* them do it, and so I know they do not believe the Christian religion."

I have mentioned this to show how universal it is, that men will gesture right, if they feel right. The only thing in the way of ministers being natural speakers is, that they do not DEEPLY FEEL. How can they be natural in elocution, when they do not feel?

7. A minister should aim to *convert his congregation*. But you will ask, Does not all preaching aim at this? No. A minister always has *some* aim in preaching, but most sermons were never aimed at converting sinners. And if sinners were converted under them, the preacher himself would be amazed. I once heard a fact on this point. There were two young ministers who had entered the ministry at the same time. One of them had great success in converting sinners, the other none. The latter inquired of the other, one day, what was the reason of this difference. "Why," replied the other, "the reason is that I *aim at* a different end from you, in preaching. My object is to convert sinners, but you aim at no such thing. And then you go and lay it to sovereignty in God, that you do not produce the same effect, when you never aim at it. Here, take one of my sermons, and preach it to your people, and see what the effect will be." The man did so, and preached the sermon, and it did produce effect. He was frightened when sinners began to weep; and when one came to him after meeting to ask what he should do, the minister apologized to him, and said, "I did not aim to wound you, I am sorry if I have hurt your feelings." O horrible!

8. A minister must *anticipate the objections* of sinners, and answer them. What does the lawyer do when pleading before a jury? O how differently is the cause of Jesus Christ pleaded from human causes! It was remarked by a lawyer, that the cause of Jesus Christ had the fewest able advocates of any cause in the

world. And I partly believe it. Does a lawyer go along in his argument in a regular train, and not explain any thing obscure, or anticipate the arguments of his antagonist? If he did so, he would lose his case, to a certainty. But no. The lawyer, who is pleading for money, anticipates every objection, which may be made by his antagonist, and carefully removes or explains them, so as to leave the ground all clear as he goes along, that the jury may be settled on every point. But ministers often leave one difficulty and another, untouched. Sinners who hear them feel the difficulty and it is never got over in their minds, and they never know how to remove it, and perhaps the minister never takes the trouble to know that such difficulties exist, and yet he wonders why his congregation is not converted, and why there is no revival. How can he wonder at it, when he has never hunted up the difficulties and objections that sinners feel, and removed them?

9. If a minister means to preach the gospel with effect he must be sure *not to be monotonous*. If he preaches in a monotonous way, he will preach the people to sleep. Any monotonous sound, great or small, if continued, disposes people to sleep. The falls of Niagara, the roaring of the ocean, or any sound ever so great or small, has this effect naturally on the nervous system. You never hear this monotonous manner from people in conversation. And a minister cannot be monotonous in preaching, if he feels what he says.

10. A minister should address the feelings enough to secure attention, and then *deal with the conscience*, and probe to the quick. Appeals to the feelings alone will never convert sinners. If the preacher deals too much in these, he may get up an excitement, and have wave after wave of feeling flow over the congregation, and people may be carried away in the flood, with false hopes. The only way to secure *sound* conversions is to deal faithfully with the conscience. If attention flags at any time, appeal to the feelings again, and rouse it up; but do your *work* with conscience.

11. If he can, it is desirable that a minister should learn the effect of one sermon, before he preaches another. Let him learn if it is understood, if it has produced any impression, if any difficulties are felt in regard to the subject which need clearing up, if any objections are raised, and the like. When he knows it all, then he knows what to preach next. What would be thought of the physician who should give medicine to his patient, and then give it again and again, without trying to learn the effect of the first, or whether

it had produced any effect or not? A minister never will be able to deal with sinners as he ought, till he can find out whether his instruction has been received and understood, and whether the difficulties in sinners' minds are cleared away, and their path open to the Savior, so that they need not stumble and stumble till their souls are lost.

I had designed to notice several other points, but time does not admit. I wish to close with a few

REMARKS.

1. We see why so few of the *leading minds* in many communities are converted.

Until the late revivals, professional men were rarely reached by preaching, and they were almost all infidels at heart.[11] People almost understood the Bible to warrant the idea, that they could not be converted. The reason is obvious. The gospel had not been commended to the consciences of such men. Ministers had not grappled with mind, and *reasoned* so as to make that class of minds see the truth of the gospel, and feel its power, and consequently such persons had come to regard religion as something unworthy their notice.

But of late years the case is altered, and in some places there have been more of this class of persons converted, in proportion to their numbers, than of any others. That is because they were made to understand the claims of the gospel. The preacher grappled with their minds, and showed them the reasonableness of religion. And when this is done, it is found that that class of minds are more easily converted than any other. They have so much better capacity to receive an argument, and are so much more in the habit of yielding to the force of reason, that as soon as the gospel gets a fair hold of their minds, it breaks them right down, and melts them at the feet of Christ.

2. Before the gospel can take general effect, we must have a class of *extempore* preachers, for the following reasons:

(1.) No set of men can stand the labor of writing sermons and doing all the preaching which will be requisite.

---

[11] Finney here and in his *Memoirs* tends to boast about the ability of his sermons to influence "professional men" and prominent society people.

(2.) Written preaching is not calculated to produce the requisite effect. Such preaching does not present truth in the right shape.

(3.) It is impossible for a man who writes his sermons to arrange his matter, and turn and choose his thoughts, so as to produce the same effect as when he addresses the people directly, and makes them feel that he *means them*. Writing sermons had its origin in times of political difficulty. The practice was unknown in the apostles' days. No doubt written sermons have done a great deal of good, but they can never give to the gospel its great power. Perhaps many ministers have been so long trained in the use of notes, that they had better not throw them away. Perhaps they would make bad work without them. The difficulty would not be for the want of mind, but from wrong training. The bad habit is begun with the school boy, who is called to "speak his piece." Instead of being set to express his own thoughts and feelings in his own language, and with his own natural manner, such as nature herself prompts, he is made to commit another person's writing to memory, and then *mouths* it out in a stiff and formal way. And so when he goes to college, and to the seminary, instead of being trained to *extempore* speaking, he is set to writing his piece, and commit it to memory. I would pursue the opposite course from the beginning. I would give him a subject, and let him first *think*, and then *speak* his thoughts. Perhaps he will make mistakes. Very well, that is to be expected — in a beginner. But he will learn. Suppose he is not eloquent, at first. Very well, he can improve. And he is in the very way to improve. This kind of training alone will ever raise up a class of ministers who can convert the world.

But it is objected to extemporaneous preaching, that if ministers do not *write*, they will not *think*. This objection will have weight with those men whose habit has always been to write down their thoughts. But to a man of a different habit, it will have no weight at all. Writing is not thinking. And if I should judge from many of the written sermons I have heard preached, I should think the makers of them had been doing any thing rather than *thinking*. The mechanical labor of writing is really a hinderance to close and rapid thought. It is true that some extempore preachers have not been men of thought. And so it is true that many men who write sermons, are not men of thought. A man whose habits have always been such, that he has thought only when he has put his mind on the end of his pen, will of course, if he lays aside his pen, at first find it difficult to think; and if he attempts to preach without writing, will, until his habits are thoroughly changed, find it difficult to throw into his sermons the same amount of thought, as if he conformed to his old habits of writing. But it should be remembered that this is only on account of his having been *trained* to write, and having always habituated himself to it. It is the training and habit that renders it so difficult for him to think without writing. Will any body pretend to say that lawyers are not men of thought? That their arguments before a court and jury, are not profound and well digested? And yet every one knows that they do not write their speeches. It should be understood, too, that in college, they have the same training with ministers, and have the same disadvantage of having been trained to write their thoughts; and it is only after they enter upon their profession, that they change their habit. Were *they* educated, as they should be, to *extempore* habits in the schools, they would be vastly more eloquent and powerful in argument than they are.

I have heard much of this objection to extempore preaching ever since I entered the ministry. It was often said to me then, in answer to my views of *extempore* preaching, that ministers who preached extemporaneously, would not *instruct* the churches, that there would be a great deal of *sameness* in their preaching, and they would soon become insipid and repetitious for want of thought. But every year's experience has ripened the conviction on my mind, that the *reverse* of this objection is true. The man who writes least may, if he pleases, *think most*, and will say what he does think in a manner that will be better understood than if it were written; and that, just in the proportion that he lays aside the labor of writing, his body will be left free to exercise, and his mind to vigorous and consecutive *thought*.

The great reason why it is supposed that *extempore* preachers more frequently repeat the same thoughts in their preaching, is because what they say is, in a general way, more perfectly remembered by the congregation, than if it had been read. I have often known preachers, who could repeat their written sermons once in a few months, without its being recognised by the congregation. But the *manner* in which extempore sermons are generally delivered is so much more impressive, that the thoughts cannot in general be soon repeated, without being remembered. We shall never have a set of men in our halls of legislation, in our courts of justice, and in our pulpits, that are powerful and overwhelming speakers, and can carry the world before them, till our system of education teaches them to *think*, closely, rapidly, consecutively, and till all their habits of speaking in the schools are extemporaneous. The very style of communicating thought, in what is commonly called a good style of writing, is not calculated to leave a deep impression on the mind, or to communicate thought in a clear and impressive manner. It is not laconic, direct, pertinent. It is not the language of nature. It is impossible that gestures should be *suited* to the common style of writing. And consequently, when they attempt to gesture in reading an essay, or delivering a written sermon, their gestures are a burlesque upon all public speaking.

In delivering a sermon in this essay style of writing, it is impossible that nearly all the fire of meaning and power of gesture, and looks, and attitude, and emphasis should not be lost. We can never have the *full meaning* of the gospel, till we throw away our notes.

3. A minister's course of study and training for his work should be *exclusively theological*.

I mean just as I say. I am not now going to discuss the question whether all education ought not to be theological. But I say education for the ministry should be exclusively so. But you will ask, Should not a minister understand science? I would answer, Yes, the more the better.[12] I would that ministers might understand all science. But it should all be in connection with theology. Studying science is studying the works of God. And studying theology is studying God.

Let a scholar be asked, for instance, this question: "Is there a God?" To answer it, let him ransack the universe, let him go out into every department of science, to find the proofs of *design*, and in this way to learn the existence of God. Let him next inquire how many Gods there are, and let him again ransack creation to see whether there is such a *unity* of design as evinces that there is *one God*. In like manner, let him inquire concerning the attributes of God, and his character. He will learn science here, but will learn it as a part of theology. Let him search every field of knowledge, to bring forward his proofs. What was the design of this

[12] Finney wrote this in the happy days before the warfare between science and theology turned most revivalists into anti-intellectuals who saw science as the tool of the devil. Finney's biographer makes the interesting but unconvincing claim that Finney would have found no objection to Darwinism and would have been a theistic evolutionist had he ever faced the problem. See Wright, *Finney*, pp. 198–199. As far as I have been able to discover Finney made no pronouncements about Darwinism, although he lived until 1875.

plan? What was the end of that arrangement? See whether every thing you find in the universe is not calculated to produce happiness, unless perverted.

Would the student's heart get hard and cold in study, as cold and hard as the college walls, if science was pursued in this way? Every lesson brings him right up before God, and is in fact communion with God, and warms his heart, and makes him more pious, more solemn, more holy. The very distinction between classical and theological study is a curse to the church, and a curse to the world. The student spends four years in college at *classical* studies, and no God in them, and then three years in the seminary, at *theological* studies; and what then? Poor young man. Set him to work, and you will find that he is not educated *for the ministry* at all. The church groans under his preaching, because he does not preach with unction, nor with power. He has been spoiled in training.

4. We learn what is *revival preaching*. All ministers should be revival ministers, and all preaching should be revival preaching; that is, it should be calculated to promote holiness. People say, "It is very well to have some men in the church, who are revival preachers, and who can go about and promote revivals; but then you must have others to *indoctrinate* the church." Strange! Do they not know that a revival indoctrinates the church faster than any thing else! And a minister will never produce a revival, if he does not indoctrinate his hearers. The preaching I have described, is full of doctrine, but it is doctrine *to be practised*. And that is revival preaching.

5. There are *two objections* sometimes brought against the kind of preaching which I have recommended.

(1.) That it is *letting down the dignity* of the pulpit to preach in this colloquial, lawyer-like style. They are shocked at it. But it is only on account of its novelty, and not for any impropriety there is in the thing itself. I heard a remark made by a leading layman in the centre of this state, in regard to the preaching of a certain minister. He said it was the first preaching he ever heard, that he understood, and the first minister he ever heard that spoke as if he believed his own doctrine, or meant what he said. And when he first heard him preach as if he was saying something that he meant, he thought he was crazy. But eventually, he was made to see that it was all true, and he submitted to the truth, as the power of God for the salvation of his soul.

What is the dignity of the pulpit? To see a minister go into the pulpit to sustain its dignity! Alas, alas! During my foreign tour, I heard an English missionary preach exactly in that way. I believe he was a good man, and out of the pulpit he would talk like a man that meant what he said. But no sooner was he in the pulpit, than he appeared like a perfect automaton — swelling, mouthing, and singing, enough to put all the people to sleep. And the difficulty seemed to be, that he wanted to maintain the *dignity of the pulpit.*

(2.) It is objected that this preaching is *theatrical*. The bishop of London once asked Garrick, the celebrated play-actor, why it was that actors, in representing a mere fiction, should move an assembly, even to tears, while ministers, in representing the most solemn realities, could scarcely obtain a hearing. The philosophical Garrick well replied, "It is because we represent fiction as a reality, and you represent reality as a fiction." This is telling the whole story. Now what is the design of the actor in a theatrical representation? It is so to throw himself into the spirit and meaning of the writer, as to adopt his sentiments, make them his own, feel them, embody them, throw them out upon the audience as living reality. And now, what is the objection to all this in preaching? The actor suits the action to the word, and the word to the action. His looks, his hands, his attitudes, and every thing are designed to express the *full meaning* of the writer. Now this should be the aim of the preacher. And if by "theatrical" be meant the strongest possible representation of the sentiments expressed, then the more theatrical a sermon is, the better. And if ministers are too stiff, and the people too fastidious, to learn even from an actor, or from the stage, the best method of swaying mind, of enforcing sentiment, and diffusing the warmth of burning thought over a congregation, then they must go on with their prosing, and reading, and sanctimonious starch. But let them remember, that while they are thus turning away and decrying the art of the actor, and attempting to support "the dignity of the pulpit," the theatres can be thronged every night. The common-sense people *will be* entertained with that manner of speaking, and sinners will go down to hell.

6. A congregation may learn how to choose a minister.

When a vacant church are looking out for a minister, there are two leading points on which they commonly fix their attention. (1.) That he should be *popular*. (2.) That he should be *learned*. That is very well. But this point should be the first in their inquiries — "Is he *wise to win* souls?" No matter how eloquent a minister is, or how learned. No matter how pleasing and popular in his manners. If it is a matter of fact that sinners are not converted under his preaching, it shows that he has not *this* wisdom, and your children and neighbors will go down to hell under his preaching.

I am happy to know that many churches will ask this question about ministers. And if they find that a minister is destitute of this vital quality, they will not have him. And if ministers can be found who *are* wise to win souls, the churches *will have* such ministers. It is in vain to contend against it, or to pretend that they are not well educated, or not learned, or the like. It is in vain for the schools to try to force down the throats of the churches a race of ministers who are learned in every thing but what they most need to know. The churches have pronounced them not made right, and they will not sustain that which is notoriously so inadequate as the present system of theological education.

It is very difficult to say what needs to be said on this subject, without being in danger of begetting a wrong spirit in the church, towards ministers. Many professors of religion are ready to find fault with ministers when they have no reason; insomuch, that it becomes very difficult to say of ministers what is true, and what needs to be said, without its being perverted and abused by this class of professors. I would not for the world say any thing to injure the influence of a minister of Christ, who is really endeavoring to do good. I would that they deserved a hundred times more influence than they now deserve or have. But, to tell the truth will not injure the influence of those ministers, who by their lives and preaching give evidence to the church, that their object is to do good, and win souls to Christ. *This* class of ministers will recognise the truth of all that I have said, or wish to say. They see it all, and deplore it. But if there be ministers who are doing no good, who are feeding themselves and not the flock, such ministers *deserve* no influence. If they are doing no good, it is time for them to betake themselves to some other profession. They are but leeches on the very vitals of the church, sucking out its heart's blood. They are useless, and worse than useless. And the sooner they are laid aside, and their places filled with those who will *exert* themselves for Christ, the better.

Finally — It is the duty of the church to pray for us, ministers. Not one of us is such as we ought to be. Like Paul, we can say, "Who is sufficient for these things?" But who of us is like Paul?

Where will you find such a minister as Paul? They are not here. We have been wrongly educated, all of us. Pray for the schools, and colleges, and seminaries. And pray for young men who are preparing for the ministry. Pray for ministers, that God would give them this wisdom to win souls. And pray that God would bestow upon the church the wisdom and the means to educate a generation of ministers who will go forward and convert the world.[13] The church must *travail* in prayer, and groan and agonize for this. This is now the pearl of price to the church, to have a supply of the *right sort* of ministers. The coming of the millenium depends on having a different sort of ministers, who are more thoroughly educated *for their work*. And this we shall have so sure as the promise of the Lord holds good. Such a ministry as is now in the church will never convert the world. But the world *is to be* converted, and therefore God intends to have ministers who will do it. "Pray ye, therefore, the Lord of the harvest, that he would send forth laborers into his harvest."

[13] At the very time Finney wrote these lines (February 1835) he was making his decision to accept a post as Professor of Theology at Oberlin in order to help create this "new race of [revival] ministers." See the letter from Finney to H. B. Stanton and George Whipple, January 18, 1835, in the Finney Papers, Oberlin College Library.

XIII

HOW CHURCHES CAN HELP MINISTERS

TEXT. — And it came to pass, when Moses held up his hand, that Israel prevailed; and when he let down his hand, Amalek prevailed. But Moses's hands were heavy: and they took a stone, and put it under him, and he sat thereon: and Aaron and Hur stayed up his hands, the one on the one side and the other on the other side: and his hands were steady until the going down of the sun. And Joshua discomfited Amalek and his people with the edge of the sword. — EXODUS xvii. 11–13.

You who read your Bibles will recollect the connection in which these verses stand. The people of God in subduing their enemies came to battle against the Amalekites, and these incidents took place. It is difficult to conceive why importance should be attached to the circumstance of Moses holding up his hands, unless the expression is understood to denote the attitude of prayer. And then his holding up his hands, and the success attending it, will teach us the importance of prayer to God, for his aid in all our conflicts with the enemies of God. The cooperation and support of Aaron and Hur have been generally understood to represent the duty of churches to sustain and assist ministers in their work, and the importance of this co-operation to the success of the preached gospel. I shall make this use of it on the present occasion. As I have spoken of the duty of ministers to labor for revivals, I shall now consider,

THE IMPORTANCE OF THE CO-OPERATION OF THE CHURCH IN PRODUCING AND CARRYING ON A REVIVAL.

There are a number of things whose importance in promoting a revival has not been duly considered by churches and ministers, which if not attended to will make it impossible that revivals should extend, or even continue for any considerable time. In my last two lectures, I have been dwelling on the duties of ministers, as it was impossible for me to preach a course of lectures on revivals, without entering more or less extensively into that department of means. I have not done with that part of the subject, but have thought it important here to step aside and discuss some points, in which the church must stand by and aid their minister, if they expect to enjoy a revival. In discussing the subject, I propose,

I. To mention several things which Christians must *avoid*, if they would support ministers.

II. Some things to which they must *attend*.

I. I am to mention several things that must be avoided.

1. By all means keep clear of the idea, both in theory and practice, that *a minister is to promote revivals alone*. Many people are inclined to take a passive attitude on this subject, and feel as if they had nothing to do. They have employed a minister and paid him, to feed them with instruction and comfort, and now they have nothing to do but to sit and swallow the food he gives. They are to pay his salary, and attend on his preaching, and they think that is doing a great deal. And he on his part is expected to preach good, sound, *comfortable* doctrine, to bolster them up, and make them feel comfortable, and so they expect to go to heaven. I tell you, THEY WILL GO TO HELL, if this is their religion. That is not the way to heaven.

Rest assured that where this spirit prevails in the church, however good the minister may be, the church have taken the course to prevent a revival. If he is ever so faithful, ever so much engaged, ever so talented and eloquent, he may wear himself out, and perhaps destroy his life, but he will have little or no revival.

Where there is no church, or very few members in the church, a revival may be promoted without any organized effort of the church, because it is not there, and in such a case, God accommodates his grace to the circumstances, as he did when the apostles went out, single-handed, to plant the gospel in the world. I have seen instances of powerful revivals, where such was the case. But where there are means, God will have them used. I had rather have no church in a place, than attempt to promote a revival in a place where there is a church which will not work. God will be inquired of by his people to bestow blessings. The counteracting influence of a church that will not work, is worse than infidelity. There is no possibility of occupying neutral ground, in regard to a revival, though some professors imagine they are neutral. If a professor will not lay himself out in the work, he opposes it. Let such a one attempt to take middle ground, and say he is going to wait and see how they come out — why, that is the very ground the devil wants him to take. Professors can in this way do his work a great deal more effectually than by open opposition. If they should take open ground in opposition, every body will say they have no religion. But by this middle course they retain their influence, and thus do the devil's work more effectually.

In employing a minister, a church must remember, that they have only employed *a leader*, to lead them on to action in the cause of Christ. People would think it strange if any body should propose to support a general, and then let him go and fight alone.[1] This is no more absurd, or destructive, than for a minister to attempt to go forward alone. The church misconceive the design of the ministry, if they leave their minister to work alone. It is not enough that they should hear the sermons. That is only the word of command, which the church are bound to follow.

2. Do not *complain of your minister* because there is no revival, if you are *not doing your duty*. It is of no use to complain of there being no revival, if you are not doing your duty. *That alone* is a sufficient reason why there should be no revival. It is a most cruel and abominable thing for a church to complain of their minister, when they themselves are fast asleep. It is very common for professors of religion to take great credit to themselves, and quiet their own consciences by complaining of their ministers. And when the importance of ministers' being awake is spoken of, this sort of people are ready to say, We never shall have a revival with such a minister, when the fact is that their minister is much more awake than they are themselves.

Another thing is true in regard to this point, and worthy of notice. When the church is sunk down in a low state, professors of religion are very apt to complain of the *church*, and of the low state of religion among them. That intangible and irresponsible being, the "church," is greatly complained of by them, for being asleep. Their complaints of the low state of religion, and of the coldness of the church or of the minister, are poured out dolefully, without seeming to realize that the church is composed of individuals, and that until each one will take *his own* case in hand, complain of *himself*, and humble himself before God, and repent, and wake up, the church can never have any efficiency, and there never

[1] Finney is reported to have said early in his career that he considered himself to be a brigadier general in the army of Jesus Christ (see the *Gospel Advocate*, Buffalo, New York, January 13, 1826, p. 5). He denied this report, but he nevertheless acted much as though he were a military commander for the New School men of the West.

can be a revival. If instead of complaining of your minister, or of the church, you would wake up as individuals, and not complain of him or them until you can say you are pure from the blood of all men, and are doing your duty to save sinners, he would be apt to feel the justice of your complaints, and if he would not God would, and would either wake him up or remove him.

3. Do not let your minister *kill himself* by attempting to *carry on the work alone*, while you refuse to help him. It sometimes happens that a minister finds the ark of the Lord will not move unless he lays out his utmost strength, and he has been so desirous of a revival that he has done this, and has died. And he was willing to die for it. I could mention some cases in this state, where ministers have died, and no doubt in consequence of their labors to promote a revival where the church hung back from the work.

I will mention one case. A minister, some years since, was laboring where there was a revival; and was visited by an elder of a church at some distance who wanted him to go and preach there. There was no revival there, and never had been, and the elder complained about their state, said they had had two excellent ministers, one had worn himself completely out and died, and the other had exhausted himself, and got discouraged, and left them, and they were a poor and feeble church, and their prospects very dark unless they could have a revival, and so he begged this minister to go and help them. He seemed to be very sorrowful, and the minister heard his whining, and at last replied by asking, Why did you never have a revival? I don't know, said the elder. Our minister labored hard, but the church did not seem to wake up, and somehow there seemed to be no revival. "Well, now," said the minister, "I see what you want; you have killed one of God's ministers, and broke down another so that he had to leave you, and now you want to get another there and kill him, and the devil has sent you here to get me to go and rock your cradle for you. You had one good minister to preach for you, but you slept on, and he exerted himself till he absolutely died in the work. Then the Lord let you have another, and still you lay and slept, and would not wake up to your duty. And now you have come here in despair, and want another minister, do you? God forbid that you should ever have another while you do as you have done. God forbid that you should ever have a minister, till the church will wake up to duty." The elder was affected, for he was a good man. The tears came in his eyes, and he said it was no more than they deserved. "And now," said the minister, "will you be faithful, and go home and tell the church what I say? If you will, and they will be faithful and wake up to duty, they shall have a minister, I will warrant them that." The elder said he would, and he was true to his word; he went home and told the church how cruel it was for them to ask another minister to come among them, unless they would wake up. They felt it, and confessed their sins, and waked up to duty, and a minister was sent to them, and a precious and powerful revival followed.

Churches do not realize how often their coldness and backwardness may be absolutely the cause of the death of ministers. The state of the people, and of sinners, rests upon their mind, they travail in soul night and day, and they labor in season and out of season, beyond the power of the human constitution to bear, till they wear out and die. The church know not the agony of a minister's heart, when he travails for souls, and labors to wake up the church to help, and still sees them in the slumbers of death. Perhaps sometimes they will rouse up to spasmodic effort for a few days, and then all is cold again. And so many a faithful minister wears himself out and dies, and then these heartless professors are the first to blame him for doing so *much*.

I recollect a case of a good minister, who went to a place where there was a revival, and while there heard a pointed sermon to ministers. He received it like a man of God; he did not rebel against God's truth, but he vowed to God that he never would rest until he saw a revival among his people. He returned home and went to work; the church would not wake up, except a few members, and the Lord blessed *them*, and poured out his Spirit, but the minister laid himself down on his bed and died, in the midst of the revival.

4. Be careful not to complain of plain, pointed preaching, *even when its reproofs fasten on yourselves*. Churches are apt to forget, that a minister is responsible only to God. They want to make rules for a minister to preach by, so as not to have it *fit them*. If he bears down on the church, and exposes the sins that prevail among them, they call it personal, and rebel against the truth. Or they say, he should not preach so plainly to the church *before the world*; it exposes religion, they say, and he ought to take them by themselves and preach to the church alone, and not tell sinners how bad Christians are. But there are cases where a minister can do no less than to show the house of Jacob their sins. If you ask, Why not do it when we are by ourselves? I answer, Just as if sinners did not know you did wrong. I will preach to you by yourselves,

about your own sins, when you will get together by yourselves to sin. But as the Lord liveth, if you sin before the world, you shall be rebuked before the world. Is it not a fact that sinners do know how you live, and that they stumble over you into hell? Then do not blame ministers, when they see it their duty to rebuke the church openly, before the world. If you are so proud you cannot bear this, you need not expect a revival. Do not call preaching too plain, because it exposes the faults of the church. There is no such thing as preaching too plain.

5. Sometimes professors take alarm, lest the minister should *offend the ungodly* by plain preaching. And they will begin to caution him against it, and ask him if he had not better alter a little to avoid giving offence, and the like. This fear is excited especially if some of the more wealthy and influential members of the congregation are offended, lest they should withdraw their support from the church, and no longer give their money to help to pay the minister's salary, and so the burden will come the heavier on the church. They never can have a revival in such a church. Why, the church ought to pray above all things, that the truth may come on the ungodly like fire. What if they are offended? Christ can get along very well without their money. Do not blame your minister, nor ask him to change his mode of preaching to please and conciliate the ungodly. It is of no use for a minister to preach to the impenitent, unless he can preach the truth to them. And it will do no good for *them* to pay for the support of the gospel, unless it is preached in such a way, that they may be searched and saved.

Sometimes church members will talk *among themselves* about the minister's imprudence, and create a party, and get into a very wrong spirit, because the wicked are displeased. There was a place, where there was a powerful revival, and great opposition. The church were alarmed, for fear that if the minister was not less plain and pointed, some of the impenitent would go and join some other congregation. And one of the leading men in the church was appointed to go to the minister, and ask him not to preach quite so hard, for if he continued to do so, such and such persons would leave the congregation. The minister asked, Is not the preaching true? "Yes." Does not God bless it? "Yes." Did you ever see the like of this work before in this place? "No, I never did." "Get thee behind me, Satan, the devil has sent you here on this errand; you see God is blessing the preaching, the work is

HOW CHURCHES CAN HELP MINISTERS

going on, and sinners are converted every day, and now you come to get me to let down the tone of preaching, so as to ease the minds of the ungodly." The man felt the rebuke, and took it like a Christian; he saw his error and submitted, and never again was heard to find fault with the plainness of preaching.

In another town, where there was a revival, a woman who had some influence, (not pious,) complained very much about plain, pointed, personal preaching, as she called it. But by and by she herself became a subject of the work. After this some of her impenitent friends reminded her of what she used to say against the preacher for "preaching it out so hot." She now said her views were altered, and she did not care how hot the truth was preached, if it was *red hot*.[2]

6. Do not *take part with the wicked* in any way. If you do it at all, you will strengthen their hands. If the wicked accuse the minister of being imprudent, or of being personal, and if the church members, without admitting that the minister does so, only admit that personal preaching is wrong, and talk about the impropriety of personal preaching, the wicked will feel themselves strengthened by such remarks. Do not unite with them at all, for they will feel that they have you on their side against their minister. You adopt their principles, and use their language, and are understood as sympathizing with them. What is personal preaching? No *individual* is ever benefited by preaching, until he is made to feel that it *means him*.[3] Now such preaching is always personal. It often appears so personal, to wicked men, that they feel as if they were just going to be called out by name, before the congregation. A minister was once preaching to a congregation, and when describing certain characters, he said, "If I was omniscient, I could call out by name the very persons that answer to this picture." A man cried out, "Name me!" and he looked as if he was going to sink into the earth. He afterwards said that he had no idea of speaking out, but the minister described him so perfectly, that he really thought he was going to call him by name. The minister did not know there was such a man in the world. It is common for men to think their own conduct is described, and they com-

---

[2] In the British Isles it is still common to speak of revivalists, particularly the more vehement sort, as "hot-gospelers."

[3] Finney was accused, and probably with justice, of having denounced certain recalcitrant sinners by name in his public sermons and prayers during his early years as a revivalist. See Ephraim Perkins, *A "Bunker Hill" Contest, A. D. 1826.* . . . (Troy, 1827). It is certain that many of his imitators did this.

plain, "Who has been telling him about me? Somebody has been talking to him about me, and getting him to preach at me." I suppose I have heard of five hundred or a thousand just such cases. Now if the church members will just admit that it is *wrong* for a minister to *mean* any body in his preaching, how can he do any good? If you are not willing your minister should mean any body, or preach to any body, you had better dismiss him. Whom must he preach to, if not to the persons, the individuals before him? And how can he preach to them, when he does not mean them?

7. If you wish to stand by your minister in promoting a revival, do not *by your lives contradict* his preaching. If he preaches that sinners are going to hell, do not give the lie to it, and smile it all away, by your levity and unconcern. I have heard sinners speak of the effect produced on their minds, by levity in Christians, after a solemn and searching discourse. *They* feel solemn and tender, and begin to be alarmed at their condition, and they see these professors, instead of weeping over them, all light and easy, as much as to say, "Don't be afraid, sinners, it ain't [4] so bad, after all; keep cool and you will do well; do you think we would laugh and joke, if you were going to hell so fast? We should not laugh if only your house was on fire, still less if we saw you burning in it." Of what use is it for a minister to preach to sinners, in such a state of things?

8. Do not needlessly *take up the time* of your minister. Ministers often lose a great deal of time by individuals calling on them to talk, when they have nothing of importance to talk about, and no particular errand. The minister of course is glad to see his friends, and often too willing to spend time in conversation with his people, as he loves and esteems them. Professors of religion should remember that a minister's time is worth more than gold, for it can be employed in that which gold can never buy. If the minister is kept from his knees, or from his Bible, or his study, that they may indulge themselves in his conversation, they do a great injury. When you have a *good reason* for it, you should never be backward to call on him, and even take up all the time that is necessary. But if you have nothing in particular to say that is important, keep away. I knew a man in one of our cities, who was out of business, and he used to take up months of the minister's time. He would come to his study, and sit for three hours at a time, and talk, because he had nothing else to do, till finally, the minister

---

[4] By 1868 it was considered bad grammar to say "ain't," and in the revised edition of these lectures Finney changed this to "is not."

had to rebuke him plainly, and tell him how much sin he was committing.[5]

9. Be sure not to sanction any thing that is calculated to divert public attention from the subject of religion. Often when it comes the time of year to work, the evenings are long, and business is light, and the very time to make an extra effort, at this moment, somebody in the church will *give a party*, and invite some Christian friends, so as to have it a *religious* party. And then some other family must do the same, to return the compliment. Then another and another, till it grows into an organized system of parties, that consume the whole winter. Abominable! This is the grand device of the devil, because it appears so innocent, and so proper, to promote good feeling, and increase the acquaintance of Christians with each other. And so, instead of prayer meetings they will have these parties.

The evils of these parties are very great. They are often got up at great expense, and the most abominable gluttony is practised in them. It is said that the expense is from one hundred to one thousand dollars. I have been told that in some instances, professed Christians have given great parties, and made great entertainments, and excused their ungodly prodigality in the use of Jesus Christ's money, by giving what was left, after the feast was ended, *to the poor!* Thus making it a virtue to feast and riot, even to surfeiting, on the bounties of God's providence, under pretence of benefiting the poor. This is the same in principle, with a splendid ball which was given some years since, in a neighboring city. The ball was got up for the benefit of the poor, and each gentleman was to pay a certain sum, and after the ball was ended, whatever remained of the funds thus raised, was to be given to the poor. Truly this is strange charity, to eat and drink and dance, and when they have rioted and feasted until they can enjoy it no longer, they deal out to the poor the crumbs that have fallen from the table. I do not see why such a ball is not quite as pious as such Christian parties. The evil of balls does not consist simply in the exercise of dancing, but in the dissipation, and surfeiting, and temptations connected with them.

But it is said they are *Christian* parties, and that they are all, or nearly all, professors of religion who attend them. And furthermore, that they are concluded, often, with prayer. Now I regard

[5] Notice that to waste a minister's time is not simply bad manners; it is a sin. There was no middle ground between right and wrong for Finney.

this as one of the worst features about them; that after the waste of time and money, the excess in eating and drinking, the vain conversation, and nameless *fooleries*, with which such a season is filled up, an attempt should be made to sanctify it and palm it off upon God, by concluding it with prayer. Say what you will, it would not be more absurd or incongruous, or impious, to close a ball, or a theatre, or a card party with prayer.

Has it come to this, that professors of religion, professing to desire the salvation of the world, when such calls are made upon them, from the four winds of heaven, to send the gospel, to furnish Bibles, and tracts, and missionaries, to save the world from death, that they should spend hundreds of dollars in an evening, and then go to the monthly concert and pray for the heathen!

In some instances, I have been told, they find a salve for their consciences, in the fact that their *minister* attends their parties. This, of course, would give weight to such an example, and if one professor of religion made a party and invited their minister, others must do the same. The next step they take, may be for each to give a ball, and appoint their minister a manager! Why not? And perhaps, by and by, he will do them the favor to play the fiddle.[6] In my estimation he might quite as well do it, as to go and conclude such a party with prayer.

I have heard with pain, that a circle of parties, I know not to what extent, has been held in ROCHESTER — that place so highly favored of the Lord.[7] I know not through whose influence they have been got up, or by what particular persons they have been patronized and attended. But I should advise any congregation, who are calculating to have a circle of parties, in the mean time to dismiss their minister, and let *him* go and preach where the people would be ready to receive the word and profit by it, and not have him stay and be distressed, and grieved, and killed, by attempting to promote religion among them, while they are engaged heart and hand in the service of the devil.

Professors of religion should never get up any thing that *may* divert public attention from religion, without first having consulted their minister, and made it a subject of special prayer. And if they find it will have this effect, they ought never to do it.

[6] Finney himself was an accomplished player of the bass viol, but he did so only in church where bass viols preceded organs as the instrumental accompaniment for the choir. See p. 256.

[7] Rochester was "favored of the Lord" because it was the scene of Finney's most successful revival in 1830–1831.

Subjects will often come up before the public which have this tendency; some course of lectures, or show, or the like. Professors ought to be wise, and understand what they are about, and not give countenance to any such thing, until they see what influence it will have, and whether it will hinder a revival. If it will do that, let them have nothing to do with it. Every such thing should be estimated by its bearing upon Christ's kingdom.

In relation to parties, say what you please about their being an innocent recreation, I appeal to any of you who have ever attended them, to say whether they fit you for prayer, or increase your spirituality, or whether sinners are ever converted in them, or Christians made to agonize in prayer for souls?

II. I am to mention several things which churches must DO, if they would promote a revival and aid their minister.

1. They must attend to his *temporal wants*. A minister, who gives himself wholly to the work, cannot be engaged in worldly employments, and *of course* is entirely dependent on his people for the supply of his temporal wants, including the support of his family. I need not argue this point here, for you all understand this perfectly. It is the command of God, that "they which preach the gospel should live of the gospel." But now look around and see how many churches do in this matter. For instance, when they want a minister, they will cast about and see *how cheap* they can get one. They will calculate to a farthing how much his salt will cost, and how much his meal, and then set his salary so low as to subject him to extreme inconvenience to get along and keep his family. A minister must have his mind at ease, to study and labor with effect, and he cannot screw down prices, and banter, and look out for the best chances to buy to advantage what he needs. If he is obliged to do this, his mind is embarrassed. Unless his temporal wants are so supplied, that his thoughts may be abstracted from them, how can he do his duty?

2. *Be honest with your minister.*

Do not measure out and calculate with how much salt and how many bushels of grain he can possibly get along. Remember, you are dealing with Christ. And he calls you to place his ministers in such a situation, that with ordinary prudence temporal embarrassment is out of the question.

3. *Be punctual with him.*

Sometimes churches, when they are about settling a minister, have a great deal of pride about giving a salary, and they will get up a subscription, and make out an amount which they never pay, and very likely never expected to pay. And so, after one, two, three, or four years, the society gets three or four hundred dollars in arrears to their minister, and then they expect he will give it to them. And all the while, they wonder why there is no revival! This may be the very reason, because the church have LIED; they have faithfully promised to pay so much, and have not done it. God cannot consistently pour out his Spirit on such a church.

4. *Pay him his salary without asking.*

Nothing is so embarrassing, often, to a minister, as to be obliged to *dun* his people for his salary. Often he gets enemies, and gives offence, by being *obliged* to call, and call, and call for his money, and then not get it as they promised. They would have paid it if their *credit* had been at stake, but when it is nothing but *conscience* and the blessing of God, they let it lie along. If any one of them had a note at the bank, you would see him careful and prompt to be on the ground before three o'clock. That is because the note will be protested, and they shall lose their character. But they know the minister will *not sue* them for his salary, and they are careless and let it run along, and he must suffer the inconvenience. This is not so common in the city as it is in the country. But in the country, I have known some heart-rending cases of distress and misery, by the negligence and cruelty of congregations in WITHHOLDING that which is due. Churches live in habitual lying and cheating, and then wonder why they have no revival. How can they wonder?

5. *Pray for your minister.* I mean something by this. And what do you suppose I mean? Even the apostles used to urge the churches to pray for them. This is more important than you imagine. Ministers do not ask people to pray for them, simply as men, nor that they may be filled with an abundance of the Spirit's influences, merely to promote their personal enjoyment. But they know that unless the church greatly desires a blessing upon the labors of a minister, it is tempting God for him to expect it. How often does a minister go into his pulpit, feeling that his heart is ready to break for the blessing of God, while he also feels that there is no room to expect it, for there is no reason to believe the church desire it! Perhaps he has been two hours on his knees in supplication, and yet because that the chuch do not desire a blessing, he feels as if his words would bound back in his face.

I have seen Christians who would be in an agony, when the minister was going into the pulpit, for fear his mind should be in a cloud, or his heart cold, or he should have no unction, and so a blessing should not come. I have labored with a man of this sort. He would pray until he got assurance in his mind, that God would be with me in preaching, and sometimes he would pray himself sick. I have known the time, when he has been in darkness for a season, while the people were gathering, and his mind was full of anxiety, and he would go again and again to pray, till finally he would come into the room with a placid face, and say, "The Lord has come, and he will be with us." And I do not know that I ever found him mistaken.[8]

I have known a church bear their minister on their arms in prayer from day to day, and watch with anxiety unutterable, to see that he has the Holy Ghost with him in his labors! When they feel and pray thus, O what feelings and what looks are manifest in the congregation! They have felt anxiety unutterable to have the word come with power, and take effect, and when they see their prayer answered, and they hear a word or a sentence come WARM from the heart, and taking effect among the people, you can see their whole souls look out of their eyes. How different is the case, where the church feel that the *minister* is praying, and so there is no need of their praying! They are mistaken. The church must desire and pray for the blessing. God says he will be inquired of *by the house of Israel*. I wish you to feel that there can be no substitute for this.

I have seen cases in revivals, where the church was kept in the back ground in regard to prayer, and persons from abroad were called on to pray in all the meetings. This is always unhappy, even if there should be a revival, for the revival must be less powerful and less salutary in its influences upon the church. I do not know but I have sometimes offended Christians and ministers from abroad, by continuing to call on members of the church in the place to pray, and not on those from abroad. It was not from any disrespect to them, but because the object was to get *that church* which was chiefly concerned, to desire, and pray, and agonize for the blessing.

[8] Finney here refers to his close friend and associate "Father" Daniel Nash, a Presbyterian minister and evangelist who worked with him during the Oneida revivals. For a description of Nash, see Cross, *Burned-Over District*, pp. 160–162 and *passim*.

In a certain place, a protracted meeting was held, with no good results, and great evils produced.[9] I was led to make inquiry for the reason. And it came out, that in all their meetings, not one member of their own church was called on to pray, but all the prayers were made by persons from abroad. No wonder there was no good done. The church was not interested. The leader of the meeting meant well, but he undertook to promote a revival without getting the church there into the work. He let a lazy church lie still and do nothing, and so there could be no good.

Churches should pray for ministers as the agents of breaking down sinners with the word of truth. Prayer for a minister is often done in a set and formal way, and confined to the prayer meetings. They will *say* their prayers in the old way, as they have always done: "Lord, bless thy ministering servant, whom thou hast stationed on this part of Zion's walls," and so on, and it amounts to nothing, because there is no heart in it. And the proof often is, that they never thought of praying for him in secret, they never have agonized in their closets for a blessing on his labors. They may not omit it wholly in their meetings. If they do *that*, it is evident that they care very little indeed about the labors of their minister. But that is not the most important place. The way to present *effectual* prayer for your minister is to take it to your closet, and when you are in secret, wrestle with God for success to attend his labors.

I knew a case of a minister in ill health, who became depressed and sunk down in his mind, and was very much in darkness, so that he did not feel as if he could preach any longer. An individual of the church was waked up to feel for the minister's situation, and to pray that he might have the Holy Ghost to attend his preaching. One Sabbath morning, this person's mind was very much exercised, and he began to pray as soon as it was light, and prayed again and again for a blessing *that day*. And the Lord in some way directed the minister within hearing of his prayer. The person was telling the Lord just what he thought of the minister's situation and state of mind, and pleading, as if he would not be denied, for a blessing. The minister went into the pulpit and preached, and the light broke in upon him, and the word was with power, and a revival commenced that very day.

6. A minister should be provided for *by the church*, and his support guaranteed, *irrespective of the ungodly*. Otherwise he may

---

[9] Finney discusses the nature and origin of protracted meetings on pp. 262ff.

be obliged either to starve his family, or to keep back a part of the truth so as not to offend sinners. I once expostulated with a minister who I found was afraid to come out fully with the truth. I told him I was surprised he did not bear down on certain points. He told me he was so situated that he *must* please certain men, who would be touched there. It was the ungodly that chiefly supported him, and that made him dependent and temporizing. And yet perhaps that very church which left their minister dependent on the ungodly for his bread, will turn round and abuse him for his want of faith, and his fear of men. The church ought always to say to their minister, "We will support you; go to work; let the truth pour down on the people, and we will stand by you."

7. See that every thing is so arranged, that people can sit *comfortably in meeting*. If people do not sit easy, it is difficult to get or to keep their attention. And if they are not attentive, they cannot be converted. They have come to hear for their lives, and they ought to be so situated that they can hear with all their souls, and have nothing in their bodily position to call for attention. Churches do not realize how important it is that the place of meeting should be made comfortable. I do not mean *showy*. All your glare and glory of rich chandeliers, and rich carpets, and splendid pulpits, is the opposite extreme, and takes off the attention just as badly, and defeats every object for which a sinner should come to meeting. You need not expect a revival *there*.

8. See that the house of God is kept *cleanly*. The house of God should be kept as clean as you would want your own house to be kept. Churches are often kept excessively slovenly. I have seen them, where people used so much tobacco, and took so little care about neatness, that it was impossible to preach with comfort. Once in a protracted meeting, the thing was charged upon the church, and they had to acknowledge it, that they paid more money for tobacco than they did for the cause of missions. They could not kneel in their pews, and ladies could not sit without all the time watching their clothes, and they had to be careful where they stepped, because the house was so dirty, and there was so much tobacco juice running all about the floor. If people cannot go where they can hear without being annoyed with offensive sights and smells, and where they can kneel in prayer, what good will a protracted meeting do? There is an importance in these things, which is not realized. See that man! What is he doing? I

am preaching to him about eternal life, and he is thinking about the dirty pew. And that woman is asking for a footstool to keep her feet out of the tobacco juice. Shame! [10]

9. It is important that the house should be *just warm enough*, and not too warm. Suppose a minister comes into a house, and finds it cold; he sees as soon as he gets in, that he might as well stay at home; the people are shivering, their feet cold, they feel as if they should take cold, they are uneasy, and he wishes he was at home, for he knows he cannot do any thing, but he must preach, or they will be disappointed.

Or he may find the house too warm, and the people, instead of listening to the truth, are fanning, and panting for breath, and by and by a woman faints, and makes a stir, and the train of thought and feeling is all lost, and so a whole sermon is wasted to no good end. These little things take off the attention of people from the words of eternal life. And very often it is so, that if you drop a single link in the chain of argument, you lose the whole, and the people are damned, just because the careless church do not see to the proper regulation of these little matters.

10. The house should be *well ventilated*. Of all houses, a church should be the most perfectly ventilated. If there is no change of the air, it passes through so many lungs it becomes bad, and its vitality is exhausted, and the people pant, they know not why, and feel an almost irresistible desire to sleep, and the minister preaches in vain. The sermon is lost, and worse than lost. I have often wondered that this matter should be so little the subject of thought. The elders and trustees will sit and hear a whole sermon, while the people are all but ready to die for the want of air, and the minister is wasting his strength in preaching where the room is just like an exhausted receiver,[11] and there they sit and never think to do any thing to help the matter. They should take it upon themselves to see that this is regulated right, that the house is just warm enough, and the air kept pure. How important it is that the church should be awake to this subject, that the minister may labor to the best advantage, and the people give their undivided attention to the truth, which is to save their souls.

It is very common, when things are wrong, to have it all laid to the sexton. This is not so. Often the sexton is not to blame. If

---

[10] For a more sustained attack upon the use of tobacco, see p. 416. To Finney using tobacco was as sinful as using "ardent spirits."

[11] An "exhausted receiver" means a retort filled with gas in a chemical experiment.

the house is cold and uncomfortable, very often it is because the fuel is not good, or the stoves not suitable, or the house is so open it cannot be warmed. If it is too warm, perhaps somebody has intermeddled when he was out, and heaped on fuel without discretion. Or, if the sexton is in fault, perhaps it is because the church do not pay him enough for his services, and he cannot afford to give the attention necessary to keep the church in order. Churches sometimes screw down the sexton's salary, to the lowest point, so that he is obliged to slight his work. Or they will select one who is incompetent, for the sake of getting him cheap, and then the thing is not done. The fault is in the church. Let them give an adequate compensation for the work, and it can be done, and done faithfully. If one sexton will not do it right, another will, and the church are bound to see it done right, or else let them dismiss their minister, and not keep him, and at the same time have other things in a state so out of order that he loses all his work. What economy! To pay the minister's salary, and then for the want of fifty dollars added to the sexton's wages, every thing is so out of order that the minister's labors are all lost, souls are lost, and your children and neighbors go down to hell!

Sometimes this uncleanliness, and negligence, and confusion are chargeable to the minister. Perhaps he uses tobacco, and sets the example of defiling the house of God. Perhaps the pulpit will be the filthiest place in the house. I have sometimes been in pulpits, that were to loathsome to be occupied by human beings. If a minister has no more piety and decency than this, no wonder things are at loose ends in the congregation. And generally it is even so.

11. People should leave their dogs, and very young children, at home. I have often known contentions arise among dogs, and children to cry, just at that stage of the services, that would most effectually destroy the effect of the meeting. If children are present and weep, they should *instantly* be removed. I have sometimes known a mother or a nurse sit and toss her child, while its cries were diverting the attention of the whole congregation. This is cruel. And as for dogs, they had infinitely better be dead, than to divert attention from the word of God. See that deacon; perhaps his dog has in this way destroyed more souls than the deacon will ever be instrumental in saving.[12]

[12] This paragraph was not included in the version of the lecture that appeared in the *New York Evangelist*, February 28, 1835, p. 24.

12. The members of the church should aid the minister by *visiting from house to house*, and trying to save souls.[13] Do not leave all this to the minister. It is impossible he should do it, even if he gives all his time, and neglects his study and his closet. Church members should take pains and qualify themselves for this duty, so that they can be useful in it.

13. They should hold *Bible classes*. Suitable individuals should be selected to hold Bible classes, for the instruction of the young people, and where those who are awakened or affected by the preaching, can be received and be converted. As soon as any one is seen to be touched, let them be invited to join the Bible class, where they will be properly treated, and probably they will be converted. The church should select the best men for this service, and should all be on the look out to fill up the Bible classes. It has been done in this congregation, and it is a very common thing, when persons are impressed, that they are observed by somebody, and invited to join the Bible class, and they will do it, and there they are converted. I do not mean that we are doing all we ought to do in this way, or all we might do. We want more teachers, able and willing to take charge of such classes.

14. Churches should sustain *Sabbath schools*, and in this way aid their ministers in saving souls. How can a minister attend to this and preach? Unless the church will take off these responsibilities, and cares, and labors, he must either neglect them, or be crushed. Let the church be WIDE AWAKE, watch and bring in children to the school, and teach them faithfully, and lay themselves out to promote a revival in the school.

15. They should *watch over the members of the church*. They should visit each other, in order to stir each other up, know each other's spiritual state, and provoke one another to love and good works. The minister cannot do it, he has not time; it is impossible he should study and prepare sermons, and at the same time visit every member of the church as often as it needs to be done to keep them advancing. The church are bound to do it. They are *under oath* to watch over each other's spiritual welfare. But how is this done? Many do not know each other. They meet and pass each other as strangers, and never ask about their spiritual

---

[13] In the 1920's and afterward home visitation became a substitute for mass revivalism, but Finney saw this method simply as a supplement to revival preaching. The problem of "following up" persons converted or awakened in a revival has always been a thorny one for the churches. Home visitation programs and Bible classes for beginners are the most popular methods.

condition. But if they hear any thing bad of one, they go and tell it to others. Instead of watching over each other for their good, they watch for their halting. How can they watch for good when they are not even acquainted with each other?

16. The church should *watch for the effect of preaching*. If they are *praying* for the success of the preached word, they will watch for it of course. They should keep a look out, and when any in the congregation give evidence that the word of God has taken hold of them, they should follow it up. Wherever there are any exhibitions of feeling, those persons should be attended to, instantly, and not left till their impressions wear off. They should talk to them, or get them visited, or get them into the anxious meeting, or into the Bible class, or bring them to the minister. If the members of the church do not attend to this, they neglect their duty. If they attend to it, they may do incalculable good.[14]

There was a pious young woman, who lived in a very cold and wicked place. She alone had the spirit of prayer, and she had been praying for a blessing upon the word. At length she saw one individual in the congregation who seemed to be affected by the preaching, and as soon as the minister came from the pulpit, she came forward, agitated and trembling, and begged him to go and converse with the person immediately. He did so, and the individual was soon converted, and a revival followed. Now one of your stupid professors would not have seen that individual awakened, and would have stumbled over half a dozen of them without notice, and let them go to hell. Professors should watch every sermon, and see how it affects the congregation. I do not mean that they should be stretching their necks and staring about the house, but they should observe, as they may, and if they find any person affected by preaching, throw themselves in his way, and guide him to the Savior.

17. Beware, and *not give away all the preaching* to others. If you do not take your portion, you will starve, and become like spiritual skeletons. Christians should take their portion to themselves. If the word should be quite searching to them, they should make the honest application, and lay it along side their heart

---

[14] Finney trained his New York congregation to be on the lookout during all of his sermons for persons in the audience who were moved by his preaching and to speak to them afterwards about their souls. Evangelists ever since Finney's day have trained "counselors" or "personal workers" before their revival meetings and scattered them through the audiences to do just the type of work Finney describes here.

and practise it, and live by it. Otherwise preaching will do *them* no good.

18. Be ready to aid your minister in effecting *his plans for doing good*. When the minister is wise to devise plans of usefulness, and the church ready to execute them, they may carry all before them. But when the church hang back from every enterprise until they are actually dragged into it, when they are opposing every proposal, because it will *cost something*, they are a dead weight upon a minister. If stoves are needed, O no, they will cost something. If lamps are called for, to prevent preaching in the dark, O no, they will cost something. And so they will stick up candles on the posts, or do without evening meetings altogether. If they stick up candles, it soon comes to pass that they either give no light, or some one must run round and snuff them. And so the whole congregation are disturbed by the candle-snuffer, their attention taken off, and the sermon lost.

I was once attending a protracted meeting, where we were embarrassed because there were no lamps to the house. I urged the people to get them, but they thought it would cost too much. I then proposed to get them myself, and was about to do it, but found it would give offence, and we went on without. But the blessing did not come, to any great extent. How could it? The church began by calculating to a cent how much it would cost, and they would not go beyond, to save souls from hell.

So where a minister appoints a meeting, such people cannot have it, because it will cost something. If they can offer unto the Lord that which costs nothing, they will do it. Miserable helpers they are! Such a church can have no revival. A minister might as well have a millstone about his neck, as such a church. He had better leave them, if he cannot learn them better, and go where he will not be so hampered.

19. Church members should make it a point to *attend prayer meetings*, and attend *in time*. Some church members will always attend on preaching, because there they have nothing to do, but to sit and hear, and be entertained, but they will not attend prayer meetings, for fear they shall be called on to do something. Such members tie up the hands of the minister, and discourage his heart. Why do they employ a minister? Is it to amuse them by preaching? or is it that he may teach them the will of God that they may do it?

20. Church members ought to *study and inquire* what they

can do, and then *do it*. Christians should be trained like a band of soldiers. It is the duty and office of a minister to train them for usefulness, to teach them and direct them, and lead them on, in such a way as to produce the greatest amount of moral influence. And then they should stand their ground and do their duty, otherwise they will be right in the way.

There are many other points which I noted, and intended to touch upon, but there is not time. I could write a book as big as this Bible, in detailing the various particulars that ought to be attended to. I must close with a few

REMARKS.

1. You see that a minister's want of success may not be wholly on account of a want of wisdom in the exercise of his office. I am not going to plead for negligent ministers. I never will spare ministers from the naked truth, nor apply flattering titles to men. If they are blameworthy, let them be blamed. And no doubt they are always more or less to blame when the word produces no effect. But it is far from being true that they are always the *principal* persons to blame. Sometimes the church is much more to blame than the minister, and if an apostle or an angel from heaven were to preach, he could not produce a revival of religion in that church. Perhaps they are dishonest to their minister, or covetous, or careless about the conveniences of public worship. Alas! what a state many country churches are in, where, for the want of a hundred dollars, every thing is inconvenient and uncomfortable, and the labors of the preacher are lost. They live in ceiled houses themselves, and let the house of God lie waste. Or the church counteract all the influence of preaching, by their ungodly lives. Or perhaps their parties, their worldly show, as in most of the churches in this city, annihilate the influence of the gospel.

2. Churches should remember that they are exceedingly guilty, to employ a minister, and then not aid him in his work. The Lord Jesus Christ has sent an ambassador to sinners, to turn them from their evil ways, and he fails of his errand, because the church refuse to do their duty. Instead of recommending his message, and seconding his entreaties, and holding up his hands in all the ways that are proper, they stand right in the way, and contradict his message, and counteract his influence, and souls perish. No doubt in most of the congregations in the United States, the minister

is often hindered so much, that he might as well be on a foreign mission a great part of the time, as to be there, for any effect of his preaching in the conversion of sinners, while he has to preach over the heads of an inactive, stupid church.

And yet these very churches are not willing to have their minister absent a few days to attend a protracted meeting.[15] "We cannot spare him; why he is *our minister*, and we like to have our minister here;" while at the same time they hinder all he can do. If he could, he would tear himself right away, and go where there is no minister, and where the people would be willing to receive the gospel. But there he must stay, though he cannot get the church into a state to have a revival once in three years, to last three months at a time. It might be well for him to say to the church, "Whenever you are determined to take one of these long naps, I wish you to let me know it, so that I can go and labor somewhere else in the mean time, till you are ready to wake again."

3. Many churches cannot be blessed with a revival, because they are *sponging* out of other churches, and out of the treasury of the Lord, for the support of their minister, when they are abundantly able to support him themselves. Perhaps they are depending on the Home Missionary Society,[16] or on other churches, while they are not exercising any *self-denial* for the sake of the gospel. I have been amazed to see how some churches live. One church that I was acquainted with, actually confessed that they spent more money for tobacco than they gave for missions. And yet they had no minister, *because they were not able* to support one. And they have none now. And yet there is *one man* in that church who is able to support a minister. And still they have no minister, and no preaching.

The churches have not been instructed in their duty on this subject. I stopped in one place last summer, where there was no preaching. I inquired of an elder in the church, why it was so, and he said it was because they were so poor. I asked him how much he was worth. He did not give me a direct answer, but said that another elder's income was about $500 a year, and I finally found out that this man's was about the same. Here, said I, are two elders, each of you able to support a minister, and be-

---

[15] It was customary in protracted meetings in rural areas for ministers in nearby towns to assist each other in carrying the burden of preaching and conducting prayer and inquiry meetings.

[16] For the Home Missionary Society, see Lecture XI, p. 191, note 10.

HOW CHURCHES CAN HELP MINISTERS 245

cause you cannot get help from abroad, you have no preaching. Why, if you had preaching, it would not be blessed, while you were thus sponging out of the Lord's treasury. Finally, he confessed that he was able to support a minister, and the two together agreed that they would do it.

It is common for churches to ask help, when in fact they do not need any help, and when it would be a great deal better for them to support their own minister. If they get funds from the Home Missionary Society, when they ought to raise them themselves, they may expect the curse of the Lord upon them, and this will be a sufficient reason for the gospel's proving to them a curse rather than a blessing. Of how many churches might it be said, "Ye have robbed God, even this whole church."

I know a church who employed a minister but half the time, and felt unable to pay his salary for that. A female working society in a neighboring town appropriated their funds to this object, and assisted this church in paying their minister's salary.[17] The result was, as might be expected. He did them little or no good. They had no revival under his preaching, nor could they ever expect any, while acting on such a principle. There was one man in that congregation who could support a minister all the time. I was informed by a member, that the church members were supposed to be worth TWO HUNDRED THOUSAND DOLLARS. Now if this is true, here is a church with an income, at seven per cent., of $14,000 a year, who felt themselves too poor to pay $200 for support of a minister to preach half the time, and would suffer the females of a neighboring town to work with their own hands to aid them in paying this sum. Among the elders of this church, I found that several of them used tobacco, and two of them who lived together signed a covenant written on the blank leaf of their Bible, in which they pledged themselves to abandon that sin for ever.

It was in a great measure for want of right instruction, that this church was pursuing such a course. For when the subject was taken up, and their duty laid before them, the wealthy man of whom I am speaking said that he would pay the whole salary himself, if he thought it would not be resented by the congregation, and do more hurt than good; and that if the church would procure

[17] A female working society was an organization of church women who banded together locally to raise money to support itinerant evangelists or home missionaries in places "destitute of the gospel." Finney's first salary as an evangelist was paid by the Female Missionary Society of the Western District of New York. See Fletcher, *Oberlin*, I, 20; Cross, *Burned-Over District*, pp. 20ff.

a minister, and go ahead and raise a part of his salary, he would make up the remainder. They can now not only support a minister half the time, but all the time, and pay his salary themselves.[18] And they will find it good and profitable to do so.

As I have gone from place to place laboring in revivals, I have always found that churches were blessed in proportion to their liberality. Where they have manifested a disposition to support the gospel, and to pour their substance liberally into the treasury of the Lord, they have been blessed both in spiritual and temporal things. But where they have been parsimonious, and let the minister preach for them for little or nothing, these churches have been cursed instead of blessed. And as a general thing, in revivals of religion, I have found it to be true that young converts are most inclined to join those churches which are most liberal in making efforts to support the gospel.

The churches are very much in the dark on this subject. They have not been taught their duty. I have in many instances found an exceeding readiness to do it, when the subject was laid before them. I knew an elder in a church, who was talking about getting a minister for half the time, because the church were poor, although his own income was considerable. I asked him if *his* income was not sufficient to support a minister all the time himself. He said it was. And on being asked what other use he could make of the Lord's money which he possessed, that would prove so beneficial to the interest of Christ's kingdom, as to employ a minister not only half but all the time in his own town, he concluded to set himself about it. A minister has been accordingly obtained, and I believe they find no difficulty in paying him his full salary.

The fact is, that a minister can do but little by preaching only half the time. If on one Sabbath an impression is made, it is lost before a fortnight comes round. As a matter of economy, a church should lay themselves out to support the gospel all the time. If they get the right sort of a minister, and keep him steadily at work, they may have a revival, and thus the ungodly will be converted and come in and help them. And thus in one year they may have a great accession to their strength. But if they employ a minister but half the time, year after year may roll away, while

---

[18] Half-time preachers were those employed to supply two churches and to preach alternate Sundays in each. Finney's complaints about the unwillingness of many western congregations to support a full-time minister were occasioned partly by the natural parsimony of New Englanders and partly by the transitional state of the frontier during this period.

sinners are going to hell, and no accession is made to their strength from the ranks of the ungodly.

The fact is, that professors of religion have not been made to feel, that all their possessions are the Lord's. Hence they have talked about *giving their property* for the support of the gospel. As if the Lord Jesus Christ was a beggar, and they called upon to support his gospel, as an act of almsgiving! A merchant in one of the towns in this state, was paying a large part of his minister's salary. One of the members of the church was relating the fact to a minister from abroad, and speaking of the *sacrifice* which this merchant was making. At this moment the merchant came in. "Brother," said the minister, "you are a merchant. Suppose you employ a clerk to sell goods, and a school-master to teach your children. You order your clerk to pay your school-master out of the store such an amount, for his services in teaching. Now suppose your clerk should give out that *he* had to pay this school-master his salary, and should speak of the sacrifices that *he* was making to do it, what would you say to this?" "Why," said the merchant, "I should say it was ridiculous." "Well," says the minister, "God employs you to sell goods as his clerk, and your minister he employs to teach his children, and requires you to pay his salary out of the income of the store. Now, do you call this *your* sacrifice, and say that *you* are making a great sacrifice, to pay this minister's salary? No, you are just as much bound to sell goods for God, as he is to preach for God. You have no more right to sell goods for the purpose of laying up money, than he has to preach the gospel for the same purpose. You are bound to be just as pious, and to aim *as singly* at the glory of God, in selling goods, as he is in preaching the gospel. And thus you are as absolutely to give up your whole time for the service of God, as he does. You and your family may lawfully live out of the avails of this store, and so may the minister and his family, just as lawfully. If you sell goods from these motives, selling goods is just as much serving God as preaching. And a man who sells goods upon these principles, and acts in conformity to them, is just as pious, just as much in the service of God, as he is who preaches the gospel. Every man is bound to serve God *in his calling*, the minister by teaching, the merchant by selling goods, the farmer by tilling his fields, the lawyer and physician by plying the duties of their profession.

"It is *equally* unlawful for any one of these to labor for the meat that perisheth. All they do is to be for God, and all they can earn, after comfortably supporting their families, is to be dedicated to the spread of the gospel and the salvation of the world."

It has long enough been supposed that ministers must be more pious than other men, that *they* must not love the world, that *they* must labor for God: they must live as frugally as possible, and lay out their whole time, and health, and strength, and life, to build up the kingdom of Jesus Christ. This is true. But although other men are not called to labor in the same field, and to give up their time to public instruction, yet they are just as *absolutely* bound to consider their whole time as God's and have no more right to love the world, or accumulate wealth, or lay it up for their children, or spend it upon their lusts, than ministers have.

It is high time the church was acquainted with these principles; and the Home Missionary Society may labor till the day of judgment to convert the people, and they will never succeed, till the churches are led to understand and feel their duty in this respect. Why, the very fact that they are asking and receiving aid in supporting their minister from the Home Missionary Society while they are able to support him themselves, is probably the very reason why his labors among them are not more blessed.

I would that the American Home Missionary Society possessed a hundred times the means that it now does, of aiding feeble churches, that are unable to help themselves. But it is neither good economy nor piety, to give their funds to those who are able but unwilling to support the gospel. For it is in vain to attempt to help them, while they are able but unwilling to help themselves.

If the Missionary Society had a ton of gold, it would be no charity to give it to such a church. But let the church bring in all the tithes to God's storehouse, and God will open the windows of heaven and pour down a blessing. But let the churches know assuredly that if they are unwilling to help themselves to the extent of their ability, they will know the reason why such small success attends the labors of their ministers. Here they are sponging their support from the Lord's treasury. How many churches are laying out their money for tea and coffee and tobacco, and then come and ask aid from the Home Missionary Society! I will protest against aiding a church who use tea and tobacco, and live without the least self-denial, and who want to offer God only that which costs nothing.[19]

---

[19] For a more sustained attack upon tea and coffee drinking, see p. 416.

FINALLY — If they mean to be blessed, let them do their duty, do all their duty, put shoulder to the wheel, gird on the gospel armor, and come up to the work. *Then*, if the church is *in the field*, the car of salvation will move on, though all hell oppose, and sinners will be converted and saved. But if a church will give up all the labor to the minister, and sit still and look on, while he is laboring, and themselves do nothing but complain of him, they will not only fail of a revival of religion, but if they continue slothful and censorious, will by and by find themselves in hell for their disobedience and unprofitableness in the service of Christ.

XIV

MEASURES TO PROMOTE REVIVALS[1]

TEXT. — "These men, being Jews, do exceedingly trouble our city, and teach customs which are not lawful for us to receive, neither to observe, being Romans." — ACTS xvi. 20, 21.

"THESE men," here spoken of, were Paul and Silas, who went to Philippi to preach the gospel, and very much disturbed the people of that city, because they supposed the preaching would interfere with their worldly gains. And so they arranged the preachers of the gospel before the magistrates of the city, as culprits, and charged them with teaching doctrines, and especially employing measures, that were not lawful.

In discoursing from these words I design to show,

I. That under the gospel dispensation, God has *established no particular system of measures* to be employed and invariably adhered to in promoting religion.

II. To show that our present forms of public worship, and every thing, so far as *measures* are concerned, have been arrived at *by degrees*, and by *a succession of New Measures*.

I. I am to show that under the gospel, God has established no particular measures to be used.

Under the *Jewish* dispensation, there were particular forms enjoined and prescribed by God himself, from which it was not lawful to depart. But these forms were all *typical*, and were designed to shadow forth Christ, or something connected with the new dispensation that Christ was to introduce.[2] And therefore

---
[1] This lecture is Finney's definitive reply to ten years of criticism by conservative Calvinists against his "new measure" revivalism. See the Introduction to this edition for the significance of this criticism.

[2] Finney like most pietists, believed in and practiced typology, the system of finding in the Old Testament customs, actions, and biographical incidents that are considered analogues or prophecies of New Testament events, doctrines, characters, or practices. (Here Christ's new dispensation provides the Christian "anti-type" to the old Jewish dispensation.) This symbolical or allegorical interpretation of the Bible seems a sharp contrast to pietistic literalism, but it is based on an unsophisticated and non-historical approach to the Bible as a unified exposition by God of His ultimate intentions that is characteristic of the pietistic outlook.

they were fixed, and all their details particularly prescribed by Divine authority. But it *was never so* under the gospel. When Christ came, the ceremonial or typical dispensation was abrogated, because the design of those forms was fulfilled, and therefore themselves of no further use. He, being the anti-type, the types were of course done away at his coming. THE GOSPEL was then preached as the appointed means of promoting religion; and it was left to the discretion of the church to determine, from time to time, what *measures* shall be adopted, and what *forms* pursued, in giving the gospel its power. We are left in the dark as to the measures which were pursued by the apostles and primitive preachers, except so far as we can gather it from occasional hints in the book of Acts. We do not know how many times they sung and how many times they prayed in public worship, nor even whether they sung or prayed at all in their ordinary meetings for preaching. When Jesus Christ was on earth, laboring among his disciples, he had nothing to do with forms or measures. He did from time to time in this respect just as it would be natural for any man to do in such cases, without any thing like a set form or mode of doing it. The Jews accused him of disregarding their forms. His object was to preach and teach mankind the true religion. And when the apostles preached afterwards, with the Holy Ghost sent down from heaven, we hear nothing about their having a particular system of measures to carry on their work, or one apostle doing a thing in a particular way because others did it in that way. Their commission was, "Go and preach the gospel, and disciple all nations." It did not prescribe any forms. It did not admit any. No person can pretend to get any set of forms or particular directions as to measures, out of this commission. Do it — the best way you can — ask wisdom from God — use the faculties he has given you — seek the direction of the Holy Ghost — go forward and do it. This was their commission. And their object was to make known the gospel in the *most effectual* way, to make the truth stand out strikingly, so as to obtain the attention and secure the obedience of the greatest number possible. No person can find any *form* of doing this laid down in the Bible. It is *preaching the gospel* that stands out prominent there as the great thing. The form is left out of the question.

It is manifest, that, in preaching the gospel, there must be *some* kind of measures adopted. The gospel must be gotten before the minds of the people, and measures must be taken so that they *can* hear it, and to induce them to attend to it. This is done by building churches, holding stated or other meetings, and so on. Without some measures, it can never be made to take effect among men.

II. I am to show that our present forms of public worship, and every thing, so far as *measures* are concerned, have been arrived at *by degrees*, and by a *succession of New Measures*.

1. I will mention some things in regard to the *ministry*.

Many years ago, ministers were accustomed to wear a *peculiar habit*. It is so now in Catholic countries. It used to be so here. Ministers had a peculiar dress as much as soldiers. They used to wear a cocked hat, and bands instead of a cravat or stock, and small clothes, and a wig. No matter how much hair a man had on his head, he must cut it off and wear a wig. And then he must wear a gown. All these things were customary, and every clergyman was held bound to wear them, and it was not considered proper for him to officiate without them. All these had doubtless been introduced by a succession of innovations, for we have no good reason for believing that the apostles and primitive ministers dressed differently from other men.

But now all these things have been given up, one by one, by a succession of innovations or new measures, until now in many churches a minister can go into the pulpit and preach without being noticed, although dressed like any other man. And when it was done in regard to each one of them, the church complained as much as if it had been a Divine institution given up. It was denounced as an *innovation*. When ministers began to lay aside their cocked hats, and wear hats like other men, it grieved the elderly people very much; it looked so "undignified," they said, for a minister to wear a round hat. When, in 1827, I wore a fur cap, a minister said, "that was too bad for a minister." [3]

When ministers first began, a few years since, to wear white hats, it was thought by many to be a sad and very undignified innovation. And even now, they are so bigoted in some places, that a clergyman told me but a few days since, in travelling through New England last summer with a white hat, he could perceive that it injured his influence. This spirit should not be looked upon as harmless; I have good reason to know that it is not harmless. Thinking men see it to be mere bigotry, and are exceedingly in danger of viewing every thing about religion in the same light

[3] This sentence and the following paragraph were not included in the version of this lecture published in the *New York Evangelist*, March 7, 1835, p. 38.

MEASURES TO PROMOTE REVIVALS

on this account. This has been the result in many instances. There is at this day scarcely a minister in the land who does not feel himself obliged to wear a black coat, as much as if it were a divine institution. The church is yet filled with a kind of superstitious reverence for such things. This is a great stumbling block to many minds.

So, in like manner, when ministers laid aside their *bands*, and wore cravats or stocks, it was said they were becoming secular, and many found fault. Even now, in some places, a minister would not dare to be seen in the pulpit in a cravat or stock. The people would feel as if they had no clergyman, if he had no bands. A minister in this city asked another, but a few days since, if it would do to wear a black stock in the pulpit. He wore one in his ordinary intercourse with his people, but doubted whether it would do to wear it in the pulpit.

So in regard to short clothes; they used to be thought essential to the ministerial character. Even now, in Catholic countries, every priest wears small clothes. Even the little boys there, who are training for the priest's office, wear their cocked hats, and black stockings, and small clothes. This would look ridiculous amongst us. But it used to be practised in this country. The time was when good people would have been shocked if a minister had gone into the pulpit with pantaloons on. They would have thought he was certainly going to ruin the church by his innovations. I have been told that some years ago, in New England, a certain elderly clergyman was so opposed to the new measures of a minister's wearing pantaloons, that he would on no account allow them in his pulpit. A young man was going to preach for him, who had no small clothes, and the old minister would not let him officiate in pantaloons. "Why," said he, "my people would think I had brought a fop into the pulpit, to see a man there with pantaloons on, and it would produce an excitement among them." And so, finally, the young man was obliged to borrow a pair of the old gentleman's clothes, and they were too short for him, and made a ridiculous figure enough. But any thing was better than such a terrible innovation as preaching in pantaloons. But reason has triumphed.[4]

[4] When Finney says that reason triumphed over the customs of former times he typifies the self-satisfaction of the age of the common man. These paragraphs on the changing dress of the Calvinist clergy are also indicative of the clergy's declining prestige and social status. And despite Finney's protests, it did reflect a secularization of religion. Finney's pleasure at the fact that ministers now

Just so it was in regard to *wigs*. I remember one minister, who, though quite a young man, used to wear an enormous white wig. And the people talked as if there was a divine right about it, and it was as hard to give it up, almost, as to give up the Bible itself. *Gowns* also were considered essential to the ministerial character. And even now, in many congregations in this country, the people will not tolerate a minister in the pulpit, unless he has a flowing silk gown, with enormous sleeves as big as his body. Even in some of the Congregational churches in New England, they cannot bear to give it up. Now, how came people to suppose a minister must have a gown or a wig, in order to preach with effect? Why was it that every clergyman was held obliged to use these things? How is it that not one of these things have been given up in the churches, without producing a shock among them? They have all been given up, one by one, and many congregations have been distracted for a time by the innovation. But will any one pretend that the cause of religion has been injured by it? People felt as if they could hardly worship God without them, but plainly their attachment to them was no part of their religion, that is, no part of the Christian religion. It was mere superstition. And when these things were taken away they complained, as Micah did, "Ye have taken away my gods." But no doubt their religious character was improved, by removing these objects of superstitious reverence. So that the church, on the whole, has been greatly the gainer by the innovations. Thus you see that the present mode of a minister's dress has been gained by a series of new measures.

2. In regard to the *order of public worship*.

The same difficulties have been met in effecting every change, because the church have felt as if God had established just the *mode which they were used to*.

(1.) *Psalm Books*. Formerly it was customary to sing David's Psalms. By and by there was introduced a version of the Psalms in rhyme. This was very bad, to be sure. When ministers tried to introduce them, the churches were distracted, people violently opposed, and great trouble was created by the innovation. But the new measure triumphed.

---

dressed like everyone else, both in and out of the pulpit, is part of the anti-clericalism which he shared with the Jacksonians. Finney carried his egalitarianism so far that even as a professor at Oberlin he asked all his students to address him simply as "Brother Finney." See *Reminiscences of Rev. Charles G. Finney* (Oberlin, 1876), p. 45.

MEASURES TO PROMOTE REVIVALS 255

Afterwards another version was brought forward in a better style of poetry, and its introduction was opposed with much contention, as a new measure. And finally Watt's version, which is still opposed in many churches. No longer ago than 1828, when I was in Philadelphia, I was told that a minister there was preaching a *course of lectures* on psalmody to his congregation, for the purpose of bringing them to use a better version of psalms and hymns than the one they were accustomed to. And even now, in a great many congregations, there are people who will go out of church, if a psalm or hymn is given out from a new book. And if Watt's Psalms should be adopted, they would secede and form a new congregation, rather than tolerate such an innovation. The same sort of feeling has been excited by introducing the "Village Hymns" in prayer meetings.[5] In one Presbyterian congregation in this city, within a few years, the minister's wife wished to introduce the Village Hymns into the female prayer meetings, not daring to go any further. She thought she was going to succeed. But some of the careful souls found out that is was made in New England, and refused to admit it. "It is a Hopkinsian thing, I dare say."[6]

(2.) *Lining the Hymns.* Formerly, when there were but few books, it was the custom to *line* the hymns, as it was called. The deacon used to stand up before the pulpit, and read off the psalm or hymn, a line at a time, or two lines at a time, and then sing, and the rest would all fall in. By and by, they began to introduce books, and let every one sing from his book. And what an innovation! Alas, what confusion and disorder it made! How could the good people worship God in singing, without having the deacon to line off the hymn in his holy tone, for the holiness of it seemed to consist very much in the tone, which was such that you could hardly tell whether he was reading or singing.

---

[5] *Village Hymns for Social Worship: Designed as a Supplement to the Psalms and Hymns of Dr. Watts* (Hartford, 1824) was a very popular compilation of hymns edited by the Rev. Asahel Nettleton. It went through many editions.

[6] Hopkinsian was the name applied generally to those neo-Edwardeans who followed the theology of the Rev. Samuel Hopkins of Newport, Rhode Island, a pupil of Jonathan Edwards. The Presbyterians of Princeton and Philadelphia had little use for Hopkinsianism and neither did Finney. Finney considered all Hopkinsians "hyper-Calvinists." Here he represents the strict Presbyterians of New York City as rejecting Nettleton's *Village Hymns* because some of the words were not in strict accord with the Westminster Confession. Nettleton was undoubtedly a Hopkinsian in most respects. For a discussion of Finney's attitude toward Hopkinsianism, see McLoughlin, *Modern Revivalism*, chaps. 1 and 2.

(3.) *Choirs.* Afterwards another innovation was carried. It was thought best to have a select choir of singers sit by themselves and sing, so as to give an opportunity to improve the music. But this was bitterly opposed. O how many congregations were torn and rent in sunder, by the desire of ministers and some leading individuals to bring about an improvement in the cultivation of music, by forming choirs of singers. People talked about innovations and new measures, and thought great evils were coming to the churches, because the singers were seated by themselves, and cultivated music, and learned new tunes that the old people could not sing. It did not use to be so when they were young, and they wouldn't tolerate such new lights and novelties in the church.

(4.) *Pitchpipes.* When music was cultivated, and choirs seated together, then the singers wanted a pitchpipe. Formerly, when the lines were given out by the deacon or clerk, he would strike off into the tune, and the rest would follow as well as they could. But when the leaders of choirs begun to use pitchpipes for the purpose of pitching all their voices on precisely the same key, what vast confusion it made! I heard a clergyman say that an elder in the town where he used to live, would get up and leave the house whenever he heard the chorister blow his pipe. "Away with your whistle," said he. "What! whistle in the house of God!" He thought it a profanation.

(5.) *Instrumental Music.* By and by, in some congregations, various instruments were introduced for the purpose of aiding the singers, and improving the music. When the bass viol was first introduced, it made a great commotion. People insisted they might just as well have a *fiddle* in the house of God. "Why, *it is* a fiddle, it is made just like a fiddle, only a little larger, and who can worship where there is a fiddle? By and by you will want to dance in the meeting house." Who has not heard these things talked of, as matters of the most vital importance to the cause of religion and the purity of the church? Ministers, in grave ecclesiastical assemblies, have spent days in discussing them. In a synod in the Presbyterian church, only a few years ago, it was seriously talked of by some, as a matter worthy of discipline in a certain church, that they had an organ in the house of God. This within a few years. And there are many churches now who would not tolerate an organ. They would not be half so much excited to be told that sinners are going to hell, as to be told that there is going to be an organ in the meeting house. O, in how many places can you get the church to do any thing else, easier than to come along in an easy and natural way to do what is needed, and wisest, and best, for promoting religion and saving souls! They act as if they had a "Thus saith the Lord," for every custom and practice that has been handed down to them, or that they have long followed themselves, however absurd or injurious.

(6.) *Extemporary Prayers.* How many people are there, who talk just as if the Prayer Book was of divine institution! And I suppose multitudes believe it is. And in some parts of the church a man would not be tolerated to pray without his book before him.

(7.) *Preaching without notes.* A few years since, a lady in Philadelphia was invited to hear a certain minister preach, and she refused, because he did not read his sermons. She seemed to think it would be profane for a man to go into the pulpit and *talk*, just as if he was talking to the people about some interesting and important subject. Just as if God had enjoined the use of notes and written sermons. They do not know that notes themselves are an innovation, and a modern one too. They were introduced in a time of political difficulties in England. The ministers were afraid they should be accused of preaching something against the government, unless they could show what they had preached, by having all written down beforehand. And with a time-serving spirit, they yielded to political considerations, and imposed a yoke of bondage upon the church. And, now in many places, they cannot tolerate extempore preaching.

(8.) *Kneeling in Prayer.* This has made a great disturbance in many parts of the country. The time has been in the Congregational churches in New England, when a man or woman would be ashamed to be seen kneeling at a prayer meeting, for fear of being taken for a Methodist.[7] I have prayed in families where I was the only person that would kneel. The others all stood, lest they should imitate the Methodists, I suppose, and thus countenance innovations upon the established form. Others, again, talk as if there was no other posture but kneeling, that could be acceptable in prayer.

3. *Labors of Laymen.*

(1.) *Lay Prayers.* Much objection was formerly made against

[7] The New England Puritans originally disliked kneeling because they considered it a Roman Catholic perversion that the Anglican Church should have reformed. It is amusing, but not without justification, that Finney should consider the New Englanders' opposition to kneeling to be based upon their fear of being compared to the socially inferior Methodists.

allowing any man to pray or to take a part in managing a prayer meeting, unless he was a clergyman. It used to be said that for a layman to pray in public, was interfering with the dignity of ministers, and was not to be tolerated. A minister in Pennsylvania told me that, a few years ago he appointed a prayer meeting in the church, and the elders opposed it and turned it out of the house. They said they would not have such work, they had hired a minister to do the praying, and he should do it, and they were not going to have common men praying.

Ministers and many others have very extensively objected against a layman's praying in public, and *especially in the presence of a minister*. That would let down the authority of the clergy, and was not to be tolerated. At a synod held in this state, there was a synodical prayer meeting appointed. The committee of arrangements, as it was to be a formal thing, designated beforehand the persons who were to take part, and named two clergymen and one layman. The layman was a man of talents and information equal to most ministers. But one doctor of divinity got up and seriously objected to a layman's being asked to pray before that synod. It was not usual, he said; it infringed upon the rights of the clergy, and he wished no innovations. What a state of things!

(2.) *Lay exhortation*. This has been made a question of vast importance, one which has agitated all New England, and many other parts of the country, whether laymen ought to be allowed to exhort in public meetings. Many ministers have labored to shut up the mouths of laymen entirely. They overlooked the practice of the primitive churches. So much opposition was made to this practice nearly a hundred years ago, that President Edwards actually had to take up the subject, and write a labored defence of the rights and duties of laymen.[8] But the opposition has not entirely ceased to this day. "What! A man that is not a minister, to talk in public! it will create confusion, it will let down the ministry; what will people think of us, ministers, if we allow common men to do the same things that *we* do?" Astonishing!

[8] As Albert Dod pointed out in his review of Finney's lectures, Finney was mistaken in stating that Edwards ever wrote a defense of the right of laymen to exhort, though he may have spoken of their right to offer prayer in the presence of a minister. Edwards abhorred lay exhorters, as did all Congregationalists and Presbyterians, and he explicitly said so in Part IV, Section 5, of his *Thoughts Concerning the Present Revival of Religion*. See *Works*, IV, 241ff. It is surprising that Finney did not correct this error in his revised edition of the lectures.

But now, all these things are gone by, in most places, and laymen can pray and exhort without the least objection. The evils that were feared, from the labors of laymen, have not been realized, and many ministers are glad to have them exercise their gifts in doing good.

4. *Female Prayer Meetings.* Within the last few years, female prayer meetings have been extensively opposed in this state.[9] What dreadful things! A minister, now dead, said that when he first attempted to establish these meetings, he had all the clergy around opposed to him. "Set women to praying? Why, the next thing, I suppose, will be to set them to preaching." And serious apprehensions were entertained for the safety of Zion, if women should be allowed to get together to pray. And even now, they are not tolerated in some churches.

So it has been in regard to all the active movements of the church. Missions, Sunday Schools, and every thing of the kind, have been opposed, and have gained their present hold in the church only by a succession of struggles and a series of innovations. A Baptist Association in Pennsylvania, some years since, disclaimed all fellowship with any minister that had been liberally educated, or that supported Missions, Bible Societies, Sabbath Schools, Temperance Societies, &c. All these were denounced as New Measures, not found in the Bible, and that would necessarily lead to distraction and confusion in the churches. The same thing has been done by some among the German churches. And in many Presbyterian churches, there are found those who will take the same ground, and denounce all these things, with the exception, perhaps, of an educated ministry, as innovations, new measures, new lights, going in their own strength, and the like, and as calculated to do great evil.

5. I will mention *several men* who have in Divine providence been set forward as prominent *in introducing these innovations.*

(1.) *The apostles* were great innovators, as you all know. After the resurrection, and after the Holy Spirit was poured out upon

---

[9] Finney's critics did not object to female prayer meetings, but they did object strenuously to permitting women to pray aloud in mixed or social prayer meetings or in public gatherings. (To use the words of the day, "audible praying of females in promiscuous assemblies" was unseemly.) Finney ignores this issue here, though there is no doubt that he permitted it in his early revivals. Some have seen in this breakdown of the restricted position of women in the church the beginnings of the movement for women's rights that became so popular in the Jacksonian era and afterwards. See Cross, *Burned-Over District,* pp. 177–178.

them, they set out to remodel the church. They broke down the Jewish system of measures and rooted it out, so as to leave scarcely a vestige.

(2.) *Luther and the Reformers.* You all know what difficulties they had to contend with, and the reason was, that they were trying to introduce new measures — new modes of performing the public duties of religion, and new expedients to bring the gospel with power to the hearts of men. All the strange and ridiculous things of the Roman Catholics were held to in the church with pertinacious obstinacy, as if they were of Divine authority.[10] And such an excitement was raised by the attempt to change them, as well nigh involved all Europe in blood.

(3.) *Wesley and his coadjutors.* Wesley did not at first tear off from the Established Church in England, but formed little classes every where, that grew into a church within a church. He remained in the Episcopal church, but he introduced so much of new measures, as to fill all England with excitement and uproar and opposition, and he was every where denounced as an innovator and a stirrer up of sedition, and a teacher of new things which it was not lawful to receive.

Whitefield was a man of the same school, and like Wesley was an innovator. I believe he and several individuals of his associates were expelled from college for getting up such a new measure, as a social prayer meeting.[11] They would pray together and expound the Scriptures, and this was such a daring novelty that it could not be borne. When Whitefield came to this country, what an astonishing opposition was raised! Often he well nigh lost his life, and barely escaped by the skin of his teeth. Now, every body looks upon him as the glory of the age in which he lived. And many of our own denomination have so far divested themselves of prejudice as to think Wesley not only a good but a wise and pre-eminently useful man. Then almost the entire church viewed them with animosity, fearing that the innovations they introduced would destroy the church.

[10] Finney's dislike for Roman Catholicism is also reflected on pp. 271 and 275. However, he did not resort to Catholic baiting in any of his revivals so far as I know. Several Catholic periodicals of the day lumped him together with other bigots (see the Boston *Jesuit*, March 13, 1830, and the New York *Truth Teller*, March 21, 1835) but the most outspoken anti-Catholic statement by Finney which I have seen appeared in the Oberlin *Evangelist*, July 30, 1845, p. 124, in a plea for support of missionaries in the West, which he signed with several other ministers at Oberlin.

[11] Finney is in error here. Whitefield was not expelled from Oxford.

(4.) *President Edwards.* This great man was famous in his day for new measures. Among other innovations, he refused to baptize the children of impenitent parents. The practice of baptizing the children of the ungodly had been introduced in the New England churches in the preceding century, and had become nearly universal. President Edwards saw that the practice was wrong, and he refused to do it, and the refusal shook all the churches of New England. A hundred ministers joined and determined to put him down. He wrote a book on the subject, and defeated them all. It produced one of the greatest excitements there ever was in New England. Nothing, unless it was the revolutionary war, ever produced an equal excitement.[12]

The General Association of Connecticut refused to countenance Whitefield, he was such an innovator. "Why, he will preach out of doors and any where!" Awful! What a terrible thing, that a man should preach in the fields or in the streets. Cast him out.

All these were devoted men, seeking out ways to do good and save souls. And precisely the same kind of opposition was experienced by all, obstructing their path and trying to destroy their character and influence. *A book*, now extant, was written in President Edwards' time, by a doctor of divinity, and signed by a multitude of ministers, against Whitefield and Edwards, their associates and their measures. A letter was published in this city by a minister against Whitefield, which brought up the same objections against innovations that we hear now. In the time of the late opposition to revivals in the state of New York, a copy of this letter was taken to the editor of a religious periodical with a request that he would publish it. He refused, and gave for a reason, that if published, many would apply it to the controversy that is going on now. I mention it merely to show how identical is the opposition that is raised in different ages against all new measures designed to advance the cause of religion.

6. *In the present generation*, many things have been introduced which have proved useful, but have been opposed on the

---

[12] Finney refers here to the battle over Edwards' refusal to abide by the Halfway Covenant, which had been adopted by the Congregational churches in 1662. After the first Great Awakening Edwards refused to admit anyone to church membership who would not make a public profession of faith testifying to his or her conversion. This was one of the causes leading to Edwards' dismissal from Northampton in 1750. As a result of the first Great Awakening most New England churches had, by the nineteenth century, given up the Halfway Covenant. See Ola E. Winslow, *Jonathan Edwards* (New York, 1941), pp. 241ff.

ground *that they were innovations*. And as many are still unsettled in regard to them, I have thought it best to make some remarks concerning them. There are three things in particular, which have chiefly attracted remark, and therefore I shall speak of them. They are *Anxious Meetings, Protracted Meetings*, and the *Anxious Seat*. These are all opposed, and are called new measures.

(1.) *Anxious Meetings.* The first that I ever heard of under that name, was in New England, where they were appointed for the purpose of holding personal conversation with anxious sinners, and to adapt instruction to the cases of individuals, so as to lead them immediately to Christ. The design of them is evidently philosophical, but they have been opposed because they were new. There are two modes of conducting an anxious meeting, either of which may effect the object of them.

1. By spending a few moments in personal conversation and learning the state of mind of each individual, and then in a address to the whole, take up all their errors and remove their difficulties together.

2. By going round to each, and taking up each individual case, and going over the whole ground with each one separately, and getting them to promise to give up their hearts to God. Either way they are important, and have been found most successful in practice. But multitudes have objected against them because they were new.[13]

(2.) *Protracted Meetings.* These are not new, but have always been practised, in some form or other, ever since there was a church on earth. The Jewish festivals were nothing else but protracted meetings. In regard to the *manner*, they were conducted differently from what they are now. But the *design* was the same, to devote a series of days to religious services, in order to make a more powerful impression of divine things upon the minds of the people. All denominations of Christians, when religion prospers among them, hold protracted meetings. In Scotland they used to begin on Thursday, at all their communion seasons, and continue until after the Sabbath. The Episcopalians, Baptists, and Methodists, all hold protracted meetings. Yet now in our day they have been opposed, particularly among Presbyterians, and called new measures, and

---

[13] As Albert Dod pointed out in his review of these lectures, Finney's critics did not object to Anxious Meetings as such, for they had been long used in New England. They merely objected to Finney's manner of conducting them, and particularly to his demand for immediate conversion by the anxious sinner.

regarded as fraught with all manner of evil, notwithstanding they have been so manifestly and so extensively blessed. I will suggest a few things that ought to be considered in regard to them.

(*a.*) In appointing them, regard should be had *to the circumstances of the people*; whether the church are able to give their attention and devote their time to carry on the meeting. In some instances this rule has been neglected. Some have thought it right to break in upon the necessary business of the community. In the country, they would appoint the meeting in harvest time, and in the city in the height of the business season, when all the men were *necessarily* occupied and pressed with their temporal labors. In defence of this course it is said that *our* business should always be made to yield to *God's* business; that eternal things are of so much more importance than temporal things, that worldly business of any kind, and *at any time*, should be made to yield and give place to a protracted meeting. But the worldly business in which we are engaged is not *our* business. It is as much *God's* business, and as much our duty, as our prayers and protracted meetings are. If we do not consider our business in this light, we have not yet taken the first lesson in religion; we have not learned to do all things to the glory of God. With this view of the subject, separating our business from religion, we are living six days for ourselves, and the seventh for God. — REAL DUTIES NEVER INTERFERE WITH EACH OTHER. Week days have *their* appropriate duties, and the Sabbath *its* appropriate duties, and we are to be equally pious on every day in the week, and in the performance of the duties of every day. We are to plough, and sow, and sell our goods, and attend to our various callings, with the same singleness of view to the glory of God, that we go to church on the Sabbath, and pray in our families, and read our Bibles. This is a first principle in religion. He that does not know and act on this principle, has not learned the A B C of piety, as yet. Now there are particular seasons of the year, in which God in his providence calls upon men to attend to business, because worldly business at the time is particularly urgent, and must be done at that season, if done at all; seed time and harvest for the farmer, and the business seasons for the merchant. And we have no right to say, in those particular seasons, that we will quit *our business* and have a protracted meeting. The fact is, the business *is not* ours. And unless God, by some special indication of his providence, indicates it to be his pleasure, that we should turn aside and have a protracted meeting at *such times*, I look upon it as tempting God to appoint them. It is saying, "O God, this worldly business is *our* business, and we are willing to lay it aside for *thy* business." Unless God has indicated it to be his pleasure to pour out his Spirit, and revive his work at such a season, and has thus *called upon* his people to quit, for the time being, their ordinary employments, and attend especially to a protracted meeting, it appears to me that God might say to us in such circumstances, "Who hath required this of your hand?"

God has a right to dispose of our time as he pleases, to require us to give up any portion of our time, or all our time, to duties of instruction and devotion. And when circumstances plainly call for it, it is our duty to lay aside every other business, and make direct and continuous efforts for the salvation of souls. If we transact our business upon right principles, and from right motives, and wholly for the glory of God, we shall never object to go aside to attend a protracted meeting, whenever there appears to be a call for it in the providence of God. A man who considers himself a steward or a clerk, does not consider it a hardship to rest from his labors on the Sabbath, but a privilege. The selfish *owner* may feel unwilling to suspend his business on the Sabbath. But the *clerk*, who transacts business not for himself but for his employer, considers it a privilege to rest upon the Sabbath. So we, if we do our business for God, shall not think it hard if he makes it our duty to suspend our worldly business and attend a protracted meeting. We should rather consider it in the light of a holiday. Whenever, therefore, you hear a man pleading that he cannot leave his business to attend a protracted meeting — that it is his duty to attend to business, there is reason to fear that he considers the business as his own, and the meeting as God's business. If he felt that the business of the store or farm was as much God's business as attending a protracted meeting, he would doubtless be very willing to rest from his worldly toils, and go up to the house of God and be refreshed, whenever there was an indication, on the part of God, that the community was called to that work. It is highly worthy of remark, that the Jewish festivals were appointed at those seasons of the year, when there was the least pressure of indispensable worldly business.

In some instances, such meetings have been appointed in the very pressure of the business seasons, and have been followed with no good results, evidently for the want of attention to the rule here laid down. In other cases, meetings have been appointed in seasons when there was a great pressure of worldly business, and have been signally blessed. But in those cases the blessing followed because the meeting was appointed in obedience to the indications of the will of God, by those who had spiritual discernment, and understood the signs of the times. And in many cases, doubtless, individuals have attended, who *really supposed* themselves to be giving up *their own* business, to attend to God's business, and in such cases they made what they supposed to be a real sacrifice, and God in mercy granted them the blessing.

(*b*.) Ordinarily a protracted meeting should be conducted through, and the labor chiefly performed, by *the same minister*, if possible.[14] Sometimes protracted meetings have been held and dependence placed on ministers coming in from day to day. And they would have no blessing. And the reason was obvious. They did not come in a state of mind to enter into the work, and they did not know the state of people's minds, so as to know what to preach. Suppose a person who was sick should call in a different physician every day. He would not know what the symptoms had been, nor what was the course of the disease or of the treatment, nor what remedies had been tried, nor what the patient could bear. Why, he would certainly kill the patient. Just so in a protracted meeting, carried on by a succession of ministers. None of them get into the spirit of it, and generally they do more hurt than good.

A protracted meeting should not, ordinarily, be appointed, unless they can secure the right kind of help, and get a minister or two who will agree to stay on the ground till the meeting is done. Then they will probably secure a rich blessing.

(*c*.) There should not be *so many public meetings* as to interfere with the *duties of the closet and of the family*. Otherwise Christians will lose their spirituality and let go their hold of God, and the meeting will run down.

(*d*.) *Families* should not put themselves out so much in entertaining strangers, as to *neglect prayer and other duties*. It is often the case that when a protracted meeting is held, some of the principal families in the church, I mean those who are principally relied on to sustain the meetings, do not get into the work at all. And the reason is, that they are encumbered with much serving. They

---

[14] This advice to have one minister or evangelist conduct the protracted meetings from beginning to end, coupled with the idea of a continuous series of services for prayer and preaching over a long period of time, was the start of the standard type revival meeting that became prevalent throughout the United States in the nineteenth century.

often take needless trouble to provide for guests who come from a distance to the meeting, and lay themselves out very foolishly to make an entertainment, not only comfortable but sumptuous. It should always be understood that it is the duty of families to have as little working and parade as possible, and to get along with their hospitality in the easiest way, so that they may all have time to pray, and go to the meeting, and to attend to the things of the kingdom.

(e.) By all means guard against *unnecessarily keeping late hours*. If people keep late hours, night after night, they will inevitably wear out the body, and their health will fail, and there will be a reaction. They sometimes allow themselves to get so excited as to lose their sleep, and become irregular in their meals, till they break down, and a reaction must come. Unless there is the greatest pains taken to keep regular, the excitement will get so great, that nature will give way, and they run down, and the work stops.

(f.) *All sectarianism* should be carefully avoided.[15] If a sectarian spirit breaks out, either in the preaching, or praying, or conversation, it will counteract all the good of the meeting.

(g.) Be watchful against *placing dependence* on a protracted meeting, *as if that of itself would produce a revival*. This is a point of great danger, and has always been so. This is the great reason why the church in successive generations has always had to give up her measures — because Christians had come to rely on them for success. So it has been in some places, in regard to *Protracted Meetings*. They have been so blessed, that in some places the people have thought that if they should only have a protracted meeting, they would have a blessing, and sinners would be converted *of course*. And so they have appointed their meeting, without any preparation in the church, and just sent abroad for some minister of note and set him to preaching, as if that would convert sinners. It is obvious that the blessing would be withheld from a meeting got up in this way.

(h.) Avoid adopting the idea that a revival cannot be enjoyed *without a Protracted Meeting*. Some churches have got into a morbid state of feeling on this subject. Their zeal has become all

---

[15] Finney often cooperated with ministers of other denominations in his revivals. In the latter part of the century it became the custom to refer to revival meetings in which more than one denomination joined as "union meetings." This type of interdenominational evangelism was made possible by Finney's emphasis upon "the fundamentals of the gospel" and his opposition to sectarianism.

spasmodic, and feverish, so that they never think of doing anything to promote a revival, *only in that way*. When a protracted meeting is held, they will seem to be wonderfully zealous, and then sink down to a torpid state till another protracted meeting produces another spasm. And now multitudes in the church think it is necessary to give up protracted meetings because they are abused in this way. This ought to be guarded against, in every church, so that they may not be driven to give them up, and lose all the benefits that protracted meetings are calculated to produce.[16]

(3.) *The Anxious Seat.*

By this I mean the appointment of some particular seat in the place of meeting, where the anxious may come and be addressed particularly, and be made subjects of prayer, and sometimes conversed with individually.[17] Of late this measure has met with more opposition than any of the others. What is the great objection? I cannot see it. The *design* of the anxious seat is undoubtedly philosophical, and according to the laws of mind. It has two bearings:

1. When a person is seriously troubled in mind, every body knows that there is a powerful tendency to try to keep it private that he is so, and it is a great thing to get the individual willing to have the fact known to others. And as soon as you can get him willing to make known his feelings, you have accomplished a great deal. When a person is borne down with a sense of his condition, if you can get him willing to have it known, if you can get him to break away from the chains of pride, you have gained an important point towards his conversion. This is agreeable to the philosophy of the human mind. How many thousands are there who will bless God to eternity, that when pressed by the truth they were ever brought to take this step, by which they threw off the idea that it was a dreadful thing to have any body know that they were serious about their souls.

2. Another bearing of the anxious seat, is to detect deception

---

[16] Finney devoted one of his "Letters on Revivals" to the evils that had grown out of the practice of protracted meetings in the decade after 1835. See Oberlin *Evangelist*, October 22, 1845, p. 171.

[17] Finney probably adopted the use of the anxious seat in his revivals from the Methodists who had used a "mourner's bench" in their camp meetings since early in the century. See Charles A. Johnson, *The Frontier Camp Meeting* (Dallas, Texas, 1955), pp. 132–142. For a discussion of the objections to the use of the anxious seat by Presbyterians and Congregationalists, see the Introduction to this edition. The practice of requiring awakened sinners to come forward publicly and express their desire or purpose to be saved at the close of a sermon became a part of all revival meetings after Finney's day.

and delusion, and thus prevent false hopes. It has been opposed on this ground, that it was calculated to create delusion and false hopes. But this objection is unreasonable. The truth is the other way. Suppose I were preaching on the subject of Temperance, and that I should first show the evils of intemperance, and bring up the drunkard and his family, and show the various evils produced, till every heart is beating with emotion. Then I portray the great danger of *moderate drinking*, and show how it leads to intoxication and ruin, and that there is no safety but in TOTAL ABSTINENCE, till a hundred hearts are ready to say, "I will never drink another drop of ardent spirit in the world; if I do, I shall expect to find a drunkard's grave." Now I stop short, and let the pledge be circulated, and every one that is fully resolved, is ready to sign it. But how many will begin to draw back and hesitate, when you begin to call on them to *sign a pledge* of total abstinence. One says to himself, "Shall I sign it, or not? I thought my mind was made up, but this signing a pledge *never* to drink again, I do not know about that." Thus you see that when a person is called upon to give a pledge, if he is found not to be decided, he makes it manifest that he was not sincere. That is, he never came to that resolution on the subject, which could be relied on to control his future life. Just so with the awakened sinner. Preach to him, and at the moment he thinks he is willing to do any thing, he thinks he is determined to serve the Lord, but bring him to the test, call on him to do one thing, to take one step, that shall identify him with the people of God, or cross his pride — his pride comes up, and he refuses; his delusion is brought out, and he finds himself a lost sinner still; whereas, if you had not done it, he might have gone away flattering himself that he was a Christian. If you say to him, "There is the anxious seat, come out and avow your determination to be on the Lord's side," and if he is not willing to do so small a thing as that, then he is not willing to do *any thing*, and there he is, brought out before his own conscience. It uncovers the delusion of the human heart, and prevents a great many spurious conversions, by showing those who might otherwise imagine themselves willing to do any thing for Christ, that in fact they are willing to do *nothing*.

The church has always felt it necessary to have something of the kind to answer this very purpose. In the days of the apostles *baptism* answered this purpose. The gospel was preached to the people, and then all those who were willing to be on the side of

Christ were called on to be *baptized*. It held the precise place that the anxious seat does now, as a public manifestation of their determination to be Christians. And in modern times, those who have been violently opposed to the anxious seat, have been obliged to adopt some substitute, or they could not get along in promoting a revival. Some have adopted the expedient of inviting the people who were anxious for their souls, to stay for conversation after the rest of the congregation had retired. But what is the difference? This is as much setting up a test as the other. Others, who would be much ashamed to employ the anxious seat, have asked those who have any feeling on the subject, to sit still in their seats when the rest retire. Others have called the anxious to retire into the lecture room. The object of all these is the same, and the principle is the same, to bring people out from the refuge of false shame. One man I heard of, who was very far gone in his opposition to new measures, in one of his meetings requested all those who were willing to submit to God, or desired to be made subjects of prayer, to signify it by leaning forward and putting their heads down upon the pew before them. Who does not see that this was a mere evasion of the anxious seat, and that it was designed to answer the purpose in its place, and he adopted this because he felt that something of the kind was important?

Now what objection is there against taking a particular seat, or rising up, or going into the lecture-room? They all mean the same thing, when properly conducted. And they are not novelties in principle at all. The thing has always been done in substance. In Joshua's day, he called on the people to decide what they would do, and they spoke right out, in the meeting, "We will serve the Lord; the Lord our God will we serve, and his voice will we obey."

REMARKS.

1. If we examine the history of the church we shall find that there never has been an extensive reformation, except by new measures. Whenever the churches get settled down into a *form* of doing things, they soon get to rely upon the outward doing of it, and so retain the form of religion while they lose the substance. And then it has always been found impossible to arouse them so as to bring about a reformation of the evils, and produce a revival of religion, by simply pursuing that established form. Perhaps it is not too much to say, that it is impossible for God himself to bring

about reformations but by new measures. At least, it is a fact that God has *always chosen* this way, as the wisest and best that he could devise or adopt. And although it has always been the case, that the very measures which God has chosen to employ, and which he has blessed in reviving his work, have been opposed as new measures, and have been denounced, yet he has continued to act upon the same principle. When he has found that a certain mode has lost its influence by having become a form, he brings up some new measure, which will BREAK IN upon their lazy habits, and WAKE UP a slumbering church. And great good has resulted.

2. The same distinctions, in substance, that now exist, have always existed, in all seasons of reformation and revival of religion. There have always been those who particularly adhered to their forms and notions, and precise way of doing things, as if they had a "Thus saith the Lord" for every one of them. They have called those that differed from them, who were trying to roll the ark of salvation forward, Methodists, New Lights, Radicals, New School, New Divinity, and various other opprobrious names. And the declensions that have followed have been uniformly owing to two causes, which should be by no means overlooked by the church.

(1.) The Old School, or Old Measure party, have persevered in their opposition, and eagerly seized hold of any real or apparent indiscretion in the friends of the work.

In such cases, the churches have gradually lost their confidence in the opposition to new measures, and the cry of "New Divinity," and "Innovation" has ceased to alarm them. They see that the blessing of God is with those that are thus accused of new measures and innovation, and the continued opposition of the Old School,[18] together with the continued success of the New School, have destroyed their confidence in the opposition, and they get tired of hearing the incessant cry of "New Lights," and "New Divinity," and "New Measures." Thus the scale has turned, and the churches have pronounced a verdict in favor of the New School, and of condemnation against the Old School.

(2.) But now, mark me: right here in this state of things, the devil has, again and again, taken the advantage, and individuals have risen up, and being sustained by the confidence of the churches in the New Measure party, and finding them sick of opposition,

---

[18] For a discussion of Finney's part in the Old School-New School controversy, see the Introduction to this volume.

and ready to do *any thing* that would promote the interests of Christ's kingdom, they have driven headlong themselves, and in many instances have carried the churches into the *very vortex* of those difficulties, which have been predicted by their opposers. Thus, when the battle had been fought, and the victory gained, the rash zeal of some well-meaning but headlong individuals, has brought about a reaction, that has spread a pall over the churches for years. This was the case, as is well known, in the days of President Edwards. Here is a rock, upon which a light-house is now built, and upon which if the church now run aground, both parties are entirely without excuse. It is now well known, or ought to be known, that the declension which followed the revivals in those days, together with the declensions which have repeatedly occurred, were owing to the combined influence of the continued and pertinacious opposition of the Old School, and the ultimate bad spirit and recklessness of some individuals of the New School.

And here the note of alarm should be distinctly sounded to both parties, lest the devil should prevail against us, at the very point, and under the very circumstances, where he has so often prevailed. Shall the church never learn wisdom from experience? How often, O, how often must these scenes be acted over, before the millennium shall come! When will it once be, that the church may be revived, and religion prevail, without exciting such opposition *in the church*, as eventually to bring about a reaction?

3. The present cry against new measures is highly ridiculous, when we consider the quarter from which it comes, and all the circumstances in the case. It is truly astonishing that grave ministers should really feel alarmed at the new measures of the present day, as if new measures were something new under the sun, and as if the present form and manner of doing things had descended from the apostles, and were established by a "Thus saith the Lord:" when the truth is, that every step of the church's advance from the gross darkness of Popery, has been through the introduction of one new measure after another. We now look with astonishment, and are inclined to look almost with contempt, upon the cry of "Innovation," that has preceded our day; and as we review the fears that multitudes in the church have entertained in by-gone days, with respect to innovation, we find it difficult to account for what appear to us the groundless and absurd, at least, if not ridiculous objections and difficulties which they made. But, my hearers, is it not wonderful, that at this late day, after the church has had so

much experience in these matters, that grave and pious men should seriously feel alarmed at the introduction of the simple, the philosophical, and greatly prospered measures of the last ten years? As if new measures were something not to be tolerated, of highly disastrous tendency, and that should wake the notes and echoes of alarm in every nook and corner of the church.

4. We see why it is that those who have been making the ado about new measures *have not been successful in promoting revivals.*

They have been taken up with *the evils*, real or imaginary, which have attended this great and blessed work of God. That there have been evils, no one will pretend to deny. But I do believe, that no revival ever existed since the world began, of so great power and extent as the one that has prevailed for the last ten years, which has not been attended with as great or greater evils. Still, a large portion of the church have been frightening themselves and others, by giving constant attention to the *evils* of revivals. One of the professors in a Presbyterian Theological Seminary, felt it his duty to write a series of letters to Presbyterians, which were extensively circulated, the object of which seemed to be to sound the note of alarm throughout all the borders of the church, in regard to the evils attending revivals.[19] While men are taken up with the evils instead of the excellences of a blessed work of God, how can it be expected that they will be useful in promoting it? I would say all this in great kindness, but still it is a point upon which I must not be silent.

5. Without new measures it is impossible that the church should succeed in gaining the attention of the world to religion. There are so many exciting subjects constantly brought before the public mind, such a running to and fro, so many that cry "Lo here," and "Lo there," that the church cannot maintain her ground, cannot command attention, without very exciting preaching, and sufficient novelty in measures, to get the public ear. The measures of politicians, of infidels and heretics, the scrambling after wealth, the increase of luxury, and the ten thousand exciting and counteracting influences, that bear upon the church and upon the world, will gain their attention and turn all men away from the sanctuary and from the altars of the Lord, unless we increase in wisdom and piety, and wisely adopt such new measures as are calculated to get the attention, of men to the gospel of Christ. I have already said,

---

[19] Perhaps these unidentified letters merely circulated in manuscript. They are obviously not Asahel Nettleton's letters to Lyman Beecher.

in the course of these lectures, that novelties should be introduced no faster than they are really called for. They should be introduced with the greatest wisdom, and caution, and prayerfulness, and in a manner calculated to excite as little opposition as possible. But new measures we *must have*. And may God prevent the church from settling down in *any* set of forms, and getting the present or any other edition of her measures *stereotyped*.

6. It is evident that we must have more exciting preaching, to meet the character and wants of the age. Ministers are generally beginning to find this out. And some of them complain of it, and suppose it to be owing to new measures, as they call them. They say that such ministers as our fathers would have been glad to hear, now cannot be heard, cannot get a settlement, nor collect an audience. And they think that new measures have perverted the taste of the people. But this is not the difficulty. The character of the age is changed, and these men have not conformed to it, but retain the same stiff, dry, prosing style of preaching that answered half a century ago.

Look at the Methodists. Many of their ministers are unlearned, in the common sense of the term, many of them taken right from the shop or the farm, and yet they have gathered congregations, and pushed their way, and won souls every where. Wherever the Methodists have gone, their plain, pointed and simple, but warm and animated mode of preaching has always gathered congregations. Few Presbyterian ministers have gathered so large assemblies, or won so many souls. Now are we to be told that we must pursue the same old, formal mode of doing things, amidst all these changes? As well might the North River be rolled back, as the world converted under such preaching. Those who adopt a different style of preaching, as the Methodists have done, will run away from us. The world will escape from under the influence of this old fashioned or rather new fashioned ministry. It is impossible that the public mind should be held by such preaching. We must have exciting, powerful preaching, or the devil will have the people, except what the Methodists can save. It is impossible that our ministers should continue to do good, unless we have innovations in regard to the style of preaching. Many ministers are finding it out already, that a Methodist preacher, without the advantages of a liberal education will draw a congregation around him which a Presbyterian minister, with perhaps ten times as much learning, cannot equal, because he has not the earnest manner of the other, and does not pour out fire upon his hearers when he preaches.[20]

7. We see the importance of having *young ministers obtain right views of revivals*. In a multitude of cases, I have seen that great pains are taken to frighten our young men, who are preparing for the ministry, about the evils of revivals, new measures, and the like. Young men in some theological seminaries are taught to look upon new measures as if they were the very inventions of the devil. How can such men have revivals. So when they come out, they look about, and watch, and start, as if the devil was there. Some young men in Princeton, a few years ago, came out with an essay upon the "evils of revivals." I should like to know, now, how many of those young men have *enjoyed* revivals among their people, since they have been in the ministry; and if any have, I should like to know whether they have not repented of that piece about the evils of revivals.[21]

If I had a voice so loud as to be heard at Princeton, I would speak to those young men on this subject. It is high time to talk plainly on this point. The church is groaning in all her borders for the want of suitable ministers. Good men are laboring and are willing to labor night and day to assist in educating young men for the ministry, to promote revivals of religion; and when they come out of the seminary, some of them are as shy of all the measures that God blesses as they are of popery itself.

Shall it be so always? Must we educate young men for the ministry, and have them come out frightened to death about new measures, as if there had never been any such thing as new measures. They ought to know that new measures are no new thing in the church. Let them GO ALONG, and keep at work themselves, and not be frightened about new measures. I have been pained to see that some men, in giving accounts of revivals, have evidently felt themselves obliged to be particular in detailing the measures used, to avoid the inference that *new* measures were introduced; evidently feeling that even the church would undervalue the revival unless it appeared to have been promoted without new measures. Besides, this caution in detailing the measures to demonstrate that there was nothing *new*, looks like admitting that new measures are wrong because they are new, and that a revival is more valuable

---

[20] Finney seems here to be asking for competition between the Presbyterians and the Methodists, but as he indicates elsewhere (see esp. p. 281), he did not advocate sectarian rivalry in connection with winning souls.

[21] I have not been able to identify this essay.

because it was not promoted by new measures. In this way, I apprehend that much evil has been done, already, and if the practice is to continue, it must come to this, that a revival must be judged of, by the fact that it occurred in connection with new or old measures. I never will countenance such a spirit, nor condescend to guard an account of a revival against the imputation of new or old measures. I believe new measures are *right*, that is, that it is no objection to a measure that it is new or old.

Let a minister enter fully into his work, and pour out his heart to God for a blessing, and whenever he sees the want of any measure to bring the truth more powerfully before the minds of the people, let him adopt it and not be afraid, and God will not withhold his blessing. If ministers will not go forward, and will not preach the gospel with power and earnestness, and will not turn out of their tracks to do any thing *new* for the purpose of saving souls, they will grieve the Holy Spirit away, and God will visit them with his curse, and raise up other ministers to do work in the world.

8. It is the *right and duty of ministers to adopt new measures* for promoting revivals. In some places the church have opposed their minister when he has attempted to employ those measures which God has blessed for a revival, and have gone so far as to give up their prayer meetings, and give up laboring to save souls, and stand aloof from every thing, because their minister has adopted what they call new measures. No matter how reasonable the measures are in themselves, nor how seasonable, nor how much God may bless them. It is enough that they are called new measures, and they will not have any thing to do with new measures, nor tolerate them among the people. And thus they fall out by the way, and grieve away the Spirit of God, and put a stop to the revival, when the world around them is going to hell.

FINALLY. — This zealous adherence to particular forms and modes of doing things, which has led the church to resist innovations *in measures, savors strongly of fanaticism*. And what is not a little singular, is that fanatics of this stamp are always the first to cry out "fanaticism." What is that but fanaticism in the Roman Catholic Church, that causes them to adhere with such pertinacity to their particular modes, and forms, and ceremonies, and fooleries? They act as if all these things were established by divine authority; as if there were a "Thus saith the Lord" for every one of them. Now we justly style this a spirit of fanaticism, and esteem it worthy of rebuke. But it is just as absolutely fanatical, for the Presbyterian church, or any other church, to be sticklish for her particular forms, and to act as if *they* were established by divine authority. The fact is, that God has established, in no church, any particular *form*, or manner of worship, for promoting the interests of religion. The scriptures are entirely silent on these subjects, under the gospel dispensation, and the church is left to exercise her own discretion in relation to all such matters. And I hope it will not be thought unkind, when I say again, that to me it appears, that the unkind, angry zeal for a certain mode and manner of doing things, and the overbearing, exterminating cry against new measures, SAVORS STRONGLY OF FANATICISM.

The only thing insisted upon under the gospel dispensation, in regard to measures, is that there should be *decency and order*. "Let all things be done decently and in order." We are required to guard against all confusion and disorderly conduct. But what is decency and order? Will it be pretended that an anxious meeting, or a protracted meeting, or an anxious seat, is inconsistent with decency and order? I should most sincerely deprecate, and most firmly resist whatever was indecent and disorderly in the worship of God's house. But I do not suppose that by "order" we are to understand any particular set mode, in which any church may have been accustomed to perform their service.

XV

HINDRANCES TO REVIVALS

TEXT. — "I am doing a great work, so that I cannot come down. Why should the work cease, whilst I leave it, and come down to you." — NEHEMIAH vi. 3.

THIS servant of God had come down from Babylon to rebuild the temple and re-establish the worship of God at Jerusalem, the city of his fathers' sepulchres. When it was discovered by Sanballat and certain individuals, his allies, who had long enjoyed the desolations of Zion, that now the temple, and the holy city were about to be rebuilt, they raised a great opposition. Sanballat and the other leaders tried in several ways to divert Nehemiah and his friends, and prevent them from going forward in their work; at one time they threatened them, and then complained that they were going to rebel against the king. Again, they insisted that their design was not pious but political, to which Nehemiah replied by a simple and prompt denial, "There are no such things done as thou sayest, but thou feignest them out of thine own heart." Finally, Sanballat sent a message to Nehemiah, requesting him to meet in the plain of Ono, to discuss the whole matter amicably and have the difficulty adjusted, but designed to do him mischief. They had found that they could not frighten Nehemiah, and now they wanted to come round him by artifice and fraud, and draw him off from the vigorous prosecution of his work. But he replied, "I am doing a great work, so that I cannot come down: why should the work cease, whilst I come down to you?"

It has always been the case, whenever any of the servants of God do any thing in his cause, and there appears to be *a probability* that they will succeed, that Satan by his agents regularly attempts to divert their minds and nullify their labors. So it has been during the last ten years, in which there have been such remarkable revivals through the length and breadth of the land. These revivals have been very great and powerful, and extensive.

It has been estimated that not less than TWO HUNDRED THOUSAND persons have been converted to God in that time.[1]

And the devil has been busy in his devices to divert and distract the people of God, and turn off their energies from pushing forward the great work of salvation. In remarking on the subject, I propose to show.

I. That a Revival of Religion is a great work.

II. To mention several things which may put a stop to it.

III. Endeavor to show what must be done for the continuance of this great revival.

I. I am to show that a Revival of Religion, *is a great work*.

It is a great work, because in it are *great interests involved*. In a Revival of Religion are involved both the glory of God, so far as it respects the government of this world, and the salvation of men. Two things that are of *infinite* importance are involved in it. The greatness of a work is to be estimated by the greatness of the consequences depending on it. And this is the measure of its importance.

II. I am to mention several things which *may put a stop to a revival*.

Some have talked very foolishly on this subject, as if nothing could injure a genuine revival. They say, "If your revival is a work of God, it cannot be stopped; can any created being stop God? Now I ask if this is common sense? Formerly, it used to be the established belief that a revival could not be stopped, because it was the work of God. And so they supposed it would go on, whatever might be done to hinder it, in the church or out of it. But the farmer might just as well reason so, and think he could go and cut down his wheat and not hurt the crop, because it is God that makes grain grow. A revival is the work of God, and so is a crop of wheat; and God is as much dependent on the use of means in one case as the other. And therefore a revival is as liable to be injured as a wheat field.

1. A revival will stop whenever the *church believe it is going to cease*. The church are the instruments with which God carries on this work, and they are to work in it voluntarily and with their hearts. Nothing is more fatal to a revival than for its friends

---

[1] Finney is referring here simply to the gains in Presbyterian church membership. The official statistics for the years 1826–1834 reveal a gain of only 120,500, however. See Herman C. Weber, ed., *Presbyterian Statistics 1826–1926* (General Council of the Presbyterian Church in the U.S.A., 1927), p. 11.

to predict that it is going to stop. No matter what the *enemies* of the work may say about it, predicting that it will all run out and come to nothing, and the like. They cannot stop it in this way. But the friends must labor and pray in faith to carry it on. It is a contradiction to say they are laboring and praying in faith to carry on the work, and yet believe that it is going to stop. If they lose their faith, it will stop, of course. Whenever the friends of revivals begin to prophecy that the revival is going to stop, they should be instantly rebuked, in the name of the Lord. If the idea once begins to prevail, and if you cannot counteract it and root it out, the revival will infallibly cease; for it is indispensable to the work, that Christians should labor and pray in faith to promote it, and it is a contradiction to say that they can labor in faith for its continuance, while they believe that it is about to cease.

2. A revival will cease *when Christians consent that it should cease.* Sometimes Christians see that the revival is in danger of ceasing, and that if something effectual is not done, it will come to a stand. If this fact distresses them, and drives them to prayer, and to fresh efforts, the work will not cease. When Christians love the work of God, and the salvation of souls so well that they are distressed at the mere apprehension of a decline, it will drive them to an agony of prayer and effort. If it does not drive them to agony and effort to prevent its ceasing, if they see the danger, and do not try to avert it, or to renew the work THEY CONSENT THAT IT SHOULD STOP. There are at this time many people, all over the country, who see revivals declining, and that they are in great danger of ceasing altogether, and yet they manifest but little distress, and seem to care but little about it. Whole churches see their condition, and see what is coming unless there can be a waking up, and yet they are at ease, and do not groan and agonize in prayer, that God would revive his work. Some are even predicting that there is now going to be a great reaction, and a great dearth come over the church, as there did after Whitefield's and Edwards' day. And yet they are not startled at their own forebodings; they are cool about it, and turn directly off to other things. THEY CONSENT TO IT. It seems as if they were the devil's trumpeters, sent out to scatter dismay throughout the ranks of God's elect.

3. A revival will cease whenever *Christians become mechanical in their attempts to promote it.* When their faith is strong,

and their hearts are warm and mellow, and their prayers full of holy emotion, and their words with power, then the work goes on. But when their prayers begin to be cold and without emotion, and their deep-toned feeling is gone, and they begin to labor mechanically, and to use words without feeling, then the revival will cease.

4. The revival will cease, whenever Christians get the idea that *the work will go on without their aid*. The church are co-workers with God in promoting a revival, and the work can be carried on just as far as the church will carry it on, and no farther. God has been for one thousand eight hundred years trying to get the church into the work. He has been calling and urging, commanding, entreating, pressing and encouraging, to get them to take hold. He has stood all this while ready to *make bare his arm* to carry on the work with them. But the church have been unwilling to do their part. They seem determined to leave it to God alone to convert the world, and say, "If he wants the world converted, let him do it." They ought to know that this is impossible. So far as we know, neither God nor man can convert the world without the co-operation of the church. Sinners cannot be converted without their own agency, for conversion *consists in* their voluntary turning to God. No more can sinners be converted without the appropriate moral influences to turn them; that is, without truth and the reality of things brought full before their minds either by direct revelation or *by men*. God cannot convert the world by physical omnipotence, but he is dependent on the moral influence of the church.

5. The work will cease when the church prefer to attend to their own concerns rather than God's business. I do not admit that men *have* any business which is properly *their own*, but they think so, and in fact prefer what they consider as their own, rather than to work for God. They begin to think they *cannot afford* sufficient time from their worldly employments, to carry on a revival. And they pretend they are obliged to give up attending to religion, and let their hearts go out again after the world. And the work must cease, of course.

6. When Christians get proud of their great revival, it will cease. I mean those Christians who have before been instrumental in promoting it. It is almost always the case in a revival, that a part of the church are too proud or too worldly to take any part in the work. They are determined to stand aloof, and wait,

and see what it will come to, and see how it will come out. The pride of this part of the church cannot stop the revival, for the revival never rested on them. It begun without them, and it can go on without them. They may fold their arms and do nothing but look on and find fault; and still the work may go on. But when that part of the church *who work*, begin to think what a great revival they have had, and how they have labored and prayed, and how bold and how zealous they have been, and how much good they have done, then the work will be likely to decline. Perhaps it has been published in the papers, what a revival there has been in the church, and how much engaged the members have been, and they think how high they shall stand in the estimation of other churches, all over the land, because they have had such a great revival. And so they get puffed up, and vain, and then they can no longer enjoy the presence of God, and the Spirit withdraws from them, and the revival ceases.

7. The revival will stop when the church gets exhausted by labor. Multitudes of Christians commit a great mistake here in time of revival. They are so thoughtless, and have so little judgment, that they will break up all their habits of living, neglect to eat and sleep at the proper hours, and let the excitement run away with them, so that they overdo their bodies, and are so imprudent that they soon become exhausted, and it is impossible for them to continue in the work. Revivals often cease, and declension follows, from negligence and imprudence, in this respect, on the part of those engaged in carrying them on.

8. A revival will cease when the church begins *to speculate about abstract doctrines*, which have nothing to do with practice. If the church turns off its attention from the things of salvation, and go to studying or disputing about abstract points, the revival will cease, of course.

9. *When Christians begin to proselyte*. When the Baptists are so opposed to the Presbyterians, or the Presbyterians to the Baptists, or both against the Methodists, or Episcopalians against the rest, that they begin to make efforts to get the converts to join their church, you soon see the last of the revival. Perhaps a revival will go on for a time, and all sectarian difficulties are banished, till somebody circulates a book, privately, to gain proselytes. Perhaps some over-zealous deacon, or some mischief-making woman, or some proselyting minister, can't keep still any longer, and begins to work the work of the devil, by attempting to gain proselytes,

and so stirs up bitterness, and raising a selfish strife, grieves away the Spirit, and drives Christians all into parties. No more revival there.

10. When Christians *refuse to render to the Lord according to the benefits received*. This is a fruitful source of religious declensions. God has opened the windows of heaven to a church, and poured them out a blessing, and then he reasonably expects them to bring in the tithes into his store house, and devise and execute liberal things for Zion; and lo! they have refused; they have not laid themselves out accordingly to promote the cause of Christ, and so the Spirit has been grieved and the blessing withdrawn, and in some instances a great reaction has taken place, because the church would not be liberal, when God has been so bountiful. I have known churches who were evidently cursed with barrenness for such a course. They had a glorious revival, and afterwards perhaps their meeting-house needed repairing, or something else was needed which would cost a little money, and they refused to do it, and so for their niggardly spirit God gave them up.

11. When the church, in any way, *grieve the Holy Spirit*.

(1.) When they *do not feel their dependence on the Spirit*. Whenever Christians get strong in their own strength, God curses their blessings. In many instances, Christians sin against their own mercies, because they get lifted up with their success, and take the credit to themselves, and do not give to God all the glory. As he says, "If ye will not hear, and if ye will not lay it to heart, to give glory unto my name, saith the Lord of hosts, I will even send a curse upon you, and, I will curse your blessings: yea, I have cursed them already, because ye do not lay it to heart." There has been a great deal of this in this country, undoubtedly. I have seen many things that looked like it, in the papers, where there seemed a disposition in men to take credit for success in promoting revivals. There is doubtless a great temptation to this, and it requires the utmost watchfulness, on the part of ministers and churches, to guard against it, and not grieve the Spirit away by vain-glorying in men.

(2.) The Spirit may be grieved *by a spirit of boasting of the revival*. Sometimes, as soon as a revival commences, you will see it blazed out in the newspapers. And most commonly this will kill the revival. There was a case in a neighboring state, where a revival commenced, and instantly there came out a letter from the pastor, telling that he had a revival. I saw the letter and said to myself, That is the last we shall hear of this revival. And so it was. In a few days, the work totally ceased. And such things are not uncommon. I could mention cases and places, where persons have published such things as to puff up the church, and make them so proud that little or nothing more could be done for the revival.

Some, under pretence of publishing things to the praise and glory of God, have published things that savored so strongly of a disposition to exalt themselves, have made their own agency to stand out so conspicuously, as was evidently calculated to make an unhappy impression. At the protracted meeting held in this church, a year ago last fall, there were five hundred hopefully converted, whose names and places of residence we knew. A considerable number of them joined this church. Many of them united with other churches. Nothing was said of this in the papers. I have several times been asked why we were so silent upon the subject. I could only reply, that there was such a tendency to self-exaltation in the churches, that I was afraid to publish any thing on the subject. Perhaps I erred. But I have so often seen mischief done by premature publications, that I thought it best to say nothing about it. In the revival in this city, four years ago, so much was said in the papers, that appeared like self-exaltation, that I was afraid to publish. I am not speaking against the *practice itself*, of publishing accounts of revivals. But the *manner* of doing it is of vast importance. If it is done so as to excite vanity, it is always fatal to the revival.

(3.) So the Spirit is grieved *by saying or publishing things* that are calculated to *undervalue the work of God*. When a blessed work of God is spoken lightly of, not rendering to God the glory due to his name, the spirit is grieved. If any thing is said about a revival, give only the plain and naked *facts* just as they are, and let them pass for what they are worth.

12. A revival may be expected to cease, *when Christians lose the spirit of brotherly love.* Jesus Christ will not continue with people in a revival any longer than they continue in the exercise of brotherly love. When Christians are in the spirit of a revival, they feel this love, and then you will hear them call each other brother and sister, very affectionately. But when they begin to get cold, they lose this warmth and glow of affection for one another, and then this calling brother and sister will seem silly and contemptible and they will leave it off. In some churches

they never call each other so, but where there is a revival, Christians naturally do it. I never saw a revival, and probably there never was one, in which they did not do it. But as soon as this begins to cease, the Spirit of God is grieved, and departs from among them.

13. A revival will decline and cease, unless *Christians are frequently re-converted*. By this I mean, that Christians, in order to keep in the spirit of a revival, commonly need to be frequently convicted, and humbled, and broken down before God, and re-converted. This is something which many do not understand, when we talk about a Christian's being re-converted. But the fact is that in a revival the Christian's heart is liable to get crusted over, and lose its exquisite relish for divine things; his unction and prevalence in prayer abates, and then he must be converted over again. It is impossible to keep him in such a state as not to do injury to the work, unless he pass through such a process every few days. I have never labored in revivals in company with any one who would keep in the work and be fit to manage a revival continually, who did not pass through this process of breaking down as often as once in two or three weeks. Revivals decline, commonly, because it is found impossible to make the church feel their guilt and their dependence, so as to break down before God. It is important that ministers should understand this, and learn how to break down the church, and break down themselves when they need it, or else Christians will soon become mechanical in their work, and lose their fervor and their power of prevailing with God. This was the process through which Peter passed, when he had denied the Savior, and by which breaking down, the Lord prepared him for the great work on the day of Pentecost. I was surprised, a few years since, to find that the phrase *"breaking down"* was a stumbling block to certain ministers and professors of religion. They laid themselves open to the rebuke administered to Nicodemus, "Art thou a master in Israel and knowest not these things?" I am confident that until some of them know what it is to be "broken down," they will never do much more for the cause of revivals.

14. A revival cannot continue *when Christians will not practice self-denial*. When the church have enjoyed a revival and begin to grow fat upon it, and run into self-indulgence, the revival will soon cease. Unless they sympathize with the Son of God, who gave up all to save sinners; unless they are willing to give up their

luxuries, and their ease, and lay themselves out in the work, they need not expect the Spirit of God will be poured out upon them. This is undoubtedly one of the principal causes of personal declension. Let Christians in a revival BEWARE, when they first find an inclination creeping upon them, to shrink from self-denial, and to give into one self-indulgence after another. It is the device of Satan, to bait them off from the work of God, and make them dull and gross, and lazy, and fearful, and useless, and sensual, and drive away the Spirit and destroy the revival.

15. A revival will be stopped *by controversies about new measures*. Nothing is more certain to overthrow a revival than this. But as my last lecture was on the subject of new measures, I need not dwell longer on the subject now.

16. Revivals can be put down *by the continued opposition of the Old School, combined with a bad spirit in the New School*. If those who do nothing to promote revivals continue their opposition, and if those who are laboring to promote them allow themselves to get impatient, and get into a bad spirit, the revival will cease. When the Old School write their letters in the newspapers, against revivals or revival men, and the New School write letters back again, against them, in an angry, contentious, bitter spirit, and get into a jangling controversy, revivals will cease. LET THEM KEEP ABOUT THEIR WORK, and not talk about the opposition, nor preach, nor print about it. If others choose to publish their slang and stuff, let the Lord's servants keep to their work, and all the writings and slander will not stop the revival, while those who are engaged in it mind their business, and keep to their work. It is astonishing how far this holds true in fact.

In one place where there was a revival, certain ministers formed a combination against the pastor of the church, and a plan was set on foot to ruin him, and they actually got him prosecuted before his Presbytery, and had a trial that lasted six weeks, right in the midst of the revival, and the work still went on. The praying members of the church laid themselves out so in the work, that it continued triumphantly throughout the whole scene. The pastor was called off to attend his trial, but there was another minister that labored among the people, and the members did not even go to the trial, generally, but kept praying and laboring for souls, and the revival rode out the storm.[2] In many other

[2] This is a reference to the trial of the Rev. Nathaniel S. S. Beman, pastor of the First Presbyterian Church of Troy, New York, in 1826. Finney was a close

places, opposition has risen up in the church, but a few humble souls have kept at their work, and a gracious God has stretched out his naked arm and made the revival go forward in spite of all opposition.

But whenever those who are actively engaged in promoting a revival get excited at the unreasonableness and pertinacity of the opposition, and feel as if they could not have it so, and they lose their patience, and feel as if they must answer their cavils and refute their slanders, then they get down into the plains of Ono, and the work must cease.

17. *Any diversion of the public mind* will hinder a revival. Any thing that *succeeds* in diverting public attention, will put a stop to a revival. In the case I have specified, where the minister was put on trial before his Presbytery, the reason why it did not ruin the revival was, that the praying members of the church *would not suffer* themselves to be diverted. They did not even attend the trial, but kept praying and laboring for souls, and so public attention was kept to the subject, in spite of all the efforts of the devil.

But whenever he succeeds in *absorbing* public attention on any other subject, he will put an end to the revival. No matter what the subject is. If an angel from heaven were to come down, and preach, or pass about the streets, it might be the worst thing in the world for a revival, for it would turn sinners all off from their own sins, and turn the church off from praying for souls, to follow this glorious being, and gaze upon him, and the revival would cease.

18. *Resistance to the Temperance Reformation* will put a stop to revivals in a church. The time has come that it can no longer be innocent in a church to stand aloof from this glorious reformation. The time was, when this could be done ignorantly. The time has been when ministers and Christians could enjoy revivals, notwithstanding ardent spirit was used among them. But

---

friend of Beman, who became a leader in the New School movement. Finney implies that the trial began after Beman had invited him to come to hold revival meetings in his church, but there is evidence that Beman knew that a trial was in the offing and invited Finney partly as a means of distracting attention from the trial. See, *A Brief Account of the Origin and Progress of the Divisions in the First Presbyterian Church in the City of Troy. Containing also Strictures upon the New Doctrines Broached by the Rev. C. G. Finney and N. S. S. Beman with a Summary Relation of the Trial of the Latter before the Troy Presbytery*, By a Member of the Late Church and Congregation, (Troy, New York, 1827).

since light has been thrown upon the subject, and it has been found that the use is only injurious, no church member or minister can be innocent and stand neutral in the cause. They must speak out and take sides. And if they do not take ground on one side, their influence is on the other. Show me a minister that has taken ground against the temperance reformation, who has had a revival. Show me one who now stands aloof from it, who has a revival. Show me one who now temporizes upon this point, who does not come out and take a stand in favor of temperance, who has a revival? It did not use to be so. But now the subject has come up, and has been discussed, and is understood, no man can shut his eyes upon the truth. The man's hands are RED WITH BLOOD, who stands aloof from the temperance cause. And can he have a revival?[3]

19. Revivals are hindered when ministers and *churches take wrong ground in regard to any question involving human rights.* Take the subject of SLAVERY for instance.[4] The time was when this subject was not before the public mind. John Newton continued in the slave trade after his conversion.[5] And so had his mind been perverted, and so completely was his conscience seared, in regard to this most nefarious traffic, that the sinfulness of it never occurred to his thoughts until some time after he became a child of God. Had light been poured upon his mind previously to his conversion, he *never could* have been converted without previously abandoning this sin. And after his conversion, when convinced of its iniquity, he could no longer enjoy the presence of God, without abandoning the sin for ever. So, doubtless, many slave dealers and slave holders in our own country, have been converted, notwithstanding their participation in this abomination, because the sinfulness of it was not apparent to their

---

[3] Whitney R. Cross makes the point in *The Burned-Over District* (p. 169) that Finney's inclusion of temperance as part of revivalism in Rochester in 1830–1831 was in itself a new measure. Previously temperance reformers had utilized only the signed pledge as the means of promoting their cause. After the Rochester revival, drinking alcoholic beverages became considered a sin only conversion could cure. From that day temperance (really teetotalism) became an inherent part of all revival preaching.

[4] For a discussion of Finney's stand on slavery, see the Introduction to this edition. The significant fact about this subject is Finney's vehement opposition to slavery in principle, as opposed to his circumspection in terms of active reform (see pp. 297–303).

[5] This is a reference to the Rev. John Newton (1721–1807), a leader of the Evangelical wing of the Church of England, who had in his early life been a sailor on ships engaged in the slave trade.

minds. So ministers and churches, to a great extent throughout the land, have held their peace, and borne no testimony against this abominable abomination, existing in the church and in the nation. But recently, the subject has come up for discussion, and the providence of God has brought it distinctly before the eyes of all men. Light is now shed upon this subject as it has been upon the cause of temperance. Facts are exhibited, and principles established, and light thrown in upon the minds of men, and this monster is dragged from his horrid den, and exhibited before the church, and it is demanded of them, "IS THIS SIN?" Their testimony *must* be given on this subject. They are God's witnesses. They are sworn to tell "the truth, the whole truth, and nothing but the truth." It is impossible that their testimony should not be given, on one side or the other. Their silence can no longer be accounted for upon the principle of ignorance, and that they have never had their attention turned to the subject. Consequently, the silence of Christians upon the subject is virtually saying *that they do not* consider slavery as a sin. The truth is, it is a subject upon which they cannot be silent without guilt. The time has come, in the providence of God, when every southern breeze is loaded down with the cries of lamentation, mourning and wo. Two milions of degraded heathen in our own land stretch their hands, all shackled and bleeding, and send forth to the church of God the agonizing cry for help. And shall the church, in her efforts to reclaim and save the world, deafen her ears to this voice of agony and despair? God forbid. The church cannot turn away from this question. It is a question for the church and for the nation to decide, and God will push it to a decision.

It is in vain for the churches to resist it for fear of distraction, contention, and strife. It is in vain to account it an act of *piety* to turn away the ear from hearing this cry of distress.

The church must testify, and testify "the truth, the whole truth, and nothing but the truth," on this subject, or she is perjured, and the Spirit of God departs from her. She is under oath to testify, and ministers and churches who do not pronounce it sin, bear false testimony for God. It is doubtless true, that one of the reasons for the low state of religion at the present time, is that many churches have taken the wrong side on the subject of slavery, have suffered prejudice to prevail over principle, and have feared to call this abomination by its true name.

20. Another thing that hinders revivals is *neglecting the claims*

of missions. If Christians do not feel for the heathen, neglect the monthly concert, and confine their attention to their own church, do not even read the Missionary Herald or use any other means to inform themselves on the subject of the claims of the world, and reject the light which God is throwing before them, and will not do what God calls them to do in this cause, the Spirit of God will depart from them.

21. *When a church rejects the calls of God upon them for educating young men for the ministry*, they will hinder and destroy a revival. Look at the Presbyterian church, look at the 200,000 souls converted within ten years, and means enough to fill the world with ministers, and yet the ministry is not increasing so fast as the population of our own country, and unless something more can be done to provide ministers, we shall become heathen ourselves. The churches do not press upon young men the duty of going into the ministry. God pours his Spirit on the churches, and converts hundreds of thousands of souls, and if then the laborers do not come forth into the harvest, what can be expected but that the curse of God will come upon the churches, and his Spirit will be withdrawn, and revivals will cease. Upon this subject no minister, no church should be silent or inactive.

22. *Slandering revivals* will often put them down. The great revival in the days of President Edwards suffered greatly by the conduct of the church in this respect. It is to be expected that the enemies of God will revile, misrepresent and slander revivals. But when *the church* herself engages in this work, and many of her most influential members are aiding and abetting in calumniating and misrepresenting a glorious work of God, it is reasonable that the Spirit should be grieved away. It cannot be denied, that this has been done, to a grievous and God-dishonoring extent. It has been estimated that in one year, since this revival commenced, ONE HUNDRED THOUSAND SOULS were converted to God in the United States.[6] This was undoubtedly the greatest number that were ever converted in one year, since the world began. It could not be expected that, in an excitement of this extent, among *human beings*, there should be nothing to deplore. To expect perfection in such a work as this, of such extent, and carried on by human instrumentality, is utterly unreasonable and absurd. Evils doubtless did exist and have existed. They were to be expected of course, and

---

[6] No statistics are available to check this estimate, but most authorities believe that it is exaggerated. Finney probably refers to the year 1831.

guarded against, as far as possible. And I do not believe the world's history can furnish one instance, in which a revival, approaching to this in extent and influence, has been attended with so few evils, and so little that is honestly to be deplored.

But how has this blessed work of God been treated? Admitting all the evils complained of to be real, which is far from being true, they would only be like spots upon the disk of the glorious sun; things hardly to be thought of, in comparison of the infinite greatness and excellence of the work. And yet how have a great portion of the Presbyterian church, received and treated this blessed work of God? At the General Assembly, that grave body of men that represent the Presbyterian Church, in the midst of this great work, instead of appointing a day of thanksgiving, instead of praising and glorifying God for the greatness of his work, we hear from them the voice of rebuke. From the reports that were given of the speeches made there, it appears that the house was filled with complainings. Instead of devising measures to forward the work, their attention seemed to be taken up with the comparatively trifling evils that were incidental to it. And after much complaining, they absolutely appointed a committee, and sent forth a "Pastoral Letter" to the churches, calculated to excite suspicions, quench the zeal of God's people, and turn them off from giving glory to God for the greatness of the blessing, to finding fault and carping about the evils. When I heard what was done at that General Assembly, when I read their speeches, when I saw their pastoral letter, my soul was sick, an unutterable feeling of distress came over my mind, and I felt that God would "visit" the Presbyterian church for conduct like this. And ever since, the glory has been departing, and revivals have been becoming less and less frequent — less and less powerful.[7]

And now I wish it could be known, whether those ministers who poured out those complainings on the floor of the General Assembly, and who were instrumental in getting up that pastoral letter, have since been blest in promoting revivals of religion — whether the Spirit of God has been upon them, and whether their churches can witness that they have an unction from the Holy One.

23. *Ecclesiastical difficulties* are calculated to grieve away the

---

[7] In the revised edition of 1868 Finney added a note here: "The strange opposition of such men as Dr. Lyman Beecher and Mr. Nettleton had much to do with provoking and sustaining this opposition."

Spirit, and destroy revivals. It has always been the policy of the devil to turn off the attention of ministers from the work of the Lord, to disputes and ecclesiastical litigations. President Edwards was obliged to be taken up for a long time in disputes before ecclesiastical councils; and in our days, and in the midst of these great revivals of religion, these difficulties have been alarmingly and shamefully multiplied. Some of the most efficient ministers in the church have been called off from their direct efforts to win souls to Christ, to attend day after day, and in some instances week after week, to charges preferred against them, or their fellow laborers in the ministry, which could never be sustained.

Look at Philadelphia; what endless and disgraceful janglings have distracted and grieved the church of God in that city, and through the length and breadth of the land.[8] And in the Presbyterian church at large, these ecclesiastical difficulties have produced evils enough to make creation weep. Brother Beman was shamefully and wickedly called off from promoting revivals, to attend a trial before his own presbytery, upon charges which, if true, were most of them ridiculous, but which could never be sustained. And since that time a great portion of his time has, it would seem necessarily, been taken up with the adjustment of ecclesiastical difficulties. Brother Duffield, of Carlisle, brother Barnes, of Philadelphia, and others of God's most successful ministers, have been hindered a considerable part of their time for years by these difficulties.[9] O, tell it not in Gath! When will those ministers and professors of religion who do little or nothing themselves, let others alone, and let them work for God?

These things in the Presbyterian church, their contentions and janglings are so ridiculous, so wicked, so outrageous, that no doubt there is a jubilee in hell every year, about the time of the meeting of the General Assembly. And if there were tears in heaven, no doubt they would be shed over the difficulties of the Presbyterian church. Ministers have been dragged from home, year by year, and perhaps have left a revival in progress, and gone up to the General Assembly, and there heard debates, and

[8] Philadelphia was considered the center of Presbyterianism in the United States, and the General Assembly met in that city every year. The presbyteries of Philadelphia were violently split over New School doctrines, and several important heresy trials originated here.

[9] N. S. S. Beman, George Duffield, and Albert Barnes were all prominent New School Presbyterians who were tried for heresy in the years 1826–1836. All of them were acquitted, but their trials were *causes célèbres* in their day.

witnessed a spirit, by which their souls have been grieved and their hearts hardened, and they have gone home ashamed of their church, and ashamed to ask God to pour out his Spirit upon such a contentious body.

24. Another thing by which revivals may be hindered, is *censoriousness, on either side,* and *especially in those who have been engaged in carrying forward a revival.* It is to be expected that the opposers of the work will watch for the halting of its friends, and be sure to censure them for all that is wrong, and not unfrequently for that which is right in their conduct. Especially is it to be expected that many censorious and unchristian remarks will be made about those that are the most prominent instruments in promoting the work. This censoriousness on the part of the *opposers* of the work, whether in or out of the church, will not, however, of itself put a stop to the revival. While its promoters keep humble, and in a prayerful spirit, while they do not retaliate, but possess their souls in patience, while they do not suffer themselves to be diverted, to recriminate, and grieve away the spirit of prayer, the work will go forward; as in the case referred to, where a minister was on trial for six weeks, in the midst of a revival. There the people kept in the dust, and prayed, not so much for their minister, for they had left him with God, but with strong crying and tears pleading with God for sinners. And God heard and blessed them, and the work went on. Censoriousness in those who are opposed to the work is but little to be dreaded, for they have not the Spirit, and nothing depends on them, and they can hinder the work only just so far as they themselves have influence personally. But the others have the power of the Holy Spirit, and the work depends on their keeping in a right temper. If they get wrong and grieve away the Spirit, there is no help, the work must cease. Whatever provocation, therefore, the promoters of this blessed work may have had, if it ceases, the responsibility will be theirs. And one of the most alarming facts, in regard to this matter, is that in many instances, those who have been engaged in carrying forward the work, appear to have lost the Spirit. They are becoming diverted, are beginning to think that the opposition is no longer to be tolerated, and that they must come out and reply in the newspapers to what they say. It should be known and universally understood, that whenever the friends and promoters of this greatest of revivals suffer themselves to be called off to newspaper janglings, to attempt to defend themselves, and reply

to those who write against them, the Spirit of Prayer will be entirely grieved away, and the work will cease. Nothing is more detrimental to revivals of religion, and so it has always been found, than for the promoters of it to listen to the opposition, and begin to reply. This was found to be true in the days of President Edwards, as you who are acquainted with his book on Revivals are well aware.

III. I proceed to mention some things *which ought to be done*, to continue this great and glorious revival of religion, which has been in progress for the last ten years.

1. *There should be great and deep repentings on the part of ministers*. WE, my brethren, must humble *ourselves* before God. It will not do for us to suppose that it is enough to call on the *people* to repent. We must repent, we must take the lead in repentance, and then call on the churches to follow.

Especially must those repent who have taken the lead in producing the feelings of opposition and distrust in regard to revivals. Some ministers have confined their opposition against revivals and revival measures to their own congregations, and created such suspicions among their own people as to prevent the work from spreading and prevailing among them. Such ministers would do well to consider the remarks of President Edwards on this subject.

"If ministers preach never so good doctrine, and are never so painful and laborious in their work, yet, if at such a day as this, they show to their people, that they are not well-affected to this work, but are very doubtful and suspicious of it, they will be very likely to do their people a great deal more hurt than good; for the very fame of such a great and extraordinary work of God, if their people were suffered to believe it to be his work, and the example of other towns, together with what preaching they might hear occasionally, would be likely to have a much greater influence upon the minds of their people, to awaken and animate them in religion, than all their labors with them: and besides their minister's opinion would not only beget in them a suspicion of the work they hear of abroad, whereby the mighty hand of God that appears in it, loses its influence upon their minds, but it will also tend to create a suspicion of every thing of the like nature, that shall appear among themselves, as being something of the same distemper that is become so epidemical in the land, and that is, in effect, to create a suspicion of all vital religion, and to put the people upon talking against it, and discouraging it, where-ever it appears, and knocking it in the head, as fast as it rises. And we that are ministers, by looking on this work, from year to year, with a displeased countenance, shall effectually keep the sheep from their pasture, instead of doing the part of shepherds to them, by feeding them; and our people had a great deal better be without any settled minister at all at such a day as this."

Others have been more public, and aimed at exerting a wider influence. Some have written pieces for the public papers. Some men in high standing in the church have circulated letters which never were printed. Others have had their letters printed and circulated. There seems to have been a system of letter writing about the country calculated to create distrust. In the days of President Edwards, substantially the same course was pursued, in view of which he says in his work on revivals:

"Great care should be taken that the press should be improved to no purpose contrary to the interest of this work. We read that when God fought against Sisera, for the deliverance of his oppressed church, *they that handle the pen of the writer* came to the help of the Lord in that affair. Judges v. 14. Whatever sort of men in Israel they were that were intended, yet as the words were indited by a Spirit that had a perfect view of all events to the end of the world, and had a special eye in this song, to that great event of the deliverance of God's church, in the latter days, of which this deliverance of Israel was a type, it is not unlikely that they have respect to authors, those that should fight against the kingdom of Satan, with their pens. Those therefore that publish pamphlets to the disadvantage of this work, and tending either directly or indirectly to bring it under suspicion, and to discourage or hinder it, would do well thoroughly to consider whether this be not indeed the work of God, and whether, if it be, it is not likely that God will go forth as fire, to consume all that stand in his way, and so burn up those pamphlets; and whether there be not danger that the fire that is kindled in them, will scorch the authors."

All these must repent. God never will forgive them, nor will they ever enjoy his blessing on their preaching, or be honored to labor in revivals, till they repent. This duty President Edwards pressed upon ministers in his day, in the most forcible terms. There doubtless have been now, as there were then, faults on both sides. And there must be deep repentance, and mutual confessions of faults on both sides.

"There must be a great deal done at confessing of faults, on both sides; for undoubtedly many and great are the faults that have been committed, in the jangling and confusions, and mixtures of light and darkness, that have been of late. There is hardly any duty more contrary to our corrupt dispositions, and mortifying to the pride of man; but it must be done. Repentance of faults is, in a peculiar manner, a proper duty, when the kingdom of heaven is at hand, or when we especially expect or desire that it should come; as appears by John the Baptist's preaching. And if God does now loudly call upon us to repent, then he also calls upon us to make proper manifestations of our repentance. I am persuaded that those that have openly opposed this work, or have from time to time spoken lightly of it, cannot be excused in the sight of God, without openly confessing their fault therein; especially if they be ministers. If they have any way, either directly or indirectly, opposed the work, or have so behaved in their public performances or private conversation, as has prejudiced the minds of their people against the work, if hereafter they shall be convinced of the goodness and divinity of what they have opposed, they ought by no means to palliate the matter, and excuse themselves, and pretend that they always thought so, and that it was only such and such imprudences that they objected against, but they ought openly to declare their conviction, and condemn themselves for what they have done; for it is Christ that they have spoken against, in speaking lightly of, and prejudicing others against this work; yea, worse than that, it is the Holy Ghost. And though they have done it ignorantly, and in unbelief, yet when they find out who it is that they have opposed, undoubtedly God will hold them bound publicly to confess it.

"And on the other side, if those that have been zealous to promote the work, have in any of the forementioned instances openly gone much out of the way, and done that which is contrary to Christian rules, whereby they have openly injured others, or greatly violated good order, and so done that which has wounded religion, they must publicly confess it, and humble themselves, as they would gather out the stones, and prepare the way of God's people. They who have laid great stumbling blocks in others' way, by their *open transgression*, are bound to remove them, by their *open repentance*." [10]

[10] These quotations from Edwards' *Thoughts Concerning the Present Revival of Religion* are from the edition previously cited, IV, 148–149, 153, 252–253.

There are ministers in our day, I say it not in unkindness but in faithfulness, and I would that I had them all here before me while I say it, who seem to have been engaged much of their time for years in doing little else than acting and talking and writing in such a way as to create suspicion in regard to revivals. And I cannot doubt that their churches would, as President Edwards says, be better with no minister at all, unless they will repent, and regain his blessing.

2. *Those churches which have opposed revivals* must humble themselves and repent. Churches which have stood aloof or hindered the work must repent of their sin, or God will not go with them. Look at those churches now, who have been throwing suspicion upon revivals. Do they enjoy revivals? Does the Holy Ghost descend upon them, to enlarge them and build them up? There is one of the churches in this city, where the session have been publishing in the newspapers what they call their "Act and Testimony," calculated to excite an unreasonable and groundless suspicion against many ministers who are laboring successfully to promote revivals.[11] And what is the state of that church? Have they had a revival? Why it appears from the official report to the General Assembly, that it has dwindled in one year twenty-seven per cent. And all such churches will continue to dwindle, in spite of every thing else that can be done, unless they repent and have a revival. They may pretend to be mighty pious, and jealous for the honor of God, but God will not believe they are sincere. And he will manifest his displeasure, by not pouring out his Spirit. If I had a voice loud enough, I should like to make every one of these churches and ministers that have slandered revivals, hear me, when I say, that I believe they have helped to bring the pall of death over the church, and that the curse of God is on them already, and will remain unless they repent. God has already sent leanness into their souls, and many of them know it.

3. *Those who have been engaged in promoting the work* must also repent. Whatever they have done that was wrong must be repented of, or revivals will not return as in days past Whenever a wrong spirit has been manifested, or they have got irritated and provoked at the opposition, and lost their temper, or mistaken Christian faithfulness for hard words and a wrong spirit, they must

---

[11] This local Act and Testimony had no direct connection with the Act and Testimony adopted by the General Assembly in 1835, although it was part of the same Old School reaction to New School views.

repent. Those who are opposed could never stop a revival alone, unless those who promote it get wrong. So we must repent if we have said things that were censorious, or proud, or arrogant, or severe. Such a time as this is no time to stand justifying ourselves. Our first call is to repent. Let each one repent of his own sins, and not fall out, and quarrel about who is most to blame.

4. *The church must take right ground in regard to politics.* Do not suppose, now, that I am going to preach a political sermon, or that I wish to have you join and get up a *Christian party* in politics. No, I do not believe in that. But the time has come that Christians must vote for honest men, and take consistent ground in politics, or the Lord will curse them. They must be honest men themselves, and instead of voting for a man because he belongs to their party, Bank or Anti-Bank, Jackson, or Anti-Jackson, they must find out whether he is honest and upright, and fit to be trusted. They must let the world see that the church will uphold no man in office, who is known to be a knave, or an adulterer, or a Sabbath-breaker, or a gambler. Such is the spread of intelligence and the facility of communication in our country, that every man can know for whom he gives his vote. And if he will give his vote only for honest men, the country will be obliged to have upright rulers.[12] All parties will be compelled to put up honest men as candidates. Christians have been exceedingly guilty in this matter. But the time has come when they must act differently, or God will curse the nation, and withdraw his spirit. As on the subject of slavery and temperance, so on this subject, the church must act right or the country will be ruined. God cannot sustain this free and blessed country, which we love and pray for, unless the church will take right ground. Politics are a part of religion in such a country as this, and Christians must do their duty to the country as a part of their duty to God. It seems sometimes as if the foundations of the nation were becoming rotten, and Christians seem to act as if they thought God did not see what they do in politics. But I tell you, he does see it, and he will bless or curse this nation, according to the course they take.

5. *The churches must take right ground on the subject of slavery.* And here the question arises, what is right ground? And First I will state some things that should be avoided.

[12] Once again Finney takes the simplistic, pietistic view that all political problems can be solved by the election of honest candidates. Notice, however, that Finney does not take the extreme view of many pietists and separatists that the Christian must withdraw from all political activity because it is worldly.

(1.) First of all, *a bad spirit* should be avoided. Nothing is more calculated to injure religion, and to injure the slaves themselves, than for Christians to get into an angry controversy on the subject. It is a subject upon which there needs to be no angry controversy among Christians. Slave-holding professors, like rum-selling professors, may endeavor to justify themselves, and may be angry with those who press their consciences, and call upon them to give up their sins. Those proud professors of religion who think a man to blame, or think it is a shame to have a black skin, may allow their prejudices so far to prevail, as to shut their ears, and be disposed to quarrel with those who urge the subject upon them. But I repeat it, the subject of slavery is a subject upon which Christians, praying men, *need not* and *must not* differ.

(2.) Another thing to be avoided is *an attempt to take neutral ground* on this subject. Christians can no more take neutral ground on this subject, since it has come up for discussion, than they can take neutral ground on the subject of the sanctification of the Sabbath. It is a great national sin. It is a sin of the church. The churches by their silence, and by permitting slaveholders to belong to their communion, have been consenting to it. All denominations have been more or less guilty, although the Quakers have of late years washed their hands of it. It is in vain for the churches to pretend it is merely a political sin. I repeat it, it is the sin of the church, to which all denominations have consented. They have virtually declared that it is lawful. The very fact of suffering slaveholders quietly to remain in good standing in their churches, is the strongest and most public expression of their views that it is not sin. For the church, therefore, to pretend to take neutral ground on the subject, is perfectly absurd. The fact is that she is not on neutral ground at all. While she tolerates slaveholders in her communion SHE JUSTIFIES THE PRACTICE. And as well might an enemy of God pretend that he was neither saint nor sinner, that he was going to take neutral ground, and pray "good Lord and good devil," because he did not know which side would be the most popular.

(3.) Great care should be taken *to avoid a censorious spirit on both sides*. It is a subject on which there has been, and probably will be for some time to come, a difference of *opinion* among Christians, as to the best method of disposing of the question. And it ought to be treated with great forbearance on both sides. A denunciatory spirit, impeaching each other's motives, is unchristian, calculated to grieve the Spirit of God, and to put down revivals, and is alike injurious to the church, and to the slaves themselves.

In the SECOND place, I will mention several things, that in my judgment the church are imperatively called upon to do, on this subject:

(1.) Christians of all denominations, should lay aside prejudice and *inform themselves* on this subject, without any delay. Vast multitudes of professors of religion have indulged prejudice to such a degree as to be unwilling to read and hear, and come to a right understanding of the subject. But Christians cannot pray in this state of mind. I defy any one to possess the spirit of prayer, while he is too prejudiced to examine this, or any other question of duty. If the light did not shine. Christians might remain in the dark upon this point, and still possess the spirit of prayer. But if they *refuse to come to the light*, they cannot pray. Now I call upon all you who are here present, and who have not examined this subject because you were indisposed to examine it, to say whether you have the spirit of prayer. Where ministers, individual Christians, or whole churches, *resist truth* upon this point now, when it is so extensively diffused and before the public mind, I do not believe they will or can enjoy a revival of religion.

(2.) Writings, containing temperate and judicious discussions on this subject, and such developments of facts as are before the public, should be quietly and extensively circulated, and should be carefully and prayerfully examined by the whole church. I do not mean by this, that the attention of the church should be so absorbed by this, as to neglect the main question, of saving souls in the midst of them. I do not mean that such premature movements on this subject should be made, as to astound the Christian community, and involve them in a broil; but that praying men should act judiciously, and that, as soon as sufficient information can be diffused through the community, the churches should meekly, but FIRMLY take decided ground on the subject, and express before the whole nation and the world, their abhorrence of this sin.

The anti-masonic excitement which prevailed a few years since, made such desolations in the churches, and produced so much alienation of feeling and ill will among ministers and people, and the first introduction of *this* subject has been attended with such commotions, that many good ministers, who are themselves entirely opposed to slavery, dread to introduce the subject among their people, through fear that their churches have not religion enough to take it up, and consider it calmly, and decide upon it in the spirit of the gospel. I know there is danger of this. But still, the subject must be presented to the churches. And if introduced with discretion, and with great prayer, there are very few churches that have enjoyed revivals, and that are at the present time any where near a revival spirit, which may not be brought to receive the truth on this subject.[13]

Perhaps no church in this country has had a more severe trial upon this subject, than this. They were a church of young and for the most part inexperienced Christians. And many circumstances conspired, in my absence, to produce confusion and wrong feeling among them. But so far as I am now acquainted with the state of feeling in this church, I know of no ill will among them on this subject. The Lord has blessed us, the Spirit has been distilled upon us, and considerable numbers added to our communion, every month since my return. There are doubtless in this church those who feel on this subject in very different degrees. And yet I can honestly say that I am not aware of the least difference *in sentiment* among them. We have from the beginning, *previous* to my going on my foreign tour, taken the same ground on the subject of slavery that we have on temperance. We have excluded slaveholders and all concerned in the traffic from our communion.[14] By some, out of this church, this course has been censured, as unwarrantable and uncharitable, and I would

---

[13] In the revised edition of these lectures in 1868 Finney added here, "Let there be no mistake here. William Morgan's exposé of freemasonry was published in 1826. The consequent excitement and discussion continued until 1830. In the meantime the churches had very generally borne their testimony against freemasonry, and resolved that they could not fellowship adhering masons. As a consequence the Masonic Lodges generally disbanded and gave up their charters. There was a general stampede of professed Christians from the lodges. This prepared the way, and in 1830, the greatest revival the world had then ever seen commenced in the center of the anti-masonic region, and spread over the whole field where the church action had been taken until its converts numbered 100,000 souls." For a brief discussion of the anti-Masonic movement in western New York, see Cross, *Burned-Over District*, pp. 114ff. In 1869 Finney published another attack upon the Masons entitled, *The Character and Claims and Practical Workings of Freemasonry*. Finney himself had been a Mason prior to his conversion.

[14] Finney and his church voted on November 3, 1834 to exclude slaveholders and slavetraders from communion. See Susan H. Ward, *The History of Broadway Tabernacle* (New York, 1901) p. 27.

by no means make my own judgment, or the example of this church, a rule for the government of other ministers and churches. Still, I conscientiously believe, that the time is not far distant, when the churches will be united in this expression of abhorrence against this sin. If I do not baptize slavery by some soft and Christian name, if I call it SIN, both consistency and conscience conduct to the inevitable conclusion, that while the sin is persevered in, it perpetrators cannot be fit subjects for Christian communion and fellowship.

To this it is objected, that there are *many ministers* in the Presbyterian church, who are slaveholders. And it is said to be very inconsistent that we should refuse to suffer a slaveholder to come to our communion, and yet belong to the same church with them, sit with them in ecclesiastical bodies, and acknowledge them as ministers. To this I answer, that I have not the power to deal with those ministers, and certainly I am not to withdraw from the church because some of its ministers or members are slaveholders. My duty is to belong to the church, even if the devil belong to it. Where I *have authority*, I exclude slaveholders from the communion, and I always will as long as I live. But where I have no authority, if the table of Christ is spread, I will sit down to it, in obedience to his commandment, whoever else may sit down or stay away.

I do not mean, by any means, to denounce all those slaveholding ministers and professors, as hypocrites, and to say that they are not Christians. But this I say, that while they continue in that attitude, the cause of Christ and of humanity demands, that they should not be recognized as such, unless we mean to be partakers of other men's sins. It is no more inconsistent to exclude slaveholders because they belong to the Presbyterian church, than it is to exclude persons who drink or sell ardent spirits. For there are a great many rum-sellers belonging to the Presbyterian church.

I believe the time has come, and although I am no prophet, I believe it will be found to have come, that the revival in the United States will continue and prevail, no farther and faster than the church take right ground upon this subject. The church are God's witnesses. The fact is that slavery is, pre-eminently, the *sin of the church*. It is the very fact that ministers and professors of religion of different denominations hold slaves, which sanctifies the whole abomination, in the eyes of ungodly men. Who does not know that on the subject of temperance, every drunkard in the land, will skulk behind some rum-selling deacon, or wine-drinking minister? It is the most common objection and refuge of the intemperate, and of moderate drinkers, that it is practised by professors of religion. It is *this* that creates the imperious necessity for excluding traffickers in ardent spirit, and rum-drinkers from the communion. Let the churches of all denominations speak out on the subject of temperance, let them close their doors against all who have any thing to do with the death-dealing abomination, and the cause of temperance is triumphant. A few years would annihilate the traffic. Just so with slavery.

It is the church that mainly supports this sin. Her united testimony upon this subject would settle the question. Let Christians of all denominations meekly but firmly come forth, and pronounce their verdict, let them clear their communions, and wash their hands of this thing, let them give forth and write on the head and front of this great abomination, SIN! and in three years, a public sentiment would be formed that would carry all before it, and there would not be a shackled slave, nor a bristling, cruel slave-driver in this land.[15]

Still it may be said, that in many churches, this subject *cannot be* introduced, without creating confusion and ill-will. This may be. It has been so upon the subject of temperance, and upon the subject of revivals too. In some churches, neither temperance nor revivals can be introduced without producing dissension. Sabbath-schools, and Missionary operations, and every thing of the kind have been opposed, and have produced dissensions, in many churches. But is this a sufficient reason for excluding these subjects? And where churches have excluded these subjects for fear of contention, have they been blessed with revivals? Every body knows that they have not. But where churches have taken firm ground on these subjects, although individuals and sometimes numbers have opposed, still they have been blessed with revivals. Where any of these subjects are carefully and prayerfully introduced, where they are brought forward with a right spirit, and the true relative importance is attached to each one of them, if in such cases, there are those who will make disturbance and resist, *let the blame fall where it ought.* There are some individuals, who are *themselves* disposed to quarrel with this subject, who are al-

---

[15] Finney's pietism led him to underrate the problem of slavery as he did the problem of politics. Or perhaps it might be said that he overrated the zeal of Christians and the power of revivalism. For a discussion of Finney's attitude toward antislavery reform, see McLoughlin, *Modern Revivalism*, pp. 108–112.

ways ready to exclaim, "Don't introduce these things into the church, they will create opposition." And if the minister and praying people feel it their duty to bring the matter forward, they will themselves create a disturbance, and then say, "There, I told you so; now see what your introducing this subject has done, it will tear the church all to pieces." And while they are themselves doing all they can to create division, they are charging the division upon the subject, and not upon themselves. There are some such people in many of our churches. And neither sabbath-schools, nor missions, nor revivals, nor anti-slavery, nor any thing else that honors God or benefits the souls of men, will be carried in the churches, without these careful souls being offended by it.

These things, however, have been introduced, and carried, one by one, in some churches with more, and others with less opposition, and perhaps in some churches with no opposition at all. And as true as God is the God of the church, as certain as that the world must be converted, this subject must be considered and pronounced sin by the church. There might, infinitely better, be no church in the world, than that she should attempt to remain neutral or give a false testimony on a subject of such importance as slavery, especially since the subject has come up, and it is impossible from the nature of the case, that her testimony should not be in the scale, on the one side or the other.

Do you ask, "What shall be done — shall we make it the all-absorbing topic of conversation, and divert attention from the all-important subject of the salvation of souls in the midst of us?" I answer, No. Let a church express her opinion upon the subject, and be at peace. So far as I know, *we* are entirely at peace upon this subject. We have expressed our opinion, we have closed our communion against slave holders, and are attending to other things.[16] I am not aware of the least unhealthy excitement among us on this subject. And where it has become an absorbing topic of conversation in a place, in most instances I believe it has been owing to the pertinacious and unreasonable opposition of a few individuals against even granting the subject a hearing.

6. If the church wishes to promote revivals, *she must sanctify the Sabbath*. There is a vast deal of Sabbath-breaking in the land. Merchants break it, travellers break it, the government breaks it.

---

[16] Finney asserted in his *Memoirs* (p. 324) that he never made such a hobby of slavery as to "divert the attention of the people from the work of converting souls."

A few years ago an attempt was made in the western part of this state, to establish and sustain a Sabbath-keeping line of boats and stages. But it was found that the *church* would not sustain the enterprise. Many professors of religion would not travel in these stages, and would not have their good forwarded in canal boats that would be detained from travelling on the Sabbath. At one time, Christians were much engaged in petitioning Congress to suspend the Sabbath Mails, and now they seem to be ashamed of it. But one thing is most certain, that unless something is done, and done speedily, and done effectually, to promote the sanctification of the Sabbath by the church, the Sabbath will go by the board, and we shall not only have our mails running on the Sabbath, and Post Offices open, but by and by our courts of justice and halls of legislation will be kept open on the Sabbath.[17] And what can the church do, what will this nation do, WITHOUT ANY SABBATH?

7. The church must take right ground on the subject of Temperance, and Moral Reform, and all the subject of practical morality which come up for decision from time to time.

There are those in the churches who are standing aloof from the subject of Moral Reform, and who are as much afraid to have any thing said in the pulpit against lewdness, as if a thousand devils had got up into the pulpit. On this subject, the church need not expect to be permitted to take neutral ground. In the providence of God, it is up for discussion. The evils have been exhibited, the call has been made for reform. And what is to reform mankind but the truth? And who shall present the truth if not the church and the ministry? Away with the idea, that Christians can remain neutral and keep still, and yet enjoy the approbation and blessing of God.

In all such cases, the minister who holds his peace is counted among those on the other side. Every body knows that it is so in a revival. It is not necessary for a person to rail out against the work. If he only keeps still and takes neutral ground, the enemies of the revival will all consider him as on their side. So on the subject of temperance. It is not needful that a person should rail at the cold-water society, in order to be on the best terms with

---

[17] One of the blackest marks against the administration of Andrew Jackson from Finney's point of view was its refusal to abandon delivery of the mail on Sundays. For this controversy in 1829, see A. M. Schlesinger, Jr., *The Age of Jackson* (Boston, 1945), pp. 138–139.

drunkards and moderate drinkers. Only let him plead for the moderate use of wine, only let him continue to drink it as a luxury, and all the drunkards account him on their side. If he refuses to give his influence to the temperance cause, he is claimed of course by the other side as a friend. On all these subjects, when they come up, the churches and ministers must take the right ground, and take it openly and stand to it, and carry it through, if they expect to enjoy the blessing of God in revivals. They must cast out from their communions such members, as in contempt of the light that is shed upon them, continue to drink or traffic in ardent spirits.

8. *There must be more done for all the great objects of Christian benevolence.* There must be much greater efforts for the cause of missions, and education, and the Bible, and all the other branches of religious enterprise, or the church will displease God. Look at it. Think of the mercies we have received, of the wealth, numbers and prosperity of the church. Have we rendered unto God according to the benefits we have received, so as to show that the church is bountiful and willing to give their money and to work for God? No. Far from it. Have we multiplied our means and enlarged our plans, in proportion as the church has increased? Is God satisfied with what has been done, or has he reason to be? Such a revival as has been enjoyed by the churches of America for the last ten years! We ought to have done ten times as much as we have for missions, Bibles, education, tracts, free churches, and in all the ways designed to promote religion and save souls. If the churches do not wake up on this subject, and lay themselves out on a larger scale, they may expect the revival in the United States will cease.

9. If Christians in the United States expect revivals to spread, and prevail, till the world is converted, they must give up writing letters and publishing pieces *calculated to excite suspicion and jealousy in regard to revivals*, and must take hold of the work themselves. If the whole church as a body had gone to work ten years ago, and continued it as a few individuals, whom I could name, have done, there would not now have been an impenitent sinner in the land. The millennium would have fully come in the United States before this day. Instead of standing still, and writing letters from Berkshire, let ministers who think we are going wrong, just buckle on the harness and *go forward, and show* us a more excellent way.[18] Let them teach us by their example how to do better. I do not deny that we have made mistakes, and committed errors. I do

---

[18] I have not been able to identify these "letters from Berkshire."

not deny that there are many things which are wrong done in revivals. But is that the way to correct them, brethren? So did not Paul. He corrected his brethren by telling them kindly that he would show them a more excellent way. Let our brethren take hold and go forward. Let us hear the cry from all their pulpits. To THE WORK. Let them lead on, where the Lord will go with them and make bare his arm, and I, for one, will follow. Only let them GO ON, and let us have the United States converted to God, and let all minor questions cease.

If not, and if revivals do cease in this land, the ministers and churches will be guilty of all the blood of all the souls that shall go to hell in consequence of it. There is no need that the work should cease. If the church will do all her duty, the millennium may come in this country in three years. But if this writing letters is to be kept up, filling the country with suspicions and jealousies, if it is to be always so, that two-thirds of the church will hang back and do nothing but find fault in time of revival, the curse of God will be on this nation, and that before long.

REMARKS.

1. It is high time there should be *great searchings of heart* among Christians and ministers. Brethren, this is no time to resist the truth, or to cavil and find fault because the truth is spoken out plainly. It is no time to recriminate or to strive, but we must search *our own* hearts, and humble ourselves before God.

2. We must repent and forsake our sins, and amend our ways and our doings, or the revival will cease. Our ecclesiastical difficulties MUST CEASE, and all minor differences must be laid aside and given up, to unite in promoting the great interests of religion. If not, revivals will cease from among us, and the blood of lost millions will be found in our skirts.

If the church would do all her duty, she would soon complete the triumph of religion in the world. But if this Act and Testimony warfare is to be kept up, and this system of espionage, and insinuation and denunciation, not only will revivals cease, but the blood of millions who will go to hell before the church will get over the shock, will be found in the skirts of the men who have got up and carried on this dreadful contention.

4. Those who have circulated slanderous reports in regard to revivals, must repent. A great deal has been said about heresy, and

about some men's denying the Spirit's influence, which is wholly groundless, and has been made up out of nothing. And those who have made up the reports, and those who have circulated them against their brethren, must repent and pray to God that they may receive his forgiveness.

5. We see the *constant tendency there is* in Christians to declension and backsliding. This is true in all converts of all revivals. Look at the revival in President Edward's day. The work went on till 30,000 souls had been converted, and by this time so many ministers and Christians got in such a state, by writing books and pamphlets, on one side and the other, that they carried all by the board, and the revival ceased.[19] Those who had opposed the work grew obstinate and violent, and those who promoted it lost their meekness, and got ill-tempered, and were then driven into the very evils that had been falsely charged upon them.

And now, what shall we do? This great and glorious work of God seems to be indicating a decline. The revival is not dead — blessed be God for that, — it is not dead! No, we hear from all parts of the land that Christians are reading on the subject and inquiring about the revival. In some places there are now powerful revivals. And what shall we do, to lift up the standard, to move this entire nation and turn all this great people to the Lord? We must DO RIGHT. We must all have a better Spirit, we must get down in the dust, we must act unitedly, we must take hold of this great work with all our hearts, and then God will bless us, and the work will go on.

What is the condition of this nation? No doubt, God is holding the rod of WAR over the heads of this nation.[20] He is waiting before he lets loose his judgments, to see whether the church will do right. The nation is under his displeasure, because the church has conducted in such a manner with respect to revivals. And now suppose war should come, where would be our revivals? How quickly would war swallow up the revival spirit. The spirit of war is any thing but the spirit of revivals. Who will attend to the claims of religion, when the public mind is engrossed by the all-absorbing topic of war. See now, how this nation is, *all at once,*

---

[19] There are no statistical records to confirm or refute this figure.

[20] Finney here refers to a possible war with France growing out of Andrew Jackson's vigorous attempts to make the French government honor its treaty of 1831 to pay damages to the United States for commercial spoliations during the Napoleonic wars. Jackson's belligerence in this matter did not endear him to Finney.

brought upon the brink of war. God brandishes his blazing sword over our heads. Will the church repent? It is THE CHURCH that God chiefly has in view. How shall we avoid the curse of war? Only by a reformation in the church. It is in vain to look to politicians to avert war. Perhaps they would generally be in favor of war. Very likely the things they would do to avert it would run us right into it. If the church will not feel, will not awake, will not act, where shall we look for help? If the church absolutely *will not* move, will not tremble in view of the just judgments of God hanging over our heads, we are certainly nigh unto cursing, as a nation.

6. Whatever is done *must be done quickly*. The scale is on a poise. If we do not go forward, we must go back. Things cannot remain as they are. If the church do not come up, if we do not have a more powerful revival than we have had, very soon we shall have none at all. We have had such a great revival, that now small revivals do not interest the public mind. You must act as individuals. *Do your own duty.* You have a responsibility. Repent quickly. Do not wait till another year. Who but God knows what will be the state of these churches, if things go on *another year* without a great and general revival of religion?

7. It is common, when things get all wrong in the church, for each individual to find fault with the church, and with his brethren, and overlook his own share of the blame. Do not let any one spend his time in finding fault with that abstract thing, "The church." But as individual members of the church of Christ, let each one act, and act right, and get down in the dust, and never speak proudly, or censoriously. GO FORWARD. Who would leave such a work, and go to writing letters, and go down into the plain of Ono, and see if all these petty disputes can't be adjusted, and let the work cease. Let us mind our work, and let the Lord take care of the rest. Do our duty, and leave the issue to God.[21]

---

[21] In the revised edition of 1868 Finney added to the end of this lecture the following note: "Since these lectures were delivered great progress has been made in all benevolent enterprises in this country. Time has settled the question of the purity and inestimable value of those revivals against which so much mistaken opposition existed in the Presbyterian church. It is now known that the great and disastrous reaction predicted by opposers has not been witnessed. It must now be admitted that the converts of those revivals have composed the strength of the churches, and that their Christian influence has been felt throughout the land. No revivals have ever existed the power and purity of which have been more thoroughly established by time and experience than that great and blessed work of God against which such a storm of opposition was raised. The

opposition was evidently a great mistake. Let it not be said that the opposition was demanded by the great evils attending that work and that those evils and errors were arrested and corrected by the opposition. The fact is that the supposed errors and evils that were made the justifications of the opposition never existed to any such extent as to justify alarm or opposition. I have written a narrative of those revivals [his *Memoirs*] in which I have considered the question more fully. The churches did take hold of temperance and other branches of reform to such an extent as to avoid those evils against which they were warned. Upon the question of slavery the church was too late in her testimony to avoid the war. But the slaveholders were much alarmed and exasperated by the constantly growing opposition to their institution throughout all that region of the north where revival influences had been felt. They took up arms to defend and perpetuate the abomination and by so doing abolished it."

XVI

THE NECESSITY AND EFFECT OF UNION

TEXT. — "Again I say unto you, That if two of you shall agree on earth, as touching any thing that they shall ask, it shall be done for them of my Father which is in heaven." — MATTHEW xviii. 19.

SOME weeks since, I used this text, in preaching on the subject of prayer-meetings. At present I design to enter more into the spirit and meaning of the text. The evident design of our Lord in this text was to teach the importance and influence of union in prayer and effort to promote religion. He states the strongest possible case by taking the number *two*, as the least number between whom there can be an agreement, and says that "where *two* of you are agreed on earth, as touching any thing that they shall ask, it shall be done for them of my Father which is in heaven." It is the fact of their *agreement*, upon which he lays the stress, and mentioning the number two, appears to have been designed merely to afford encouragement to the smallest number between whom there can be an agreement. But what are we to understand by being "agreed as touching" the things we shall ask? I will answer this question under the two following heads:

I. By showing that we are to be "agreed" in *prayer*.

II. We are to agree in every thing that is essential to obtaining the blessing that we seek.

I. In order to come within this promise, we are to be agreed in prayer. This is particularly taught in the text. That is,

1. We should *agree in our desires* for the object. It is necessary to *have desires* for the object, and to be agreed in those desires. Very often individuals pray *in words* for the same thing, when they are by no means agreed in desiring that thing. Nay, perhaps some of them, in their hearts desire the very opposite. People are called on to pray for an object, and they all pray for it in words, but God knows they often do not desire it, and perhaps he sees that the hearts of some may, all the while, be resisting the prayer.

2. We must *agree in the motive* from which we desire the object. It is not enough that our desires for an object should be

the same, but the *reason why* must be the same. An individual may desire a revival, for the glory of God and the salvation of sinners. Another member of the church may also desire a revival, but from very different motives. Some, perhaps, desire a revival in order to have the congregation built up and strengthened, so as to make it more easy for them to pay their expenses in supporting the gospel. Another desires a revival for the sake of having the church increased so as to be more numerous and more respectable. Others desire a revival because they have been opposed or evil spoken of, and they wish to have their enemies know that whatever *they* may think or say, *God* blesses them. Sometimes people desire a revival from mere natural affection, so as to have their friends converted and saved. If they mean to be so united in prayer as to obtain a blessing, they must not only desire the blessing, and be agreed in desiring it, but they must also agree in desiring it for the same reasons.

3. We must be agreed in desiring it *for good reasons*. These desires must not only be united, and from the same motives, but they must be from *good* motives. The supreme motive must be *to honor and glorify God*. People may even desire a revival, and agree in desiring it, and agree in the motives, and yet if these motives are not good, God will not grant their desires. Thus parents may be agreed in prayer for the conversion of their children, and may have the same feelings and the same motives, and yet if they have no higher motives than because they are *their children*, their prayers will not be granted. They are agreed in the reason, but it is not the *right* reason.

In like manner, any number of persons might be agreed in their desires and motives, but if their motives are selfish, their being *agreed* in them will only make them more offensive to God. "How is it that ye have *agreed together* to tempt the Spirit of the Lord?" I have seen a great deal of this, where churches have been engaged in prayer for an object, and their motives were evidently selfish. Sometimes they are engaged in praying for a revival, and you would think by their earnestness and union that they would certainly move God to grant the blessing, till you find out the reason. And what is it? Why, they see *their* congregation is about to be broken up, unless something can be done. Or they see some other denomination gaining ground, and there is no way to counteract them but by having a revival in *their* church. And all their praying is only an attempt to get the Almighty in to help them out of their difficulty, and is purely sefish and offensive to God. A woman in Philadelphia, was invited to attend a female prayer-meeting at a certain place. She inquired what they met *there* for, and for what they were going to pray? She was answered that they were going to pray for the outpouring of the spirit upon the city. "Well," said she, "I shan't go, if they were going to pray for *our congregation* I would go, but I am not going there to pray for other churches!" O, what a spirit!

I have had a multitude of letters and requests that I should visit such and such places, and endeavor to promote a revival, and many reasons have been urged why I should go, but when I came to weigh their reasons, I have sometimes found every one of them selfish. And God would look upon every one with abhorrence.

In prayer-meetings, how often do we hear people offer such reasons why they desire such and such blessings, as are not right in the sight of God. Such reasons, that if they are the true ones, and if Christians are actually excited by those reasons, it would render their prayers not acceptable to God, because their motive was not right.

There are a great many things often said in favor of the cause of missions, which are of this character, appealing to wrong motives. How often are we told of six hundred millions of heathens, who are *in danger* of going to hell, and how little is said of the *guilt* of six hundred millions engaged and banded together as rebels against God, or of the *dishonor* and contempt poured upon God our Maker by such a world of outlaws. Now I know that God refers to those motives which appeal to our mere natural sympathies, and compassion, and uses them, but always in subordination to his glory. If these lower motives are placed foremost, it must always produce a defective piety and zeal, and a great deal that is false. Until the church will look at the dishonor done to God, little will be done. It is this which must be made to stand out before the world, it is this which must be deeply felt by the church, it is this which must be fully exhibited to sinners, before the world can ever be converted.

Parents never agree in praying for the conversion of their children in such a way as to have their prayers answered, until they feel that their children are rebels. Parents often pray very earnestly for their children because they wish God to save them, and they almost think hard of God if he does not save *their* children. But if they would have their prayers prevail, they must come to take

THE NECESSITY AND EFFECT OF UNION

God's part against their children, even though for their perverseness and incorrigible wickedness he should be obliged to send them to hell. I knew a woman who was very anxious for the salvation of her son, and she used to pray for him with agony, but still he remained impenitent, until at length she became convinced that her prayers and agonies had been nothing but the fond yearnings of parental feeling, and were not dictated at all by a just view of her son's character as a wilful and wicked rebel against God. And there was never any impression made on his mind until she was made to take strong ground against him as a rebel, and to look on him as deserving to be sent to hell. And then he was converted. The reason was, she never before was influenced by the right motive in prayer, desiring his salvation with a supreme regard to the glory of God.

4. If we would be so united as to prevail in prayer, *we must agree in faith*. That is, we must concur in expecting the blessing prayed for. We must understand the reason why it is to be expected, we must see the evidence on which faith ought to rest, and must *absolutely believe* that the blessing will come, or we do not bring ourselves within the promise. Faith is always understood as an indispensable condition of prevailing prayer. If it is not expressed in any particular case, it is always implied, for no prayer can be effectual but that which is offered in faith. And in order that *united* prayer may prevail, there must be united faith.

5. So, again, we must be agreed as to the *time when we desire the blessing to come*. If two or more agree in desiring a particular blessing, and one of them desires to have it come *now*, while others are not ready to have it quite yet, it is plain they are not agreed. They are not united in regard to one essential point. If the blessing is to come in answer to their united prayer, it must come as they prayed for it. And if it comes, it must be *at some time*. But if they disagree as to the time when they will have it, plainly it can never come in answer to their prayer.

Suppose a church should undertake to pray for a revival, and should be all agreed in desiring a revival, but not as to the time when it shall be. Suppose some wish to have the revival come now, and are all prepared, and their hearts waiting for the Spirit of God to come down, and are willing to give time and attention and labor to it NOW; but others are not quite ready, they have something else to attend to just at present, some worldly object which they want to accomplish, some piece of business in hand and want just to finish this thing, and *then* — but they cannot possibly find time to attend to it now, they are not prepared to humble themselves, to search their hearts and break up their fallow ground, and put themselves in a posture to receive the blessing. Is it not plain that here is no real union, for they are not agreed in that which is essential? While one part are praying that the revival may come now, the others are praying with equal earnestness that it *may not* come now.

Suppose the question were now put to *this* church, whether you are agreed in praying for a revival of religion here? Do you all desire a revival, and would you all like to have it come now? Would you be heartily agreed now to break down in the dust, and open your hearts to the Holy Ghost if he should come to-night? I do not ask what you would *say*, if I should propose the question. Perhaps if I should put it to you now, you would all rise up and *vote* that you were agreed in desiring a revival, and agreed to have it now. You know how you ought to feel and what you ought to say, and you know you ought to be ready for a revival *now*. But, I ask, would GOD see it to be so in your hearts, that you are agreed on this point? Has there been a time, since I came back from the country,[1] that this church were all agreed in desiring and praying for a revival, and in wishing to have it come now? Have *any two* of you agreed on this point, and prayed accordingly. If not, when will you be agreed to pray for a revival? And if this church cannot be agreed among yourselves, how can you expect a revival? It is of no use for you to take the outward attitude, and stand up here and *say* you are agreed, when God reads the heart, and sees that you are not agreed. Here is the promise — "Again I say unto you, That if two of you shall agree on earth, as touching any thing that they shall ask, it shall be done for them of my Father which is in heaven." Now this is either true, or it is false. Which ground will you take? If it is true, then it is true that you are not agreed, and never have been, except in those cases where you have had a revival.

But we must agree not only upon *a time*, but it must be the *present time*, or we are not agreed in every thing essential to the work. Unless we agree to have the revival *now*, we shall not *now* use the means. But until the means are used, it cannot come. It is plain then, that we must be agreed upon the present time, that is,

---

[1] It was Finney's custom in these years to take a long summer vacation in Whitestown, New York, the home of his wife's parents.

we are not agreed in the sense of the text, until we agree that *now* we will have the blessing, and conduct accordingly. To agree upon a future time is of no use, for when that future time comes we must *then* be agreed upon *that present time*, and use means accordingly, so that you see you are never properly agreed until you agree that *now* is the time.

II. We are to agree in every thing that is essential to obtaining the blessing that we seek.

You see the language of the text, "If two of you shall agree *as touching* any thing that they shall ask." Many people seem to read it as if it referred merely to an agreement *in asking*, and they understand it to promise, that whenever two are agreed *in asking* for any blessing, it shall be given. But Christ says there must be an agreement "as touching" the thing prayed for. That is, the agreement or union must comprise every thing that is essential to the bestowment and reception of the blessing.

1. If Christians would enjoy the benefits of this promise in praying for a revival, they must be *agreed in believing revivals of religion to be a reality*. There are many individuals, even in the church, who do not in their hearts believe that the revivals which take place are the work of God. Some of them may pray in words for an outpouring of the Spirit and a revival of religion, while in their hearts they doubt whether there are any such things known in modern times. In united prayer there must be no hypocrisy.

2. They must agree *in feeling the necessity of revivals*. There are some who believe in the reality of revivals, as a work of God, while at the same time, they are unsettled as to the necessity of having them in order to the success of the gospel. They think there is a real work of God in revivals, but after all, perhaps it is quite as well to have sinners converted and brought into the church in a more quiet and gradual way, and without so much excitement. Whenever revivals are abroad in the land, and prevail, and are popular, they may appear in favor of them, and may put up their cold prayers for a revival, while at the same time they would be sorry on the whole, to have a revival come among them. They think it so much safer and better, to indoctrinate the people, and spread the matter before them in a calm way, and to bring them in gradually, and not run the danger of having animal feeling or wildfire in their congregations.

3. They must be agreed *in regard to the importance of revivals*. Men are not blessed with revivals, in answer to prayers that

are not half in earnest. They must feel the infinite importance of a revival, before they will pray so as to prevail. Blessings of this kind are not granted but in answer to such prayers as arise from a sense of their importance. As I have shown before, when preaching on the subject of prevailing prayer, it is when men desire the blessing with UNUTTERABLE AGONY, that they offer such prayer as will infallibly prevail with God. Those who feel less of the importance of a revival may pray for it in words, but they will never have the blessing. But when a church has been united in prayer, and really felt the importance of a revival, they never have failed of having one. I do not believe a case can be found, of such a church being turned empty away. Such an agreement, when sincere, will secure an agreement also on all other subjects that are indispensable.

4. They must be agreed also, in having *correct scriptural notions about several things connected with revivals.*

(1.) *The necessity of divine agency* to produce a revival. It is not enough that they all hold this *in theory*, and pray for it *in words*. They must fully understand and deeply feel this necessity, they must realize their entire dependence on the Spirit of God, or the whole will fail.

(2.) *Why* divine agency is necessary. There must be an agreement on correct principles in regard to the reason that divine agency is so indispensable. If they get wrong ideas on this point, they will be hindered. If Christians get the idea that this necessity of divine influence in the *inability* of sinners, or if they feel as if God was under obligation to give the Holy Spirit, in order to make sinners *able* to obey the gospel, they insult God, and their prayers will not avail. For in that case they must feel that it is a mere matter of comomn justice for God to pour out his Spirit, before he can justly require Christians to work, or sinners to repent.

Suppose a church get the idea that sinners are poor, unfortunate creatures, who come into the world with such a nature that they can't help sinning, and that sinners are just as unable to repent and believe the gospel as they are to fly to the moon, how can they feel that the sinner is a rebel against God, and that he deserves to be sent to hell? How can they feel that the sinner is *to blame*? And how can they take God's part when they pray? If they do not take God's part against the sinner, they cannot expect God will regard their prayers, for they do not pray with right motives. No doubt one great reason why so many prayers are not answered, is that those who pray do in fact take the sinner's part against God. They pray as if the sinner was a poor unfortunate being, to be pitied, rather than as if he was a guilty wretch, to be blamed. And the reason is that they do not believe sinners are able to obey God. If a person does not believe that sinners are *able* to obey their Maker, and really believes that the Spirit's influences are necessary to make him *able*, it is impossible, with these views, to offer acceptable and prevailing prayer for the sinner, and it is not wonderful that persons with these views should not prevail with God, and should doubt about the efficacy of the prayer of faith.

How often do you hear people pray for sinners in this style, "O Lord, *help* this poor soul to do what he is required to do — O Lord, *enable* him to do so and so." Now this language implies that they take the sinner's part, and not God's. If it was understood by those who use it, as it is sometimes explained, and if people meant by it what they ought to mean when they plead for sinners, I would not find so much fault with it. But the truth is, that when people use this language, they often mean just what the language itself would be naturally at first sight, understood to mean, which is just as if they should pray. "Lord, thou commandest these poor sinners to repent, when, O Lord, thou knowest they cannot repent unless thou givest them thy Spirit, to *enable* them to do it, though thou hast declared that thou wilt send them to hell if they do not, whether they ever receive the Spirit or not; and now, Lord, this seems very hard, and we pray thee to have pity upon these poor creatures, and do not deal so hardly with them, for Christ's sake." Who does not see that such a prayer, or a prayer which *means* this, whatever language it may be couched in, is an insult to God, charging him with infinite injustice, if he continues to exact from sinners a duty which they are unable to perform without that aid which he will not grant. People may pray in this way till the day of judgment, and never obtain a blessing, because they take the sinner's part against God. They cannot pray successfully, until they understand that the sinner is a rebel, and obstinate in his rebellion — so obstinate that he never will, without the Holy Spirit, do what he might do as well as not, instantly, and this obstinacy is the reason, and the only reason, why he needs the influence of the Holy Spirit for his conversion. The only ground on which the sinner needs divine agency is to overcome his obstinacy, and make him willing to do what he *can* do, and what God justly requires him to do. And a church are never in an attitude in which God will hear their united prayer, unless they are agreed in so understanding their dependence on God, as to feel it in perfect consistency with the sinner's blame. If it is the other way, they are agreed in understanding it wrong, and their prayers for divine help to the unfortunate instead of divine favor to make a rebel submit, are wide of the mark, are an insult to God, and they never will obtain favor in heaven.

(3.) They must be agreed in understanding that *revivals are not miracles, but that they are brought about by the use of means* like other events. No wonder revivals formerly came so seldom and continued so short a time, when people generally regarded them as miracles, or like a mere shower of rain, that will come on a place and continue a little while, and then blow over; that is, as something over which we have no control. For what can people do to get a shower of rain? Or how can they make it rain any longer than it does rain? It is necessary that those who pray should be agreed in understanding a revival as something to be brought about by means, or they never will be agreed in using them.

(4.) They must be agreed in understanding that *human agency is just as indispensable to a revival as divine agency*. Such a thing as a revival of religion, I venture to say, never did occur without divine agency, and never did occur without human agency. How often do people say, "God *can*, if he pleases, carry on the work *without* means." But I have no faith in it, for there is no evidence of it. What is religion? Obedience to God's law. But the law cannot be obeyed unless it is known. And how can God make sinners obey but by making known his commandments? And how can he make them known but by revealing them himself, or sending them by others — that is, by bringing THE TRUTH to bear upon the person's mind till he obeys it. God never did and never can convert a sinner except with the truth. What is conversion? Obeying the truth. He may communicate it himself, directly to the sinner. But then, the sinner's own agency is indispensable, for conversion consists in the right employment of the sinner's own agency. And ordinarily, he employs the agency of others also, in printing, writing, conversation, and preaching. God has put the gospel treasure in earthen vessels. He has seen fit to employ *men* in preaching the word. That is, he has seen that human agency is that which he can best employ in saving sinners. And if there ever was a case, of which we have no evidence, there is not one in a thousand, if one in a million, converted in any other way than through the truth, made known and urged by human instrumentality. And as the church must be united in using those means, it is plainly necessary that they should be united in understanding the true reason why means are to be used, and the true principles on which they are to be governed and applied.

5. It is important that there should be union in regard to the *measures essential to the promotion of a revival*. Let individuals agree to do any thing whatever, and if they are not agreed in their measures, they will run into confusion, and counteract one another. Set them to sail a ship, and they never can get along without agreement. If they attempt to do business as merchants when they are not agreed in their measures, what will they do? Why, they will only undo each other's work, and thwart the whole business of the concern. All this is preeminently true in regard to the work of promoting a revival. Otherwise the members of the church will counteract each other's influence, and they need not expect a revival.

(1.) The church must be agreed in regard to *the meetings which are held*, as to what meeting shall be held, and how many, and where, and when they shall be held. Some people always desire to multiply meetings in a revival, as if the more meetings they had, the more religion. Others are always opposed to *any* new meetings in a revival. Some are always for having a protracted meeting, and others are never ready to hold a protracted meeting at all. Whatever difference there may be, it is essential that the church should come to a good understanding on the subject, so that they can go on together in harmony, and labor with zeal and effect.

(2.) They must be agreed as to *the manner of conducting meetings*. It is necessary that the church should be united and cordial on this subject, if they expect to offer united prayer with effect. Sometimes there are individuals who want to adopt every new thing they can hear of or imagine, while others are totally unwilling to have any thing altered in regard to the management of the meeting, but would have every thing done precisely as they are accustomed to. They ought to be *agreed* in some way, either to have the meetings altered, or to keep them on in the old way. The best possible way is, for the church to agree in this, that they will let the meetings go on and take their course, just as the Spirit of God shapes them, and not even attempt to make two meetings just alike. The church never will give the fullest effect to the truth, until they are agreed in this principle, — That in promoting a revival they will accommodate their measures to circumstances, and not attempt to interrupt the natural course which pious feeling and sound judgment indicate, but cast themselves entirely upon the guidance and direction of the Holy Spirit, introducing any measure, at any time, that shall seem called for in the Providence of God, without laying any stress upon its being new or old.

6. They must be agreed *in the manner of dealing with impenitent sinners*. This is a point immensely important, that the church should be agreed in their treatment of sinners. Suppose that they are not agreed, and one will tell a sinner one thing and another another. What confusion! How can they agree in prayer, when it is plain that they are not agreed as to the things they shall pray for. Go among such a church, and hear them pray for sinners. Attend a prayer-meeting and listen. Here is one man prays that the sinners present may repent. Another prays that they may be convicted, and perhaps, if he is very much engaged, will go so far as to pray that they may be *deeply* convicted. Another prays that sinners may go home solemn, and pensive, and silent, meditating upon the truths they have heard. Another prays in such a manner, that you can see he is afraid to have them converted now. Another prays very solemnly that they may not attempt to do any thing in their own strength. And so on. How easy it is to see that the church are not agreed *as touching* the things they ask for, and of course they have no interest in the promise.

If you set them to talk with sinners, their courses would be just as discordant, for it is plain that they are not agreed, and have no clear views in regard to what a sinner must do to be saved, or of what ought to be said to sinners, to bring them to repent. And the consequence is, that sinners who are awakened and anxious, presently get confounded, and do not know what to do, and perhaps give it all up in despair, or conclude there is in reality nothing rational or consistent in religion. One will tell the sinner he must *repent*, immediately. Another will give him *a book*, Doddridge's *Rise and Progress* perhaps, and tell him to read that book.[2] Another will tell him he must pray and persevere, and in God's time he will obtain the blessing. A revival can never go on, for any length of time, amidst such difficulties. If it begins, it must soon run out;

---

[2] Philip Doddridge, *The Rise and Progress of Religion in the Soul* (London, 1745). Doddridge was an English Congregational minister who was a favorite writer among New England Calvinists for many years.

unless, perhaps, the body of the church will keep still and say nothing at all, and let others carry on the work. And there the work will suffer materially for want of their co-operation and support. A church ought to be agreed. Every Christian ought to have a clear understanding of this subject, and all speak the same thing, and give the same directions. And then the sinner will find no one to take his part, and can get no relief or comfort till he repents.

7. They must be agreed *in removing the impediments to a revival*. If a church expects a revival, they must take up the stumbling blocks out of the way.

(1.) In the *exercise of discipline*. If there are rotten members in the church, they should be removed, and the church should all agree to cut them off. If they remain in the church, they are such a reproach to religion, as to hinder a revival. Sometimes when an attempt is made to cast them out, this creates division, and thus the work is stopped. Sometimes the offenders are persons of influence, or they have family friends who will take their part, and make a party, and thus create a bad spirit, and prevent a revival.

(2.) In *mutual confessions*. Whenever wrong has been done to any, there should be a full confession. I do not mean a cold and forced acknowledgment, such as saying, "*If* I have done wrong, I am sorry for it." But a hearty confession, going the full length of the wrong, and showing that it comes out of a broken heart.

(3.) *Forgiveness of enemies*. A great obstruction to revivals is often found in the fact that active and leading individuals harbor a revengeful and unforgiving spirit towards those who have injured them, which destroys their spirituality, makes them harsh and disagreeable in their manner, and prevents them from enjoying either communion with God in prayer, or the blessing of God to give them success in labor. But let the members of a church be truly agreed, in breaking down and confessing their own faults, and in cherishing a tender, merciful, forgiving, Christ-like spirit toward those who they think have done them wrong, and then the Spirit will come down upon them not by measure.

8. They must be agreed *in making all the necessary preparations for a revival*. They should be agreed in having all necessary preparation made, and agreed in bearing their part of the labor or expense of making it. There should be an equality, and not let a few be burthened and the rest do little or nothing, but every one his proportion, according to his several ability. Then there will be no

envying nor jealousy, nor any of those mutual recriminations and altercations and disrespectful remarks about one another, which are so inconsistent with brotherly love, and such a stumbling block in the way of sinners.

9. They must be agreed in *doing heartily whatever is necessary to be done for the promotion of the revival.* Sometimes a slight disagreement about a very little thing will be allowed to break in and destroy a revival. A minister told me that he once went to labor in a place as an evangelist, and the Spirit of God was evidently present, and sinners began to inquire, and things looked quite favorable, until some of the members in the church began to agitate the inquiry how they should pay him for his services. They said "If he stays among us any longer, he will expect we should give him something," and they did not see how they could afford it. And they talked about it until the minds of the brethren got distracted and divided, and the minister went away. Look at it. There God stood in the door of that church, with his hands full of mercies but these parsimonious and wicked professors thought it would cost something to have a revival, and their expenses were about as much as they felt willing or able to bear. And so they let him depart and the work ceased. The minister would not have left, at the time, whether they gave him any thing or not, for what he should receive, or whether he should receive any thing from them, was a question about which he felt no concern. But the church by their parsimonious spirit got into such a state as to grieve the Spirit, and he saw that to stay longer with them would do no good. O, how will those professors feel when they meet sinners from that town in judgment, when it will all come out, that God was ready and waiting to grant them a blessing, but they allowed themselves to get agitated and divided by inquiring how much they should have to pay!

10. They must be agreed *in laboring to carry on the work.* It is not enough that they should agree to pray for a revival, but they should agree also in laboring to promote it. They should set themselves to systematically, and as a matter of business, to visit and converse and pray with their neighbors, to look out for opportunities of doing good, to watch the effect of the word, and watch the signs of the times, that they may know when any thing needs to be done, and do it.

(1.) They should be agreed *to labor.*
(2.) They should be agreed *how* to labor.

(3.) They should be agreed to live *accordingly*.

11. They must agree in a *determination to persevere*. It will not answer for some members of the church to-day to begin to move and bluster about, and then as soon as the least thing turns up unfavorable, to get discouraged, and faint, and one-half of them give over. They should be all united and agree to persevere, and labor, and pray, and hold on, until the blessing comes.

In a word, if Christians expect to unite in prayer and effort, so as to prevail with God, they must be agreed in speaking and doing the same things, in walking by the same rule, and maintaining the same principles, and in persevering till they obtain the blessing, so as not to hinder or thwart each other's efforts. All this is evidently implied in being agreed *"as touching"* the things for which they are praying.

REMARKS.

1. We see why it is that so many of the children of professing parents are not converted.

It is because the parents have not been agreed *as touching* the things they should pray for in behalf of their children. Perhaps they never had any kind of agreement respecting them. Perhaps they were never agreed even as to what was the very *best thing* they could ask them. Sometimes parents are not agreed in any thing, but their opinions clash and they are perpetually disagreeing, and their children see it, and then no wonder they are not converted.

Or perhaps they may not be agreed as touching *the salvation* of their children. Are they sincere in desiring it? Do they agree to desire it, and agree from right motives? Do they agree in regard to the importance of it? Are they agreed how their children ought to be dealt with, to effect their conversion — what shall be said to them — how it shall be said — when — by whom. Alas! in how many cases is it evident they are not agreed. Probably few cases will be found, where children remain unconverted, but what it will prove that the parents were never truly agreed as touching the things they should ask for the salvation of their children.

Often there is such disagreement that we could not expect any good to result, or any thing but ruin to the children. The husband and wife often disagree entirely and fundamentally in regard to the manner of bringing up their children. Perhaps the wife is fond of dress, and display, and visiting, while the husband is plain and humble, and is grieved and distressed and mourns and prays to see how his children are puffed up with vanity. Or it may be that the father is ambitious, and wants to have his daughters fashionably educated and make a display, and his sons become great men, and so he will send his daughter to a polite boarding-school where they may learn any thing but their duty to God, and will be all the time pushing his sons forward, and goading their ambition, while the mother grieves and weeps in secret to see her dear children hurried on to destruction, and all her own influence counteracted, and her sons and daughters trained up to serve the god of this world, and go to hell.

2. We see the hypocrisy of those who profess to be praying for a revival while they are doing nothing to promote it. There are many who appear to be very zealous in *praying* for a revival, while they are not *doing* any thing at all for one. What do they mean. Are they agreed *as touching* the things they ask for? Certainly not. They cannot be agreed in offering acceptable prayer for a revival until they are prepared TO DO what God requires them to do to promote it. What would you think of the farmer who should pray for a crop and not plough or sow? Would you think such prayers pious, or an insult to God?

3. We see why so many prayers offered in the church are never answered. It is because those who offered them never were agreed *as touching* the things they asked for. Perhaps the minister never laid the subject before them, never explained what it is to be agreed, nor showed them its importance, nor set before them the great encouragement which the promise before us affords to churches that will agree. Perhaps the members of the church have never conferred together, and compared their views, to see whether they understood the subject alike, whether they were agreed in regard to the motives, grounds, and importance of being united in prayer and labor for a revival. Suppose you were to go through the churches in this city, and learn the precise views and feelings of the members on this subject. How many would you find who were agreed even in regard to the essential and indispensable things, concerning which it is necessary Christians should be agreed in order to unite in prevailing prayer? Perhaps no two could be found who are agreed, and if two were found, whose views and desires were alike, it would probably be ascertained that they are unacquainted with each other, and of course neither act nor pray together.

4. We see why it is that this text has been generally under-

stood to mean something different from what it says. People have first read it wrong. They have read it as if it was, "If any two of you shall agree *to ask* any thing, it shall be done." And as they have often agreed to ask for things and the things were not done, they have said, "The literal meaning of the text cannot be true for we have tried it and know it is not true. — How many prayer meetings have we held, and how many petitions have we put up, in which we have perfectly agreed in asking for blessings, and yet they have not been granted." Now the fact is, that they have never yet understood what it is to be agreed *as touching* the things they are to ask for. I am sure this is no strained construction of the text, but is its true and obvious meaning, as a plain, pious reader would understand it, if he inquired seriously and earnestly the true import. They must be agreed not only *in asking*, but in every thing else that is indispensable to the existence of the thing prayed for. Suppose two of you were agreed in desiring to go to London together. If you were not agreed in regard to the means, what route you shall take, and what ship you will go in, you will never get there together. Just so in praying for a revival, you must be agreed in regard to the means and circumstances, and every thing essential to the existence and progress of a revival.

5. We may ordinarily expect a revival of religion to prevail and extend among those without the church, just in proportion to the union of prayer and effort within. If there is a general union within the church, the revival will be general. If the union continues, the revival will continue. If any thing begins to break in upon this perfect union in prayer and effort, it will begin to limit the revival. How great and powerful would be the revival in this city, if all the churches in the city were thus united in promoting it.

There is another fact, which I have witnessed, worthy of notice. I have observed, that a revival will prevail out of the church, among persons in that *class of society*, amongst whom it prevails in the church. If the females in the church are most awake and prayerful, the work may ordinarily be expected to prevail mostly among females out of the church, and more women will be converted than men. If the youth of either, or of both sexes, in the church are most awake, the work is most likely to prevail among youth, male or female, or both, as the work may be in the church, in this respect. If the heads of families and the principal men in the church are awake, the revival is, I have observed, more likely to prevail among that class out of the church. I have known a revival mostly confined to females, and few males converted, apparently because the male part of the church did not take hold and work. Again I have repeatedly known the greatest number of converts among *men*, owing apparently to the fact that the male part of the church were most engaged. When the revival does not reach a particular class of the impenitent, pains should be taken to arouse that portion of the church who are of their own age and standing, to make more direct efforts for their conversion. There seems to be a philosophy in this fact, which has often been witnessed. Different classes of professors naturally feel a sympathy for the impenitent of *their own sex* and *age* and *rank*, and more naturally pray for them, and have more intercourse with them, and more influence over them, and this seems to be at least one of the reasons why revivals are apt to be the most powerful and general in that class without the church who are the most awake in the church. Christians should understand this, and feel their responsibility. One great reason why so few of the principal men are sometimes converted in revivals, doubtless is, that that class in the church are often so worldly, they cannot be aroused. The revival will generally prevail mostly in those families where the professors belonging to them are awake, and the impenitent belonging to those families where the professors are not awake, are apt to be left unconverted. One principal reason, obviously is, that when the professors in a family or neighborhood are awake, there is not only prayer offered for sinners in the midst of them, but there are corresponding influences acting upon the impenitent among them. If they are awake, their looks and lives and warnings, all tend to promote the conversion of their impenitent friends. But if they are asleep, all their influences tend to prevent their conversion. Their coldness, grieves the Spirit, their worldliness contradicts the gospel, and all their intercourse with their impenitent friends is in favor of impenitence, and calculated to perpetuate it.

6. We see why different denominations have been suffered to spring up in the church, and under the government of God.

Christians often see and deplore the evils that have arisen to the church of God, from the division of his people into jarring sects. And they have wondered and been perplexed, to think that God should suffer it to be so. But in the light of this subject we can see, that considering what diversities of opinions and feelings and views actually exist in the church, much good results from this division of sects. Considering this diversity of opinion, many would never agree to pray and labor together, so as to do it with success, and so it is better they should separate, and let those unite who are agreed. In all cases where there cannot be a cordial agreement in labor, it is better that each denomination should labor by themselves, so long as this difference exists. I have sometimes seen revivals broken up by attempting to unite Christians of different denominations in prayer and labor together, while they were not agreed as to the principles or measures by which the work was to be promoted. They would then undo each other's work, and destroy each other's influence, perplex the anxious, and give occasion to enemies to blaspheme, and soon their feelings would get soured, and the Spirit of God is grieved away, and the work stops, and perhaps painful confusion and controversy follow.

7. We see why God sometimes suffers churches to be divided. It is because he finds that the members are so much at variance that they *will not* pray and labor together with effect. Sometimes churches that are in such a state, will still keep together from worldly considerations and worldly policy, because it is so much easier for the whole to support public worship. Perhaps both parties want to keep the meeting-house, or both want to retain the minister, and they cannot agree which shall go off, and so they continue along, jealous and jangling for years, accomplishing little or nothing for the salvation of sinners. In such cases, God has often let something turn up among them, that would *tear them asunder*, and then each party would go to work in their own way, and perhaps both would prosper. While they were in the same church, they were always making each other trouble, as they did not think nor feel alike, but as soon as they were separated, every thing settled down in peace, and made it evident that it was better they should divide. I have known some cases in this state, where this has been done with the happiest results, and both churches have been speedily blessed with revivals.

8. It is evident that many more churches need to be divided.[3] How many churches there are, who are holding together, and yet are doing no good, for the simple reason that they are not sufficiently agreed. They do not think alike nor feel alike on the subjects connected with revivals, and while this is so, they never can work together. Unless they can be brought to such a change of views and feelings on the subject as will unite them, they are only

[3] Finney here refers to an amicable division of a congregation, which results in the building of a new church of the same denomination in the vicinity.

a hindrance to each other and to the work of God. In many cases they see and feel that it is so, and yet they keep together, conscientiously, for fear a division should dishonor religion, when in fact the division that now exists may be making religion a by-word and a reproach. Far better would it be if they would just agree to divide amicably, like Abraham and Lot. "If thou wilt take the left hand, I will go to the right; or if thou depart to the right hand, then I will go to the left." Let them separate, and each work in his own way, and they may both enjoy the blessing.

9. We see why a few individuals, who are perfectly united may be successful in gathering and building up a new church, and may do so much better than a much larger number who are not agreed among themselves. If I were going to gather a new church in this city, I should rather have five persons, or three, or even two that were perfectly agreed *as touching* the things they were to pray for, and the manner in which they should labor for them, and in all that is essential to the prosperity of a church, and who would stand by me, and stand by each other, than to have a church to begin with, or five hundred members who were not agreed.

10. We see what glorious things may be expected for Zion, whenever the churches generally shall be agreed on these subjects. When ministers shall lay aside their prejudices, and their misconstructions, and their jealousies, and shall see eye to eye, and when the churches shall understand the Bible alike, and see their duty alike, and pray alike, and shall be "agreed *as touching* the things they shall ask for," a nation shall be born in a day. Only let them feel as the heart of one man, and be agreed as to what ought to be done for the salvation of the world, and the millennium will come at once.

11. There is vast ignorance in the churches on the subject of revivals. After all the revivals that have been enjoyed, and all that has been said and written and printed concerning revivals, there are very few who have any real, consistent *knowledge* on the subject. And when there is a revival, how few are there who can take hold to labor and promote it as if they understood what they were about. How few persons are to be found, who have ever taken up revivals of religion as a subject to be studied and understood. Every body knows, that in a revival Christians must pray, and must do some things which they have not been in the habit of doing. But multitudes know nothing of the REASON WHY they should do this, or why one thing is better than another, and of

course they have no principles to guide them, and when any thing occurs which they did not expect, they are all at a fault and know nothing what to do. If men should go to work to build a house of worship, and know as little how to proceed as many ministers and professors know how to build the spiritual temple of God, they never would get up a house in the world. And yet people make themselves believe they are building the church of God, when they know nothing at all what they are about, and are utterly unable to give a reason why they are doing as they do, or why one thing should be done rather than another. There are multitudes in the church who never seem to suppose that the work of promoting revivals of religion is one that requires study, and thought, and knowledge of principles, and skill in applying the word of God, so as to give every one his portion in season. And so they go on, generally doing little or nothing because they are attempting nothing, and if they ever do awake, go headlong to work, without any system or plan, as if God had left this part of our duty out of the reach of sound judgment and good sense.

12. There is vast ignorance among ministers upon this subject, and one great reason of this ignorance is, that many get the idea that they already understand all about revivals, when in reality they know next to nothing about them. I once knew a minister come in where there was a powerful revival, and blustered about and found fault with many things, spoke of his knowledge of revivals, that he had been in seventeen of them and so on, when it was evident that he knew nothing as he ought to know of revivals.

13. How important it is that the church should be trained and instructed, so as to know what to do in a revival. They should be trained and disciplined like an army; each one having a place to fill, and something to do, and knowing where he belongs, and what he has to do, and how to do it. Instead of this, how often do you see a church in a time of revival take hold of the work to promote it, just like a parcel of children taking hold to build a house. How few are there that really know how to do — what? — Why, the very thing for which God suffers Christians to live in this world, the very thing for which ALONE he would ever let them remain away from heaven a day, is the very thing of all others that they do not study and do not try to understand.

14. We see why revivals are often so short, and why they so often produce a reaction. It is because the church do not understand the subject. Revivals are short, because professors have been

stirred up to a spasmodical kind of action. They have gone to work by impulse rather than from deliberate conviction of duty, and have been guided by their feelings rather than by a sound understanding of what they ought to do. The church did not know what to do, what they could do, and what they could not, nor how to husband their strength, nor what the state of things would bear, and perhaps their zeal led them into some indiscretions, and they lost their hold on God, and so the enemy prevailed. The church ought to be so trained as to know what to do, so as never to fail, and never to suffer defeat or re-action, when they attempt to promote a revival. They should understand all the tactics of the devil, and know where to guard against his devices, so that they may know him when they see him, and not mistake him for an angel of light come to give them lessons of wisdom in promoting the revival, and so that they can co-operate wisely with the minister, and with one another, and with the Holy Ghost, in carrying on the work. No person who has been conversant in revivals can overlook the fact, that the ignorance of professors of religion concerning revivals, and their stupid blunders are among the most common things that put revivals down, and bring back a fearful reaction upon the church. Brethren, How long shall this be so? It ought not to be so, it need not be so, shall it always be so?

15. We see that every church is justly responsible for the souls that are among them. If God has given such a promise, and if it is true that where so many as two are agreed, *as touching* the things they ask for, it shall be done, then certainly Christians are responsible, and if sinners are lost, their blood will be found upon the church. If the churches can have what they ask, as soon as they are agreed as touching it, then certainly the damnation of the world will be required at the hands of the church.

16. We see the guilt of ministers, in not informing themselves, and rightly and speedily instructing the churches upon this momentous subject. Why, what is the end of the Christian ministry! What have they to do, but to instruct and marshal the sacramental host, and lead them on to conquest. What! let the church remain in ignorance upon the very subject, and the only point of duty, for the performance of which they are in the world, the salvation of sinners. Some ministers have acted as *mysteriously* about revivals, as if they thought Christians were either incapable of understanding how to promote them, or that is was of no importance

that they should know. But this is all wrong. No minister has yet begun to understand, or do his duty, if he has neglected to teach his church to work for God in the promotion of revivals. What is he about? What does he mean? Why is he a minister? To what end has he taken the sacred office? Is it that he "may eat a piece of bread?"

17. We see that pious parents can render the salvation of their children certain. Only let them pray in faith, and be agreed *as touching* the things they shall ask for, and God has promised them the desire of their hearts. Who can be agreed so well as parents? Let them be agreed in prayer, and agreed what to do, and agreed in doing all their duty, let them thus train up their children in the way they should go, and when they are old, they *will not* depart from it.

And now, brethren, do you believe you are agreed, according to the meaning of this promise? I know that where a few individuals may be agreed in some things, they may produce some effect. But while the body of the church are not agreed, there will always be so many things to counteract, that they will accomplish but little. THE CHURCH MUST BE AGREED. O, if we could find one church that were perfectly and heartily agreed in all these points, so that they could pray and labor together, all as one, what good would be done! But now, while things are as they are, we see colony after colony peopling hell, because the church are not agreed. O, what do Christians think, how can they keep still, when God has brought down his blessings so that if any two were agreed, as touching the things they ask for, it would be done. Alas! alas! how bitter will be the remembrance of these janglings in the church, when Christians come to see the crowds of lost souls that have gone down to hell, because *we* were not agreed to labor and pray for their salvation.

FINALLY. — In the light of this promise we see the awful guilt of the church. God has given it to be the precious inheritance of his people at all times, and in all places. If his people *agree*, their prayers will be answered. We see the *awful guilt of this church*, who come here and listen to lectures about revivals and then go away and *have no revival*, and also the guilt of members of other churches who hear these lectures and go home and *refuse to do their duty*. How can you meet the thousands of impenitent sinners around you, at the bar of God, and see them sink away into everlasting burnings? Have you been united in heart to pray for them? If you have not, why have you disagreed? Why have you not prayed with this promise until you have prevailed?

You will now either be agreed, and pray for the Holy Ghost, and receive him before you leave the house, or the anger of the Lord will be upon you. Should you now agree to pray in the sense of this promise, for the Spirit of God to come down on this city, the heavenly dove would fly through the city in the midst of the night and would rouse the consciences and break up the guilty slumbers of the wicked. What then is the crimson guilt of those professors of religion who are *sleeping in sight of such a promise*! They seem to have skipped over, or to have entirely forgotten it. Multitudes of sinners going to hell in all directions, and yet this blessed promise is neglected; yea, more, is *practically despised by* the church. There it stands in the solemn record, and the church might take hold of it in such a manner that vast numbers might be saved, but they are not agreed. Therefore souls will perish. And where is the responsibility? Who can take this promise and look the perishing in the face at the day of judgment?

XVII

FALSE COMFORTS FOR SINNERS[1]

TEXT. — "How then comfort ye me in vain, seeing in your answers there remaineth falsehood." — JOB xxi. 34.

JOB's three friends insisted on it that the afflictions which he suffered were sent as a punishment for his sins, and were evidence conclusive that he was a hypocrite, and not a good man as he professed to be. A lengthy argument ensued, in which Job referred to all past experience, to prove that men are not dealt with in this world according to their character, that the distinction is not observed in the allotments of Providence. His friends maintained the opposite, and intimated that this world is also a place of rewards and punishments, in which men receive good or evil, according to their deeds. In this chapter, Job shows by appealing to common sense and common observation, and experience, that this cannot be true, because it is a matter of fact that the wicked are often prosperous in the world and through life, and hence infers that their judgment and punishment must be reserved for a future state. "The wicked is *reserved* to the day of destruction," and "they shall be brought forth to the day of his wrath." And inasmuch as his friends came to comfort him, but being in the dark on this fundamental point, had not been able to understand his case, and so could not afford him any comfort, but rather aggravated his grief, Job insisted upon it that he would still look to a future state for consolation, and rebukes them by exclaiming, in the bitterness of his soul, "How then comfort ye me in vain, seeing in your answers there remaineth falsehood?"

My present purpose is, to make some remarks upon the various methods employed in comforting anxious sinners, and I design,

I. To notice briefly the necessity and design of instructing anxious sinners.

[1] This lecture is a direct assault upon the psychology, theology, and stereotyped procedure of Calvinist ministers in regard to the practical work of converting sinners.

II. To show that anxious sinners are always seeking comfort. Their supreme object is to get comfort in their distress.

III. To notice some of the false comforts often administered.

I. The necessity and design of instructing anxious sinners.

The very idea of anxiety implies some instruction. A sinner would not be anxious at all about his future state, unless he had light enough to know that he is a sinner, and that he is in danger of punishment and needs forgiveness. But men are to be converted, not by physical force, or by a change wrought in their nature or constitution by creative power, but by the truth, made effectual by the Holy Spirit. Conversion is yielding to the truth. And therefore, the more truth can be brought to bear on the mind, *other things being equal*, so much the more probable is it that the individual will be converted. Unless the truth is brought to bear upon him, it is certain he *will not* be converted. If it is brought to bear, it is not absolutely certain that it will be effectual, but the probability is in proportion to the extent to which the truth is brought to bear. The great design of dealing with an anxious sinner is to clear up all his difficulties and darkness, and do away all his errors, and sap the foundation of his self-righteous hopes, and sweep away every vestige of comfort that he could find in himself. There is often much difficulty in this, and much instruction is required. Sinners often cling with a death grasp to their false dependences. The last place to which a sinner ever betakes himself for relief is to Jesus Christ. Sinners had rather be saved in any other way in the world. They had rather make any sacrifice, go to any expense, or endure any suffering, than just to throw themselves as guilty and lost rebels upon Christ alone for salvation. This is the very last way in which they are ever willing to be saved. It cuts up all their self-righteousness, and annihilates their pride and self-satisfaction so completely, that they are exceedingly unwilling to adopt it. But it is as true in philosophy as it is in fact, that this is, after all, the only way in which a sinner *could* find relief. If God should attempt to relieve sinners, and save them without humbling their pride and turning them from their sins, he could not do it. Now the object of instructing an anxious sinner should be to lead him by the shortest possible way to do this. It is to bring his mind, by the shortest rout, to the practical conclusion, that there is, in fact, no other way in which he can be relieved and saved, but to renounce himself and rest in Christ alone. To do this with effect, requires great skill. It requires a thorough knowledge of the human heart, a clear understanding of the plan of salvation, and a precise and definite idea of the very thing that a sinner MUST DO in order to be saved. To know how to do this effectually is one of the rarest qualifications in the ministry at the present day. It is distressing to see how few ministers, and how few professors of religion there are who have in their own minds that distinct idea of *the thing to be done*, that they can go to an anxious sinner, and tell him exactly what he has to do, and how to do it, and can show him clearly that there is no possible way for him to be saved, but by doing that very thing which they tell him, and can make him feel the certainty that he *must* do it, and that unless he does that very thing, he will be damned.

II. I am to show that anxious sinners are always seeking comfort.

Sinners often imagine they are seeking *Jesus Christ*, and seeking *religion*, but this is a mistake. No person ever sought religion, and yet remained irreligious. What is religion? It is obeying God. Seeking religion is seeking to obey God. The soul that hungers and thirsts after righteousness is the soul of a Christian. To say that a person can seek to obey God, and yet not obey him, is absurd. For if he is seeking *religion* he is not an impenitent sinner. To seek *religion*, implies a willingness to obey God, and a willingness to obey God is religion. It is a contradiction to say that an impenitent sinner is seeking religion. It is the same as to say, that he seeks and actually longs to obey God, and God will not let him, or that he longs to embrace Jesus Christ, and Christ will not let him come. The fact is, the anxious sinner is seeking a hope, he is seeking pardon, and comfort, and deliverance from hell. He is anxiously looking for some one to comfort him, and make him feel better, without being obliged to conform to such humiliating conditions as those of the gospel. And his anxiety and distress continue, only because he will not yield to the terms. Unfortunately, anxious sinners find comforters enough to their liking. Miserable comforters they all are, too, "seeing in their answers there remaineth falsehood." No doubt, millions and millions are now in hell, because there were those around them who gave them false comfort, who had so much false pity, or were themselves so much in the dark, that they would not let them remain in anxiety till they had submitted their hearts to God, but administered falsehood, and relieved their distress in this way, and now their souls are lost.

III. I am to notice several of the ways in which false comfort is given to anxious sinners.

I might almost say, there is an endless variety of ways in which this is done. The more experience I have, and the more I observe the ways in which even good people deal with anxious sinners, the more I feel grieved at the endless fooleries and falsehoods with which they attempt to comfort their anxious friends, and thus, in fact, deceive them and beguile them out of their salvation. It often reminds me of the manner in which people act when any one is sick. Let any one of you be sick, with almost any disease in the world, and you will find that every person you meet with has a remedy for *that* disorder, a certain cure, a specific, a panacea; and you will find such a world of quackery all around you, that if you do not take care and SHUT IT ALL OUT, you will certainly lose your life. A man must exercise his own judgment, for he will find as many remedies as he has friends, and each one is tenacious of his own medicine, and perhaps will think hard if it is not taken. And no doubt this miserable system of quackery kills a great many people.

This is true to no greater extent respecting the diseases of the body than respecting the diseases of the mind. People have their specifics and their catholicons and their panaceas to comfort distressed souls, and whenever they begin to talk with an anxious sinner, they will bring in their false comforts, so much that if he does not TAKE CARE, and mind the word of God, he will infallibly be deceived to his own destruction. I propose to mention a few of the falsehoods that are often brought forward in attempting to comfort anxious sinners. Time would fail me, even to *name them all*.

The direct object of many persons is to *comfort* sinners, and they are often so intent upon this that they do not stick at means or kind of comfort. They see their friends distressed, and they pity them, they feel very compassionate, "Oh, oh, I cannot bear to see them so distressed, I must comfort them somehow," and so they try one way, and another, and all to *comfort* them! Now, God desires they should be comforted. He is benevolent, and has kind feelings, and his heart yearns over them, when he sees them so distressed. But he sees that there is *only one way* to give a sinner real comfort. He has more benevolence and compassion than all men, and wishes to comfort them. But he has fixed the terms as unyielding as his throne, on which he will give a sinner relief.

And he will not alter. He knows that nothing else will do the sinner effectual good, for nothing can make him happy, until he repents of his sins and forsakes them, and turns to God. And therefore God will not yield. Our object should be the same as that of God. We should feel compassion and benevolence, just as he does, and be as ready to give comfort, but be sure that it be of the right kind. The fact is, our prime object should be, to induce the sinner to *obey God*. His comfort ought to be with us, and with him, but a secondary object, and while we are more anxious to *relieve* his *distress* than to have him cease to abuse, and dishonor God, we are not likely, by our instructions, to do him any real good. This is a fundamental distinction, in dealing with anxious sinners, but it is evidently overlooked by many, who seem to have no higher motives, than sympathy or compassion for the sinner. If in preaching the gospel, or instructing the anxious, we are not actuated by a high regard to the honor of God, and rise no higher, than to desire to relieve the distressed; this is going no farther than a constitutional sympathy, or compassion, would carry us. Overlooking this principle, has often misled professors of religion, and when they have heard others dealing faithfully with anxious sinners, they have accused them of cruelty. I have often had professors bring anxious sinners to me, and beg me to *comfort* them, and, when I have probed their consciences to the quick, they have shuddered, and sometimes taken the sinners' part. It is sometimes impossible to deal effectually with youth who are anxious, in the presence of their parents, because they have so much more compassion for their children, than regard to the honor of God. This is all wrong, and with such views and feelings you had better hold your tongue, than to say any thing to the anxious.

1. One of the ways in which people give false comfort to distressed sinners, is, by asking them "What have you done? you are not so bad." They see them distressed, and cry out, "Why, what have you done?" as if they had never done any thing wicked, and had in reality no occasion to feel distressed at all. I have before mentioned the case of a fashionable lady, who was awakened in this city, and was going to see a minister to converse with him, when she was met by a friend, who turned her back, and drove off her anxiety, by the cry, "What have you done, to make you feel so? I am sure you have never committed any sin, that need to make you feel so."

I have often met with cases of this kind. A mother will tell her son, who is anxious, what an obedient child he has always been, how good and how kind, and she begs him not to take on so. So a husband will tell his wife, or a wife her husband, how good they are, and ask, "What have you done?" When they see them in great distress, they begin to comfort them, "Why you are not so bad. You have been to hear that frightful minister, that frightens people, and you have got excited. Be comforted, for I am sure you have not been bad enough to feel so much distressed." When the truth is, they have been a great deal worse than they think they have. No sinner ever had an idea that his sins were greater than they are. No sinner ever had an adequate idea of how great a sinner he is. It is not probable that any man could live under the full sight of his sins. God has, in mercy, spared all his creatures on earth that worst of sights, a naked human heart. The sinner's guilt is much more deep and damning than he thinks, and his danger is *much greater* than he thinks it is, and if he should see them as they are, probably he would not live a moment. A sinner may have some false notions on the subject, that creates distress, which have no foundation. He may think he has committed the unpardonable sin, or that he has grieved away the Spirit, or sinned away his day of grace. But to tell the most moral and naturally amiable person in the world that he is good enough, or that he is not *so bad* as he thinks he is, is not giving him rational comfort, but is deceiving him, and ruining his soul. Let those who do it, take care.

2. Others tell awakened sinners that "Conversion is a progressive work," and in this way ease their anxiety. When a man is distressed, because he sees himself to be such a sinner, and that unless he turns to God, he will be damned; it is a great relief to have some friend hold out the idea that he can get better by degrees, and that he is *now* coming on, by little and little. They tell him, "Why you cannot expect to get along all at once; I don't believe in these *sudden* conversions, you must wait and let it work, you have begun well, and by and by you will get comfort." All this is false as the bottomless pit. The truth is, Regeneration, or conversion, is *not* a progressive work. What is regeneration? What is it but the *beginning* of obedience to God? And is the beginning of a thing progressive? It is the first act of genuine obedience to God — the first voluntary action of the mind that is what God approves, or that can be regarded as obedience to

God. That is conversion. When persons talk about conversion as a progressive work, it is absurd. They show that *they know* just as much about regeneration or conversion, as Nicodemus did. They know nothing about it, as they ought to know, and are no more fit to conduct an anxious meeting, or to advise or instruct anxious sinners, than Nicodemus was.

3. Another way in which anxious sinners are deceived with false comfort, is by *being advised to dismiss the subject for the present.*

Men who are supposed to be wise and good, have assumed to be so much wiser than God, that when God is dealing with a sinner, by his Spirit, and endeavoring to bring him to an *immediate* decision; they think God is crowding too hard, and that it is necessary for them to interfere; and they will advise the person to take a ride, or go into company, or engage in business, or something that will relieve his mind a little, at least for the present. They might just as well say to God, in plain words, "O God, you are too hard, you go too fast, you will make him crazy, or kill him, he can't stand it, poor creature, if he is so pressed, he will die." Just so they takes sides against God, and do the same as to tell the sinner himself, "God will make you crazy if you do not dismiss the subject, and resist the Spirit, and drive him away from your mind."

Such advice, if it be truly conviction of sin that distresses the sinner, is in no case, either safe or lawful. The strivings of the Spirit, to bring a sinner to himself, will never hurt him, nor drive him crazy. He may make himself deranged by resisting, but it is blasphemous, to think, that the blessed, wise and benevolent Spirit of God, would ever conduct with so little care, as to derange and destroy the soul he came to sanctify and save. The proper course to take with a sinner, when the striving of the Spirit throws him into distress, is, to *instruct* him, to clear up his views, correct his mistakes, and make the way of salvation so plain that he can see it right before him. Not to dismiss the subject, but to fall in with the Spirit, and thus hush all those dreadful agonies which are produced by resisting the Holy Ghost. REMEMBER, if an awakened sinner voluntarily dismiss the subject once, probably he will never take it up again.

4. Sometimes an awakened sinner is comforted by being told that *religion does not consist in feeling bad.* I once heard of a Doctor of Divinity, giving an anxious sinner such counsel, when

he was actually writhing under the arrows of the Almighty. Said he, "Religion is cheerful, religion is not gloomy, don't be distressed, be comforted, dismiss your fears, you should not feel so bad," and such like miserable comforts, when, in fact, the man had infinite reason to be distressed, for he was resisting the Holy Ghost, and in danger of grieving him away for ever.

It is true, religion does not consist in feeling bad. But the sinner has reason to be distressed, because *he has no* religion. If he had religion, he would not feel so. Were he a Christian, he would rejoice. But to tell an impenitent sinner to be cheerful! why, you might as well preach this doctrine in hell, and tell them there, "Cheer up here, cheer up, don't feel so bad."

The sinner is on the very verge of hell, he is in rebellion against God, and his danger is infinitely greater than he imagines. O, what a doctrine of devils! to tell a rebel against heaven not to be distressed. What is all his distress but rebellion itself? He is not comforted, because he refuses to be comforted. God is ready to comfort him. You need not think to be more compassionate than God. He will fill him with comfort, in an instant, if he will submit. But there he stands, struggling against God, and against the Holy Ghost, and against conscience, until he is distressed almost to death, and still he will not yield; and now some one comes in, "Oh, I hate to see you feel so bad, don't be so distressed, cheer up, cheer up, religion don't consist in being gloomy, be comforted." Horrid!

5. Whatever involves the subject of religion in mystery, is calculated to give a sinner false comfort.

When a sinner is anxious on the subject of religion, very often, if you becloud it in mystery, he will feel relieved. The sinner's distress arises from the pressure of present obligation. Enlighten him on this point, and clear it up, and if he will not yield, it will only increase his distress. But tell him that regeneration is all a mystery, something he cannot understand; and leave him all in a fog of darkness, and you relieve his anxiety. It is his clear view of the nature and duty of repentance, that produces his distress. It is the light that brings agony to his mind, while he refuses to obey. It is that, which will make up the pains of hell. And it will almost make hell in the sinner's breast here, if only made clear enough. But only cover up this light, and his anxiety will immediately become far less acute and thrilling. But if you lift up a certain and clear light, and flash it broad upon his soul, and if he will not yield, you kindle up to the tortures of hell in his bosom.

6. Whatever *relieves the sinner from a sense of blame*, is calculated to give him false comfort.

The more a man feels himself to blame, the deeper is his distress. But any thing that lessons his sense of blame, of course lessons his distress, but it is a comfort full of death. If any thing will help him divide the blame, and throw off a part of it upon God, it will afford comfort, but it is a relief that will destroy his soul.

7. To *tell him of his inability*, is false comfort. Tell an anxious sinner "What can you do? you are a poor feeble creature, you can do nothing." You will make him feel a kind of despondency. But it is not that keen agony of remorse, with which God wrings the soul, when he is laboring to cut him down and bring him to repentance.

If you tell him he is unable to comply with the gospel, he naturally falls in with it as a relief. He says to himself, "Yes, I *am* unable, I am a poor feeble creature, I cannot do this, and certainly God cannot send me to hell for not doing what I cannot do." Why, if I believed that the sinner was *unable*, I would tell him plainly, "Don't be afraid, you are not to blame for not complying with the call of the gospel: for you are unable, and God will never send you to hell for not doing what you have no strength to do. "Will not the Judge of all the earth do right?" I know it is not common for those who talk about the sinner's being unable, to be so consistent, and carry out their theory. But the sinner *infers* all this, and so he feels relieved. It is all false, and all the comfort derived from it, is only treasuring up wrath against the day of wrath.

8. Whatever makes the impression on a sinner's mind that he is to be *passive in religion*, is calculated to give him false comfort.

Give him the idea he has nothing to do but to wait God's time; tell him conversion is the work of God, and he ought to leave it to him; and that he must be careful, not to try to take the work out of God's hand; and he will *infer*, as before, that he is not to blame, and will feel relieved. If he is only to hold still, and let God do the work, just as a man holds still to have his arm amputated, he feels relieved. But such instruction as this, is all wrong. If the sinner is thus to hold still and let God do it, he instantly infers that *he* is not to blame for not doing it himself. And the inference is not only natural but legitimate, for he is not to blame.

It is true that there is a sense in which conversion is the work of God. But it is false, as it is often represented. It is also true that there is a sense, in which conversion is the sinner's own act. It is ridiculous, therefore, to say, that a sinner is passive in regeneration, or passive in being converted, for conversion is his own act. The thing to be done is that which cannot be done for him. It is something which *he must do*, or it will never be done.

9. Telling a sinner to *wait God's time*.

Some years ago, I met a woman in Philadelphia, who was anxious about her soul, and had been a long time in that state. I conversed with her, and endeavored to learn her state. She told me a good many things, and finally said she knew she ought to be willing to wait on God as long as he had waited upon her. She said, God had waited on her a great many years, before she would give any attention to his calls, and now she believed it was her duty to wait God's time to show mercy and convert her soul. And she said, this was the instruction she had received. She must be patient, and wait God's time, and by and by he would give her relief. O amazing folly!

Here is the sinner in rebellion. God comes with pardon in one hand, and a sword in the other, and tells the sinner to repent and receive pardon, or refuse and perish. And now here comes a minister of the gospel, and tells the sinner to "wait God's time." Virtually he says, that God is not ready to have him repent *now*, and is not ready to pardon him *now*, and thus, in fact, throws off the blame of his impenitence upon God. Instead of pointing out the *sinner's* guilt, in not submitting at once to God, he points out *God's* insincerity in making the offer, when, in fact, he was not ready to grant the blessing.

I have often thought such teachers needed the rebuke of Elijah when he met the priests of Baal. "Cry aloud, for he is a God; either he is talking, or he is pursuing, or he is in a journey; or peradventure he sleepeth, and must be awaked." The minister who ventures to intimate that God is not ready, and that tells the sinner to wait God's time, might almost as well tell him, that now God is asleep, or gone on a journey, and cannot attend to him at present. Miserable comforters indeed! It it little less than outrageous blasphemy of God. How many have gone to the judgment, red all over with the blood of souls, that they have deceived and destroyed, by telling them God was not ready to save them, and they must wait God's time. No doubt, such a doctrine is exceedingly calculated to afford present relief to an anxious sinner. It warrants him to say, "O, yes, God is not ready, I must wait God's time, and so I can live in sin, and take it out a while longer, till he gets ready to attend to me, and then I will get religion."

10. It is false comfort to tell an anxious sinner to do any thing for relief, *which he can do, and not submit his heart to God.*

An anxious sinner is often willing to do any thing else, but the very thing which God requires him to do. He is willing to go to the ends of the earth, or to pay his money, or to endure suffering, or any thing, but full and instantaneous submission to God. Now, if you will compromise the matter with him, and tell him of something else that he may do, and yet evade *that point*, he will be very much comforted. He likes that instruction. He says, "O, yes, I will do that, I like that minister, he is not so severe as others, he seems to understand my particular case, and knows how to make allowances."

It often reminds me of the conduct of a patient, who is very sick, but has a great dislike for a certain physician and a particular medicine, but that is the very physician, who, alone understands treating his disease, and that the only remedy for it. Now the patient is willing to do any thing else, and call in any other physician; and he is anxious and in distress, and is asking all his friends if they can't tell him what he shall do, and he will take all the nostrums and quack medicines in the country, before he will submit to *the only course* that can bring him relief. By and by, after he has tried every thing without any benefit, if he does not die in the experiment, he gives up his unreasonable opposition, calls in the physician, takes the proper medicine, and is cured. Just so it is with sinners. They will eagerly do any thing, if you will let them off from this intolerable pressure of present obligation to submit to God. I will mention a few of the things which sinners are told to do.

(1.) Telling a sinner he must *use the means*. Tell an anxious sinner this — You must use the means, and he is relieved. "O, yes, I will do that, if that is all. I thought that God required me to repent and submit to him now. But if using the means will answer, I will do that with all my heart." He was distressed before, because he was cornered up, and did not know which way to turn. Conscience had beset him, like a wall of fire, and urged him to repent *now*. But this relieves him at once, and he feels better, and is very thankful, he says, that he found such a good adviser in his distress. But he may use the means, as he calls it, till the day of judgment, and not be a particle the better for it, but will only hasten his way to death. What is the sinner's use of means, but rebellion against God? God uses means. The church uses means, to convert and save sinners, to bear down upon them, and bring them to submission. But what has the sinner to do with using means? Will you set him to use means back upon God, and so make an offset in the matter? Or is he to use means to make himself submit to God? How shall he go to work with his means to make himself submit? It is just telling the sinner, "You need not submit to God now, but just use the means awhile, and see if you cannot melt God's heart down to you, so that he will yield this point of unconditional submission." It is a mere cavil, to evade the duty of immediate submission to God. It is true, that sinners, actuated by a regard to their own happiness, often give attention to the subject of religion, attend meetings, and pray, and read, and many such things. But in all this, they have no regard to the honor of God, nor do they so much as *mean* to obey him. Their design, is not obedience, for if it were, they would not be impenitent sinners. They are not, therefore, using means to *be christians*, but to obtain pardon, and a hope. It is absurd to say, that an impenitent sinner is using means to repent, for this is the same as to say, that he is willing to repent, or in other words, that he does repent, and is not an impenitent sinner. So, to say that an unconverted sinner uses means with design to become a christian, is a contradiction, for it is saying, that he is willing to be a christian, which is the same as to say, that he is a christian already.

(2.) Telling the sinner to *pray for a new heart*. I once heard a celebrated Sunday-school teacher do this. He was almost the father of Sunday-schools in this country. He called a little girl up to him, and began to talk to her. "My little daughter, are you a Christian?" No, Sir. "Well, you cannot be a Christian, yourself, can you?" No, Sir. "No, you cannot be a Christian, you cannot change your heart yourself, but you must pray for a new heart, that is all you can do, pray to God, God will give you a new heart." He was an aged and venerable man, but I felt almost disposed to rebuke him openly in the name of the Lord, I could not bear to hear him deceive that child, telling her she could not be a Christian. Does God say "Pray for a new heart?" Never. He says, "Make you a new heart." And the sinner is not to be told to pray to God to do his duty, for him, but to go and do it himself. I know the Psalmist, *a good man*, prayed. "Create in me a clean heart, and renew a right spirit within me." He had *faith* and prayed in faith. But that is a very different thing from setting an obstinate rebel to pray for a new heart. No doubt, an anxious sinner will be delighted with such instruction. "Why, I knew I needed a new heart, and that I ought to repent, but I thought I must do it myself, I am very willing to ask God to do it, I hated to do it myself, but have no objection that God should do it, if he will, and I will pray for it, if that is all that is required."

(3.) Telling the sinner *to persevere*. And suppose he does persevere. He is as certain to be damned as if he had been in hell ever since the foundation of the world. His anxiety arises only from his resistance, and if he would submit, it would cease. And now, will you tell him to persevere in the very thing that causes his distress? Suppose my child should, in a fit of passion, throw a book or something on the floor. I tell him "Take it up," and instead of minding what I say, he runs off and plays. "Take it up!" He sees I am in earnest, and begins to look serious. "Take it up, or I shall get a rod." And I put up my arm to get the rod. He stands still. "Take it up, or you must be whipped." He comes slowly along to the place, and then begins to weep. "Take it up my child, or you will certainly be punished." Now he is in distress, and sobs and sighs as if his bosom would burst, but still remains as stubborn as if he knew I could not punish him. Now I begin to press him with motives to submit and obey, but there he stands, in agony, and at length bursts out, "O, father I do not feel so bad, I think I am growing better." And now, suppose a neighbor to come in and see the child standing there, in all this agony of stubbornness. The neighbor asks him what he is standing there for, and what he is doing. "O, I am using means to pick up that book." If this neighbor should tell the child, "Persevere, persevere, my boy, you will get it by and by," What should I do? Why I would turn him out of the house. What does he mean, by encouraging my child in his rebellion.

Now, God calls the sinner to repent, he threatens him, he draws the glittering sword, he persuades him, he uses motives, and the sinner is distressed to agony, for he sees himself driven to the dreadful alternative of giving up his sins or going to hell. He ought instantly to lay down his weapons, and break his heart at once. But he resists, and struggles against conviction, and that creates his distress. Now will you tell him to persevere? Persevere in what? In struggling against God! That is just the direction the devil would give. All the devil wants is to see him persevere in just the way he is going on, and his destruction is sure. Satan may go to sleep.

(4.) Telling the sinner to *press forward*. That is, "You are in a good way, only press forward, and you will get to heaven." This is on the supposition that his face is towards heaven, when in fact his face is towards hell, and he is pressing forward, and never more rapidly than now, while he is resisting the Holy Ghost. Often have I heard this direction given, when the sinner was in as bad a way as he could be. What you ought to tell him is, "STOP — sinner, stop, do not take another step that way, it leads to hell." God tells him to stop, and because he does not wish to stop, he is distressed. Now, why should you attempt to comfort him in this way?

(5.) Tell a sinner that he must *try to repent, and give his heart to God*. "O, yes," says the sinner, "I am willing to try. I have often tried to do it, and I will try again." Ah, does God tell you to try to repent? All the world would be willing to try to repent, in their way. Giving this direction implies that it is very difficult to repent, and perhaps impossible, and that the best thing a sinner can do, is to *try*, and see whether he can do it or not. What is this, but substituting your own commandment in the place of God's. God requires nothing short of repentance and a holy heart. Any thing short of that, is comforting him in vain, "seeing in your answers there remaineth falsehood."

(6.) To tell him to *pray for repentance*. "O yes I will pray for repentance, if that is all. I was distressed because I thought God required *me* to repent, but if *he* will do it, I can wait." And so he feels relieved, and is quite comfortable.

(7.) To tell a sinner to *pray for conviction*, or *pray for the Holy Ghost* to show him his sins, or to *labor to get more light* on the subject of his guilt, in order to increase his conviction.

All this is just what the sinner wants, because it lets him off from the pressure of *present* obligation. He wants just a little more *time*. Any thing that will defer that *present pressure* of obligation to repent immediately, is a relief. What does he want more conviction for? Does God give any such direction to an impenitent sinner? God takes it for granted that he has conviction enough already. And so he has. Do you say, he cannot realize all his sins? If he can realize *only one* of them, let him repent of that one, and he is a Christian. Suppose he could see them all, what reason is there to think he would repent of them all, any more than that he would repent of that one that he does see? All this is comforting the sinner by setting him to do that which he can do, and still not submit his heart to God.

11. Another way in which false comfort is given to anxious sinners, is to tell them *God is trying their faith by keeping them in the furnace*, and they must wait patiently upon the Lord. Just as if God was in fault, or stood in the way, of his being a Christian. Or as if an impenitent sinner had faith! What an abomination! Suppose somebody should tell my child, while he was standing by the book, as I have described, "Wait patiently, boy, your father is trying your faith." No. The sinner is trying the patience and forbearance of God. God is not setting himself to torture a sinner, and teach him a lesson of patience. But he is waiting upon him, and laboring to bring him *at once* into such a state of mind as will render it consistent to fill his soul with the peace of heaven. And shall the sinner be encouraged to resist by the idea that God is bantering? TAKE CARE. God has said his Spirit shall not always strive.

12. Another false comfort is telling a sinner, *Do your duty, and leave your conversion with God*.

I once heard an elder of a church say to an anxious sinner, "Do your duty, and leave your conversion to God, he will do it in his own time and way." That was just the same as telling him, that it was not his duty to be converted *now*. He did not say, Do your duty, and leave your *salvation* with God. That would have been proper enough, for it would have been simply telling him to submit to God, and would have included conversion as the first duty of all. But he told him to leave his *conversion* to God. And this elder, that gave such advice, was a man of liberal education too. How absurd! Just as if he could do his duty and not be converted. Just as if God was going to convert a sinner and let the sinner sit calmly under it in the use of means. Horrible! No. God has required him to make him a new heart, and do you beware how you comfort him with an answer of falsehood.

13. Sometimes professors of religion will try to comfort a sinner, by telling him, "*Do not be discouraged; I was a long time in this way* before I found comfort." They will tell him "I was under conviction so many weeks — or perhaps so many months, or sometimes years, and have gone through with all this, and know just how you feel, your experience is the same with mine, precisely, and after so long a time I found relief, and I don't doubt you will find

it, by and by. Don't despair, God will comfort you soon." Tell a sinner to take courage in his rebellion! O, horrible. Such professors ought to be ashamed. Suppose you were under conviction so many weeks, and afterwards found relief, it is the very last thing you ought to tell to an anxious sinner. What is it but encouraging him to hold on, when his business is to submit. Did you hold out so many weeks while the Spirit was striving with you. You only deserved so much the more to be damned, for your obstinacy and stupidity.

Sinner! it is no sign God will spare *you* so long, or that his Spirit will remain with you to be resisted. And remember, if the Spirit is taken away, you will be sent to hell.

14. "I have faith to believe you will be converted."

You have faith to believe! On what does your faith rest? On the promise of God? On the influences of the Holy Ghost? Then you are counteracting your own faith. The very design and object of the Spirit of God, is, to tear away from the sinner, his last vestige of a hope, while remaining in sin; to annihilate every crag and twig he may cling to. And the object of your instruction should be the same. You should fall in with the plan of God. It is only in this way, that you can ever do any good, by crowding him right up to the work, to submit at once and leave his soul in the hands of God. But when one that he thinks is a Christian, tells him, "I have faith to believe you will be converted," it upholds him in his false expectation. Instead of tearing him away from his false hopes, and throwing him upon Christ, you just turn him off to hang upon your faith, and find comfort because you have faith for him. This is all false comfort, that worketh death.

15. "I will pray for you." Sometimes professors of religion try to comfort an anxious sinner in this way, by telling him, "I will pray for you." This is false comfort, for it leads the sinner to trust in those prayers, instead of trusting in Christ. The sinner says, "He is a good man, and God hears the prayers of good men, no doubt his prayers will prevail some time, and I shall be converted, I don't think I shall be lost." And his anxiety, his agony, is all gone. A woman said to a minister, "I have no hope now, but I have faith in your prayers." Just such faith, this is, as the devil wants them to have — faith in prayers instead of faith in Christ.

16. "I rejoice to see you in this way, and I hope you will be faithful, and hold out." What is that but rejoicing to see him in rebellion against God? For that is precisely the ground on which

FALSE COMFORTS FOR SINNERS 349

he stands. He is resisting conviction, and resisting conscience, and resisting the Holy Ghost, and yet you rejoice to see him in this way, and hope he will be faithful and hold out. There is a sense, indeed, in which it may be said that his situation is more hopeful than when he was in stupidity. For God has convinced him, and may succeed in turning and subduing him. But that is not the sense in which the sinner himself will understand it. He will suppose that you think him in a hopeful way, because he is doing better than formerly. When his guilt and danger are, in fact, greater than they ever were before. And instead of rejoicing, you ought to be distressed and in agony, to see him thus resisting the Holy Ghost, for every moment he does this, he is in danger of being left of God, and given up to hardness of heart and to despair.

17. "You will have your pay for this, by and by, God will reward you." Yes, sinner, God *will* reward you, if you continue in this way, he will put you in the fires of hell. Reward for all this distress! Yes, if you are ever rewarded for it, it will be in hell. I once heard a sinner say, "I feel very bad, I have strong hopes that I shall get my reward." But that individual afterwards said, "Nowhere can there be found so black a sinner as I am, and no sin of my life seems so black, and damning as that expression." He was overwhelmed with contrition, that he should ever have had such an idea, as to think God would reward him for suffering so much distress, when he brought it all upon himself, needlessly, by his wicked resistance to the truth. The truth is, what such people want, is to *comfort* the sinner, and being all in the dark themselves on the subject of religion, they of course give him false comfort.

18. Another false comfort, is to tell the sinner *he has not repented enough*. The truth is, he has not repented at all. God always comforts the sinner as soon as he repents. This direction implies that his feelings are right as far as they go. To imply that he has any repentance, is to tell him a lie, and cheat him out of his soul.

19. People sometimes comfort a sinner by telling him "If you are elected, you will be brought in." I once heard of a case where a person under great distress of mind, was sent to converse with a neighboring minister. They conversed a long time. As the person went away, the minister said to him, "I should like to write a line by you, to your father." His father was a pious man. The minister wrote the letter, and forgot to seal it. As the sinner was going home, he saw that the letter was not sealed, and he thought to himself, that probably the minister had written about him, and his curiosity

at length led him to open and read it. And there he found it written to this purport: "Dear Sir, I find your son under conviction, and in great distress, and it seems not easy to say any thing to give him relief. But, if he is one of the elect, he will surely be brought in." He wanted to say something to comfort the father. But now, mark. That letter had well-nigh ruined his soul. He settled down on the doctrine of election; "If I am elected, I shall be brought in," and his conviction was all gone. Years afterwards he was awakened and converted, but only after a great struggle, and never until that false impression was obliterated from his mind, and he was made to see that he had nothing at all to do with the doctrine of election, but if he did not repent, he would be damned.

20. It is very common for some people to tell an awakened sinner, "You are in a very prosperous way, I am glad to see you so, and feel encouraged about you." It sometimes seems, as if the church was in league with the devil, to help sinners resist the Holy Ghost. The thing that the Holy Ghost wants to make the sinner feel, is, that all his ways are wrong, and that they lead to hell. And every body is conspiring to make the opposite impression. The Spirit is trying to discourage him, and they are trying to encourage him; the Spirit to distress, by showing him he is all wrong, and they to comfort him by saying he is doing well. Has it come to this, that the worst counteraction to the truth, and the greatest obstacle to the Spirit, shall spring from the church? Sinner! Do not believe any such thing. You are not in a hopeful way. You are not doing well, but ill; as ill as you can, while resisting the Holy Ghost.

21. Another very fatal way, in which false comfort is given to sinners, is by applying to them *certain scripture promises*, which were designed only for saints. This is a grand device of the devil. It is much practised by the Universalists. But Christians often do it. For example:

(1.) "Blessed are they that mourn, for they shall be comforted." How often has this passage been applied to anxious sinners, who were in distress because they would not submit to God; blessed are ye that mourn. Indeed! That is true, where they mourn with godly sorrow. But what is this sinner mourning about? He is mourning because God's law is holy and his terms of salvation so fixed that he cannot bring them down to his mind. Tell such a rebel — Blessed are they that mourn! You might just as well apply it to those that are in hell. There is mourning there too. The sinner is mourning because there is no other way of salvation, because God is so holy that he requires him to give up all his sins, and he feels, that the time has come, that he *must* either give them up, or be damned. Shall we tell him, he shall be comforted? Go and tell the devil, "Poor devil, you mourn now, but the Bible says you are blessed if you mourn, and you shall be comforted by and by."

(2.) "They that seek shall find." This is said to sinners in such a way, as to imply that the anxious sinner is seeking religion. This promise was made in reference to Christians, who ask in faith, and seek to do the will of God, and is not applicable to those who are seeking hope or comfort; but to holy seeking . To apply it to an impenitent sinner, is only to deceive him, for his seeking is not of this character. To tell him "You are seeking, are you? Well, seek, and you shall find," is to cherish a fatal delusion. While he remains impenitent, he has not a desire, which the devil might not have, and remain a devil still.

If he had desire to do his duty, if he was seeking to do the will of God, and give up his sins, he would be a Christian. But to comfort an impenitent sinner, with such a promise, you might just as well comfort Satan.

(3.) "Be not weary in well doing, for in due time you shall reap if you faint not." To apply this to a sinner for comfort, is absurd. Just as if he was doing something to please God. He has never done well, and never has done more ill, than now. Suppose my neighbor, who came in while I was trying to subdue my child, should say to the child, "In due time you shall reap, if you faint not," what should I say? "Reap, yes, you shall reap, if you do not give up your obstinacy, you shall reap indeed, for I will apply the rod." So the struggling sinner shall reap the damnation of hell, if he does not give up his sins.

22. Some professors of religion, when they attempt to converse with awakened sinners, are very fond of saying, "I will tell you my experience." This is a dangerous snare, and often gives the devil a handle to lead him to hell, by trying to copy your experience. If you tell it to him, and he thinks it is a Christian experience, he will almost infallibly be trying to imitate it, and instead of following the gospel, or the leadings of the Spirit in his own soul, he is following your example. This is absurd as well as dangerous. He never will have just such feelings as you had. No two persons were ever exercised just alike. Men's experiences are as much unlike as their countenances. Such a course is very likely to mislead him.

The design, is often, nothing, but to encourage him, at the very point where he ought not to be encouraged, *before* he has submitted to God. And it is calculated to impede the work of God in his soul.

23. How many times will people tell an awakened sinner that *God has begun* a good work in him, and he will carry it on. I have known parents talk so with their children, and as soon as they saw their children awakened, give up all former anxiety about them, and settle down at their ease, thinking that now God had begun a good work in their children, he would carry it on. It would be just as rational for a farmer to say so about his grain, and as soon as it comes up out of the ground, say, "Well, God has begun a good work in my field, and he will carry it on." What would be thought of a farmer who should neglect to put up his fence, because God had begun the work of giving him a crop of grain? If you tell a sinner so, and he believes you, it will certainly be his destruction, for it will prevent his doing that which is absolutely indispensable to his being saved. If, as soon as the sinner is awakened, he is taught that now God has begun a good work, that only needs to be carried on, and that God will surely carry it on, he sees that he has no further occasion to be anxious, for, in fact, he has nothing more to do. And so he will be relieved from that intolerable pressure of present obligation, to repent and submit to God. And if he is relieved from his sense of obligation to do it, he will never do it.

24. Some will tell the sinner, "Well, you have broken off your sins, have you?" "O, yes," says the sinner. When it is all false, he has never forsaken his sins for a moment, he has only exchanged one form of sin for another; only placed himself in a new attitude of resistance. And to tell him, he has broken them off, is to give him false comfort.

25. Sometimes this direction is given for the purpose of relieving the agony of an anxious sinner, "Do what you can, and God will do the rest," or "Do what you can, and God will help you." This is the same as telling a sinner, "You can't do what *God requires* you to do, but if you will do what you can, God will help you, as to the rest." Now sinners often get the idea that they *have done* all they can, when, in fact, they have done nothing at all, only resisted God with all their might. I have often heard them say, "I have done all I can, and I get no relief, what can I do more?" Now, you can see how comforting it must be to such a one to have a professor of religion come in and say, "If you will do what you can,

FALSE COMFORTS FOR SINNERS 353

God will help you." It relieves all his keen distress at once. He may be uneasy, and unhappy, but his agony is gone.

26. Again they say, "You should be thankful for what you have, and hope for more." If the sinner is convicted, they tell him he should be thankful for conviction, and hope for conversion. If he has any feeling, he should be thankful for what feeling he has, just as if his feeling was religious feeling, when he has no more religion, than Satan. He *has* reason to be thankful, indeed; thankful that he is out of hell, and thankful that God is yet waiting on him. But it is ridiculous to tell him he should be thankful in regard to the state of his mind, when he is all the while resisting his Maker with all his might.

ERRORS IN PRAYING FOR SINNERS.

I will here mention a few errors in praying for sinners in their presence, by which an unhappy impression is made on their minds, in consequence of which, they often obtain false comfort in their distress.

1. People sometimes pray for sinners, as if they deserved TO BE PITIED more than BLAMED. They pray for them as MOURNERS, "Lord help these pensive mourners," as if they were just mourning, like one that had lost a friend, or met some other calamity, and they could not help it, and were very sorry for it, but death would come, and so they were greatly to be pitied, as they were sitting there, sad, pensive, and sighing. The Bible never talks so. It pities sinners, but it pities them as mad and guilty rebels, guilty, and deserving to go to hell, not as poor pensive mourners, that can't help it, that want to be relieved, but can do nothing but sit and mourn.

2. Praying for them as *poor sinners*. Does the Bible ever use any such language as this? The Bible never speaks of them as "poor sinners," as if they deserved to be pitied more than blamed. Christ pities sinners in his heart. And so does God pity them. He feels in his heart, all the gushings of compassion for them, when he sees them going on, obstinate and wilful in gratifying their own lusts, at the peril of his eternal wrath. But he never lets an expression escape from him, as if the sinner was just a "poor creature" to be pitied, as if he could not help it. The idea that he is poor, rather than wicked, unfortunate, rather than guilty, relieves the sinner greatly. I have seen the sinner writhe with agony under the truth,

in a meeting, until somebody begun to pray for him as a *poor* creature. And then he would gush out into tears, and weep profusely, and think he was greatly benefited by such a prayer. "O, what a *good* prayer that was." If you go now and converse with that sinner, you will find he is pitying himself as a poor unfortunate creature, perhaps weeping over his unhappy condition, but his CONVICTIONS OF SIN, his deep impressions of AWFUL GUILT, are all gone.

3. Praying that God would *help the sinner to repent.* "O Lord, *enable* this poor sinner to repent *now.*" This conveys the idea to the sinner's mind, that he is now trying with all his might to repent, and that he cannot do it, and therefore Christians are calling on God to help him, and enable him to do it. Most professors of religion pray for sinners, not that God would make them WILLING to repent, but that he would ENABLE them, or make them able. No wonder their prayers are not heard. They relieve the sinner of his sense of responsibility, and that relieves his distress. But it is an insult to God, as if God had commanded a sinner to do what he could not do.

4. People sometimes pray, "Lord, these sinners are *seeking thee, sorrowing.*" This language is an allusion to what took place at the time when Jesus was a little boy, and went into the temple to talk with the rabbies and doctors. His parents, you recollect, went a day's journey towards home, before they missed him, and then they turned back, and after looking all around, they found the little Jesus standing in the temple and disputing with the learned men, and his mother said to him, "Son, why hast thou thus dealt with us? behold, thy father and I *have sought thee sorrowing.*" And so this prayer represents sinners as seeking Jesus, and he hides himself from them, and they look all around, and hunt, and try to find him, and wonder where Jesus is, and say, "Lord, we have sought Jesus these three days, sorrowing." It is a LIE. No sinner ever sought Jesus with all his heart three days, or three minutes, and could not find him. There Jesus stands at his door and knocks, there he is right before him pleading with him, and facing him down with all his false pretences. Seeking him! The sinner may whine and cry, "O, how I am sorrowing, and seeking Jesus." It is no such thing; Jesus is seeking you. And yet how many oppressed consciences are relieved and comforted by hearing one of these prayers.

5. "Lord, have mercy on these sinners, who are *seeking thy love to know.*" This is a favorite expression with many, as if sinners

were seeking to know the love of Christ, and could not. No such thing. They are not seeking the love of Christ, but seeking to get to heaven without Jesus Christ. Just as if they were seeking it, and he was so hard-hearted that he would not let them have it.

6. "Lord, have mercy on these *penitent souls*;" calling anxious sinners penitent souls. If they are penitent, they are Christians. To make an impression on an unconverted sinner that he is penitent, is to make him believe a lie. But it is very comforting to the sinner, and he likes to take it up, and pray it over again, "O Lord, I am a poor penitent soul, I am very penitent, I am so distressed, Lord have mercy on a poor penitent." Dreadful delusion!

7. Sometimes people pray for anxious sinners as *humble souls*. "O Lord, these sinners have humbled themselves." Why, that is not true, they have not humbled themselves; if they had, the Lord would have raised them up and comforted them, as he has promised. There is a hymn of this character, that has done great mischief. It begins,

> Come HUMBLE sinner in whose breast
> A thousand thoughts revolve.[2]

This hymn was once given by a minister to an awakened sinner, as one applicable to his case. He began to read, "Come humble sinner." He stopped, "Humble sinner, that is not applicable to me, I am not a *humble* sinner." Ah, how well was it for him that the Holy Ghost had taught him better than the hymn. If the hymn had said, Come *anxious* sinner, or *guilty* sinner, or *trembling* sinner, it would have been well enough, but to call him a *humble* sinner would not do. There are a vast many hymns of the same character. It is very common to find sinners quoting the false sentiments of some hymn, to excuse themselves in rebellion against God.

A minister told me he heard a prayer, quite lately, in these words, "O Lord, these sinners have humbled themselves, and come to thee as well as they know how. If they knew any better, they would do better, but O Lord, as they have come to thee, in the best manner they can, we pray thee accept them and shew mercy." Horrible!

8. Many pray, "Father, forgive them, they know not what they do." This is the prayer which Christ made for his murderers.

---

[2] This hymn was written by the English Baptist, Edmund Jones. It first appeared in Jones's book *Sacred Poems* (1760). Finney doubtless became acquainted with it through Nettleton's *Village Hymns*, of which it was number 77 in the edition of 1824.

And, in that case, it was true, they did not know what they were doing, for they did not believe that Jesus Christ was the Messiah. But it cannot be said of sinners under the gospel, they do not know what they are doing. They *do know* what they are doing. They do not see the full extent of it, but they do know that they are sinning against God, and rejecting Christ, and the difficulty is, that they are unwilling to submit to God. But such a prayer is calculated to make him feel relieved, and make him say, "Lord, how can you blame me so, I am a poor ignorant creature, I *don't know* how to do what is required of me. If I knew how, I would do it."

9. Another expression is, "Lord, direct these sinners, who are inquiring the way to Zion, with their faces thitherward." But this language is only applicable to Christians. Sinners have not their faces toward Zion, their faces are set toward hell. And how can a sinner be said to be "inquiring the way" to Zion, when he has no disposition to go there. The real difficulty is, that he is unwilling to WALK in the way in which he knows he ought to go.

10. People pray that sinners may *have more conviction*. Or, they pray that sinners may *go home solemn* and tender, and take the subject into consideration, instead of praying that they may *repent now*. Or, they pray as if they supposed the *sinner was willing* to do what is required. All such prayers, are just such prayers, as the devil wants. He wishes to have such prayers, and I dare say he does not care how many such are offered.

Sometimes I have seen in an anxious meeting, or when sinners have been called to the anxious seats, and the minister has made the way of salvation all plain to them, and taken away all the stumbling blocks out of their path, and removed the darkness of their minds on the several points, and when they are just ready to YIELD, some one will be called on to pray, and instead of praying that they may *repent now*, he begins to pray, "O Lord, we pray, that these sinners may be solemn, that they may have a deep sense of their sinfulness, that they may go home impressed with their lost condition, that they may attempt nothing in their own strength, that they may not lose their convictions, and that, in thine own time and way, they may be brought out into the glorious light and liberty of the sons of God."

Instead of bringing them right up to the point of IMMEDIATE submission, on the spot, it gives them time to breathe, it lets off all the pressure of conviction, and he breathes freely again and feels relieved, and sits down at his ease. Thus, when the sinner is brought up, as it were, and stands at the gate of heaven, such a prayer, instead of pushing him in, sets him away back again, — "There, poor thing, sit there till God helps you."

11. Christians sometimes pray in such a manner as to make the impression that CHRIST IS THE SINNER'S FRIEND, in a different sense from what God the Father is. They pray to him, "O, thou friend of sinners," as if God was full of wrath, and stern vengeance, just going to crush the poor wretch, till Jesus Christ comes in and takes his part, and delivers him. Now this is all wrong. The Father and the Son are perfectly agreed, their feelings are all the same, and both are equally disposed to have sinners saved. And to make such an impression, deceives the sinner, and leads to wrong feelings towards God. To represent God the Father as standing over him, with the sword of justice in his hand, eager to strike the blow, till Christ interposes, is not true. The Father is as much the sinner's friend as the Son. His compassion is equal. But if the sinner gets this unfavorable idea of God the Father, how is he ever to love him with all his heart, so as to say "Abba, Father."

12. The impression is often made by the manner of praying, that you do not expect sinners to repent NOW, or that you expect God to do THEIR duty, or that you wish to encourage them to trust in your prayers. And so, sinners are ruined. Never pray so as to make the impression on sinners, that you secretly hope they are Christians already, or that you feel a strong confidence they will be, by and by, or that you half believe they are converted now. This is always unhappy. Multitudes are deceived with false comfort, in this way, and prevented, just at the critical point, from making the final surrender of themselves to God.

Brethren, I find this field so broad that I cannot possibly mention all I wished to say. There are many other things that I intended to touch upon this evening, but the time is too far spent. I must close with a few brief

REMARKS.

1. Many persons who deal in this way with anxious sinners, do it from false pity. They feel so much sympathy and compassion, that they cannot bear to tell them the truth, which is necessary to save them. As well might a surgeon, when he sees that a man's arm must be amputated, or he will die, indulge this feeling of false pity, and just put on a plaster, and give him an opiate.

There is no benevolence in that. True benevolence would lead the surgeon to hide his feelings, and to be cool and calm, and with a keen knife, cut the limb off, and save the life. It is false tenderness to do any thing short of that. I once saw a woman under distress of mind, who had been well nigh driven to despair for months. Her friends had tried all these false comforts without effect, and they brought her to see a minister. She was emaciated, and worn out with agony. The minister set his eye upon her, and poured in the truth upon her mind, and rebuked her in a most pointed manner. The woman who was with her, interfered, she thought it cruel, and said, "O, do comfort her, she is so distressed, don't trouble her any more, she cannot bear it." He turned, and rebuked *her*, and sent her away, and then poured in the truth upon the anxious sinner like fire, and in five minutes she was converted, and went home full of joy. The plain truth swept all her false notions away, and in a few moments she was joyful in God.

2. This treatment of anxious sinners, administering their false comfort, is, *in fact, cruelty*. It is cruel as the grave, as cruel as hell, for it is calculated to send the sinner down to its burning abyss. Christians feel compassion for the anxious, and so they ought. But the last thing they ought to do, is to flinch just at the point where it comes to a crisis. They should feel compassion, but they should show it just as the surgeon does, when he deliberately goes to work, in the right and best way, and cuts off the man's arm, and thus cures him and saves his life. Just so Christians should let the sinner see their compassion and tenderness, but they should take God's part, fully and decidedly. They should lay open to the sinner, the worst of his case, expose his guilt and danger, and then lead him right up to the cross, and insist on instant submission. They must have firmness enough to do his work thoroughly, and if they see the sinner distressed and in agony, still they must press him right on, and not give way in the least, however much he may be in agony, but still press on till he yield.

To do this often requires nerve. I have often been placed in circumstances, to know this by experience. I have found myself surrounded by anxious sinners, in such distress, as to make every nerve tremble, some overcome with emotion and lying on the floor, some applying camphor to prevent their fainting, others shrieking out as if they were just going to hell. Now, suppose any one should give false comfort in such a case as this. Suppose he had not nerve enough to bring them right up to the point of instant and absolute submission. How unfit is such a man to be trusted in a case like this.

3. Sometimes sinners become deranged through despair and anguish of mind. Where this is the case, it is almost always because those who deal with them try to encourage them with false comfort, and thus lead them to such a conflict with the Holy Ghost. They try to hold them up, while God is trying to break them down. And by and by, the sinner's mind gets confused with this contrariety of influences, and he either goes deranged, or is driven to despair.

4. If you are going to deal with sinners, remember that you are soon to meet them in judgment, and be sure to treat them in such a way that if they are lost, it will be their own fault. Do not try to comfort them with false notions now, and have them reproach you with it then. Better suppress your false sympathy, and let the naked truth cleave them asunder, joints and marrow, than to soothe them with false comfort, and beguile them away from God.

5. Sinner! if you converse with any Christians, and they tell you to do anything, first ask, "If I do *that*, shall I be saved?" You may be anxious, and not be saved. You may pray, and not be saved. You may read your Bible, and not be saved. You may use means, in your way, and not be saved. Whatever they tell you to do, if you can do it and not be saved, do not attend to such instructions. They are calculated to give you false comfort, and divert your attention from the main thing to be done, and beguile you down to hell. Do not follow any such directions, lest you should die while doing it, and then there is no retrieve.

FINALLY. — Never tell a sinner any thing, or give him any direction, that will lead him to stop short, or that does not include absolute submission to God. To let him stop at any point short of this, is infinitely dangerous. Suppose you are at an anxious meeting, or a prayer-meeting, and tell a sinner to pray, or to read a book, or any thing short of saving repentance, and he should fall and break his neck that night, of whom would his blood be required? A youth in New England once met a minister in the street, and asked him what he should do to be saved. The minister told him to go home and go into his chamber, and kneel down and give his heart to God. "O, sir," said the boy, "I feel so bad, I am afraid I shall not live to get home." The minister saw his error, and felt the rebuke, thus unconsciously given by a child, and he told him, "Well, then, give your heart to God here, and go home to your chamber and tell him of it."

Oh, it is enough to make one's heart bleed, to see so many miserable comforters for anxious sinners, in whose answers there remaineth falsehood. What a vast amount of spiritual quackery there is in the world, and how many "forgers of lies" there are, "physicians of no value," who know no better than to comfort sinners with false hopes, and delude them with their "old wives' fables," and nonsense, or who give way to false tenderness and sympathy, till they have not firmness enough to see the sword of the spirit applied, to cut men to the soul, and lay open the sinner's naked heart. Alas! that so many are ever put into the ministry, who have not skill enough to administer the gospel remedy, nor firmness enough to stand by and see the Spirit of God do its work, in breaking up the old foundations, and crushing all the rotten hopes of a sinner, and breaking him all down at the feet of Jesus.

XVIII

DIRECTIONS TO SINNERS

Text. — "What shall I do to be saved." — Acts xvi. 30.

These are the words of the jailor at Philippi, the question which he put to Paul and Silas, who were then under his care as prisoners. Satan had, in many ways, opposed these servants of God in their work of preaching the Gospel, and had been as often defeated and disgraced. But here, at Philippi, he devised a new and peculiar project for frustrating their labors. There was a certain woman at Philippi, who was possessed with a spirit of divination, or in other words, the spirit of the devil, and brought her masters much gain by her soothsaying. The devil set this woman to follow Paul and Silas about the streets, and as soon as they had begun to gain the attention of the people, she would come in and cry, "These men are the servants of the most high God, which show unto us the way of salvation." That is, she undertook to second the exhortations of the preachers, and added her testimony, as if to give additional weight to their instructions. The effect of it was just what Satan desired. The people all knew that this was a wicked, base woman, and when they heard her attempting to recommend this new preaching, they were disgusted, and concluded it was all of a piece. The devil knew that it would not do him any good, but would help their cause, to set such a person to oppose the preaching of the apostles, or to speak against it. The time had gone by, for that to succeed. And, therefore, he comes round the other way, and takes the opposite ground, and by setting her to praise them as the servants of God, and to bear her polluted testimony in favor of their instructions, he led people to suppose the apostles were of the same character with her, and had the same spirit that she had, and thus all their efforts were defeated. Paul saw that if things went on so, he should be totally baffled, and never succeed in establishing a church at Philippi. And he turns round to her, and commands the foul spirit, in the name of Jesus Christ, to come out of her. When her masters saw that the hope of their gains was gone, they raised a great persecution, and caught Paul and

Silas, and made a great ado, and brought them before the magistrates, and raised such a clamor that the magistrates shut them up in prison, and made their feet fast in the stocks.

Thus, they thought they had put down the excitement. But at midnight Paul and Silas prayed and sang praises, and the prisoners heard them. This old prison that had so long echoed to the voice of blasphemy and oaths, now resounded with the praises of God, and these walls, that had stood so firm, now trembled under the power of prayer. The stocks were unloosed, the gates thrown open, and every one's bands broken. The jailor was aroused from his sleep, and when he saw the prison doors opened, as he knew, that if the prisoners had escaped, he must pay for it with his life, he drew his sword, and was about to kill himself. But Paul, who had no notion of escaping clandestinely, cried out to him instantly. "Do thyself no harm, for we are all here." And the Jailor called for a light, and sprang in, and came trembling, and fell down before his prisoners, Paul and Silas, and brought them out, and said, "Sirs, what must I do to be saved?"

In my last lecture, I dwelt at some length on the false instructions given to sinners under conviction, and the false comforts too often administered, and the erroneous instructions which such persons receive. It is my design, to-night, to show *what are the instructions* that should be given to anxious sinners in order to their speedy and effectual conversion. Or, in other words, to explain to you, what answer should be given to those who make the inquiry, "What must I do to be saved?" In doing it, I propose,

I. To show *what is not a proper direction* to be given to sinners, when they make the inquiry in the text.

II. Show *what is a proper answer* to the inquiry. And

III. To *specify several errors*, which anxious sinners are apt to fall into.

1. I am to show *what are not proper directions* to be given to anxious sinners.

No more important inquiry was ever made than this, "What must I do to be saved?" Mankind are apt enough to inquire "What shall I eat, and what shall I drink," and the question may be answered in various ways, with little danger. But when a sinner asks in earnest, "What must I do to be saved?" it is of infinite importance that he should receive the right answer. It is my desire, to-night, to tell you, professors of religion, what to answer to this inquiry, and to tell you, who are sinners, what you must do to be saved.

I. No direction should be given to a sinner, that *will leave him still in the gall of bitterness* and the bonds of iniquity. No answer is proper to be given, with which, if he complies, he would not go to heaven, if he should die the next moment.

2. No direction should be given, that does not include a change of heart, or a right heart, or hearty obedience to Christ. In other words, nothing is proper, which does not imply actually becoming a Christian. Any other direction, that falls short of this, is of no use. It will not bring him any nearer to the kingdom, it will do no good, but will only lead him to *defer the very thing* which he must do, in order to be saved. The sinner should be told plainly, at once, what he must do or die; and he should be told nothing that does not include a right state of heart. Whatever you may do, sinner, that does not include a right heart, is sin. Whether you read the Bible or not, it is sin, so long as you remain in rebellion. Whether you go to meeting, or stay away, whether you pray or not, it is nothing but rebellion, every moment. It is surprising, that a sinner should suppose himself doing God's services, when he prays, and reads his Bible. Should a rebel against this government, read the statute book, while he continues in rebellion, and has no design to obey; should he ask for pardon, while he holds on to his weapons of resistance and warfare, would you think him doing his country a service, and laying them under obligation to show him favor. No, you would say that all his reading and praying, were only an insult to the majesty both of the lawgiver and the law. So you, sinner, while you remain in impenitence, are insulting God and setting him at defiance, whether you read his word and pray or let it alone. No matter what place or what attitude your body is in, on your knees, or in the house of God, so long as your heart is not right, so long as you resist the Holy Ghost, and reject Christ, you are a rebel against your Maker.

II. I am to show *what is a proper* answer to this inquiry. "What must I do to be saved."

And, generally, you may give the sinner any direction, or tell him to do any thing, that includes a right heart, and if you make him understand it, and do it, he will be saved. The Spirit of God, in striving with sinners, suits his strivings to the state of mind in which he finds them. His great object in striving with them, is, to dislodge them from their hiding-places, and bring them to submit to God, at once. Now these objections, and difficulties, and states of mind, are as various as the circumstances of mankind, as many as there are individuals. The characters of individuals, affords an endless diversity. What is to be done with each one, and how he is to be converted, depends on his particular errors. It is necessary to ascertain his errors, to find out what he understands, and what he needs to be taught more perfectly, to see what points the Spirit of God is pressing upon his conscience, and to press the same things and thus bring him to Christ. The most common directions are the following:

1. It is generally in point, and a safe, and suitable direction, to tell a sinner to *repent*. I say, *generally*. For sometimes the Spirit of God seems not so much to direct the sinner's attention to *his own sins* as to some other thing. In the days of the apostles, the minds of the people seem to have been agitated mainly on the question, whether Jesus was the true Messiah. And so the apostles directed much of their instructions to this point, to prove that he was the Christ. And whenever anxious sinners asked them what they must do, they most commonly exhorted them to "Believe in the Lord Jesus Christ." They bore down on this point, because here was where the Spirit of God was striving with them, and this was the subject that especially agitated people's minds, and, consequently, this would probably be the first thing, a person would do on submitting to God. It was the grand point at issue between God and the Jew and Gentile of those days, whether Jesus Christ was the son of God. It was the point in dispute, to bring a sinner to yield this controverted question, was the way the most effectually to humble him.

At other times, it will be found, that the Spirit of God is dealing with sinners chiefly in reference to their own sins. Sometimes he deals with them, in regard to a particular duty, as prayer, perhaps family prayer. The sinner will be found to be contesting that point with God, whether it is right for him to pray, or whether he ought to pray in his family. I have known striking cases of this kind, where the individual was struggling on this point, and as soon as he fell on his knees to pray, he yielded his heart, showing that this was the very point which the Spirit of God was contesting, and the hinge on which his controversy with God all turned. That was conversion.

The direction to repent is always *proper*, but will not always be effectual, for there may be some other thing that the sinner needs to be told also. And where it is the pertinent direction, sinners need not only, to be told, to repent, but to have it explained to them, what repentance is. Since there has been so much mysticism, and false philosophy, and false theology, thrown around the subject, it has become necessary, to tell sinners not only what you mean by repentance, but also to tell them what you *do not* mean. Words that used to be plain, and easily understood, have now become so perverted that they need to be explained to sinners, or they will often convey a wrong impression to their minds. This is the case with the word repentance. Many suppose that *remorse*, or a sense of guilt, is repentance. Then, hell is full of repentance, for it is full of remorse, unutterable and eternal. Others feel *regret* that they have done such a thing, and they call that repenting of it. But they only regret that they have sinned, because of the consequences, and not because they abhor sin. This is not repentance. Others suppose that convictions of sin and strong fears of hell are repentance. Others consider the remonstrances of conscience as repentance; they say, "I never do any thing wrong but that I repent; that I always feel sorry, I did it." Sinners must be shown, that all these things, are not repentance. They are not only consistent with the utmost wickedness, but the devil might have them all, and doubtless has them all, and yet remains a devil. Repentance is a change of mind, as regards sin itself. It is not only a change of views, but a change of feelings. It is what is naturally understood by a change of mind on any subject of interest and importance. We hear that such a man has changed his mind on the subject of Abolition, for instance, or that he has changed his views in politics. Every body understands that he has undergone a change in his views, his feelings, and his *conduct*. This is repentance, on that subject, it is a change of mind.

Repentance, always implies abhorrence of sin. It is feeling towards sin just as God feels. It always implies forsaking sin. Sinners should be made to understand this. The sinner that repents does not feel as impenitent sinners think they should feel, at giving up their sins if they should become religious. Impenitent sinners look upon religion just like this, that if they become pious, they shall be *obliged* to stay away from balls and parties, and obliged to give up theatres, or gambling, or other things that they now take delight in. And they see not how they could ever enjoy themselves, if they should break off from all those things. But this is very far from being a correct view of the matter. Religion does not make them unhappy, by shutting them out from things in which they delight, because the first step in it, is, to repent, to change their mind in regard to all these things. They do not seem to realize, that the person who has repented has no disposition for these things, they have given them up, and turned their mind away from them. Sinners feel as if they should *want* to go to such places, and want to mingle in such scenes, just as much as they do now, and that it will be such a continued sacrifice, as to make them unhappy. This is a great mistake.

I know there are some professors, who would be very glad to betake themselves to their former practices, were it not that they feel constrained, by fear of losing their character, or the like. Now, mark me. If they feel so, it is because they have no religion, they do not hate sin. If they desire their former ways, they have no religion, they have never repented, for repentance always consists in a change of views and feelings. If they were really converted, instead of *desiring* such things, they would turn away from them with loathing. Instead of lusting after the flesh-pots of Egypt, and desiring to go into their former circles, parties, balls, and the like, they find their highest pleasure in obeying God.

2. Sinners should be told to *believe the gospel*. Here, also, they need to have it explained to them, and to be told what *is not* faith, and what is. Nothing is more common, than for a sinner, when told to believe the gospel, to say, "I do believe it." The fact is, he has been brought up to admit the fact, that the gospel is true, but he does not *believe* it, he knows nothing about the evidence of it, and all his faith is a mere admission without evidence. He holds it to be true, in a kind of loose, indefinite sense, so that he is always ready to say, "I do believe the Bible." It is strange they do not see that they are deceived in thinking that they believe, for they must see that they have never acted upon these truths, as they do upon those things that they do believe. Yet it is often quite difficult to convince them that they do not believe.

But the fact is, that the careless sinner does not believe the gospel at all. The idea, that the careless sinner is an *intellectual* believer, is absurd. The devil is an intellectual believer, and that is what makes him tremble. What makes a sinner anxious is, that he begins to be an intellectual believer, and that makes him feel. No being in heaven, earth, or hell, can intellectually believe the truths of the gospel, and not feel on the subject. The anxious sinner has faith of the same kind with devils, but he has not so much of it, and, therefore, he does not feel so much. The man that does not feel nor act at all, on the subject of religion, is an infidel, let his professions be what they may. He that feels nothing and does nothing, believes nothing. This is a philosophical fact.

Faith does not consist in an intellectual conviction that Christ died for you in particular, nor in a belief that you are a Christian, or that you ever shall be, or that your sins are forgiven. But faith is that trust, or confidence, in the scriptures, that leads the individual to act as if they were true. This was the faith of Abraham. He had that confidence in what God said, which led him to act as if it were true. This is the way the apostle illustrates it in the eleventh of Hebrews. "Faith, is the substance of things hoped for, the evidence of things not seen." And he goes on to illustrate it by various examples. "Through faith we understand that the worlds were made," that is, we believe this, and act accordingly. Take the case of Noah. Noah was warned of God of things not seen as yet, that is, he was assured that God was going to drown the world, and he believed it, and acted accordingly, he prepared an ark to save his family, and by so doing, he condemned the world that would not believe; his actions gave evidence that he was sincere. Abraham, too, was called of God to leave his country, with a promise that he should be the gainer by it, and he obeyed and went out, without knowing where he should go. Read the whole chapter, and you will find many instances of the same kind. The whole design of the chapter is to illustrate the nature of faith, and to show that it invariably results in action. The sinner should have it explained to him, and be *made to see* that the faith which the gospel requires, is just that confidence in Christ, which leads him to act on what he says as a certain fact. This is believing in Christ.

3. Another direction, proper to be given to the sinner is, that he should *give his heart to God*. God says, "My son, give me thine heart." But here also there needs to be explanation, to make him understand what it is. It is amazing that there should be any darkness here. It is the language of common life, in every body's mouth, and every body understands just what it means, when we use it in regard to any thing else. But when it comes to religion, they seem to be all in the dark. Ask a sinner, no matter what may be his age, or education, what it means to give the heart to God, and, strange as it may appear, he is at a loss for an answer. Ask a woman, what it is to give her heart to her husband, or a man, what it is to give his heart to his wife, and they understand it. But then they are totally blind as to giving their hearts to God. I suppose I have asked more than a thousand anxious sinners this question. When I have told

them, they must give their hearts to God, they would always say they were willing to do it, and sometimes, that they were anxious to do it, and even seem to be in an agony of desire about it. Then I have asked them, what they understood to be giving their hearts to God, as they were so willing to do it. And very seldom have I received a correct or rational answer from a sinner of any age. I have sometimes had the strangest answers that can be imagined — any thing but what they ought to say. Now, to give your heart to God, is the same thing as to give your heart to any body else; the same as for a woman to give her heart to her husband. Ask that woman if she understands this? "O yes, that is plain enough, it is to place my affections on him, and strive to please him in every thing." Very well, place your affections on God, and strive to please him in every thing. But alas, when they come to the subject of religion, people suppose there is some wonderful mystery about it. Some talk as if they supposed it was to take out this bundle of muscles, or fleshy organ, in their bosom, and give it to God. Sinner, what God asks of you, is, that you should love him supremely.

3. *Submit to God*, is also a proper direction to anxious sinners. And, O, how dark sinners are here too. Scarcely a sinner can be found, who will not tell you he is willing to submit to God. But they do not understand it. They need to be told what true submission is. Sometimes they think it means that they should be willing to be damned.[1] Sometimes they place themselves in this attitude, and call it submission; they say, if they are elected, they shall be damned. This is not submission. True submission, is yielding obedience to God. Suppose a rebel, in arms against the government, was called on to submit. What would he understand by it? Why, that he should yield the point, and lay down his arms, and obey the laws. That is just what it means, for a sinner to submit to God. He must cease his strife and conflict against his Maker, and take the attitude of a willing and obedient child, willing to be and do whatever God requires. "Here, Lord, am I; Lord, what wilt thou have me to do?"

---

[1] Samuel Hopkins once stated that it was a good sign that a man was converted if he could honestly say that he loved God so much that he would willingly let himself be damned to hell if it were for the greater glory of God. Hopkinsianism became identified as the "willing to be damned" school of Calvinism. Finney here repudiates this idea, although elsewhere he makes statements very similar to it. Finney was much closer to Hopkins in many of his views than he ever admitted or perhaps realized. The best discussion of Hopkinsianism is in Joseph Haroutunian, *Piety versus Moralism* (New York, 1932), *passim*.

Suppose a company of soldiers had rebelled, and government had raised an army to put them down, and had driven them into a strong hold, where they were out of provisions, and had no way to escape, and they should not know what to do. Suppose the rebels to have met in this extremity, to consider what is to be done? and one rises up, and says, "Well, comrades, I am convinced we are all wrong from the beginning, and now the reward of our deeds is like to overtake us, and we cannot escape, and as for remaining here to die, I am resolved not to do it, I am going to throw myself on the mercy of the commander-in-chief." That man submits. He ceases, from that moment, to be a rebel in his heart, just as soon as he comes to this conclusion. So it is with the sinner when he yields the point, and consents in his heart to do, and be, whatever God shall require. The sinner may be in doubt what to do, and may feel afraid to put himself in God's hands, thinking that if he does, perhaps God will send him down to hell, as he deserves. But it is his business to leave all that question with God, and not resist his Maker any longer, but give all up to God, make no conditions, and trust it wholly to God's benevolence and wisdom to decide what shall be done, and to appoint his future condition. Until you do this, sinner, you have done nothing to the purpose.

5. Another proper direction to be given to sinners, is to *confess and forsake your sins*. This means that they should both confess and forsake them. They must confess to God their sins against God, and confess to men their sins against men, and forsake them all. A man does not forsake his sins till he has made all the reparation in his power. If he has stolen money, or defrauded his neighbor out of property, he does not forsake his sins by merely resolving not to steal any more, or not to cheat again; he must make reparation to the extent of his power. So, if he has slandered any one, he does not forsake his sin by merely saying he will not do so again. He must make reparation. So, in like manner, if he has robbed God, as all sinners have, he must make reparation, as far as he has the power. Suppose a man has made money in rebellion against God, and has withheld from him his time, talents and service, has lived and rioted upon the bounties of his providence, and refused to lay himself out for the salvation of the world; he has robbed God. Now, if he should die feeling that this money *was his own*, and should he leave it to his heirs — why, he is just as certain to go to hell as the highway robber. He has never made any satisfaction to God. With all his whining and pious talk, he has never confessed HIS

SIN to God, nor forsaken his sin, for he has never felt nor acknowledged himself to be the steward of God. If he refuses to hold the property in his possession, as the steward of God; if he accounts it his own, and as such gives it to his children, he says, in effect, to God, "That property is not yours, it is mine, and I will give it to my children." He has continued to persevere in his sin, for he does not relinquish the ownership of that of which he has robbed God.

What would a merchant think, if his hired clerk should take all the capital and set up a store of his own, and die with it in his hands? Will such a man go to heaven? "No," you say, every one of you, "If such a man does not go to hell, there might just as well be no hell." God would prove himself infinitely unjust, to let such a character go unpunished. What, then, shall we say of the man who has robbed God all his life? Here God set him to be his clerk, to manage some of his affairs, and he has gone and stolen all the money, and says it is his, and he keeps it, and dies, and gives it to his children, as if it was all his own lawful property. Is that man going to heaven? Has that man forsaken sin? I tell you, no. If he has not surrendered himself and all to God, he has not taken the first step in the way to heaven.

6. Another proper direction to be given to sinners is, *"Choose ye this day, whom ye will serve."* Under the Old Testament dispensation, this or something equivalent to it, was the most common direction given. It was not common to call on men to *believe in Christ* until the days of John the Baptist. He baptized those who came to him, with the baptism of repentance, and directed them to believe on him who should come after him. Under Joshua, the text was something which the people all understood more easily than they would a call to believe on the distant Messiah; it was "Choose ye, this day, whom ye will serve." On another occasion, Moses said to them, "I call heaven and earth to record this day against you, that I have set before you life and death, blessing and cursing: therefore choose life, that both thou and thy seed may live." The direction was accommodated to the people's knowledge. And it is good now, as it was then. Sinners are called upon to choose — what? Whether they will serve God or the world — whether they will follow holiness or sin. Let them be made to understand what is meant by choosing, and what is to be chosen, and then if the thing is done from the heart, they will be saved.

Any of these directions, if complied with, will constitute true conversion. The particular exercises may vary in different cases. Sometimes the first exercise in conversion, is submission to God, sometimes repentance, sometimes faith, sometimes the choice of God and his service, in short, whatever their thoughts are taken up with at the time. If their thoughts are directed to Christ at the moment, the first exercise will be faith. If to sin, the first exercise will be repentance. If to their future course of life, it is choosing the service of God. If to the Divine government, it is submission. It is important to find out just where the Holy Spirit is pressing the sinner at the time, and then take care to push that point. If it is in regard to Christ, press that; if it is in regard to his future course of life, push him right up to an immediate choice of obedience to God.

It is a great error to suppose that any one particular exercise is always foremost in conversion, or, that every sinner must have faith first, or submission first. It is not true, either in philosophy or in fact. There is a great variety in people's exercises. Whatever point is taken hold of, between God and the sinner, when the sinner YIELDS that, he is converted. Whatever the particular exercise may be, if it includes *obedience of heart to God on any point*, it is true conversion. When he yields one point *to God's authority*, he is ready to yield all. When he changes his mind, and obeys in one thing, *because it is God's will*, he will obey in other things, so far as he sees it to be God's will. Where there is this right choice, then, whenever the mind is directed to any one point of duty, he is ready to follow. It matters very little which of these directions is given, if it is only made plain, and if it is to the point, so as to serve as a test *of obedience to God*. If it is to the point that the Spirit of God is debating with the sinner's mind, so as to fall in with the Spirit's work, and not to divert the sinner's attention from the very point in controversy, let it be made perfectly clear, and then pressed till the sinner yields, and he will be saved.

III. I am to mention several errors which anxious sinners are apt to fall into, respecting this great inquiry.

1. The first error is, in supposing that they must make themselves better, or prepare themselves, so as in some way to recommend themselves to the mercy of God. It is marvelous, that sinners will not understand, that all they have to do is to *accept* salvation from God, all prepared to their hands. But they all, learned or unlearned, at first, betake themselves to a legal course to get relief. This is one principal reason why they will not become Christians

at once, just as soon as they begin to attend to the subject. They imagine that they must be, in some way or other, *prepared* to come. They must change their dress, and make themselves look a little better; they are not willing to come just as they are, in their rags and poverty. They must have something more on, before they can approach to God. They should be shown, at once, that it is impossible they should be any better, until they do what God requires. Every pulse that beats, every breath they draw, they are growing worse, because they are standing out in rebellion against God, so long as they *don't do the very thing* which God requires of them as the first thing to be done.

2. Another error is, in supposing that they must *suffer a considerable time under conviction*, as a kind of punishment, before they are ready properly to come to Christ. And so they will pray for conviction. And they think, that if they are ground down to the earth, with distress, for a sufficient time, then God will pity them, and be more ready to help them, when he sees them so very miserable. They should be made to understand clearly, that they are thus unhappy and miserable, *merely because* they refuse to accept the relief which God offers. Take the case of the stubborn child, when his parent stands over him with the rod, and the child shudders and screams. Should that child imagine he is gaining any thing by his agony? His distress arises from his conviction, and shall he pray for more conviction? Does that make him any better? Does his father pity him any more, because he stands out? Who does not see that he is all the while growing worse?

3. Sometimes sinners *imagine that they must wait for different feelings*, before they submit to God. They say, "I do not think I feel right yet, to accept of Christ; I do not think I am prepared to be converted yet." [2] They ought to be made to see that what God

---

[2] In the revised edition of 1868 Finney rewrote the last part of this paragraph to read: "They ought to be made to see what God requires of them is to *will* right. If they obey and submit with the *will* the feelings will adjust themselves in due time. It is not a question of *feeling* but of *willing* and *acting*. The *feelings* are voluntary and have no moral character except what they derive from the action of the will, with which action they sympathize. Before the will is right, the feelings will not be, of course. The sinner should come to Christ by accepting him at once; and this he must do, not in obedience to his *feelings* but in obedience to his *conscience*. Obey, submit, trust. Give up all instantly and your feelings will come right. Do not wait for better feelings but commit your whole being to God at once and this will soon result in the feelings for which you are waiting. What God requires of you is the present act of your own mind in turning from sin to holiness and from the service of Satan to the service of the living God."

requires of them is to *feel* differently. And to say they must feel differently before they obey God, is to say they must feel differently before they feel differently; or to say, "I don't feel right, because I don't feel right." God tells the sinner to love him, and the sinner replies, "Lord, I must wait till I feel differently." That is, you must wait till you love God before you will begin to love him. Why, sinner, you are not to wait for these feelings, as if they were to come into your mind from some other quarter. What God requires of you, is the present act of your own mind, in turning from sin to holiness, and from the service of Satan to the service of the living God. The very thing required, is to *feel right*; and do you wait for these feelings, as if they were not to be exercises of your own?

4. Another error of sinners, is to suppose they *must wait* till their *hearts are changed*. "What?" say they, "am I to believe in Christ before my heart is changed? Do you mean that I am to repent before my heart is changed?" Now, the simple answer to all this is, that the change of heart is the very thing in question. God requires sinners to love him. *That is* to change their heart. God requires the sinner to believe the gospel. *That is* to change his heart. God requires him to repent. *That is* to change his heart. God does not tell him to wait till his heart is changed, and then repent and believe, and love God. The very word itself, *repent*, signifies a change of mind or heart. To do either of these things, is to change your heart, and to make you a new heart, just as God requires.

5. Sinners often get the idea that they are perfectly willing to do what God requires. Tell them to do this thing, or that, to repent, or believe, or give God their hearts, and they say, "O yes, I am perfectly willing to do that, I wish I could do it, I would give any thing if I could do it." They ought to understand, that, being truly *willing* is doing it, but there is a difference between willing and desiring. People often *desire* to be Christians, when they are wholly *unwilling* to be so. When we see any thing, which appears to us to be a good, we are so constituted that we desire it. We necessarily desire it when it is before our minds. We cannot help desiring it in proportion as its goodness is presented to our minds. But yet we may not be *willing* to have it, under all the circumstances. It may be that, we prefer upon the whole, that the present possessor should continue to possess it still. Or that *we* choose to have our friend or child possess it, instead of ourselves. A man may desire to go to Philadelphia on many accounts, while,

for still more weighty reasons, he *chooses* not to go there. So the sinner may desire to be a Christian. He may see many good things in being a Christian. He may see that if he were a Christian he would be a great deal more happy, and that he should go to heaven when he dies, but yet, he is not willing to be a Christian. WILLING to obey Christ is to be a Christian. When an individual actually *chooses* to obey God, he is a Christian. But all such desires, as do not terminate in actual choice, are nothing.

6. The sinner will sometimes say, that he *offers* to give God his heart, but he intimates that God is unwilling. But this is absurd. What does God ask? Why, that you should love him. Now, for you to say you are willing to give God your heart, but God is unwilling, is the same as saying, that you are willing to love God, but God is not willing to be loved by you, and will not suffer you to love him. It is important to clear up all these points in the sinner's mind, that he may have no dark and mysterious corner to rest in, where the truth will not reach him.

7. Sinners sometimes get the idea that they repent, when they are only convicted. Whenever the sinner is found resting in any LIE, let the truth sweep it away, however much it may pain and distress him. If he has any error of this kind, you must tear it away from him, if you do not mean that he shall stumble into the depths of hell.

8. Sinners are often wholly taken up with *looking at themselves*, to see if they cannot find something there, some kind of feeling or other, that will recommend them to God. Evidently, for want of proper instruction, David Brainard,[3] was a long time taken up with his *state of mind*, looking for some *feelings* that would recommend him to God. Sometimes he imagined that he had such feelings, and would tell God in prayer, that now he felt as he ought, to receive his mercy; and then he would see that he had been all wrong, and be ashamed that he had told God that he felt right. Thus, the poor man, for want of correct instruction, was driven almost to despair, and it is easy to see, that his Christian exercises through life, were greatly modified, and his comfort and usefulness much impaired by the false philosophy he had adopted on this point. You must turn the sinner away from himself, to

---

[3] David Brainerd (1718–1747) was a devout Congregational missionary to the Indians. At the time of his death he was engaged to marry a daughter of Jonathan Edwards. Brainerd was a favorite hero of nineteenth-century pietists, and his famous diary was often republished. Edwards wrote an eloquent biography of him in 1749.

something else. Suppose he keeps poring over himself, until he is going into a state of despair. The proper course then is, to turn off his attention from looking at himself, and make him look at some duty to be performed, or make him look at Christ, and, perhaps, before he is aware, he will find that he has submitted to God. His attention was diverted away from himself, to contemplate the reasonableness of God's requirements, or the sufficiency of Christ's atonement, or something of this kind, and as he dwelt upon it, he just gave up his heart, and the agony was over.

REMARKS.

1. The labor of ministers is greatly increased, and the difficulties in the way of salvation are greatly multiplied, by the false instructions that have been given to sinners. The consequence has been, that directions which used to be plain are now obscure. People have been taught so long, that there is something awfully mysterious and unintelligible about conversion, that they do not try to understand it. Sinners have been taught these false notions, till now they are every where entrenched behind these sentiments, such as "cannot repent," "must wait for God," and the like. It was once sufficient, as we learn from the Bible, to tell sinners to repent, or to tell them to believe on the Lord Jesus Christ. But now faith has been talked about as a *principle*, instead of an act, and repentance as something put into the mind, instead of an exercise of the mind, and sinners are perplexed. Ministers are charged with preaching heresy, because they presume to teach that faith is an exercise, and not a principle, and that sin is an act, and not a part of the constitution of man. And sinners have become so sophisticated, that you have to be at great pains in explaining, not only what you do not mean, but what you do mean, otherwise they will be almost sure to misunderstand you, and either gain a false relief from their anxiety, by throwing their duty off upon God, or else run into despair, from the supposed impracticability of doing what is requisite for their salvation. It is often the greatest difficulty to lead them out of these theological labyrinths and mazes, into which they have been deluded, and to lead them along the straight and simple way of the gospel. It seems as if the greatest ingenuity had been employed, to mystify the minds of people, and weave a most subtle web of false theology, calculated to involve a sinner in endless darkness.

Who that has been in revivals, has not encountered that endless train of fooleries, which have been inculcated, till it has become necessary to be as plain as A B C, and the best educated have to be talked to just like children. So much have your D. D.'s done to mystify and befool people's minds, in the plainest matters. Tell a sinner to *believe*, and he turns round to you, and stares, "Why, how you talk; is not faith a principle, and how am I to believe until I get this principle?" So, if a minister tells a sinner the very words that the apostles used, in the great revival at the day of pentecost, "Repent and be converted, every one of you," and they reply as they have been taught, "O, I guess you are an Arminian; I don't want any of your Arminian teaching for me; don't you deny the Spirit's influences?" It is enough to make humanity weep, to see the fog, and darkness, that have been thrown around the plain directions of the gospel, till many generations have been emptied into hell.

2. These false instructions to sinners, are infinitely worse than none. The Lord Jesus Christ found it more difficult to get the people to yield up their false notions of theology, than any thing else. This has been the great difficulty with the Jews to this day, that they have received false notions in theology, have perverted the truth on certain points, and you cannot make them understand the plainest points in the gospel. So it is with sinners, the most difficult thing to be done is to get away these refuges of lies, which they have gotten from false theology. They are so fond of holding on to these refuges, because they are called orthodox, and because they excuse the sinner, and condemn God, that it is found to be the most perplexing, and difficult, and discouraging part of a minister's labor, to drive them away.

3. No wonder the gospel has taken so little effect, encumbered as it has been with these strange dogmas. The truth is, that very little of the gospel has come out upon the world, for these hundreds of years, without being clogged and obscured by false theology.[4] People have been told that they must repent, and, in the same breath, told that they could not repent, until the truth itself has been all mixed up with error, so as to produce the same

---

[4] Finney had to accept the fact that the gospel was preached by Edwards and Whitefield because God blessed their work by a great revival. But as Finney said in his sermon, "The Traditions of the Elders," Calvinists who had revivals did so only when "they were inconsistent enough to lay aside" the doctrines of Calvinism "and come out with the pressure of the gospel upon the hearts and consciences of men." Finney, *Sermons on Various Subjects*, p. 80.

practical effect with error, and the gospel that is preached has been another gospel, or no gospel at all.

4. You can understand what is meant by healing slightly the hurt of the daughter of God's people, and the danger of doing it. It is very easy, when sinners are under conviction, to say something that shall smooth over the case, and relieve their anxiety, so that they will either get a false hope, or will be converted with their views so obscure, that they will always be poor, feeble, wavering, doubting, inefficient Christians.

5. Much depends on the manner in which a person is dealt with, when under conviction. Much of his future comfort and usefulness depends on the clearness, and strength, and firmness, with which the directions of the gospel are given, when he is under conviction. If those who deal with him are afraid to use the probe thoroughly, he will always be a poor, sickly, doubting Christian. If converted at all, he will never do much good. The true mode, is to deal thoroughly and plainly with a sinner, to tear away every excuse he can get up, and show him plainly what he is, and what he ought to be, and he will bless God to all eternity, that he fell in with those who would be so faithful to his soul. For the want of this thorough and searching management, many are converted who seem to be stillborn. And the reason is, they never were faithfully dealt with. We may charitably hope they are Christians, but still it is uncertain and doubtful. Their conversion seems rather a change of opinion, than a change of heart. But if, when a sinner is under conviction, you pour in the truth, put in the probe, break up the old foundations, and sweep away his refuges of lies, and use the word of God, like fire and like a hammer, you will find that they will come out with clear views, and strong faith, and firm principles, not doubting, halting, irresolute Christians, but such as follow the Lord wholly. This is the way to make strong Christians. This has been eminently the case in many revivals of modern days. I have heard old Christians say of the converts, "These converts were *born* men and women, full grown, they never were children, but have, at the very outset, all the clearness of view, and strength of faith, of old Christians. They seem to understand the doctrines of religion, and to know what to do, and how to take hold, to promote revivals, better than one in a hundred of the old members in the church."

I once knew a young man who was converted, away from home. The place where he lived had no minister, and no preaching, and no religion. He went home in three days after he was converted, and immediately set himself to work, to labor for a revival. He set up meetings in his neighborhood, and prayed and labored, and a revival broke out, of which he had the principal management through a powerful work, which converted most of the principal men of the place. The truth was, he had been so dealt with, that he knew what he was about. He understood the subject, and knew where he stood himself. He was not all the while troubled with doubts, whether he was himself a Christian.[5] He knew that he was serving God, and that God was with him, and so he went boldly and resolutely forward to his object. But if you undertake to make converts, without cutting up all their errors, and tearing away their false hopes, you may make a host of hypocrites, or of puny, dwarfish Christians, always doubting, and easily turned back from a revival spirit, and worth nothing. The way is, to bring them right out to the light. When a man is converted in this way, you can depend on him, and know where to find him.

7. Protracted seasons of conviction are generally owing to defective instruction. Wherever clear and faithful instructions are given to sinners, there you will generally find that convictions are *deep and pungent*, but *short*.

8. Where clear and discriminating instructions are given to convicted sinners, if they do not soon submit, their convictions will generally leave them. Convictions in such cases are generally short. Where sinners are deceived by false views, they may be kept along for weeks, and perhaps months, and sometimes for years, in a languishing state, and at last, perhaps, be crowded into the kingdom and saved. But where the truth is made perfectly clear to the sinner's mind, and all his errors are torn away, if he does not soon submit, his case is hopeless. Where the truth is brought to bear upon his mind, and he directly resists the very truth that must convert him, there is nothing more to be done. The Spirit will soon leave him, for the very weapons he uses, are resisted. Where instructions are not clear, and are mixed up with errors, the Spirit may strive even for years, in great mercy, to get sinners through the fog of false instruction. But not so, where their duty is clearly explained to them, and they are brought right up to the

---

[5] Finney may be referring here to his own conversion, for in his *Memoirs* he tells of returning to his hometown of Henderson shortly afterward and converting not only his parents but many others in the village.

single point of immediate submission, and have all their false pretences exposed, and the path of duty made perfectly plain. Then, if they do not submit, the Spirit of God forsakes them, and their state is well nigh hopeless.

If there be sinners in this house, and you see your duty clearly, TAKE CARE how you delay. If you do not submit, you may expect the Spirit of God will forsake you, and you are LOST.

8. A vast deal of the direction given to anxious sinners amounts to little less than the popish doctrine of indulgences. The pope used to sell indulgences to sin, and this led to the reformation under Luther. Sometimes people would purchase an indulgence to sin for a certain time, or to commit some particular sin, or a number of sins.[6] Now, there is a vast deal in protestant churches, which is little less than the same thing. What does it differ from this, to tell a sinner to wait? The amount of it is, telling him to continue in sin a while longer, while he is waiting for God to convert him. And what is that but an indulgence to commit sin? Any direction given to sinners, that does not require them *immediately* to obey God, is an indulgence to sin. It is in effect, giving them liberty to continue in sin against God. Such directions are not only wicked, but ruinous and cruel. If they do not destroy the soul, as no doubt they often do, they *defer*, at all events, the sinner's enjoyment of God and of Christ, and he stands a great chance of being lost for ever, while listening to such instructions. O, how dangerous it is, to give a sinner reason to think he may wait a moment, before giving his heart to God.

9. So far as I have had opportunity to observe, those conversions which are most sudden have commonly turned out to be the best Christians. I know the reverse of this has often been held and maintained. But I am satisfied there is no reason for it, although multitudes, even now, regard it as a suspicious circumstance, if a man has been converted very suddenly. But the Bible gives no warrant for this supposition. There is not a case of protracted conviction recorded in the whole Bible. All the conversions recorded there, are sudden conversions. And I am persuaded there never would have been such multitudes of tedious convictions, and often ending in nothing after all, if it had not been for those theological perversions which have filled the world with *cannot-ism*.[7] In Bible days, they told sinners to repent, and they

---

[6] Finney obviously had been misinformed about the meaning of indulgences.
[7] For a discussion of "cannot-ism," see the Introduction to this volume, p. xxviii.

did it *then*. Cannot-ism had not been broached in that day. It is this speculation, about the inability of sinners to obey God, that lays the foundation for all the protracted anguish and distress, and perhaps ruin, through which so many are led. Where a sinner is brought to see what he has to do, and he takes his stand at once, AND DOES IT, he generally does so afterwards, and you generally find that such a person will hold out so, and prove a decided character. You will not find him one of those that you always have to *warp up* to duty, like a ship, against wind and tide. Look at those professors who always have to be dragged forward in duty, and you will generally find that they had not clear and consistent directions when they were converted, and most likely they will be very much "afraid of these sudden conversions."

Afraid of sudden conversions! Some of the best Christians of my acquaintance were convicted and converted in the space of a few minutes. In one quarter of the time that I have been speaking, many of them were awakened, and came right out on the Lord's side, and have been shining lights in the church ever since, and have generally manifested the same decision of character in religion, that they did when they first came out and took a stand on the Lord's side.

XIX

INSTRUCTIONS TO CONVERTS

Text. — "Feed my lambs." — John xxi. 15.

You, who read your Bibles, recollect the connection in which these words are found, and by whom they were spoken. They were addressed by the Lord Jesus Christ to Peter, after he had denied his Lord, and had professed repentance. Probably one of the designs which Christ had in view, in suffering Peter to sin so awfully as to deny his master, was to produce a deeper work of grace in him, and thus fit him for the peculiar duty to which he intended to call him, in laying the foundations of the Christian Church, and watching over the spiritual interests of the converts. It needed a peculiar work of grace in his soul, to fit him to lead others through those scenes of trial and temptation to which the early Christians, in particular, were exposed.

It is evident, that, though Peter had special *natural* qualifications for such a work, yet he was quite a superficial *saint*. He was probably converted before this, but he was weak, and there was left so much of his natural roughness and turbulence of temper, that he was still ready to bristle up on any occasion, and take offence at every thing that crossed him, so that he was still quite unfit for that particular work to which he was destined. Christ designed him for such a peculiar service, that it seems something was indispensable to fit him for it, and make him such a saint, that future opposition would not irritate him, nor difficulties dishearten him, nor success and honor spoil him, by lifting up his heart with pride. And, therefore, Christ takes the effectual method recorded before us, of dealing with him once for all, to secure a thorough work in his soul.

He asked him this question, to remind him, in an affecting manner, at once of his sin and of the love of Christ, "Simon, son of Jona, lovest thou me more than these?" Strongly implying a doubt whether he did love him. Peter answers, "Yea, Lord, thou knowest that I love thee." He said unto him, "Feed my lambs." He then repeated the question, as if he would read his inmost soul, "Simon, son of Jona, lovest thou me?" Peter was still firm, and promptly answers again, "Yea, Lord, thou knowest that I love thee." Jesus still asked him the question again, the third time, emphatically. He seemed to urge the point, as if he would search his inmost thoughts, to see whether Peter would ever deny him again. Peter was touched, he was grieved, it is said; he did not fly into a passion — he did not boast, as he did on a former occasion, "Though I should die with thee, yet would I not deny thee," but he was grieved, he was subdued, he spoke tenderly, he *appealed* to the Savior himself, as if he would implore him not to doubt his sincerity any longer, "Lord, thou knowest all things, thou knowest that I love thee." Christ then gave him his final charge, "Feed my sheep."

By the terms sheep and lambs here, the Savior undoubtedly designated Christians, — members of his church; the lambs probably represented young converts, those that have but little experience and but little knowledge of religion, and therefore, need to have special attention and pains taken with them, to guard from harm, and to train them for future usefulness. And when our Savior told Peter to feed his sheep, he doubtless referred to the important part which Peter was to perform in watching over the newly formed churches in different parts of the world, and in training the young converts, and leading them along to usefulness and happiness.

My last Lecture was on the subject of giving right instruction to anxious sinners. And this naturally brings me along, in this Course of Lectures, to consider the manner in which young converts should be treated and the instructions that should be given to them.

INSTRUCTIONS TO YOUNG CONVERTS.

In speaking on this subject, it is my design,

I. To state several things that ought to be considered, in regard to the hopes of young converts.

II. Several things respecting their making a profession of religion, and joining the church.

III. The importance of having correct instruction given to young converts.

IV. What should not be taught to young converts.

V. What particular things are specially necessary to be taught to young converts.

VI. How young converts should be treated by church members.

I. I am to state several matters in regard to *the hopes of young converts.*

1. Nothing should be said to them *to create a hope.* Nothing should ordinarily be intimated to persons under conviction, calculated to make them think they have experienced religion, till they find it out themselves. I do not like this term, "experienced religion," and I use it only because it is a phrase in common use.[1] It is an absurdity in itself. What is religion? Obedience to God. Suppose you should hear a good citizen say he had experienced obedience to the government of the country. You see it is nonsense. Or suppose a child should talk about experiencing obedience to his father. If he knew what he was saying, he would say he had *obeyed his father*, just as the apostle Paul says to the Roman believers, "Ye have *obeyed from the heart* that form of doctrine which was delivered you."

What I mean to say is, that ordinarily, it is best to let their hope or belief that they are converted spring up spontaneously in their own minds. Sometimes it will happen that persons may be really converted, but owing to some notions which they have been taught about religion, they do not realize it. Their views of what religion is, and its effect upon the mind, are so entirely wide of the truth, that they do not think that they have it. I will give you an illustration on this point.

Some years since, I labored in a place where a revival was in progress, and there was in the place a young lady from Boston. She had been brought up a Unitarian, she had considerable education, and was intelligent on many subjects, but on the subject of religion she was very ignorant. At length she was convicted of sin. She became awfully convinced of her horrible enmity against God. She had been so educated as to have a sense of propriety, but her enmity against God became so great, and broke out so frightfully, that it was horrible to hear her talk. She used to come to the anxious meetings, where we conversed with each one separately. And her feelings of opposition to God were such that she used to create disturbance. By the time I came within two or three seats from her, where she could hear what I said in a low voice to the others, she would begin to make remarks in reply,

---

[1] Finney may seem to object to the term "experienced religion" here, but see pp. 392–393.

so that they could be heard. And she would say the most bitter things against God, and against his providence, and his method of dealing with mankind, as if God was an infinite tyrant. She would speak of him as the most unjust and cruel being in the universe. I would try to hush her, and make her keep still, because she distracted the attention of others. Sometimes she would stop and command her temper awhile, and sometimes she would rise and go out. I have seldom seen a case, where the enmity of the heart rose so high against God. One night at the anxious meeting, after she had been very restless, as I came towards her, she began as usual to reply, but I hushed her, and told her I could not converse with her there, but invited her to my room the next morning, and then I would talk with her. She promised to come, but, says she, "God is unjust, he is infinitely unjust. Is he not almighty? Why then has he never shown me my enmity before? Why has he let me run on so long? Why does he let my friends at Boston remain in this ignorance? They are the enemies of God, as much as I am, and are going to hell. Why does he not show them the truth in regard to their condition?" And in this temper she left the room.

The next morning she came to my room, as she had promised. I saw as soon as she came in that her countenance was changed, but I said nothing about it. "O," said she, "I have changed my mind, as to what I said last night about God, I don't think he has done me any wrong, and I think I shall get religion sometime, for now I love to think about God. I have been all wrong; the reason why I had never known my enmity before, was, that I would not. I used to read the Bible, but I always passed over the passages that would make me feel as if I was a lost sinner, and those passages that spoke of Jesus Christ as God, I passed over without consideration, and now I see that it was my fault, not God's fault, that I did not know any more about myself; I have changed my mind now." She had no idea that this was religion, but she was encouraged now to expect religion at some future time, because she loved God so much. I said nothing to make her imagine that I thought her a Christian, but left her to find it out. And, for a time, her mind was so entirely occupied with thinking about God, that she never seemed to ask whether this is religion or not.

It is a great evil, ordinarily, to encourage persons to hope they are Christians. Very likely you may judge prematurely. Or if not, it is better they should find it out for themselves, suppose they do not see it at once. They may break down lower than ever, and then they will come out so clear and decided, that they will know where they are.

2. When you see persons expressing a hope, and yet they express doubts too, it is generally because the work is not thorough. It they are convicted, they need breaking up. They are still lingering around the world, or they have not broken off effectually from their sins, and they need to be pushed back, rather than urged forward. If you see reason to doubt, or if you find that they have doubts, most probably there is some good reason to doubt. Sometimes persons express a hope in Christ, and afterwards remember some sin, that needs to be confessed to men, or some case where they have slandered, or defrauded, where it is necessary to make satisfaction, and where either their character, or their purse, is so deeply implicated that they hesitate, and refuse to perform their duty. This grieves the Spirit, brings darkness over their minds of course, and justly leads them to doubt whether they are truly converted. If a soul is truly converted, it will generally be found when there are doubts, that on some point they are neglecting duty. They should be searched as with a lighted candle, and brought up to the performance of duty, and not suffered to hope until they do it. *Ordinarily* it is proper just there to throw in some plain and searching truth, that will go through them, something that will wither their hopes like a moth. Do it while the Spirit of God is dealing with them, and do it in the right way, and there is no danger of its doing harm.

To illustrate this: I knew a person, who was a member of the church, but an abominable hypocrite, proved to be so by her conduct, and afterward fully confessed to be so. In a revival of religion she was awakened and deeply convicted, and after a while she got a hope. She came to a minister to talk with him about her hope, and he poured in the truth to her mind in such a manner as to annihilate all her hopes. She then remained under conviction many days, and at last she broke out in hope again. The minister knew her temperament, and knew what she needed, and he tore away her hope again. And then she broke down, clear to the ground, so that she could not stand or go. So deeply did the Spirit of God PROBE her heart, that, for a time, it took away all her bodily strength. And then she came out subdued. Before, she had been one of the proudest rebels against God's government that ever was, but now she became humbled, and was one of the most modest, tender, lovely Christians I have ever known. And such she remained. No doubt that was just the way to deal with her. It was just the treatment that her case required.

It is often useful to deal with individuals in this way. Some persons are *naturally* unamiable in their temper, and unlovely in their deportment. And it is particularly important that such persons should be dealt with most thoroughly whenever they first begin to express hope in Christ. Unless the work with them, is, in the first place, uncommonly deep and thorough, they will be vastly less useful, and interesting, and happy, than they otherwise would have been, had the probe been thoroughly and skilfully applied to their heart. If they are encouraged at first without being thoroughly dealt with, if they are left to go right along, and not sufficiently probed and broken down, these unlovely traits of character will remain unsubdued, and will be always breaking out to the great injury, both of their personal peace, and their general influence and usefulness as Christians.

It is important to take advantage of such characters while they are just in these peculiar circumstances, so that they can be moulded into proper form. Do not spare, though it should be a child, or a brother, or a husband, or a wife. Let it be a thorough work. If they express a hope, and you find they bear the image of Christ, they are Christians. But if that appears doubtful — if they do not appear to be fully changed, just tear away their hope, by searching them with the most discriminating truth, and leave the Spirit to do the work more deeply. If still the image is not perfect, do it again — break them down into a child-like spirit, and then let them hope. They will then be clear and thorough Christians. By such a mode of treatment, I have often known people of the crookedest and hatefulest natural character, so transformed in the course of a few days, that they appear like different beings. You would think the work of a whole life of Christian cultivation had been done at once. Doubtless this was the intent of our Savior's dealing with Peter. He had been converted, but became puffed up with spiritual pride and self-confidence, and then he fell. After that, Christ broke him down again, by three times searching him with the inquiry, "Simon, son of Jona, lovest thou me?" after which, he seems to have been a stable and devoted saint the rest of his days.

3. There is no need of young converts *having or expressing doubts as to their conversion*. There is no more need of a person

doubting whether he is now in favor of God's government, than there is for a man to doubt whether he is in favor of our government or another. It is, in fact, on the face of it, absurd, for a person to talk of doubting on such a point, if he is intelligent and understands what he is talking about. It has long been supposed to be a virtue, and a mark of humility, for a person to doubt whether he is a Christian, and this notion that there is virtue in doubting is a device of the devil. "I say, neighbor, are you in favor of our government, or do you prefer that of Russia?" "Why, I have some hopes that I love our own government, but I have many doubts." Wonderful! "Woman, do you love your children?" "Why, sir, I sometimes have a trembling hope that I love them, but you know the best have doubts." "Wife, do you love your husband?" "I don't know — I sometimes think I do, but you know the heart is deceitful, and we ought to be careful and not be too confident." Who would have such a wife? "Man, do you love your wife, do you love your family?" "Ah, you know we are poor creatures, we don't know our own hearts. I think I do love them, but perhaps I am deceived." Ridiculous!

Ordinarily, the very idea of a person's expressing doubts, renders his piety truly doubtful. A real Christian has no need to doubt. And when one is full of doubts, ordinarily you ought to doubt for him and help him doubt. Affection to God is as much a matter of consciousness as any other affection. A woman *knows* she loves her child. How? By consciousness. She is conscious of the exercise of this affection. And, then, she sees it carried out into action every day. In the same way a Christian may know that he loves God, by his consciousness of this affection, and by seeing that it influences his daily conduct.

In the case of young converts, truly such, these doubts generally arise from their having been wrongly dealt with, and not sufficiently taught, or not thoroughly humbled. In any case, they should never be left in such a state, but should be brought, if possible, to such a thorough change, that they will doubt no longer. It is inconsistent with the greatest usefulness, for a Christian to be always entertaining doubts. It not only makes him gloomy, but it renders his religion a stumbling block to sinners. What do sinners think of such religion? They say, "These converts are always afraid to think they have got any thing real. They are always trembling, and doubtful whether it is a reality, and they ought to know whether there is any thing in it or not; for if it is any thing, these people seem to have it, and I am inclined to think it rather doubtful. At any rate, I will let it pass for the present; for I don't believe God will damn me for not attending to what appears so uncertain." No, a cheerful, settled hope in Christ, is indispensable to usefulness, and therefore you should deal so with young converts, as to lead them to a consistent, well-grounded, stable hope. Ordinarily this may be done, if pursued wisely, at the proper time, and that is at the commencement of their religious life. And they should not be left till it is done.

I know there are some exceptions, there are cases where the best instructions will be ineffectual, but these generally depend on the state of the health, and the condition of the nervous system. Sometimes you find a person incapable of reasoning on a certain topic, and so their errors will not yield to instruction. But most commonly they mistake the state of their own hearts, because they judge under the influence of a physical disease. Sometimes persons under a nervous depression will go almost into despair. I will not take time now to show the connection, but persons who are acquainted with physiology will easily explain the matter, and this will make it plain that the only way to deal with such cases is first to recruit their health, and get their nervous system in a proper tone, and thus remove the physical cause of their gloom and depression, and then they will be able to receive and apply your instructions to the state of their minds. But if you cannot remove their gloom and doubts and fears in this way, you can at least avoid doing any positive harm, by giving them wrong instructions. I have known, even experienced Christians, to have the error fastened upon them, thinking it was necessary, or was virtuous, or a mark of humility to be always in doubt, and Satan would take advantage of it, and of the state of their health, to drive them almost into despair. You ought to guard against this, by avoiding the error in teaching young converts. Teach them that instead of there being any virtue in doubting, it is a sin to have any reason to doubt, and a sin if they doubt without any reason, and a sin to be gloomy, and disgust sinners with their despondency. And if you teach them thoroughly what religion is, and make them SEE CLEARLY what God wishes to have them do, and lead them to do it promptly and decidedly, ordinarily they will not be harrassed with doubts and fears, but will be clear, openhearted, cheerful and growing Christians, an honor to the religion they profess, and a blessing to the church and the world.

II. I proceed to mention some things worthy of consideration in regard to their making a profession of religion, or joining the church.

1. Young converts should, ordinarily, *offer themselves for admission to some church of Christ immediately*.[2] By immediately, I mean that they should do it the *first* opportunity they have. They should not *wait*. If they set out in religion by waiting, most likely they will always be waiting, and never do any thing to much purpose. If they are taught to wait under conviction, before they give themselves up to Christ, or if they are taught to wait after conversion, before they give themselves publicly to God, by joining the church, they will probably go halting and stumbling along through life. The first thing they should be taught, always is, NEVER TO WAIT WHERE GOD HAS POINTED OUT YOUR DUTY. We profess to have given up the waiting system, let us carry it through and be consistent.

While I say it is the duty of young converts to offer themselves to the church immediately, I do not say that they should, in all cases, *be received* immediately. But the church may, and have an undoubted right to assume the responsibility of receiving them immediately or not. If the church are not satisfied in the case, they have the power to bid candidates wait till they can make inquiries, or in any other way obtain satisfaction, as to their character and their sincerity. This is more necessary in large cities than it is in the country, because the church is liable to receive so many applications from persons that are entire strangers, where it is necessary to make inquiries before admitting them to communion. But if the church think it necessary to postpone an applicant, the responsibility is not his. *He* has not postponed obedience to the dying command of Christ, and so he has not grieved the Spirit away, and so he may not be essentially injured if he is faithful in other respects. Whereas, if *he* had neglected the duty voluntarily, he would soon get into the dark, and very likely backslide.

If there is no particular reason for delay, ordinarily the church ought to receive them when they apply. If they are sufficiently in-

---

[2] It was common practice in Calvinist churches to make persons converted in a revival wait six to twelve months before admitting them to the church. Meanwhile they were given careful instruction in the doctrines of Calvinism and often required to memorize the Shorter Catechism of the Westminster Confession. Here again Finney is a true pietist in putting "experimental religion" ahead of creedal confession of faith.

structed on the subject of religion to know what they are doing, and if their general character is such that they can be trusted as to their sincerity and honesty in making a profession, I see no reason why they should delay. But if there are sufficient reasons, in the view of the church, for making them wait a reasonable time, let them do it, on their responsibility to Jesus Christ. They should, however, remember, what is the responsibility they assume, and that if they keep those out of the church who ought to be in it, they sin, and grieve the Holy Spirit.

It is impossible to lay down particular rules on this subject, applicable to all cases. There is so great a variety of reasons which may warrant keeping persons back, that no general rules can reach them all. Our practice, in this church, is to propound persons for a month after they make application, before they are received to full communion. The reason of this is, that the Session may have opportunity to inquire respecting individuals who offer themselves, as so many of them are strangers. But in the country, where there are regular congregations, and all the people have been instructed from their youth in the doctrines of religion, and where every body is perfectly known, the case is different, and ordinarily I see no reason why persons of fair character should not be admitted immediately. If a person has not been a drunkard, or otherwise of bad character, let him be admitted at once, as soon as he can give a rational and satisfactory account of the hope that is in him.

That is evidently the way the apostles did. There is not the least evidence in the New Testament, that they *ever* put off a person that wanted to be baptised and join the church. I know this does not satisfy some people, because they think the case is different. But I do not see it so. They say the apostles were inspired. That is true; but it does not follow that they were inspired to read the characters of men, so as to prevent their making mistakes in this matter. On the other hand, we know they *were not inspired* in this way, for we know they did make mistakes, just as ministers may do now, and, therefore, it is not true that their being inspired men alters the case on this point. Simon Magus was supposed to be a Christian, and was baptised and admitted to the communion, and remained in good standing till he undertook to purchase the Holy Ghost with money. The apostles used to admit converts from Heathenism immediately, and without delay. If they could receive persons who, perhaps, never heard more than one gospel sermon, and who never had a Bible, nor attended a Sabbath-school or Bible-class in their lives, surely it is not necessary to wake up such an outcry and alarm, if a church thinks proper to receive persons of fair character who have had the Bible all their lives, and been trained in the Sabbath-school, and sat under the preaching of the gospel, and who, therefore, may be supposed to understand what they are about, and not to profess what they do not feel.

I know it may be said that persons who make a profession of religion now, are not obliged to make such sacrifices for their religion as the early believers were, and, consequently, people may be more ready to play the hypocrite. And, to some extent, that is true. But then, on the other hand, it should be remembered, that, with the instructions which they have on the subject of religion, they are not so easily led to deceive themselves, as those who were converted without the previous advantages of a religious education. They may be strongly tempted to deceive others, but I insist upon it, that, with the instructions which they have received, the converts of these great revivals are not half so liable to deceive themselves, and take up with a false hope, as they were in the days of the Apostles. And on this ground I believe that those churches who are faithful in dealing with young converts, and who exhibit habitually the power of religion, are not likely to receive so many unconverted persons, as the Apostles did.

It is important that the churches should act wisely on this point. Great evil has been done by this practice of keeping persons out of the church a long time to see if they were Christians. This is almost as absurd as it would be to throw out a young child into the street, to see whether it will live; to say, if it lives and promises to be a healthy child, we will take care of it, when that is the very time it wants nursing, and taking care of, at the moment when the scale is turning, whether it shall live or die. Is that the way to deal with young converts? Should the church throw her newborn children out to the winds, and say, if they live there, let them be raised; but if they die, they ought to die. I have not a doubt that thousands of converts, in consequence of this treatment, have gone through life, and never have joined any church, but have lingered along, full of doubts, and fears, and darkness, and in this way have spent their days, and gone to the grave without the comforts or the usefulness which they might have enjoyed, simply because the church, in her folly, has suffered them to wait outside of the pale, to see whether they would grow and thrive, without those ordinances which Jesus Christ established particularly for their benefit.

Jesus Christ says to his church, "Here, take these lambs, and feed them, and shelter them and watch over them, and protect them:" and what does the Church do? Why, turn them out alone upon the cold mountains, among the wild beasts, to starve or perish, to see whether they are alive or not. This whole system is as unphilosophical as it is unscriptural. Did Jesus Christ tell his churches to do so? Did God of Abraham teach any such doctrine as this, in regard to the children of Abraham? Never. He never taught us to treat young converts in such a barbarous manner. It is the very best way that could be taken to render it doubtful whether they are converts. The very way to lead them into doubts and darkness, is to keep them away from the church, from its fellowship, and its ordinances.

I have understood there is a church, not very far from here, who have passed a resolution that no young converts shall be admitted till they have had a hope for at least six months. Where did they get any such rule? Not from the Bible, nor the example of the early churches.

3. In examining young converts for admission to the church, their consciences should not be ensnared by examining them too extensively or minutely *on doctrinal points*. From the manner in which examinations are conducted in some churches, it would seem as if they expected that young converts would be all at once acquainted with the whole system of divinity, and able to answer every puzzling question in theology. The effect of it is, that young converts are perplexed and confused, and give their assent to things they do not understand, and thus their conscience is ensnared, and consequently weakened. Why, one great design of receiving young converts into the church, is to teach them doctrines, but if they are to be kept out of the church till they understand the whole system of doctrines, this end is defeated. Will you keep them out till one main design of receiving them is accomplished by other means? It is absurd. There are certain cardinal doctrines of Christianity, which are embraced in the experience of every true convert. And these, young converts will testify to them, on their examination, if they are questioned in such a way as to draw out their knowledge, and not in such a way as to puzzle and confound them. The questions should be such, as are calcu-

lated to draw out from them, what they have learned by experience, and not what they may have got in theory before or since their conversion. The object is, not to find out how much they know, or how good scholars they are in divinity, as you would examine a school, or a number of young men striving for a premium. It is to find out whether they have a *change of heart*, to learn whether they have experienced the great truths of religion by their power in their own souls. You see therefore how absurd, and injurious too, it must be, to examine as is sometimes done, like a lawyer at the bar, cross-examining a suspicious witness. It should rather be like a faithful physician anxious to find out his patient's true condition, and therefore leading his mind, by inquiries and hints, to disclose the real symptoms of his case.

You will always find, if you put your questions right, that real converts will see clearly those great fundamental points, the divine authority of the scriptures, the necessity of the influences of the Holy Spirit, the divinity of Christ, the doctrine of total depravity and regeneration, the necessity of the atonement, justification by faith, and the eternal punishment of the wicked.[3] By a proper course of inquiries you will find all these points come out, as a part of their experience, if you put your questions in such a way that they understand them.

A church session in this city have, as we are informed, passed a vote, that no person shall join that church till he will give his assent to the whole Presbyterian Confession of Faith, and adopt it as his "rule of faith and practice and Christian obedience." That is, they must read the book through, which is about three times as large as this hymn-book, and must understand it, and agree to it all, before they can be admitted to the church, before they can make a profession of religion, or obey the command of Christ. By what authority does a church say that no one shall join their communion till he understands all the points and technicalities of this long confession of faith? Is that their charity, to cram this whole confession of faith down the throat of a young convert, before they let him so much as come to the communion? He says, "I love the Lord Jesus Christ, and wish to obey his command." "Very well, but do you understand and adopt the confession of Faith?" He says, "I don't know, for I never read

---

[3] This definition of the "great fundamental points" of the gospel became the basis of evangelicalism in most denominations during the latter part of the nineteenth century.

that, but I have read the Bible, and I love that, and wish to follow the directions in it, and to come to the table of the Lord." "Do you love the confession of faith? If not, YOU SHAN'T COME," is the reply of this charitable session, "you shan't sit down at the Lord's table, till you have adopted all this confession of faith." Did Jesus Christ ever authorise a church session to say this — to tell that child of God, who stands there with tears, and asks permission to obey his Lord, and who understands the grounds of his faith, and can give a satisfactory reason of his hope, to tell him he cannot join the church till he understands the confession of faith? No doubt, Jesus Christ is angry with such a church, and he will show his displeasure in a way that admits of no mistake, if they do not repent. Shut the door against young converts till they swallow the confession of faith! And will such a church prosper? Never.

No church on earth has a right to impose its extended confession of faith on a young convert, who admits the fundamentals of religion. They may let the young convert know their own faith on ever so many points, and they may examine him, if they think it necessary, as to his belief; but suppose he has doubts on some points not essential to Christian experience, as the doctrine of Infant Baptism, or of Election, or the Perseverance of the Saints, and suppose he honestly and frankly tells you he has not made up his mind concerning these points. Has any minister or church a right to say, he shall not come to the Lord's table, till he has finished all his researches into these subjects? That he shall not obey Jesus Christ till he has fully made up his mind on every such point, on which Christians, acknowledged and devoted ones too, differ among themselves? I would sooner cut off my right hand than debar a convert under such circumstances. I would teach a young convert as well as I could in the time before he made his application, and I would examine him candidly as to his views, and after he was in the church, I would endeavor to make him grow in knowledge as he grows in grace. And by just as much confidence as I have that my own doctrines are the doctrines of God, I should expect to make him adopt them, if I could have a fair hearing before his mind. But I never would bid one, whom I charitably believed to be a child of God, to stay away from his Father's table, because he did not see all I see, or believe all I believe, through the whole system of divinity. The thing is utterly irrational, ridiculous and wicked.

4. Sometimes persons who are known to entertain a hope, *dare not make a profession* of religion for fear they should be deceived. I would always deal decidedly with such cases. A hope that will not warrant a profession of religion, is manifestly worse than no hope, and the sooner it is torn away the better. Shall a man hope he loves God, and yet dares not obey Jesus Christ? Preposterous. Such a hope had better be given up at once.

5. Sometimes persons professing to be converts will make an excuse for not joining the church, that they can *enjoy religion just as well* without it. This is always suspicious. I should look out for such characters. It is almost certain they have no religion. Ordinarily, if a person does not desire to be associated with the people of God, he is rotten at the bottom. It is because he wants to keep out of the responsibilities of a public profession. He has a feeling within him, that he had rather be free, so that he can by and by go back to the world again if he likes, without the reproach of instability or hypocrisy. Enjoy religion just as well without obeying Jesus Christ! It is false on the face of it. He overlooks the fact that religion *consists* in obeying Jesus Christ.

III. I am to consider the importance of giving right instruction to young converts.

Ordinarily, their Christian character through life is moulded and fashioned according to the manner in which they are dealt with when first converted. There are many who have been poorly taught at first, but have been afterwards *re-converted*, and if they are *then* dealt with properly, they may be made something of. But the *proper* time to do this is when they are first brought in, when their minds are soft and tender, and easily yield to the truth. Then they may be led with a hair, if they think it is the truth of God. And whatever notions in religion they get then, they are apt to cleave to for ever afterwards. It is almost impossible to get away a man's notions that he got when he was a young convert. You may reason him down, but he cleaves to them. How often is it the case where persons have been taught certain things when first converted, and they afterwards get a new minister, who teaches somewhat differently, these people will perhaps rise up against him as if he was going to subvert the faith and carry away the church to error, and throw every thing into confusion. Thus you see that young converts are thrown into the hands of the church, and it depends on the church to mould them, and form them into Christians of the right stamp. — Much of their future comfort and usefulness depends on the manner in which they are instructed at the outset. The future character of the church, the progress of revivals, the coming of the millennium, depend on having right instruction given, and a right direction of thought and life to those who are young converts.

IV. I am to mention some things which *should not be taught* to young converts.

1. "You won't always feel as you do now." When the young convert is rejoicing in his Savior, and calculating to live for the glory of God and the good of mankind, how often is he met with this reply, "You won't always feel so." Thus preparing his mind to expect that he shall backslide, and not to be much surprised when he does. This is just the way the devil wants young converts dealt with, to have old Christians tell them your feelings will not last, and that by and by you will be as cold as we are. It has made my heart bleed to see it. When the young convert has been pouring out his warm heart to some old professor, and expecting to meet the warm burstings of a kindred spirit responding to his own, what does he meet with? This cold answer, coming like a northern blast over his soul, "You won't always feel so." SHAME! Just preparing the young convert to expect that he shall backslide as a matter of course; so that when he begins to decline, as under the very influences of this instruction it is most likely he will, it produces no surprise or alarm in his mind, but he looks at it just as a thing of course, doing as every body else does.

I have heard it preached as well as prayed, that seasons of backsliding are necessary to test the church. They say, "when it rains, you can find water any where: it is only in seasons of drought that you can tell where the deep springs are." Wonderful logic! And so you would teach that Christians must get cold and stupid, and backslide from God, and for what reason? Why forsooth, to show that they are not hypocrites. Amazing! You would prove that they *are* hypocrites in order to show that they are not.

Such doctrine as this is the very last that should be taught to young converts. They should be told that now they have only begun the Christian life, and that their religion is to consist in *going on in it*. They should be taught to go forward all the time, and grow in grace continually. Do not teach them to taper off their religion, let it grow smaller and smaller till it comes to a point. God says, "The path of the just, is as the shining light, that shineth more and more to the perfect day." Now whose path is that, which grows dimmer and dimmer until the perfect night? They should be brought to such a state of mind, that the first indications of decay in spirituality or zeal will alarm them and spur them up to duty. There is no need that young converts should backslide as they do. Paul did not backslide. And I do not doubt that this very doctrine, "You won't always feel so," is one of the grand devices of Satan to bring about the result which it predicts.

2. "Learn to walk by faith and not by sight." This is sometimes said to young converts in reference to their continuing to exhibit the power of religion, and is a manifest perversion of scripture. If they begin to lose their faith and zeal, and to get into darkness, some old professor will tell them, "Ah, you can't expect to have the Savior always with you, you have been walking by sight, you must learn to walk by faith and not by sight." That is, you must learn to get as cold as death, and then hang on to the doctrine of the Saint's Perseverance, as your only ground of hope that you shall be saved. And that is walking by faith. *Cease to persevere and then hold on to the doctrine of perseverance.* "One of guilt's blunders, and the loudest laugh of hell." And living in the enjoyment of God's favor and the comforts of the Holy Ghost, they call walking by sight! Do you suppose young converts *see* the Savior at the time they believe on him? When they are so full of the enjoyments of heaven, do you suppose they see heaven, and so walk by sight? It is absurd on the face of it. It is not faith, it is *presumption*, that makes a backslider hold on to the doctrine of perseverance as if that would save him, without any sensible exercises of godliness in his soul. Those who attempt to walk by faith in this way had better take care, or they will walk into hell with their faith. Faith indeed! Faith without works is dead. — Can dead faith make the soul live?

3. "Wait till you see whether you can hold out." When a young convert feels zealous and warm-hearted, and wants to lay himself out for God, some *prudent* old professor will caution him not to go too fast. "You had better not be too forward in religion, till you see whether you can hold out; for if you take this high ground and then fall, you will disgrace religion." That is, in plain English, "Don't do any thing that *constitutes* religion, till you see whether you have religion." Religion consists in obeying God. Now these wise teachers tell a young convert, "Don't obey God till you see" — what? — till you see whether you have obeyed

him — or, till you see whether you have gotten that substance, that mysterious thing which they imagine is created and put into a man, like a lump of new flesh, and called religion. This waiting system is all alike, and all wrong. There is no scripture warrant for telling a person to wait, when the command of God is upon him, and the path of duty before him. Let him go along.

Young converts should be fully taught that this is the only consistent way to find out whether they have any religion. — The only evidence they can have is to find that they are heartily engaged in *doing* the will of God. To tell him to wait, therefore, *before* he does these things, till he first gets his evidence, is reversing the matter, and is absurd.

4. "Wait till you get strength, before you take up the cross." This is applied to various religious duties. Sometimes it is applied to prayer, just as if prayer was a cross. But I have known young converts advised not to attempt to pray in their families, or not to attempt quite yet to pray in meetings and social circles. "Wait till you get strength." Just as if they would get strength without exercise. Strength *comes* by exercise. You cannot get strength by lying still. Let a child lie in the cradle all his life, and he would never have any strength, he might grow in size, but he never could be any thing more than a great baby. This is a law of nature. There is no substitute for exercise in producing strength. The body as every one knows, can be strengthened *only* by exercise. — It is so in the nature of things. And it is just so with the mind. It is so with the affections, so with the judgment, so with conscience. All the powers of the soul are strengthened by exercise. I need not now enter into the philosophy of this. — Every body knows it is so. If the mind is not exercised, the brain will not grow, and the man will become an idiot. If the affections are not exercised he will become a stoic. To talk to a convert about neglecting Christian action till he gets strength, is absurd. If he wants to gain strength, let him go to work.

5. Young converts *should not be made sectarian* in their feelings. They should not be taught to dwell upon sectarian distinctions, or to be sticklish about sectarian points. They ought to examine these points, at a proper time, and in a proper way, and make up their minds for themselves, according to their importance. But they should not be taught to dwell upon them, or to make much of them in the outset of their religious life. Otherwise there is great danger that their whole religion will run into sectarian-

ism. I have seen some most sad and melancholy exhibitions of the effects of this upon young converts. And whenever I see professed converts taking a strong hold of sectarian peculiarities, no matter of what denomination of Christians, I always feel in doubt about them. When I hear them asking, "Do you believe in the doctrine of election?" or, "Do you believe in sprinkling?" or, "Do you believe in plunging?" I feel sad. I never knew such converts to be worth much. Their sectarian zeal soon sours their feelings, eats out all the heart of their religion, and moulds their whole character into sinful sectarian bigotry. They generally become mighty zealous for the traditions of the elders, and very little concerned for the salvation of souls.

V. I proceed to mention some of the things which it is important should be taught to young converts.

1. One of the first things young converts should be taught is to distinguish between emotion and principle in religion. Do you understand me? I am going to explain what I mean, but I want you to get hold of the words, and have them fixed in your mind. What I want is to have you distinguish between *emotion* and *principle*.

By emotion, I mean that state of mind of which we are conscious, and which we call *feeling*, an involuntary state of mind, that arises of course when we are in certain circumstances or under certain influences. There may be high-wrought feelings, or they may subside into tranquillity, or disappear entirely. But these emotions should be carefully distinguished from religious principle. By principle I do not mean any substance or root or seed or sprout implanted in the soul. But I mean the voluntary decision of the mind, the firm determination to act out duty and to obey the will of God, by which a Christian should always be governed. When a man is fully determined to obey God, because it is RIGHT that he should obey God, I call that principle. Whether he feels any lively religious emotion at the time or not, he will do his duty cheerfully, and readily, and heartily, whatever may be the state of his feelings. This is acting upon principle, and not from emotion. Many young converts have mistaken views upon this subject, and depend almost entirely upon the state of their feelings to go forward in duty. Some will not lead in a prayer-meeting, unless they *feel* as if they could make an eloquent prayer. Multitudes are influenced almost entirely by their emotions, and they give way to this, as if they thought themselves under no obligation to duty, unless urged on by some strong emotion. They will be very zealous in religion when they feel like it, when their emotions are warm and lively, but they will not act out religion consistently, and carry it into all the concerns of life. They are religious only as they are impelled by a gush of feeling.

Young converts should be carefully taught, when duty is before them to *do it*. However dull their feelings may be, if duty calls, DO IT. Don't wait for feeling, but DO IT. Most likely the very emotions for which you would wait will be called into exercise when you begin to do your duty. If the duty is prayer, for instance, and you have not the feelings you would wish, do not wait for emotions before you pray, but pray, and open your mouth wide. And in doing it, you are most likely to have the emotions for which you were inclined to wait, and which constitute the conscious happiness of religion.

2. Young converts should be taught that they have *renounced the ownership of all their possessions, and of themselves, or if they have not done this they are not Christians.* They should not be left to think that any thing is their own, their time, property, influence, faculties, bodies or souls. "Ye are not your own;" all belongs to God; and when they submitted to God they made a free surrender of all to him, to be ruled and disposed of at his pleasure. They have no right to spend one hour as if their time was their own. No right to go any where, or do any thing, for themselves, but should hold all at the disposal of God, and employ all for the glory of God. If they do not, they ought not to call themselves Christians, for the very idea of being a Christian is to renounce self and become entirely consecrated to God. A man has no more right to withhold any thing from God, than he has to rob or steal. It is robbery in the highest sense of the term. It is an infinitely higher crime than it would be for a clerk in a store to go and take the money of his employer, and spend it on his own lusts and pleasures. I mean, that for a man to withhold from God, is a higher crime against HIM, than a man can commit against his fellow man, inasmuch as God is the owner of all things in an infinitely higher sense than man can be the owner of any thing. If God calls on them to employ any thing they have, their money, or their time, or to give their children, or to dedicate themselves, in advancing his kingdom, and they refuse, because they want to use them in their own way, or prefer to do something else, it is vastly more blamable than for a clerk or an agent to go and em-

bezzle the money that is intrusted him by his employer, and spend it for his family, or lay it out in bank stock or in speculation for himself.

God is, in an infinitely higher sense, *the owner* of all, than any employer can be said to be the owner of what he has. And the church of Christ never will take high ground, never will be disentangled from the world, never will be able to go forward without these continual declensions and backslidings, until Christians, and the churches generally, take the ground, and hold to it, that it is just as much a matter of discipline for a church member practically to deny his stewardship as to deny the divinity of Christ, and that covetousness fairly proved shall just as certainly exclude a man from communion as adultery.

The church is mighty orthodox in *notions*, but very heretical in practice, but the time must come when the church will be just as vigilant in guarding orthodoxy in practice as orthodoxy in doctrine, and just as prompt to turn out heretics in practice as heretics that corrupt the doctrines of the gospel. In fact, it is vastly more important. The only design of doctrine is to produce practice, and it does not seem to be understood by the church, that *true faith* "works by love and purifies the heart," that heresy in *practice*, is proof conclusive of heresy in sentiment. The church are very sticklish for correct doctrine and very careless about correct living. This is preposterous. Has it come to this, that the church of Jesus Christ is to be satisfied with correct notions on some abstract points, and never reduce her orthodoxy to practice? Let it be so no longer.

It is high time these matters were set right. And the only way to set them right, is to begin right with those who are just entering upon religion. Young converts must be told that they are just as worthy of damnation, and that the church cannot and will not hold fellowship with them, if they show a covetous spirit, and turn a deaf ear when the whole world is calling for help, as if they were living in adultery, or in the daily worship of idols.

3. Teach them *how to cultivate a tender conscience*. I have often been amazed to find how little conscience there is, even among those who we hope are Christians. And here we see the reason of it. Their consciences were never cultivated. They never were taught and told how to cultivate a tender conscience. They have not even a natural conscience. They have dealt so rudely with their conscience, and resisted it so often, that it has got

blunted, and does not act. The usefulness of a Christian, greatly depends on his knowing how to cultivate his conscience. Young converts should be taught to keep their conscience just as tender as the apple of the eye. They should watch their conduct and their motives, and let their motives be so pure and their conduct so disinterested as not to offend or injure or stifle conscience. They should maintain such a habit of listening to conscience, that it will be always ready to give forth a stern verdict on all occasions. It is astonishing to see how much the conscience may be cultivated by a proper course. If rightly attended to, it may be made so pure, and so powerful, that it will always respond exactly to the word of God. Present any duty to such a Christian, or any self-denial, or suffering, and only show him the word of God and he will do it without a word. In a few months if properly taught and attended to, young converts may have a conscience so delicately poised that the weight of a feather will turn them. Only bring a "Thus saith the Lord," and they will be always ready to do that, be it what it may.

4. Young converts should be taught *to pray without ceasing*. That is, they should always keep up a watch over their minds, and be all the time in a prayerful spirit. They should be taught to pray always, whatever may take place. For the want of right instruction on this point many young converts suffer loss and get far away from God. For instance, sometimes it happens that a young convert will fall into some sin, and then he feels as if he could not pray, and instead of overcoming this he feels so distressed that he waits for the keen edge of his distress to pass away. Instead of going right to Jesus Christ in the midst of his agony, and confessing his sin out of the fulness of his heart and getting a renewed pardon and peace restored, he waits till all the keenness of his feelings have subsided, and then his repentance, if he does repent, is cold and half-hearted. Let me tell you beloved, never to do this, but when your conscience presses you, go then, right to Christ, confess your sin fully, and pour out your heart to God.

Sometimes people will neglect to pray because they are in the dark, and feel no desire to pray. But that is the very time when they need prayer. That is the very reason why they ought to pray. You should go right to God and confess your coldness and darkness of mind. Tell him just how you feel. Tell him "O Lord, I have no desire to pray, but I know I ought to pray." And the first you will know, the Spirit may come, and lead your heart out in prayer, and all the dark clouds will pass away.

5. Young converts should be faithfully warned against adopting *a false standard in religion*. They should not be left to fall in behind old professors, and keep them before their minds as a standard of holy living. They should always look at Christ as their model. Not aim at being as good Christians as the old church members, and not think they are doing pretty well because they are as much awake as the old members of the church. But they should aim at being holy, and not rest satisfied till they are as perfect as God.[4] The church has been greatly injured for the want of attention to this matter. Young converts have come forward, and their hearts were warm and their zeal ardent enough to aim at a high standard, but they were not directed properly, and so they soon settle down into the notion that what is good enough for others is good enough for them, and therefore they never aim higher than those who are before them. And in this way the church instead of rising with every revival higher and higher in holiness, is kept nearly stationary.

6. Young converts should be taught *to do all their duty*. They should never make a compromise with duty, nor think of saying "I will do *this* as an offset for neglecting *that*." They should never rest satisfied till they have done their duty of every kind, in relation to their families, the church, Sabbath Schools, the impenitent around them, the disposal of their property, the conversion of the world. Let them do their duty, as they feel it when their hearts are warm; and never attempt to pick and choose among the commandments of God.

7. They should be made to feel that *they have no separate interest*. It is time Christians were made actually to feel that they have no interest whatever, separate from the interest of Jesus Christ and his kingdom. They should understand that they are incorporated into the family of Jesus Christ, as members in full, so that their whole interest is identified with his. They are embarked with him, they have gone on board, and taken their all. And henceforth they have nothing to do, or nothing to say, except as it is connected with this interest and bearing on the cause and kingdom of Christ.

8. They should be taught to *maintain singleness of motive*.

---

[4] The views expressed here and on pp. 415–416 and 419–420 contain the seeds that later sprouted into Finney's "Oberlin Perfectionism."

Young converts should not begin to have a double mind, on any subject, or let selfish motives mingle in with good motives in any thing they do. But this can never be, so long as Christians are allowed to hold a separate interest of their own, distinct from the interest of Jesus Christ. If they feel that they *have* a separate interest, it is impossible to keep them from *regarding* it, and having an eye to it as well as to Christ's interest, in many things that they do. It is only by becoming entirely consecrated to God, and giving up all to his service, that they can ever keep their eye single and their motives pure.

9. They should set out with a determination to *aim at being useful in the highest degree possible.* They should not rest satisfied with merely being useful, or remaining in a situation where they can do *some* good.[5] But if they see an opportunity where they can do more good, they must embrace it, whatever may be the sacrifice to themselves. No matter what it may cost them, no matter what danger or what suffering, no matter what change in their outward circumstances, or habits, or employments it may lead to. If they are satisfied that they will on the whole do more good, they should not even hesitate. How else can they be like God? How can they think to bear the image of Jesus Christ, if they are not prepared to do all the good that is in their power? When a man is converted he comes into a new world, and should consider himself as a new man. If he finds he can do the most good by remaining in his old employment, let it be so. But if he can do more good in some other way, he is bound to change. It is for the want of attention to this subject, in the outset, that Christians have got such low ideas on the subject of duty. And that is the reason why there are so many useless members in our churches.

10. They must be taught *not to aim at comfort but usefulness in religion.* There are a great many spiritual epicures in the churches, who are all the while seeking to be happy in religion, while they take very little pains to be useful. They had much rather spend their time in singing joyful hymns, and in pouring out their happy feelings in a gushing tide of exultation and triumph, than to spend it in agonizing prayer for sinners, or in going about and pulling dying men out of the fire. They seem to feel as if they were born to enjoy themselves. But I do not think such

---

[5] The connection between Finney's theology and the social reform spirit of the era is epitomized in these lines. See also pp. 425–426 and 452–453.

Christians show such fruits as to make their example one to be imitated. Such was not the temper of the apostles. They travailed for souls, and laboured in weariness and painfulness, and in deaths oft, to save sinners. Nor is it safe. Ordinarily, Christians are not qualified to drink deep at the fountain of joy. In ordinary cases, a deep agony of prayer for souls is more profitable than high flights of joy. Let young converts be taught, plainly, not to calculate upon a life of joy and triumph. They may be called to go through fiery trials. Satan may sift them like wheat. But they must go forward, not calculating so much to be happy as to be useful, not talking about comfort but duty, not desiring flights of joy and triumph, but hungering and thirsting after righteousness, not studying how to create new flights of rapture, but how to know the will of God, and do it. They will be happy enough in heaven. There they may sing the song of Moses and the Lamb. And they will in fact enjoy a more solid and rational happiness here, by thinking nothing about it, but patiently devoting themselves to do the will of God.

11. They should be taught *to have moral courage*, and not to be afraid of going forward in duty. The Bible insists fully on Christian boldness and courage, in action as a duty. I do not mean that they should indulge in their bravadoes, like Peter, telling what they will do, and boasting of their courage. The boaster is generally a coward at heart. But I mean moral courage, a humble and fixed decision of purpose, that will go forward in any duty, unangered and unawed, with the meekness and firmness of the Son of God.

12. They should be so instructed as to be *sound in the faith*. That is, they should be early made, as far as possible, complete and correct in regard to their doctrinal belief. As soon as may be, without turning their minds off from their practical duties, in promoting the glory of God and the salvation of men, they should be taught fully and plainly, all the leading doctrines of the Bible. Doctrinal knowledge is indispensible to growth in grace. Knowledge is the food of the mind. "That the soul be without knowledge," says the Wise Man, "It is not good." The mind cannot grow without knowledge, any more than the body without food. And therefore it is important that young converts should be thoroughly indoctrinated, and made to understand the Bible. By indoctrinating I do not mean teaching the catechism, but teaching them to draw knowledge from the fountain head. Create in their

minds such an appetite for knowledge that they will eat the Bible up, will devour it, will love it and love it all. *All* scripture is profitable, that the man of God may be perfect, thoroughly furnished unto all good works.

13. Great pains should be taken to *guard young converts against censoriousness*. Young converts, when they first come out on the Lord's side, and are all warm and zealous, sometimes find old professors so cold and dead that they are strongly tempted to be censorious. This should be corrected immediately, otherwise the habit will poison their minds and destroy their religion.

14. They must *learn to say, No*. This is a very difficult lesson to many. See that young woman. Formerly she loved the gay circle, and took delight in its pleasures. She joined the church, and then found herself aloof from all her old associates. They ask her not now, to their balls and parties, because they know she will not join them, and perhaps they keep entirely away for a time, for fear she should converse with them about their souls. But by and by they grow a little bold, and some of them venture to ask her just to take a ride with a few friends. She does not like to say, No. They are her old friends, only a few of them are going, and surely a ride is so innocent a recreation, that she accepts the invitation. But now she has begun to comply, the ice is broken, and they have her again as one of them. It goes on, and she begins to attend their social visits — "only a few friends," you know, till by and by the carpet is taken up for a dance, and the next thing, perhaps, she is gone to a sleigh ride, on Saturday night, and comes home after midnight, and then sleeps all the forenoon on the Sabbath to make up for it, perhaps communion Sabbath too. All for the want of learning to say, No.

See that young man. For a time he was always in his place, in the Sabbath school and in the prayer meeting. But by and by his old friends begin to treat him with attention again, and they draw him along step by step. Every one seems a very small thing, and it would look like rudeness to deny so small a thing. He reasons that if he refuses to go with them in things that are innocent, he will lose his influence with them. And so he goes on, till prayer meeting, Bible class, and even Bible and closet are neglected. Ah, young man, stop there! Go only a little farther without learning to say, No, and you are gone. If you do not wish to hang up the cause of Christ to scorn and contempt, learn to resist the beginnings of temptation. Otherwise it will come upon you, by and by, like the letting out of water.

15. They should be taught, *what is and what is not Christian experience*. It is necessary, both for their comfort and their usefulness, that they should understand this, so that they need not run themselves into needless distress for the want of that which is by no means essential to Christian experience, nor flatter themselves that they have more religion than they really exercise. But I cannot dwell on this topic to-night.

16. Teach them not to count any thing *a sacrifice which they do for God*. Some persons are always telling about the sacrifices they make in religion. I have no confidence in such piety. Why keep telling about their sacrifices, as if every thing they did for God was a sacrifice If they *loved* God they would not talk so. If they considered their own interests and the interest of Christ, identical, they would not talk of making sacrifices for Christ; it would be like talking of making sacrifices for *themselves*.

17. It is of great importance that young converts should be taught *to be strictly honest*. I mean more by this than perhaps you would think. It is a great thing to be strictly honest. It is being very different from the world at large, and very different even from the great body of professors of religion. The holiest man I ever knew, and one who had been many years a Christian and a minister, once made the remark to me, "Brother, it is a great thing to be strictly honest, upright, straight, in every thing, so that God's pure eye can see that the mind is perfectly upright." [6]

It is of the utmost importance that young converts should understand what it is to be strictly honest *in every thing*, so that they can maintain a conscience void of offence, both towards God and towards men. Alas, alas! how little conscience there is. How little of that real honesty, that pure, simple uprightness, which ought to mark the life of a child of God. How little do many regard even an express promise. I heard the other day of a number of individuals who subscribed to the Anti-Slavery Society, and not half of them will pay their subscriptions. The plea is, that they signed when they were under excitement and they don't choose to pay. Just as if their being excited released them from the obligation to keep their promise. Why it is just as dishonest as it would

---

[6] Finney is probably referring here to Daniel Nash. See Lecture XIII, p. 235, note 8.

be to refuse payment of a note of hand. They promised, signed their names, did they, and now won't pay? And they call that honesty!

I have heard that there are a number of men in the city who have signed hundreds of dollars for the Oneida Institute,[7] promising to pay the money when called on; and when they were called on they refused to pay the money. And the reason was, they had all turned abolitionist in the Institute. Very well. Suppose they have. Does that alter your promise? Did you sign on the condition that if they got Abolitionism introduced there you should be clear? If you did, then you are clear. — But if you gave your promise without any condition, it is just as dishonest to refuse as if you had given a note of hand. — And yet some of you might be almost angry if any body should charge you with refusing to pay money when you promised it.

Look at this seriously. Who does God say will go to heaven? Read the 15th Psalm, and see. "He that sweareth to his own hurt, and *changeth not*." What do you think of that? If a man has promised any thing, *except it be to commit sin*, let him keep his promise, if he means to be honest or to go to heaven. But here these people will make promises, and because they cannot be prosecuted, will break them as easily as if they were nothing. They would not let a note be protested at the bank. Why? Because they would lose credit, and would be sued. But the Oneida Institute, and the Anti-Slavery Society, and other societies, will not sue for the money, and therefore these people take some offence at something, and refuse to pay. Is this honest? Will such honesty as this get them admitted to heaven? What? Break your promises, and go up and carry a lie in your hand before God? If you refuse or neglect to fulfill your promise you are a *liar*, and if you persist in this, you shall have your part in the lake that burns with fire and brimstone. I would not for ten thousand worlds, die with money in my hands, that I had unrighteously withheld from any other object to which I had promised it. Such money will "eat like a canker."

If you are *not able* to pay the money, that is a good excuse. But then say so. But if you refuse to pay what you have promised,

---

[7] Oneida Institute was a manual labor school founded in 1827 in Whitesboro, New York, "to educate young men who have ultimately in view the gospel ministry." It was founded by Finney's former pastor, George W. Gale, and Theodore Weld was for a time a pupil and agent for the school. See Fletcher, *Oberlin*, I, 35ff.

because you have altered your mind, rely upon it, you are guilty. You cannot pray till you pay that money. — What will you pray? "O Lord, I promised to give that money, but I altered my mind, and broke my promise, but still, O Lord, I pray thee to bless me, and forgive my sin, although I keep my money, and make me happy in thy love." Will such prayers be heard? Never.

But, brethren, I find it impossible to touch upon all the points I intended to speak upon, and so I will break off here, and finish this subject another time.

XX

INSTRUCTION OF YOUNG CONVERTS

Text. — "Feed my lambs." — John xxi. 15.

I remarked on this text in my last lecture, and was obliged, for want of time, to omit many of the points which I wished to present in regard to the

INSTRUCTION OF YOUNG CONVERTS.

To-night I propose to continue the subject by noticing.

I. Several other points upon which young converts ought to be instructed.

II. To show the manner in which young converts should be treated by the church.

III. Mention some of the evils which naturally result from defective instructions given in that stage of Christian experience.

I. I shall pursue the subject, taking it up where I left off, by mentioning some further instructions which it is important should be given to young converts.

1. It is of great importance that young converts should early be made to understand *what religion consists in*. Perhaps you will be surprised at my mentioning this. "What! Are they converts, and do they not know what religion consists in?" I answer, They would know, if they had had no instruction but such as is drawn from the Bible. But multitudes of people have imbibed such *notions* about religion, that not only young converts, but a great part of the *church* do not know what religion consists in, so as to have a clear and distinct idea of it. There are many ministers who do not. I do not mean to say that they have no religion, for it may be charitably believed they have; but what I mean is, that they do not discriminate as to what it consists in, and cannot give a correct statement of what does and what does not constitute real religion. It is important that young converts should be taught.

INSTRUCTION OF YOUNG CONVERTS

Negatively, what religion does not consist in

(1.) Not in *doctrinal knowledge*. Knowledge is essential to religion, but it is not religion. The devil has doctrinal knowledge, but he has no religion. A man may have doctrinal knowledge to any extent, without a particle of religion. Yet some people have very strange ideas on this subject, as though having doctrinal knowledge indicated an increase of piety. I once heard a remark of this kind. In a certain instance, where some young converts had made rapid progress in doctrinal knowledge, a person who saw it said, "How these young converts grow in grace." Here he confounded improvement in knowledge with improvement in piety. The truth was, that he had no means of judging of their growth in grace, and it was no evidence of it because they were making progress in doctrinal knowledge.

(2.) They should be taught that religion is *not a substance*. It is not any root, or sprout, or seed, or any thing else in the mind, as a *part of the mind itself*. Persons often speak of religion as if it was something that may be covered up in the mind, just as a spark of fire may be covered up in the ashes, which does not show itself, and which produces no effects, but yet lives and is ready to act as soon as it is uncovered. And in like manner they think they may have religion, as something remaining *in* them, although they do not manifest it by obeying God. But they should be taught that this is not the nature of religion. It is no part of the mind itself, or of the body, nor is it a root, or seed, or spark, that can exist and yet be hid and produce no effects.

(3.) Teach them that religion does not consist in raptures, or ecstacies, or high flights of feeling. There may be a great deal of these where there *is* religion. But it ought to be understood that they are all involuntary emotions, and may exist in full power where there *is no* religion. They may be the mere workings of the imagination, without any truly religious affection at all. Persons may have them to such a degree as actually to swoon away with ecstacy, even on the subject of religion, without having any religion. I have known one person almost carried away with rapture, by a mere view of the natural attributes of God, his power and wisdom, as displayed in the starry heavens, and yet the person had no religion. Religion is obedience to God, the voluntary submission of the soul to the will of God.

(4.) Neither does religion consist in going to meeting or reading the Bible, or praying, or any other of what are commonly called *religious duties*. The very phrase, "religious duties," ought to be stricken out of the vocabulary of young converts. They should be made to know that these acts are not religion. Many become very strict in performing certain things, which they call religious duties, and suppose that is being religious; while they are careless about the ordinary duties of life, which in fact constitute A LIFE OF PIETY. Prayer may be an expression and an act of piety, or it may not be. Going to church or to a prayer meeting, may be considered either as a means, an act, or an expression of pious sentiment; but the performance of these, does not constitute a man a Christian, and there may be great strictness and zeal in these, without a particle of religion. If young converts are not taught to discriminate, they may be led to think there is something peculiar in what are called religious duties, and to imagine they have a great deal of religion because they abound in certain actions that are commonly called *religious* duties, although they may at the same time be very deficient in honesty or faithfulness or punctuality, or temperance, or any other of what they choose to call their common duties. They may be very punctilious in some things, may tithe mint, annis and cummin, and yet neglect the weightier matters of the law, justice and the love of God.

(5.) Religion does not consist in *desires to do good actions*. Desires that do not result in choice and action are not virtuous. Nor are such desires necessarily vicious. They may arise involuntarily in the mind, in view of certain objects, but while they produce no voluntary act, they are no more virtuous or vicious than the beating of the pulse, except in cases where we have indirectly willed them into existence, by voluntarily putting ourselves under circumstances to excite them. The wickedest man on earth may have strong desires after holiness. Did you ever think of that? He may see clearly that holiness is the only and indispensable means of happiness, he naturally desires it. It is to be feared, that multitudes are deceiving themselves with the supposition, that a desire for holiness, as a means of happiness, is religion. Many doubtless, give themselves great credit for desires that never result in *choosing* right. They feel desires to do their duty, but do not choose to do it, because upon the whole they have still stronger desires not to do it. In such desires, there is no virtue. An action or desire to be virtuous in the sight of God, must be an act of the will. People often talk most absurdly on this subject, as though their desires had any thing good, while they remain mere desires. "I think

I desire to do so and so." But do you do it. "O no, but I often feel a desire to do it." This is practical Atheism.

Whatever desires a person may have, if they are not carried out into actual *choice* and action, they are not virtuous. And no degree of desire is itself virtuous. If this idea could be made prominent, and fully riveted in the minds of men, it would probably annihilate the hopes of half the church, who are living on their good desires, while doing nothing for God.

(6.) They should be made to understand that nothing which is selfish, is religion. Whatever desires they may have, and whatever choices and actions they may put forth, if after all the reason of them is selfish, there is no religion in them. A man may just as well commit sin in praying, or reading the Bible, or going to meeting, as in any thing else, if his motive is selfish. Suppose a man prays simply with a view to promote his own happiness. Is that religion? What is it, but attempting to make God his almighty servant? It is nothing else but to attempt a great speculation, and put the universe, God and all, under contribution to make him happy. It is the sublime degree of wickedness. It is so far from being piety, that it is in fact superlative wickedness.

(7.) Nothing is acceptable to God, as religion, unless it be performed heartily, to please God. No outward action has any thing good, or any thing that God approves, unless it is performed from right motives, and from the heart.

(*b*) Young converts should be taught fully and positively that all religion consists in obeying God from the heart. All religion consists in voluntary action. All that is holy, all that is lovely in the sight of God, all that is properly called religion, consists in voluntary action, in voluntarily obeying the will of God from the heart.

2. Young converts should be taught that the duty of *self-denial* is one of the leading features of the gospel. They should understand that they are not pious at all, any farther than they are willing to take up the cross daily, and deny themselves, for Christ. There is but very little self-denial in the church, and the reason is, that the duty is so much lost sight of, in giving instruction to young converts. How seldom are they told that self-denial is the leading feature of Christianity. In pleading for benevolent objects, how often will you find, that ministers and agents do not even ask Christians to *deny themselves* for the sake of promoting the object. They only ask them to give what they can spare as well as not, or in other words, to offer unto the Lord that which costs

them nothing. What an abomination! They only ask for the surplus, for what they do not want, for what they can give just as well as not. There is no religion in this kind of giving. A man may give to a benevolent object, a hundred thousand dollars, and there would be no religion in it, if he could give it as well as not, and there was no self-denial in it. Jesus Christ exercised self-denial to save sinners. So has God the Father exercised self-denial in giving his Son to die for us, and in sparing us, and in bearing with our perverseness. The Holy Ghost exercises self-denial, in condescending to strive with such unholy beings to bring them to God. The angels exercise self-denial, in watching over this world. The apostles planted the Christian religion among the nations by the exercise of self-denial. And are we to think of being religious without any self-denial? Are we to call ourselves Christians, the followers of Christ, the temples of the Holy Ghost, and to claim fellowship with the apostles, when we have never deprived ourselves of any thing that would promote our personal enjoyment for the sake of promoting Christ's kingdom? Young converts should be made to see that unless they are willing to lay themselves out for God and ready to sacrifice life and every thing else for Christ, they have not the spirit of Christ, and are none of his.

3. They must be taught *what sanctification is*. "What!" you will say, "do not all who are Christians know what sanctification is?" No, many do not. Multitudes would be as much at a loss to tell intelligibly what sanctification is, as they would be to tell what religion is. If the question were asked of every professor of religion in this city, What is sanctification? I doubt if one in ten would give a right answer. They would blunder just as they do when they undertake to tell what religion is, and speak of it as something dormant in the soul, something that is put in, and lies there, something that may be practised or not, and still be in them. So they speak of sanctification as if it were a sort of washing off of some defilement, or a purging out of some physical impurity. Or they will speak of it as if the faculties were steeped in sin, and sanctification is taking out the stains. This is the reason why some people will pray for sanctification, and practise sin, evidently supposing that sanctification is something that *precedes* obedience. They should be taught that sanctification is not something that precedes obedience, some change in the nature or the constitution of the soul. But sanctification *is obedience*, and, as a

progressive thing, consists in obeying God more and more perfectly.[1]

4. Young converts should be taught so as to understand *what perseverance is*. It is astonishing how people talk about perseverance. As if the doctrine of perseverance was "Once in grace, always in grace," or "Once converted, sure to go to heaven." This is not the idea of perseverance. The true idea is, that if a man is truly converted, HE WILL CONTINUE TO OBEY GOD. And as a *consequence*, he will surely go to heaven. But if a person gets the idea, that because he is converted, *therefore* he will assuredly go to heaven, that man will almost assuredly go to hell.

5. Young converts should be taught *to be religious in every thing*. They should aim to be religious in every department of life and in all that they do. If they do not *aim* at this, they should understand that they have no religion at all. If they do not intend and aim to keep all the commandments of God, what pretence can they make to piety? Whosoever shall keep the whole law and yet offend in one point, he is guilty of all. He is justly subject to the whole penalty. If he disobeys God habitually in one particular, he does not in fact obey him in any particular. Obedience to God *consists* in the state of the heart. It is being willing to obey God; willing that God should rule in all things. But if a man habitually disobeys God, in any one particular, he is in a state of mind, that renders obedience in any thing else impossible. To say that in some things a man obeys God, out of respect to his authority, and that in some other things he refuses obedience, is absurd. The fact is, that obedience to God consists in an obedient state of heart, a preference of God's authority and commandments to every thing else. If, therefore, an individual *appears* to obey in some things, and yet perseveringly and knowingly disobeys in any one thing, he is deceived. He offends in one point, and this proves that he is guilty of all; in other words, that he does not, *from the heart*, obey at all. A man may pray half of the time and have no religion; if he does not keep the commandments of God, his very prayer will be hateful to God. "He that turneth away his ear from hearing the law, even *his prayer* shall be abomination." Do you hear that? If a man refuses to obey God's law, if he refuses to comply with

---

[1] This doctrine of progressive sanctification eventually became Finney's concept of perfectionism. For a discussion of Oberlin Perfectionism, see Wright, *Finney*, pp. 203ff., and Frank H. Foster, *A Genetic History of the New England Theology* (Chicago, 1907), pp. 453ff.

any one duty, he cannot pray, he has no religion, his very devotions are hateful.

6. Young converts, by proper instructions, are easily brought to be "temperate in all things." Yet this is a subject greatly neglected in regard to young converts, and almost lost sight of in the churches. There is a vast deal of intemperance in the churches. I do not mean intemperate *drinking*, in particular, but intemperance in eating, and in living generally.[2] There is in fact but little conscience about it in the churches. And therefore the progress of reform in the matter is so slow. Nothing but an enlightened conscience can carry forward a permanent reform. Ten years ago, most ministers used ardent spirit, and kept it in their houses to treat their friends and their ministering brethren with. And the great body of the members in the churches did the same. Now there are but few of either, who are not actual drunkards, that will do it. But still there are many that indulge without scruple in the use of wine. There are some ministers, and many professors, who will drink down wine that has as much spirit in it as brandy and water. This is intemperance. Chewing and smoking tobacco are mere acts of intemperance. If they use these mere stimulants when there is no necessity for it, what is that but intemperance? That is not being temperate in all things. Until Christians shall have a conscience on this subject, and be made to feel that they have no right to be intemperate in any thing, they will make but little progress in religion. It is well known, or ought to be, that TEA AND COFFEE have no nutriment in them.[3] They are mere stimulants. They go through the system without being digested. The milk and sugar you put in them are nourishing. And so they would be just as much so, if you mixed them with rum, and made milk punch. But the tea and the coffee afford no nourishment. And yet I dare say, that a majority of the families in this city give more in a year for their tea and coffee, than they do to save the world from hell. Probably this is true respecting entire churches. Even agents of benevolent societies will dare to go through the

---

[2] This emphasis upon proper eating and drinking led Finney in the early 1840's to become an ardent advocate of the dietary reforms of Sylvester Graham, the inventor of the Graham cracker. Finney tried to impose Grahamism upon all the students at Oberlin but eventually gave it up. See Fletcher, *Oberlin*, I, 316ff.

[3] It is amusing to note that this sentence and the eight sentences that follow it were omitted from the English edition of these lectures published in London in 1840 by Simpkin, Marshall, and Co. No Englishman could see the sinfulness of drinking tea.

churches soliciting funds, for the support of missionary and other institutions, and yet use tea, coffee, and in some cases tobacco. Strange! There is now in this city, an agent employed in soliciting funds, who uses all three of these worse than useless stimulants. And he is, moreover, a minister of the gospel! No doubt many are giving *five times* as much for mere intemperance, as they give for every effort to save the world. If the church could be made to know how much they spend for what are mere poisons and nothing else, they would be amazed. Sit down and talk with many persons, and they will strenuously maintain that they cannot get along without these stimulants, these poisons, and they cannot give them up — no, not to redeem the world from eternal damnation. And very often they will absolutely show anger if argued with, just as soon as the argument begins to pinch their consciences. O, how long shall the church show her hypocritical face at the Monthly Concert, and pray God to save the world, while she is actually *throwing away* five times as much for sheer intemperance, as she will give to save the world. Some of you may think these are little things, and that it is quite beneath the dignity of the pulpit to lecture against tea and coffee. But I tell you it is a great mistake of yours, if you think these are little things, when they make the church odious in the sight of God, by exposing her hypocrisy and lust. Here is an individual who pretends he has given himself up to serve Jesus Christ, and yet he refuses to deny himself any darling lust, and then he will go and pray, "O Lord, save the world; O Lord, thy kingdom come." I tell you it is hypocrisy. Shall such prayers be heard? Unless men are willing to deny themselves, I would not give a groat for the prayers of as many such professors as would cover the whole United States.

These things must be taught to young converts. It must come to this point in the church, that men shall not be called Christians, unless they will cut off the right hand, and pluck out the right eye, and deny themselves for Christ's sake. A little thing? See it poison the spirit of prayer? See it debase and sensualize the soul! Is that a trifle beneath the dignity of the pulpit? When these intemperate indulgencies, of one kind and another, cost the church five times if not fifty times more than all they do for the salvation of the world.

An estimate has recently been made, showing, that the United States consume seven millions of dollars worth of coffee yearly; and who does not know, that a *great* part of this is consumed by the *church*. And yet, grave ministers and members of Christian churches are not ashamed to be seen countenancing this enormous waste of money; while at the same time, the poor heathen are sending upon every wind of heaven, their agonizing wail for help. Heaven calls from above, "go preach the Gospel to every creature." Hell groans from beneath, and ten thousand voices cry out from heaven, earth and hell, "*Do something to save the world!*" *Do it now*! O, NOW, or millions more are in hell through your neglect. And, O, tell it not in Gath, the church, the *ministry*, will not deny even their lusts, to save a world. Is this Christianity? What business have you to use Christ's money for such a purpose? Are you a steward? Who gave you this liberty? Look to it, lest it should be found at last, that you have preferred self-gratification to obedience, and made a "god of your belly."

The time to teach these things with effect, is when they are young converts. If they are not properly taught then, if they get a wrong habit, and begin with an easy, self-indulgent mode of living, it is rare that they are ever thoroughly reformed. I have conversed with old professors on these subjects, and have been astonished at their pertinacious obstinacy in indulging their lusts. And I am satisfied that the church never can rise out of this sloth until young converts are faithfully taught in the outset of their religious course to be temperate *in all things*.

7. They should be taught to have just as *much religion in all their business*, as they have in prayer, or in going to meeting. They should be just as holy, just as watchful, aim just as singly at the glory of God, be just as sincere and solemn, in all their daily employments, as when they come to the throne of grace. If they are not, their Sabbath performances will be an abomination.

8. They should be taught that it is necessary for them to be *just as holy as they think ministers ought to be*. There has for a long time been an idea that *ministers* are bound to be holy and practice self-denial. And so they are. But it is strange they should suppose that ministers are bound to be *any more* holy than other people. They would be shocked to see a minister show levity, or running after the fashions, or getting out of temper, or living in a fine house, or riding in a coach. O, that is dreadful. It does not look well in a minister. Indeed! For a minister's wife to wear such a fine bonnet, or such a silk shawl. O, no. But they think nothing of all this in a layman, or a layman's wife. That is no offence at all. I am not saying that these things do look well in a minister;

I know they do not. But they look in God's eyes, just as well in a minister as they do in a layman. *You* have no more right to indulge in vanity and folly and pride than a minister. Can you go to heaven without being sanctified? Can you be holy without living for God, and doing all that you do to his glory? I have heard professedly good men speak against ministers' having large salaries, and living in an expensive style, when they themselves were actually spending a great deal more money for the support of their families, than any ministers. What would be thought of a minister, living in the style in which many professors of religion, and elders of churches are living in this city. Why, every body would say that they were hypocrites. But, it is just as much an evidence of hypocrisy in a layman to spend God's money to gratify his lusts, or to please the world, or his family, as it is for a minister to do the same. It is distressing to hear some of our foremost laymen talk of its being dishonorable to religion, to give ministers a large salary, and let them live in an expensive style, when it is a fact that *their* own expenses, are, for the number of their families and the company they have, far above that of almost any minister. All this arises out of fundamentally wrong notions imbided while they were young converts. Young converts have been taught to expect that ministers will have all the religion, especially all the self-denial, and so long as this continues there can be no hope that the church will ever do much for the glory of God, or for the conversion of the world. There is nothing of all this in the Bible. Where has God said, "You, ministers, love God with all your heart and soul and mind and strength," or "You ministers do all that you do to the glory of God?" This is said to all alike, and he who attempts to excuse himself from any duty or self-denial, from any watchfulness or sobriety, by putting it off upon ministers do all that you do to the glory of God?" This is said to all alike, and he who attempts to excuse himself from any duty or self-of proving himself a hypocrite, and paying the forfeit of his foolishness in hell.

Much depends on the instructions given to young converts. If they once get into the habit of supposing that they may indulge in things which they would condemn in a minister, it is ten to one if they ever get out of it.

8. They should *aim at being perfect*. Every young convert should be taught, that if it is not his *purpose* to live without sin, he has not yet began to be religious. What is religion, but a su-

preme purpose of heart or disposition to obey God? If there is not this, there is no religion at all. It is one thing to *profess to be perfect*, and another thing to profess and feel that you *ought to be* perfect. It is one thing to say, that men ought to be perfect, and can be if they are so disposed, and another thing to say that *they are* perfect. If any are prepared to say that they are perfect, all I have to say is, Let them prove it. If they are so, I hope they will show it by their actions, otherwise we can never believe they are perfect.

But it is the duty of all to *aim* at being perfect. It should be their constant purpose, to live wholly to God, and obey all his commandments. They should live so, that if they should sin it would be an inconsistency, an exception, an individual case, in which they act contrary to the fixed and general purpose and tenor of their lives. They *ought not* to sin at all, they are bound to be as holy as God is, and young converts should be taught to set out in the right course, or they will never be right.

9. They should be taught *to exhibit their light*.

If the young convert does not exhibit his light, and hold it up to the world, it will go out. If he does not bestir himself, and go forth and try to enlighten those around him, his light will go out, and his own soul will soon be in darkness. Sometimes young converts seem disposed to be still and not do any thing in public till they get a great deal of light, or a great deal of religion. But this is not the way. Let the convert use what he has, let him hold up his little twinkling rush-light, boldly and honestly, and *then* God will pour in the oil and make him like a blazing torch. But God will not take the trouble to keep a light burning that is hid. Why should he? Where is the use?

This is the reason why so many people enjoy so little in religion. They do not exert themselves to honor God. They keep what little they do enjoy, so entirely to themselves, that there is no good reason why God should bestow blessings and benefits on them.

10. They should be taught *how to win souls to Christ*. Young converts should be taught particularly what to do for this, and how to do it, and then taught to live for this end as the great leading object of life. How strange has been the course sometimes pursued. These persons have been converted, and there they are. They get into the church and then they are left to go along in their business just as they did before; they do nothing and are

taught to do nothing for Christ, and the only change is that they go more regularly to church on the Sabbath, and let the minister *feed them* as it is called. But suppose he does feed them, they do not grow strong, for they cannot digest it, because they take no exercise. They become spiritual dyspeptics. Now the great object for which Christians are converted and left in this world, is to pull sinners out of the fire. If they do not effect this, they had better be dead. And young converts should be taught this as soon as they are born into the kingdom. The first thing they do should be to go to work for this end, to save sinners.

II. I am to show how young converts should be treated by the church.

1. Old professors *ought to be able* to give young converts a *great deal of instruction*, and they *ought to give it*. The truth is, however, that the great body of professors in the churches do not know how to give good instruction to young converts, and if they attempt to give them instruction, give only that which is false. The church ought to be able to teach her children; and when she receives them, she ought to be as busy in training them to act, as mothers are in teaching their little children such things as they will need to know and do hereafter. But this is far enough from being the case generally. And we can never expect to see young converts habitually taking right hold of duty, and going straight forward without declension and backsliding, until young converts shall be intelligently trained by the church.

2. Young converts should not be kept back behind the rest of the church. How often is it found that the old professors will keep the young converts back behind the rest of the church, and prevent them from taking any active part in religion, for fear they should become spiritually proud. Young converts in such churches, are rarely or never called on to take a part in meetings, or set to any active duty, or the like, for fear they should become lifted up with *spiritual pride*. Thus the church become the *modest keepers* of their humility, and teach them to file in behind the old, stiff, dry, cold members and elders, for fear that if they are allowed to do any thing for Christ, it will make them proud. Whereas, the very way to make young converts humble and keep them so, is to put them to their work and keep them there. That is the way to keep God with them, and as long as God is with them, *He* will take care of their humility. Keep them constantly engaged in religion, and then the Spirit of God will dwell with them, and then they

will be kept humble by the most effectual process. But if young converts are left to fall in behind the old professors, where they never can do any thing, they will never know what spirit they are of, and this is the very way to run them into danger of the worst species of spiritual pride.

3. They should be watched over, by the church, and warned of their dangers, just as a tender mother watches over her young children. Young converts do not know at all the dangers by which they are surrounded. The devices of the devil, the temptations of the world, the power of their own passions and habits, and the thousand forms of danger, they do not know; and if not properly watched and warned, they will run right into danger. See that mother watching her little child. Does she let it put its little hand in the candle, or allow it to creep where it will fall, because its own blindness and ignorance does not prevent it from desiring to do so? The church should watch over and care for her young children, just as mothers watch their little children in this great city, for fear the carts may run over them, or they may stray away and be lost; or as they watch them while growing up, for fear they may be drawn into the whirlpools of iniquity. The church should watch over all the interests of her young members, know where they are, and what are their habits, temptations, dangers, privileges, state of religion in their hearts, spirit of prayer. Look at that anxious mother, when she sees paleness gather round the little brow of her child. "What is the matter with you, my child? Have you eaten something improper? Have you taken cold? What ails you?" O, how different it is with the children of the church, the lambs that the Savior has committed to the care of his churches. Alas! Instead of restraining her children, and taking care of them, the church lets them go any where, and look out for themselves. What should we say of a mother who should knowingly let her little child totter along to the edge of a precipice? Should we not say she was horribly guilty for doing so, and that if the child should fall and be killed, its blood would rest on the mother's head? What then is the guilt of the church, in knowingly neglecting her young converts? I have known churches, where young converts were first totally neglected, and regarded with suspicion and jealousy; nobody went near them to strengthen or encourage or counsel them; nothing was done to lead them to usefulness, to teach them what to do, or how to do it, or open to them a field of labor. And then — what then? Why, when they find that young converts

cannot stand every thing, and find them growing cold and backward under their own treatment, they just turn round and abuse them, because they did not hold out. This is all wrong.

4. *Be tender in reproving them.* When Christians find it necessary to reprove young converts, they should be exceedingly careful of their manner in doing it. Young converts should be faithfully watched over by the elder members of the church, and when they begin to lose ground, or to turn aside, they should be promptly admonished, and if necessary, reproved. But to do it in a wrong manner is worse than not to do it. It is sometimes done in a manner that is abrupt, harsh, coarse, and apparently censorious, more like scolding than like brotherly admonition. Such a manner, instead of inspiring confidence, or leading to reformation, is just calculated to harden the heart of the young convert, and confirm him in his wrong courses, while at the same time it closes his mind against the influence of such censorious guardians. The heart of a young convert is tender, and easily grieved, and sometimes a single unkind look will set them into such a state of mind as will fasten their errors upon them and make them grow worse and worse.

You who are parents know how important it is when you reprove your children, that they should see that you do it from the best of motives, for their benefit, because you wish them to be good, and not because you are angry. Otherwise they will soon come to regard you as a tyrant, rather than a friend. Just so with young converts. Kindness and tenderness, even in reproof, will win their confidence, and attach them to you, and give an influence to your brotherly instructions and counsels, so that you can mould them into finished Christians. Instead of this, if you are severe and critical in your manner, that is the way to make them think you wish to lord it over them. Many persons, under pretence of being *faithful*, as they call it, often hurt young converts in such a severe and overbearing manner, as to drive them away, or perhaps crush them into despondency and apathy. Young converts have but little experience, and are easily thrown down. They are just like a little child when it first begins to walk. You see it tottering along, and there it stumbles over a straw. You see the mother take up every thing from the floor, when her little one is going to try to walk. Just so with young converts. The church ought to take up every stumbling block, and treat them in such a way as to make them see that if they are reproved, Christ is in it, and then they will receive it as it is meant, and it will do them good.

5. Kindly *point out things that are faulty in the young convert* which he does not see. He is but a child, and knows but little about religion, and will of course have a great many things that he needs to learn, and a great many that he ought to mend. Whatever there is that is wrong in spirit, or unlovely in his deportment, or uncultivated in manner, that will impede his usefulness or impair his influence as a Christian, ought to be kindly pointed out and corrected. To do this in the right way, however, requires great wisdom. Christians ought to make it a subject of much prayer and reflection, that they may do it right, so as not to do more hurt than good. If you rebuke him merely for the things that he did not see, or did not know to be improper, it will grieve and disgust him. Such instruction should be carefully timed, often it is well to take the opportunity after you have been praying together, or after a kind conversation of religious subjects, calculated to make him feel that you love him, and seek his good, and earnestly desire to promote his sanctification, his usefulness, and his happiness. Then a mere hint will often do the work. Just suggest that "Such a thing in your prayer" or "your conduct so and so, did not strike me pleasantly. Had you not better think of it, and perhaps you will judge better to avoid the same thing again." Do it right, and you will help and do him good. Do it wrong and you will do ten times more hurt than good. Often young converts will err, through ignorance, their judgment is unripe, and they need time to think and make up an enlightened judgment, on some point that at first appears to them doubtful. In such cases the church should treat them with great kindness and forbearance. Should kindly instruct them and not denounce them at once for not seeing, at first, what perhaps they did not themselves understand, for years after they were converted.

6. Do not *speak of the faults of young converts*, behind their backs. This is quite too common among old professors, and by and by they hear of it; and what an influence it must have to destroy the confidence of young converts in their elder brethren, to grieve their hearts and discourage them, and perhaps drive them away from the good influence of the church.

III. I am to mention some of the evils of defective instruction to young converts.

1. If not fully instructed, they never will be fully grounded in right principles. If they have right fundamental principles, this will lead them to adopt a right course of conduct in all particular

cases. In forming a Christian character, a great deal depends on establishing those fundamental principles which are correct on all subjects. If you look at the Bible you will see there, that God teaches right principles which we can carry out in detail in right conduct. If the education of young converts is defective, either in kind or degree, you will see it in their character all their lives. This is the philosophical result, just what might be expected, and must be always so. It could be shown, if I had time, that almost all the practical errors that have prevailed in the church, are the natural results of certain false dogmas, which have been taught to young converts, and which they have been made to swallow as the truth of God, at a time when they were so ignorant as not to know any better.

2. If the instruction given to young converts is not correct and full, they will not grow in grace, but their religion will dwindle away and decay. Their course instead of being like the path of the just, growing brighter and brighter to the perfect day, will grow dimmer and dimmer, and decay and finally perhaps go out in darkness. Wherever you see young converts let their religion taper off till it comes to nothing, you may understand that it is the proper result of defective instruction. The philosophical result of teaching young converts the truth, and the whole truth, is that they grow stronger and stronger. Truth is the food for the mind — it is what gives the mind strength. And where religious character grows feeble, rely upon it, in nine cases out of ten it is owing to their being neglected or falsely instructed, when they were young converts.

3. They will be left justly in doubt whether they are Christians. If their early instruction is false, or defective, there will be so much inconsistency in their lives, and so little real evidence of real piety, that they themselves will finally doubt whether they have any. Probably they will live and die in doubt. You cannot make a little evidence go a great ways. If they do not see clearly they will not live consistently, if they do not live consistently they can have but little evidence, and if they have not evidence they must doubt, or live in presumption.

4. If young converts are rightly instructed and trained, it will generally be seen that they will take the right side on all great subjects that come before the church. Subjects are continually coming up before the churches, on which they have to take ground, and on many of them there is often no little difficulty to make all

the church take right ground. Take the subject of Tracts, or Missions, or Sabbath schools, or Temperance, for instance, and what cavils, and objections, and resistance, and opposition, have been encountered from members of the church in different places. Go through the churches, and where you find young converts have been well taught, you never find *them* making difficulty, or raising objections, or putting forth cavils. I do not hesitate to charge it upon pastors and older members of churches, that there are so many who have to be dragged up to the right ground on all such subjects. If they had grounded them well in the principles of the gospel at the outset, when they were first converted, they would have seen the application of their principles to all these things. It is curious to see, and I have had great opportunity to see, how ready young converts are to take right ground, on any subject that may be proposed. See what they are willing to do for the education of ministers, for missions, for moral reform, for the slaves. If the great body of young converts from the late revivals had been well grounded in gospel principles, you would have found in them, throughout the church, but one heart and one soul in regard to every question of duty that occurs. Let their early education be right, and you have got a body of Christians that you can depend on. If it had been general in the church, O, how much more strength there would have been in all her great movements for the salvation of the world.

5. If young converts are not well instructed they will inevitably backslide. If their instruction is defective, they will probably live in such a way as to disgrace religion. The truth, kept steadily before the mind of a young convert, in proper proportions, has a natural tendency to make him grow up into the *fullness* of the stature of a perfect man in Christ Jesus. If any one point is made too prominent in the instruction given, there will probably be just that disproportion in his character. If he is fully instructed on some points and not in others, you will find a corresponding defect in his life and character.

If the instruction of young converts is greatly defective, they will press on in religion no further than they are strongly propelled by the emotions of their first conversion. As soon as that is spent they will come to a stand, and then they will decline and backslide. And ever after you will find that they will go forward *only* when aroused by some powerful excitement. These are your periodical Christians, that are so apt to wake up in a time of revival, and bluster about as if they had the zeal of an angel, a few days, and then die away as dead and cold as a northern winter. O how desirable, how infinitely important it is, that young converts should be *so* taught, that their religion will not depend on impulses and excitements, but that they will go steadily onward in the Christian course, advancing from strength to strength, giving forth a clear and safe and steady light all around.

REMARKS.

I. The church is verily guilty for her past neglect, in regard to the instruction of young converts.

Instead of bringing up their young converts to be working Christians, the churches have generally acted as if they did not know how to employ young converts, or what use to make of them. They have acted like a mother, who has a great family of daughters, and knows nothing how to set them to work, and so suffers them to grow up idle and untaught, useless and despised, and to be the easy prey of every designing villain.

If the church had only done her duty in training up young converts to work, and labour for Christ, the world would have been converted long ago. But instead of this, how many churches even oppose young converts, when they attempt to set themselves at work for Christ. Multitudes of old professors look with suspicion upon every movement of young converts, and talk against them, and say, "They are too forward, they ought not to put themselves forward, but *wait* for those who are older." There is *waiting* again. Instead of bidding young converts "God speed," and cheering them on when they take hold with warm hearts and strong hands, very often they hinder them and perhaps put them down. How often have young converts been stopped from going forward, and turned in behind a formal, lazy, inefficient church, till their spirit is crushed, and their zeal extinguished, and after a few ineffectual struggles to throw off the cords, they conclude to sit down with the rest and WAIT. In many places, young converts cannot even attempt to hold a prayer-meeting by themselves, but what the pastor, or some of the deacons, rebukes them for being so forward, and charges them with spiritual pride. "Oh, ho! you are *young converts*, are you? and so you want to get together and call all the neighbors together to look at you, because you are young converts." You had better turn preachers at once. A celebrated Doctor of Divinity in New England boasted at a public table of his success in keeping all his converts still. He had great difficulty, he said, for they were in a terrible fever to do something, to talk, or pray, or get up meetings, but by the greatest vigilance he had kept it all down, and now his church was just as quiet as it was before the revival.[4] Wonderful achievement for a minister of Jesus Christ! Was that what the blessed Savior meant when he told Peter, "Feed my lambs?"

2. Young converts should be *trained to labour*, just as carefully as young recruits in an army are trained for war.

Suppose a captain in the army should get his company enlisted, and then take no more pains to teach and train and discipline them, than are taken by many pastors to train and lead forward their young converts. Why, the enemy would laugh at such an army. Call them soldiers! Why, as to any effective service, they are in a mere state of babyhood, they know nothing what to do or how to do it, and if you bring them up to the CHARGE, where are they? Such an army would resemble the church that does not train her young converts. Instead of being trained to stand shoulder to shoulder in the onset, they feel no practical confidence in their leaders, no confidence in their neighbors, no confidence in themselves, and they scatter at the first shock of battle. Look at the church now. Ministers are not agreed as to what shall be done, and many of them will turn and fight back against their brethren, quarreling about New Measures, or the Act and Testimony, or something. And as to the members, they cannot feel confidence when they see their leaders so divided. And then if they attempt to do any thing — Alas! alas! what ignorance, what awkwardness, what discord, what weakness, what miserable work they make of it. And so it must continue, until the church shall train up young converts to be intelligent, single-hearted, self-denying, working Christians. Here is an enterprise now going on in this city, which I rejoice to see. I mean the *Tract* enterprise — a blessed work.[5] And the plan is to train up a body of devoted Christians to do — what? — why to do what all the church ought to have been trained to do long ago, to know how to pray, and how to converse with people

---

[4] This is doubtless a reference to Lyman Beecher, but the occasion is unknown.

[5] The "tract enterprise" was an effort to spread the gospel among the unconverted by lending or giving away gospel tracts. This was an activity newly converted Christians often engaged in.

about their soul's salvation, and how to attend anxious meetings, and how to deal with inquirers, and how to SAVE SOULS.

3. The church has entirely mistaken the manner in which she is to be sanctified.

The experiment has been carried on long enough, of trying to sanctify the church, without finding any thing for them to do. But holiness consists in obeying God. And sanctification, as a process, means obeying him more and more perfectly. And the way to promote it in the church, is to give every one something to do. Look at these great churches, where they have 500 or 700 members, and get a minister to *feed* them from Sabbath to Sabbath, while there are so many of them together that the great part have nothing at all to do, are never trained to make any direct efforts for the salvation of souls. And in that way they are expecting to be sanctified and prepared for heaven. They never will be sanctified *so*. That is not the way God has appointed. Jesus Christ has made his people co-workers with him in saving sinners, for this very reason, because sanctification *consists in* doing those things which are required to promote this work. This is one reason why he has not employed angels in the work, or carried it on by direct revelation of truth to the minds of men. It is because it is necessary as a means of sanctification, that the church should sympathize with Christ in his feelings and his labours for the conversion of sinners. And in this way the entire church must move, before the world will be converted. When the day comes, that the whole church shall realize that they are here on earth as a body of missionaries, and shall live and labor accordingly, then will the day of man's redemption draw nigh.

Christian! if you cannot go abroad to labour why are you not a missionary in your own family? If you are too feeble even to leave your room, be a missionary there in your bedchamber. How many unconverted servants have you in your house? Call in your unconverted servants, and your unconverted children, and be a missionary to them. Think of your physician, perhaps, who is laying himself out to save your body, while he is losing his own soul, and you receive his kindness and never make him the greatest return in your power.

It is necessary that the church should take hold of her young converts at the outset, and set them to work, and set them to work right. The hope of the church is in the young converts.

4. We see what a responsibility rests on ministers, and elders,

and all who have opportunity to assist in training young converts. How distressing is the picture which often forces itself upon the mind, where multitudes are converted, and yet so little pains taken with the young converts, that in a single year you cannot tell the young converts from the rest of the church. And then to see the old church members turn round and complain of these young converts, and perhaps slandering them, when in truth these old professors themselves are most to blame. O, it is too bad. This *reaction* that people talk so much about after a revival, as if reaction was the necessary effect of a revival, it would never come, young converts never would backslide as they do, if the church were prompt and faithful in attending to their instruction. If they are truly converted, they *can be made* thorough and energetic Christians. And if they are not such, Jesus Christ will require it at the hands of the church.

XXI

BACKSLIDERS[1]

TEXT. — "The backslider in heart shall be filled with his own ways." — PROVERBS xiv. 14.

In remarking on this text I shall inquire,
I. Who are backsliders?
II. Mention some of the causes of backsliding. And
III. Some of the consequences of backsliding.
I. Who are backsliders?
1. The term backslide means to go back from a point. In its widest signification when applied to religion, it may mean the declension of any class of persons who *profess* religion, whether they *possess* it or not. If they have professed religion, and have at any time conformed their lives to its rules so far as to appear to be religious, and if they then go back from even the appearance of religion, they are called backsliders, although their profession may have been a mere form. So it is equally customary to call them backsliders, whether they apostatize wholly from all religion, or change to another religion. In this sense it is often used under the Old Testament dispensation. God's people used to be spoken of as backsliders, when they went off to idolatry, as well as when they grew lax and unprincipled in the duties of religion. In the sense in which I use the term to-night, I mean by a backslider to denote a person who is truly converted and is a Christian, but has left his first love. His zeal has grown cold. The ardor of his feelings and the depth of his piety are abated. Such a person is a "backslider in heart." He may keep up all the forms of religion, attend to worship, public and private, and read his Bible, and go through all these exercises regularly, but the spirit of it is gone — all the fine edge of pious feelings is blunted. He is a backslider in heart. Probably this applies to some of you who hear me to-night. God knows whether it does or not. Your own consciences will tell you,

[1] For the revised edition of 1868 Finney completely rewrote and slightly enlarged this lecture. He wrote it on the same text, however, and it does not differ significantly in its content from this original lecture.

if you will let them speak. Have you less ardor of feeling, less fixedness of purpose, less faithfulness in duty? If you have, then I mean *you*. God means you. He calls you backslider. That is your name — you, elder in the church; or you minister, if there be any such here; you woman — no matter what is your standing in the church, if that is the description of your character, then you are a backslider. And so you stand entered on the book of God.

2. The backslider is any one who was once converted, but who does not *enjoy secret prayer*, and hold daily communion with God. A man may keep up the form of prayer, he may be on his knees a great deal, and yet have no communion with God — not feel that God is present with him. He may pray ever so much, in form, and yet have no spirit of prayer. If in your secret prayer you do not actually draw near to God, you are either a backslider in heart or a hypocrite. No matter to what church you belong, or what office you hold, or what character you may bear in the sight of men; God regards you as a backslider, if you do not enjoy the spirit of prayer.

3. If you do not *enjoy the word of God*, you are a backslider in heart. If you do not habitually form your practical views from it, you are a backslider. If you do not delight in the Bible more than in any other book, if you find you can relish reading any commentary as well as you do the naked text itself, you have begun to backslide. I do not hesitate to say, that the man who finds he can relish the best commentary that ever was written, as well as he does the simple word of God, has begun to backslide. If he has gone still farther, and thinks he has read the Bible about enough, and that now he will take up other things and study, he is far gone. TAKE CARE, professor! If you find that when you read a chapter it is dark and uninteresting, your name before God is Backslider.

4. If you are *worldly minded*, you are a backslider. If you find the things of the world are uppermost in your mind, and occupy your first thoughts in the morning, or press spontaneously upon your attention as soon as you are alone, if your associations and thoughts and feelings are earthly, you are a backslider in heart.

5. If you do not feel your heart drawn out in *painful anxiety and prayer in view of the state of the church*, it is because you are a backslider. If you can look at the state of the churches in this city without pain, and grief of heart, and deep anxiety, you must be a backslider in heart.

6. If you are insensible how low the state of religion is, you

are a backslider. Many people, when they see congregations as large as usual, and when there are no dissensions among them, will say, "There is a very pleasant state of things among that people; it is a very prosperous parish; how quiet and peaceful every thing is there; it is delightful." And all this, notwithstanding there may be no conversions there, no souls saved. A person who can call that a pleasant and prosperous state for a congregation, must be either a backslider or a hypocrite. If he was not, he would never rest in such a state of things, he would never be satisfied until he knew that sinners were turning from their sins. The man that can rest satisfied with any thing short of this, must have, to say the least, but a very superficial piety.

7. When the wickedness of sinners does not distress and grieve you, it is a sign of backsliding. If any one can hear sinners profane the name of God, and see them break the Sabbath, or do other abominations, and not groan and sigh and pray and grieve for them, he must be a backslider. How little you feel like the Psalmist, when he says in regard to the wicked, "Rivers of waters run down mine eyes, because they keep not thy law." "Horror hath taken hold upon me, because of the wicked, that forsake thy law." "I beheld the transgressors and was grieved, because they kept not thy word." So does every Christian, who is not a backslider, grieve at the transgressions of the wicked.

8. A person may be known as a backslider, when his *secret prayers are short, and far between.* Persons who *enjoy* prayer, pray very frequently. If you pray but seldom, or if you do not pray as often as you eat, or do not spend as much time in communion with God as you do in gratifying your appetite, it is a sign you have backslidden. You did not do so when you enjoyed your first love. *Then* you had rather pray than eat. Your feeling was, that if you must cut short one, you would say, Let the body fast, but my soul must be fed. It is to be feared that very many in the church do not pray as much as they eat. They are not so frequent, nor so regular, and do not spend as much time. Let them take care. Depend upon it, if they do so, their table will prove a snare and a trap to them. He is a glutton, or worse, who spends more time in eating, than he spends with God in prayer.

9. When you *can perform secret prayer in a slight manner.* If a person can go to his closet and pray slightly, without any honest fervency of soul before God, or any wrestling with God for a blessing, it is proof that he is a backslider.

10. When you *suffer trifling excuses* to prevent your praying, either in secret, or in public. Point me to a man who absents himself from his closet for trifling reasons, or who is kept from the house of God by frivolous excuses, that man's name is backslider. If not, he would make eating and every thing else give way to his regular hours of devotion; and the reason would be, that he enjoyed more in prayer and the word of God, than in his daily food. Job says, "I have esteemed the words of his mouth more than my necessary food." If you find that a slight indisposition or inconvenience will keep you from the house of God, and lead you to set aside private duties, you are a backslider.

Perhaps I ought here to ask each one of you who hear me tonight, whether this is your case. Have I mentioned facts that apply to you, and that *you know* refer to you? Beloved, do any of you do these things? If you do, let the truth reach your hearts. Do not apply it to your neighbor, do not give it away, but take it home to yourself. You need it, it will do you good, if you will let it. If these things belong to you, just be honest with yourself, and write your name "Backslider," and act accordingly.

II. I am to mention some of the principal causes of backsliding.

1. *Ill will towards any person.* If ill will is harbored towards any being that God has made, you cannot continue to enjoy the presence of God. No matter how wicked that being may be, or how worthless, if you *hate* that being, you are the same as a murderer in the sight of God, and the spirit of God cannot dwell with you. You must be a backslider. Sometimes persons who are perhaps really injured, will let it fester in their minds, and rankle there, till it eats out all their piety. You cannot pray, when you have any ill will towards any. I defy you to pray with such a spirit in you. God will not hear your prayer. If you think you pray, you are deceived. You cannot have the spirit of prayer, nor hold communion with God, in such a state. "When ye stand praying, FORGIVE, if ye have aught against any, that your Father, also, which is in heaven may forgive you your trespasses."

2. Another fruitful source of backsliding is *having too much worldly business.* If you have so much worldly business as to absorb your thoughts, and take up too much of your time, you will backslide. You ought not to have so much business that you cannot pray. And you need not. God does not require it. He does not wish *his clerks* to have so much work to do that they cannot get time to confer with him, to tell him their situation and progress,

and ask his direction. If you accumulate so much business that you cannot attend on God, it is evident that you have no right views of business. If you really considered it as God's business, you would not think that this was the best way to please and honor God, to plunge into such a mass of worldly business that you cannot pray nor read your Bible. Business is a duty. I have always inculcated this, as you know, that it is a duty which God requires, to be busy, always usefully employed in some way. But to get into business that will encroach upon secret prayer and eat out religion, is all wrong. God never requires it. Men are God's stewards, and HE never employs them so that they cannot have time to commune with him. And if they run themselves into such a press of worldly business and cares, it is a sure sign that they have set up to do business for themselves, and not for God, and are now hastening to be rich. Otherwise they would never think of doing so, for they would have no motive. Love to God never shows itself in that way. And he who sets up business on his own account will surely backslide.

3. Another frequent cause of backsliding is being associated in business with an unconverted partner. Whoever forms such a connection after he is converted, will infallibly taper off his religion, his piety will decay, and he will backslide. — The reason is obvious. The unconverted man never pursues his business on Christian principles. He has not the beginning of such a principle. And therefore the business of the concern can never be conducted on such principles as God requires. And if you consent to have it conducted on any other principles, you are ruined. You will backslide, and your religion is ruined. God requires that business to be carried on for his glory, and if you do not have your business conducted in this way, you will backslide. I could mention a multitude of facts here, some of which you are acquainted with, where Christians have formed business connections with the unconverted and have been greatly injured, and often injured not only in their piety but their reputation also. I do not mean to say, that unconverted men are not honest, in the sight of men, and so far as men are concerned. But they are not honest in the sight of God, unless they do business *for him*. God requires them to carry on their business for his glory, and to be as faithful in it as if God was standing by, overlooking and directing it. Now where you find a man doing this, you have found an excellent Christian. But if you associate yourself with one who will do nothing of the kind, you do in fact go with him and adopt his principles. And then you will backslide. I do not

believe an instance to the contrary can be found, of a Christian who has taken a worldly partner, and has continued to enjoy religion. You must either offend your partner or offend God. You offend God at first by placing yourself in these circumstances. And no doubt you will continue to do so.

4. The *influence of worldly companions*, is a common cause of backsliding. When a person is converted, if he *continues* to associate as before with unconverted companions, he will backslide.

5. Taking a *worldly partner for life* is a cause of backsliding. In fact it is a proof that the individual is already a backslider. Before a Christian can give the heart to one who is not the friend of God, there must certainly be a departure from first love, which may be expected to grow worse till God gives him up to be filled with his own ways.

6. The fear of *giving offence to worldly friends* by being strictly religious, often produces backsliding. If you are so much afraid of hurting the feelings of your friends, that you will let them abuse God in your presence without reproof, you will soon be a backslider. Some will even go so far as to abuse God themselves, or break his laws for fear of giving offence, or for the sake of being civil to their ungodly companions.

7. When you begin to neglect or slightly perform the duty of secret prayer, you are on the brink of backsliding. I have mentioned this as one of the evidences of backsliding. It is also a cause. Backsliding often takes its rise here. I will mention the case of Mr. Oliphant of Auburn, whose memoir is recently published, by the title of "OLIPHANT'S REMAINS." [2] It is to be found at the bookstores, and I wish you would all read it, for you will find it to contain much that is useful. He was an excellent man, I knew him well. In the "Remains" you will find a letter which he wrote to his son, giving an account of his own backsliding. He says:

"I think I enjoyed religion for two years, or two and a half years, after my marriage. It then became evident, that I had lost nearly all sweet enjoyment of God. I had greatly relaxed in secret prayer — was off my guard, and began to fall an easy prey to sin. I began to associate with vain companions, and, of course, did not reverence the Sabbath, as I had formerly done. The cares of the world loaded me down, and I sought comfort in that which I

---

[2] John Oliphant (1771–1831). See *Memoirs and Remains of John Oliphant of Auburn, New York* (Auburn, N.Y., 1835), ed. Matthew LaRue Perrine.

knew was offensive to God. My conscience often smote me; but I still retained the form of prayer, with my wife and children. My spiritual father, Mr. Thomas Wills, died — I did not love his successor at Silver street — I became a rambler, on the Sabbath — and having 'itching ears,' I became fond of a variety in preaching; and sought it to my hurt. I injured my wife and children, by my example, and became involved in the fashion and pleasures of the world. I could distinctly perceive, how greatly I had forsaken my own mercy; but was so entangled that I had no heart to turn."

Here you see the starting point was a want of honest fervency in secret prayer. So it is often. Persons begin to pray shorter, and with less fervency and frequency, and then, the less they pray the less they desire to pray, and they still grow shorter and less frequent. The shorter the prayer, the shorter the next is like to be, until perhaps he gets where he can hardly be reclaimed. The way is to resist the beginnings. Take the alarm at the very outset. Just as soon as you see an inclination this way, shut down the gate and stop there, or your name will soon be Backslider.

8. Neglecting the Bible is another precursor of backsliding. This also is not only an evidence but a cause of backsliding. No individual, who has a Bible, can enjoy religion unless he reads it. And if he reads his Bible carelessly, he will backslide. It is amazing to see how little genuine Bible knowledge there is in the church. It shows how little they read the Bible, and how little real confidence they have in the Bible, how little they care about knowing its contents, and how little they believe in it, as the word of God.

9. A *want of strict honesty* is another prevailing cause of backsliding. A want of strict honesty will assuredly undermine all your religion. If you allow yourself to over-reach a little in business, or to take advantage of others in any way, you will backslide. You must not indulge the *least degree* of dishonesty. Unless you are as honest as if you had but another day to live, you cannot maintain your ground in religion. Almost all professors of religion in great cities do backslide. It is very seldom that you find any of the spirit of prayer in this city. I mean as I say, exactly. There are multitudes who are called praying people, and very good people too, but let any one talk to them about prayer, as the Bible talks on this subject, and they will not understand it: they will ask a thousand unmeaning questions, which they never would think of asking if they knew any-thing of the subject by experience. On this subject no man is right in theory, who has no experience. And the reason why

there is so little of the purest kind of piety in New York is, that so large a proportion of the church, almost every one, indulge in some kind of dishonesty, which eats out their religion. They do little things which are not purely honest. I know they pretend not to call them dishonest. They say every body understands it, and so on. But it is dishonest. And, furthermore, every body does not understand it. If every body did understand it, they would not do it. There would be no temptation to do it. Thus when a man asks a certain price for his goods, and afterwards takes less, showing that it was worth less to him, he will tell you he did not expect any body would take it at the first price. But, let me ask him, if any body *should* offer you the price you asked, would you not take it? If any body should suppose you were an honest man, who would not ask more for a thing than it was worth, would you take it, or would you tell him plainly that you intended to cheat him by getting an extra price for the article, if you found him ignorant or careless enough to be taken in? Or would you say, I will take less, I only asked more because I expected to be beaten down in the price; and would you, if what you at first asked, was offered, put the article down to its real value? [3]

I have been amazed at my own experience among professors of religion. Why, I hardly dare offer a man what he asks for a thing, for fear he is asking more than it is worth, and I hate to offer less for fear of appearing to desire to get the article for less than the real value, and because I refused to banter, I have found, that for some things I have given about double their value. They may say, it is generally understood. Suppose it is. Suppose it was generally understood that professors of religion would get drunk, or swear, or go to brothels, would that make it any better? Would that sanctify such things? But the purchaser, is often as much in fault, as the vender. Here is a customer comes in, and asks the lowest price of an article, and when told, he says, I will not give that, but offers you less. Now, although you offered it at the lowest price, at which you could well afford to sell it, rather than lose his custom, you let him have it, at his own price. In this case, he sins by tempting you, if he knows the value of the article, and you sin in letting him have it in that way, for you tempt him to banter and serve you so again.

[3] Part of Finney's great admiration for Lewis and Arthur Tappan was based on the fact that these merchants had adopted the one-price system in their dry goods store in New York. But the one-price system was exceptional at that time.

If you think you can practice a little dishonesty, and yet continue to enjoy the presence of God, you deceive yourselves. Any one who begins to do those things is either an arrant hypocrite, or he will backslide. The churches in this city never can enjoy religion steadily, they never can take hold of the work strongly, they never can know the power of prayer, until there is a reformation on this subject. Professors of religion must have conscience enough to be honest, and faith enough to believe in a judgment to come, and to believe that God listens to every bargain and every lie they tell behind the counter. You never can have much religion in New York, until you mend your ways. Go into that store, and hear a professor of religion bantering about a price, lowering down, and lowering down, because he has a sharp customer to deal with. I set that man down as a backslider. He is not honest. He is not doing business for God. He is not dealing like a steward. Do you suppose he is trying to make a good bargain for God? I tell you he is not speculating for God, but for himself. God does not need him to cheat on his account. All such persons will be filled with their own ways.

10. *Covetousness* is a fruitful cause of backsliding. Covetousness is idolatry. Withholding more than is meet, not only tendeth to poverty in outward things, but it produces spiritual leanness and poverty. Nothing has such a tendency to deaden religion. Such professors are always the most difficult to wake up, or to keep awake. Show me a man who holds the world with a close grasp, and you need not expect he will ever do much in religion. Sometimes you find a minister that loves money. He is good for nothing. He never will be of any use, as a minister, till he gives up that passion. Is he an elder in the church? Appoint no such man to the eldership. You might as well appoint the devil an elder, as a covetous man. He will only do hurt, he will hold the church back from all advancement. If you have any such elders, my counsel is, that you get rid of them as soon as you can. They are backsliders, and will always stand in the way. God expressly forbids having men for deacons who are "greedy of filthy lucre," and no church will prosper that tolerates such officers.

11. Another frequent cause of backsliding is the *want of perfect truth and sincerity in conversation*. People do not exactly call it *lying*, but yet it is so much like it that I know not what else to call it. A man cannot have a conscience void of offence, who is in the habit of exaggeration, coloring and reaching after the marvel-

lous in his stories. He will backslide. The only way to avoid it, is to tell always the naked, simple truth, just as carefully as if you was under oath, or as if you believed that God was listening to every word you say. Let your conversation be Yea, Yea, and Nay, Nay; for whatsoever is more than these, cometh of evil.

12. *Tale-bearing.* Show me a man or a woman, that loves to hear a secret and tell it, and I will show one who is already a backslider, and who will grow worse and worse, unless he repents. Any person that is always eager to tell the first news, will live and die a backslider, unless there is a reformation in this respect.

13. *Levity.* This is so obviously a cause of backsliding, that I need not dwell upon it.

14. *An intemperate way of living* causes a great deal of backsliding. I do not refer merely to the use of intoxicating liquor, but to every excess or intemperance in eating and drinking. I do not mean sitting at the table after dinner and drinking glass after glass of wine, till highly excited. Any one who will do this is too openly a backslider, to require remark. But I speak of those individuals who eat so much as to take off the edge of their feelings, and stupify their minds, so that they are not as bright and active after eating as before. He who allows himself to do this will certainly backslide. Show me a man who sits at his table and eats till he is more inclined to sleep than pray, and there is one who is beginning to be a glutton already. He cannot maintain himself in religion. Even if the articles of food are proper in themselves, it is impossible a man should indulge in such excess, and keep from backsliding. He is intemperate, God looks upon him so.

III. I proceed to mention some of the *consequences* of backsliding.

1. Backsliders become *the most unhappy people* in the world.

There are many who have known what it was to enjoy God, but now they neither enjoy God nor the world. They are away from home every where. They are unhappy when they rise up and when they lie down. They are like a bird that has no rest. They have too much religion to enjoy the world, and too much of the world to enjoy God. You who are in this state, know that this is true. You are filled with your own ways.

2. They will be the *most guilty people* on earth.

(1.) Their temper will be bad. Such persons are always full of complaining and out of humor. They are a stumbling block to sinners all around them. If it is a merchant, he is a stumbling block to his clerks. If it is a woman, she is a stumbling block to her servants.

(2.) They are more guilty, because they have a *clearer knowledge of duty*. Responsibility increases with a knowledge of duty, as every one knows, and as backsliders have had more light, they have of course more guilt.

(3.) They sin against *peculiar obligations*. They know what it is to feel the delight of pardoned sin. They have known what it was to feel the love of God shed abroad in the heart. If such a man backslides, his guilt is infinitely great.

(4.) They are *covenant breakers*, and are the more guilty on that account. They are not only under their responsibility to God's law, but they are perjured. To profess religion, and receive the sacraments, is to take an oath of allegiance to God. To backslide, is to break this oath, and in the eye of God, is perjury.

(5.) They *bring up an evil report* against religion itself. — By going after the world, its amusements, or its honors, or its riches, they say to sinners, "We have tried religion, and we have found out that you were right all the time; for religion will not answer by itself, and now we are coming back to enjoy the world again; we must have the world to make us happy." Thus, they are traitors to the cause of Christ. Who shall measure the guilt of such a course?

3. Backsliders render themselves the *most despicable of all people*.

Both sides condemn a backslider, and both despise him. And they have good reason for it, for he is a deserter from both. He first deserted from the world to join the church, and then he went back and tried to join the world again. Who can trust such a character? Who can help despising him. The ungodly despise him, he never can recover his former standing among them. The church distrust him and set him aside as a broken reed.

I know that the ungodly will sometimes praise a backsliding professor. They puff him up, and say, "We like such a Christian as that; he is consistent, he is charitable, he is a liberal man, such a Christian, is what we like." But they are not sincere in this. Let a man be as bad as the devil, if he is sick, which will he send for to come and pray with him, one of those backsliders, or a consistent Christian? Mark that man who puffs up the backsliders, and at another time you will hear him call them all hypocrites, and laugh at them; "Pretty Christians these, they love the world as well as

I do!" Whatever they may *say*, when it suits their turn, it is plain they do not respect backsliders. You are greatly deceived if you think you will get the good graces of the world by conformity to their ways. You are despised, and must be. It is not in the nature of man to respect such conduct.

4. They are the *most inconsistent people* in the world.

They adhere consistently to neither party. Their theory contradicts their practice, and their practice contradicts their theory. They pretend to believe in their hearts, what they notoriously contradict by their lives.

5. They are the *most difficult to please*.

No class of people make so much trouble for a minister. If he preaches so as to commend himself to their conscience, he hurts their feelings, and they oppose him. If he preaches so as to satisfy their feelings, then their conscience condemns him, and they have no confidence in his honesty. You come down to their standard and they know you are wrong. There is no such thing as pleasing them by preaching. If you crowd the truth home to them, they will grumble, and call it harsh and personal. If you do not preach so as to cut them to the quick, they know that it is wrong, and they will say, "That will never do, we shall never get awake by such preaching as this, the minister is as much asleep as we are, and we never can get along so." Thus they will always feel uneasy, let the preaching be as it may. If the preacher temporizes for the sake of pleasing, they will have no hearty confidence in him. They may pretend to be pleased, and may praise him, and tell what a great preacher he is, and what an agreeable man, may extol him to the clouds for a scholar or an orator. But they are not satisfied in conscience, for they know there cannot be any reasonable expectation of getting any good to themselves, or having a revival, under such preaching. They know that the minister *ought* to preach differently, and they feel that he *must* preach differently, or they must get another minister, or there never will be a revival. A minister ought not to conciliate the feelings of professors who are in a backslidden state, by any compromise, but he ought to tear open their hearts, and pour in the burning truth, till he can drive them out from their bed of slumber and death.

5. Very often, backsliders are the *most hardened people* to be found. They are so used to the gospel and all its motives, that they cease to be moved by it. You may hold up the most solemn and piercing truths, you may roll a world of responsibility upon

their consciences, and they do not feel. And after a while, the more you use the means to arouse them, the more they will be hardened, until it seems impossible to move them.

6. They are the *most loathsome people in the world*. Christ uses language in regard to backsliders, in his epistle to the church at Laodicea, which fully expresses this. "I would thou wert either cold or hot. So then, because thou art neither cold nor hot, I will spew thee out of my mouth." God seems to loathe them, he cannot endure them, and threatens to spew them out as a most loathsome thing. Backslider! How can you attempt to go near to God, when he feels so? Perhaps I am speaking to some here who *know* you are backsliders. You know that if you go before God he will loathe you and spew you out, he cannot bear you.

7. They are *most injurious* to the cause of religion. A backslider does more hurt to the cause than an infidel. He does more to prejudice the world against religion, more to prevent the conversion of sinners, more to favor the designs of the devil, than any other person in the world.

8. Backsliders are the *most hypocritical* of all people. They serve neither God nor the devil, sincerely. They have forsaken the devil, so that they no longer serve him with singleness of heart, and have given themselves to God, but now they do not serve him. They are hypocrites on both sides. Neither God nor the devil can trust them.

9. When an individual backslides, if he continues in that way without reformation, sooner or later the very same thing will come upon him which he dreaded, and which was the occasion of his backsliding. Suppose it was a regard to reputation that made him backslide. He is a politician, perhaps, and he became a backslider in heart, because he wanted to get some office. By and by you will see that man put down in politics, and lose his office, and so the very thing comes upon him that he was eager to avoid. God will order it, somehow or other, so as to bring the very curse upon him that he dreaded, and he is filled with his own ways. Instead of being lifted up and kept up, as he expected, God has lifted him up to let him fall and make his fall more signal.

Suppose the individual desires to be rich, and in the pursuit of riches backslides from God. As certain as he is a Christian, God will blast his riches. God values his soul a great deal more than his wealth, and HE will not hesitate to burn up all that property, if there is no better way to deliver him from it.

If he has backslidden through fear of getting the ill will of his friends, or through fear of persecution, very likely he will in some other way lose the good will of those very persons. Most marvelous instances could be pointed out, if I had time, where backsliders have thus been filled with their own ways. Their course has resulted in the entire loss of those very objects which they prized more than the favor of God, and in the suffering of those very evils which they dreaded more than his frown and curse.

10. If you continue in your backslidden state, you may expect that by and by God will let you fall into some iniquity or some disgrace, that will be a source of vexation and trial to you as long as you live. I have known men who have blackslidden to get rich, and they have got into debt and failed, and gone down to their graves loaded with anxiety and reproach. I knew a man, perhaps he is now living, who to gratify an ungodly and ambitious son, entered upon a course of speculation that first destroyed his piety, and then he failed in his speculation and became a bankrupt, and got into such a sea of trouble and toil as will harass him to the day of his death. He used to give liberally to missions, and every good cause, but now he can hardly give a shilling at the monthly concert, because he feels that he owes it, and perhaps it is wronging his creditors. All this is simply being filled with his own ways.

Sometimes, when backsliding is occasioned by an idolatrous attachment to a wife or a child, God takes away the desire of their eyes at a stroke. All this is because God is faithful. He sees one of his children leaning on an idol, and he puts forth his hand and withers away the idol in an instant, rather than let a child of his live and die in sin, and go to hell.

REMARKS.

1. There is no way for young converts to keep from being backsliders, but by guarding against the beginning of decline.

Backsliding comes on very much like intemperance, gradually, from the smallest beginning, in a way that is overlooked. No man ever commenced the career of becoming a drunkard with his eyes open, intending to do it. He first, perhaps, takes a glass on some public day. By and by he begins to keep it in his house to treat his friends, or to take it with bitters, or as a medicine. Next he takes a few drops with his dinner, to help digestion. And so he goes on, without suspecting his danger, till he is a drunkard before he is aware. Nine-tenths of those who become drunkards, are led on from small beginnings, in some such way as this. In much the same way, persons become backsliders by little and little. They do not intend to backslide, but they take the first step without knowing where it will lead, and then they more easily take the second, and so on. The only security is in adopting the principle of TOTAL ABSTINENCE FROM SIN. Avoid those *little things*, as they call them, which lead the way. If they begin to allow themselves in some such "little thing" they are gone. They may continue to keep up the show of godliness, but it will be without the power, and they overlook the fact, that they have become loathsome backsliders in the sight of God. See that woman. If you could listen at the door of her closet, you would be convinced at once that she is not half in earnest. She keeps up the form of secret prayer very strictly, but there is no heart in it. Prays in secret? She mocks God in secret! She is a backslider.

2. You see the duty of church members to watch over young converts in love, and put them on their guard against the beginnings of backsliding. They should watch them, just as a mother watches her little child, to see that it does not go near where it will fall. Look out for them, and if you see them verging near the lines, warn them, "Beware! go not near that brink — hell is there." Ask them, early and frequently, "Do you pray now as frequently and fervently as you did? Do you love the Bible as much as you did?" And keep them on the guard, and thus prevent them from backsliding.

3. There is great reason to praise God for all that he does with his people when they backslide.

He follows them with stripes, till they return. He says, "If they break my statutes, and keep not my commandments, then will I visit their transgression with a rod, and their iniquity with stripes; nevertheless, my loving kindness will I not utterly take from him, nor suffer my faithfulness to fail."

4. If any of you are in a backslidden state, or if you are a professor of religion and have these marks, and if God does not chastise you, and if you are still prosperous, you have reason to fear that you are given up of God. You have great reason to fear that you never were a child of God, and never knew the love of God, but are a hypocrite on the way to hell. How long have you been in this state? How long is it since you left what you call your first love? If it is long, and you are not yet chastised, you have reason

to believe it is because you are a hypocrite. God is faithful, and he *will* chastise his children when they backslide. He has promised to do it, and he will not fail.

Or does God chastise you? If so, repent, before he chastises you any more. Do not wait for him to chastise you to death, or till he lets you fall into the snares of the devil, and into some grievous sin that shall disgrace and torment you as long as you live. Come back, O Backslider, come back to God. Seek his face, renounce your sin, and he will heal your backslidings, and forgive your transgressions, and bless your soul.

XXII

GROWTH IN GRACE[1]

TEXT. — "Grow in grace." 2 PET. iii. 18.

THIS evening I must conclude all that I have to say at present on the subject of Revivals. There are several other subjects which I designed to discuss, but have not had time. It is possible that I may resume the subject in the fall if I live to return to the city, according to my present intention. One of the subjects which I fully intended to discuss, was that of EVANGELISTS, the importance of having such a class of ministers to be employed in revivals — their relation to the church and the ministry, the manner in which they are to be received and treated, both by pastors and churches, and the principles on which they ought to govern themselves in discharging the appropriate duties of their office. But at present, I have concluded that it would be better to conclude this course of lectures with a sermon on

GROWTH IN GRACE.

The term grace is used in the Bible in several different senses. When applied to God its meaning is not the same as when applied to man. Grace, in God, is synonymous with beneficence. It is undeserved favor. This is the sense in which the term is used by theologians in reference to God. In men, grace means *holiness*, that is the sense in which it is used in the text, and to grow in grace is the same as to grow in holiness, or to increase in conformity to God. In discussing this subject, I design to pursue the following order:

I. Show what is meant by growing in grace.

II. Mention some things which are *not* evidences of growth in grace.

[1] In the revised edition of 1868 this lecture was completely rewritten and slightly enlarged, though its text and title remained the same. In the revision Finney referred to some of the views on sanctification he expounded in his *Systematic Theology*, and he took to task certain ministers who seemed to doubt that "every step of progress in the Christian life is taken by a fresh and fuller appropriation of Christ by faith, a fuller baptism of the Holy Spirit."

III. What are some of the evidences of growth in grace.

IV. Show how it is to be done, or in what way Christians may grow in grace.

V. Mention some of the evidences of a decline in piety or grace.

VI. How to escape or recover from a state of decline in piety.

I. What is meant by growing in grace?

To grow in grace is to increase in a spirit of conformity to the will of God, and to govern our conduct more and more by the same principles that God does. God has one great absorbing object, that controls every thing he does. It is the promotion of his own glory by seeking to fill the universe with holiness and happiness. He does this by exhibiting his own character. And our object should be the same, to exhibit the character of God more and more, to reflect as many rays of the image of God as possible. That is, we must aim constantly to be more and more like God. To do this more and more is to grow in grace. In other words, it is to obey more and more perfectly and constantly the law of God. That is growing in grace, becoming more holy, or obeying God more fully and constantly.

II. I will mention some things that *are not evidences* of growth in grace, although they are sometimes supposed to be such.

1. It is not a certain evidence that an individual grows in grace, because he grows in gifts.

A professor of religion may increase in gifts, that is, he may become more fluent in prayer, and more eloquent in preaching, or more pathetic in exhortation, without being any more holy. We naturally increase in that in which we exercise ourselves. And if any person often exercises himself in exhortation, he will naturally, if he makes any effort or lays himself out, increase in fluency and pungency. But he may do all this, and yet have no grace at all. He may pray ever so engagedly, and increase in fluency and apparent pathos, and yet have no grace. People who have no grace often do so. It is true, if he has grace, and exercises himself in these things, as he grows in grace he will grow in gifts. No person can exercise himself in obeying God, without improving in those exercises. If he *does not* improve in gifts, it is a true sign he *does not* grow in grace. But on the other hand it is not evidence that he grows in grace, because he improves in certain exercises, for they will naturally improve by practice, whether he is a sinner or a hypocrite.

2. *Growing in knowledge* is not evidence of growth in grace.

Knowledge is indispensable to grace, and growth in knowledge is essential to growth in grace, but knowledge is not grace, and growth in knowledge does not constitute growth in grace. A person may grow ever so much in knowledge and yet have no grace at all. In hell no doubt they grow in knowledge but never in grace. Their growth in knowledge constitutes hell. They know more and more of God and his law and their own guilt, and the more they know the more wretched they are. They have more and more experience of God's wrath, but they never learn piety from it.

3. It is not evidence that a person grows in grace, because *he thinks he is doing so*. A person may be favorably impressed with regard to his progress in religion, when it is evident to others that he is not only making no progress, but is in fact declining. An individual who is growing worse is not ordinarily sensible of the fact. It is common for both impenitent sinners and those who are pious to think they are growing better, when they are no better. This is so, from the nature of the mind, as any one who will attend to the philosophy of the mind can see. If a person is growing worse, his conscience will become more and more seared, and his mind more and more dark, as he stifles conscience and resists light. Then he may think he is growing better, just because he has less and less sense of sin, and while his conscience continues to sleep, he may continue under a fatal delusion.

It is manifest that where a professor gets the idea that he is growing *rapidly* in grace, it is a supicious circumstance. For the best of reasons. To grow better implies a more clear and distinct knowledge of the breadth of God's law, and a growing sense of the sinfulness of sin. But the more clear an individual's views become of the standard, *the lower* will be the estimate which he forms of himself, because the clearer will be his views of the distance at which he still is from that pure and perfect standard of holiness to which God requires him to conform all his conduct. If he compares himself with a low standard, he will think he is doing pretty well. This is the reason why there is such a difference in people's views of their own state, and of the state of the church. They compare themselves and the state of the churches with different standards. Hence, when one complains of the church, and thinks his brethren are cold, another thinks it censorious, and thinks it strange that the other should find so much fault with the church, when they appear to *him* to be doing pretty well. — The reason why he does not think the church is cold is that he is cold himself, and he does not feel his own state because he does not judge by the right standard, for he does not look at his life in the light of God's holy law. If a man shuts his eyes, he does not see the defilement on his person, and may think he is clean while to all around he appears to be loathsome. I have always observed this to be true, that when persons are making, in reality, the most rapid advances in holiness, they have the most debasing views of themselves, and the humblest sense of their state. I do not mean, that those who understand the subject, and who know what are evidences of growth in grace, may not *by reasoning* or by comparing their present with their former views, feelings, and character, come to the conclusion that they are growing in grace. But that, if they should determine simply by their present views of what they are, and what God requires, if they should not reason on the subject, they would come to the conclusion that they were growing worse and worse. Individuals who were making rapid progress have often felt so, because they saw more and more clearly the standard with which they are to compare themselves. But yet, if they understand well what growth in grace is, and what are the evidences of it, when they set themselves down to reason about the matter, they may become convinced that *they are* growing in grace, although at the same time they will feel more and more humbled under a sense of their sins.

III. I will mention some things that are evidences of growth in grace.

1. When an individual finds he has more singleness of heart and more purity of motive in his conduct, it is evidence that he is growing in grace. I will explain what I mean. Even religious men are apt to be influenced in their conduct by a variety of motives, and some of them may be merely selfish. These motives together make up the complex whole that influences the individual to do a certain act. For instance, suppose a man is asked to give money to build a church in some particular place. He may have a variety of reasons for doing it. He may wish to see a more respectable house there on some account, or it may be so located that if built it will increase the value of his property, or he wishes to be thought liberal, or it may be an object with him to obtain the favor of that church and people. All or any of these may have some influence in determining his mind, and still, after all, a motive of greater weight than the whole may be a desire to save souls and to build up the kingdom of God. Here it is easy to see that some of the considerations which make up the complex whole, are selfish,

and so far are wrong and wicked. Now sinners are *only* selfish in all that they do. And when men are converted, although their *leading* object then is to glorify God and save souls, yet when they are young in the Christian life, and weak in religion, ignorance and the force of habit will still keep them more or less under the influence of private considerations, and they will be exceedingly apt to perform right things from wrong motives. To grow in grace is to grow in purity of motive, more and more to exclude selfish reasons, and to act more exclusively from a regard to the glory of God.

You that are here can tell whether from year to year your motives are more single, more pure, more free from selfishness. How is it? Are you growing more and more free from selfishness? Do you act more with a single reference to God's glory, leaving self more and more out of view?

2. An individual who grows in grace is more and more actuated by principle, and less and less by emotion or feeling. I do not mean that such a person *has* less feeling, but that he *acts* less under the influence of feeling or emotion. He does things less because he feels so, and more because it is RIGHT. By principle I do not mean a seed, or sprout or root, or any thing created and put into the soul. It is all nonsense to talk about such kind of holiness, or such a principle as that. By principle in contradistinction from feeling or emotion, I mean a controlling determination in the mind to *do right*.

Young converts are seldom actuated at first so much by principle, but are borne along by the tide of their feelings, and unless they feel deeply, it is sometimes difficult to get them to *act* as they ought. But if they grow in grace, they will learn to go forward, and obey the commandments of God, whatever their feelings may be. Young converts are apt to imagine that all religion consists in emotion or feeling, and that whatever regard a man may have to the *authority* of God, however much regard he may have to what is *right*, still his conduct is not acceptable unless it be done under the full tide of emotion. He will therefore often wait till these emotions first exist in his mind, before he addresses himself to the performance of duty. But converts should know that the way to call emotion or feeling into exercise, is to engage, *from principle*, in the performance of duty. And that whenever a man engages in the performance of duty, from a regard to the authority of God, he may expect, in this way, to call into exercise those feelings for which young converts are so apt to wait. A growing regard to the authority of God, a strengthening of the purpose of obedience, a more firm and constant adherence to what is right, and to what God requires because it is right, at once constitutes, and is an evidence of, growth in grace.

3. Another important evidence of growth in grace is *more love to God*. By this I do not mean that there will be in all cases a conscious increase of *emotions* of love to God. But that there will be a strengthening of real attachment to God's character and government. This may be illustrated by the operation of a growing attachment to our country, or to our families. Very young persons are apt to have but little love for their country. But as they grow older, and have more experience, if the government is good, their attachment to it increases, until in the decline of life you will see an aged patriot with his crutch and his gun, ready to turn out and hobble to the field of battle, to repel the invaders of his country's peace. I do not mean by this that increasing love to God leads individuals to use carnal weapons, in either building up or defending his government. — But that if they are true friends to God, the longer they live under his government, the more confidence they have in him, and the more attachment to him. And this increased attachment will evince itself in a growing veneration for all the institutions of religion, for the Sabbath, and for all the commands of God.

It is true, where there is a growth in principle, there is commonly a proportionate increase of feeling. But this is not always so. There may be various causes for the mind's exercising less of *felt* emotion, while it actually increases in the strength of holy principle. But let there be no mistake on this subject. I have said that by principle I mean a regard to what is right, and a fixed determination to do that which is duty. Let no one say, therefore, *while he neglects his duty*, and his heart is cold, that he is growing in principle, although he has less feeling than others. To grow in principle *is* to grow in obedience. And it is in vain for a man who neglects his duty, to profess to be growing in grace.

4. Another evidence of growth in grace is when a person increases in love to men as well as love to God. Growing Christians show by their lives that they become continually more and more inclined to do good to men. Their hearts become more and more enlarged in benevolence to all men. Young converts are apt to be chiefly influenced by a special and partial regard to individuals, their relations, or their former companions or neighbors. But as they grow in grace these circumstances make less and less differ-

ence in their feelings, towards their friends and towards others. Their hearts expand, they have more and more feeling for the heathen, and for all the world. As they increase in piety, they feel more and more a desire that the *world* should be converted to God. They have more and more heart-breaking agony at the dreadful state of men in their sins. And their views and affections rise and expand, until they feel, like God, their bowels of compassion yearn for all men that they might repent and be saved.

Beloved does it appear so to you? Is this your state of mind? Are you more and more weighed down with the idea that men are going to hell? And have you greater and greater desires that the world should be converted to God?

5. Those who grow in grace feel more and more self-loathing. They have greater humility and self-abasement. I suppose the saints will increase in this to all eternity. I see nothing in this inconsistent with the happiness of *heaven*. It seems to me that to all eternity as the ages roll round, the saints will feel constantly, more and more, how much they deserve to be sent to hell for their wickedness. As they see the development of God's government, and the displays of his infinite goodness, they will be more and more impelled to exclaim, "O how wicked I was, what an infinite wretch, how much I deserve to lie in hell rather than to be in heaven." It is so here in this world. Growing Christians more and more loathe themselves, and wonder how God could have spared such wretches. Job, when he was in darkness, justified himself throughout. He declared that his prayer was pure, and that he did not deserve these calamities. And God had said he was a perfect and an upright man. He did not mean that Job was perfectly sinless, for it was not true that he was perfect in this sense. But God meant to say, he was *sincere*. This is the meaning of the word perfect here. And it is generally the meaning of it in the Bible. He meant to say that Job was honest in religion. Job remained in this darkness, and all the while justifying himself, for a long time, but by and by he had clear views of God, and all his self-justification was gone, and he cried out, "I have heard of thee by hearing of the ear, but now mine eye seeth thee; wherefore I abhor myself, and repent in dust and ashes." Such deep self-abasement was the natural result of clear views of God.

So it was with Isaiah. I have been confounded when I have heard some persons talk of their purity, and of being entirely pure from their sins, and of being perfect. They must have vastly different views of themselves from what Job and Isaiah had. What did Isaiah see? He says, "I saw the LORD sitting upon a throne, high and lifted up, and his train filled the temple. Above it stood the seraphim; each one had six wings, with twain he covered his face, and with twain he covered his feet, and with twain he did fly. And one cried unto another, and said, Holy, HOLY, HOLY, is the Lord of hosts; the whole earth is full of his glory." What was the effect of a view of God on his mind? "Wo is me!" said Isaiah, "Wo is me, for I am undone, because I am a man of unclean lips, and I dwell in the midst of a people of unclean lips; for my eyes have seen the King, the Lord of Hosts!" Hear that man saying that he is perfect, that he is pure from his sins. Is he? I ask again, Is he? I doubt that man. What! When Isaiah had but a glimpse of God, and of heaven, it was so holy that he was overwhelmed, he could not endure it, his self-abasement was so great that until an angel took a live coal from off the altar and touched his lips, and assured him his sins were forgiven, he was in despair. This is the natural result of having a clear view of God. It makes a person sink down in self-abasement *lower*, and LOWER, and LOWER, so that when he comes into the presence of God, he wants to find a place so infinitely low before God, words cannot express it.

Beloved, do you know any thing of this? Do you grow in grace in this respect? Do you feel day by day as if you wanted to get lower and lower in the dust before God? Have you ever felt so that you could say in truth, as President Edwards did: "O that I could get infinitely low before God!"

6. An increased abhorrence of sin is another mark of growth in grace. When a person feels day by day less and less disposed to compromise with sin, with any sin, in himself or in others, it is a sign that he is growing in grace. Is it so with you, beloved? Have you daily less and less fellowship with sin in all shapes, in YOURSELF and in others? Do you feel more as God feels towards sin?

7. He who grows in grace has less relish for the world. — He has less and less desire for its wealth, its honors, its pleasures. A desire for these things has less and less influence, as a motive, in his mind. He seeks wealth and honor *only* as instruments of glorifying God and of doing good to men.

A person who is growing in grace becomes less fond of worldly company and worldly conversation, and reading worldly books, or newspapers. You see a growing Christian engaged in holiness, and you will find he cares very little for intelligence of any kind, unless it has a bearing some way or other, upon the kingdom of God. You will find him rather seeking after the most spiritual things he can get hold of. He will seize hold of the most spiritual books to read. He will love the company and conversation of the most spiritual Christians. He will relish, and if possible attend the most pungent, and searching spiritual preaching.

8. Increasing delight in the fellowship of the saints, is another evidence of growth in grace. The growing Christian loves to *unite* with others in acts of devotion, and other religious exercises, and loves to enjoy *religious* intercourse. Do you know what this is, beloved? Do you *increase* in this?

9. He who grows in grace finds it more and more easy to exercise a forgiving spirit, and to pray for his enemies. There is nothing in which men, who are in their natural state, more resemble the devil, than in their harboring angry and revengeful feelings toward those who have injured them. A young convert often finds it hard to forgive. When he feels himself injured, very often he finds he cannot pray. That wrong comes right up before his mind, and he cannot pray. Now if he lets it rankle in his bosom, till he gets angry, it is most likely he will backslide. He does not mean to be angry, but if he does not heartily forgive the one that he thinks has done him wrong, it will run on till darkness fills his soul, and his revengeful feelings will destroy his religion. If a person is growing in grace, he will find it more and more easy to forgive. He will find that he is less apt to lay up any thing against another, and that it costs him less trouble to get over supposed injuries, so as to be able to pray. Do you find this to be so, you who hear me to night; is it easier for you to forgive, can you forgive the greatest injuries at once, so that nothing of the kind can come up between you and God, to hinder your prayers?

10. Growing more charitable is an evidence of growth in grace. I do not mean by charitable, that he should be more ready to believe every body a Christian who professes to be so. But he is more ready to ascribe a person's apparently wrong conduct to mistake, or misapprehension, or some other cause, than to direct evil intention. Nothing more satisfactorily shows the Christian. If you find an individual inclined to put the best construction on actions, whenever they are susceptible of two constructions; as, for instance, if an act appears on the face of it to be unkindness or neglect, and the individual is apt to think it was not designedly wrong, but only done through a mistake, or some other motive of

that kind, you have evidence that such a person is growing in grace.

11. Having less and less anxiety about worldly things is an evidence of growth in grace. A growing Christian will more and more perfectly obey the command, "Be careful for nothing," that is, Be not anxious, "but in every thing by prayer and supplication with thanksgiving, let your requests be made known unto God." All *anxiety* about the world is wicked. Persons who grow in grace have more and more confidence in God, and less and less love for the world, and of course will be less liable to feel anxiety about worldly things.

12. Becoming *more ready to bestow property* is a sign of growth in grace. If a person is growing in grace he will be more and more ready to give, and willing to give ALL that is in his power. He will rejoice to be called on. He will give more and more yearly. If he gives from right motives he will be glad when he has given. And the more he gives, the more he loves to give. His giving will be a part of his religion, and he will grow in it just as in prayer. Now you know, the more a persons prays, the more he loves to pray. Do you find this evidence that you are growing in grace? Is it more and more a pleasure to you to give, according to your ability, for every good object, according as you have opportunity? Do you give *according* to your ability, or do you give only just as much as is necessary to keep up appearances?

13. He feels less and less as if he had any separate interest. It is a great thing, in regard to growth in grace, to feel that *all you have* is Christ's, and that you have absolutely no separate interests, no private interest in living, or in dying, or in holding property, or children, or character. "Whether we live, we live unto the Lord, and whether we die, we die unto the Lord; whether we live, therefore, or die, we are the Lord's." This is a great and solemn lesson to learn. Persons who grow in grace feel that their time, talents, property, life itself, have value, only in their relation to Christ's kingdom.

14. It is an evidence of growth in grace where a person becomes more willing to confess faults before men. It is a great thing to be ready to confess to men. It is a point often hard to learn. Men are willing to confess to God, because they have not so far to stoop, to do this. But to confess fully and frankly to men is a great stoop for a proud heart. But when they grow in grace, they would just as soon confess a fault, and confess as frankly, to a servant, or an enemy, or the lowest member of society, as to the most exalted in-

dividual. Do you know this? Do you feel it less and less painful to confess a fault? There is no man who knows his own heart, that has not found a struggle necessary to bring his mind to confess to individuals. A man can confess to God, but many cannot without a struggle confess a fault to a friend, or a servant, or an enemy. But as he grows in grace, he will become ready to confess, if he has done wrong to any body, yes, to the entire universe. If he is perfectly humble, he will be willing to confess, if all the universe should hear. If you cannot do this, be sure you are not growing in grace, if you have any grace.

15. Growing in grace raises a person more and more above the world. The growing saint regards less and less either the good or ill opinions of men. He feels that it is of little importance, only as it may affect his usefulness. I do not mean by this, that a person should have a proud contempt for the opinions of his fellow men. He may feel and manifest this, and instead of having more evidence of weanedness from the world, he will have evidence of his consummate pride. But if a person is growing in grace, only let him see his DUTY, and he will not turn aside although public opinion should be all against him. He will not do, or omit to do, any thing, but from a regard to the glory of God. The frowns or the flatteries of the world will not be taken into the account when he sees his duty. It is amazing to see how much of what appears to be religion, is, after all, a mere obsequious yielding to public opinion, instead of yielding obedience to God. Public opinion requires that those who have made a profession of religion should do so and so, and *therefore* they do so.

IV. I am to show you how to grow in grace.

This is a highly important subject to young converts, that they should know how it is done.

1. They should *watch*. They should watch against their besetting sins.

(1.) Levity. I need not enlarge on this any farther than to say, that it is the besetting sin of many persons, and unless they place a tenfold watch at the door of their lips, they will never grow in grace. Once yielding to a spirit of levity, may grieve the spirit and put out your light for a day, and giving way once, but makes way for a repetition, so that unless you begin with decision and continue with great prayer and watchings, to keep down the spirit of levity, you are undone.

(2.) Censoriousness. Young converts are particularly in danger of this. They enter upon religion full of ardor, and they are soon amazed at the coldness and apathy of old professors. And they have room to be amazed. Heaven and earth are amazed at the manner in which old professors lay stumbling blocks before young converts. And it is no wonder that young converts, when they see such things, should imagine, in the warmth of their feeling, that such professors have no religion. And so they are liable to say hard and censorious things. But they ought to learn carefully to distinguish between the deep *principles* of ripe Christians, and the lively *feelings* of young converts. If they keep this in mind, they will not be so likely to misjudge. And whatever may be their sober judgment about the state of others, young converts ought to be very careful what they say of them. Don't keep talking about the faults of others. Do not speak censoriously of any. If you do, you will grieve away the Holy Spirit, and you will not grow in grace.

(3.) Anger. How many Christians are injured by letting their temper rise. If they are women, they fret at their servants. Men fret at their clerks, or at those who are in their employ, or they get angry with the government, or with their neighbors, go to finding fault in some way or other, that shows they do not watch their temper. How can they grow in grace?

(4.) Pride. Guard against pride and vanity in all their forms. Be very careful never to purchase an article of dress, or furniture, or any thing calculated to foster vanity in your mind. Woman, you are going to buy a bonnet, be careful not to get one that will make you think of it when you wear it. Alas! how much pains some people take to foster their own bad passions. The devil might go to sleep, in regard to some Christians; he has no need to lie in wait to tempt them, they tempt themselves, they are doing the very things that are calculated to puff them up with pride. Such foolishness is enough to make them the ridicule of Satan. Young females, young men, be careful, watch against this. In how many places has this been the history. During the winter a revival, many converted, all engaged; spring comes, and somebody sets them all agog for some new fashion, and then where is your prayer-meetings? Here are these young converts taken in the snare, and all gone off to worship the goddess of fashion. I mean that by degrees the young ladies and others are drawn off from conversation and thinking upon religion, to conversing and thinking of something new in dress or equipage, or some vain thing that eats up their spirituality, and leaves them in great darkness.

(5.) Selfishness in all its forms. Here is the great root of all the difficulty. This is the foundation, the fountain, the substance and sum total of all the iniquity under heaven. Watch here, look out constantly, see where self comes out in your conduct, and there set a guard. If you are making a bargain, see to it that you do not act from selfish motives. Deal just as you would do if you were dying. Do as you would be done by.

If you find you are disposed to act selfishly, shut down the gate, stop there. If you are about to deal in any other way than you would if God stood visibly before you — STOP. The devil is in that bargain. You never will grow in grace unless you are exceedingly on your guard against self in your bargains. If you find this mighty self coming in to interfere, bid him to stand away. "Stand away, self, you are not to speak here, I am doing business for God." You cannot grow in grace, until you stop the mouth of this "self."

(6.) Sloth. This is an evil, great enough to ruin the world. How many converts stop and decline by sloth. In plain terms, they get lazy. Like idle servants, they saunter about as if they had nothing to do, they will not take hold of the work, they are mere eye-servants, unprofitable enough, a moth to the church.

(7.) Envy. If you see others going ahead of you in prosperity, in influence or in talents, examine your feelings, and see whether you are pleased at it. If the sight gives you pain, or make you uneasy, beware.

(8.) Ambition. By this sin angels fell, and it is impossible to grow in grace without suppressing it.

(9.) Impure thoughts. We are so much under the influence of sensible objects that unless we watch diligently, before we are aware, we are perverted with impure thoughts. It is necessary to make a covenant with our eyes, and with our ears too, and all our senses, or they will prove the inlet of temptation and sin. If you find yourself in danger, *turn your thoughts away instantly*. If you let your mind run on, it is impossible you should avoid impure thoughts. Here is the responsibility, the will can control the thoughts, you can think of one thing or you can think of another, as you please, and thus control your emotions, and therefore you are responsible for them. Let an individual suffer his thoughts to dwell on a subject, and he *cannot but* be affected by it, and he is responsible for the effect because he can govern his thoughts. In all such cases, I tell you, GO AWAY, turn off your mind, or impure thoughts will fester in your soul, till they prove a gangrene.

2. Another direction for growing in grace, is *Take care to exercise all the Christian graces*. If a little child does not exercise its faculties, it will never be any thing but a child.

Rock it in a cradle till it grows to man's size, and it is still in a state of babyhood. It is impossible that the muscles should have strength but by exercise. It is equally impossible that the graces of a Christian should grow and have strength if they are not exercised. Here I wish to suggest a thought for you to dwell upon. The soul thinks by using the brain, just as it sees by using the eyes, or hears by using the ears. And the brain needs exercise, in order to have strength, just as much as any other part of the body. What is it that gives power to the mind that studies. The exercise of the brain. Any power of the mind, intellectual or moral, increases by exercise. You know that the more you use your arm, the more powerfully you can use it, and with the more ease. See that musician, how he moves his fingers on his instrument, with what precision, and almost with the rapidity of thought. So it is with the mind that uses the brain. By exercise it gains the brain so entirely under control, that it can throw itself at once into any act, exercise, or attitude, and is never at a loss, or taken by surprise. Just so with the Christian graces, they must grow and be cultivated by exercise. It is just as absurd to expect that the mind can readily and powerfully throw itself into *them*, without practice, as to expect that it shall throw itself readily and powerfully into any intellectual operation without practice.

Exercise yourself especially in those things where you find yourself most deficient, whether the defect arises from your previous habits, or constitutional temperament, or circumstances of life. If you are exposed to a particular sin, guard there. If you are deficient in a particular grace, exercise that.

(1.) Suppose you are naturally worldly minded, and in danger of being carried away by the love of the world. Shut down the gate, and determine that you will on no account add to your wealth, or lay field to field. Do nothing of the kind.

What would you think of any body who should go to reclaiming a drunkard by filling his cellar with wine and all sorts of tempting liquors? You would say he was deranged. Not a particle more beside himself than is that professor of religion, who knows he is inclined to love the world, and yet will go on adding to his wealth. He needs no devil, he tempts himself, he takes the most effectual course to destroy himself. If you are tempted to indulge a worldly spirit, pour out more and more, give often, give liberally, give heartily, bountifully, increase your gifts, give to every object, give away every thing you have on earth, if that is necessary to knock on the head this hateful spirit. Relieve yourself from the temptation to hoard up the wealth of this world. Carry this out, and you will find that the more you give, the more you gain advantage, and your soul will grow in grace.

(2.) Suppose you are in danger of being flattered and lifted up with pride. As a reasonable being you are bound to know this, and be on your guard. There is a woman who has a husband, doating on her, and wants to dress her up like a graven image and worship her. Be firm and say, "I am not going to be worshipped. I worship God myself, and will not be an idol for man." I have known some Christian women, who, when asked how they could wear such and such expensive dresses, say, "O, it is to please my husband, he is a worldly man, and loves to see me wear them, and he can afford it, and so I gratify him." Suppose now he should build a temple, and set up an altar in it, and then wish you to stand up there and be his goddess, and let him offer incense, and some one should say, "How is this? I thought you professed to worship Jehovah, and do you stand up here to be worshipped yourself?" You should reply, "O, I do it to please my husband, he is an ungodly man, and wishes to do so, and I like to gratify him, I hope in this way to lead him along, and retain an influence on his mind, that in God's time I hope to make him a Christian." Why, you have just as much right to say this, as you have to be decked out in all this gaudy drapery of fashion, and made an idol of in the way you are. REMEMBER, you are a servant of Jesus Christ, and you have no right to yield to any mortal, that authority which belongs to HIM. And besides, this pretence of doing it to please your husband, is, in nine cases out of ten, all a sham. You do it to please yourself. Beware. If you are inclined to be proud, guard against it as against the gates of death.

(3.) If you find that you are reluctant to confess your faults, break right over it, and confess to every body that you have injured. Practice it on all occasions, till you get the victory. Victory will come at last, if you are thorough. But there is no other way to get the upper hand of your evil propensities. If you indulge the feeling, you are just as certainly ruined, as a man who loves liquor is sure to become a drunkard, if he continues to drink. If he does not deny himself of every thing that can intoxicate or excite his appetite, he is gone. So with you, if you do not resist where you are exposed, you will just as surely go to hell as there is a hell.

5. Exercise decision of character. In nothing is decision of character so indispensable as in religion. In nothing else are there so many influences bearing against a man, and so many things that are calculated to turn him back from his purpose. To walk with God a man must walk contrary to the course of this world. He must face public sentiment, and go abreast, not unfrequently, of the opinions of all the world, and nearly of all the church. If on the one hand, he can be awed by opposition, or on the other courted by smiles and flattery, he will be certain not to make headway, and stem the tide that is bearing him away from God. Very few persons exercise sufficient decision to maintain a spirit of prayer. No person can enjoy the spirit of prayer, who does not maintain a conscience void of offence, towards God and man. He must be willing to know, and do, all his duty. If he draws back from doing what he sees to be duty, or if he neglects to search and know what his duty is, he cannot enjoy the spirit of prayer. But most men are so much the creatures of public sentiment, so easily deterred by enemies, or kept away from duty by the flatteries and persuasion of friends, that they grieve the Spirit of God, get into a temporizing, man-pleasing, man-fearing spirit, that dishonors God, and freezes the soul. A man must maintain great firmness of purpose, and great decision of character, to be undeviating in the performance of *secret* duties. Men are so apt to neglect secret prayer and private duties, when they do not at the time *feel* like engaging in them, that without uncommon energy of character, even the form of private duties will be more or less punctually attended to, according to the state of feeling in which the Christian finds himself at the time.

6. To grow in grace, a man must possess *great meekness*.

Meekness is patience under injuries. If a man suffers himself to be fretted by opposition, and thrown into a passion by obstacles that are thrown in his way, he may rest assured that Satan will manage to keep him in such a state of mind, that he will by no means grow in grace. A want of meekness is a sad defect in Christian character. A spirit to *resent* every thing is extremely unlovely, unchrist-like, and wicked. And perhaps there are few things that more disarm professors of religion, and nullify their influence as Christians, than a disposition to fret. If a Christian does his duty, he must take it for granted that he will meet with opposition. And as long as the church is in such a state as it now is, he must expect often to receive the most determined opposition from those from whom much better things ought to have been expected. In such cases he must learn to possess his soul in patience, and let patience have its perfect work. When he is reviled, he must learn not to revile again. And if he is persecuted, to threaten not.

Many individuals seem to attach great importance to their own *reputation*, and suppose themselves obliged to defend their character, for the honor of religion. I am afraid of this spirit. It seems to me exceedingly unlike the spirit of Christ, who made himself of NO REPUTATION. He was reviled and slandered, and all manner of evil spoken against him, and yet he seems to have manifested no disposition to spend his time in going about, hunting up the authors of those slanders. He never acted as if he supposed that his honor, or the success of his gospel, required him to do so. And why the servant should be thought above his master, I do not know.

V. I will mention some things that are evidences of declension.

Those of you who were present at the last lecture will recollect that I preached on backsliding, and in the course of it mentioned several things that are evidences of backsliding, or declension. I will now mention several others, that ought to be kept in view, as evidences of declension.

1. The person who grows weary of being asked to give for promoting the kingdom of Christ, is evidently declining. He says, "Now I think I have given about enough, there seems to be no end to it, and I mean to stop; there are so many agents constantly begging, it is time to break it up." You hear a man talk in that style, depend upon it he is either a hypocrite, and has never given from right motives at all, or he is a backslider, and is declining rapidly in piety. It is plain, that where a man gives from right motives, the more he gives, the more he loves to give. This holds just as true in regard to giving, as praying. If you find a man sick of giving to promote the kingdom of Christ, are you to call that man pious? Suppose he should get sick of praying, and say,

"There is no end to this, I may as well stop first as last, for if I go on in this way, by and by I shall have to pray all the days of my life." Would any body pretend to give him the character of a pious man?

2. Becoming backward to converse on the subject of religion, and particularly to converse on spiritual and experimental, and heart-searching points, is evidence of declension. Young converts, when they are in the ardor of their first love, delight to pour out their hearts in spiritual conversation. They love to talk of the things of the kingdom. And when they lose their relish for this, you may be sure they are declining in piety.

3. When a person is less disposed to engage in the duties of devotion, public, social, or private, it is a sign of declension. If he does not love so well to pray, and read his Bible, and draw near to God, he must be declining in piety.

4. Taking more delight in public meetings than in private duties and secret communing with God, is another evidence of a declining state. Those who enjoy religion enjoy themselves nowhere so well as in secret. If you find it necessary to have the excitement of a meeting to stir up your feelings and create an interest in devotion, it is certain you are declining.

5. Feeling less delight in revivals of religion, is a sad token of declension. The young convert delights in revivals. How eagerly he seizes the newspaper to see where there are revivals. How he dwells on such blessed outpourings of the spirit. But when he declines in piety, he becomes less anxious to know about revivals. Revival intelligence no longer gives such joy, or causes such bounding of heart, as it once did. When you see a professor of religion uninterested in accounts of revivals and in hearing of the conversion of sinners, be sure he is in a state.

6. A person that becomes captious about measures used in promoting revivals, is in a declining state. If you find yourself growing very much afraid of the measures that good men pursue, and that God owns and blesses, for promoting revivals, you are evidently declining. If your heart was set on the object, then so long as you saw the object was gained, and sinners were brought in, the particular means by which it was done would give you no manner of concern unless they were manifestly wicked, and certainly you would not be disposed to take it for granted that they are wicked and unscriptural. But where you see people, I do not care who they are, beginning to be suspicious and captious and

fretful about the means by which revivals are carried on, their heart is in a bad state. I do not mean to speak it unkindly, or disrespectfully, but I say it is a simple matter of fact that it is so. Men never act in this way when they are greatly engaged in promoting an object. They do not spend all their strength in finding fault with the means. See that man who is deeply engaged in carrying on an electioneering campaign. Do you find him captious about measures? What does he ask? "Is our candidate elected?" Not, "Was the vote carried by new or old measures?" You would laugh at any man who should pretend to be zealously engaged in promoting a cause, if his first question and greatest concern was about the measures, and if he lost all his interest in the *event* unless it was accomplished by new or old measures. No doubt the devil laughs, if they can laugh in hell, to hear a man pretend to be very much engaged in religion, and a great lover of revivals, and yet all the time on the look-out for fear some new measures would be introduced. Such conduct is not natural, and people will not believe such professions of zeal for revivals.

VI. I am to show how to escape from a state of declension.

1. You must admit the conviction that you are in a state of declension. One of the greatest difficulties with backsliders is to make them feel that they are backsliders. You continually hear them making excuses. They will not admit that *they* are in this sad state. When the condition of the backslider is described ever so plainly, they are exceedingly loth to admit that it means them. And until they admit this, there is no remedy.

2. Apply to yourself all that God says to backsliders, just as if you were the only individual in the world in that condition.

3. Find out the point where you began to decline. See what was the first cause of you backsliding, and give that up. You will often find this first cause where you did not expect it, in some things that you called a little matter, or that you tried to make yourself believe was not a sin. Multitudes have been kept down in this way, and perhaps have been trying hard for sanctification while holding on to some darling idol or some sensual indulgence. I knew a man who stood out in defending the use of tobacco, till it became a lust that eat out his spirit of prayer. Using some soft word, calling it a comfort or a medicine, or even baptizing it by a Christian name, and calling it a blessing of Providence, will not answer. God does not call it so. How many keep themselves in a state of decline and pretend not to know why

it is so: "O, no, I cannot tell why I should be so long in the dark;" when they are laying out God's money to indulge their own appetite or pride. God will always hold them at arm's length, and will frown upon them when they pray, unless they search out and remove the cause of their declension.

4. Give up your idols. Whatever you find occupies your thoughts, and calls you off from serving God, get rid of it, if you can. If it is any article of property, dispose of it in some way, give it away, sell it, burn it, away with it, rather than have it stand between you and God.

5. Be careful to apply afresh to the Lord Jesus Christ, for pardon and peace with God. Go to him just as you did at first, as a guilty, condemned sinner, more deserving of hell than ever. Apply to this fountain, which is set open in the house of David for sin and uncleanness. Confess your sins fully, and forsake them, and thus return to God, and he will have mercy on you, and will heal your backslidings, and remember your iniquities no more.

REMARKS.

1. There is no such thing as standing still in religion.

People talk as if religion was something they could cover up and keep, just as people cover up fire to keep it when they want to go to sleep, and then when they wake up in the morning, find a good bed of coals, all ready to kindle up again. This is all a mistaken idea. Religion is not such a kind of thing as they suppose. Religion consists in obedience to God. And when a man has no obedience he has no religion.

2. The idea that persons grow in grace during seasons of declension, is abominable. I have often heard people say, that it is necessary that revivals should pass away, in order to give religion time to take deep root. Nothing can be more ridiculous than to suppose a person can be making advances in religion, when in a state of declension. Their whole progress is the other way.

3. There are but few persons that do grow in grace.

It is astonishing to see how little the generality of professors grow in grace. I have no doubt, that if persons would do as they might, and give the attention to it that they ought, the generality of professors might grow more in six months than they now do in all their lives. They might do more to counteract and remove all that is bad and to cultivate all that is good. One great reason why people do not grow in grace, is the erroneous idea they have of religion itself. Religion has been too much looked upon as something separate from obedience to God. And hence people set themselves down in inaction, and wait for God to do a work in them, instead of setting themselves at work to obey God. This notion of physical depravity, and physical regeneration, and physical sanctification is the great curse of the church. It leads Christians astray, and hinders their growth in grace. How many, instead of setting themselves resolutely to obey God, and setting their faces as a flint against all sin, with a determination to break up all old habits and associations, by repeated acts of resistance, passively commit themselves to the stream, and expect to be wafted home to glory in this lazy way, without the trouble of a conflict.

5. We see the great fault of ministers.

How much they are to blame. How little pains they take to train up young converts. Go now over the ground where there have been some of the greatest revivals, and what will you see? Instead of finding the young converts built up in their most holy faith, growing in grace, and adorning the doctrine of God our Savior, you hear all, old and young, complaining of general coldness.

"O 'tis a time of great stupidity, our church seem to be fast asleep, I do not know what we are coming to." Whereas, if ministers had only gone to work, when there was a revival, and when young converts were brought in, had trained them up to work, taught them how to grow in grace, pointed out their dangers, rebuked their sins in season and in love, they might still have been growing Christians, an honor to Christ, and the strength of the cause, and the revival might have been prolonged, and souls converted, to this day. Now where is their blood, and at whose hands will it be required? One great reason why ministers do so little to make young converts grow in grace, is because they grow so little in grace themselves. I say it in kindness, but my duty requires that I should say it plainly to my brethren. Their studies are intellectual, and of course their progress is intellectual, and often they do not grow in grace, as it is necessary they should, in order to lead the church forward in Christian experience. They do not go into the subject at all lengths so that they can come forth from the very depths of spiritual experience, and teach the church. I do not mean to say, that this is so with all Ministers, but it is evidently so with many.

6. Unless ministers grow in grace, it is impossible for the church to grow. Ministers may preach the truth, but they will not enter into the experience of Christians, so as to meet their wants, or tell them what to do in their various spiritual circumstances, or warn them of their danger, or tell them how to meet or escape it. The minister must have experience, or he will be a blind leader of the blind. Like people like priest, is a maxim founded on principles of correct philosophy.

7. Great pains should be taken by young ministers to grow in grace.

I have found that many young men have been stopped from entering on a preparation for the ministry by witnessing the experience of others in this respect. Others have been driven to the conviction that they must stop studying or lose their piety. There is no need of this, if they would start right. O that I could make all young men hear this. There is no necessity that young men, preparing for the ministry, should decline. And yet how many do we find, that come out of college with hearts as hard as the college walls, and by the time they are through the seminary, their piety is well nigh all gone. They may keep up certain appearances because they are ministers, when it is manifest to all that their piety is nearly extinct. This is a grievous thing, but it needs to be told. If I could come in contact with the young men preparing for the ministry, and found them not growing in grace, I would advise them by all means to stop studying, and give up all idea of entering the ministry, unless they would recover their spirit of growing piety. They will only do hurt. They are worse than no ministers, — They will lead the church back, rather than forward. The church will follow the minister, and if the minister leads them back from God, they had better have no minister. The churches must be on their guard against this evil. I would tell young men, firmly but kindly, not to be ministers, unless they are growing Christians.

When Christians generally shall feel this, and shall watch over young men, and when young men shall feel this watch of the church in every step of their path, pressing them up to duty, and urging them to be holy, then there will be a set of ministers to convert the world. And not until then. As long as the great effort is to give young men intellectual strength, to the almost entire neglect of cultivating their moral feelings, the church never can convert the world. Do you see in our seminaries of learning any great effort to cultivate the moral feelings of young men? I appeal to every young man who has been there. The race is an intellectual one. The excitement, the zeal, are all for the intellect. The young man who enters the lists, from the nature of the case, soon loses the firm tone of spirituality. And if he does not take the alarm in time, and break up his habits, he will lose his piety. His intellect improves, and his heart lies waste. While in college, he is sensible that he does not feel right, but he says to himself, "When I come to study theology, then I shall wake up and be all piety."

But alas! when he comes to take up theology in a cold abstract way he finds his spirituality as little promoted as if he was studying Euclid. Then he goes on, learns to write a pretty sermon, and to stand and gesture according to rule, and preach his cold, formal writing, that has no more of God in it than the molten calf. The reason is, he has no Holy Ghost. — God is not with him, nor is it possible that he should be, when he has more brains than heart. How can such a ministry convert the world? There must be a general understanding on this subject. The Education Society [2] must see to it, the ministers must see to it, the churches must see to it, young men themselves must see to it, and must be made to feel that the church has her eye on them, and *expects* them to maintain deep piety, or the world never can be converted.

7. It is just as indispensable in promoting a revival, to preach to the church, and make them grow in grace, as it is to preach to sinners and make them submit to God. Many seem to think that if they can only get people converted, the whole ground is gained, and that they will grow in grace of course without any special aid. But the fact is, that young converts will no more grow in grace, without being properly preached to, than sinners will turn to God without being preached to. The truth, in the hands of the Holy Ghost, is just as essential to the one as to the other. If he converts a sinner, it is by employing truths preached, which are adapted to that. And if he causes a convert to grow in grace, he must employ truths preached, which are adapted to that. The perseverance of the saint depends just as entirely upon having truth adapted to his state, as the repentance of a sinner depends on having truth adapted to his state. Until Christians give up entirely the idea of a physical

---

[2] Finney here refers to the American Education Society organized in Boston in 1815 to help educate "pious youth for the gospel ministry." This Plan of Union enterprise was dominated by Congregationalists and after 1837 the Presbyterians withdrew from its support. See Williston Walker, *A History of the Congregational Churches in the United States* (New York, 1897), pp. 326–327.

religion, and understand that sanctification consists in obeying the truth, the church never will go along. There has been an oversight on this subject, in many protracted meetings, where almost all the preaching has been aimed for the conversion of sinners. In such meetings, at least half the preaching should be to the church. And it should be adapted to their state. The church must be preached to, *where they are*, just as sinners must be preached to where *they are*.

8. See why revivals cease.

When there is a revival, and Christians are awake, and get to a certain point, and then are carried no farther, the revival will cease of course. If the church is kept advancing, the revival will not cease. If the instructions given, and the measures pursued, keep the church going ahead, and the young converts growing in grace, the revival will go on. Let the minister keep pouring in the truth where they are, let him know fully, from time to time, the state of the church, and find out just what they need, and treat them thoroughly, and not suffer them to stand still for the want of being searched, and probed, and urged along in their course, and the revival may gain strength and power all the time. If the means could be made to bear upon the church, and upon the young converts, to keep them out of the way of sinners, and to keep them continually advancing in holiness, the revival would never cease.

O, brethren, I wish you had patience, and I had strength enough to go on farther. There are so many points I wished to dwell upon before I closed this important subject. But if the Lord spares my life, I hope to have another opportunity of bringing them before you, when I return to the city in the fall.[3]

THE END.

[3] Finney did not continue his lectures on revivals in the fall of 1835. Instead he delivered a series of lectures to professing Christians, which appeared as *Sermons on Important Subjects* in 1836. The sequel to *Lectures on Revivals* was the series of "Letters on Revivals" that appeared in the Oberlin *Evangelist* from January 29, 1845, to June 24, 1846.

THE JOHN HARVARD LIBRARY

*The intent of
Waldron Phoenix Belknap, Jr.,
as expressed in an early will, was for
Harvard College to use the income from a
permanent trust fund he set up, for "editing and
publishing rare, inaccessible, or hitherto unpublished
source material of interest in connection with the
history, literature, art (including minor and useful
art), commerce, customs, and manners or way of
life of the Colonial and Federal Periods of the United
States . . . In all cases the emphasis shall be on the
presentation of the basic material." A later testament
broadened this statement, but Mr. Belknap's interests remained constant until his death.*

*In linking the name of the first benefactor of
Harvard College with the purpose of this later,
generous-minded believer in American culture the
John Harvard Library seeks to emphasize the importance of Mr. Belknap's purpose. The John Harvard
Library of the Belknap Press of Harvard University
Press exists to make books and documents
about the American past more readily
available to scholars and the
general reader.*

DATE DUE			
RESERVE			
JUN 28 1995			
GAYLORD			PRINTED IN U.S.A.